JESS STACY

THE QUIET MAN OF JAZZ

JESS STACY

The Quiet Man of Jazz

A Biography and Discography
by
Derek Coller

Jess Stacy

JAZZology press

Jazzology Press
1206 Decatur Street, New Orleans, LA 70116, U.S.A.
© 1997 by Jazzology Press, New Orleans

First printing October 1997
Printed in the United States of America by Wendel Printing, New Orleans, Louisiana

Library of Congress Cataloging-in-Publication Data

Derek Coller, 1926 -
Jess Stacy: The Quiet Man of Jazz

Biography: p
Discography: p
Includes index.

1. Jess Stacy, 1904–1995
2. Jazz musician – United States.

Library of Congress Catalog Card Number 97-76582

ISBN 0-9638 890-4-4

Back cover photo by Ray Avery

Contents

To Phyllis

Introduction

I have been an admirer of Jess Stacy's piano playing for more than 50 years. As one of the thousands of youngsters who came to jazz in the early 1940s, influenced by the burgeoning interest in traditional jazz – the jazz revival – I was drawn to the recordings of the Bob Crosby orchestra, in which Stacy was a featured player.

In 1969 I scoured the available literature for information about Jess, incorporating the results into a circulating file, which became the basis for this book. To the file was added data obtained when exchanging letters with musicians and collectors. There was also the pleasure of corresponding with Jess and Pat Stacy, and then meeting them in 1979 and 1992. Jess was not always happy to answer questions about obscure players in obscure bands; he thought that it was the music that counted. It does, indeed, but perhaps history has its place as well.

From 1974 on, after Stacy had played at the Newport Jazz Festival, he was often interviewed and many articles about him were printed, culminating in the publication in 1989 of "Oh, Jess!", a biography by Keith Keller. Keller made available a lot of information about Stacy's career. This book aims to add to that information and to tell the story in chronological order, as well as commenting upon the musicians who were associated with him during his career.

Jess Stacy was one of the great jazz pianists, but despite the acclaim he received during the 1930s and 1940s, winning popularity polls in the major music magazines and receiving praise from the best critics, he remains sadly underrated. But then he was never flamboyant, he was strictly a musician. He did not have the technical wizardry of Art Tatum, the showmanship of Earl Hines or the entertainment skills of Fats Waller – all musicians he admired. Yet he contributed much to the early days of jazz and swing.

Even if he had not been such a brilliant jazzman, his story would still have been a fascinating one, following as it does the history of jazz, riverboats on the Mississippi, gangsters and prohibition in Chicago, the birth of the Swing Era, and the famous Benny Goodman Carnegie Hall concert.

There are few books dealing with any part of the first 50 years of jazz which do not mention Stacy in the index. Like so many fine musicians, his name is usually to be found, for example, in a list of players who worked with Benny Goodman, were members of the Chicago Jazz school, or were part of the Eddie Condon gang.

Jess Stacy maintained an astonishingly consistent level of performance throughout his career, until his retirement in the 1960s. This consistency is most marked during the 1940s, as his recordings with Bob Crosby, Eddie Condon and Benny Goodman testify, but it applies to so much he recorded between 1935 and 1969. Readers are urged to use the discography at the end of this book to seek out the records.

There is no difficulty in finding praise for Jess Stacy, as the following quotations indicate. James Lincoln Collier said Stacy was one of the hardest swinging band pianists of the entire swing era. Bob Rusch wrote that he was one of the finest swing pianists, with a great sense of rhythm, bouncing off the keys in a Hinesian manner. Bobby Hackett considered that a pianist in a band should first accept the role of an accompanist, saying, "Jess Stacy with Benny Goodman was so wonderful at that. Everything he'd play would be relative to the arrangement they were playing. He would be in the right place at the right time."

But the reader should not accept these writers' opinions, or mine. He or she should discover the true value of Jess Stacy's art by *listening* to as many of his recordings as possible. This is what Jess would have wanted.

Truly the quiet man of jazz, but a jazz giant nevertheless.

Derek Coller
England
July 1997

Foreword

Derek Coller very kindly asked me to write a few words about the life Jess (a loving, funny, modest, darling man) and I shared together for 45 years.

I began listening to jazz and collecting records when I was in junior high school. Since the Goodman and the Commodore records were my early favorites, I became a fan of Jess' music right from the start and went to see and hear him at every opportunity. But I first met Jess when he was playing with the Bob Crosby band at the Blackhawk Restaurant in Chicago. I was seventeen years old.

Jess' first marriage proposal to me was in 1941 at the Panther Room of the Sherman Hotel, Chicago, where I had gone with college friends to hear the Crosby band. Jess kissed my cheek and said, jokingly, "Will you marry me when you grow up?" We all laughed. His serious proposal came on August 3, 1950, after we had been dating for about six months in Los Angeles. We were very much in love and were married on September 8, 1950, at my parents' home in Winnetka, Illinois.

Early in 1951 we bought our little house located in a small canyon in the Hollywood Hills. Here I'm tempted to say, "and we lived happily ever after," which is really the truth. Jess and I were always content to be alone together but we discovered a group of very congenial neighbors, shortly to become good friends, with whom we celebrated all birthdays, anniversaries, Halloween, Christmas, 4th of July, etc. It would take only a few phone calls to assemble a lively group for spur-of-the-moment cocktails.

After all his years on the road, Jess loved having a home of his own and through the years happily built a six-foot redwood fence, painted the interior and exterior of the house, planted citrus trees, a vegetable garden as well as a rose garden, camellias and irises. Together we did all the garden and house maintenance work, supervised by a series of beloved cats (two at a time).

Before Jess and I were married I worked for a business manager whose clients were in the motion picture business (producers, directors, writers, and actors) and therefore I was able to continue working on a part-time basis, at night when Jess was working in clubs and during the day after he took his job with Max Factor.

Up until the last five years of his life when he had serious health problems, Jess continued to practice the piano every day, as he said, "to keep arthritis out of my hands." In addition, we took daily walks on top of our hill, feeding the wild quail and enjoying the panoramic view of the city.

I had just left the hospital at 6.35 p.m. on January 1, 1995, when Jess' heart stopped beating. His wonderful son Fred and darling daughter-in-law Beverly were at his bedside when Jess peacefully slipped away.

Pat Stacy,
Los Angeles,
March 1997

9

Acknowledgements

Firstly, I must acknowledge the invaluable help of Jess Stacy, and his wife, Pat. Secondly, there was the help and encouragement of my old friends, Bert Whyatt and Pete Goulding, who also made valuable suggestions after reading the manuscript. In Cape Girardeau R.F. Peg Meyer was always helpful, and proved a generous host. Mary and Paula Kempe, Walter Kempe, Dutch Estes and Albert Uhl also provided useful background information on Stacy's days in Cape. In Los Angeles John Lucas was another fine host and ever willing to talk and write about his old friend. Keith Keller was helpful with information and constantly spurred me towards completion. Also my appreciation to Mike Hazeldine for his guidance and dedication in the preparation of this book for publication.

My thanks go to the following musicians, whether they answered two questions while rushing from one bandstand to another or wrote lengthy letters in reply to my endless questions: Steve Allen, Byron Baxter, Heinie Beau, Buddy Bergman, Earl Bergman, Noni Bernardi, Pud Brown, Benny Carter, Dick Cary, Buck Clayton, Wild Bill Davison, Pee Wee Erwin, Bud Freeman, Bill French, Murray Gaer, Don Goldie, Bob Greene, Chris Griffin, Marty Grosz, Bob Haggart, Horace Heidt, Bob Higgins, Gardner Hitchcock, Art Hodes, Ed Hubble, Hugh Hudgings, Dean Kincaide, Mannie Klein, Ed Kusby, Joyce Lacey (McDonald), Frankie Laine, Yank Lawson, Dan Lipscomb, Donny McDonald, Rosy McHargue, Marian McPartland, Eddie and Gerry Martin (Di Martino), George Masso, Eddie Miller, Bill Mitchell, Art Nielsen, Tom Pletcher, Nelson Riddle, Bob Ringwald, Arthur Rollini, John Setar, Ray Sherman, Zoot Sims, Ray Skjelbred, Hal Smith, George Snurpus, Ralph Sutton, Mario Toscarelli, Warren Vache, Sr., Gus Van Camp, Bus Watson, Dick Wellstood, Bill Williams, Zeke Zarchy.

And to the following collectors, researchers and record producers: Les Airey, Richard B. Allen, Walter C. Allen, Ernie Anderson, Jeff Atterton, Harry Avery, Sidney D. Brown, Bob Byler, Dave Carey, Peter Carr, Mark Cantor, John Chilton, Michael Coates, Paul Copeland, Henry Donaldson, Jack Dormand, Frank Dutton, Don Eagle, Phil Evans, Mary Jo Frere (of Time-Life Records), Milt Gabler (of Commodore Records), Norman Gentieu, Jim Gordon, John Hammond, Merrill M. Hammond, Norman Harrison, Karl Gert zur Heide, Bob Hilbert, Franz Hoffman, Steve Holzer, Trevor Huyton, Catherine Jacobson, William Kenney, Larry Kiner, Karl Emil Knudsen (of Storyville Records), Bob Krune, Gus R. Kuhlman, Len Kunstadt, Steve Lane, John Leifert, Floyd and Lucille Levin, William Love, Jim Lowe, Dan Mahony, Harry Mackenzie, Mack McCormick, David Meeker, Tony Middleton, Geoffrey Minish, Alun Morgan, Cody Morgan, Bob Morris, John R. Nelson, Helen Oakley (Dance), Florence O'Brien, Hank O'Neal (of Chiaroscuro Records), John A. Payne, Brian Peerless, Art Pilkington, Bert Rehnberg, Dick Reimer, Don Richardson, Bob Rusch, Priscilla Rushton, William Russell, Howard Rye. Len Salmon, Barry Schneck, Rolf Schmidt, Robert J. Schoenberg, Walter Scott, Manfred Selchow, Jim Shacter, Paul B. Sheatsley, Bernard Shirley, Daniel M. Simms, Peggie Snyder, Ruth Spanier, John Steiner,

Jack Stine, John Stock, Klaus Stratemann, Mike Sutcliffe, John Todd, Mike Tovey, Iris Town, Jim Weaver, Derek Webster, C.K. Bozy White and Ken Wilson, as well as all the authors of the books which are cited for each chapter.

Thanks are also due to the following organizations: Chicago Federation of Musicians (Ed Ward); The Department of the Navy; Hogan Jazz Archive, Tulane University; The Institute of Jazz Studies, Rutgers University; Max Factor Co.; National Jazz Foundation Archive (Loughton, England: Ken Jones); Recorded Sound Reference Center, Library of Congress (Sam Brylawski and Edwin Matthias); Streckfus Steamers.

Jess Stacy, Chicago, 1927   *Photo: courtesy of Mrs. Pat Stacy*

1
The Early Days

At 2,340 miles the longest river in the U.S.A., the Mississippi has its source in northern Minnesota. By the time it reaches the Gulf of Mexico it has taken water from dozens of tributaries, including the Illinois, Missouri, and Ohio rivers, and has drained one-third of America. It is estimated that in a year it discharges 785 million cubic yards of water and 406 million tons of mud into the Gulf.

Inevitably this mighty river became a major means of transportation for much of the central U.S.A. For over a 100 years the day-to-day routines of the towns built along the banks of the Mississippi were enlivened by the arrival of a steamboat to load and unload cargo and passengers, to provide a show or, in later years, a moonlight dance. Such distraction was bound to delight the youngsters at any port-of-call, and particularly so in the early years of the twentieth century, when jazz was being created.

This new, exciting music was filtering northwards from New Orleans, near the mouth of the Mississippi, and the excursion steamers coming from that city were making their contribution to the spread of jazz.

North of New Orleans, 550 miles as the crow flies, there was a hamlet in Missouri called Bird's Point. It was about two hundred miles south of St. Louis, across the river from Cairo, remembered as being "right out of Charleston, Missouri, over on the Mississippi River. There's a ferryboat there and it took passengers, cars, wagons and teams across and landed at a little place called Wickliffe, Kentucky. It saved many a mile round." It was also a train layover, at the end of the St. Louis Southwestern ("Cotton Belt") Railway, with a population of about 200. Here, in 1904, Fred and Vada Stacy were living in a converted boxcar.

It was not uncommon for boxcars, with their wheels removed, to be used as a form of housing. Later the Mississippi, always changing its course, washed away Bird's Point and the pasture on which this temporary home had stood.

Frederick Lee Stacy, born April 6, 1862 in De Soto, Illinois, started work with the Illinois Central Railroad in 1880. As a railroad engineer, one of his exploits was driving the first express train from Centralia, Illinois, to New Orleans in 1898, touching 85 miles an hour. Five years before that his train was carrying gold from Centralia to the Chicago World Fair when he was involved in an attempted hijacking. The gold was in a car behind the coal tender. The hijackers disconnected the rest of the train and told Fred Stacy to drive to a point where their transport was waiting. While the train was racing along Stacy turned suddenly, hit the man holding the pistol on him, knocking him down. The robber fell from the cab and lost both his legs. Fred Stacy received a medal from the railroad and some shares of stock.

His wife, Sarah Alexander, always known as Vada, had been born December 24, 1875, of Scottish-Irish descent. An excellent seamstress, she was later able to use this skill to supplement the family income, but times were very hard in the early years of the century. Squirrel was not unknown on the Stacy table. "Respectable, Irish and poor" was one description of the family.

Jess Stacy was born in Bird's Point on August 11, 1904, Fred and Vada Stacy's only child. He was christened Jesse Alexandria, the first name for his fraternal grandfather, the second a revised spelling of his mother's surname. As Jess Stacy told his wife, Pat, his middle name was originally 'Alexander', but there was a very unpleasant family in town whose name ended '. . .der', so Jess' mother decided to change his name to Alexandria. As Pat Stacy says, "A strange whim, but that was Jess' explanation."

A sidelight on the lack of official records in remote areas at that time is provided by Pat Stacy: "In 1904, Bird's Point did not issue birth certificates. Many years after we were married Jess applied for a 'Delayed Birth Certificate' with affidavits from his mother and aunt. Since Bird's Point no longer existed, Jess insisted on listing his place of birth as Cape Girardeau. The certificate was required for Social Security purposes."

"Poor as Job's turkeys" the Stacy family may have been but it provided a secure and loving background for the young Jess, and one to which he would regularly return from his musical travels across America.

Jess Stacy, aged 2
Photo: courtesy of Mrs. Pat Stacy

Jess Stacy as Huckleberry Finn. c.1908
Photo: courtesy of Mrs. Pat Stacy

A few months after Jess' birth the family moved inland to the village of Malden, 68 miles south of Cape Girardeau. At this time Malden had a population of about 2,000, and here Stacy's first tentative steps towards a musical career were taken. At eleven years old he played both snare and bass drum in the Malden Masons' Military Band. When this unit made an appearance at a convention in nearby Caruthersville the local newspaper reported that Stacy was "a manly and talented little man."

As a boy he was still called Jesse. On one occasion his infant teacher, Miss Carrie Machem, put the class names on the blackboard, but wrote "Jessie Stacy". Jess said: "I wish you'd take the ball [ie, the dotted i] from over my name. The kids will think I'm a girl."

During those Malden years he helped out by taking various jobs, cutting lawns, delivering for Western Union, jerking sodas in a drug store, and selling melons on a percentage basis for a Mr. Mert Waggle. "If you made 50 cents a day, it was darn good money," Jess said.

Jess' parents were not musical, so the first music he heard was from a neighbor, an ex-music teacher, who played songs like *Memphis Blues* and *The Trail of The Lonesome Pine*. When he was 12, Vada became a foster mother to an abandoned girl named Jeannette McCombs. Her mother had died and her father had disappeared. With Jeannette came a piano, and Jess would listen when she was being given lessons. Afterwards he would play what he had heard by ear. "When my mother caught me doing that, she said I should have lessons."

However, Vada Stacy has also written that her son learned on a Monarch Cabinet Grand made by Baldwin. "We bought it new for Jess when he was six years old for $500.00." Then again, family friend Mary Kempe wrote, "We are under the impression that the piano belonged to Ruth Cully, a cousin of Jess'." But Pat Stacy only remembers Jess talking of the piano that Jeanette McCombs brought with her.

The lessons were given by Mrs. Florina (or Florine) Morris, and Jess' main memory was of being hustled in and out as fast as possible. A lesson cost 50 cents, which included a piece of pie "to keep my hands occupied. I guess I learned a smattering of music there, but nothing complicated like harmony . . . I didn't much care. I was playing by ear most of the time anyway . . . More or less I'm self-taught."

Some ten years later Joyce Lacey took lessons from Mrs. Morris. She went on to play piano with the Doc Evans band during the 1940s, alongside her husband, clarinetist John McDonald. During the 1980s she played with Jim Joseph's Tailgate Ramblers. Her recollections of Mrs. Morris

Jess Stacy (in uniform!) c.1909
Photo: courtesy of Mrs. Pat Stacy

are kinder: "My lessons from her were some of the happiest times of my life. She was a marvellous teacher, a wonderful person . . . Mrs. Morris realized jazz music is truly creative and encouraged my efforts." Mrs. Morris obviously mellowed in those ten years!

Stacy had no problems with practicing. From his earliest days sitting at a piano for scales or exercises was not drudgery. His mother told a reporter that he was at the piano almost all the time. Unlike other boys who invented excuses to escape from the keyboard, he had to be paid to stop. "I had to pay that boy a quarter to keep him from practicing so his Uncle Will Duncan next door could rest. The quarters I've given that boy!"

Another version of this story is that the uncle disliked music intensely and he would pay his nephew not to practice.

Boyhood friend Raymond 'Peg' Meyer has recalled how after school Stacy would hurry home and practice arpeggios by the hour. He was never heard to complain about having to practice. In fact when he said he was "going to go practice" he said it with the same enthusiasm that the other boys used when talking about playing pool or going fishing.

Friend Florence O'Brien remembered that Vada Stacy, a very down-to-earth person, old-fashioned, countryish, talkative, told her some 30 years later that she sat with her son, day after day, while sewing, and made him learn the piano. Mrs. O'Brien wisely commented, "But I think he would have done it anyway. He was a born musician."

So by 1918, when the Stacy family moved to Cape Girardeau, Jess was already a capable pianist, well able to play by ear, and with some awareness of written music. The arrival in the river town meant contact with like-minded youngsters and with the music which was to be his vocation.

Cape Girardeau, in Cape Girardeau County, Missouri, on the bluffs of the Mississippi River is 131 miles SSE of St. Louis. It is the most northerly point of the Mississippi Delta, the alluvial plain of the Mississippi valley. The town's name derives from a French ensign trader by the name of Jean B. Girardot, who is believed to have settled there about 1720. Louis Lorimier, an Indian agent for the Spanish government, set up a trading post about 1792 at the site of the present city, which has grown steadily over the years to its population in excess of 40,000. In 1920 the official population was 10,252, and, according to Stacy, "every one of them was as square as a bear."

The family's first residence was on the corner of Independence and Lorimer, followed by a small frame two-story house at 14 North Fountain, where they lived for many years. Both buildings have since been demolished. Finally the family moved, a few years after Jess had left home, to 139 South Park.

After 20 years with the Illinois Central, Fred Stacy worked a further fifteen with the Cotton Belt Railroad,

Fred & Vada Stacy outside 139 So. Park Avenue
Photo: courtesy of Mrs. Pat Stacy

before failing eyesight meant he was unable to continue as an engineer. Unworried, carefree – "the exact opposite of my mother", said Jess – he spent a lot of time hunting. Peg Meyer recalled that Fred worked as a clerk in a clothing store for a time, then "in the summer, he was lifeguard at the municipal swimming pool." An excellent swimmer, Fred Stacy spent 14 years as the pool's lifeguard.

Of Mrs. Stacy, Peg Meyer said that when the family first came to Cape she worked for stores downtown, altering clothes, probably at J.C. Finlay's. Later she worked from home, still making alterations, and also making clothes. "She made all the clothes for everybody here in town who had money. She was busy all the time." Pat Stacy confirmed that her mother-in-law "was a darling little person and an expert dressmaker. She welcomed me warmly and I was devoted to her."

And of the family ties, Mary and Paula Kempe, contemporaries of Stacy's in the Cape, said: "They were a closely knit family. Jess was an only child and his parents were very proud of him. He too was devoted to his parents and they came first by him. He was most concerned about their welfare and was a really dutiful son." (Mary and Paula Kempe were twins, two years younger than Jess, and they attended High School with him) .

By 1919 Stacy was becoming known to his fellow pupils for his musical ability. He started work at the Orpheum theater, playing accompaniment to the silent movies being shown. "I would look at the picture and make up my own tunes – sort of instant music. They liked me very well, but I was too young."

Too young, as reported in *The South East Missorian* for June 23, 1919:

> Since the visit of the state labor inspector, John P. Eagan, last week, Jessie Stacy, 14 years old, who has been playing piano at the Orpheum Theater at night, has been compelled to quit his work to comply with the child labor laws.

Another contemporary, Albert Uhl, said that his first recollection of Jess Stacy was seeing and hearing him play piano in a gymnasium at Central High School during noon hour. Dancing was permitted for girl students only. "He was about 14 then and could improvise and 'jazz up' a piece of sheet music at that age."

1922: left to right: Bergman Snider, Peg Meyer, Jess Stacy, Martell Lovell. (The original "Agony Four")

Photo: courtesy of Mrs. Pat Stacy

On one of these occasions in the gym a small group decided to play for their fellow students before classes restarted. As Peg Meyer described it, "Our orchestra was born. It was quickly dubbed The Agony Four by the students, and they were not far wrong." The four players involved were Jess Stacy, piano; Peg Meyer, soprano sax; Martell Lovell, violin; and Bergman Snider, drums. Rehearsals followed and they began to look for engagements outside school. Originally they played for nothing, or perhaps for a banana split when they performed at Bluebird Confectionery (at Broadway and Fountain) or the Sweet Shop on Main Street. The place which really got The Agony Four going during the winter of 1921–22 was the Ideal Hall, a dance floor over Jim Brodtman's restaurant, patronized by the high school and college students. Here the band played for Friday night dances.

"Jess had played a little with different outfits around here, but not very much. I did all the bookings, I bought all the music. We'd get three dollars for those school dances. Then we decided to get so much for the orchestra. There were four of us; I'd charge $15.00. I'd take three dollars and put it in the music fund for the music and anything else we had to have. In my book I give Jess credit for what success I've had in music because he got me interested in playing. If Jess hadn't interested me in music in the first place I'd never have spent my whole life in music."

Peg Meyer was the "Music Man" of Cape Girardeau. Born Raymond Frederick Meyer in 1900, his family moved to Cape in 1912. His wife persuaded him to stop being a bandleader in 1927; thereafter he ran a music store for many years, and continued repairing instruments until well into his eighties. Through the years he was responsible for training and organizing dozens of school bands. His autobiography, "Backwoods Jazz in the Twenties", is full of information and stories about those early days. Mr. Meyer died in 1995.

Meyer switched from soprano to tenor, later adding alto. A new student named Bill Gadbois, from Cairo, Illinois, joined as clarinetist, and the band became Peg Meyer's Melody Kings. The leader recalled that they played in every town in Southeast Missouri, and all over Southern Illinois, using an old Model T Ford. "Our suits were made like white pajamas, had big fluff collars and cuffs and big red pompoms down the front. Mrs. Stacy made them."

That Model T Ford took the band to towns and villages within a 30 mile radius of Cape; places in Missouri such as New Hamburg, Oran, Charleston, Sikeston, and Schumer Springs, or Anna in Illinois. There were locations further afield, 60 miles to Campbell or 80 miles to Hayti, although travelling even ten miles was fraught with difficulties in the early 1920s. There was then no bridge across the river at Cape Girardeau, which posed problems for dates on the west side of the Mississippi. On the eastern side there were still the dirt roads, with their rocks, ruts and chuckholes, with the attendant problems of punctures and overheating radiators. Yet all these setbacks were taken in their stride by these carefree young men, enjoying their escape from home restrictions and their opportunity for music-making.

Peg Meyer said, "We just had a show from the time we left until we got home. There was never a dull moment. We were just kids and looked forward to the next day with anticipation and had no worries. Our folks were all feeding us, we had no financial worries. We just had a hell of a good time. I've seen Stacy laugh so damn much as to almost fall off the piano stool. Gadbois was a nut, and Lovell was a clown, he was crazy

Peg Meyer's Original Melody Kings. Left to right: Bergman Snider, Peg Meyer, Jess Stacy, Bill Gadbois, Martell Lovell

Photo: courtesy of Mrs. Pat Stacy

too. This crazy drummer we had, he had a good sense of rhythm, and Stacy's got that rhythm. Like a metronome. He and Snider, you couldn't rock them off that rhythm. Lovell and I and Gadbois, we used to get together and say, 'OK, in the middle of this piece, we'll slow down or we'll pick-up', [but] do you think we could rock those guys? Hell, no. Stacy just dug down like this, they would listen to each other. You couldn't rock them off that. Stacy and Snider just had that beat, that rhythm. It was so perfect."

The Melody Kings played the popular tunes of the day – numbers like *Tiger Rag*, *Darktown Strutters' Ball*, *Margie*, *Chinatown*, *Japanese Sandman*, and *Panama*.

One recording not included in the discography was made at the Stacy home in the days of the Agony Four, when they played to an "aluminium disc that was soft enough to take the imprint of vibrations off an ordinary phonograph reproducer and record it." When the disc was replayed the music was barely audible, but what was very clear, after a sour note from Lovell's violin, was Fred Stacy's exclamation "Now you played hell!"

As the band's confidence grew they advertised in the show-business magazine, *Billboard*, seeking new outlets for their talent. A telegram from Juarez in Mexico offered them work with a medicine show, but when news arrived a few days later of Pancho Villa's latest attack, in which Americans were killed, their plans for foreign travel were cancelled.

One of Peg Meyer's ventures, in 1922, was to produce a show at the Broadway Theatre in Cape Girardeau for two nights. Supported by his band he had six chorus girls, five vocalists, a dance team, and a drama. Later the show played in Illmo and Chaffee. At the latter location Meyer made an unfortunate joke about the local ball team and the atmosphere at the dance which followed the show was distinctly frosty. Stacy's recollection was that "Probably we were lucky to get out of Chaffee alive!"

It was not long after his arrival in Cape that Jess Stacy began to take formal piano lessons. Professor J. Clyde Brandt was appointed professor of piano and violin at Cape Girardeau University on August 16, 1919. He was head of the music department until he retired in 1957. And it was Professor Brandt who became Stacy's tutor.

Mary Kempe was told by Mr. Brandt of the first time he saw Jess. The professor, who had just moved to Cape Girardeau, lived near the Stacys. He was in his front yard when the youngster came running across the street to see him, excitedly asking, "My name is Jess Stacy and would you give me piano lessons? No one else will because my

R.F. "Peg" Meyer, October 1979
Photo: Derek Coller

fingers are so long, and also I like jazz." Mr. Brandt recalled that at the time Stacy was barefoot.

Stacy himself told Whitney Balliett that Professor Brandt had him playing Beethoven sonatas and Mozart and Bach partitas. "I think it was then I realised that Bach was the first swing pianist." He regretted not practicing more, but he wanted to play in a dance band "and get the hell out of Cape Girardeau."

Peg Meyer was eloquent on the subject of Stacy's behavior and ability in those early days. "Jess was never complacent about his musical knowledge. Besides being a jazz advocate Jess was always a serious and fundamentally sound musician. His great interest in life was always the piano, and he pursued it in a quiet and hard-working manner. He was born with a natural talent and fingers that could span 13 piano keys (five notes over an octave) and developed a determination that he would not just play the piano, he would excel at it."

Meyer said that Jess was outstanding even in the early days of the Agony Four. At their performances there was always a group of admirers standing near the piano listening to him. His improvisations were never the same; his tempo and rhythm were even as a metronome.

Perhaps surprisingly, Stacy still played drums with the Central High School band, under the direction of a Miss Smith. The pianist in the band was Ruth Shivelbine. In later years it was Shivelbine's music store in which Peg Meyer worked as an instrument repairer.

The first steamboat built specifically for the lower Mississippi was the *New Orleans* of 1811. Five years later Henry Miller Shreve launched the *Washington*, a boat of his own design which set the pattern for all future Mississippi steamboats. After the Civil War the rapid expansion of the railways meant that trade increasingly switched from river to rail. As the 19th century came to a close so did the golden era of these "swimming volcanoes", but the age of the excursion boat was about to begin.

Captain John Streckfus, Sr., began carrying freight and passengers on the *Freddie*, a small sternwheeler, in 1884. His company expanded, and in 1901 the steamer *J.S.* was launched. This was the first vessel to be built expressly for excursion service. It was 175 feet long, had a maple dance floor which measured 100 feet by 27 feet, and could carry 2,000 passengers. With the *J.S.*, Streckfus Steamers pioneered and dominated the excursion trade, and its period of greatest popularity coincided with the exodus of jazz from New Orleans.

Joe Streckfus, John's eldest son, was responsible for music on his family's boats. One of his captains, Clarence Elder, wrote, "Capt. Joe, in my opinion, was the man who

The Gordon C. Greene. Peg Meyer played on this boat in 1924

Photo: courtesy of Peg Meyer

did most to exploit music in my day. The men themselves were talented, but it was Capt. Joe who provided them the place to start. He personally trained some of them, always insisted on regular rehearsals, and strove for perfection. He had an uncanny sense when appraising a musician, and in audience reaction. You may note that I harp on the Streckfus excursion boats. None of the others had what was called good solid beat rhythm music with the dixieland flavor."

Pianist Fate Marable began working for Streckfus Steamers about 1907, but it was not until 1917 that he used New Orleans musicians for weekend excursions out of that city. The following year he employed the young Louis Armstrong in place of trumpeter Peter Bocage for weekend dances on the *S.S. Sidney*, and in 1919 the Marable band, with Armstrong, sailed on the *St. Paul* from St. Louis for excursions up and down the river.

In 1920 Marable, again with Louis Armstrong, was on the *S.S. Capitol*. On board was the band which made such an impression upon the young musicians who heard it. Jess Stacy never forgot its impact. He has told of the *Capitol* visiting Cape Girardeau three times a year to play excursions, and how he went down to the levee to be astounded by this new band with its new trumpet player. "It was like nothing I had heard in my life." Stacy recalled the personnel as Henry Allen, Sr., Louis Armstrong, trumpets; Johnny Dodds, clarinet; Fate Marable, piano; Baby Dodds, drums; and possibly Pops Foster, bass. He remembers them playing *Skeleton Jangle*, *Tiger Rag*, *Whispering* and, most exciting of all, *Railroad Man*. "You can't imagine such energy, such musical fireworks as Louis Armstrong on that boat." As he told Bob Rusch, "The music sounded so good out on the river. They'd go out in the middle . . . and the paddlewheel would be turning slowly to keep it from drifting downstream. People danced there. That band carried me away. When I heard that band, I said, 'That's what I want to be. I want to play on the riverboats.'"

An advertisement in Cape Girardeau's paper, *The South East Missourian*, for May 1921 still conveys, more than 70 years on, something of the excitement the boats aroused:

STEAMER CAPITOL EXCURSION
Thursday, June 2nd, 1921

The boat that set New Orleans wild for 7 consecutive months. Your last opportunity to ride this marvelous Excursion Palace. It leaves for the upper Mississippi immediately after this trip. Music by 10 – Capitol Harmony Syncopators. Captain Cornelius McGee. Crew of 125.　　　　　Can accomodate 1200 couples　　　　　Adm. 75c

Both Jess Stacy and Peg Meyer have emphasised Fate Marable's skill as a band pianist. When the *Capitol* was in port Stacy would go on board to play for him, and to be given advice on how to play with a band. In the evening during the excursion Jess would stand by the piano absorbing everything that Marable played. As Stacy told Marian McPartland, "He was one of the best band piano players I've ever known. I listened to him a lot." And to Whitney Balliett he said, "I marvelled at the way he held everything together."

"In 1921," Peg Meyer recalled, "the steamer *Majestic* was in Alton, Illinois, for an excursion and the orchestra went swimming in the Mississippi. The piano player drowned and the sax man got water on the lungs and could no longer play. They picked up temporary members in St. Louis but dance musicians were scarce in those days and they could not find permanent replacements. Three days later the boat was in Cape Girardeau and Jess and I finished out the season. This was the Harvey Berry orchestra out of Davenport, Iowa, and the first group that Jess played with on Mississippi riverboats. We played nothing but stock arrangements."

Meyer has given the personnel as Bill Bieberback, trumpet; unknown trombone; Jimmy Cannon, clarinet; Peg Meyer, tenor; Harvey Berry, violin, leader; Jess Stacy, piano; Johnny Day, drums. He and Stacy were with the band for about two months. For the last two weeks of the season Bieberback's place was taken by Carl 'Pickles' Cullison, recalled as "a wild bastard. He was always broke." Cullison carried a telegram from Paul Whiteman, offering him a job, until it was just a rag. Jimmy Cannon achieved a modest fame with the Ray Miller and Ray Noble orchestras. Of the Berry band Stacy said, "It was a bad, awful band. I don't recall anybody in it. Berry played violin; looked like Valentino; all the girls adored him."

The *Majestic*, owned by the General Excursion Company (D.W. Wishard Line), went down the Mississippi, up the Ohio as far as Paducah, Kentucky, and then back to St. Louis. Peg Meyer remembered excursions being made from many river towns, including Cairo and Shawneetown in Illinois, from Hickman, Paducah and Henderson in Kentucky.

This summer season of 1921 was excellent training for the young musicians, despite their suffering many of the problems associated with riverboats; being stranded on sandbars, the danger of fire (in fact the *Majestic* was burnt to the hull at the start of the 1922 season in Havana, Illinois, its first port of call), and fights on board. The band played *Ain't We Got Fun?* throughout a battle between a gang and the crew during an excursion from Peoria. Stacy said they kept a slapstick style musical background going and when the boat docked all the police in town were waiting for them.

On Labor Day, September 1921, in St. Louis, the *Majestic* had a private excursion. After listening to the top local bands of Charlie Creath and Dewey Jackson, which had been booked for that evening, Stacy and Meyer went to the *J.S.* to hear Louis Armstrong with Fate Marable. This was Armstrong's final season with Marable.

One must stress again the extraordinary effect that Louis Armstrong's playing had upon all the young musicians who heard him during the 1920s. He was the genius who ensured that jazz moved on from its ragtime origins, who was so far ahead of other musicians in technique, tone and rhythmic freedom.

Playing with the Berry band also gave Stacy an incentive to improve his reading ability. His ear was fast enough to catch such popular tunes of the day as *Whispering* and *Margie*, but not the intricate introductions the band liked to use.

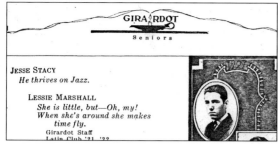

MISS SMITH - - - Director.
RUTH SHIVELBINE, Piano   LENORA OCHS, Violin
HOLLY ROBINSON. Violin   OTILLIA EGGIMANN, Violin
OHN POPP, Cornet   ALBERTA MEYSTEDT, Cor
KELLY BROWN, Trombone   LORENZ FISHER, Saxophone
JESSIE STACY, Drums

Extracts from the School Annuals for 1921 and
1922 Central High School, Cape Girardeau,
Missouri

Courtesy of Mr. Albert Uhl

With the excitement of the river trips behind them, Stacy and Meyer returned to the more mundane routine of Cape Girardeau – school, graduation and the Agony Four. The 1922 High School Yearbook stated, beneath a photograph of Stacy, "He thrives on jazz." Stacy graduated in May 1922, and that same month Walter Kempe, Sr, and Claude Judas arrived to take charge of Clark's Music Store, at 116 North Main Street. It was here that Stacy began work, sweeping floors, tending the boiler and playing sheet music for the customers. After the store closed he would sweep it out to the sounds of the latest jazz records. "Clark's was unquestionably the best-swept music store in the country at the time."

Stacy's appreciation of the new music was encouraged by listening to records, although there was little classic jazz being issued in 1922. What was generally available was jazz-flavored dance or novelty music, much of it influenced by the Original Dixieland Jazz Band. First recorded in 1917, the O.D.J.B. was a link between ragtime and New Orleans jazz.

Stacy recalled playing a one-nighter on the *St. Paul* steamer, as well as spending a month on the *G.W. Hill*, with a poor band whose leader he did not remember. It is possible that these events took place during the summer of 1922.

Reedman George Snurpus, who was born in 1906 in Evansville, Indiana, recalled: "I met Jess Stacy and Bix Beiderbecke when the steamboat *Verne Swain* stopped at Evansville. I was 16, just got my union card, and the union called, said they needed a clarinet player for two cruises. I didn't play sax and the steward on board loaned me his C-melody sax. I took it home and the next night I played everything on it. I had a write-up in the Evansville paper – 'Local Clarinet Jams With Calliope.' Of course you couldn't hear me, but Jess and I became very friendly."

Snurpus thinks the Evansville stay actually lasted several days. This is the only mention of Jess playing on the *Verne Swain*. Bix did not play in a riverboat band with Stacy, but he could have been in town with the steamer *Michigan City*.

Work with Peg Meyer's Original Melody Kings continued, enlivened by a domestic celebration. The local paper reported that "Jesse Stacy plays wedding march" when Selma Meyer, Peg's sister, was married in October 1922.

Early in 1923 the band lost the services of Martell Lovell, as *The South East Missourian* of March 2, 1923, reported:

Raymond 'Peg' Meyer, Bergman Snider and Jesse Stacy entertain with farewell party at Ideal Hall for Martell Lovell, who will leave soon for California; the young musicians have been playing together four years.

Lovell went on to play trumpet with Walter Davidson's Louisville Loons. When he died sometime in the 1960s he was playing trumpet with Vincent Lopez. Bergman Snider continued to play with Peg Meyer until 1927. In 1988 he was living in St. Louis, but in a nursing home, sadly too ill to be interviewed.

When the summer of 1923 arrived, Stacy continued to spread his wings. He recalls playing with Peg Meyer and Berg Snider on the packet boat, the *Bald Eagle*. This job was probably short-lived because Stacy was out of town for part of the summer, playing with another unidentified band. *The South East Missourian* for August 8, 1923:

Jesse Stacy is back in Cape Girardeau after a sojourn in Cincinati and Springfield; will be at Clark Music store to give special attention to sheet music department.

It has been reported that Stacy played winter residencies at the Coliseum Ballroom in Davenport during this period, but Stacy himself said this was incorrect.

A Streckfus advertisement in 1924 listed the following bands on the company's boats:

Polk Burke's Syncopating Artists
Tony's Famous Iowan Band
Jules Buffano and his Famous Montmartre Orchestra of Chicago
New Orleans Harmony Serenaders
Max Newby's Melody Makers
Schaefer's Melody Kings

Tony's Famous Iowan Band from Davenport was featured on the *Capitol*. It was led by trumpeter Tony Catalano, an early admirer of pioneer jazzman Joe 'King' Oliver. Catalano had been a bandleader since 1907, and had employed Fate Marable in a trio on the *J.S.* in 1908. His whole band had been influenced by Papa Celestin's Tuxedo Jazz Band during a visit to New Orleans in 1923. As Duncan Schiedt commented, "For at least 20 years a Catalano band on any of the Streckfus Line boats guaranteed good jazz indeed."

Tony's Famous Iowans,
April 1923 (Pre-Jess Stacy)

Photo: courtesy of Streckfus Steamers, Inc.

Streckfus Steamers could provide little data on the Tony Catalano band. As they explained, "We lost all our records on these and other bands in a fire aboard one of our wharf boats years ago." However, a few itinerary details were available.

Catalano "played on the Steamer *Capitol* in 1922-24. The *Capitol* would spend the winter in New Orleans offering excursions and moonlight dances and would 'tramp' north and would operate out of St. Paul during the summer months. Tony's band would work the off-season in cities like Chicago and play on the boat in the summer. The *Capitol*, when cruising north in the Spring or back to New Orleans in the fall, would stop to make about 60 excursions in the various river towns along the way."

The excursion season ran from Memorial Day in late May to Labor Day in early September. The furthest the steamers travelled north on the Mississippi was to St. Paul, Minnesota; up the Illinois as far as Peoria; and along the Ohio to Pittsburgh, Pennsylvania.

Jess Stacy recalled the *Capitol* reaching Cape Girardeau early one evening. When he got there the band was not playing and Catalano was looking for a pianist. Stacy, wearing knickerbockers, was pointed out to Catalano, who said, "Kid, get some long pants and get back here right away, you've got a job for tonight only." The job lasted a little longer than that.

In a 1938 *Down Beat* article Catalano was reported as saying that he had wanted to hear "Jimmy Stacy" because Jimmy Cannon and Dick Hoffmeister had said he was pretty darn good. "And he was more than good, bashful though. Scared stiff the first time he played for Tony."

Stacy gave the personnel as Tony Catalano, cornet; Tal Sexton, trombone; Jimmy Cannon, clarinet; Nate Marblestone, alto; Dick Hoffmeister, tenor and violin; Jess Stacy, piano; Paul Miltlina, banjo; Pat Pattison, bass; Paul Smith, drums. As he said, "This band came close to playing a little. We played all the dixieland tunes. These guys were all pros. I was lucky to get to play in a good band. This was a very good jazz band. Had to be to play on that riverboat." He did not have to read too much with Tony's Iowans. One of the band's jobs was to play a half-hour or so before the boat sailed, performing its hottest

Calliope being played on the "Natchez",
New Orleans
Photo: Derek Coller

numbers, like *Skeleton Jangle* and *Sensation Rag*, to get people to buy a ticket.

Another task on the steamers which Stacy hated, although he was paid an extra five dollars a week for it, was playing the steam calliope. The calliope is a combination of steam whistles activated from a two-octave metal keyboard. It was located near the smokestack. Playing it meant coping with cinders from the stack, clouds of steam and very hot keys. Stacy wore a raincoat and hat, as well as either gloves or tape on his fingers. The whooper, as it was called, was used to attract people to the boat trips. Even if it was 5 a.m. when the boat reached a town Stacy would have to get up and "play the damn calliope" to let people know the boat had arrived. The one advantage was that the view from the top deck was a good one!

A typical Stacy comment when talking about this was, "I guess you could say that calliope players were the original hot keyboard artists."

It was probably on the *Capitol* that Jess, after losing at cards, threw them overboard and remarked "I must be a whiz at love!"

At a stopover in Davenport Stacy saw Bix Beiderbecke for the first time when the cornetist came aboard the *Capitol*. Jimmy Cannon and Tal Sexton welcomed Bix by singing his chorus from *Riverboat Shuffle*, which he had just recorded with The Wolverines. Bix borrowed Catalano's cornet and sat in with the band. Then, "Bix sat down at the piano and played the kind of stuff I'd always had in the back of my mind, but had never been able to express. He played a song called *Baby Blue Eyes* with the same impressionistic harmony he used years later on *In A Mist*."

Beiderbecke had a powerful influence on Stacy's approach to his piano compositions, as can be heard in many of his later solo recordings for the Commodore label. Throughout his career Stacy was the major performer to retain the Bix Beiderbecke piano pieces in his repertoire.

On another occasion the *Capitol* had docked in Dubuque, Iowa, and the band was heard by Joe Kayser, the drummer-leader of a territory group. Stacy played the Zez Confrey composition *Poor Buttermilk*, impressing Kayser to the extent that he offered the pianist a job.

Joe Kayser's Band. Chicago, early 1925. Jess is at the piano, age 21. His first job in Chicago.
Photo: courtesy of Mrs. Pat Stacy

Zez Confrey has been unjustly denigrated by jazz enthusiasts, his piano pieces being written off as 'novelty ragtime', but there can be no doubting the longevity of compositions like *Kitten On The Keys* or the dexterity required to play them. Pianist Dick Wellstood considered *Poor Buttermilk* the most difficult number in his repertoire during the 1970s. As he said, "*Jim Jams* [by Roy Bargy] is hard, but it comes second to *Poor Buttermilk*."

Joe Kayser became a bandleader in 1920. Following the example of the Jan Garber-Milton Davis orchestra, he was one of the first to undertake onenighters on a regular basis. Kayser's offer of a job came at an opportune moment for Stacy. The season with Catalano was coming to an end, whereas Kayser held out the promise of a booking at the Arcadia Ballroom in Chicago. To quote Stacy on his reasons for joining Kayser in August 1924, "It was a desire to see the big city. I was full of dreams and hoping I would make good."

Not that the band was an ideal one for an aspiring jazz pianist. Stacy's memories were: "We played stock arrangements – fair dance band. Three saxes, three brass, four rhythm. This was a no place band. Jimmy Cannon, clarinet, was the only one any good." Trombonist Jack Read was possibly present, as perhaps was bassist Pat Pattison, with Kayser still playing drums. Phil Wing on saxophone was certainly a member, he and Stacy becoming good friends.

The band played many small towns in Wisconsin and Iowa and Illinois, before playing in Chicago's Arcadia Ballroom (at Wilson and Broadway) for six months. After a summer job in Duluth the band broke up "and I found myself back in Chicago, stranded and on my own. It was the beginning of a ten year scuffle."

2

Chicago

In 1925, when Jess Stacy's ten year scuffle began, President Coolidge was starting his second term of office, Scott Fitzgerald's "The Great Gatsby" was published, and mobsters Al Capone and Johnny Torrio escaped separate assassination attempts organized by Hymie Weiss. New songs published included *Dinah, Riverboat Shuffle, Sleepytime Gal* and *Sweet Georgia Brown*.

National prohibition of the sale of alcohol in the U.S.A. had come into effect at 12:01 a.m. on January 17, 1920, with the 18th Amendment (the Volstead Act). The Act came after 100 years of continual and growing propaganda against the demon drink, but its effect was the opposite of that intended by the temperance lobby. A majority of the population considered it bad law and were content to be supplied illegally by bootleggers, rum-runners, or gangsters under any other name. Enormous profits were generated in meeting this public demand, laying the basis for organised crime for years ahead. It also meant that there were thousands of saloons, cafes and speakeasies which sold the beer and bath-tub gin that the gangsters provided. Some 5,000 of these establishments operated in New York City alone in 1923, and no doubt Chicago could rival that figure. In 1927 Al Capone was reported to be earning $60 million from booze. Federal estimates for 1928 and 1929 were that profits from bootlegging were close to $350 million a year. For the budding jazzmen it was good fortune that these dives provided work for a pianist or for a small band, and that the mobsters liked such music. Jess Stacy was to see a lot of these speakeasies and these gangsters during the next few years.

One of his first outings on arrival in Chicago was to see trumpeter King Oliver and his Dixie Syncopators at the Plantation Cafe. Oliver had just begun what was to prove to be a two year engagement there. Stacy was duly impressed by Oliver's playing and he became a frequent visitor to the Plantation.

He spent the Easter holiday in Cape Girardeau, with his parents, presumably on leave from the Joe Kayser band. That same month he joined the American Federation of Musicians in Chicago, Local 208, on April 21, 1925.

It may have been during this particular stay at the Arcadia ballroom that Stacy visited Alan Spencer at the American Conservatory of Music for piano lessons, but Spencer wanted him to stop playing jazz for six months, which Stacy could not afford to do.

After the Kayser band broke up that summer Stacy's activities are untraced. No doubt work in speakeasies kept him occupied through the fall and winter. It may have been around this time that he worked briefly with the Maurie Sherman orchestra for tea-dances at the College Inn of the Sherman Hotel. Stacy said of Sherman, "I suppose I used to give him a lot of trouble. He was the leader and I was always trying to play the way I wanted." Finally, despite his misgivings about "cornball bands", he joined Al Katz and his Kittens at the start of 1926.

Billed as a "novelty dance orchestra", it could be said that the Kittens pandered to the public's desire for mickey-mouse music. The Katz catchphrase, captured on their recording of *Ace In The Hole*, went as follows:

Katz: Are you ready, kittens?
Band: Meow.
Katz: Let's go!

Stacy worked with Katz for about six months, quoting January to July, and his memories were, "The band was very commercial – a poor man's Fred Waring. It was a show band. Funny hats, etc. We had a good jazz trumpet and trombone, but in those days you were lucky if you got to take a chorus. It was just another unhappy job for me. This band would just barely pass, but one had to make a living."

Al Katz and his Kittens at the Million Dollar Pier, 1926.
Stacy is second from the right.

The trumpet and trombone players mentioned were Fred Rollison and Jerry Bump, who had achieved a modicum of local fame playing with Hitch's Happy Harmonists during the early years of the decade. The Harmonists, a pioneer white jazz band, were best known for the inclusion of Hoagy Carmichael, with his early compositions, in their ranks.

Basic information about the Katz band at this period comes from a review in *Variety* for April 28, 1926, when it was appearing at Young's Million Dollar Pier in Atlantic City. After closing there on May 16, dates in Cincinnati and Chicago were scheduled. A recording session for Victor is mentioned in the review and this duly took place on May 3. Three titles were recorded but only *Ace In The Hole* was released. Stacy cannot be heard on this title, and Rollison's strong lead is the sole contribution of interest.

When asked by Bill Mitchell what became of Katz, Stacy remarked

Al Katz and his Kittens (Only eight-pieces now).
Jess Stacy in rear centre
Photo: courtesy of Mrs. Pat Stacy

in typical manner, "He's probably gone to that big sandbox in the sky."

Variety again, July 28, 1926, indicated that Stacy was back with Joe Kayser. A full page advertisement reported that Joe Kayser and His Gang were at The Pier in Gordon State Park, Lake St. Mary's, Ohio, for the summer season. Readers were invited to "Meet the Gang", though only names, no instruments, were listed. The personnel was: Joe Kayser, drums; Leo 'Fuzzy' Lambertz, trumpet; Jess Stacy, piano; Cobby Elsner, bass, tuba; Jimmy Ray, Arch Cole, Mutt Alesworth, Bill Smith, George Dodge, and Charles Smith, instruments unknown.

Back in Chicago, Stacy's next known engagement was with the Sig Meyer band, at the White City Ballroom, where violinist Meyer led a second band on two nights a week, Thursday and Saturday. Jimmy McPartland, who was in the resident band, recalled Meyer's personnel as including Muggsy Spanier, cornet; Rosy McHargue, clarinet; Jess Stacy, piano; and, he thought, George Wettling, drums.

Jess and Helen Stacy c. 1925
Photo: courtesy of Mr. R.F. "Peg" Meyer

It was about this time that Stacy met and married Helen Robinson. "She seemed very nice," said Iris Town. Stacy recalls it as a young, romantic affair, with little thought behind it. They had no money; he worked nights and slept days. Stacy's dedication to his music is shown by his comments to Keith Keller: "She didn't have any heart for jazz. Especially as long as jazz didn't yield more money."

The Stacys' only child, a son, was born in Chicago on June 2, 1927, and christened Frederick Jess. He too went on to a successful career in music, as will be seen as this story unfolds.

Somewhere in the story one must insert the first time that Stacy met Eddie Condon. Condon recalled it in the following words: "Every once in a while a musician finds himself in some unmusical company. That is, if he wants to eat regularly. My appetite forced me to take a club date at the Palmer House in Chicago one night some years ago. The band was one of those salt-mine combinations. I was planning to spend a very miserable evening until I heard the piano player. It was a case of love at first sight. He was showing me some new chords on *China Boy* and I asked his name. His name turned out to be Jess Stacy."

It was also about this time (1926) that Stacy first met pianist Joe Sullivan. "When we were both struggling around Chicago trying to make a living with our own style of music, we helped each other get jobs. If he heard of an opening he would call me, and I would do the same for him. Believe me, the going was rough."

In late 1926, tenor player Floyd Town organized a unit for an engagement at the Midway Gardens ballroom at 60th and Cottage Grove Avenue. For most of its life, the Midway – "Where Better Dancers Meet" – was owned by the Edelweiss Brewing Company. It occupied an entire city block, with a large interior court. Eddie Condon said it was the biggest dance hall on the South Side until the Trianon was built. "It had terraces and a balcony; the band sat in a shell on the balcony and poured it down on the people."

Muggsy Spanier was in the band and he recalled how Danny Altier was soon added on alto sax, followed by Stacy. "Jess played our kind of music and fell right in with the mood of the band. Jess and I got along fine, we always have, because we have the same tastes in music . . . We certainly couldn't have asked for a better piano man in that band. That was some band we had!"

Stacy's own account was that he was terribly hard up and badly needed the job with Town. "It was the middle of winter . . . snow everywhere and awfully cold. I didn't have an overcoat, but I did have a tuxedo, so I put it on and started out from the North Side where I lived for the Midway Gardens on the South Side. I had to take the L train and when I got to the Midway Gardens I was freezing cold, shivering and my hands were blue! Muggsy remembered me . . . took me up to the band room and gave me a pint of bathtub gin. I drank the whole pint and, the next set, played with the band. I remember the tune we played – *Poor Little Rich Girl*. After we finished Muggsy said, 'That's our man! Hire him!' And they did. Boy, I needed that job.

"This was the first good, hot band I had played with since the riverboat days and it was wonderful for me to be playing with such a band. Muggsy was the sparkplug and swung the whole band."

There are two known photographs of this group, the presumed earliest showing nine musicians: Muggsy Spanier, cornet; Cy Simadel, trombone; Frank Teschemacher, clarinet, alto; Danny Altier, alto; Floyd Town, tenor; Jess Stacy, piano; Earl Wright, banjo, guitar; George Tupper, tuba; Al (Wop) Waller, drums. (Reproduced in "Muggsy Spanier: The Lonesome Road.") In the second photograph (see below) an unknown cornet player is added. The personnel seems to have been reasonably stable throughout the engagement.

Floyd Town and the Midway Garden Band. Left to right: Muggsy Spanier, cornet; Al Waller, Drums; Danny Altier, reeds; Cy Simadel, trombone; Jess Stacy, piano; Frank Teschemacher, clarinet; Earl Wright, banjo; George Tupper, tuba; unknown, cornet; Floyd Town, reeds, leader   *Photo: courtesy of the late Mrs. Iris Town*

An advertisement for the Midway Gardens gave the playing schedule:

The Midway Dancing Gardens afford lovers of dancing an opportunity to keep step to Floyd Town and his Midway Orchestra every Tuesday, Thursday, Saturday and Sunday nights, with the special matinee session on Sunday afternoon.

Floyd Town, early 1930s?
Photo: courtesy of the late Mrs. Iris Town

Around this period the ballroom had a series of dates featuring 'band battles'. One night Floyd Town, Husk O'Hare, Charlie Pierce, Louis Armstrong, Del Delbridge, Verne Buck, Herbie Mintz, Elmer Kaiser and Doc Cook were on hand. Perhaps this was the night that Muggsy Spanier persuaded Louis Armstrong to sing a number with the Town band.

On November 7, 1927, the famous jam session at Sam Beer's "My Cellar", known as the Three Deuces, 222 North Street, took place. Paul Whiteman's orchestra had opened that day at the Chicago Theatre, and after the show Bix Beiderbecke, Tommy and Jimmy Dorsey and Hoagy Carmichael went to the Three Deuces. Up to 100 musicians moved in and out during the night, including Jess Stacy, Joe Sullivan, George Wettling and Eddie Condon.

Stacy has recalled sitting in the balcony of the Chicago Theatre listening to Bix with Paul Whiteman: "I was a jitterbug over Bix. He was my idol. I wanted to play like that. I wanted to think like that." Listening to Bix was just one of the musical pleasures which Stacy enjoyed during these years. Bessie Smith's voice was another, Stacy considering her the greatest blues singer who ever lived. Naturally Stacy also admired Louis Armstrong and Earl Hines.

Carrol Dickerson had been leading the orchestra at the Sunset Cafe. Featured with the band were Armstrong and Hines. But early in 1927 Joe Glaser, whose mother owned the Sunset, decided to feature Louis, and the resulting 11-piece Louis Armstrong Stompers included Hines on piano, Honoré Dutrey, trombone; Boyd Atkins, clarinet, alto; Joe Walker, alto; Pete Briggs, tuba; Tubby Hall, drums; and Willie Hamby, second pianist. No doubt the young Chicagoans heard Armstrong and Hines with both Dickerson's orchestra and with the Stompers. Stacy, Muggsy Spanier, and Frank Teschemacher "lived" in the Sunset Cafe. After finishing at the Midway Gardens about 1 a.m. they would rush over to the Cafe on 35th and Calumet, which did not close until about 6 a.m., to hear these great musicians. They knew most of the tunes the Sunset Cafe band played and would sit in to give the regular members a rest.

Stacy liked Earl Hines "an awful lot", but said that, stylistically, this wasn't the way he wanted to go. He often told the story of listening intently to Hines at the Sunset Cafe when Jelly Roll Morton tapped him on the shoulder and said, "'That boy can't play piano.' Jelly, of course, had more of a simple style; he didn't get all over the keyboard like Earl."

Other magnets for these young men were The Nest, where Jimmie Noone was playing, and the Plantation, where King Oliver was featured.

32

During these years there was a mutual respect among the young pianists struggling to survive in the music business. Art Hodes, Tut Soper and Roy Wasson have spoken of this and of their appreciation for Jess Stacy's help. Veteran Chicago pianist Dan Lipscomb said, "Jess Stacy has been my idol for many, many years. During the '20s Jess was working in a band directed by Floyd Town at the Midway Gardens, which was only a few blocks from where I was working at the Pershing Ballroom. Our paths crossed quite often."

Roy Wasson frequently visited Stacy at home. They would play all afternoon, then go to the Midway. "I sat in for Jess a couple of times, and I remember Benny Goodman, in short pants, sitting in with the band."

The Floyd Town engagement at the Midway Gardens finally ended early in 1928. Muggsy Spanier says they left because the boss decided they should wear funny hats and play waltzes. Town then obtained a booking at the Triangle Café.

The Triangle Café, on Des Plaines Avenue at Harrison Street, was in Forest Park. Iris Town described the Café: "It was put up where two streets came together, so the red brick building was in the shape of a triangle. It was quite old but had been kept in good repair. The inside was a large dining room, with a good sized dance floor." Ray Reynolds was the master of ceremonies for the floor show.

Everyone was enthusiastic about their part in this band, the settled personnel of which was: Muggsy Spanier, cornet; Floyd O'Brien, trombone; Frank Teschemacher, clarinet, alto; Danny Altier, alto; Floyd Town, tenor; Jess Stacy, piano; Pat Pattison, bass; George Wettling, drums. Spanier called it the best band he ever played in. Wettling said much the same, while Stacy's comments were, "We played dance music and swung like mad . . . this band was a swinger. I was very happy."

In June 1928 Teschemacher left the Triangle to go to New York with Eddie Condon. His replacement was Rosy McHargue, who had been with Stacy in the Meyer band. Iris Town, Floyd's widow, also remembered pianist Dave Rose and trombonist John Carsella being in the band. As she did not meet her husband until May 1928, at the Triangle, it is possible that Rose worked as a substitute for Stacy, with Carsella replacing O'Brien towards the end of the Triangle engagement.

Unfortunately no recordings exist of this all-star Chicagoan orchestra, though George Wettling did suggest that a recording session had taken place, but was unissued. The nearest we can get now to the sound of the Town orchestra are the two titles, *I'm Sorry, Sally*/*My Gal Sal*, recorded for Vocalion on October 22, 1928, under Danny Altier's name. Spanier, Stacy, Pattison, Wettling, and Altier (and Carsella?) from the Town band are on the record, and despite a period vocal on the first title, the front line soloists acquit themselves well. Stacy backs the vocal in what was to become his trademark style, and on *My Gal Sal* contributes his first recorded solo. (Danny Altier told Jim Gordon that the sides were to have been released under Muggsy Spanier's name, but Jack Kapp refused to have a name like "Muggsy" on the label).

Richard Hadlock, in his highly recommended "Jazz Masters of the Twenties", points out that Stacy had already formed his mature style. "Stacy displays superb control and an advanced sense of dynamics throughout his solo on *My Gal Sal* and behind the dismal vocal on *I'm Sorry, Sally*."

An unidentified newspaper clipping, containing a radio station listing, shows:

208M WNBA 1440K 7:30 p.m.
Floyd Town and his Air Kings
Ray Reynolds; Frank Frederick Basso
The wrecking crew, Jess Stacy,
Danny Altier, Muggsy Spanier

Reynolds was the m.c., Basso presumably a singer, but the exact purpose of 'The wrecking crew' is a mystery. Could it be the first example of a band-within-a-band?

The owner of the Triangle Café, Mickey Rafferty, was either a gangster himself or a close associate of such hoodlums. It was he who believed that five letters in both one's first and last names was lucky. So he had Town's name changed to Towne for all the Triangle advertising, and Town continued this variation for a time after the band left the Café.

Various stories have been told about Rafferty and this particular Town band. Eddie Condon tells of Spanier and Wettling being asked to take a break without pay, to which they mildly protested. Rafferty took them for a ride in his car, closed the windows and exploded a tear-gas gun – "a small weapon disguised as a fountain pen" – on them. But Stacy thought that "George embellished a lot," and Stacy's version of this story sounds more reasonable: "One night at Forest Park, George Wettling got juiced. A mob guy took him out in his car, fired off a tear-gas bomb, closed the car door and left George there. George cried for a month."

Left to right: Jess Stacy, Frank
Teschemacher and George Wettling. c.1928

Muggsy Spanier and Jess Stacy,
probably at Lake Delavan, c.1928

Both photos: courtesy of the late Mrs. Ruth Spanier and Bert Whyatt

Then there was the time that Rafferty was told by the union to raise the musicians' wages. "What union?" he asked. "Give me the address and I'll bomb it."

The most famous story is another told by Wettling: "We could see those rods come up – and duck. At the Triangle Club, the boss was shot in the stomach one night, but we kept on working. After that he walked sort of bent over."

Iris Town told it a little differently. During the week which the band had free after leaving the Triangle and before starting work at the Cinderella, Rafferty was in a fight. Trying to escape from the hoodlum over a parking lot fence, Rafferty was shot in the stomach. He was lucky to survive and he never did regain full use of one of his legs. Mrs. Town thought it was Joe Saltis, a Polish psychopath, who shot Rafferty.

Her view of Rafferty was a little kinder than that of the musicians, probably because she and her husband were on friendlier terms with him. Her comment was: "He had a background of working with some gangsters. Mickey was a tough, feisty, little Irishman. He liked nothing better than to do his little dance routine for the customers every night. He was shot a week after the band left – much to everyone's surprise. I know he never danced again."

The Town band left the Triangle during the summer of 1928. Muggsy Spanier said they were there for six months, which fits better than Stacy's claim that the engagement lasted nine. On leaving the Triangle, Stacy and Spanier joined Joe Kayser at the Merry Garden Ballroom. Spanier has spoken of the value of a good friend, saying that he and Stacy always managed to make the best of any situation, enjoying themselves no matter what.

The personnel for the Joe Kayser band at the Merry Garden and Municipal Pier is reputed to have included, in addition to Spanier and Stacy, Marty Marsala, trumpet; Floyd O'Brien, trombone; Bud Jacobson, clarinet, tenor; George Wettling, drums. Danny Alvin who may have played drums in the band for a time, suggested that bassist Steve Brown; and even Benny Goodman on clarinet were also present. Another possible member was tenor player Joe Masek. Teschemacher has been named, but Spanier contradicted this: "Joe Kayser and I tried to get Tesch in there but they wouldn't have him and I was pretty sore. The job with Kayser lasted four months, then we separated. Jess toured the gin mills, it was hard getting a job, and I joined Ray Miller." Spanier went into the Miller orchestra about October, 1928.

The musicians in the Floyd Town and Joe Kayser bands were all members of that elite group of young jazzmen known as the Chicagoans. Bud Freeman, a founder member, said: "We, the Austin High Gang, were very much influenced by Louis and King Oliver and Bix, and so what we played was our impression of what we heard, and that was later to be called Chicago style. But the real inventors of the Chicago style were King Oliver and Louis. That was the melting pot – that was the place to be if you wanted to hear good jazz . . . you had to go to Chicago." Freeman should also have quoted the New Orleans Rhythm Kings as an early influence upon himself and his friends.

Bud Freeman, Frank Teschemacher, Jimmy McPartland and his brother, Dick, were students at Austin High School in Chicago, and this association led to the informal grouping of young jazz musicians called the Austin High Gang. Like-minded players, including Eddie Condon, Muggsy Spanier, Floyd O'Brien, Dave Tough, Gene Krupa and

Joe Sullivan, were soon honorary members. Stacy played with all these jazzmen, though remaining on the outer fringes of the gang.

George Avakian has written of the tension, urgency and fire which is found in Chicago style jazz, with its various stylistic features, such as the Chicago shuffle (the rhythm section plays double-time while the soloist remains in the original tempo), explosions (sudden flares) and double endings (two extra bars added to the final chorus).

The most influential Chicago style recordings were organized by Eddie Condon and Red McKenzie. Their first records were made in December 1927, under their names, with Jimmy McPartland, a Bix Beiderbecke disciple, on cornet, Frank Teschemacher clarinet, Bud Freeman tenor, Joe Sullivan piano, Condon, banjo; Jim Lanigan, bass; Gene Krupa drums, and McKenzie, vocal. These records, for the OKeh Phonograph Corporation, introduced the Chicagoans to a far wider audience and remain today as leading examples of the style. The tunes put on wax were *Sugar, Liza, China Boy* and *Nobody's Sweetheart.*

In the early months of 1928 there was a flurry of recording activity for the Chicagoans. Spanier and Teschemacher recorded twice with Charlie Pierce at the start of the year. In April and May, with Joe Sullivan, they recorded as the Chicago Rhythm Kings, The Louisiana Rhythm Kings and The Jungle Kings – all very regal! The two Chicago Rhythm Kings titles, *There'll Be Some Changes Made/I've Found A New Baby,* are considered the epitome of Chicago style.

None of these recordings included Jess Stacy, as Joe Sullivan always seemed to get the first call for these dates. Much has been made of the fact that Frank Teschemacher cut so few records prior to his untimely death, and how this restricted an appreciation of his true talents. If Jess Stacy had died in 1932 he would have left behind just three band titles, only one of which contained a piano solo. As a result he would have been consigned to musical oblivion.

Spanier's remark that Jess toured the gin mills probably accounts for Stacy's employment during the end of 1928 and the start of 1929, though Max Kaminsky did recall a job as a 21-year-old on Christmas Eve in 1928 which included the pianist. "Jess went out of his way to make sure I reached home safely from the South Side, which was especially wide open on Christmas Eve . . . I first met Stacy on a date for which Charlie Pierce had optimistically booked for me to lead a band with Muggsy Spanier, Wingy Manone, Stacy and Wettling. How I managed it I'll never know."

Pianist Art Hodes recalled playing with a band led, he believed, by Doc Rudder – "played sax; and not too harmful" – at a large dance hall on the South Side. "I believe it was located on Cottage Grove near 63rd." This would have been the Pershing Ballroom, and the band *was* Ralph (Doc) Rudder's. Hodes said that Rudder "had taste in sidemen. Spanier on cornet; O'Brien on trombone; I think Tesch worked there, and I'm pretty sure I followed Jess on this gig (seems like this got to be a habit with me). That was one fine band, but again, we weren't attracting a hell of a lot of customers. At the same time we weren't gettin' paid regular either."

Pat Pattison may have been the bassist with Rudder. Bert Whyatt dates the Spanier stay at the Pershing Ballroom, which was actually at East 64th Street, west of

South Cottage Grove Avenue, as mid-1929, when Spanier had a four-week break from the Ted Lewis band. Stacy's time with Rudder would have been brief also, possibly a short spell of leave from the Louis Panico engagement reported below.

A last comment on Doc Rudder, from Iris Town. Doc was so-called because he was an orthodontist, and music was more of a hobby. He was a diabetic and had lost a leg.

Another 1929 job for Stacy was with Gene Kerwin and his band at the Canton Tea Gardens, a Chinese chop suey restaurant, at Van Buren and Wabash, where they had daily broadcasts over KYW. Kerwin told John Steiner that the group was stable, except for the rhythm section: Marty Marsala, trumpet; Floyd O'Brien, trombone; Joe Marsala, Eddie Miller, Bud Hunter, reeds; Gene Kerwin, first piano; Eddie Condon, banjo; Harry Goodman, bass. In the rhythm section the second pianist was Dave Rose, replaced by Jess Stacy, and then by Art Hodes. Gene Krupa, Dave Tough and George Wettling followed each other on drums. The band worked seven days a week from noon to 2 p.m., 6 to 8 p.m., and 10 p.m. to 1 a.m., "a not uncommon routine for that period." Kerwin also remembered that Louis Panico followed him into the Canton with an excellent local "businessman's band".

Louis Panico was a trumpet player who had been featured with the Isham Jones orchestra for many years. He became well-known after being featured on the 1923 Jones' version of *Wabash Blues*, which he played in a corny, wa wa fashion. In fact Panico was a better player than the hit record suggested, but because of it he was probably the first jazz musician whose career was restricted by performing on a hit record. On the other hand it did enable him to become a bandleader at the Canton Tea Gardens, from late 1924 onwards, for an engagement which lasted many years.

Stacy said that he joined Panico at that venue in 1929, staying for about a year. He remembered it as a very good dance band, with Panico not telling him how to play. Also in the band, for some of the time at least were Frank Teschemacher, Eddie Condon and George Wettling. Panico, describing the first time they played with him, said, "I've never heard anything like those four. They turned the house upside down." The story which Panico told, to John Steiner, was that Condon approached him to ask if Tesch, Stacy, Wettling and he (Condon) could play the next set as a quartet, ostensibly to give the rest of the band members a break. Panico quoted Condon as saying, "And, Louie, nothing personal, but no trumpet, OK?" They played the set, the audience ate it up, and afterwards the Chinese proprietor approached Louis and suggested, that since the audience response was so enthusiastic, Panico join the quartet and dismiss the rest of the orchestra. They could play every night with five men instead of the usual ten. "That," said Panico, "was the last time I had a jam session."

Others in the band were probably Don Jones, trombone; Herb 'Putty' Nettles, alto; and Andy Panico, bass. Rod Cless is reported to have been the replacement when clarinetist Teschemacher left.

Towards the end of 1929 Stacy was back with Joe Kayser, this time at the Coconut Grove, another Chinese restaurant. *Orchestra World* for January, 1930, listed the personnel as, Bob LeCarr, Charlie Attier, trumpets; Ed Kurzborsko, trombone; Larry Lyons, Gene Yates, Frank Teschemacher, reeds; Jess Stacy, piano; Ced Spring, banjo; Richard Patterson, tuba, bass; Joe Kayser, drums.

"Attier" was Charlie 'Nosey' Altiere, and "Richard Patterson" was Pat Pattison, while "Ed Kurzborsko" was 17-year-old Ed Kuzborski. As Ed Kusby he became a studio musician, recording prolifically with Billy May and Nelson Riddle. He recalled Altiere as reminiscent of Bix, and that "Tesch was enthralling, so was Jess Stacy. We were playing the popular songs of the day. Folks used to dance near where Jess was playing 'cause he was in front of the band, on a lower level. Jess used to call me 'Cubs Park', in good humor. When the owner of the cafe couldn't pay us we all met at union headquarters. President Petrillo bawled hell out of him and I think we got paid off in chop suey!"

If life was a struggle for jazz musicians prior to October 1929, the months and years immediately following were to be even worse.

Various "Black days" have been nominated for the date of the Wall Street Crash and the beginning of the Great Depression; Thursday, October 24, 1929 was one of them. On that date *The New York Herald Tribune's* headline stated, "STOCKS OFF 5 BILLION IN SEVEREST BREAK IN WALL STREET HISTORY." The stock market rallied briefly, to be followed by Black Tuesday, October 29th. As *Variety* reported the following day, "WALL STREET LAYS AN EGG."

The results were catastrophic. By the end of the year $15,000,000,000 had disappeared and 25 million people were affected. Until the New Deal of Franklin D. Roosevelt in the mid-1930s, this was the period of the breadline, the soup kitchen – and the dance marathon.

Dance marathons were started in the early 1920s, but they became a phenomenon during the depression years. Anyone who has seen the Jane Fonda film, "They Shoot Horses, Don't They?", will remember the organization and the rules which governed the marathons, in which couples danced week in and week out until only the winning pair were left on their feet. Musical accompaniment for the "dancing" varied from solo piano through various size combos up to medium-sized bands for the big occasions.

Stacy's Aces, 1931. Left to right: Vic Abbs, Jess Stacy, LeRoy Buck and Frank Teschmacher
Photo: courtesy of Mrs. Pat Stacy

Singer Anita O'Day has written of being a professional "walkathon contestant" for two years, estimating that 15,000 people, including nurses, judges, trainers, cooks and musicians obtained their main source of income from these endurance shows.

Frankie Laine, born Frank LoVeccio, was also a professional contestant, and in 1932 won a marathon at Young's Million Dollar Pier in Atlantic City. He and Ruthie Smith, his partner, won $1,000 each, after 145 days. Prior to this, Laine had entered a contest at the Merry Garden in Chicago.

After the Coconut Grove engagement (of about six weeks, Ed Kusby estimated) Stacy and Teschemacher played a dance marathon at the Merry Garden under the name "Stacy's Aces". Stacy said, "Trumpet, clarinet, tenor, piano, drums. Tesch on clarinet, and sometimes drums, Vic Abbs, trumpet, Bud Freeman, tenor. This was a good outfit, if I do say so myself. This lasted eight months. We played that gig only in-between. Frankie Laine was one of the contestants. We used to let him sing with us."

Bud Freeman's memory was, "I played in that band about a month. I had just come back from New York . . . I was always off to New York and back. There was a very good trumpet player by the name of Vic Abbs. We just had the two horns." Tut Soper remembered Abbs as a Bix stylist.

Freeman thought that Laine won the marathon, though Laine himself mentioned only the win in Atlantic City. Note that Freeman says just two horns, though Stacy gives three. On another occasion Stacy did not mention Freeman, which probably indicates the comings and goings of these strolling players, rather than lapses in memory. A photograph of the Aces shows Vic Abbs, trumpet; Frank Teschemacher, clarinet; Jess Stacy, piano; and LeRoy Buck, drums.

In his autobiography, "That Lucky Old Son", Frankie Laine recalls that Stacy's quartet at the Merry Garden, owned by Jack Lund and Ethel Kendall, included Abbs, Leroy (sic) Buck, and an unknown bass player. To fill a gap in the entertainment the ballroom manager, Eddie Gilmartin, called upon Laine to sing. "I was one nervous 17-year-old as I walked over to Jess, who smiled at me reassuringly and asked, 'What would you like to sing, kid?' " Laine chose *Beside An Open Fireplace* and *Coquette*. He remembered the evening as "one of those rare occasions that you can look back on and clearly recognize as a turning point in your life."

Other reported changes in the Aces personnel include Frank Snyder replacing Buck, and Rod Cless "briefly" for Teschemacher. Wingy Manone, in his autobiography, tells of playing a dance marathon at the Merry Garden with Jess, Tesch and George Wettling. He was criticised by the boss for playing open horn. "We played three weeks more, and then all of us were out."

Artie Shaw visited Chicago with the Irving Aaronson orchestra around this time, and he was impressed with Teschemacher and Floyd O'Brien. About 4 a.m. he and his fellow musicians "wound up in some dance hall where they were holding one of the marathon dance contests that were always taking place in those days. Different musicians floated in and out, sat in for a while, played a few choruses, and then got up to let some other guy blow. There was a piano player named Jess Stacy, and another named Joe Sullivan."

In Bud Freeman's autobiography there is a photograph, taken in 1930 at Dowagiac, Michigan, showing Vic Abbs, Jess Stacy, Bud Freeman, Dick McPartland and drummer Sleepy Kaplan at the lakeside. It is useless to speculate now if this was taken at the time of another engagement or during a break from the Merry Garden.

1930 seems the likely date for the Aces stay at the Merry Garden Ballroom, but 1931 has also been quoted. The given length of the engagement has varied from three months to eight to nine, but perhaps eight or nine months was excessive even for a marathon?

Across the Atlantic, unknown to Stacy, his name was being spread outside the U.S.A. Towards the end of April, 1930, the Ted Lewis orchestra, with Muggsy Spanier in the trumpet section, sailed for Europe. In France Spanier talked with the doyen of jazz critics, Hugues Panassie. Later when reviewing Stacy's first recorded piano solo, Panassie wrote "*Barrelhouse* proves that I was right in having full confidence in Muggsy on the subject of Jess Stacy. In 1930 Muggsy had told me that there was an extraordinary white pianist named Jess Stacy in Chicago, who was only surpassed by Earl Hines."

◄

It was probably early 1931 (though 1932 has also been suggested) when drummer Danny Alvin returned to Chicago and took a band into the 100 Club on Superior Street. The personnel included Charlie Altiere, trumpet; Bud Freeman, tenor; Jess Stacy, piano; Ray Biondi, guitar; Danny Alvin, drums. Bud Freeman confirmed a few details. "Yes, that was a band – I remember that. We played a show, a few acts, and then played for dancing. It was not really a jazz band. We had a trombone player who was so funny and so drunk all the time he used to fall off the bandstand. He'd come to work every night with a new bandage on. It was so funny, but I don't remember his name to save my soul. Danny did a little act in the show, an imitation of Ted Lewis, because he'd worked for him. Danny was a good drummer . . . cannot remember the pianist [which is surprising], and there was a very good guitarist, Ray Biondi. I cannot remember the other people, but this is the little band that played in this club owned by one of the Capone lieutenants."

This lieutenant was Jack 'Machine-Gun' McGurn, another psychopath. By 1927 he had joined Al Capone's "board of directors", and he is believed to have planned the 1929 St. Valentine's Day Massacre. Stacy commented, "It was glamorous to see these guys, the way they dressed. They were good looking guys. McGurn looked like a college graduate. He wore the most expensive clothes and, well, it was glamorous to see them." On one occasion the band was about to take a break and McGurn said, "Keep playing. I want to dance." They kept playing! Jess would hunch over the piano and look neither to left or right. When they went into the gangster's office for their pay, it was like entering an arsenal. There were machine-guns, rifles and hand grenades all over the place.

Stacy recalled, "Sometimes Capone's gang would come in, have a good time, put their guns on the table. There was no trouble. Those gangsters all liked jazz."

In a phrase he liked to use, Stacy would say that if one worked on the South Side it was for Capone, on the North Side it was for Bugs Moran, and on the West Side it was for Mickey Rafferty. (Again, Rafferty was hardly in the same league as Capone and Moran; he was never on the Public Enemy list. In any case, the West Side was predominantly Jewish and controlled by the Miller gang). The gangsters were good employers as long the musicians gave good measure and didn't get drunk. But getting drunk was an occupational hazard and many musicians became alcoholics. Stacy did his share of drinking, until he became a teetotaler around 1960, and also briefly experimented with marijuana.

Speaking generally of the Chicago days, Stacy said, "Jazz musicians had no respect at all. You were looked down on as a drunkard. We had to eke out a living in boring dance bands. I was out of work a lot. So were all the rest of the jazzmen. Musicians lived on hopes, figuring someday they'd hit it big and make records and attain fame. For me, it happened – for lots of others it didn't."

Next follow a few engagements for which no dates are known. They help to illustrate the nomadic kind of musical life which Stacy, and so many like-minded colleagues, had to live. He was faced with the classic dilemma of the jazz musician; the need to earn a living conflicting with the desire to play hot music. A problem throughout the music's history, it was at its worst during the pre-swing era. It was a particularly bad situation for white musicians, whose audiences were generally unsympathetic to jazz. Work in the speakeasies gave greater freedom, but pay was low. So, despite his ideals, Stacy would take work in "boring dance bands" to pay his bills, only for the employment to be shortlived when he soon despaired of the kind of music he had to play.

No details are available for a short stay with the Charlie Straight orchestra, but a little is known about his brief sojourn with Art Kassel. Clarinetist Kassel was another dance band leader who occasionally employed jazz refugees. Described by George Simon as a "friendly, hand-shaking maestro", Kassel later became popular with his "Kassels in the Air". Jess said, "I remember when I played with him at the Marsden Hotel, he told the drummer, 'I want you to pick out the lousiest dancer on the floor and follow him.' Sometimes we'd either start running away with everything or stop."

Another undated engagement was a short fling with Eddie Neibaur and his Seattle Harmony Kings at the gigantic Trianon Ballroom. "I gave my notice the first week. That made three weeks altogether with this conformist, clumsy bad-awful band. Would much rather play alone in some honky-tonk."

Wingy Manone said that he and many musicians existed on Jewish and Italian weddings. A wedding each weekend provided both pay and food. People would sit-in just to share in the buffet. He recalled one time when he, Bud Freeman, Jess Stacy, and Muggsy Spanier all had bands at the same audition to play at the Bamboo Cafe at Randolph and Clark Streets. "A cornball band wound up getting the job." At least Stacy could return to playing solo – Manone had to find a band.

In the summer of 1931 Stacy was playing at the summer resort of Lake Delavan, Wisconsin, where there were two dance halls and a large band stage. Tickets for the stage were ten cents each, or 12 for a dollar. It was there, as drummer Wop Waller told John Steiner, that they heard the news of Bix Beiderbecke's death. Bix, the golden boy of white jazz, died August 6, 1931, aged 28, directly of lobar pneumonia, indirectly of his addiction to alcohol.

Seven months later Frank Teschemacher was to die tragically. He was being driven by Wild Bill Davison, with whose big band he was rehearsing. The car was involved in an accident; Tesch was thrown from his seat and fatally injured.

In the early hours of

Frank Teschemacher marker at Woodlawn Cemetry
Photo: Derek Coller

the morning of March 1st, 1932, Bill Chandler called George Wettling, telling him to get to Ravenswood Hospital. Wettling collected Stacy and they rushed to Teschemacher's bedside. Tesch did not regain consciousness and died at about 6 a.m. He was just short of his 26th birthday. Many years later Stacy told Bob Rusch, "It affected me severely. I loved Frank Teschemacher, we were dear friends. I worked with him for over a year, a year and a half, and he played great." The friendship must have been deep, for Stacy called Tesch's name on his death-bed.

The main headline in *The Chicago Tribune* for March 2, 1932 was: "LINDBERG BABY IS STOLEN." Tucked away on page 20, in the death notices, was the announcement that Frank M. Teschemacher had died March 1, and was to be interred at Woodlawn Cemetery on Thursday, the 3rd. Pall-bearers at the funeral were Jess Stacy, Muggsy Spanier, Danny Altier, Floyd Town, Floyd O'Brien and George Wettling.

Bill Chandler, who "played real loud" trumpet, was with Jess Stacy's quartet at this time. At the end of 1931 the four, including Teschemacher, had been working at a dime-a-dance hall on the North Side and perhaps this job lasted into the early part of 1932. (Florence O'Brien actually called the hall the Dime-A-Dance Palace, though there has been no mention elsewhere of a venue with this name). Chandler and Stacy are the only known quartet members for 1932.

By 1932 the U.S.A. had 12,000,000 unemployed. Musicians struggled like everyone else, unless they were in radio, which offered well-paid, stable employment to those with the technical ability and willingness to accept the boredom. Recording work had all but disappeared as record sales fell 94 per cent in just five years. Art Hodes claimed that Chicago became a jazz desert area in the '30s. "The accordion came in, the strolling quartets . . . and all the good musicians had left."

Stacy commented several times in similar vein. "It was hard going all the time. It was not easy to try to get a job, and when the Depression came on it got worse. It was a scuffle all the way through. I lived on the North Side, on Wilson Avenue, which was a bad neighborhood even then. When the Depression hit, people like Eddie Condon and Gene Krupa and Dave Tough went on to New York, but . . . it was all I could do to keep my family alive where I was."

"I played for a lot of singers 1931–1932–1933 when I played intermission piano in the speakeasies. I was out of work a lot, so were all the rest of the jazzmen. The panic was on . . . I picked up anything I could get, mostly playing alone. These are years I would especially like to forget."

Another job reported for 1932 had Stacy and Wettling in the band accompanying the dance team of Norman and Arlene Selby at the Rendez-Vous. Apparently Norman Selby was able to dance and play trumpet simultaneously, though it is not known if this was the reason for what was probably a short engagement. Less certain is the report that Stacy and Wettling were working in the pit band of Chicago's Folies Bergere when they first worked with the Selbys.

It may have been about this time that pianist Dan Lipscomb bumped into Stacy: "I recall meeting Jess one time at Wabash Avenue and Van Buren Street in the loop, and he had his portable piano keyboard, which he carried with him always. He demonstrated it to me. At that time he was playing in a downtown Chinese restaurant."

Towards the end of 1932 an economic ray of hope appeared. A November 9, 1932 headline read; "ROOSEVELT WINNER IN LANDSLIDE." The New Deal was on its way.

It was probably 1932 when Stacy went into a studio at 940 Lyon and Healy Building to accompany trumpeter Bill Alamshah on two 13-inch aluminium-based discs. It was nearly 50 years later when these recordings were found by collector John Leifert in a trunk in a Staten Island antiques shop. Alamshah, whose professional name was Bill Shaw, was a limited trumpet player, who greatly admired Louis Armstrong. The discs are believed to have been made as mementos to be given to singer Bee Palmer, so it is possible that both musicians played a date, or dates, with her. However, the important part of this find is the lengthy piano solo on *All Of Me*, an enlightening example of Stacy's playing at this time, clearly showing the improvisational skills he had developed. These titles were released on the Arcadia label in 1983.

Early in 1933 Floyd Town (still advertised as Towne) led the band at the Casino Moderne, at 913 East 63rd Street, owned by Herb Shutter, for an engagement which lasted at least from April until sometime in June. (Town's next job began July 1st at the Triangle Cafe, with a different personnel).

The band at the Casino Moderne was Dick Feige, —— Graham, trumpets; Floyd O'Brien, trombone; Rod Cless, Cal Green, Floyd Town, reeds; Jess Stacy, piano; Dick McPartland, guitar; Pat Pattison, bass; George Wettling, drums. Part of their duties included playing for an all-girl floor show.

Stacy and Wettling were together again in another dance band, led by someone with a name sounding like "Rothschild", tenor saxophonist Buzz Knudsen recalled. The job was on Diversey Avenue, for about four weeks, and they had a hell of a time getting their last two weeks pay – yet another occupational hazard of being a musician in Chicago – or anywhere! Besides Stacy and Wettling, Knudsen could remember only Art Hansen, alto; and Volly De Faut, lead alto and clarinet.

By 1933 the number of unemployed had grown to over 13 million, 25 per cent of the working population. It also saw marijuana made illegal and, on December 5th, the repeal of the 18th Amendment. Prohibition was over; the U.S. was no longer dry.

Sometime in 1934 Helen and Jess Stacy were divorced. Helen then married Phil Wing, who was probably with Wayne King's orchestra at the time. She passed away not long after.

During the summer Stacy worked for $21.00 a week at the Subway Cafe at 507 North Wabash Avenue. Johnny Paterson had opened the Subway during Prohibition in two rooms below street level and had gradually improved it until he could claim 'the longest bar in the world'. This claim was accepted, rightly or wrongly, by the syndicated Ripley column, "Believe It Or Not".

Down Beat for August and September 1934 listed the Subway band as: Carl Rinker, trumpet; George Sugg, trombone; Charley Johnson, sax; Jess Stacey, piano; and Frank Snyder, drums. Charley Johnson is a mystery, as Bud Jacobson was the clarinetist with the band during its run at the Cafe, from sometime in 1933 to January 1936. (Catherine Jacobson said, "The personnel *never* changed", though she overlooked the comings and goings at the piano, with Art Hodes, Tut Soper and Art Gronwall taking their turn). Sugg was actually George Lugg. And when Stacy's name began to appear in print it was frequently misspelled Stacey. Despite the errors and misprints, these reports were another indication of better times to come. *Down Beat* in the U.S. and *Jazz Hot* in France, both concerned with hot music, commenced publication in 1934 and 1935 respectively.

The leader of the Subway band was Frank Snyder, who had been the original drummer with the New Orleans Rhythm Kings. Tut Soper, who took Stacy's place in September 1934, said, "Frank was not a great drummer. He was too lazy. Once in a while he'd put it together and lay down a swinging beat, but his energies were directed elsewhere . . . into outdoor sports, golf, fishing, hunting, and the pleasant habit of tilting glass after glass . . . I especially loved his human qualities and his compassion and understanding. Very frustrating musically but very secure and safe socially."

Soper also commented to Bert Whyatt on the work itself: "It was an interesting job. There were five pianos going at one time – all about 50 feet apart. Each player had his own girl singer to play for. We in the band would start work at 11 p.m. and finish at 7 a.m. We would work hard from start to about 1:30 or 2 a.m., then business would mostly go to the bars."

Frank Snyder, ? late 20s?
Photo from his widow, Mrs Peggie Snyder

Peggie Snyder, Frank's widow, remembered that he had three bands at the Subway, as Johnny Paterson wanted live music almost 24 hours a day. One of the bands came in at 5 p.m. and played until the group led by Snyder himself took over. She gave three singers, one male and two female, with Kyle Pierce, composer of *I Get The Blues When It Rains*, as their regular accompanist. (Pierce's jazz credentials included sharing the piano work with Jelly Roll Morton on the July 1923 New Orleans Rhythm Kings recordings for Gennett).

Catherine Jacobson agreed there were three bands playing around the clock, 3 p.m. to 11 p.m., 11 p.m. to 7 a.m. and 7 a.m. to 3 p.m. Scope for exaggeration is shown by George Lugg's quoting two bands at the Subway, while Wild Bill Davison mentioned ten bands playing around the clock! Davison said he played with Stacy on several occasions in Chicago, including at The Subway. "The place was open all day and night, they never closed. We had Nappy Lamare with us, and Ray Bauduc, and they were wild sessions." Undoubtedly Davison was referring to jam sessions. Lugg confirmed the personnel of himself, Rinker, Jacobson, Stacy and Snyder.

Helen Oakley, an early, influential worker for jazz, later to marry British critic Stanley Dance, remembers first hearing Stacy in The Subway, calling it "a dark, damp cellar." It was Helen Oakley who persuaded John Hammond to visit The Subway to hear Stacy.

Hammond was the jazz-loving son from a wealthy family who devoted much of his energy to promoting the musicians he admired. During the 1930s he was to bring Count Basie and Billie Holiday, among many others, to the public's attention. In 1934 he was mainly concerned with Benny Goodman. He came to Chicago to persuade drummer Gene Krupa to leave the Buddy Rogers band to join Goodman's on the "Let's Dance" radio

Subway Cafe, 507 N. Wabash Ave.
Photo: courtesy of Mrs. Peggie Snyder

show. Hammond has said that while he was in Chicago, "I heard Jess Stacy, who was playing at an enormous speakeasy known as the Subway. Because of union regulations it wasn't possible for Jess to join the radio band, but he was a wonderful guy to remember for the future."

This *Down Beat* story seems more feasible than the one Hammond told in his autobiography, repeated in a letter to this writer, in which he says he first heard Stacy on a Paul Mares record. His Chicago visit was late 1934; the Mares' records were recorded and released in 1935.

After the job at The Subway, which lasted about two months, Stacy found work with another New Orleans Rhythm Kings original, the leader and trumpet player, Paul Mares.

The Frank Snyder Band at the Subway cafe in 1934 (After Stacy left). Tut Soper,p; Carl Rinker, tp; Bud Jacobson, ts; Frank Snyder, d; George Lugg, tb.   *Photo: courtesy of Peggie Snyder*

This was at Harry's New York Bar, run by Charles 'Harry' Hepp. Stacy has quoted a five week stay, but it was probably a little longer than that, from October 1934 to early January 1935. The personnel was Paul Mares, trumpet; Santo Pecora, trombone; Boyce Brown, alto; Jess Stacy, piano; Marvin Saxbe, guitar; Pat Pattison, bass; George Wettling, drums.

Boyce Brown told George Hoefer that his happiest days in the music business were spent with Paul Mares and his Friar's Society Orchestra at this bar. The horseplay and relaxed manner of working so prevalent at the Friar's Inn in the 1920s was repeated on this job. The band was stationed on a balcony where their feet were not visible to the customers. Towards the middle of the evening Mares would go out for 'some stuff'. When he returned, each member of the band had a pint of juice at his feet. Mares would then turn to the band and say, "All right, you so-and-so's, what shall we play?" (If a customer wanted *Tiger Rag*, which the band had played already, Mares would say that they had a request to play *Take Your Finger Out of Grandma's Ear*. The 'boys' would then play any dixieland number that took their fancy).

"The Esquire Jazz Book" confirmed that Saxbe was a regular member of the band, although he is omitted from a review in *Down Beat's* November issue. Stacy did say that the band consisted of seven pieces, and that, "This was a good group. I loved playing with this outfit." Written in hipster fashion, the *Down Beat* review reported that "Jess Stacy plays plenty of rhythm piano."

45

On January 7, 1935, the band recorded four titles for OKeh, thanks to the efforts of Helen Oakley, who was working for Irving Mills' Music Publishing Company at the time. Due to the sorry state of the market the records were not pressed and distributed in a manner to attract much attention, though they continue to be reissued today in compilations of Chicago jazz recordings.

For the OKeh session Omer Simeon was added. Simeon was a creole clarinetist, one of the finest New Orleans players, who was working, as he did for many years, with the Earl Hines big band. He replaced another New Orleans clarinet player, Lester Bouchon, who was scheduled to play the date, but couldn't make it.

Mares contacted Simeon at the Grand Terrace ballroom, where Hines had his residency, and Simeon rehearsed at Mares' house that evening – the night before the recording session. Stacy recalled that Simeon frequently sat-in with the Mares band, which would explain why he was the one chosen to replace Bouchon.

Stacy also said that, "Paul Mares' band folded because they [the audience] didn't like our type of music . . . I must repeat, jazz music was looked down on. They wanted commercialism, funny hats, etc." However, the replacement band was another Floyd Town unit, which include Bill Dohler on alto, Johnny Lane on clarinet, and Art Hodes on piano, so it had some jazz credentials. The Town band opened on January 20, 1935, but it is possible that Harry's New York Bar underwent renovation between Mares' departure and Town's opening.

John Hammond reported, in the April 1935 issue of *Jazz Hot*, "Jess Stacy, that marvelous Chicago pianist, has just joined Earl Burtnett's band, along with Ray Biondi, who plays guitar, trumpet and swell fiddle. I had wanted Ray and Jess to make records in Chicago, but [Irving] Mills never got round to sending me out there." Stacy said, "I worked for Earl Burtnett, who had fiddles and a harp, and needed an Eddy Duchin piano player instead of me." (Duchin was a society-type performer. One member of his band told George Simon, "I'll say this for the man, he was the only musician I've ever known who could play a 32 bar solo with 32 mistakes and get an ovation for it afterwards.")

Again, the outcome was inevitable. As with Eddie Neibaur, Stacy gave Burtnett two weeks' notice at the end of his first week with another "clumsy outfit."

The spring and early summer of 1935 were spent with a Maurie Stein unit. "I worked with Stein in a five-piece band at a gangster-owned night club called the Paramount. We played the floor shows and for dancing in-between. No jazz in this outfit."

Stein, who played clarinet and alto, was the brother of pianist Julius Stein, who later became famous as Jule Styne, composer of such Broadway hit shows as "Gipsy", "Funny Girl" and "The Bells Are Ringing". *Down Beat* listed the Stein personnel as: Fred Taylor, trumpet; Maurie Stein, reeds; Benny Gill, violin; Kappy Kaplin, guitar; and Pat Pattison, bass. No piano or drums were shown, but Stacy was with Stein at the Paramount when Benny Goodman telephoned.

"I got a call from New York from somebody who said he was Benny Goodman and wanted me to come to New York to join his band. I just thought it was somebody playing a practical joke on me, so I told him if he was really Goodman to send me a wire confirming the offer. The next day the wire arrived and I left for New York."

3

Benny Goodman

$\mathcal{I}$t is not the intention here to retell in detail the often-told Benny Goodman story, but the basic facts are necessary to set the scene. For the details the reader is referred to Goodman's autobiography ("The Kingdom of Swing"; 1939), two biographies ("Benny Goodman and The Swing Era", by James Lincoln Collier; and "Swing, Swing, Swing" by Ross Firestone), and an encyclopedic bio-discography ("Benny Goodman: Listen to His Legacy" by D. Russell Connor).

Benny Goodman loomed large in Stacy's life from 1935 onwards. The pianist worked with him, on and off, for the next 30 years, and despite his major contributions to other bands, (such as Bob Crosby's), Stacy's name will always be associated with Goodman's.

Born in 1909, Benny Goodman, a native Chicagoan and a clarinet prodigy, had learned his jazz by association with the Austin High Gang and by listening to black clarinetist Jimmie Noone. He was in the pioneer orchestra of drummer Ben Pollack, alongside Jimmy McPartland, Jack Teagarden and Glenn Miller. In the early 1930s he became a highly-paid studio musician. Towards the end of 1934 he was one of three leaders chosen to appear on a new, weekly radio show on NBC called *Let's Dance*. Favorable reaction to these broadcasts, between December 1, 1934 and May 25, 1935 and to the band's recordings, led to plans for a nationwide tour.

The band, with Frank Froeba on piano, played one week at the Stanley Theatre in Pittsburgh, commencing July 5, returning to New York for the Trio (Goodman, clarinet, Gene Krupa, drums, and Teddy Wilson, piano) to make its first recordings on the 13th.

Stacy joined Goodman in New York as the replacement for Froeba. He arrived about the middle of July, for some hasty rehearsals, no doubt, and to leave on the tour which was to keep the band away from the city for the next ten months. As he told Bob Rusch, "Frank Froeba met me in New York and he said, 'You're not going to get along with this guy'." Stacy had an early indication of this when he met Goodman, who asked him to play a tune Stacy had never heard of. Goodman said, "Well, try it anyway!"

Not all members of the band had wished to leave New York, to suffer the difficulties and uncertainties of life on the road. Froeba was one, thus giving Stacy the chance to display his talent beyond the confines of Chicago. However, joining the Goodman band at this time was no great deal. To fellow musicians it was a recognition of one's ability, but in financial terms, security of employment and popular appeal it was no sinecure.

In fact, securing Stacy's services was of greater benefit to the Goodman orchestra than it was to Stacy. In place of a man who, according to John Hammond, "had a prodigious technique, but couldn't hold a steady tempo," the band had acquired an original and inventive soloist, a brilliant accompanist, and a rock-steady rhythm man.

"Needless to say," wrote Goodman in his autobiography, "that's another change that I've never regretted."

George Frazier Jr., in *Hot News* for August 1935, gave a different slant in his report: "Goodman, by the way, has made several changes in his band. Frank Froba *(sic)* has been replaced by Jess Stacy. Frank's a good swing man, but he's too moody to turn in consistently able work. Even at his best though, he's simply not in a class with Jess . . . . [who's] definitely a gain for the Goodman gang."

The personnel of the orchestra for the tour was: Nate Kazebier, Bunny Berigan, Ralph Muzzillo, trumpets; Red Ballard, Jack Lacey, trombones; Hymie Schertzer (Shertzer), Bill DePew, altos; Art Rollini, Dick Clark, tenors; Jess Stacy, piano; Allan Reuss, guitar; Harry Goodman, bass; Gene Krupa, drums; Helen Ward and Joe Harris, vocals.

Goodman, Berigan and Krupa were the stars of the band. Berigan, a powerful, masterly musician in the Louis Armstrong tradition, was described by Stacy as "a wonderful man and an electrifying trumpet player." Gene Krupa was the gum-chewing extrovert showman, the man who made the drummer a key figure in the swing bands.

Information from a variety of sources, but mainly Bozy White's researches into Bunny Berigan's career, suggests that the itinerary was as follows:

Clark Lake, MI	(Ocean Beach Pier)	(one night, July 16, 1935)
Columbus, OH.	(Olentangy Park)	(one night, July 17)
Columbus, OH.	(Valley Dale Ballroom)	(one night, July 18) (unconfirmed)
Lakeside, MI.	(Luna Pier)	(one night, July 19)
Grand Rapids, MI.	(Mile-A-Away Ballroom)	(one night, July 20)
Milwaukee, WI.	(Modernistic Ballroom)	(two nights, July 21/22))
Denver, CO.	(Elitchs' Gardens)	(three weeks, July 26-August 15)
Grand Junction, CO.	(Mile-A-Away Ballroom)	(one night, August 16)
Salt Lake City, UT.	(Coconut Grove)	(one night, August 17)
Oakland, CA.	(McFadden's Ballroom)	(one night, August 19)
Pismo Beach, CA.	(Pismo Pavilion)	(one night, August 20)
Los Angeles, CA.	(Palomar Ballroom)	(August 21 onwards)

The story of the tour is one of the legends of jazz. As the motorcade (BG could not afford a band bus) crossed America, musicians and fans helped to turn a few engagements into moderate successes, but the road to Los Angeles gave little indication of the triumph to come.

Stacy recalled, "Bunny Berigan, Nate Kazebier, Mort Davis (the road manager) and I drove across the country in Benny's old Pontiac. I helped drive because Bunny was stoned all the time. He was drinking 'Old Quaker' then (that was one of the cheapest bottles you could buy) and it seemed like every 100 miles we'd have to stop and buy a pint for him. And it was only a pint – if we'd bought a fifth or a quart, he'd have finished all of that in the same distance. He'd just sit back and get stoned out of his mind. And all the while we were doing the one-nighters across the country, laying eggs 'til we got to the Palomar in Los Angeles."

Stacy told Bob Rusch, "The first place we played was Jackson, Michigan, [Clark Lake is nearby]. There were 36 people there and they were all musicians from different surrounding towns." He also mentioned a gig at Lansing, a location not given elsewhere ("18 people there, and they were all musicians from Detroit"), though it is not clear where this would fit into the itinerary.

In the August issue of *Down Beat*, Helen Oakley reviewed Goodman's Milwaukee date, commenting: "A splendid thing all around has been Jess Stacy's addition to the band . . . Judging from the point of view of swing and sincerity, Jess is a somebody that has to be listened to." A "good attendance" was reported.

Not so good was a three week date at Elitchs' Gardens in Denver. It was a disaster. Because the band didn't play like Kay Kyser's, which was filling a rival dancehall, the Elitchs' Gardens manager wanted to cancel the booking. As a compromise, Goodman's agent, Willard Alexander, persuaded him to play some waltz sets, using a small group with Helen Ward on piano. Stacy said: "In Denver we had to play dime-a-dance music, with a waltz every third number." Somehow they survived, but it had been a desperate struggle. If the Elitchs' Gardens job had been cancelled it is highly unlikely that the tour would have continued.

In fact, after this fiasco, Goodman contemplated giving up and returning to studio work in New York. Stacy was one who persuaded him to carry on, to see what happened when they got over the mountains to California. As he said, "I liked the band and I wanted to stay with it. I was being selfish."

Stacy said that at Grand Junction, Colorado, there was chicken wire in front of the bandstand to protect them from bottles thrown by drunken Indians. This was the night that news came through of the death of comedian Will Rogers and pilot Wiley Post. (They were killed in a plane crash August 15). He also recalled that, prior to California, it was only in Salt Lake City that they were given an inkling that they might have a wider audience than they imagined.

Typical of touring conditions for an unknown band was the overnight drive from Grand Junction to Salt Lake City, followed by a journey of some 700 miles to Oakland. "Oh, it was rough, you know. You had to be really young to be able to hold up."

The Oakland location has often been given as Sweets' Ballroom, the usual venue for touring bands in that town, but Goodman actually played at MacFadden's. The late Harry Avery, a veteran collector, remembered it as a public dance hall on Broadway in downtown Oakland. "The crowd was unusually enthusiastic, and reasonably large, considering the fact that it was a Monday night, when the place would normally have been closed."

Attendance at Pismo Beach was poor, then on to Los Angeles and the Palomar at the corner of Vermont and Third Avenue.

The rest, as they say, is history. Recollections of the event vary, but whatever the details, whatever the reasons, sometime during the evening Goodman called for the band's instrumentals, many of them arranged by Fletcher Henderson, and the large crowd reacted with wild enthusiasm. Goodman, in his autobiography, said: "When we opened at the Palomar we had a 'what've we got to lose' attitude and decided to let loose and shoot the works with our best things like *Sugar Foot Stomp, Sometimes I'm Happy*, and the others . . . From the moment I kicked them off, the boys dug in with some of the best playing I'd heard since we left New York. I don't know what it was, but the crowd went wild, and then – boom!"

Gene Krupa remembered: "We played the first couple of sets under wraps. We weren't getting much reaction, so Benny, I guess, decided to hell with playing it safe and we started playing numbers like *King Porter Stomp*. Well, from then on, we were in!"

In, indeed. The swing era was born. For the next ten years the big bands were to be the kingpins of popular music.

As a 17-year-old, John Lucas was greatly impressed by Goodman and the band. Lucas, who to became a name trumpeter on the Los Angeles revivalist scene, was able to recall, 50 years later, the excitement of hearing and meeting Benny Goodman at the Palomar. He remembered "the huge, huge dance floor. That Palomar was big enough to hold a blimp or two." Goodman was kind to Lucas and his two schoolfriends, and Lucas recalls celebrities like Jackie Cooper, Andy Devine, Isabel Jewel and Pinky Tomlin in the audience. "When we drove home back to Pasadena our whole car was about three or four feet off the ground . . . I guess I didn't sleep for three or four days."

It was not until the following year that Lucas became friendly with Jess Stacy, a friendship which endured until Stacy's death.

Originally a four-week booking, the Palomar engagement was increased to seven weeks, ending October 1, 1935. In September there was a recording session for Victor, Stacy's first with the band, and his first recorded solo, on a Jimmy Mundy original called *Madhouse*.

Benny Goodman and His Orchestra at the Congress Hotel, late 1935. Left to right: Jess Stacy, Helen Ward, Harry Goodman, Alan Reuss, Gene Krupa, Benny Goodman; reeds: Dick Clark, Bill Depew, Hymie Shertzer, Art Rollini; trombones: Joe Harris, Red Ballard; trumpets (uncertain order): Nate Kazebier, Harry Geller and Ralph Muzzillo.

Photo: courtesy of Mrs. Pat Stacy

A week at the Paramount Theatre in Los Angeles was followed by one-nighters in Texas, then November 6 the band opened at the Urban Room of the Congress Hotel in Chicago. It was here that the Palomar success was consolidated.

Stacy says that Goodman was offered the two largest ballrooms in Chicago, the Trianon or the Aragon, but Stacy warned him against these "Wayne King" waltz citadels, telling him to take the Congress Hotel instead. That this suggestion was the right one is confirmed by the fact that the booking at the Congress Hotel, which was originally for four weeks, was extended to May 23, 1936, a total of 19 weeks.

A few days after returning to Chicago Stacy was recording again, on November 16, 1935, this time under the aegis of John Hammond, who was supervising the records for English Parlophone. These included the famous trio session with Israel Crosby on bass and Gene Krupa on drums, followed three days later by a Gene Krupa band date. Parlophone R2187, which paired *Barrelhouse*, a Stacy original, with the Meade Lux Lewis version of *Honky Tonk Train Blues*, created a stir when it was issued in England, remaining in catalogue for many years.

John Hammond recalled: "Jess was a big fan of Bix Beiderbecke and that was why I made the solo Stacy recordings for Parlophone . . . I even turned the pages on *In The Dark* and *Flashes* because it was impossible for Jess to memorize them. I also had a ball recording him in the Gene Krupa sessions." (Stacy was in excellent form on this Krupa session, also recorded in November for Parlophone. *Blues For Israel* is frequently and justly cited as a prime example of his playing).

50 years later British trumpet player and writer, Humphrey Lyttelton was to say of *Barrelhouse*: "This is a Stacy masterpiece . . . Jess Stacy makes his mark with that wonderfully buoyant piano solo, playing largely in octaves, à la Earl Hines, but with a very distinctive melody line inspired more by, I would say, Bix Beiderbecke than by Louis Armstrong."

On Sunday, December 8, 1935, the Chicago Rhythm Club, with Helen Oakley and attorney Squirrel Ashcraft III to the fore, organized a 'tea dance' at the Congress Hotel to feature the Benny Goodman orchestra. This was the first of several jazz concerts presented by the Club. The second, also by the Goodman band, was on March 8, followed by a third on Easter Sunday, which featured pianist Teddy Wilson. Wilson had recorded with the Trio in July 1935, but it was only from this concert onwards that he became a regular member of the Goodman organization, playing with Goodman and Krupa, and also as intermission pianist.

The relationship between Teddy Wilson and Jess Stacy has been the subject of debate over the years. Generally there seems to have been a mutual respect and appreciation between them, though it would have been natural for Stacy to feel a certain amount of jealousy at the way Wilson featured with the Trio and, later, the Quartet.

To quote Otis Ferguson, Wilson said: "Jess plays one more time like that, I'll never touch a piano again," while Stacy said: "Anybody I *really* admire, it's that little old Wilson." In later years Stacy was to say: "There was no animosity between Teddy Wilson and me at anytime. We were together for three years. He did his job, I did mine and that was it. I didn't get many solos, because Benny featured Teddy Wilson so much, but Teddy and I had a friendly relationship – in my heart I knew he fit better in that trio than I would have. I was more of a band pianist. Teddy played lots of runs. Did you ever notice that Teddy would never attack a note? It's pretty piano. I played more barrelhouse style.

If I tried to play like Teddy Wilson I'd make an ass out of myself. So I can only do what I do. If people like it, fine."

Trumpeter Chris Griffin was just one who considered Stacy a better band pianist than Wilson, although he felt that Stacy did resent the attention which Wilson received.

Another sidelight on those hard-drinking days came from Pee Wee Erwin: "[Jess and I] would split a bottle of Seagram's Ancient Age Whiskey very often, and keep it in a lattice work, in a room not being used, next to the Joseph Urban Room in the Congress Hotel, Chicago."

It was at the Congress Hotel that Goodman seems to have realized that real success could be his. As a result, his determination to succeed was intensified. Musicians spoke of him becoming more serious, more inward looking and remote. His aloofness grew, as did his search for perfection.

Jess Stacy's recollections confirm this. "Even at the beginning Benny was a task-master. And after we went into the Congress and he had some success, he got tougher.

"I was fooling around with a little blues before a set started, and he came over and stood next to me and listened awhile, and then said, 'That's the blues?' I hadn't been with him very long, and I was crushed.

"Benny was a terrific leader, but I took a lot of guff off him. If I'd had any spunk instead of being the naive, easygoing young man I was, I'd probably have thrown the piano at him. Still, how could I leave? It was the top band in the country."

At the end of May 1936 the band returned briefly to New York, but late in June it was en route to California again, this time to appear in the film "The Big Broadcast of 1937" starring Jack Benny. They doubled at the Palomar, the fee being three times that of a year earlier. On June 30 the band made its 'Camel Caravan' broadcasting debut, the first in a series which was to continue until the end of 1939. All of this was confirmation that Benny Goodman and his Orchestra had truly arrived as one of the major box-office attractions in the U.S. It also meant that the band was now settling down into the relentless grind of work and more work. They were playing in theatres during the day, and for dancing at hotels at night, in addition to rehearsals, recording sessions and broadcasts. Only those young and enthusiastic could have survived such a schedule.

Pee Wee Erwin, who came in as one of the replacements for Berigan, recalled that period: "To begin with we were playing at the Palomar every night except Sunday from 9 p.m. to 2 a.m. Then when we began work on the picture we had to get up early enough to be in the make-up room at the studio at 8 a.m. and on the set by 9, where we put in a full day until 5 p.m."

For a pianist, in addition to the long hours and hard work, there was the perennial problem – the piano on which he was expected to play. Stacy told Keith Keller: "I have played on some terrible instruments in my time. Back on the road with Goodman, you came off the bus late, and you just played whatever ugly thing with sticky surfaces and broken keys that they had at your disposal."

Other major events during 1936 were the introduction of another name soloist, trumpeter Ziggy Elman; the band's first engagement at the prestigious Madhattan Room of the Hotel Pennsylvania in New York, commencing October 1; and, in November, the addition of vibraphonist Lionel Hampton. For Stacy himself there was further recognition when he was, listed seventh, to Teddy Wilson's first, in the "Pianists" section of the *Down Beat* Readers' Poll.

French critic Hugues Panassie published his book 'Hot Jazz' in 1936, again quoting Muggsy Spanier and John Hammond in praise of Stacy.

At the end of 1936 Otis Ferguson, a die-hard supporter of the Goodman band, and of Jess Stacy, wrote of the stay at the Madhattan Room, with some interesting comments about the Room, Goodman, Teddy Wilson, the Quartet and the band. Of the last he wrote: "Swing in, swing out, the band is up again and drawing the people out like the sun in the fable. With Krupa, Reuss (guitar), and the inspired, quiet Stacy (piano) laying down a thick rhythmic base, it plays on through whatever songs are the demand of the day, making most of them sound like something. This is an organization in the line of the great jazz bands – Jean Goldkette, Fletcher Henderson, McKinney's Cotton Pickers, Ellington, Kirk, et al. – a little lighter than some of these but more beautifully rehearsed and economical, and with cleaner edges."

Jazz Hot continued to promote Stacy, with Joost Van Praag writing in the Christmas, 1936, issue: "Jess Stacy is probably the greatest white piano player, perhaps almost up to the level of Earl Hines. Teddy Wilson is a good pianist, but he is decidedly inferior to Earl and he can often be rather monotonous in his delicate and simple playing. Stacy seems . . . to have ideas that are never exhausted; he has a far greater variety than Teddy Wilson. It is clear that Bennie *(sic)* Goodman does not like Stacy so much."

Stacy's comment about solo space in the arrangements was: "Solo areas were marked out in the score – eight or 16 bars, with the soloist indicated. But it was Benny's band and he hogged all the choruses. If you got eight bars, you were damned lucky."

Chris Griffin confirmed that Stacy was not featured with Goodman, just eight bars here and there, saying that Goodman was commercial in the sense that he featured the musicians the kids wanted to hear – Harry James, Gene Krupa. Stacy was not a flashy player. He was a hard-working pianist who spent his time bent over the piano. So the musicians and the jazz fans admired him, but he meant little to the jitterbugs.

1937 began with the arrival of trumpeter Harry James from the Ben Pollack band, and now the famous section of Harry James, Chris Griffin and Ziggy Elman was in place. James quickly established himself, alongside Goodman and Krupa, as one of the band's main attractions. But the major event of the year was Goodman's opening on March 3 at the Paramount Theater in New York. The reaction of the teenagers at seeing the band on stage was one of the publicity events of the year.

When the band arrived at the Paramount for an early morning rehearsal before the first show they found, in Goodman's words, "a couple of hundred kids lined up in front of the box office at about 7 a.m." "In fact, by 3 p.m., 11,500 people had paid for tickets and the first day's attendance was 21,000." There was general hubbub and whistling during the showing of the film, Claudette Colbert's "Maid of Salem". "The theater was completely full an hour before we were supposed to go on, and when we finally came up on the rising platform, the noise sounded like Times Square on New Year's Eve. The reception topped anything we had known up to that time, and because we felt it was spontaneous and genuine, we got a tremendous kick out of it."

Reviewing a show at the Paramount, critic Stanley Dance noted: "The swell Jess Stacy sits unobtrusively at the piano, seldom taking a solo and seldom getting any of the limelight. That's more than likely his own fault, since I believe he would rather be working in the rhythm section back of the orchestra than as a soloist. It's a pity because he does play so wonderfully."

In June the band was off to Hollywood again, to appear in its second film, "Hollywood Hotel" with Dick Powell. Stacy is seen only briefly and in long shot in the band sequences.

Earlier in the year Lionel Hampton began making small band records for Victor. As Hampton recalled: "In 1937, Eli Oberstein, who was recording director at RCA Victor, came and told me that anytime I wanted to record, I had an open invitation."

Between February 1937 and January 1938 Stacy appeared on five sessions with Hampton, from which came a number of gems, including the romping *Buzzin' Around With The Bee*, the superb Johnny Hodges feature, *On The Sunny Side Of The Street*, and the exciting *Ring Dem Bells*, on which Hampton salutes the pianist with his cry, "Mister Stacy, ring dem bells!"

Then in December there began a short series of recordings by Harry James, using men from the Goodman and Count Basie orchestras. Stacy was the pianist, notably on the intro and fadeout of *One O'Clock Jump*. On *Life Goes To A Party* (named in tribute to feature about the Goodman band in the national photomagazine *Life*) Jo Jones reported that "Jess had a quart-and-a-half of whiskey in him when he cut this solo." If true, it does not show on the record. John Hammond brought singer Helen Humes to the session, having heard her at the Renaissance Casino in New York. Hammond wrote: "I always thought that Jess did a marvelous job in those first Harry James recordings with Basie's rhythm section and Herschel Evans and Buck Clayton."

When touring Harry James and Stacy shared rooms. Stacy told Keith Keller that James "smoked too much, but he was always very neat!"

During 1937 Stacy could afford to rent a Tudor City apartment in Manhattan, where he and Otis Ferguson would throw darts at Benny Goodman's photograph. (Note that the same story was told about Stacy and Berigan back in 1935!) Stacy also remembered the band's new singer: "Martha (Tilton) used to come over to my apartment in Tudor City in New York and go over the new tunes with me. Of course, when she first joined the band she was scared to death."

Goodman too rehearsed with Stacy: "He liked to go over tunes with me alone, so he could hear the chords, for his own security and to keep both of us together."

Ernie Anderson has written: "[Stacy] was the great romantic of jazz. He did love the ladies. When I first knew Jess he was living in the Claridge Hotel on 43rd Street just east of Times Square. This was an old time theatrical establishment and I'm sure the reason Jess stayed there was because it was much favored by the strippers from the burlesque houses just around the corner on 42nd Street. Jess had a tiny suite on one of the upper floors. He had a small upright plus three silent keyboards situated around the room: one across the arms of the only easy chair, one on the dresser, one on the window sill. Jess practiced endlessly, which is how he accomplished and then maintained that delicate and startling technique."

On November 30, 1937, an issue of *The New Republic* appeared, containing "Piano In The Band", a Jess Stacy feature. This was an extremely perceptive and stylishly written article by Otis Ferguson.

In it Ferguson referred to an event earlier in the year: " . . . much later they were playing some sad backwater where the bloods were yelling for *Casa Loma Stomp* and failed to get the idea of a solo and bawled for brass. And Jess dug in and took about five in a row, so mad they couldn't get him out of it, and it was beautiful – they didn't want to

54

take him out. All he said after that was: 'I'll teach them what to holler for, the icky bastards.'"

An indication of what could happen is suggested on a broadcast from November 30, 1937, issued by CBS. When the band comes to the coda of *St. Louis Blues*, it is actually a false ending. Harry James keeps going, he and Stacy jamming more choruses, so that the usual three minute performance lasts four-and-a-half. Note how, despite James' dramatic solo, Stacy's solo brings no lessening of tension. One of Stacy's great gifts was to be able to swing, to compete using rhythm and melody, without recourse to flashiness.

Throughout the year the recordings with Benny Goodman, mainly of popular songs with vocals, plus an occasional instrumental, continued on a monthly basis, as they did through 1938. It was on the vocal records that Stacy had his most consistent opportunities to play, with songs like *It's Wonderful* and *The Dreamer In Me* becoming virtually vocal/piano duets.

Benny Goodman and Jess Stacy in 1938
Photo: courtesy of Mrs. Pat Stacy

Other recordings with Goodman which can safely be named as examples of Stacy's best work with the orchestra include *The Glory of Love, You Can't Pull The Wool Over My Eyes, Goody, Goody, This Year's Kisses, You Can Tell She Comes From Dixie, Goodnight My Love* and *T'Ain't No Use. I Want To Be Happy* is notable for a clarinet with piano and rhythm interlude which was as close as Stacy got to the Trio at that time. Add to these his contributions to the band's instrumentals, numbers like *Big John Special, One O'Clock Jump* and *Madhouse.*

Note too the backings which he gives to the Johnny Mercer parody numbers on the Camel Caravan broadcasts (*Class of '39, Indianapolis Speedway Race*, for example), where he is given the room to spread out. Further examples of fine accompaniments include *That Feeling Is Gone, Blue Interlude, When I Go A Dreamin'*, and *Why'd You Make Me Fall In Love.*

As Stacy told Keith Keller about the singers: "I tried to hear them as little as possible, they were so tinny sounding, they were either missing out on intonation or beat or they were downright off-key. So I just took the melodic line into consideration, I heard *that* inside my head, and built from there, putting lace around it, adding bounce where I could, and otherwise getting in my own licks whenever the girls had to pause for breath."

On another occasion he said: "I imagine all those vocalists hated my guts. That's one place where I got a chance to play . . . the bandleader didn't say a word; I got by with murder."

Murder perhaps, but even Goodman, in his autobiography, admitted that, "As for the way [Stacy] plays behind a vocalist, that's just tops."

Jess Stacy and Ziggy Elman, Atlantic
City, 1938   *Photo: courtesy of Mrs. Pat Stacy*

Helen Ward, singer with Goodman from late 1934 to late 1936, is quoted by Ross Firestone on the subject of Stacy: "He had such feeling and delicacy, and he was a heavenly accompanist. And he was such a sweet, easygoing guy. I don't think I ever saw him lose his temper or get out of sorts."

However, in his *New Republic* article, Otis Ferguson highlighted Stacy's greatest ability: "Jess Stacy is above everything else a band pianist, the hands powerful on the full heavy chords, the fingers trained down to steel in bringing out both ends of an octave at once through any din, wrists, hands and fingers quick and skimming in a working musician's economy of motion . . . His own summing up of it . . . 'What I try to do' – Jess says, 'Look, I try to melt with the band.'"

That same month, November 1937, *Down Beat* published a feature on Stacy by Sharon Pease, though still spelling his name incorrectly: "STACEY GOT IDEAS FROM RIVER BOAT BANDS".

The event of 1938 took place on January 16th, when the orchestra played at Carnegie Hall, another legendary occasion in jazz annals. Plagued with doubts about being the first jazz artist to appear at Carnegie Hall, Goodman tried to get comedienne Beatrice Lillie to appear on the programme. Fortunately, Miss Lillie declined. A short 'history of jazz' was included, with guests Bobby Hackett, Johnny Hodges, Harry Carney and Cootie Williams. For a jam session some of Count Basie's band were added, including Basie himself, Buck Clayton and Lester Young. But these additional attractions were unnecessary; the show was sold out.

The notes to the CBS issue of the concert recording, written by Irving Kolodin, detail the background, though with a couple of errors. The main slip is not to credit Albert Marx, the man whose initiative resulted in the concert being recorded – and thus allowing us to hear one of the great piano solos in jazz.

There was one microphone on the stage, and the music was carried by telephone line to recordist Harry Smith's studio in the R.K.O. Building, where he used two turntables to capture the entire concert. Albert Marx arranged everything with Harry Smith, as Goodman expressed no interest at all. It was not until some months later that Goodman asked to borrow the acetates to copy. The Marx acetates were lost during a house move, and Goodman's copies languished in a cupboard. 12 years later, Benny's sister-in-law, Rachel Breck, moved into Goodman's old apartment and uncovered the acetates. She queried her brother-in-law about them. He listened to them and then arranged with CBS, via John Hammond, to be issued on microgroove. The resulting double-album became one of the biggest-selling jazz records ever.

John Hammond always acknowledged that Albert Marx was responsible for the recording, but it was not until several years after the release on microgroove that Goodman did.

Demand for tickets was such that Goodman himself had to buy tickets for his family from touts. Stacy said: "They even had to put chairs up on the stage. I barely had elbow room to play with . . . Chairs all round the back of the piano." This can be seen in the very brief Movietone newsreel clip of the concert which has survived.

The planned finale of the concert (there were two encores) was *Sing, Sing, Sing*, a Louis Prima tune, originally arranged by Jimmy Mundy, with a vocal by Helen Ward, which had grown since its introduction in early 1936 in both length and pretentiousness. There was no longer a vocal, but Gene Krupa and Harry James were heavily featured. (James later said that one of the reasons he left Goodman was to escape his chair next to the drums when *Sing, Sing, Sing* was being played!)

Stacy was not scheduled to solo in this final number, and he has told the story of what happened on many occasions: "Anyway, before I went on stage I'd had four scotch and sodas, and I was flying high through most of the concert. While we were playing the *Sing, Sing, Sing* number Benny seemed to like what I was doing behind his solo, and with no warning at all he turned to me when he ended his chorus and said, 'Take it, Jess.'

"If I'd known it was coming, I would have probably screwed it up. It just happened. I think Benny liked what I was doing behind him that night. I wasn't getting in his way, but I was still goosing him a little."

"It was just one of those things. I didn't know it was going to happen . . . and all of a sudden I was playing and that was all. I just kept playing and years later I heard it on a record."

"When I started to play, I figured, good Lord, what with all the circus-band trumpet playing we've heard tonight and all the Krupa banging, I might as well change the mood and come on real quiet. So I took the A minor chord *Sing, Sing, Sing* is built around and turned it this way and that. I'd been listening to Edward McDowell and Debussy, and I think some of their things got in there, too."

In later years Goodman expressed admiration for Stacy's "brilliant" solo. To Peter Clayton he said: "I remember being amazed at Jess – who was always a great musician – but I thought in the particular environment of that evening, with all the stars . . . I was just riveted by this piano solo. But Jess was that kind of player . . . He could rise to those occasions and to those heights."

Many times Stacy said that his solo at Carnegie Hall was his first ever on *Sing, Sing, Sing*, but that would seem to be a memory lapse. In his November 24, 1937 article Otis Ferguson wrote: "About the best of all is the way he used to eat up the choruses on *Sing, Sing, Sing*, getting higher with each one and beyond himself, truly wonderful piano . . . The first time I heard it was at the New York Paramount, and when I began cheering afterwards backstage, all Jess would say was: 'Oh, you mean that old A-minor-chord thing; it's alright, that chord.'"

Ferguson also deplored the absence of the piano solo on the double-sided Victor recording of *Sing, Sing, Sing*, made in June 1937. Chris Griffin confirmed that Stacy's solo was not a completely spontaneous effort.

In his review of the concert (*Metronome*, February 1938), George Simon was perceptive enough to write: "Came the full band, and then suddenly soft, church music from Jess Stacy at the piano. It was wonderful contrast."

When the album was released the reaction to the solo was rhapsodic, and has continued to be so: "High spot of the evening was clearly Jess Stacy's five-chorus solo on the last scheduled on the program, *Sing, Sing, Sing,* though those of us who were there that night didn't realize it. In recorded retrospect, those delicate measures stand way out, as Jess makes his simple, developed way through as lovely a piece of construction as Swing ever offered."

". . . the single classic stroke of the concert; Jess Stacy's unscheduled two-minute solo, an airy, calm, circular improvisation that rises angelically into the noisy air."

Although "The Famous 1938 Carnegie Hall Jazz Concert" recording has stayed in catalog since its release more than 40 years ago, not all contemporary reviews of the concert were complimentary. Olin Downes, the classical music critic of *The New York Times*, wrote, in a generally adverse review: "Nor did we hear a single player, in the course of a solid hour of music, invent one original or interesting musical phrase, over the persistent rhythm."

However, the following day's editorial was mildly approving of Goodman, the Carnegie Hall concert, and swing in general.

An interesting offshoot from the concert was reported in 1987. Loren Schoenberg, tenor saxophonist and bandleader, was collating the Benny Goodman library of arrangements and found one called *Jess's Theme.* It was an arrangement by Jimmy Mundy of Stacy's *One O'Clock Jump* solo from Carnegie Hall scored for the band.

Milt Gabler in his study in October 1979.
(Note Stacy in collage display on wall)   *Photo by Daniel L. Mahony*

On January 17, 1938, the day following the Carnegie Hall triumph, Stacy took part in the first recording session for Milt Gabler's Commodore label, although his hands were still sore from the previous evening's work. He was in an Eddie Condon group which included Bobby Hackett, George Brunis (Brunies), Pee Wee Russell, Bud Freeman, Art Shapiro and George Wettling. It has even been said that Goodman postponed a recording session by his own band so that Jess would be free to play with Condon.

Whatever the truth of that story, the date was to mark the beginning of a fruitful association with both Condon and Gabler. This occasion was a milestone for Milt Gabler, the inauguration of his own jazz recording company.

After five numbers with Condon, Stacy and Wettling completed the Bud Freeman trio to record three more titles. There were two more sessions by the Trio to come, with the same personnel, in April and November. (Stacy has said that Freeman wanted to call one of the originals, *The King Of Swing Who Couldn't Swing!)*

A rush of recording outside the Goodman band came to an end on January 18th, 1938, with a session by Lionel Hampton. There is a dynamic Stacy accompaniment to *Buzzin' Around With The Bee,* behind Cootie Williams and Johnny Hodges.

58

Eight days later Goodman opened at the Paramount Theater, repeating the chaotic scenes of the previous year. A news item from *The New York Times* for January 27 reported: "Long before the scheduled opening hour at 8 a.m. yesterday crowds filled the lobby of the Paramount Theatre, overflowed onto Broadway and down the 43rd Street side of the theatre to hail the return of Benny Goodman and his swing orchestra and to welcome the new Mae West comedy, "Every Day's A Holiday." Lines started forming at 5 o'clock and the management reported that 1,500 persons were on hand when the doors opened at 7:30, an hour *(sic)* earlier than had been planned. Shortly after 8 o'clock the management put in a call to the West 47th Street police station and ten patrolmen were detailed to assist the ushers in handling the crowd . . . all seats and all available standing room inside the 3,664-seat house had been sold by 9 o'clock. When the Goodman band appeared on stage the audience, composed in the main of high school students, roared a hearty greeting and couples danced in the aisles. As a precautionary measure the doors of the Paramount will open this morning and tomorrow morning at 7:30."

The band was at the Paramount for three weeks, playing six shows a day, and breaking all previous attendance records.

An interesting sidelight was Stacy playing with the revived Original Dixieland Jazz Band on the February 15, 1938, Camel Caravan broadcast. With Eddie Edwards, trombone; Larry Shields, clarinet; and Tony Sbarbaro, drums; from the original group, plus Bobby Hackett on cornet, the band played *Dixieland One-Step*.

On March 3rd Gene Krupa played his last date with the Benny Goodman orchestra. There had been ill-feeling between the two men for many weeks, much of it due to Krupa's increasing popularity with the fans. So Krupa quit without notice to form his own band. Lionel Hampton briefly subbed for him, and then Stacy's old friend, Dave Tough, came in as replacement. Stacy and Tough then persuaded Bud Freeman to leave Tommy Dorsey for Goodman, though this reunion of the three Chicagoans lasted only a

Benny Goodman's Orchestra in 1938

few months. Tough was fired in October and Freeman left in November.

There is no doubt that Gene Krupa made a tremendous contribution to Benny Goodman's success, and it was this popularity which enabled Krupa to achieve his own rapid success as a leader. He was a great showman. Stacy told Dan Mahony, "When Krupa went through his bag of tricks people went wild. 99.9 per cent of the people don't hear, they just see." But there were reservations about Krupa's time-keeping and his loudness. Benny Goodman's comment was: "Gene had excitement. If he gained a little speed, so what? Better than sitting on your ass just getting by."

Jess Stacy always had strong views on drummers and was fond of repeating comedian Steve Allen's wisecrack that you never had to ask a drummer to play louder. He told James Collier: "Krupa, you had to hold him back, too. I had the bass going down there. I played rhythm piano . . . He'd go faster, perpetual motion or something. There'd be no end to it."

Krupa himself admitted that he did not believe in a strict metronomic tempo.

Six days after Krupa left, Goodman recorded a trite song called *OooOO-OH BOOM!* He shared the vocal with Martha Tilton, singing lyrics which referred to trombonist Vernon Brown, tenor saxist Babe Russin, Harry James and Jess Stacy, perhaps trying to promote these members of his band. The Stacy lyrics were:

First, Mr. Stacy
Jess is gonna play something racey.
First the treble, then the bass-y.   Take it!

The main events during the spring and summer of 1938 were, chiefly, recording dates. In April Stacy recorded with Harry James, Bud Freeman, Eddie Condon, and made his first piano solos for Commodore. Jack Teagarden was featured trombonist with the Condon band, as Stacy recalled: "I thought he was the best trombonist who ever lived. When I made those Commodore sides with him in 1938 – *Diane* and *Serenade To A Shylock* – he just walked in, warmed up, and hit out, and he played like an angel."

Commenting on his Commodore recordings, Condon told Max Jones: "What really made the band though, was Jess Stacy on piano and George Wettling on drums. A good band is based on good drums and good piano."

The two piano solos, both originals, were recorded at the beginning of the Condon session, though only *Ramblin'* was issued at the time.

A rarity on the June 7th Camel Caravan broadcast was a piano duet version of *She's Funny That Way* by Stacy and Teddy Wilson. Two other Camel Caravan events, three months later, were another piano duet, *China Stomp*, with Stacy providing the bass notes for Lionel Hampton's single-finger style (September 20), and a solo by Stacy, playing *In A Mist* (September 6).

One particularly fine recording session took place July 12, 1938. The band was Bud Freeman and his Gang, which included Bobby Hackett on cornet, Pee Wee Russell on clarinet and Dave Matthews on alto. Stacy and Condon were part of the rhythm section. Stacy is in excellent form on *What's The Use*, while two versions of *Memories Of You* merit special attention. That originally released is played slow, while the version which was issued for the first time in "The Complete Commodore Jazz Recordings" set on Mosaic is taken at a brisk tempo.

In The Otis Ferguson Reader there are two articles about the Goodman orchestra, written in 1938 but not previously published. The first is entitled, "Goodman Band: Road Discipline," and tells of the band bus travelling from Cranston, Rhode Island, to Philadelphia, leaving in the early hours and arriving the following afternoon. [Goodman had travelled by train.] Perhaps this piece was unpublished because it gives an unglamorous picture of the band, and an insight into Goodman's discipline: "You're in the band and the band is up at 8:30. So you're there at 8:30 with a good clean note, or else. Never mind the subway tie-up or somebody sat on your horn, or there's no stool for this piano."

(Also on the subject of travelling, Stacy commented that in one period the band did 51 one-niters in a row. Arthur Rollini recalled that, "Jess was a moderate drinker. One morning we got on the bus at a very early hour. Jess said, 'This morning I got up too early to puke!' He had a dry sense of humor." Rollini also said that Stacy was "the last of the ragtime swing pianists with a tremendous drive to his playing." He too recalled the pianist practising on the band bus on a small silent keyboard. Of Goodman, Rollini wrote: "Benny was a great player but hogged all the solos. My meager solos consisted of *When Buddha Smiles* [G-flat concert], *Blue Skies* [D concert], *Stompin'* [D-fla, and several other solos that were not enough to keep me warm.")

Why Ferguson's second article did not appear is unclear. Entitled "Goodman Band: The Finest Nights", it explains why the band members endured the traveling, the discipline and the other hardships. It is because it is a great band and because of what happens on a great night: "And suddenly, when the number has (you think) been about milked dry after 15 minutes or so, they pass the coda and take up again, the band drops out, and the first piano chords are heard – Jess Stacy, among the greatest, is off again, sitting by himself and playing in the faraway land of his inner ear, which mingles the deep strong feeling for music with the ringing beauty of the musicians whose work he has admired. And when Jess plays, the boys listen . . ."

A contrary view of the band at this time is given by Gunther Schuller in his book, 'The Swing Era': "By 1938 the Goodman band had reached an artistic nadir, clearly reflected in its recordings. Of some 50-odd released sides, very few offer more than an occasional moment of interest: a Harry James-led trumpet trio here, a Jess Stacy solo there, sometimes some real rhythmic ensemble drive (as on Henderson's *Wrappin' It Up*) – this is in contrast to the generally listlessly mechanical performances that abound."

The first chapter of 'The Swing Era', entitled 'The King of Swing', is a brilliant 43-page essay on Benny Goodman, his music, his arrangers and his

Benny Goodman, Lionel Hampton, Teddy Wilson and Jess Stacy. c.1938
Photo: courtesy of Mrs. Pat Stacy

bands. This is another source of information which can be recommended to the reader.

In November 1938 Stacy participated in two broadcast jam sessions. One, on the 5th, was held at the St. Regis Hotel. Organized by clarinetist Joe Marsala and compered by Alistair Cooke, the session was relayed to the BBC in London and featured a wide range of New York musicians – Max Kaminsky, Mezz Mezzrow, Hot Lips Page, Yank Lawson, Tommy Dorsey and Bud Freeman among them. The second was a WNEW Martin Block radio show, on the 11th, which again featured Lawson and Dorsey, plus Artie Shaw clarinet; and Chu Berry, tenor.

At the end of the month the Bud Freeman Trio (with Stacy and Wettling) recorded four more titles for Commodore. During the session veteran stride pianist Willie The Lion Smith and his pupil, Joe Bushkin, walked in. When the Freeman sides were finished, Milt Gabler took advantage of the two pianos and the celeste which were in the studio to record a trio of Stacy, Smith and Bushkin, as well as a Smith-Bushkin duet, with Smith on celeste.

Down Beat's readers poll for 1938 had Teddy Wilson first, Bob Zurke second and Jess Stacey *(sic)* was third.

And so to 1939, a tumultuous year for both Stacy and for Goodman. The first blow for Goodman was the departure, in January, of Harry James, although this was, unlike Krupa's, an amicable affair. James too formed his own orchestra, with financial help from Goodman, which was eventually successful, after a lengthy struggle.

By the time the Goodman band played at The Paramount that month, Stacy was getting front-of-house billing alongside James (just before he left), Hampton, Wilson, Elman, Griffin and Martha Tilton. He also recorded three more solos for Commodore, including another Beiderbecke composition (*Candlelights*), and two distinctive originals, *Complainin'* and *Ain't Goin' Nowhere* blues playing of the highest calibre.

The next blow was the departure, in late February, of Teddy Wilson, also to form his own orchestra. But the loss of Wilson was a gain in appreciation for Stacy, who immediately took his place in the trio and quartet. Trombonist Vernon Brown, who wrote a column for *Orchestra World*, reported in the April 1939 issue: "Jess Stacy has taken Teddy Wilson's place in the quartet. Jess has always played well and he improves all the time."

It was unfortunate that there was no Victor recording session by the trio at this time and one only by the quartet, from which just one title, *Opus 3/4*, was issued.

A fan letter from a Miss P.J.A. appeared in the April issue of *Metronome*: "On different days I've seen Benny Goodman at the Paramount Theater; 18 shows in all. I sat through "Zaza" 18 times just because of Benny's pianist. I don't even know his name and here I've got the worst crush on the man! I don't mean Teddy Wilson but the one who plays in the entire band. He has dark hair, is fairly tall and is awfully good-looking. Any information you can give me about him will be appreciated. I'd at least like to know his name."

On May 1st the Goodman orchestra played at the Green Key Prom of Dartmouth College in Hanover, NH, and the April 27th issue of the college newspaper *The Dartmouth* contained an article about Stacy, headlined:

Stacy, Goodman Pianist, Hides Light of Ability under Band's Bushel of Swing

Little-Known Key Man of Band's Rhythm Section Labelled 'Greatest White'

The article itself seemed to be based upon the Hugues Panassie and John Hammond comments from the previous year.

Three months passed routinely, and then, early in June, an event outside the Goodman organization was to have its impact upon Jess Stacy's future. After two decades as a bandleader, Fletcher Henderson disbanded. Although a brilliant arranger, he had never been a forceful leader, and the quality of his band had deteriorated to the stage where he felt unable to continue. When this happened, Goodman immediately asked Henderson, who had continued to supply arrangements to him since the Let's Dance days, to become his chief arranger. Henderson joined Goodman on June 8, 1939.

On June 13 Stacy recorded again for Commodore, in a particularly interesting session. One title is a duet with Bud Freeman, and the other three are piano solos. The first, an interpretation of *She's Funny That Way*, is one of those rare instances, up to this time, of a pure improvisation, without the customary statement of the theme at the beginning. *The Sell Out* and *Ec-Stacy* are 12" recordings of blues improvisations, with the titles later allocated by Milt Gabler. Of *Ec-Stacy*, Gabler wrote: "As a one-take improvisation of almost five minutes' duration, it is a remarkable work."

Shortly after Henderson joined the staff, Goodman began to give him features at the piano, and to use him in the trio and quartet. This naturally upset Stacy. As Walter C. Allen, Henderson's biographer, put it: "But to Stacy's dismay Benny started to spot Fletcher Henderson on piano. Fletcher was definitely present on the first Saturday Camel Caravan broadcast, July 8th . . . Jerry Jerome recalls that Benny started 'conducting' Jess, who started drinking and became upset, leaving the piano chair for Fletcher. Benny had The Ray working, but would not fire Jess." It is revealing that the Camel Caravan broadcast of June 20 includes a version of *China Boy* by the Quintet, with Stacy, but he does not have a solo and is not announced; only Goodman and Hampton have that privilege.

The Ray was Goodman's famous 'glare', which some musicians ignored, but which caused many others to quit. Definitions of The Ray have included:

"The Ray is best described as 'a fish stare', with which Benny seems to be not so much looking at a person as looking through him."   (George Simon)

"[Benny's reaction] was to glare at the perpetrator, his face expressionless, his eyes boring like laser beams, a devastating, silent reprimand which no recipient has ever forgotten."   (John Hammond)

"Well, that 'ray' was pretty fearsome, all right. Benny could really nail you with a look. Maybe it was astigmatism. I don't know."   (Jess Stacy)

Finally, Stacy resigned. *Metronome*, in its August 1939 issue, continued the story: "It is understood that Jess quit the band in very much of a huff. There had been some friction, friends say, but it wasn't until Benny put Fletcher Henderson in the Trio and Quartet in place of Stacy, then asked him to take Jess' chorus on *Stealin' Apples* [Henderson's arrangement] with the full band that the quiet Chicagoan flared up."

Benny Goodman was an enigma. "At best," said Stacy, "Benny was a mystery man." Many others, too, failed to understand the mystery, and through his 50-odd years of bandleading Goodman built a legend about the occasions when he was rude, miserly or just plain forgetful. Particularly after his death the number of such stories grew, a short selection of which are given in an Appendix. They show his failings and the love-hate relationship he had with so many of those who worked for him. Not all musicians disliked him and he was given to moments of generosity which he did not publicize.

On the question of money, Goodman himself said: "I've always been fairly frugal and sensible. A lot of people in our business make very simple and stupid mistakes. They go bankrupt."

Or, to put it in Jess Stacy's quietly humorous way: "He was always on the verge of being cautious with a buck."

Bob Wilber took a psychological viewpoint: "I think Benny had problems stemming from his . . . poor background. He worked hard and he hit it very big, all of a sudden. I think he never could quite believe he was as wealthy as he was."

Perhaps the best summary of the complex character of Benny Goodman comes from his daughter, Rachel: "My father was an extremely self-absorbed man. This self-absorption enabled him to go where he needed to go, but also drove everybody else crazy."

Given such a character it is not surprising that his attitude to Stacy in June of 1939 continues to mystify. Six months later Goodman was still to claim: "Maybe Fletcher isn't the best pianist going but at least he knows what we want." Then shortly after this he employed pianist Johnny Guarnieri, telling *Down Beat*: "We feel Fletcher is more valuable working strictly as an arranger!"

What did Goodman want? Whatever it was, causing Stacy to leave made no sense musically. Few rated Henderson very highly as a jazz pianist. His biographer Walter C. Allen wrote: "It seems strange now that [Goodman] would have in effect driven as great a pianist as Jess Stacy out of the band in favour of one who – let's face it! – didn't have a tenth of Jess' soloistic ability."

Johnny Guarnieri's comment was, "Fletcher was a wonderful arranger, but he wasn't much of a piano player."

One of the few not to be dismayed was a writer named Lillian Johnson. Writing in the *Afro-American* (August 19, 1939), in an example of reverse Jim Crow, she appeared to claim that Henderson was indeed a better pianist than Stacy.

Understandably bitter at this turn of events, Stacy told George Simon: "I never want to play with Benny Goodman's band again . . . There were no hard feelings between Benny and me. He's a fine guy. But it was too much of a strain. You never knew just where you were with Benny and I feel terribly relieved that it's all over." He told Keith Keller that he got along with Goodman, but their relationship was built on politeness, rather than friendliness.

Reflecting on Goodman's success, Stacy said: "It was a hell of a god-damned band, wasn't it? Now that I'm retired, I look back with a lot of fond memories. Benny had a band that played by itself. We all wanted to play those arrangements. We loved them. He was lucky to have such good men." "With [Goodman] the timing was right, first of all. Then his guys loved to play that music. It was a complete devotion. The word 'swing' came in then, too; that helped a lot. On the whole Benny was very, very lucky. That's what you have to have in the music business – luck. It's like a crap game. Of course, Benny had the men, too . . . The very best."

Stacy called John Hammond the unsung hero. "Benny was playing lousy arrangements until John hipped him to Fletcher Henderson, who began to write for the band." And of Henderson he noted: "That man could sure write for a band. Nowadays the arranger fills every hole himself. He leaves nothing for the piano player's imagination. [Henderson] left a lot of gaps in the arrangement for the piano to fill in."

In his autobiography, which was published early in 1939, Benny Goodman paid a tribute to Stacy which sat uneasily alongside the way he treated him later that year: "Jess has sharpened up his playing a lot from the time when he first joined the band . . . the way Jess plays now, sincere and deep and with wonderful rhythm – it's more like the spirit of the old jazz days than anything you can hear any place . . . He's also about the most modest guy in the world, a good-hearted Irishman who has worked plenty hard to obtain whatever has come to him in these last few years."

Three years later, Stacy was to rejoin Goodman, and the 1939 upset became a part of history. In the 1970s Stacy told Mort Goode: "As for Benny, I hate him but I still don't hate him. At all times I did my level best, and though I felt then that he didn't seem to appreciate me, I guess some of the things he's said since sort of changed that feeling. Benny is a funny guy. I don't know how to explain him. I always felt he sorta looked down on me – sorta said: 'You're lucky to be here, kid.' That's the way I looked at it then, though I must admit I just assumed that."

But Harry Goodman, Benny's bass playing brother, told Goode: "[Stacy] got it all wrong, because Benny liked him very much."

Liked or not, Jess Stacy was now unemployed, but in a very different musical world to that of Chicago a few years previously.

4

Bob Crosby

*A*s he began to consider his future plans, Stacy's first thoughts turned to the possibility of forming his own band. He was now a name musician, and he had seen Harry James, Gene Krupa and Teddy Wilson leave Goodman to become leaders. It is likely that the first approach for such a project came from a band agent, anxious to persuade Stacy to take the plunge.

An interesting sidelight on Stacy's departure from the Goodman organisation was that he promoted Chicago blues pianist Art Hodes as his replacement. In his auto-biography, "Hot Man", Hodes recalls Stacy bringing Goodman, John Hammond and a singer, into the 5100 Club where Hodes was working. The audition was a failure, with Hodes blaming the singer, presumably Louise Tobin. It is difficult to imagine how Hodes' blues-laden piano style would have blended with the Goodman ensemble.

Metronome for August, 1939, reported: ". . . Stacy stated he's definitely through with the [Goodman] band and interested in starting his own outfit. (Willard Alexander of the Wm. Morris office announces that he has been communicating with Stacy and may help him build a seven- or eight-piece band.")

Down Beat for the same month said that Stacy was to take a month's vacation, then form his own band of about eight-pieces.

After his rest in the peace of Cape Girardeau, Stacy was back in New York in August but, despite help from Harry Goodman, the plans for his own band were soon shelved.

On August 29th he recorded again with Ziggy Elman, and about this time he began sitting in for pianist Joe Sullivan with the Bob Crosby Orchestra.

The pianist in the Crosby band was a featured performer, a tradition established when Bob Zurke joined late in 1936. Zurke was a star in the band, a favorite for his boogie woogie features (*Honky Tonk Train Blues*, for example), and his own compositions (*Eye Opener, Big Foot Jump*). When Zurke left early in 1939 to form his own big band, Joe Sullivan returned as his permanent replacement. (Sullivan had been with Crosby in 1936, but left when he contracted tuberculosis). Although reported to be recovered from this illness, Sullivan was still not in perfect health, though this was due more to strong drink than to strictly medical problems.

His first wife, Mary Ann Dean, recalled that Sullivan and Crosby did not get along; Joe was drinking and being unfaithful, which the band did not like. Stacy said: "I took Sullivan's place because Sullivan had a drink problem, they liked him in the band, but they couldn't put up with his deportment."

The saga continued, as reported by *Jazz Information*, for September 8, 1939, "Although Stacy subbed in Crosby band several time recently, it was learned that Stacy, impatient with three weeks runaround, has been listening favorably to overtures from Tommy Dorsey."

Jan Garber was another leader reported to be interested in signing Stacy, but finally the Crosby situation was sorted out, and a week later *Jazz Information* could report that, due to ill-health, Joe Sullivan could not meet the heavy schedule of the Crosby band and would lead a small group at Cafe Society. He was given notice September 10, 1939, with Stacy named as replacement

In "Stomp Off, Let's Go", his book about the Bob Crosby Orchestra, John Chilton gives the background to the confusion surrounding Sullivan's departure. Sullivan had told Gil Rodin, the band manager, that he was thinking of leaving, so Rodin suggested the recruitment of a second pianist to ease Sullivan's work load. The pianist agreed to stay while this was being considered.

When Jess Stacy became available, Rodin approached him as Sullivan's replacement. Learning of this, Sullivan queried Rodin, and then Stacy complicated matters by accepting Rodin's offer. Rodin prevaricated, which only upset both pianists. To quote Chilton: "This forced Rodin to act. He explained to Joe Sullivan that he would like to make a firm offer to Stacy. Accordingly Joe handed in his notice on September 10, 1939. Jess Stacy officially joined the Crosby band on October 3, 1939, but during the previous weeks had played several gigs with them."

However it would seem that Stacy actually joined sometime between the 4th and 10th of September, despite the fact that *Jazz Information* for Tuesday, October 3, 1939 reported: "Jess Stacy, whose joining the Crosby band has been held for two weeks, will play on the Camel Caravan Tuesday night with the Dixieland outfit, it was announced by CBS." But it sounds like Joe Sullivan on the October 3rd broadcast, and the Stacy style is not heard until the following week's broadcast, October 10th. Possibly the *Jazz Information* news item was actually referring to the 10th.

The Bob Crosby orchestra was the outcome of a "palace revolution" within the Ben Pollack band. Pollack, a brilliant talent-spotter, had been the leader of the foremost white big band of the 1920s, employing future stars like Jack Teagarden, Glenn Miller, Jimmy McPartland and Bud Freeman. In 1926 he had recruited a 16-year-old clarinet player called Benny Goodman. But by the early 1930s his personnel was very different. His musicians were now young unknowns who were to become famous as members of the Crosby unit.

Pollack had fallen in love with the singer Doris Robbins (later to be his wife) and devoted more time to unsuccessfully promoting her film prospects than he did to promoting the band. As a result of the unrest and lack of work which this caused, the musicians left Pollack in late 1934, and found what jobs they could, but working together whenever possible.

In 1935 a nucleus of the musicians formed a cooperative to run a big band, with

Gil Rodin, a mediocre saxophone player but an excellent organizer, to manage it. The main criticism of Rodin's management is that he was never content with the band's dixieland style, despite the individuality it bestowed. Frequently he tried to modify the style, which just resulted in the band sounding like any other. For a time there was an emphasis on country-and-western songs. Later he employed vocal groups, followed by the hiring of Phil Moore and Buddy Baker to write "new-style" arrangements. Fortunately the band survived all such tinkering.

A front-man was sought for the band, and from the short-list they chose Bob Crosby, singer with the Dorsey Brothers' Orchestra.

As Bob Haggart put it, "Gil made all the decisions on hiring and firing. Bob was just a figurehead, but he was a good storyteller and loved to introduce all the guys in the band and go into detail about where they came from, etc. So he was a very important part in the band's success."

Crosby proved the ideal choice. He was Bing's younger brother, which gave him a certain status, and he had a pleasant, attractive personality. He was not, by any means, in the same class as his brother as a singer, and he was aware of this. Comparing his voice to Bing's in a 1934 *Down Beat* he said: "You will see that my voice is much deeper, a lot smoother, and doesn't sound half as good."

He might also have mentioned his wavering vibrato which came and went. Or, as Stacy told Leonard Feather: "Bob was easy to work for, but he was always feeling sorry for himself because he had a brother named Bing. And Bob couldn't sing and he knew it."

The full story of the formation and history of the Bob Crosby orchestra may be found in John Chilton's "Stomp Off, Let's Go", with a chapter in George Simon's "Simon Says" as as an interesting back-up. For now, let it be said that the band which played under Bob Crosby's baton and Gil Rodin's management, went a long way towards living up to its publicity as "the Best Dixieland Band in the Land."

When Jess Stacy joined, the other featured men were Billy Butterfield on trumpet; Warren Smith, trombone; the great New Orleans clarinetist Irving Fazola; Eddie Miller, tenor; Nappy Lamare, guitar and vocals; Bob Haggart, bass and arranger; and Ray Bauduc, drums. Shorty Sherock, trumpet; and Ray Conniff, trombone; were also members at this time. Miller, Lamare, Bauduc, all from New Orleans, and Haggart had been with the band since its inception, as had clarinetist Matty Matlock, now sidelined as one of the band's arrangers.

Stacy's first recording session with Crosby was on October 23, and only two weeks later, on November 6, the band recorded its first Stacy feature, Bob Haggart's arrangement of Stacy's solo, *Complainin'*. Three other Stacy compositions were recorded during the band's life, as Bob Haggart recalled: "We recorded *Complainin'*, *Ec-Stacy*, and *Ain't Goin' Nowhere* . . . I made those arrangements from piano solos Jess had made for Commodore. *Burnin' the Candle At Both Ends* was sort of a satire on Muggsy Spanier." (However, Matty Matlock told Ian Crosbie that he arranged *Complainin'*. There was also a comment in *The Melody Maker* that Bill Challis transcribed the Stacy piano solos for the Crosby band, but Challis has said that this was not so).

In the October 1939 issue of *Metronome* George Simon's diary mentions two occasions when he met Stacy. In the first he visited Harry Goodman's Pick-A-Rib restaurant: "Jess Stacy dropped in; he and B.G. were surprisingly curt. What a shame." The second reported: "Spent the evening with Jess Stacy. He bought all the Crosby jazz records and most of their stocks so that he'd know just what was what when he joins the band. Smart beanwork. In his small hotel room he's crowded a piano (stuffed with towels so he can play at 6 a.m.) plus a celeste and a practice keyboard."

Billy Butterfield recalled Stacy practising on his silent keyboard on the Crosby band bus. As Butterfield put it, "Stacy was keener than most on practice."

Not all was sweetness and light however. This was how Barry Ulanov, in *Swing* for November 1939, reported an early appearance by Stacy with Bob Crosby: "When reviewed, Jess Stacy had just joined the band. The former Goodman pianist sounded entirely wrong in this section. After playing so many years in a section devoted to beating out four quarters to the bar, Jess seemed lost among these boys, just as Joe Sullivan did, in spite of the latter's experience with them . . . Stacy may develop into an able part of the Crosby rhythm; at least it is pleasant that he will be accorded a great slice of solo time, something Goodman never had the grace or sense to do. And when the genius is as marked as Jess', that time will be gratefully received by jazz lovers."

A period of adjustment was required for the rhythm section to become a cohesive unit, as members of the band agreed. Nappy Lamare said: "When he first came with the band we had to sort of feel our way around because he [Stacy] was used to working with . . . a special rhythm section. But it worked out fine. We got together real good. He's just a fine piano player."

Bob Crosby and his Orchestra, 1940.

Left to right: (back five) Bob Peck, tp; Ray Bauduc, d; Nappy Lamare, g; Bob Haggart, b; Bill Stegmeyer, as.

(middle five) Jess Stacy, p; Doc Rando, as; Ray Coniff, tb; Billy Butterfield, tp; Gil Rodin, bar.

(front five) Max Herman, tp; Eddie Miller, ts; Irving Fazola, cl; Bob Crosby; Warren Smith, tb; Doris Day in front of Fazola.

69

Bob Crosby's view, some months after Stacy joined, was: "For one thing the band is playing cleaner, the arrangements are better and the enthusiasm is greater. Jess Stacy is one of the factors. A year ago when Bob Zurke suddenly pulled out, leaving a piano chair open, we faced one of the toughest problems that has yet confronted the boys and myself. But Jess came along, finally, and put us back in the right groove. His work with the band has been one of most revitalizing things ever. Jess is playing today like he never did before. Don't take my word – ask Jess. All I can say is that his presence has helped the band immensely, not only from a strictly performance standpoint, but also inspirationally."

In the same issue of *Down Beat*, Gil Rodin said: ". . . when Jess Stacy came in from Goodman's band in the fall of 1939, our piano troubles were over."

Bob Haggart recalled: "Jess Stacy was a marvelous 'time-keeper' and his octave (Earl Hines) right hand, plus the occasional 'stride' left hand, using tenths effectively, a la Teddy Wilson, Joe Sullivan, Fats Waller, James P. Johnson or Willie (The Lion) Smith – they were all stylists and very different from one another."

The rhythm section itself had its failings, although it had an all-around ability which suited the band. Nappy Lamare was an average rhythm guitarist, able to sing the required novelties and blues. Bob Haggart was an excellent bassist and a very talented composer and arranger. (His major hit, *What's New?*, with lyrics by Johnny Burke, was originally the instrumental *I'm Free*, a feature for trumpeter Billy Butterfield). Ray Bauduc, grounded in New Orleans style drumming, was an essential part of the Crosby band style. But he had his faults. "Ray Bauduc was good with the big Crosby band, but he, too, ran amok with the smaller group and couldn't keep a steady beat for all the cowbells he had to tinkle."

There is a story which trumpeter Danny Alguire tells of the Crosby orchestra playing a location in San Francisco. Stacy was fed up with Bauduc's rushing of the

Bob Haggart and Ray Bauduc. Two of Stacy's compatraiots in the rhythm section.

tempo, and his temper got the better of him. He stood up on his solo, banged the piano's music rack, and shouted, "ONE-TWO-THREE-FOUR, THERE'S THE BEAT, GOD-DAMMIT!"

Another story concerns the St. Louis Festival in 1985, which starred a Bobcats reunion group, including Yank Lawson, Eddie Miller and Ray Bauduc. During one set, experiencing Bauduc's proneness to "spotlight-itis", Lawson asked Miller, "Was it always as bad as this?" To which Miller replied, "Yes."

John Chilton tells another story indirectly concerning Ray Bauduc. "Jess Stacy's sensitivity extended beyond his piano playing, and during one Crosby session he thought he was the target for some vicious glances emanating from Hank D'Amico. With worry written all over his face Jess apologized to a non-plussed D'Amico, who later explained that the hard looks were directed at drummer Ray Bauduc."

A habit which Stacy brought from the Goodman band was to frequently hit an 'A' to allow Benny to check pitch. Crosby told him, "If you don't cut that out I'll give you six years notice!"

Once the teething problems had been resolved Stacy was able to enjoy the relaxed atmosphere of the Crosby organisation. This was one of the most settled and successful musical periods of his life. As he has said, " . . . we played all the best jobs, too."

And they did. There were fewer one-nighters. Instead the band played week-long theater dates, plus longer residencies at prestige hotels, concentrating on the three major centers – New York, Chicago and Los Angeles.

In March, 1939, Eli Oberstein left RCA Victor to form the U.S, Record Corporation, and it was for his Varsity label that Stacy recorded the first band titles under his own name. There were two sessions, with the featured soloists coming from the Crosby orchestra – Billy Butterfield, and Eddie Miller on both, and with Irving Fazola on the first. The September 26 date was produced by George Simon, with arrangements by Noni Bernardi, while the November 30th session was produced by Warren Scholl, with arrangements by Bob Haggart.

Otis Ferguson wrote a short piece about the second session for *The New Republic*. Its beginning suggests the strange hours at which jazzmen usually recorded: "A few weeks ago, along toward midnight, Jess Stacy got some of the boys from the Bob Crosby and other bands up to the recording studio in a dark building off Columbus Circle."

By the standard of these musicians the records are not exceptional, yet still contain fine playing. *Breeze* achieved a certain notoriety, as it was recorded in two versions, one slow, one medium-tempo, and they were released back-to-back as Blues and Foxtrot. For an as yet unknown reason, the labels of the four titles from the first session contained the statment: "Playing In The Honky Tonk." Perhaps Oberstein felt this added a touch of exotica?

On November 3 Jess sat in with Muggsy Spanier's Ragtime Band at Nick's, as one of the pianists who helped out until a replacement for George Zack was found. The Ragtime Band would soon fold, and before long Spanier would be joining Stacy in the Bob Crosby orchestra.

When *Down Beat* for January 1, 1940 appeared, the piano section of the 1939 Readers' Poll listed Stacy in second position, 79 votes behind Bob Zurke. (Count Basie, Fletcher Henderson, Earl Hines and Fats Waller were in the first nine, but Art Tatum was 14th.) The Crosby band was third in the Swing Band section, behind Benny Goodman and Glenn Miller. (Jess also won the *Metronome* poll in 1940, 1941 and 1944).

The band opened at the Terrace Room of the New Yorker Hotel on January 8, and this particular three month engagement in New York gave rise to much fine recording. On January 16 Stacy was in good form on a notable date for Decca records organized by a young jazz enthusiast, George Avakian, for a "Chicago Jazz" album. The band was led by George Wettling, and also featured old friend Floyd O'Brien, clarinetist Danny Polo, and Joe Marsala on tenor. Avakian has said that Muggsy Spanier was originally scheduled to appear in the album, but then he signed with Victor. Muggsy's version of *Sister Kate*, Avakian claimed, was that scheduled for the Decca album, but speeded-up in order to include the George Brunis vocal without cutting the arrangement. However, any similarity is not too evident.

Two weeks later came the famous Bob Cats session which produced *Spain* and

Jazz Me Blues, with lovely Stacy, Butterfield, Miller and, especially, Fazola. Then, the following day, Stacy was a member of the Metronome All Stars, recording *King Porter Stomp* for Columbia with other poll winners. The second title cut was *All Star Strut* by the Metronome All Star Nine, with Harry James, trumpet; Jack Teagarden, trombone; Benny Goodman, clarinet; Benny Carter, alto; Jess Stacy, piano; Charlie Christian, guitar; Bob Haggart, bass; and Gene Krupa, drums. Of this title, producer George Simon wrote: "The small band side, a Hammond suggestion, was mapped out in advance by Metronome (ie, Simon) . . . Jess Stacy set the exact tempo via his piano intro . . . By the way, there wasn't any sign of the expected friction between Jess and Benny . . ."

On February 27, 1940 Bob Crosby recorded his brother's signature tune, *Where The Blue Of The Night*, with Stacy, heavily featured, demonstrating his ability to fashion fine music from unlikely material. *Drummin' Boy* is another such example.

Recording with the Bob Crosby orchestra and Bob Cats continued through March, and there was another Varsity date, with a Bud Freeman group backing a popular singer of the time, Buddy Clark. Stacy is not featured behind Clark, but he is heard to greater effect on a March 23 session called Jam Session at Commodore Number 3. This is a four-part version of *A Good Man Is Hard To Find*, using two front-lines, issued on two 12" 78rpm records. Milt Gabler recorded Part 4 early in the session, to ensure that the Brad Gowans arranged section could be played before the musicians had too much to drink. He recalled that during a break George Wettling fell into his drum kit. But Stacy remembered it a little differently: " . . . after we made the four sides we were out of wax, and that was it. George (Wettling) just made it up to about the last six bars and just fell over into the drums."

An indication of the status which Stacy had achieved within the Crosby organization can be found on the Aircheck 17 album, containing a broadcast from the New Yorker on March 25. This heavily features Stacy, even more than the ubiquitous Eddie Miller. Through the year Stacy was spotlighted playing his own compositions, as well as the specialties played by his predecessors, typically, Joe Sullivan's *The World Is Waiting For The Sunrise*, and Bob Zurke's *Honky Tonk Train Blues, Boogie Woogie Maxixe*, and *Yancey Special*. Stacy himself was not interested in boogie woogie, but the style was a feature of the Crosby band.

When the band left New York for an engagement commencing April 12 at the Blackhawk Cafe in Chicago, to be followed by one week at the Oriental theater, it was ending a period of seven months in the New York area.

Pat Stacy, then Patricia Peck, remembers that she went with some girl friends, from the New Trier High School in Winnetka, along with Joe Rushton to attend a tea dance at the Blackhawk. (One of the friends, Priscilla, was later to marry Rushton, an admirable bass saxophonist and clarinetist, who played with Stacy in the 1943 Benny Goodman band). Joe introduced the girls to the musicians, and Pat was attracted to Stacy. She saw him again with Crosby and later with Goodman and at Nick's, and then not until early 1950.

Mary Kempe was librarian at Sullins College in Bristol, Virginia between 1934 and 1944. She recalled: "One Sunday morning at breakfast Pat Peck and Priscilla 'Prissy' Boyden came excitedly to my table and said they heard that I was from Cape (Girardeau) and knew Jess Stacy. They wanted me to tell them all about him. They said they came from Winnetka, a suburb of Chicago, and that they and other teenagers often went to

Patricia Peck, 1940
Photo: courtesy of Mrs. Pat Stacy

Chicago to the big ballroom where the Crosby band had a long engagement. Pat, Prissy and I became good friends, and I became a V.I.P., not as the librarian but as a person from Jess' home town."

Among the Crosby band's biggest hits was *The Big Noise From Winnetka*, played by Bob Haggart on bass and whistling, and Ray Bauduc on drums, recorded in 1938. It was named for an enthusiastic group of students from the New Trier High School, but not the Peck/Rushton party. Priscilla Rushton recalled that the 'Big Noise' group preceded them by a year.

Noted comedian Steve Allen was also a high school student when he visited the Blackhawk. His resulting admiration for Stacy was to have repercussions nearly 20 years later.

By the time the band opened at the Oriental on June 1, there were several new members. Irving Fazola, Billy Butterfield, and Warren Smith were among those who departed, to be replaced by Hank D'Amico (though he had originally joined as a section player), and two old friends of Stacy's from Chicago, Muggsy Spanier on cornet and Floyd O'Brien on trombone.

A June 1940 *Down Beat* published details of the Bob Crosby payroll. This placed Stacy at about midway point in the annual salary hierarchy, earning $10,000 a year.

Doris Day had joined Crosby at the Blackhawk as a 16-year-old, auditioning at a Sunday afternoon jam session. In her autobiography she recalled the encouragement which Stacy and Haggart gave her during her short stay with the band. Due to commercial radio politics she was compelled to leave after a few weeks but, with Gil Rodin's help, she joined the Les Brown orchestra. The hit song *Sentimental Journey* and future Hollywood stardom lay ahead.

That June issue of *Down Beat* also contained a Robbins Music Corporation advertisement for sheet music for *Ec-Stacy* and *The Sell Out*, price 40 cents each. Years later Stacy said that he had screwed Milt Gabler without knowing it. He had accepted the offer from Robbins Music, but as a result Gabler had then to pay royalties to the publisher. "Why did you do that?" Gabler asked!

There had been earlier Stacy sheet music. Robbins had published his transcriptions of *Camel Hop* (by Mary Lou Williams) and *Don't Be That Way* (by Edgar Sampson) in 1938, while in 1939 Bregman, Vocco and Conn, Inc. had published Stacy's own *Ramblin'*. This same company was also to publish *Complainin'*, and *Ain't Goin' Nowhere*. More detail will be found in the Appendix listing Stacy's compositions.

After returning to New York for a Strand theatre engagement, the band started to work its way across America for an August 17th opening at the Catalina Island Casino, the start of a lengthy stay on the west coast. During this time Crosby and the band were featured in two films. Shooting on the first, R.K.O.'s "Let's Make Music", began on October 1. Bob Crosby is the 'hero' in the film, playing alongside Jean Rogers and

Ray Bauduc, Bob Haggart, Jess Stacy, Bob Crosby and unknown dancer, 1941.

Elizabeth Risden. The band is seen in two numbers, *Fight On For Newton High* and *Big Noise From Winnetka*, both with vocals by Crosby and the Bob-O-Links, and with Stacy occasionally on camera.

The second film, "Sis Hopkins", a Judy Canova feature made for Republic Studios, with songs by Jule Styne and Frank Loesser, was made towards the end of the year, though the band did not record songs from the movie, *Well, Well* and *Look At You, Look At Me*, until March 1941 – and even then the latter was rejected.

1941 began with Jess Stacy winning the piano section of the 1940 *Down Beat* readers' poll, with 4,916 votes to Bob Zurke's 1,190. The figures underline the importance of being featured with a name band.

February 1941 saw the end of the west coast sojourn, with a booking at the Paramount theater in Los Angeles. Around the 20th the band set off for Chicago, opening in the Panther Room of the Sherman Hotel on March 7, for an eight week stay. On the first Sunday, March 9, Stacy was featured in a Sunday afternoon jam session, organized by jazz enthusiast Harry Lim, alongside Muggsy Spanier, cornet; Bud Freeman, tenor; Bob Casey, bass; and Baby Dodds, drums. (Spanier had left Crosby at the end of January, to form his own band, and was in Chicago for discussions with his brother, Bill, and with C.W. Kraft, one of his band's backers).

The March 9 session was privately recorded by Chicago jazz expert John Steiner, who recalled: "One of the most thrilling performances of Stacy which I attended was his participation in a jam session with Muggsy, Bud Freeman, Baby Dodds and Bob Casey . . . in one of the many concerts which Harry Lim ran in the Old Town Room of the Sherman Hotel. The Old Town Room was in the west side of the basement of the Sherman Hotel (across from the Panther Room on the east side) at the northwest corner of Randolph and LaSalle Streets." Both rooms were part of the College Inn. (Demolition of the Sherman, a 1700-room hotel, began in 1979).

Patricia Peck saw the Crosby band at the Sherman Hotel and it was there that Jess asked her, "Will you marry me when you grow up?"

Stacy was kidding, of course. At this time his romantic attention was turned elsewhere. *Down Beat* had reported: "Stacy walking round with a love light in his eyes." The unnamed target of this love light was singer Lee Wiley, and a year later George Simon was to mention, in a report on the Crosby band: "That's really getting to be some

Jess Stacy, April 1941, whilst appearing with Bob Crosby
at the Panther Room of the Sherman Hotel in Chicago.
Photo by Art Banning, courtesy of Mrs. Jean Carter

Left to right: Bob Haggart, Yank Lawson and
Eddie Miller in Chicago, 1978,
Photo: courtesy of Jim Gordon

romance between song-stress Lee Wiley and one of the gentlemen of the orchestra, isn't it?" But it was not until 1943 that the Stacy-Wiley marriage took place.

By April 1941 the band had returned to New York, continuing its theater engagements and its recording for Decca Records and Standard transcriptions. What is surprising is that despite Stacy's success with the band and in the polls, he was not taking part in recording sessions outside the Crosby fold.

The Crosby band and the band-within-a-band, the Bob Cats, recorded many dixieland and swing numbers, as well as feature numbers for individual instrument-alists. But they also recorded a great deal of dross. In addition to second-rate love songs, country-and-western tunes were introduced, with Crosby having to make the best of lyrics such as, "How he sang when he sprang on his old mustang." Fortunately the musicians were sometimes able to inject a spot of jazz into such uninspiring material. Regardless of these restrictions, Stacy always had fond memories of the Bob Crosby orchestra. He liked to call it a fun band, with the members getting along well together, while all the time it had a deeply musical feel.

During June 1941 there were two particular examples recorded of Stacy's ability to turn ordinary pop song material into little gems of jazz playing. *Mexicali Rose* is one and, even more surprisingly, the novelty *Elmer's Tune* is the other. To quote John Chilton on the latter: "The Crosby band's version juxtaposes a commercial reading of the melody with some unrestricted piano work from Jess Stacy. The pianist's 24 bar solo is a pearl within a Tin Pan Alley oyster . . ." Humphrey Lyttelton too was impressed by *Elmer's Tune* as an example of a novelty song transformed, albeit briefly, by a musician with a clearly identifiable voice and enormous swing.

After an engagement at the Strand theater in New York, the band played various out-of-town dates during June, in the course of which Stacy had a fortunate escape: "Speeding along the highway 20 miles outside Philly a few days ago, Jess Stacy lost control of his motor car on a slippery pavement and crashed into a tree. Stacy, pianist with Bob Crosby's band, said the only thing hurt were his feelings. 'It shook hell out of me,' he added. Jess was on the road with the band and it was raining hard."

For most of July the band was on holiday, then once more it set off across the country, heading for Los Angeles again. It was to remain on the west coast, until the final tour a year later. During the holiday there had been further personnel changes. Hank D'Amico was one of those who departed, and this enabled Matty Matlock to again combine his arranging duties with the role of featured clarinetist. Another who left was trumpeter Bob Goodrich, Muggsy Spanier's replacement, and this allowed the return of Yank Lawson, whose powerful, driving playing had contributed so much to the band's early success.

Lawson considered that, "Jess Stacy played much lighter than Zurke or Sullivan. I always liked to play with him as he had excellent taste and good judgement."

Jess' son, Fred, travelled with his father to Catalina Island for his summer vacation. He, Eddie Miller's son, E.J. (Edward), and Matty Matlock's son, Julian, had a great time together, climbing and swimming.

Back on the west coast the routine continued – broadcasts, recordings, and ballroom and theater engagements. The venues were the familiar names, including Catalina Island Casino, the Trianon Ballroom, the Casa Manana Ballroom (in Culver City), and the Rendezvous Ballroom (in Balboa).

Overshadowing all future events for the next four years, and to have a profound effect upon the swing band business, was the attack by the Japanese on Pearl Harbor on December 7, 1941. The impact on the Crosby band was to become clear as 1942 proceeded.

Late in 1941, or early in 1942, there was another flurry of film-making, the most prestigious of which was recording the soundtrack for the Paramount film of Irving Berlin's "Holiday Inn" – the *White Christmas* movie, with Bing Crosby and Fred Astaire. The band did not appear on screen. However, they were to be seen in two films shot early in 1942, probably about April, when the Wilde Twins joined. In Columbia's "Reveille With Beverly", starring Ann Miller, the band played *Big Noise From Winnetka*, with vocals by Bob Crosby and the Wilde Twins. Stacy can barely be seen.

Fortunately he is more in evidence in MGM's "Presenting Lily Mars", a Judy Garland feature. In a nightclub sequence the band plays *When You Think Of Lovin'*, with

Dorothy Lamour, Bob Crosby and Jess Stacy.
Jess receives his *Down Beat* award.
Photo: courtesy of Mrs. Pat Stacy

a vocal by Crosby, the Wilde Twins and the band, and then backs Garland for *When I Look At You*. Strings, harp, etc, have been added, but the band members can be clearly seen. Stacy is well on camera, though unsmiling most of the time.

The piano section of *Down Beat* readers' poll was again won by Jess Stacy, ahead of Mel Powell, with Art Tatum third. (In June Stacy also came first in *The Melody Maker* "Collectors Corner" poll).

At the end of January the band recorded 16 titles at three Decca recording sessions, with Stacy well featured on several titles, including the two-part *Brass*

76

Boogie, Vultee Special, Sugar Foot Stomp, and *Tin Roof Blues.* The following month his composition *Ec-Stacy* was recorded by the band.

During July the band and the Bob Cats recorded another 13 titles, six of them martial tunes. This was to provide a small backlog in readiness for the recording ban which had been called as from August 1 by James Caesar Petrillo, president of the American Federation of Musicians. The Musicians' Union was trying to obtain fees for records played on juke boxes and radio stations.

In September Gil Rodin and Ray Bauduc decided to enlist, rather than wait for call-up, and on September 28th they joined the Coast Artillery Band. It was the loss of these two key players which started the countdown to disbandment. A final tour, ten weeks of theater engagements, was organized, to begin the last week in September.   This took them to Omaha, Minneapolis, Milwaukee, Chicago, Detroit, Cleveland, Buffalo, Philadelphia, Newark and Boston. A few days after the tour started the Government, on October 4th, introduced stringent travel restrictions. These were a severe problem to all the big bands, but the major blow, amid all the uncertainty, came with Bob Crosby's decision to accept an M.G.M. movie contract.

The band's last week, December 11–17, was at the RKO theatre in Boston. When the final notes were played on the 17th, the band members went their own ways, most of them travelling to their homes in Los Angeles. Jess Stacy, Bob Haggart and Yank Lawson made the shorter journey to New York, Lawson to join the pit band of the show "Something For The Boys" and Stacy to re-join Benny Goodman. On December 18th he replaced Jimmy Rowles in the Goodman orchestra at the Hotel New Yorker.

Bob Crosby's Orchestra, Casino Ballroom, Catalina, California, 1941.
Standing: Jess Stacy, Ray Bauduc, Elmer Smithers, Yank Lawson, Bob Crosby, Liz Tilton, Bob Haggart, Lyman Vunk, Buddy Morrow, Tony Paris. Below: Nappy Lamare, Eddie Miller, Art Mendelsohn, Max Herman, Doc Rando, Floyd O'Brien, Matty Matlock and Gil Rodin.   *Photo: courtesy of Mrs. Pat Stacy*

5

B.G., Horace Heidt & Tommy Dorsey

In the three-and-a-half years since Stacy's departure, Benny Goodman's orchestra had undergone numerous changes. Before his premature death from TB, guitarist Charlie Christian had revolutionised the Sextet, while the full band, starring Cootie Williams and Billy Butterfield, trumpets; Lou McGarity, trombone; Mel Powell, piano; and the arrangements of Eddie Sauter, had evolved into something very different from the Harry James/Gene Krupa unit. By the end of 1942, however, various factors, but mainly the draft, had resulted in a far from settled band. Even D. Russell Connor is unable to give a definite personnel for the time when Stacy rejoined. It seems probable that it did include Lee Castle, trumpet; Miff Mole, trombone; Joe Rushton, bass-sax; Dave Barbour, guitar; Sid Weiss, bass; Louie Bellson, drums; Peggy Lee, vocals.

Writing of Rushton's membership of the band, John Lucas has said: "Joe (Rushton) loved Benny Goodman; (BG) put him in the band without any bass sax parts! 'Cause Joe was broke."

Shortly after joining Goodman, Stacy was involved in another famous musical occasion.

Frank Sinatra had left the Tommy Dorsey orchestra to embark on a solo career the previous September. Not much happened until he began a CBS radio series, followed by a booking at the Mosque theater in Newark, New Jersey. In November Harry Romm of G.A.C. persuaded Bob Weitman, MD of the Paramount theater, to hear Sinatra at the Mosque. As a result, Sinatra was booked for the Paramount.

The *New York Times* for December 28, 1942 carried an advertizement for the Paramount, where the film showing was "Star Spangled Rhythm". The announcement included:

> Benny Goodman and his Famous Orchestra
> Extra added attraction   Frank Sinatra

The show opened on December 30. The band completed its part by playing *Sing, Sing, Sing*. Then, as Frank Sinatra recalled it, Benny Goodman announced, " 'Ladies and

Paramount Theatre,
New York, 1943

Photo: courtesy of
Mrs. Pat Stacy

gentlemen, Frank Sinatra.' . . . and the biggest yell went up in the theatre, and it scared me and scared everybody in the room . . . and with his back to the audience and his arms upraised ready for a downbeat, Goodman turned around and looked at nobody, he said, 'What the hell is that?'"

Drummer Louie Bellson's recollection of that moment was: "I never seen anything like that in my life."

Whether or not Goodman said "hell" is open to question, but the answer to his query might well have been that it was the sound of the beginning of the end of the big band era. The solo singers were going to take center stage in the very near future.

Another of Stacy's early engagements with Goodman was a December appearance in the film "Stage Door Canteen", wherein the band played its current hit, *Why Don't You Do Right?*, sung by Peggy Lee. The pianist is in the foreground for this sequence, which was filmed in New York. He is also seen and heard briefly when the band plays *Bugle Call Rag*.

Down Beat readers again voted Jess Stacy as their favorite pianist of 1942 (3064 votes), ahead of Mel Powell (1416) and Art Tatum (939).

In February the band was in Chicago, then Goodman and some key members, including Stacy, flew to the west coast for a lengthy booking at the Hollywood Palladium. The personnel was completed with local musicians.

One of these was reedman Heinie Beau, who worked with the band for two weeks while the Tommy Dorsey orchestra was taking a vacation. Beau said, "BG phoned and asked me to work with him. I did accept and enjoyed it with Jess, Miff Mole, Herbie Haymer, Hymie Shertzer, etc. Jess Stacy is one of my personal favorites, both as a musician and as a person."

Shortly after the band took part in the filming of "The Gang's All Here", a Technicolor production from 20th Century-Fox, with Alice Faye and Carmen Miranda. The musicians are well featured, visually. One of the songs was called *Minnie's In The Money*, and in typical manner Stacy drives this dog-tune along as if it is a classic hot number.

When shooting of the film was over, Goodman seems to have been inactive for five or six weeks, following the birth of his first daughter, Rachel, on May 2 in Los Angeles. This break suited Jess Stacy's plans, and on June 3 he married Lee Wiley at the Beverly Hills home of her sister, Pearl, just before the Goodman band left to play at the Golden Gate theater in San Francisco. *Down Beat* reported: "Singer Wiley nixed plans for a similar altar trek the following day with wealthy Lieut. Charles Boettcher II in Arrowhead."

Charles 'Chuck' Boettcher later denied that he and Lee Wiley had been engaged.

Don Richardson, the Lee Wiley biographer, has reported that the guests at Pearl Pegler's home included Bing Crosby, Bob Hope, Paulette Goddard, Zazu Pitts, Adolphe Menjou, and Victor and Rida Young. The presence of such stars was a tribute to Lee Wiley's standing in the film colony.

Lee Wiley and Jess Stacy. c.1943/44

Photo: courtesy of Mrs. Pat Stacy

Lee Wiley was born in Fort Gibson, Oklahoma, on October 9, 1915. At 16 she was singing with Leo Reisman's orchestra. Through the 1930s she did a great deal of radio work, with her own shows, and with Paul Whiteman. She enjoyed working with jazz musicians, and was associated with the Eddie Condon clique. Max Jones called her a chanteuse, a singer of quality songs. She was the first to record albums (78 rpm) of songs by composers of the standing of Cole Porter, Harold Arlen, and George Gershwin.

The following quotations may help to explain the high regard in which she was held by musicians and the more discerning public: "Wiley was among the first white singers to build on the stylistic advances made by Ethel Waters. She had a husky, smoky contralto voice that was made more expressive by a pronounced vibrato."   (Dick Sudhalter)

"She was always absolutely correct musically and there was always a high sexual quotient in her voice. Musicians were all mad about her . . ."   (Ernie Anderson)

"Her look was that of a lady of exceptional refinement. Not a snob by any means, but at first rather distant. As for her jazz time, she was one of those improvisers who didn't have to even think about swinging. The pulse, the flow and flexibility of her beat were as natural a part of her as the discreetly erotic vibrato that, in certain wordless passages, promised initiation into incomparable rites."   (Nat Hentoff)

"She was not a beautiful woman, nor was her figure divine, but she had a hard-to-define appeal. I remember her walking into Condon's one night, quietly and unobtrusively. And yet, she attracted all eyes and drew an accompanying hush in nightclub noise."
          (Henry Donaldson)

Photographs both confirm and deny the comment that Lee Wiley was not beautiful. In some she looks quite ordinary, in others quite stunning. Similarly, her look may have been ladylike, but she did not suffer fools gladly and was known to use her fist to emphasise her point of view. Her affairs with Victor Young, Bunny Berigan and other musicians were well known.

This was the lady that Jess Stacy married and who was to feature in what in later years he called "The Wiley Incident". But for now, all was well, and the work and applause continued with the ever-popular Benny Goodman orchestra.

A holdover from his Bob Crosby sojourn found Stacy playing *Honky Tonk Train Blues* on a June 26, 1943 broadcast. Two days later, as D. Russell Connor reported: "Benny and the band began a lengthy engagement at the Astor Roof, Hotel Astor, Manhattan. George Wettling joined, and together with Stacy, Reuss and Weiss, gave Benny the best rhythm section he'd had for more than a year."

Connor then raves, justifiably, about Goodman's playing on an air check of *Stealin' Apples*, but he could have stressed Stacy's very worthy contribution rather more. Also strongly recommended is a trio version of *Oh, Lady Be Good*, with Stacy well featured.

A similar view to Connor's was expressed by Frank Stacy in *Down Beat*: "Particularly noteworthy was the way Jess Stacy sent the rhythm section rocking its way down long stretches of the intricate passages which keep creeping into B.G.'s arrangements . . . Benny's duetings with Jess Stacy are the *ne plus ultra* for this reviewer's dough."

Another old friend rejoined the band September 21. This was Gene Krupa, just released from a short spell in prison "for contributing to the delinquency of a minor." Here was another example of Goodman immediately helping a friend. The full story is told in "Listen To His Legacy" by D. Russell Connor. Of the three months that Krupa stayed with BG, Connor says: "The rhythm section, three-quarters of it the same as that of Benny's standard, the Victor-era section, was outstanding. Krupa . . . never worked harder. Stacy rarely played more melodiously. Reuss never more rhythmically. Joined with Sid Weiss, a bassist superior to Harry Goodman of 1935-1939, they were a formidable foursome."

Making a similar observation, James Lincoln Collier remarks on the fact that Goodman was increasingly featuring himself. "Only Jess Stacy was getting any reasonable solo space." Worse still, "Goodman had also come to think of himself as a singer."

An unusual event took place in photographer Gjon Mili's studio the last week in September. Stacy and his wife were participants in a jam session sponsored by *Life* magazine which featured 31 of the finest players and singers then in New York. Details are given in the discography.

During 1943 Hugues Panassie's book, "The Real Jazz", was published. In his original volume, "Hot Jazz", the French critic emphasized the achievements of the white jazzmen. His new book gave credit to the black creators of jazz, and of Stacy he now wrote: "There are no white pianists who have the ability of Earl Hines, James P. Johnson or Fats Waller. The two best known are Jess Stacy and Joe Sullivan, both representatives of the Chicago style. Jess Stacy took his inspiration from Earl Hines and Bix. He has a good attack and a punch which is rare among white musicians; his harmonic ideas are original but he has none of that supreme abandon of the greatest Negro pianists."

On October 6 Decca signed an agreement with the American Federation of

Musicians, the first of the major record companies to do so. RCA Victor and Columbia continued to hold out against the strike for another year, not signing until November 11, 1944. This strike proved to be one of the contributory factors in the decline of the big bands in popular esteem. Unable to record the orchestras, the recording companies switched the emphasis to singers, backing them with vocal groups. Indeed, if it had not been for the AFRS transcriptions or the rare airshot the exciting qualities of the Goodman band of this period would not have been appreciated.

Jam sessions were becoming a feature of Sundays on 42nd Street, and Stacy may have appeared at some of these. He was scheduled to attend a Milt Gabler session at Jimmy Ryan's on October 24, 1943, with Bobby Hackett, Miff Mole, Rod Cless and Sidney and Wilbur DeParis.

On radio, on November 1, 1943, Benny Goodman featured Stacy on Stacy's own composition, *Complainin'*. Shortly afterwards, on November 16, the Goodman band was filmed for a March of Time short called "Upbeat In Music". On screen the band is seen playing part of *Henderson Stomp*.

In the December, 1943 section of his brilliantly detailed survey of Goodman's career, Connor refers to a highlight at the Hotel New Yorker: "One night, when the band had finished a set and dispersed on Benny's 'Take five', Gene remained on his drummer's throne, regarding his tubs almost meditatively. All alone, he began a brush beat, for he wanted to play. Jess, ever Gene's good friend, slid back onto the piano bench and joined in. Then Goodman returned, and finally it was eight pieces jamming for 'what seemed about 20 minutes.'"

Gene Krupa left the band in mid-December, before it travelled again to California. Around the same time, on December 15, one of Stacy's early influences, Thomas 'Fats' Waller, died at the age of 39.

January 1944 began with Goodman's participation in the *Esquire* Jazz Concert broadcast, having been chosen best jazz clarinetist by the magazine's forum of critics. The concert was held at the Metropolitan Opera House in New York, but Goodman's contribution, a trio version of *Rachel's Dream* was broadcast from Hollywood. Jess Stacy, who had won the *Down Beat* poll as favorite pianist, and drummer Morey Feld completed the trio.

Sharon Pease, writing in *Down Beat*, was particularly impressed by Stacy's backing of Benny Goodman's solo on the *Esquire* broadcast. "In that performance, he took on the proportions of a one-man rhythm section. So, maybe, Walter Winchell wasn't too far off the beam when, during a broadcast a few nights later, he referred to Jess as 'The drummer with Benny Goodman's orchestra.'"

Little is known about *The 88 Rag*, a mimeographed magazine edited by Mary Peart. Apparently the publication of a fan club for pianists, Jess Stacy was its honorary president. The only issue seen was undated and unnumbered, but posted to subscribers in January, 1943.

In 1944, came the main reason for the trip to the west coast: Goodman's participation in the film "Sweet and Lowdown". Made for 20th Century Fox, it starred Linda Darnell and Jack Oakie. Both Goodman and the band are well featured. This is the film which gives the greatest opportunity to observe Jess Stacy, although he is rather ill-at-ease in front of the camera. It was also planned that he would speak his first words on screen. There is a scene, following a lumbering foot chase, in which the hero, a trombonist (dubbed by Bill Harris), auditions for Goodman, playing *I'm Making Believe*, accompanied by the pianist. Goodman asks Stacy, "Jess, see if you can fake an introduction for him, will ya?", and Stacy was intended to say something like, "What tempo?", but that was omitted from the film as released.

Of particular note is the quartet version of *The World Is Waiting For The Sunrise*, with Goodman, Stacy, Sid Weiss and Morey Feld.

A typical review for the period, in the Motion Picture Herald, began: "The good news for the followers of Benny Goodman and his band is that "Sweet and Lowdown" gives the boys plenty of room for 'solid sending' and still weaves a plot around them which is in partnership rather than competition with the music."

While the film was in production the first reports of early marital disharmony between the Stacys appeared in magazines for February 1944. *The Capitol News* said: "Lee Wiley awaiting split with Stacy. Friends reported that Lee Wiley is now in Nevada awaiting a divorce from Stacy, whom she married here last spring." And *Metronome*: ". . . reports are that Lee Wiley is in Nevada, where she last month filed suit for divorce from Jess Stacy."

But the March issue of *Metronome* noted: "Lee Wiley and Jess Stacy are back together in Hollywood in spite of Lee's weeks in Nevada awaiting a divorce."

This was followed by a report in *Down Beat* for April 1, 1944, that Stacy had been ill, under the heading, "STACY WEATHERS PNEUMONIA TIFF", commenting "Jess Stacy's illness improved, maybe he was just lonesome for Lee?" *Metronome* for the same month said: "Jess was critically ill for two weeks, but recovered and then announced he would organize a band of his own . . ."

Goodman had been trying for months to cancel his long-term contract with M.C.A. (Music Corporation of America) without success, so on March 9 he disbanded. *The International Musician* (April 1944) indicated: "He will tour army camps after the picture is completed. He stated that the calling of five of his men in the draft in a week was partly responsible for his decision to disband."

The "I want to lead a band" stories began again, with *Down Beat* reporting: "Jess Stacy, with 15 men and Lee Wiley, opens April 25 at the Chanticleer in Baltimore." And *The Capitol News*: "Stacy, renowned jazz pianist, at first planned to organize his own orchestra in New York and bookings for his new group were being set up by General Amusement Corp. to which Stacy was signed. But on March 26 he announced, instead, that he would join Horace Heidt at the Trianon in Culver City. Apparently his plans as a leader will wait."

Metronome for May contained the headline:

JESS JOINS HEIDT; JILTS GAC

Hollywood – Jess Stacy, slated to take over the remnant of the Benny Goodman band when Benny quit band business last month, reneged at the last moment and accepted a lucrative offer with Horace Heidt instead . . . Jess had been booked as far East as the Baltimore Chanticleer by GAC (Dick Webster of the Los Angeles office); he was set for a full career as a band-leader. He averred a preference for sunshine and the soft California life as a major reason for giving up band.

Down Beat's report (April 15, 1944) said:

JESS STACY HALTS PLANS FOR BAND

Los Angeles – Jess Stacy, ex-Goodman pianist who signed a contract with GAC here last month to head his own band, changed his mind after the first few days of good old California springtime sunshine and accepted an offer from Horace Heidt, who is paying the biggest dough for sidemen in the music business. Basking in the sun on the roof of the Hollywood apartment in which he resides with his wife, singer Lee Wiley, Stacy said, "You see how it is, this is just too nice. I like it here so much I can't leave. Yes, I still plan to have a band of my own one of these days, but not just yet. My contract with GAC is still good and sometime in the future I'll go through with the band idea." GAC officials here were unhappy about the outcome of the deal, but didn't show any bitterness. Local spokesman said, "Naturally we're disappointed. We had dates lined up for Jess in New England and were getting a swell band together for him in New York. We could collect on his earnings with Heidt but don't intend to do it because it would not be keeping the spirit of our relationship."

So ended Stacy's second spell with Benny Goodman, but it was not to be the end of their association.

Horace Heidt
Photo: courtesy of Buddy Bergman

Horace Heidt had been a bandleader since 1923, and by 1944 he was a major name in the entertainment business. His 1930s "Pot of Gold" giveaway radio programme had made him nationally famous, and his show band had been highly popular thereafter. Along with other property, he owned the Trianon Ballroom in South Gate, California. The Musical Knights, as his band was known, featured almost anything which would appeal to the general public – a singer, a glee club, a dancer, a whistler; even a skit or a quiz show.

Since the late 1930s Heidt had, from time to time, employed a solitary jazz soloist, notably cornetist Bobby Hackett in 1939 and clarinetist Irving Fazola in 1943. Bill Finegan scored for the band in 1943, and Neal Hefti did so a little later. In 1944 Heidt began to move closer to the swing band style, encouraged by his band manager, the late Hugh Hudgings. Hudgings said: "I was in charge of many things on the Heidt band and brought many of my friends and acquaintances on the band in the hope of changing the image completely. Among those were [Jess] Stacy, [Shorty] Sherock, [Joe] Rushton, Irving Fazola, Tony Johnson, Frankie Carlson, Abe Aarons, Charley Parlotta *(sic)*, Tony Terran and many others. I also brought in Bill Finegan as arranger. This band did not record but did make many transcriptions to send overseas."

Finegan had made his name as arranger with Glenn Miller, and later co-founded the Sauter-Finegan orchestra. Trumpeter Shorty Sherock had been featured with Gene Krupa, while Frankie Carlson had been the drummer with Woody Herman for many years. Sherock, Rushton and Carlson had joined early in 1944, shortly before Stacy was tempted by the salary and by Heidt's offer to back him with his own band at a later date. The band offer was more than a empty inducement, for Heidt had supported pianist

84

Frankie Carle when he left to form his own group, and he was to finance the Shorty Sherock band in 1945.

Stacy was recruited as the regular replacement for Frankie Carle, a flashy piano entertainer, when the latter departed.

Asked in later years about his reasons for joining Heidt, Stacy said: "He promised to finance the band . . . but it didn't work out. It was not the kind of band I wanted to play in, anyway, but it was a job at the time."

To Whitney Balliett he said: "After that came a low point in my life. I joined Horace Heidt . . . He paid me 300 a week and tried to make a showman out of me, which is ridiculous." And to Don Chichester: "I went with Horace Heidt, I'm ashamed to say . . . I was only with him about six months. I didn't enjoy it at all . . . it was a commercial band."

Hugh Hudgings remembered Heidt as "quite a smiler", saying: "Jess once said to me, 'Look at him smiling at me – at intermission he's going to take me out and chop my head off.'"

Heidt himself said: "I asked Jess to play a solo every show, but he didn't like it, and never took a bow. He'd say he was an organization man, not a soloist." But on the one transcription of a broadcast by the band with Stacy, he does have a long solo feature, *Rosetta*, which is vintage Stacy.

Horace Heidt Orchestra at The Trianon, 1944, includes: Bert Moncrief, Shorty Sherock, Charlie Parlota, tps; Russ Brown, tb; Tony Johnson, Fred Worrell, Don Raffel, Joe Rushton, reeds; Bob Bauer, p; Gus van Camp, b; Frankie Carlson, d; Bob Matthews, v.

Probably just before Stacy joined.

Photo: courtesy of the late Hugh Hudgings

Stacy's debut with Heidt was on, or shortly after, March 26. He was featured on broadcasts from the Trianon on April 5 and 7. A review in *Metronome* of the April 7 radio show on KNX-CBS commented: ". . . the new and streamlined Heidt crew, an outfit which has undergone a profound psychological metamorphosis since Jess Stacy joined as pianist. Heidt himself reflects the enthusiasm of the musicians with his announcements . . . not that Heidt has a phenomenally exciting band. It is still a long way from the best, but the improvement is so obvious that due credit should be granted the man who for more than two decades emphasized almost everything but musicianship. Buzz Adlam's arrangements, the Stacy Steinway stylings, Shorty Sherock's tasty trumpeting, Frank Carlson's virile drumming, bass sax by Joe Rushton, Jim Sims' sly sliphorn – these are the factors which have improved the Heidt standard to hitherto-unreached heidts."

In the same issue the following comment appeared: "Horace Heidt honoured his newly-acquired Jess Stacy on piano with a 'Jess Stacy Week' at Heidt's Trianon Ballroom. The pay ain't bad either, bub." *The Capitol News* for May reported that Stacy was being heavily featured and that, "On every radio program over KNX-CBS Heidt has allocated Stacy a solo spot and heavy billing."

Bassist Gus Van Camp recalled the band's routine and Stacy's presence: "We usually worked theaters about five months a year, then a few one-nighters, and the rest of the time at Heidt's ballroom, The Trianon in South Gate, Calif. Dance band practically all the time at the Trianon. Heidt had a few arrangements built around Jess. It was a pleasure to work with Jess (he was with Goodman while I was with the band). You could always feel him there at all times with just the right ideas. I admired him years before I ever met him."

Murray Gaer, a drummer who later replaced Carlson, had similar memories: "Basically a show band, playing theatres. Stacy was featured, as well as everyone for solos during the stage show. Not too much jazz, but a good solid orch, with a good beat."

The band's stay at the Trianon ended May 7, and it embarked on a series of one-nighters in California, in addition to its regular broadcasts from Hollywood. Then, early in July, they began working their way across country to New York, playing one-week theater dates in Milwaukee, Chicago, Detroit, Cleveland and Boston. The International Musician gave the band's New York destination as the Pennsylvania Hotel, but this date appears to have been cancelled. Instead the band's New York venue became the Capitol theater. (One problem with the early part of this chronology is that The International Musician quotes Heidt playing a date as far east as the Armory, Wilmington, Delaware on May 31).

On the screen at the Capitol was the film "Sweet and Lowdown", so patrons had a double helping of Stacy. The New York engagements also gave Stacy his first opportunity to appear on an Eddie Condon 'Blue Network' broadcast, on August 5.

The full background to these broadcasts is contained in "The Eddie Condon 'Town Hall' Broadcasts 1944-45", compiled by C.K. Bozy White. In summary, the broadcasts ran for nearly a year, from May 1944 to April 1945. As a general rule they lasted 30 minutes, were unsponsored, and took place on Saturday afternoons, commencing 1 p.m. Fortunately, most of the broadcasts were recorded by AFRS (the Armed Forces Radio Services), and 16-inch $33\frac{1}{3}$rd rpm transcriptions of this music were sent to overseas radio stations. The most complete collection of this music is the 11 volumes which have been issued on the "Jazzology" label.

These broadcasts featured most of the best jazzmen appearing in New York at the time. Regulars included Billy Butterfield, Max Kaminsky, trumpets; Muggsy Spanier, cornet; Lou McGarity, Benny Morton, Miff Mole, trombones; Pee Wee Russell, Ed Hall, clarinets; Ernie Caceres, baritone; and Gene Schroeder, piano. Sidney Bechet, Willie The Lion Smith, Earl Hines, Tommy Dorsey, Jack Teagarden, Wingy Manone, and Gene Krupa were just a few of the guests. The recordings from these broadcasts afford the opportunity to hear some of the finest Jess Stacy, playing behind his wife, Lee Wiley, in solos and in a band context. Condon obviously enjoys Stacy's presence, and the broadcasts are peppered with remarks like, "Jess, I want you to really fly into this thing," "Take it, Jess," "Jess, you wanna take two bars?" "Give us the Gaelic touch, Jess," and, a little rashly perhaps, "Thank you, Jess – you never made a mistake in your life."

On the August 5 broadcast Condon said of Stacy: "He's working with some fellow named Horace Heidt. I think Jess replaced the dog." This is a reference to the fact that in his early bandleading days Heidt had featured a trained dog named Lobo!

Trumpeter Buddy Bergman's memories of the band were: "Horace Heidt went to a jazz band in 1944. Musicians like Shorty Sherock, Charlie Parlota and myself on trumpets . . . Joe Rushton on bass saxophone. He was the best in the business on that instrument, which had been considered too unyielding to be flexible, but Joe had fitted an E-flat baritone mouthpiece and neck to the horn and he played it like it was a toy. Jimmy Sims, a trombonist, had the most beautiful sound I have ever heard on any man's trombone. Jimmy was having a marital problem at the time. He was married to the most gorgeous creature I have ever seen. He was badly broken up over this lost love, and four times a day he had to play a solo at the theater dates. He had to play *A Stranger In Paradise* . . . it hurt him deeply to do this, and we often wondered if Jimmy was finally going to break down.

Buzz Adlam traveled with the band, writing all the charts for Horace. The band was big: four trumpets, four trombones, six saxophones, four rhythm, a quintet of male voices, and a female quartet, and a tap dancer. When the band was given the beat off, the first notes sounded like a shot out of a cannon . . . that was a spectacularly brilliant band."

Murray Gaer recalled, "*The Bells of St. Mary's* was Heidt's theme song for radio shows, and in closing he used it again, featuring Jess Stacy, Shorty Sherock, myself, and various other men in 8 bar solos." Of the three known broadcast versions of *The Bells of St. Mary's*, two are played straight, and one is used to introduce the singers, the sections and the soloists, these being Fred Lowery, whistler; Bob Matthews, Virginia Reece, vocals; The Glee Club, The Swingsters, vocal groups; Jess Stacy, piano; Murray Gaer, drums; Shorty Sherock, trumpet; and Jimmy Sims, brother of tenor player, Zoot Sims, trombone. Sherock usually had his own, Harry James-style, feature number. Altoist Tony Johnson is named as leader of the reed section.

The plans for a Jess Stacy band were revived towards the end of the summer, and *Down Beat* (September 1, 1944) even reported that Stacy had handed in his two weeks notice, but the next issue (September 15, 1944) headlined, from New York:

STACY STALLS ON PLANS FOR A BAND

Jess Stacy is holding up his own band plans again to play the Capitol theater here with Horace Heidt's crew. Originally set to organize his own outfit several months ago, Stacy has made two false starts to date, although GAC confirms the pianist's plans. As it stands now, Stacy will confab with GAC at the end of Heidt's Capitol run, deciding at that time how large and what kind of band he'll have. It's undetermined whether or not Stacy's wife, jazz singer Lee Wiley, will chirp with the planned orch.

Metronome (September 1944) reported a mix-up in the bookings for the Capitol, with Heidt unable to play there as planned. Instead he worked at Loew's theaters in Washington, Buffalo and Rochester, before finally appearing at the Capitol. On the Eddie Condon radio show for September 16, 1944, announcing that Stacy will appear the following week it is said, "Jess is in Syracuse right now with Horace Heidt."

Chilton says that Stacy left Heidt on September 18, 1944, but it should be noted that Horace Heidt did not close at the Capitol until October 25. When Stacy did leave his replacement was Mel Henke.

To let Murray Gaer have the final words on the Heidt period: "Jess was a wonderful musician to work with. He had a beautiful disposition and was so cordial and never complained. Just a great guy . . . "

In New York Jess Stacy had renewed contact with Eddie Condon and Milt Gabler, fitting in concerts and broadcasts with the former, recordings with the latter. Stacy noted of this period: "Went back to N.Y., goofed around and joined Tommy Dorsey in Chicago, Sherman Hotel, December 1944."

This "goofing around" in New York can be summarised as follows:

	recordings	broadcasts	concerts
Sep. 23	Bobby Hackett (Commodore)	Eddie Condon	
30	Pee Wee Russell (Commodore)	Eddie Condon	
Oct. 5	Red McKenzie (Commodore)		
6	piano solos (World)		
14		Eddie Condon	
16			Eddie Condon
17	Muggsy Spanier (V-Disc)		
21		Eddie Condon	
24	Eddie Condon (Associated)		
28		Eddie Condon	
Nov. 4		Eddie Condon	Eddie Condon
11		Eddie Condon	
18		Eddie Condon	
25	piano solos (Commodore)	Eddie Condon	

Typically stylish, swinging piano playing, some of Stacy's finest work, can be heard on these recordings and broadcasts. The reader is recommended to sample the Pee Wee Russell Quartet titles and the two piano solo sessions.

The broadcasts are full of top-class Stacy. That of November 4 deserves mention for the opportunity it provides to hear Jess Stacy and fellow pianist Gene Schroeder in the same ensemble, while that of November 11 has Stacy in particularly good form.

Reports of the concerts by the musical press were less than enthusiastic. Barry Ulanov's report of the October 16 concert was headed: "CONDON'S CARNEGIE CONCERT DEEPLY DISAPPOINTING", though it did say that: "Ed Hall, Joe Thomas, Maxie Kaminsky, Lips Page, Jess Stacy, Ernie Caceres, Gene Schroeder played consistently on a professional level", and that, "There were several good moments. Lee Wiley sang three songs, *Someone To Watch Over Me, You're Lucky To Me*, and *Somebody Loves Me*, with typical good taste and feeling and understanding, all successfully communicated." Her accompaniment was Billy Butterfield, trumpet; Miff Mole, trombone; Joe Marsala, clarinet; Ernie Caceres, baritone; Jess Stacy, piano; Sid Weiss, bass; and George Wettling, drums. Ralph Berton, in *The Jazz Record* for November, felt that "Jess Stacy added little to his richly deserved laurels, except for a few moments in *Rosetta.*"

An indication of the all-star nature of the Carnegie Hall concerts can be judged by the list of performers on October 16, as listed in *The Jazz Record* (November 1944):

trumpeters: Hot Lips Page, Billy Butterfield, Yank Lawson, Max Kaminsky, Muggsy
    Spanier, Joe Thomas

trombones: Miff Mole, Benny Morton
clarinets: Joe Marsala, Ed Hall, Pee Wee Russell
baritone: Ernie Caceres
pianos: Jess Stacy, James P. Johnson, Willie The Lion Smith, Gene Schroeder, Sammy
        Price, Art Hodes
basses: Bob Haggart, Sid Weiss, Bob Casey, Jack Lesberg
drums: George Wettling, Eddie Dougherty, Kansas Fields
vocalists: Lee Wiley, Red McKenzie

George Simon was not impressed with the November 4 concert either. His report was headed: "POOR PRODUCTION PULVERIZES NICKSIELAND CONCERT."

In addition to all these activities, Stacy's "goofing around" included trying to organize his own big band. On Eddie Condon's radio show for October 7 announcer Fred Robbins introduced his report that Stacy would appear the following week by saying: "Jess Stacy, who's in New York to organize his own orchestra . . ."

Down Beat (15 Nov 1944) reported: "Jess Stacy's new band may be master-minded by Andy Weinberger, the attorney who has handled Artie Shaw's affairs."

The plans and rehearsals were to come to nought, as the following *The Jazz Record* item tells:

> Jess Stacy joins Tommy Dorsey – and here's the story. For two weeks he rehearsed a band of his own and then auditioned. What with expenses piling up, everything goin' out and nothing comin' in, Jess was pretty flat by this time. But the ten per-centers (booking agents to you) were well pleased with his band, and gave him a wonderful offer, one of New York's best ballrooms, *the spot* for a new band to get a name. The only catch was that in order to work this job Jess would have to go in the hole at the rate of $600 a week – and J.S. didn't even have 600 drachmas.

Leonard Feather related the same story in *The Melody Maker*, while *Down Beat* provided extra details:

> ### LOW SCALE ENDS STACY'S EFFORT
> Pianist Jess Stacy's decision to junk big-band plans in favor of a chair with Tommy Dorsey points up the current battle here (New York) concerning location spot scales. Dope is that Stacy refused bookings which would require him to operate at a loss, specifically, a date at Roseland Ballroom. Many band-leaders have been griping about the need for financial backing to keep a band going but until Stacy's explanation for disbanding came out, the maestri had kept their squawks under their hats. Local 802 here is still waiting word from Washington on a proposal before the WLB to raise location scales.

No details have been uncovered of the personnel for the band which was in rehearsal.

In 1945 Tommy Dorsey, "The Sentimental Gentleman of Swing", was at the peak of his popularity. A successful bandleader since 1935, after walking out of the band he had co-led with his brother, alto-saxophonist Jimmy, he had early hits like *I'm Getting Sentimental Over You, Song Of India, Marie* and *Boogie Woogie* behind him. He was known for his fluent, sweet-styled trombone playing, and for a succession of popular singers with his band, including Jo Stafford, Dick Haymes, Frank Sinatra, and The Pied Pipers vocal group. Thanks to arranger Sy Oliver, who had been enticed from the Jimmy Lunceford Orchestra, the Dorsey band now had big hits with *On The Sunny Side Of The Street, What Is This Thing Called Love?* and *Opus One*.

Greatly admired by his fellow musicians, Dorsey had no high opinion of himself as a jazz player, though he was better than many critics gave him credit for. He always admired the best jazzmen and would employ them where possible, sometimes tolerating personal faults which he would not have accepted for a moment in lesser musicians.

Of his playing Gunther Schuller has written: ". . . as a lyric player and romantic balladeer Dorsey had no equal. Indeed he virtually invented the genre."

Clarinetist Buddy De Franco was in the band at the same time as Stacy and has been quoted as saying that Dorsey was "very strict; no room for error". He "had fines for everything." For example, $10 if you were not in the theatre 30 minutes before the show. For about two months there was a "no laughing or smiling on stage" rule, otherwise it was a $5 fine.

Bassist Bill Cronk recalled: "We had so many changes with Tommy because he fired guys very fast, if they screwed up one way or another . . . he was a tough guy to work for, very disciplined, very exacting, but there was nothing that he would ask you to do that he wasn't doing. In other words, as far as playing, he played perfect, so he expected you to do the same, otherwise he'd be screaming at you."

The Dorsey band opened at the Sherman Hotel in Chicago, on December 1, following a week at the Chase Hotel in St. Louis. Singer Bob Allen had been called upon to front the band, with violinist Al Beller conducting, because Dorsey was compelled to stay in Hollywood for a hearing arising from a brawl he had with film star Jon Hall. He rejoined the band during the Chicago engagement.

It is assumed that Stacy was in Chicago for the December 1 opening, though Chilton quotes November 29 as his date of joining. Perhaps he arrived on the 29th in preparation for the College Inn engagement.

Stacy's view of the Dorsey organisation was not a complimentary one: "Dorsey used to call the band 'the Big Bertha'. No swing at all, you know."

To Eddie Martin he said, "That Dorsey, he put me behind a harp and I looked like I was in prison all the time." And to Bob Rusch, commenting on the band's size: "It was big – there was a string section and a harp and two basses. It was a 36-piece orchestra. And I don't even know why they had a piano. Everything was arranged, there were no openings. In the Benny Goodman band at that time there were openings behind vocals and little spots here and there to fill in. But there was no chance in the Tommy Dorsey orchestra."

As so often happened, Stacy underestimated himself. The broadcasts show that his opportunities were minimal, but for a few seconds on a tune like *Let Me Love You Tonight* he can be heard striving as hard as he did with Goodman and Crosby. However, considering the few bars he is allocated on such titles as *Fresh Money, Minor Goes A-Muggin', Opus One, Sunny Side Of The Street* and *Buster's Gang Comes On*, it is not surprising that the thought of leading his own band should seem so attractive.

Closing at the Sherman Hotel on December 14, the band headed east to open at the Capitol theater in New York on December 21. Arriving in New York, Stacy was again available for the Eddie Condon broadcasts and Carnegie Hall concerts. On Christmas

Day he was at Carnegie Hall in a typical all-star line-up, and again on January 20, alongside Muggsy Spanier and Jack Teagarden. He was on nine Condon broadcasts between December and March, details of which are shown in the discography, and he was in brilliant form throughout. From the January 20, 1945 broadcast, *At Sundown*, a band number, *Dear Old Southland*, a Sidney Bechet feature, and *Don't Blame Me*, a Lee Wiley vocal, can be recommended as prime examples. One just has to smile with pleasure at Stacy's work throughout *I've Found A New Baby* from a March 3, 1945 broadcast. That same day he provided the only bright spot on a turgid version of *Just Friends*, recorded by Red McKenzie for Commodore.

Jess Stacy in 1945
with the Tommy Dorsey Orchestra.
Photo: courtesy of Walter Scott

While at the Capitol the musical press reviewed the band, confirming the lack of exposure given to the pianist: "Tommy Dorsey's string section seems as pointless as ever, but his band has improved since last reviewed here. Tunes played at show caught were representative of TD; *Well, Get It, Sunny Side Of The Street, Boogie Woogie*, and a handful of pops." [Then, after reviewer's praise for Buddy Rich and Buddy De Franco] "Jess Stacy's sole contribution to the show was a boogie-woogie bass to TD's version of *Boogie Woogie*."

A reviewer in *Variety* wrote: "Dorsey's forte has always been, in addition to intelligence applied to his arrangements and manner of presenting his band, the talent he surrounds himself with. It shows up in this 55-minute show constantly. There's pianist Jess Stacy to take the spotlight in *Boogie Woogie* . . ." Some spotlight!

The *Down Beat* Readers' Poll had Stacy in fourth place in the piano section.

Eddie Condon's concert at Carnegie Hall on Saturday, January 20, began at 5:30 p.m., featuring, typically, eight trumpets, five trombones, six clarinets, eight pianists, four basses, and seven drummers. The singer was Lee Wiley, as reported by *The Record Changer*: "Miss Lee Wiley (now Stacy), assisted by Max Kaminsky, McGarity, Caceres, Casey, Stacy, and Al Seidel *(sic)*, sang *Ghost Of A Chance*, and took an encore with *How Long Has This Been Going On?* The background for *Ghost* was arranged by Dick Carey *(sic)*, and when the paper was passed out it brought a gasp from some die-hards in the audience."

Later to achieve fame as an arranger and conductor for singers like Frank Sinatra and Nat 'King' Cole, Nelson Riddle was a trombonist in the Tommy Dorsey band at this time: "I remember little of Jess, except that he was always very pleasant to work with. He replaced Dodo Marmarosa, who, though very talented, was very eccentric, and aloof from most of us."

The short working relationship which Stacy and Riddle enjoyed in 1945 was to result, thirty years later, in an unexpected screen credit for the pianist.

After the final show at the Capitol theater on January 24, the Dorsey orchestra continued working in the New York area. Two weeks at the Meadowbrook Ballroom in Cedar Grove, New Jersey, were followed by six weeks at the 400 Club restaurant in New York City, and a week at the Palace theater in Albany, N.Y., ending April 4.

Dorsey was signed to RCA Victor, which had agreed terms with the AFM in November, but it took almost two months for Victor to get Dorsey into the studios. This was on February 7, 1945, Unfortunately the half-dozen recording sessions which took place during Stacy's employment consisted mostly of popular songs of the day or of Strauss waltzes. Just two swing numbers, *After Hour Stuff* and *That's It* were recorded, with Stacy allocated a tiny spot on the first.

The April issue of *The International Musician* included the following comment in discussing the problems facing dance and swing bands: "Lack of one-nighters to bolster incomes, transportation problems, cuts in air-time, and sidemen scarcity. However this may be, new bands keep coming on with all the freshness of lilacs in May."

Words of foreboding which Jess Stacy probably didn't see!

April and May saw the band touring, playing one, three, or seven nights in towns and cities in Ohio, Massachusetts and Michigan, and in Canada. On May 23 it appeared at the Maple Leaf Gardens in Toronto, and Geoffrey Minish recalled that Charlie Shavers, Buddy de Franco and Buddy Rich were highlighted, but that "Jess was not allowed a single note of solo space. Those of us who were there specifically to hear Jess were bitterly disappointed."

At the end of May the band stopped-over in Chicago to record for Victor. Two titles were cut on the 26th. Presumably it left the Windy City the following day to travel west, for it was in Hollywood by June 1, while Stacy headed east, his big band plans about to come to fruition.

As *The Capitol News* for July 1945 reported:

Tommy Todd replaced Jess Stacy as pianist with the Tommy Dorsey band last month in Los Angeles.

6

The Big Band

*L*eading his own big band occupied a year of Jess Stacy's life, a year he was always reluctant to discuss, and one about which little has been written. Those comments he did make were curt and critical. This is understandable. It was the worst possible time at which to form a big band, complicated by the fact that his marriage was in trouble.

Why did Stacy become the leader of a big band? He said: "I married Lee Wiley in 1943 . . . She had million-dollar taste and I didn't have any money. She got me to form a big band and she wanted equal billing, and it was a disaster, what with the bum wartime bookings, and so many good musicians being in the service." "She touted me into getting my own band. That was such a rotten band! The class of musicians you could get then were just bums; all the good ones were in the service." "I was less than a hit as a leader."

Stacy told Bill Mitchell that Lee Wiley was anxious for him to have a big band which would feature her as vocalist. Perhaps Stacy did not need excessive persuasion; the thought of being a leader had been with him, on and off, since leaving Benny Goodman in 1939. It only needed Wiley's prodding to turn the thought into action.

Stacy was not bandleader material. Perhaps if he had taken the plunge earlier or if he had had luck with a hit record he might have been successful. (Freddie Slack's *Cow Cow Boogie* and Ralph Flanagan's *Hot Toddy* are two examples of hits for new leaders who were able to continue for longer than most because they had such luck).

Other leaders who, like Stacy, were not so fortunate, included many well-known jazz names. Just a few were Bobby Hackett, Teddy Wilson, Bob Zurke, George Auld, Eddie Miller, Muggsy Spanier, Vido Musso, Coleman Hawkins, Shorty Sherock, Roy Eldridge and Billy Butterfield.

Billy Butterfield told John Chilton: "I suppose it cost me about 35,000 dollars, which in the 1940s was a lot of money. The bottom was falling out of the big band market. We just couldn't get that big breakthrough. Our last tour ended fairly abruptly out in Indiana. Being stranded is a bandleader's nightmare and it happened to me."

While Roy Eldridge said: "Business began to go down the drain for the big bands that year. I noticed a lot of dates getting cancelled, and I saw the handwriting on the wall . . . after all the money I lost, you couldn't give me a big band. I didn't have anyone backing me. I did it all myself . . . I just blew all my bread, man, and I ain't had nothing since!"

Back in New York, Stacy set about putting his and Lee Wiley's plans for their big band into operation. The only dated engagements during June were two recording sessions, both of excellent quality. On June 14 Stacy was a member of an Eddie Condon septet which cut two titles for Decca. These were for inclusion in Condon's 78 rpm album, a tribute to George Gershwin. The second session, a big band date under Stacy's name, took place on June 29. Two titles were made, *Daybreak Serenade* and *It's Only A Paper Moon*, the latter sung by Wiley. This orchestra consisted of studio musicians and it included old friends Billy Butterfield and Pee Wee Erwin on trumpets; and Bob Haggart on bass. On drums was Mario Toscarelli, of whom more anon. Stacy has said: "I made recordings for Victor, but I used house [musicians] – my men weren't up to making a record." But it is doubtful that there was a regular band formed by the end of June. Some park dates may have been played, but these would have been more auditions than anything else, with a fluctuating personnel.

Initially *Down Beat* reported that a small band was in preparation: "Jess Stacy is organizing a small combo, featuring Buddy De Franco . . . on clarinet. GAC will book it . . ."

Mario Toscarelli, the drummer, was playing at Nick's with Bobby Hackett when Stacy, who was still with Tommy Dorsey, sat in one night. He and Toscarelli were chatting, and Stacy spoke of forming his own band. It was agreed that Toscarelli would be a member. Stacy said he would be in town in a couple of weeks, and asked Toscarelli, who was also to be band manager, to start getting musicians together.

This conflicts with the following Art Hodes report: "Jack Bland tells me Jess Stacy is getting a band of his own – and the Growler (Bland to you) is goin' to be manager." Bland, who played guitar, was with the band for only a few weeks, and probably not as manager.

Another early member was a tenor saxophonist from Scotland. Benny Winestone had played with the short-lived Heralds of Swing before emigrating to Canada in 1939. *The Melody Maker* reported:

> Benny Winestone, now a familiar figure around every New York bandstand, and a friend of hundreds of New York jazzmen, has been in rehearsal with Jess Stacy's new orchestra with which Mrs Stacey *(sic)* (Lee Wiley) will probably be featured. This is Benny's first US job since his arrival here from Canada. He still has a broad Glasgow accent.

In fact, Winestone was an illegal immigrant, and his stay with the band was also a brief one.

July finally found the band working regularly, as reported by *Down Beat*:

STACY BAND AND LEE WILEY DEBUT

> NY – Jess Stacy's band was ready to open July 6 at Seaside Park, Virginia Beach, for its debut. The pianist-bandleader had a bad break at the last minute when clarinetist Buddy De Franco, his key man, left to go back to the Tommy Dorsey fold on the west coast. Stacy's wife, Lee Wiley, handles vocals and Benny Winestone, ex-Ambrose tenorman, is featured. Band books through GAC which set the Seaside Park date for four weeks.

The Virginia Beach resort was south of Norfolk, Virginia, about 300 miles south of New York.

Mario Toscarelli said the band was on a low budget, so the aim was to achieve good quality with young men who would accept the travelling and the pay. He remembered that the band at Virginia Beach included Al Aarons, trumpet; Benny Winestone, tenor; Jack Bland, guitar; Lloyd Springer, bass; Lee Wiley, vocal; and himself on drums. The band was based upon Goodman's, with Fletcher Henderson-type arrangements, such as *Don't Be That Way* and *Air Mail Special.* Instrumentation was three trumpets, two trombones, four reeds, four rhythm. They also played a few service dates.

However, Toscarelli erred in listing Al Aarons, who did not join until a few weeks later. (This trumpeter is not the one who played with Count Basie.)

One of the trombonists was probably Ed Hubble. As a seventeen-year old he was a member of the Stacy band, though only briefly, before joining the Alvino Rey orchestra.

After Virginia Beach, Toscarelli believed the band had several weeks on the road, but he had overlooked the fact there were park dates in New York first, as the following news item indicates:

TWO TOP-FLIGHT NAME-BANDS TO PLAY IN PARKS
Johnny Long's Orchestra,
Maestro Jess Stacy Ready
To Make 'Em Swing 'n' Sway

Two more top-flight Name Bands will play for dancing in the parks this week as part of the program of fifty-four Name Band Dances which Consolidated Edison Systems Company is sponsoring for the entertainment and enjoyment of New Yorkers in co-operation with the Department of Parks . . . Jess Stacy, another top-ranking maestro, will be on hand for three dances, playing on Wednesday, August 8, at Poe Park, 193 Street and Grand Concourse, Bronx; Thursday, August 9th at the Mall in Central Park, Manhattan; and on Friday, August 10, at the Prospect Park Dance area, 11 Street and Prospect Park West, Brooklyn. The Stacy Orchestra is a versatile musical unit, with a long line *(sic)* of successful ballroom, theater and hotel engagements to its credit. Stacy will present an added attraction in Lee Wiley, vocalist, who has sung at several jazz concerts in Carnegie Hall.
All dances start at 8.30 p.m. and will continue to be held on Mondays through Fridays until September *[date unclear]*

There was another park date in Ridgewood, Queens, on which tenor player Eddie Di Martino (professional name, Eddie Martin) played, but first let us see how he and others came to be singled out for special mention during appearances by the Stacy orchestra.

Before Pearl Harbor, saxophonist Saxie Dowell (1904-1974) had led a successful dance band, based upon that of Hal Kemp, his previous employer. He became well-known when he composed a trite novelty song, *Three Little Fishes.* In 1943 he joined the navy, recruiting a band to play at the Naval Air Station in Norfolk, Virginia. All the musicians were enlisted as 1st Class Seamen. Eddie Martin joined the Navy from the Bob Allen orchestra, and recalled: "The band when recruited was promised permanent station at the Naval Air Station." Be that as it may, the band was later transferred to the aircraft carrier, *USS Franklin.* Martin's comment on this was: "I don't know why they placed such a great band in battle. To this day I can't figure it out." Neither, apparently, can The

Naval Historical Center at The Department of The Navy, which is "unable to confirm that combatant ships carried bands."

But whatever the reason, on October 30, 1944, the USS Franklin was a thousand miles off Samar. While its planes flew against northern Luzon, it was attacked by three kamikazes, led by Rear-Admiral Masafumi Arima. His plane, hit by anti-aircraft fire, crashed so close to the carrier that it exploded and a large part of the aircraft skidded across the flight deck. The gallery deck was pierced and 56 of the crew were killed. The damaged Franklin proceeded to Puget Sound Navy yard for repairs.

Before the carrier returned to the war zone, Eddie Martin and other band members were discharged. As he said, "All released for different reasons, but it was generally nerves and battle fatigue."

Saxie Dowell Navy Band aboard USS Franklin, South Pacific, 1944

(For personnel, see page 171)

Photo: courtesy of Eddie di Martino

Among those who remained in the Saxie Dowell band when the Franklin sailed for Japanese waters, in February 1945, were saxophonist Earl Bergman, bassist Bus Watson, and arranger Deane Kincaide. A few weeks later, on March 19, planes from the Franklin and other carriers were attacking airfields on Okinawa. A lone Japanese bomber, diving out of overhanging cloud, undetected by radar, dropped two bombs, both of which hit the Franklin, exploding below decks and causing tremendous damage. The crew suffered 724 killed and 265 wounded. Incredibly, the vessel did not sink, but was able to make her way to Pearl Harbor, and then on to the Brooklyn Navy Yard.

Very little has been written about this Dowell episode, though *Down Beat* for June 1, 1945 did report: "Five of the 15 men in the Saxie Dowell band lost their lives on the carrier Franklin." It also reported that the band helped "to fight the fires which threatened to destroy the ship, helped to care for the wounded, and then went back to their regular job of dishing out jive to spur morale on the stricken Big Ben." Bergman, Watson and Kincaide survived. *Down Beat* did not list the five musicians who died, though trumpeter Ray Dorney is now known to have been one.

Martin, Bergman and Watson were to become regular members of the Jess Stacy orchestra, while it is possible that Kincaide provided some of that band's arrangements.

It was Eddie Martin, Earl Bergman and Bus Watson who were introduced to the Stacy band's audiences as survivors of the attack upon the *U.S.S. Franklin*.

When discharged, Eddie Martin had joined trumpeter Lee Castle's band, but bookings were scarce and he was looking for other opportunities. While playing with Castle at Palisades Park in New Jersey, his friend, trumpeter Al Aarons, told Martin that Stacy was forming a band, and that he was playing a park date in Ridgewood, Queens, Long Island. "If you come out there, Jess'll let you sit in." Martin continues: "This was in August, 1945. I remember two distinctive things that night. There was a tenor man on the band by the name of Benny Winestone, who was from the old Bert Ambrose band. He told me he was in the country by sneaking across the river. He didn't have permanent citizenship, so he was always on the run, so a travelling band was good for him. And Danny Banks was on the band that night. Fine baritone player. And a drummer by the name of Mario Toscarelli. And there was a bunch of mostly New York kids. There was a kid named Larry who was having a little drug problem. He finally got off the band. In fact he got lost somewhere; we couldn't find him."

Danny Banks remembered playing with Stacy groups at this time, with Lee Wiley singing, and told collector Jim Lowe he thought the band played only at the weekends.

Martin confirmed that Stacy was forming his band by jobbing around New York and trying different men out. "So anyhow, I sat in with the band and Jess liked my playing. [Jess said] 'We just got these few park dates and I'll use these kids I'm using now,' and when I leave New York you'll join the band.' I got a telegram when he was forming. We left New York [in] an old bus, because it was right after the war and the tires were bald. We kept blowing out tires all the way to Pennsylvania."

The war with Japan ended on August 15, and the tour probably began shortly afterwards, as it is known a one-nighter was played August 19 at the Danceland Ballroom at Ocean Beach, New London, Conneticut. A date in Hazelton, Pennyslvania may have been earlier, as it was here that John Setar replaced Larry, who had failed to catch the bus. Setar was a 20-year-old when he was invited to the local ballroom to try out for the band, as Eddie Martin recalled: "He played lead alto and beautiful jazz clarinet. In fact he played a lot like Benny. Just wonderful. He sat in and Jess hired him."

Alto-player Earl Bergman joined around this time, preceding his trumpet playing brother, who arrived on September 21, when the band had a long stay at the Band Box. But before the Band Box there were more one-nighters, and then two weeks starting September 7 at the Casa Loma Ballroom in St. Louis. It was around this time that Stacy broke his finger. *Down Beat* reported: "Jess Stacy broke the little finger of his right hand, just taking off his shirt. It was in a cast for four weeks, but he kept on pounding the keyboard with nine fingers."

Peg Meyer's recollection was: "When playing in St. Louis he started to change shirts, swung his arm around, hit the door and broke a finger." The *Down Beat* report places this incident during August. Later, the October 15, 1945 issue told of Stacy and Wiley being interviewed on a St. Louis radio show: "Jess' right hand, encased in a cast due to a broken bone, which forced him to discontinue his 88ing for a couple of months."

Trumpeter Buddy Bergman remembered: "The broken bone in Jess's hand

Jess Stacy's Band with Lee Wiley, 1945   *Photo: courtesy of Mrs. Pat Stacy*

happened before I joined the band at the Band Box in Chicago. Jess's hand was in a cast. Floyd Bean played Jess's book for him until it healed. It happened while he was putting on a shirt. The sleeves were starched together and when Jess forced his hand through it, he hit the closet door and broke the bone in his hand behind the little finger."

For Jess Stacy it was typical bad luck that this should happen at this particular time. A piano-playing band-leader, one who was the only major soloist in his newly formed orchestra, could hardly suffer worse luck than to break a finger.

It is doubtful that Stacy "kept pounding the keyboard" as *Down Beat* put it, but it would appear that he did try to play, as a St. Louis review will show. Only in Chicago, apparently, when pianist Floyd Bean joined, did he restrict himself to conducting.

The January 1946 issue of *The Jazz Record* reported: "Jess Stacy's hand now well enough for an hour or two of practice daily." This news was late, for Stacy would have been playing again by the end of November. But back to the engagement of September 7 to 20, starting with Eddie Martin: "We hit St. Louis and we played the Casa Loma Ballroom. [The band] got a very good reception down there."

Though this does not entirely match the review by Lynn Foersterling: "Jess Stacy and his Orchestra were a sadly poor group of old men and frank adolescents. Jess himself had a bandaged finger and played only now and then, mostly to accompany the singing of his wife, Lee Wiley. He turned out to be a most surprising chap, and if he was not an established piano genius, you might take him for the most dyed-in-the-wool hipster. The music was more typically Wiley than typically Stacy. Jess was a mixture of Missouri farm boy and the big city bandsman. On arrival at the Club he looked around and in an indistinct voice said, 'Hi, cats!' Such jivisms turned out to be the common thing, and after this one night everyone answered to 'Jack!' Lee, on the other hand, was the exact opposite; quiet, as Jess was, she spoke plainly and in a precisely grammatical manner." So Stacy was at least *trying* to play the role of bandleader.

The good news was that the band was to play a lengthy engagement in Chicago. *Down Beat* (August 15, 1945) had the following under a Chicago deadline: "Jess Stacy and his band, with Lee Wiley, on vocals, will replace Jimmy Jackson in the Band Box September 21 for ten weeks or longer. Simultaneously, a coast to coast wire will be installed, giving Stacy plenty of air time."

With the usual optimism associated with such announcements, there were suggestions that Stacy's might be the house band for many months, but as usual these were unfounded. Eddie Martin again: "At first they said he might stay a year at the Band Box, because they wanted a house band there, and Jess thought it would be a good place to get the band organized."

Chicago jazz historian, John Steiner, remembers the Band Box as a basement joint on Randolph Street, under the Brass Rail. His memory of the band is: "The Jess Stacy band was mainly Jess Stacy. The band didn't have great arrangements, that I can recall . . . Wiley always got the last three numbers, so that narrowed the band down to those two people as being the featured performers. I don't know that anybody else in the band got anymore than eight bars now and then. My biggest impression was Wiley, who was pretty attractive at that time."

There were several changes in the personnel for the Band Box job, as the following quotations show:

Buddy Bergman: "I joined Jess on the day he opened at the Band Box. So for a while we had four trumpets on the bandstand, as the trumpet player I was replacing didn't leave for nearly two weeks."

Could the unnamed trumpet player be the one mentioned by Eddie Martin? "When we came into Chicago, first of all we dropped one of the kid trumpet players from New York. He got in a fight. The manager told Jess to get rid of him. Benny Winestone, they found out he was in Chicago and he had to go over the river again. So we picked up Johnny Lewis from Harry Cool's band. Then our drummer, Mario Toscarelli, left. We picked up a very fine drummer here by the name of Jerry Rosen."

Down Beat for November 15, 1945 advised, "Sam Skolnik, formerly with several top bands, has brought his fine trumpet to Jess Stacy's band, best musical news for that outfit – outside of the fact that Jess' hand will be ready soon – in a long time."

Eddie Martin echoed the *Down Beat* view of Skolnik's playing, recalling that he had a white streak in his hair, "always looked like a skunk." While to Buddy Bergman: "[He] was one of those strong-lipped solid lead men who never seem to get tired."

The top bands Skolnik had played with included Tommy Dorsey, Charlie Barnet and Paul Whiteman. John Setar said: "Sam Skolnik was a good trumpet player, [though] he was more interested in where he could screw someone out of some money. What a con-artist! It's funny now but at that time it wasn't."

While Bus Watson thought, "Sam was a helluva trumpet man. He really rocked the brass section. A real power house, but only in Chicago. It sure was a blast."

Of bassist Bobby Mann and drummer Mario Toscarelli, who both departed in Chicago, John Setar reminisced: "Bobby Mann was the first bass player I heard that got a great sound – made it ring through the whole beat so that it was part of the orchestra that added both pitch and time. Mario Toscarelli was a good drummer [with] absolutely no patience. He had a quick fuse and would ignite rapidly – what anger! But was so contrite afterwards. I remember him throwing his sticks on the floor and calling me a 'beatless S.O.B.' because I played so badly out of time. But he took me aside later and showed me what it was to play in time."

As Setar says: "I learned a lot on the band, since it was my first time on the road. Eddie Martin was a beautiful man who really extended himself to me. Played good tenor sax – a cross between Vido Musso & Charlie Ventura."

Elmer Jerome (Buddy) Bergman, 1945   Earl Bergman, c.1941   Sam Skolnick, 1945

Photos: courtesy of Buddy Bergman

Bus Watson recalled: "I was discharged from Saxie Dowell's Navy Band at Glenview Naval Air Station, near Chicago. Jess was at the Band Box and needed a bass man, so I auditioned and got the job."

The result of all these changes was that the personnel for the Band Box engagement settled down as follows, confirmed by Eddie Martin:

Trumpets:	Buddy Bergman, Eddie Downs, Sam Skolnick,
Trombones:	Ray Thomas, J.C. Wilson
Altos:	Earl Bergman, John Setar
Tenors:	Eddie Martin (Di Martino), Johnny Lewis
Baritone:	Dick Vogt
Piano:	Jess Stacy (with Floyd Bean substituting)
Bass:	Bus Watson
Drums:	Jerry Rosen
Vocalist:	Lee Wiley

Arrangements for the band appear to have been obtained from a variety of sources. To quote Eddie Martin: "We had a lot of arrangements by Fletcher Henderson. We had some Benny Goodman and . . . Bob Crosby charts."

The only arranger John Setar could recall was Deane Kincaide, but Bus Watson said Deane did not write for the band! Kincaide himself was uncertain, saying, "Number and title of my arrangements unknown."

Floyd Bean and Buzz Adlam contributed, and *Down Beat* mentioned that trumpeter Justin Stone was arranging for Stacy, among other bands. And Eddie Martin also noted: "We had two of the trombone players from the Boyd Raeburn band, Ray Thomas and J.C. Wilson. Ray Thomas was writing some things – *One For The Book* and *Call You Day*(sp?). I think Floyd Bean wrote that theme [ie; the Stacy band's unidentified theme tune]. It was sort of like an Artie Shaw type thing, *Nightmare* almost."

John Steiner's review of the Stacy band appeared in *The Jazz Record*: "Floyd

Bean, pianist pro tem for the Stacy band at the Band Box, has changed with surprising ease from the fluid, flowery style he recently used on solo jobs to a driving and rhythmic manner (whipped octaves, rolled chords, full, steady bass). Perhaps no one else could sound more like Jess at the piano. Stacy himself fronts the band with his right hand in a sling, his most significant tasks are calling repertoire and fumbling with the mike stand to adjust it for Lee Wiley. Wiley, convalescing from a touch of laryngitis, has a very charming double huskiness. Band is better than could be expected, not bad at all."

Down Beat was more critical. Don Haynes briefly commented: "The Band Box currently boasts of Jess Stacy's new band and chantress Lee Wiley. They can boast of the name, though not particularly of the band. A ten-week booking will undoubtedly find Jess' crew dishing out better music."

Later in the same issue a staff man wrote: "Jess Stacy's debut at the Band Box was something of a bringdown to most jazz fans, though the trouble wasn't entirely that of the famous 88er. Jess had a broken bone in his right hand, making it necessary for the capable Floyd Bean to sub, while Lee Wiley, vocal feature of the band, was suffering from a bad case of laryingitis, making singing an almost impossible task. Band is far from exceptional though it does exhibit possibilities of rounding into a good unit once personnel is set and better arrangements are available."

A stable personnel and a settled location were beneficial to any orchestra, and some accounts would suggest that Stacy's gained from its Band Box stay.

When the time came to leave the Band Box, *Down Beat's* reason was surprising: "Promised air time didn't materialize for Stacy, so the band will go on the road for a short time before their important Panther Room engagement."

After the nine weeks in Chicago, one might have expected the band to stay there, rather than travel again, if they had the option. Joe Sanders opened at the Band Box on November 23, while the Stacy unit travelled to the Colony Club in Cape Girardeau.

Down Beat listed the Stacy orchestra at the Colony Club (night club), November 23 – December 9, but from a report in the local paper one can deduce that it was just a one week booking, starting on the 24th. Eddie Martin recalls that The Colony was a gambling casino, across the river from Cape Girardeau. He also remembers: "We stayed in a motel, and Lee and Jess stayed with his mother and father. Jess' folks were country

Above: Jess Stacy Band includes Bus Watson on bass and Eddie Downs on trumpet.

Right: Bus Watson on bass and Johnny Setar (right) on alto.

Location possibly Cape Girardeau

Photos: courtesy of Bus Watson

folk. They were very fine people. In fact, everybody in Cape Girardeau, they were crazy about Jess. He was the home-town favorite down there."

Martin was sure that Lee was unhappy in Cape Girardeau. It was too unsophisticated; her tastes were to be found in the city. As Jess always had the highest regard for his parents, and a nostalgia for his hometown, this was another source of friction between them.

The South East Missourian had the following reports during the week:

November 24: Having achieved fame elsewhere, Jess Stacy brought his dance band back to his own home town today. The famed pianist, who got his early training here and in playing for river excursions during summers while still in high school, is combining business with pleasure, business being a week's engagement with his band at the Colony Club and pleasure being a week to be spent with his parents, Mr. and Mrs. F.L. Stacy, 130 South Park Avenue. With him is Mrs. Stacy (Lee Wiley) headline vocalist with the band. From Cape Girardeau the band will tour Oklahoma and Iowa, the next engagement being at Enid, Okla.

November 27: They . . . are finishing out an engagement at the Colony Club. There are 14 men in the band, including Jess. Coming to the Colony Club from Chicago, they will follow the engagement with one-nighters in Oklahoma, Kansas, Missouri and Iowa before opening Dec. 14 in the Panther Room of the Sherman Hotel in Chicago.

STACYS WELCOMED AT JUNIOR CHAMBER DINNER

An honorary life membership and pin were presented to Jess Stacy, Cape Girardeau pianist, at a ladies night meeting of the Junior Chamber of Commerce Monday night at the Colonial Tavern. [after Lee Wiley was presented with a corsage] Mr. Stacy played several piano selections and accompanied his wife, who sang.

Down Beat for November 1 had announced:

Chicago – One of the real booking surprises of the year is Jess Stacy's forthcoming two weeks stint at the Inn, following the Krupa band. The pianist opens December 14, winds up on New Year's Eve. Jess' new band – currently at the Band Box – has been giving a better account of itself lately. Lee Wiley has recovered from her throat infection to knock out Band Box patrons with her wonderful vocals.

But before Chicago, there were the one nighters mentioned in *The South East Missourian*. The only one traced is the first, in Enid, Oklahoma, which took place on December 7. (A provisional listing of the band's itinerary during its year of existence is included as appendix 6).

Charlie Dawn, in an undated and unsourced clipping, wrote:

JESS STACY'S BAND STARS AT COLLEGE INN

The Stacy band made its initial appearance at the Sherman Friday. [Lee Wiley was unable to appear at the opening, due to illness.] Band numbers highlighting the key-board ramblings of Stacy include *The World Is Waiting For The Sunrise, Rosetta, Boogie-Woogie* and *Donkey Serenade*.

It was during the the College Inn engagement that the only known recording of the orchestra took place. A radio engineer at the Sherman Hotel made an acetate for Eddie Martin, which is now heavily worn, but through the noise can be heard *Air Mail Special*; the band's unidentified theme; and *Sweet Lorraine*. It is perhaps unfair to judge the band on this evidence, but it sounds efficient, if anonymous.

Eddie Martin recalled one on stage incident: "We were playing the College Inn one night. Jess got a hand on one of the numbers. Then [Lee Wiley] sang a number. Nobody clapped, and she got mad. Jess got up [and said], 'Everybody clap for Lee.'"

A news story in *Down Beat*, for December 1, was corrected in the following issue:

Jess Stacy and his band, with his wife, Lee Wiley, as vocalist, which opened yesterday (December 14) in the Panther Room of the Hotel Sherman here, is set for the west coast next month, although the facts in the last issue of the beat were slightly garbled. Larry Finley of Hollywood bought the Stacy band from Bob Weems of the GAC office, but will play it at the Casino Gardens for four weeks, instead of the Mission Beach ballroom for 26 weeks as stated. Opening date will be January 17.

Unfortunately, Mr. Finlay's plans fell through. The band played in the main ballroom of the Sherman Hotel on New Year's Eve, and then the bookings ran out. The band folded, albeit temporarily.

An omen that the start of 1946 was to be no better than the end of 1945 appeared in the first issue of *Down Beat* for the year, in which Jess Stacy was unlisted in the pianist section of the Readers' Poll.

The Stacys returned to Cape Girardeau, while the rest of the band scuffled around Chicago. *Down Beat* for January 28, 1946 reported:

STACY PLANS FOR ANOTHER BAND

Jess Stacy, who is home in Missouri taking a well-earned rest, is thinking about fronting another band. Whether his vocalist-wife Lee Wiley, who was featured with the previous ill-fated band, and who had a featured part in the break-up of that outfit, will be with Stacy in the new venture is not certain. Several of the men in his band have formed a small group to job out of here on their own. A new band would take an entirely new personnel, though a fair book is there.

Buddy Bergman spoke for those who remained in Chicago when he said, "I didn't have anything coming up so I stayed in Chicago. We all took jobbing dates to assist ourselves financially." While Bus Watson recalled, "We hung around Chicago waiting for a call from Jess. Some guys did rehearse a small combo, but no work. Chicago local members did some club dates while waiting for the call from Jess, but it didn't happen in January or February. We kept waiting for a call from Jess to go to work. It took so long I finally went broke and went back home to Oil City, Pa. where he finally called."

Eddie Martin (Eddie Di Martino), 1946

Eddie Martin remembered: "Ray Thomas said to me 'I have a book for seven men.' I took several members of the band and we signed with M.C.A. We didn't know whether Jess was going to reform or not. They didn't want the name Eddie Martin as a band leader, so they suggested I change it to Eddie Mason. We took Ray Thomas, Bus Watson, John Setar, Eddie Downs, Jerry Rosen; (Mousie Alexander, drums, played one date with us); and I can't remember who we had on piano. We jobbed around here, played South Bend, Indiana, and a couple of spots around here. We didn't play too much. It was a good little band, so we were going to continue doing that, except that Jess wired us, 'OK, we're getting together. I'm coming into Chicago.'"

Stacy signed with the Shribman brothers, and Martin recalled that Stacy had bought a trailer to go on the back of the car. Lee Wiley had pawned a mink coat to help raise funds to restart the band.

Down Beat for February 11, 1946, continued the story: "Jess Stacy and Lee Wiley, after a rest in the pianist's home in Cape Girardeau, will go to New York, organize a new band and break in around Boston. Lee, who owns half the band under a corporate set-up, definitely will continue as vocalist."

The Shribmans, Si and Charlie, were the major bookers in New England, controlling a number of ballrooms in Massachusetts, Maine, New Hampshire and Connecticut. They regularly booked Duke Ellington in his early band leading days and gave financial support to Glenn Miller when he was struggling.

Bus Watson said that the new band was made up of a good number of the men that were at the Hotel Sherman: "Most of the guys were very faithful to Jess and strived to make it successful. (Lee didn't help that). In New England we stayed in Boston and did one-nighters by car to ballrooms in that area. Weekly payments were late but the music seemed to be compensation. Most thrilling for me was a dance/concert at the Symphony Ballroom in Boston, with Billie Holiday and her accompanist, Horace Henderson."

It is surprising that the Billie Holiday concert was not remembered by the other musicians queried.

Trumpeter Byron Baxter joined the band for its New England dates, which started March 1st. He asked Stacy for a guaranteed $150 a week as first trumpet, a good salary at that time. Jess agreed – but Baxter never once received this amount. The band did not work too frequently and the only pay was a couple of dollars when they wanted to eat. Buddy Bergman said that "Jess paid about $95.00 a week."

Baxter's recollection of the band personnel during his stay was:

Trumpets:	Eddie Downs, Buddy Bergman, Byron Baxter
Trombones:	Ray Thomas, Paige Palmer
Altos:	John Setar, Earl Bergman
Tenors:	Eddie Martin, Bob Knatse
Baritone:	Dick Vogt
Piano:	Jess Stacy
Bass:	Bus Watson
Drums:	Ernie West

Bus Watson remembered Ernie West joining the band in Boston in March 1946. "He was a Boston 'cat', a good drummer and very personable." And Eddie Martin recalled an incident involving West, who had lost an ear during the war: "He was playing a drum solo and the audience went crazy. It wasn't that great, but they went crazy. He started to sweat and [his ear] was hanging like mozzarella cheese."

While Byron Baxter had exaggeratedly uncomplimentary comments about two of his colleagues: "Dick Vogt was a masochist and his wife a sadist, so he came down each morning with a broken arm or leg! Paige Palmer was almost blind and a near half-wit. He was always saying how good he was, but he was lousy."

Kinder was John Setar, in his comments on Byron Baxter: "Byron Baxter was a great leveling influence on the later band, during our starving days in the New England states [called the Shribman circuit] . . . Byron played with great time and pitch and precision and had a great sound throughout the range of his instrument. He was a great lead trumpet."

And he was grateful to tenor saxist Bob Knatse: "Bob Knatse took me aside one day and taught me how to relax and play on the beat or even a little behind, according to the piece, instead of rushing ahead at times. This he got me to do by listening to Miles Davis, Dizzy Gillespie, Parker, Getz, etc. I have many fond memories of this band."

Buddy Bergman wrote resignedly of the first date the band didn't play when it was scheduled to reconvene in Boston in March: "Hardship is hardly an adequate word! If you can imagine driving from Chicago all the way to Boston on a continuous sheet of ice, and arriving so late we found the others were already on their way to our first one nighter 200 miles north of Boston – and when we arrive the date had been cancelled and we drove back to Boston to check in the hotel for our first night's sleep in three days! Union rules? Sure! But do you want to work? Or do you enjoy reciting union rules without a job and without an audience"

Byron Baxter was no doubt referring to this incident when he recalled it being bitterly cold and the band leaving for an engagement in a car and estate wagon, the latter driven by Ray Thomas. They drove non-stop, except to eat. Thomas just napped in the car when everyone else took a break. When they arrived at the Gardiner(?) Hotel in Boston someone ran from the hotel and redirected them to a date in Maine. They were too late arriving in Maine and the engagement was cancelled. The weather situation was confirmed by Bus Watson when he wrote, "I met the band in Boston in a helluva sleet storm."

For the next two weeks or so the band played a few dates in towns like Salem, Lowell, and Dover. One night Byron Baxter split his lip and Max Kaminsky replaced him for a day or two until Baxter recovered.

The Enid Morning News (December 2, 1945)
Courtesy of Prof. Sidney Brown, University of Oklahoma

The Free Press, London, Ontario, Canada. (Left) Wednesday May 29, 1946 and (below) Thursday May 30, 1946

Courtesy of Art Pilkington

Eddie Martin's wife, Gerry, believed it was in Dover, New Hampshire, that: "Lee and Jess were arrested because they didn't have plates on their '46 station wagon. They were in jail for a day."

Bookings dried up at the end of March, and the band again folded temporarily. Buddy Bergman remembered the final engagement at this time, and his final appearance with the band: "Our last job was at a ballroom in Boston. Imagine if you will, this giant ballroom, filled to capacity, and because of the Shribner Brothers' flim-flamming, Jess didn't have enough money to pay for the boys' transportation home. Jess went to the microphone as he usually did to say 'Good night', and the following is what Jess said: 'I want to thank all you beautiful people for coming out to see us tonight, and I would like to come back soon to play for you again, but before I can, I've got to find some new thieves to book the band!'"

The band reformed in mid-April, rehearsing in New York for about ten days. The Stacys presence in New York on April 10, 1946 was confirmed by a news item in *American Jazz Review*: "Jess Stacy and his wife Lee Wiley dropped in [to Eddie Condon's] to say hello."

There were more bookings in the Boston area, followed by college proms around New York in May. The Stacys visited Condon's again around this time. At the end of that month there followed a series of one-nighters, which spilled over into June, coupled with two week-long engagements. It was May, perhaps, that Bus Watson referred to when he wrote: "I remember one-nighters out of there as far as Presque Isle, Maine [near the Canadian border]. There's more potatoes up there than Idaho, Long Island or Ireland ever saw. All the potato farmers' daughters wanted a ride back to New York."

Reporting a conversation with Lee Wiley, Hank O'Neal wrote: "She recalls one time when the bus they were travelling in went through the Holland Tunnel and they did not have enough money to pay the toll. She paid the toll in stamps out of her stationery folder. I guess that is really kind of poor."

About this time Eddie Martin recalled that Cliff Leeman [drums] was in the band a couple of times, up in Vermont. "He'd got his orange juice and vodka, whatever it was, on the side of him, sipping it with a straw. Great drummer."

Martin also remembers fresh arrangers being used. Marty Schwartz, who was working on the Frank Sinatra Show, did some arrangements for Lee Wiley, while Earl (or Jimmy?) Blue and Fred Norman wrote charts for the band.

For the week of June 15–21 the band played an amusement park, Chippewa Lake Park in Ohio. Trumpeter Joe Caputo joined here, as reported in *Down Beat* (July 15, 1946). The previous week another trumpeter, Leon Gabys, had been recruited, and around this time Bill Bushey replaced Dick Vogt on baritone.

Gerry Martin remembered: "Once, in Chippewa Lake [Lee Wiley] said to me, 'There's a new tune out called *Shoo-Fly-Pie and Apple Pan Dowdy*, recorded by some snip with the Stan Kenton orchestra.' I wrote the lyrics out for her. She sang them back to me 50 times, and said, 'I can sing this better than June Christy, and I'll show them.' I sat in the ballroom that night and watched her sing [that song], and thought to myself, 'My goodness . . . what are you trying to prove. You are not June Christy.' But that was Lee and you accepted Lee for what she was. I think she had a lot of guts. I think she knew what she wanted. I just don't think she went about it the right way. I'm not ever going to put her down."

Singing June Christy's mindless hit was Lee Wiley's way of trying to make the Stacy orchestra more commercial and therefore more successful. A laudable ambition, but doomed to fail. Wiley's forte was singing songs of the quality of *But Not For Me, A Cottage For Sale* and *I've Got A Crush On You.*

Bookings appear to have been satisfactory for August, but these are deceptive. There was a week on the dance floor of a carnival in Trenton, New Jersey – "the Catholic Fair down there," as Eddie Martin called it, followed by two weeks, August 9–22, at the Sea Girt Inn, at Sea Girt, New Jersey.

Jazz collector Dewey P. Jeannette saw the band: "I lived in Trenton also and my first experience of seeing Lee and Jess was with that Carnival. I guess I was about 14 years old at the time. I must say that Jess Stacy impressed me most; not the band, but Jess. I had a chance to meet both of them when my father met them at one of the cabarets in Trenton and brought them to my house. In fact, I had a wire recording of Jess playing and Lee singing in our living room. Unfortunately the biggest mistake I made was to sell both the wire recorder and the recording. I also went down to Sea Girt to hear them. Again, they were great; the band was not. And they did very little business. There were not very many arrangements for Lee and she was forced to do the same tunes over a number of times during the evening."

Another collector, Frank H. Trolle, also saw the band at both locations. "It was a dance band that Jess had at both gigs. I can assure you that as far as I know there was not one hot jazzman in the bunch."

At Sea Girt Stacy asked Eddie Martin if he knew a place to eat that was open: "There was a little diner near the Inn that Gerry and I used to go to after the job. I had already told him that I was going to leave the band because I didn't think it was going to stay together anyhow. He didn't have any bookings. Lee got violently mad at me. She was boiling, but she wouldn't say anything. She wanted me just to hang around New York with the band, but I decided to work my New York card out this time. Gerry and I decided to get married and live in New York. Jess was really depressed that night. He just drank his coffee and Lee did all the talking (making derogatory remarks about her husband)."

"That particular night", said Gerry Martin, "the band was playing real good and everybody was taking solos. It came to Jess' turn, and I don't know what possessed him but he decided he was going to play. Played *Candlelights* like for 20 minutes. He played just so beautifully – you get very few moments like that in your life."

"Everybody realised that there were no more bookings." recalled Eddie Martin. "They all came to him [Stacy] one by one, said 'Where are we going?' He said, 'I have nothing.' But Lee was mad. She wanted everybody to work for nothing and hang around for nothing. They went back to New York, and I heard that they did the same thing they did when they started the band – get a few New York musicians and play a couple of park dates – but then it just fizzled out."

The one known date by this last-ditch band was at Danceland on Ocean Beach, New London in Connecticut, on September 8.

Why did the Stacy big band fail? Reasons have been touched upon in its story, but let us consider the question, and possible answers, in more detail. Stacy himself tended to stress two factors; the fact that gas was rationed, in addition to its high price, and the quality of his musicians. He has referred to them in harsh terms, talking of "dregs" and "inferior musicians" and "all the good men were in the service."

The remarks about his sidemen are unfair. They were inferior if compared with the star players Stacy had worked with in the Benny Goodman, Bob Crosby and Tommy Dorsey orchestras, but Stacy was in no position to employ men of this caliber, as Mario Toscarelli's comment has already indicated. Stacy was really complaining about the lack of individual jazz voices, because he could not afford to recruit proven jazzmen like Max Kaminsky or Irving Fazola or Eddie Miller. Most of the young men he did use were capable, or more than capable, big band players, as their previous experience must have shown. Many continued in the big band business, working for leaders like Ray Anthony, Hal McIntyre, Buddy Morrow, and Boyd Raeburn, as well as on staff in radio and television studios. But not one of them was a Bunny Berigan, a Harry James or a Bud Freeman.

Freeman himself had decided views on leaders: "You've got to be a strong, tough character to run [a big band]. A succesful bandleader doesn't give a damn about his musicians – he can't afford to; he's got to be as tough as nails." To quote from Keith Keller's book: "Pat Stacy will often remind her husband that 'if Benny had been easygoing like you, he would never have made it as a bandleader.' Stacy admits: 'I have always let people run all over me.'"

Or as some of the musicians recalled, starting with Bus Watson: "Jess was really easygoing. He seemed to feel if you worked for him you must be talented enough to 'cut the mustard' the first time around – or at least the second time. If not, he wanted a qualified replacement. Off stage (or on) he was a real musicians' musician. As long as you produced on stage, he could care less about your off stage antics.

"Jess was very humble on stage as were many leaders of that era. He did some announcing but not commercial. He liked to announce band members that he considered musicians' musicians. Lee liked to do announcements but she was so barrelhouse. I liked it but I'm not so sure about the audience." (Bus Watson). Note that this comment on the announcing is at odds with the review of Stacy's St. Louis engagement in September 1945.

"Jess was like most of us were in those days – musicians – period! Not any business acumen at all – expecting the world to come to us. I realise now it was wrong, but it took a lot of living and experience to understand that. Jess was a beautiful, harmless, benign individual who was close to the musicians – who idolized him for what he was as a musician – but certainly was not geared for the rough, realistic world of survival in a rough business. In my opinion, if Jess had been coached by someone how to act as a leader, the band might have had a chance. (John Setar)

"Everything good about a person I have ever said I would have to say about Jess. He was a sensitive, gentle, terrific human being. I have never heard Jess bawl out a musician no matter how bad he goofed. Jess rarely commented on how we played, except when he thought our 'time' was good. He never criticized us. He knew as professionals we knew what it ought to sound like and if it didn't we'd request our own section rehearsals. Jess had been a sideman too long not to remember that a musician doesn't play badly on purpose. Jess's attitude towards his sidemen earned a special kind of loyalty. And that's the kind you can't buy. We had all worked for bastards and when a guy like Jess is the boss, 90 per cent of the pressure is gone." (Buddy Bergman)

"I never heard anyone in the time the band was formed to the time it broke up, that said one word against Jess. Plenty against Lee, but nothing against Jess. [He was] very, very easy going . . . if you did something wrong he'd say, 'Gee, could you watch it, please?' But he'd say it so polite you could hardly tell that he was upset." (Eddie Martin)

Opinions conflict a little on the question of whether Stacy featured himself enough. Earl Bergman, commenting on the band's repertoire, wrote that it was "Mostly instrumentals, lots of piano solos, the band mainly ensemble playing, and vocals by Lee Wiley."

Whereas John Setar thought: "[The band] played basically standards, very few pop tunes. My recollection could be distorted but it seemed we had more vocal numbers than jazz that featured Jess. He seemed reluctant to feature himself. Lee had quite an influence on the band. At the time I was antagonistic toward her, but as I look back on the scene, I think she was right. She wanted Jess to feature himself more, but he felt it was a band and should be a band. I feel if he would have featured himself much more and thereby given the band an identity, he might have made a success of it. As it turned out, he had one of many, many bands attempting to make it and failed."

There was also the fact that Stacy did not have the drive to be a bandleader. "I don't think Jess had the ambition to lead a band, and bands were dying out . . ." (Earl Bergman)

"When we were with him in 1945 and '46 he was tired of [the music business] . . . it was Lee who kept him going . . . As far as Jess was concerned he'd just as soon go back to Girardeau and fish in the Mississippi River." (Eddie Martin)

Another factor may have been the strained relations between Jess Stacy and Lee Wiley, greatly due to Wiley's volatile nature. Ernie Anderson considered that Jess and Lee were partners in the big band, but also rivals. While Bus Watson felt that Lee Wiley, in his words, "let Jess run the musical part but interfered with everything else. One of the biggies of hers was to get top billing in the ads and marquees. This bugged the promoters and bookers. Lee Wiley used to get loaded and fight, not only with Jess, but with the ballroom promoters and booking agents."

Hank O'Neal said that Lee Wiley told him the band ". . . broke up largely because of financial reasons. She remembers that audiences were generally very receptive to the band and that bookers were usually stinkers." Those "financial reasons" just about cover it all, though other views of Lee Wiley's part in the story of Jess Stacy and his Orchestra are set out in the next chapter.

7
Lee Wiley

To continue the story of 'The Wiley Incident', as told in the last chapter and in that of the 1943 Benny Goodman orchestra, it should be clear that as a singer Lee Wiley was stylish and consistent, but as a person she had a mercurial temperament. Ernie Anderson, promoter and publicist for Eddie Condon, knew and admired Wiley. He has spoken of her beauty, grace, vivacity and intelligence, and how, at a party or in a bar, people would gather around her to listen and enjoy her company.

Deane Kincaide, however, had another view: "Lee was a very strong-willed, tyrannical, 'swinginger-than-thou' sort . . . Jess and Lee were about as compatible as two cats, tails tied together, hanging over a clothesline."

Lee Wiley gave her version of how the big band started and ended to Leonard Feather in *Down Beat* (January 11, 1945): "[Jess] wanted a very high price to work for anybody as a sideman, so nobody could hire him, and we agreed that the only thing to do was to start his own band. I hocked my jewelry to get things going. And I did more than that – the physical work, like driving a car; you can't imagine what it's like driving a car for hours and then having to get up and sing all night. It was a waste of time and years."

Lee Wiley may have pawned her jewels to help finance the band initially, but her husband shared in the overall losses, as Stacy is quoted in "Jazz Greats": "I saved a little when I was playing regularly, but when I tried to have my own band, I lost it all."

It was with the 1946 version of the band that the pawnbroker came into his own. Byron Baxter, who joined the band in March 1946, said that the money situation was very bad. The only time there was cash was when Lee hocked a fur coat.

Jess Stacy expressed a different view to Keith Keller: "It was a thoroughly unhappy affair. She wanted fur coats and for us both to become rich and famous in a hurry. She was a good singer, I guess, a professional chanteuse rather than a jazz person."

Wiley agreed about her singing: "I don't sing gutbucket, I don't sing jazz. I just sing. I've been wrongly labeled as a Dixieland singer."

Many years later she discussed her ex-husband with Hank O'Neal, who recalled: "Lee is of the opinion that Jess was just about the finest soloist she ever heard. She said the only person she felt was really any better was Earl Hines and that Jess would probably count Hines as one of his genuine favorites. As an accompanist she felt Jess to be without a peer."

Buddy Bergman was impressed by more than her singing: "Her voice had grown hoarse from years of overwork, but it gave her a special sound and we liked it. She was statuesque, beautiful, with the most enviable bosom I have ever seen on anyone. In spite of her dimensions she could go without a bra . . . She was down to earth, one of the guys, and was the kind of gal that musicians in 1945 gave their highest compliment and said, 'She is a great chick!' [She] had a temper but you had to provoke her in order for her to get short with them. Several of us had a terrific relationship with her, and I was one of them."

His brother, Earl, agreed about her 'great body', and also wrote: "As I rode in the car on tour with Lee and Jess and Bus Watson and Ed Martin, I remember Lee, being part Indian, liked her booze and uppers, and would never share until she felt high, then we had fun. Lots of laughs. I remember Lee was a striking woman . . . Jess, very quiet and gentlemanly, sort of an American-British type."

While John Setar commented: "I don't think Lee Wiley had too much influence on the selling of the band – she was more of a musicians' singer in the phrasing she used, and she was near the end of her career in both looks and singing. Too much booze can send anyone down the tubes."

Byron Baxter felt there was little organization and no leadership with the band, but he was not aware of this at the time, being young and inexperienced. Lee Wiley did the booking ahead of rooms and suchlike, but she never booked a room for Baxter's wife; she always booked him a single room, or a double with another musician. "Lee was jealous of a beautiful young wife," Baxter said. (He would have left, but he never had the car fare until they reached New York and he joined Alvino Rey.)

One incident involving the Stacys, which Baxter remembered, occurred when the band stopped to eat at a restaurant, where Lee and Jess started fighting. They began to spit at one another. (Baxter and his wife sat apart from them, trying to pretend they were not with the Stacys). Lee was spitting into Jess' face, but Jess could not raise enough spittle. Outside the restaurant they began throwing stones at each other, before driving off together, still fighting.

And Eddie Martin: "Lee was always the aggressive one. She was a very strong personality. She was very nice if she liked you, but if she thought you were going to cross her, she was rotten. She'd punch you right in the mouth . . . she could get so vicious. I have to give the devil her due. She put everything into the band." And Eddie Martin's wife, Gerry: "I got along famously with her, but she was a strange person."

On one occasion Eddie Martin got into a row with Lee Wiley, defending one of the other musicians: "She said things that were so rotten I started to get a little tear in my eye. Then she started to cry. This will give you an idea what kind of woman she is – she said, 'You cried first!'"

Another incident recalled by Martin was somewhat hazardous. "We had our shirts off and riding in the sunshine along a New Hampshire road. She says, 'I want you guys to know something. I *own* this band. It's my money that's keeping this band going. I own this car, I own everything this man has.' Right in front of Jess. 'As a matter of fact, I can do anything I want. And I can take these keys out [of the ignition]': and stops the car. This big semi-trailer's behind us and the guy's honking his horn. So the car stops, because the motor's off, and the guy screeches and squeals and just made it around us. He comes back to Jess and called him every name under the sun. And she says to the truck driver, 'You're exactly right. That's exactly the kind of person he is.'"

112

"Another time she pulled the same thing. She says, 'I can do anything I want and I'm the boss.' She kicked her foot through the windshield!"

There were more joint ventures by Mr. & Mrs. Stacy in 1946 and 1947, and these will be covered shortly, but by 1948 the marriage had completely broken down. They were divorced in that year. Stacy was always reticent in talking about this marriage, but he did tell Keith Keller: ". . . I divorced her. That made her furious. 'What will Bing Crosby be thinking about *you* divorcing *me!*' That was actually her reaction."

After the divorce Lee Wiley continued to work in night clubs, and in 1949 she made several appearances on Eddie Condon's Floor Show television series. She made a number of admired recording sessions, including dates for Columbia (1950/51), and for Victor (1956/57). In the 1960s she was inactive, and she married retired businessman Nat Tischenkel in 1966.

A 1971 recording session for Monmouth-Evergreen brought her out of retirement, and the following year she appeared at a Carnegie Hall concert as part of the Newport Jazz Festival. By this time age had taken its toll and her voice was no longer the stylish and individual instrument it had once been.

Lee Wiley, c. early 1950s
Photo: courtesy of the late Helene Chmura

Speaking to Bob Rusch, Stacy summarized the background to his marriage to Lee Wiley: "It was on and off all the time . . . It just didn't work out. She had a different temperament to mine. It was just a mistake all the way 'round."

Lee Wiley died in New York on December 11, 1975. Jess Stacy said: "She drank a lot and she died of cancer of the stomach in 1975, but I had no business at her funeral."

8

Eddie Condon
. . . and Goodman again

$\mathcal{A}$s their big band fizzled out, the Stacys remained in New York, and Eddie Condon again took the chance to add them to his gang of strolling players. *Down Beat* reported in its October 7, 1946 issue that Eddie Condon was scheduled for 60 concerts starting October 12 at Town Hall, and the first Saturday afternoon of each month thereafter.

Of this October 12 concert *The New York Times* said:

A crowd of 1,000 turned out at 5:30 yesterday afternoon for the jazz concert by Eddie Condon at Town Hall. The concert inaugurated Mr. Condon's sixth year as a jazz impresario. There will be seven more during the season, as well as sixty concerts on tour. Thirteen musicians assisted Mr. Condon in the two hour program. Sidney Bechet, veteran Negro saxophonist, aroused by far the greatest enthusiasm. The others who wandered on and off, appearing in different instrumental groupings, included Gene Schroeder, Jess Stacy and Joe Sullivan, pianists; George Wettling and Dave Tough, drummers; Bobby Hackett and Max Kaminsky, trumpeters; Bill Wood, clarinet; Ernie Caceres, clarinet and baritone saxophone; Freddie Ohms, trombone; Jack Lespard *(sic)* [Jack Lesberg], bass; and Lee Wiley, singer.

American Jazz Review reported the items played, with Stacy listed on the following:

Jess Stacy and George Wettling: *Love Is Nothing But The Blues; Keepin' Out Of Mischief Now*

Bobby Hackett, Jess Stacy, Jack Lesberg, George Wettling: *September In The Rain; She's Funny That Way*

Sidney Bechet, same rhythm: *The Blues; Jelly Roll*

Hackett, Freddie Ohms, Caceres added: *Royal Garden Blues*

Lee Wiley, with Hackett, Stacy, Lesberg, Wettling: *Sugar; How Long Has This Been Going On?*

Ohms, Wood, Caceres added: *Baby*

Perhaps Eddie Condon played the guitar when he wasn't talking.

Another reviewer was Clyde H. Clark: "Caught the first Condon concert on the 12th, with Maxie and Schroeder carrying the Condon band, uninspired Stacy and Caceres, poor Hackett, fair Wiley, exciting Sullivan, fine Wettling, wonderful Bechet. Condon is touring with a group including Jess and Lee, Hackett, Freeman, Caceres and Cliff Jackson."

In *The Melody Maker* there was another report by Clark in which he commented further on Bechet's performance: "Bash really brought down the house with a beautiful blues [about ten choruses] on soprano, with Stacy, Lesberg and a very exciting and excited Wettling backing."

Clark's Jazz Notes column advised that Eddie Condon was still in town on October 14, and that the tour was due to start the following day. Tour venues included Detroit, Chicago, St. Louis, Cleveland, and Ottawa. The Detroit concert was held in the Masonic Temple on October 18, the cast including Bobby Hackett and Wild Bill Davison, cornets; Bud Freeman, tenor; Ernie Caceres, baritone; Jess Stacy and Lee Wiley.

Ottawa Evening Citizen, October 26, 1946   *Courtesy of Art Pilkington*

October 25 was the date of the Chicago concert. Some of the musicians were Joe Thomas, trumpet; Bobby Hackett, cornet; Charlie Castaldo, trombone; Buster Bailey, clarinet; Ernie Caceres, baritone; Jess Stacy, Cliff Jackson, pianos; Al Hall, bass; Al Sidell, drums; and Lee Wiley. George Hoefer's review included: "Musical highlights were Jess Stacy's *Sweet Lorraine*, Ernie Caceres' *The Man I Love* and the closing *Blues in E-Flat* by the entire company." On the 28th a similar group appeared at the Technical Auditorium in Ottawa. The group was back in New York for the second Town Hall concert of the season on November 2:

CONDON BAND IN CONCERT

FEATURES LEE WILEY IN SONGS BY GERSHWIN AT TOWN HALL

Eddie Condon and his band gave the second jazz concert of their sixth season at the Town Hall late yesterday afternoon. A feature of the informal entertainment – there were no printed programs – was a group of Gershwin songs sung by Lee Wiley. The musicians taking part were Dave Tough and George Wettling, drummers; Jess Stacy, Pat Flowers, Joe Bushkin and Gene Schroeder, pianists; Al Hall and Jack Lesberg, bassists; Bobby Hackett and Max Kaminsky, trumpeters; Peewee *(sic)* Russell, Billy Woods *(sic)* and Buster Bailey, clarinetists; Ernie Caceres, baritone saxophone; Fred Ohms, trombone.

American Jazz Review reported that the Condon entourage had returned the night before the concert "from a two week stint of one-nighters." It listed the programme, with Stacy participating as follows:

> Jess Stacy and George Wettling: *Sweet Lorraine ; Rosetta.*
> Buster Bailey, with Stacy, Al Hall, Wettling: *Night and Day*
> Lee Wiley, with Bobby Hackett, Stacy, Lesberg, Wettling:
>   *Wherever There's Love*
> Buster Bailey, Freddie Ohms, Ernie Caceres added; *Somebody Loves Me*

Twelve days after this concert Stacy joined the Benny Goodman Orchestra again, but he made one more Town Hall appearance with Condon. It was on December 7 that Stacy played what was to be his last concert with Eddie Condon for some time. He was featured on the following tunes:

> Sidney Bechet, clarinet; Jess Stacy, piano; Trigger Alpert, bass; George
>   Wettling, drums: *Blues*
> Bobby Hackett, Jess Stacy, Trigger Alpert, bass; Al Sidell, drums: *Sugar;*
>   *Rose Room.*
> Jess Stacy and George Wettling: *St. Louis Blues*
> Lee Wiley with Stacy, Wettling: *You're Lucky To Me*
> Bobby Hackett, Freddie Ohms, Ernie Caceres, Jack Lesberg; added: *Baby*

And everyone in the 'traditional jamout,' which included Max Kaminsky, Billy Butterfield, Pee Wee Russell, and Gene Schroeder. Also on the bill were pianist Pat Flowers and Jack Bland, as raconteur, not guitarist.

Stacy replaced Joe Bushkin in the Benny Goodman Orchestra at the 400 Restaurant in New York on November 14, though the stay in the Big Apple was to be a short one. In mid-December NBC radio switched 'The Victor Borge Show, Starring Benny Goodman' back to Hollywood, and Goodman, with a nucleus of his musicians, traveled to the west coast. This was probably on December 12, in view of a press report: "BG will break up on Dec. 11th." They were in Hollywood for the Victor Borge broadcast of December 16, with the nucleus including Jess Stacy; Nate Kazebier, trumpet; Lou McGarity, trombone; Skeets Herfurt, Heinie Beau, Babe Russin, reeds; Barney Kessel, guitar; Harry Babasin, bass; and Johnny White, vibes.

In passing it should be noted that television was just beginning to make its impact on the entertainment business. As we now know, the box in the corner was to revolutionise the business, with more disastrous consequences for the big bands.

January 1947 arrived and with it the Readers' Polls. Inexplicably, Stacy was back in favor in *Down Beat*, third (572 votes) in the pianist's section, behind Mel Powell (1249) and Teddy Wilson (1081). Inexplicable because he had been out of the mainstream for most of 1946. In *Metronome* he was 14th, with 46 votes! (Nat Cole was first, with 299). *American Jazz Review* also had a poll, in which Stacy came 5th (273 votes), behind Joe Sullivan (448), Gene Schroeder (417), James P. Johnson (304), and Art Hodes (288).

Yet another poll in the collectors' magazine, *The Record Changer*, for February, had Stacy in 5th position, ahead of James P. Johnson, and behind Art Hodes, Joe Sullivan, Don Ewell and Buster Wilson.

In January Goodman began recording for Capitol, with Stacy present on three sessions, a total of ten titles. Four were with the orchestra, five with the Quintet, and one with the Trio. The small groups feature exemplary piano, with *Sweet Lorraine* a fine example, though all should be heard. Alongside Goodman in the Quintet's frontline is Ernie Felice, an accomplished accordionist, who does not intrude excessively.

Connor lists this big band as the start of Benny Goodman's 'bop band', though it was not until a year later that tenor player Wardell Gray and other musicians associated with the bebop style became Goodman employees. Of Stacy's participation Connor noted that he was uninfluenced by the trend to bop, and played beautifully, as he always had.

The band played an engagement at the Meadowbrook Gardens, and appeared at a number of one-nighters in the Los Angeles area.

In this part of his book Connor writes of Stacy's style, telling the following story: ". . . his conception and 'sound' are unmistakable in both big band and sextet renditions. As much as any pianist's, Jess's timbre, his *Klangfarbe*, is unique. The author once persuaded a very accomplished pianist, both an accompanist and teacher of some repute, to try to duplicate a Stacy solo. Although he could 'play like' Hines and Wilson and Waller, and gave a fairly good representation of Tatum and Peterson, he simply could not simulate that solo. He played all the notes easily enough – it simply sounded different. He said he thought there must be something in the bone-and-muscle structure of Jess's hands that enabled him to play as he did, and that anyone with a different manual formation would produce a different timbre. Interestingly, the author once asked Jess if he could account for his unexampled sound; Jess, a modest man, said he thought it had something to do with his hands . . ."

9

Los Angeles

In his autobiography trumpeter Wingy Manone wrote that he had to report to Monogram Pictures in Hollywood on Tuesday, March 4, 1947, for the film "Sarge Goes To College," a musical directed by Will Jason and including June Preisser. Manone was to lead what was, stylistically, a strangely mixed band consisting of Jerry Wald, clarinet; Joe Venuti, violin; Jess Stacy, piano; Les Paul, guitar; Candy Candido, bass; and Abe Lyman, drums. Monogram, one of the Hollywood studios which was run on a shoestring, churned out second features. Reporting the event, *The Jazz Record* referred to: ". . . the rather hybrid musical crew which Wingy fronts for the pic, and which considering the varied backgrounds of its members, blew some pretty good jazz."

"Sarge goes to College." Left to right: Jerry Wald, Abe Lyman, Pat Goldin, Wingy Manone, Joe Venuti, Candy Candido and Jess Stacy.

Lasting four minutes, this is an excellent jazz sequence, despite the obligatory eccentric dancer who appears towards the end of the scene. Stacy has an extended solo, and this movie rivals "Sweet and Low-down" for the best presentation of his talent on film.

Stacy remembered that at the recording Joe Venuti suggested they play the blues in C-sharp, knowing that Wingy Manone couldn't play in that key. (Venuti's gag wasn't mentioned when Wingy wrote, in his book, that they performed the *B-flat Blues*.)

It was typical of Monogram's production methods that the film was ready for release on May 17, 1947!

Despite the recording sessions, the broadcasts and the greater exposure, Stacy decided to leave Goodman, though his reasons for doing so are unclear.

119

It is D. Russell Connor who lists early March as the date when Stacy left Goodman, but this is based upon lack of piano solos between March 10 and April 5. Jimmy Rowles' presence is not confirmed until a Capitol recording date on April 6, so it is possible that Stacy did not leave Goodman until late March or even early April. In fact, the little piano to be heard on *Linda*, from an April 7 broadcast, could be called Stacy-like, so the exact date for his leaving must remain open.

This stay of four months was Stacy's third and final period with The King of Swing, though they were to play together on special occasions in the future.

The next news report traced is from *Down Beat*, dated May 21, 1947: "Jess Stacy has left Benny Goodman's radio orchestra and is now heading his own band, an eight-piece unit, on one-nighters. Stacy is restricted to casual engagements until he attains full membership in Local 47. Under union regulations he had to resign from BG's ork before he could apply for local union status."

The same issue advised: "Lee Wiley has a 'Saturday Night Club' at Henri's on the Sunset Strip with small unit. (Husband Jess Stacy cannot work here with Lee because of certain union restrictions.") Henri's was shortlived; the following issue reported that the club had folded.

No details have been traced of this particular Stacy eight-piece band, but it does not seem to be related to the small group which toured a few weeks later.

Majestic was a short-lived New York label, which had Jimmy Walker, ex-New York City mayor, as president, and Ben Selvin, a famous name in early recording history, as vice-president. John Hammond worked for the label in 1946, and Ernie Anderson in 1947. It is presumed that the Stacys travelled to New York to record for Majestic.

Down Beat for June 4, 1947 reported: "It is understood that Miss Wiley will sign for Majestic and will be backed on that label by her husband, pianist Jess Stacy, and a band under his leadership."

It is likely that Lee Wiley's single session for Majestic was held during May. At the time they appeared the records were not considered a success, but in retrospect are held in higher regard. Wiley told Leonard Feather that she had had a bad throat; the records didn't sound right, but were released anyway; and she never got paid. Metronome referred to poor recording, bad balance with the accompanying orchestra, and something less than Lee's best voice, though Mike Levin in *Down Beat* could ask: "What is there about the Jess Stacy right hand which sounds so well behind a vocal?"

Back in Los Angeles sometime in June, Stacy took a small band on tour, as reported in *The Capitol News*:

STACY ON ROAD WITH NEW BAND

Jess Stacy flew the coop and tried his wings as a bandleader last month, taking a small combo into Nevada and Northern California for one-nighters booked by the McConkey agency. Stacy, who has led bands of his own before, but always in the east, was featuring several well-known sidemen when he left Hollywood in early June. Art Lyons, former Teagarden clarinet; Ernie Figueroa, trumpet; Zoot Sims, tenor; Bill Williams, trombone; Benny Bennett, bass; and Dwight Towne, drums, departed town with the veteran Missouri pianist . . . Lee Wiley said he would be gone 'a couple of months.'

This report seems more credible than that in *Down Beat*: "Jess Stacy enlarged his unit to 14 men for a jaunt into the northwest starting June 5 at Jantzen Beach."

Trombonist Bill Williams had worked in Chicago in the 1920s. He moved to Los Angeles to work in the studios, mainly as a music copyist at Warner Brothers, and led dixieland units around town. His recollections of the tour were: "I first met Jess at a few jam sessions. At that time I had a seven piece group using a fairly well rounded library. So Jess, who was jobbing around at the time, got a call for a job in Winnemucca, Nevada, to open a deluxe Greyhound Bus terminal, complete with a very nice combination gambling and dining room, along with a coffee shop. He asked if I would be interested, I was, and assembled a group . . . While in Winnemucca, which was for several weeks, we had a good reception, due to the fact that we were not stereotyped as to the variety of music we could play. My main remembrance of this tour was that Jess was married to Lee Wiley at this time. Lee was back in Hollywood, and Jess checked in with her regularly at about 6 p.m. His end of the conversation was invariably, 'Yes, honey,' 'No, honey,' and finally, 'All right, honey.' The other highlight was that an old acquaintance of most of us, a piano player that we used to jam with . . . showed up the second night we were there . . . He invited us out to his place [a little club] after work. We finished at 2 a.m. So we went out there almost every night, and had some jam sessions I would love to have on tape. It was such a relief to get away from requests and the stuff we had to play, that we all really cut loose. Plus the fact that the owner never left an empty jug on the piano. So for a couple of quarts of booze this cat had several hundred dollars worth of entertainment. The sessions never broke up till dawn. . .

"After the Winnemucca date we played a series of one-nighters and short engagements through the northwest."

This band, whose personnel Williams remembered, except for Lyons and Bennett, returned to Los Angeles, and then Stacy went out with another. It was not long after this tour that Zoot Sims joined Woody Herman, the famous Four Brothers orchestra. Zoot

Jess Stacy Band
with unknown
personnel. c.1947

*Photo: courtesy of
Mrs. Pat Stacy*

Sims had been with Benny Goodman at the New Yorker Hotel in 1943, aged 17, playing alongside Stacy. Recalling the 1947 tour, Sims said they played a version of dixieland – not the traditional kind, he couldn't play that.

Bill Williams did participate in the second tour, though his memory of it was not as clear: "The next engagement followed shortly after, starting with a gig in Salt Lake City, in a very nice club. This time Lee came with us. The personnel of the band I have completely forgotten, except that we had a much less exciting group. This club was supposedly the best in town and Jess wouldn't play anything except the usual night club tunes. After about a week of this, and I had been bugging him to play some two-beat, or Dixie, he acquiesed. He had been afraid that the people wouldn't accept this type of music. However, I called for *High Society*. There were a few couples on the floor, and when we started the number, they left. So Jess looked over his shoulder at me and said, 'See.' But after we finished the number, the customers gave us a real ovation, and, thank God, gave us a lot more leeway. Another contributing factor to the success of this tour was that Lee would, as a courtesy, sing once in a while. What a singer."

Perhaps it was on one of these dates that the trumpeter was Bob Higgins, who remembers a six-piece band: "The Jess Stacy – Lee Wiley connection was only a one-nighter . . . I believe they were separated shortly after that. I don't remember anything about who was in the band, other than it was a job up in northern California somewhere."

The next known engagement was in Chicago, in October 1947. Down Beat had listed Stacy as appearing at a club called Jump Town during October 7-19, but no record of this engagement has been found. However, the Stacys did appear at the Rag Doll, opening on October 21.

A typical newspaper column in the *Chicago Sunday Tribune* advised:

IT'S JAZZ WEEK IN CITY'S CAFES AND CONCERT HALLS
Stacy group opens Tuesday at Rag Doll (by Will Davidson)

The very tough job of following Louis Armstrong will be essayed Tuesday night at the Rag Doll by one of the wonderful veterans of jazz, Jess Stacy, and a group of shining lights. Naturally, Lee Wiley will be there, with her husky, marvellous singing. Also there will be Edmund *(sic)* Hall, the great clarinetist; Buck Clayton and his powerful trumpet; Nick Caiazza's clarinet *(sic)*; Buzzy Drootin, bass *(sic)*; and as a special feature, Wingy Manone, who blows a trumpet like few men do. With that group the far north Western Ave. spot shouldn't go into any Rag Doldrums.

The line-up should have read: Buck Clayton, trumpet; Edmond Hall, clarinet; Nick Caiazza, tenor; Jess Stacy, piano; unknown, bass; Buzzy Drootin, drums; Lee Wiley, vocal; with Wingy Manone, trumpet and vocal; as guest star. Buck Clayton said there was "a Chicago boy on bass."

A long report by John Steiner, printed in "Profoundly Blue", said the band was in good form, with no surprises, though Wingy Manone was a vulgar, clownish guest. Wingy played all right, but his lyrics and behavior were reprehensible.

The Louis Armstrong All Stars, with Jack Teagarden, Barney Bigard and Earl Hines, had closed on the 19th, after a very successful engagement. Jess Stacy "didn't attract big crowds as had Louis . . ."

122

Buck Clayton, in his autobiography, said that Joe Glaser had called him for the Rag Doll engagement. He describes the excitement generated during Louis Armstrong's final show, continuing: "That great line of musicians was just too much for us to follow as we hadn't as yet even had a rehearsal. Anyway, the following week we opened in there and we died in there. When we were playing on the stand we could just feel Louis all over the place. Too, Wingy Manone and Lee Wiley didn't like each other and it wasn't long before Lee threw a glass of whiskey in Wingy's face. In a couple of hours they had chosen sides and were going to battle in the alley behind the Rag Doll." Fortunately the threatened brawl never happened. Clayton wasn't invited to participate, and it is difficult to imagine either Stacy or Hall indulging in fisticuffs.

Manone said the Rag Doll engagement lasted four weeks, though Clayton's account suggests it may have finished early: "that was on a Halloween night and after a few days more I think the club folded." Whenever it ended, the Stacys may have stayed on in Chicago for a few days, as Clyde H. Clark heard them on the Dave Garroway show on November 16. Later they made their way back to New York, as *Down Beat* for December 3 reported: "[Jess Stacy and Lee Wiley] tipped into New York together to see what is cooking on the apple. They had no definite plans for the formation of another unit."

Lee Wiley found work at the Village Vanguard, but there is no mention of Stacy until a Town Hall date on January 3, 1948. Ernie Anderson and Eddie Condon, who was m.c., organized the concert to feature Lee Wiley. To quote *Down Beat*: "Lee Wiley postponed her trip to Hollywood to remain an extra day for this [concert]."

The same issue contained a long report of the event, including the following on Stacy's appearance: "Jess Stacy turned in an excellent account of himself at the keyboard early in the first half, scoring particularly strong with his own composition *Complainin'*, then remained to accompany Lee, his wife, on all her numbers. He did no solos in the second half. The afternoon's proceedings were opened by Max Kaminsky's group from the Vanguard as was the second half. Max also joined Lee and Jess (plus bass and drums) for the finale."

Nick's, 1948. L-r: Jess Stacy, Tony Scott (subbing for Pee Wee Russell), Billy Butterfield, Joe Grauso, Freddie Ohms. *Photo: courtesy of the late Max Jones*

When the *Down Beat* poll results appeared, Stacy was ninth in the piano section.

Nick's Tavern in the Village, Seventh Avenue South, at 10th Street, had been founded by Nick Rongetti. He had died in July 1947, but his wife, Grace, kept the saloon going. Nick's had been a home for dixieland bands for many years, usually centred around Eddie Condon. In November 1947 Billy Butterfield had become the nominal leader, and this was the band which Jess Stacy joined, replacing Teddy Napoleon; Billy Butterfield, trumpet; Freddie Ohms, trombone; Pee Wee Russell, clarinet; Jess Stacy, piano;

Bob Casey, bass; Joe Grauso, drums.

The New Yorker gave this information when it referred to the band "merrily rattling the windowpanes." "Jess Stacy will be added to the cast on Saturday, Feb. 21. Visiting performers drop in here on Sunday afternoons. Closed Mondays."

Down Beat gave the news under a headline, "JESS JUNKS BAND FOR NICKSIELAND", though the 'junks band' news seems rather out-of-date.

Stacy was at Nick's for about six weeks, and during that time Jack Lesberg replaced Bob Casey on bass at the end of March, and Bob Haggart took over from Lesberg shortly before Stacy departed. *The New Yorker* for April 10, 1948, is the last to show Jess Stacy at Nick's.

Jess Stacy's activities are not documented for the next few weeks. Freelancing in New York before moving to Los Angeles has been mentioned, as has "playing solo piano throughout the midwest." Stacy himself said that one job was playing solo in Defiance, Ohio. He was in New York late in April when *Down Beat*, May 19, 1948, reported: "Lee Wiley flew from Hollywood to rejoin her husband". A May 22, 1948 Town Hall concert, with Muggsy Spanier, Wild Bill Davison, George Brunies, and Stacy has been listed. If Stacy was present it would mean that he left for California shortly afterwards.

Jess and Fred Stacy at Lake Manitou, near Rochester, Indiana. 1948.
Photo: courtesy of Gardner Hitchcock

It is not known exactly when, but sometime during 1948 Stacy spent a few days at Lake Manitou, just outside Richmond, Indiana. To quote drummer Gardner Hitchcock: "I was working in Don Ragon's big band, with Jess's son, Fred, playing trumpet. Jess came to visit Fred. During this time he would sit in with the rhythm section. I remember how impressed I was with not only his piano playing, but his ongoing feud with the instrument. We would play something way up in tempo and if, after the number he was satisfied, while bowing, he would murmur asides to the piano, like 'I beat you that time, you [various curse words].'"

In similar vein, in a discussion on piano playing with Teddy Wilson, Stacy commented that the 88 keys sometimes turn into 88 teeth!

Apropos Fred Stacy playing trumpet, Peg Meyer recalled the time that "Jess came home and his son talked him into playing with a bunch in a town close to here. Freddy was playing bop, and next morning Jess came into my store raising hell, saying he was paying big money to make a trumpet player out of Fred. He said he was going to take [his] damn horn and throw it in the river and never let him play again. If ever there was anyone who could not take bop it was Jess. He hated it."

It was, of course, almost inevitable that a young musician in 1948 would experiment with bebop. Despite this, Stacy remained extremely proud of his son's achievements. Fred Stacy received his degree in music from Washington University in St. Louis. After service in the Marine Corps he taught music in the St. Louis school system. He was on trumpet with the St. Louis Symphony Orchestra, and later conductor of youth

Fred Stacy wearing the gold medal given to his grandfather in 1898 for foiling a train robbery.
Photo: courtesy of Mrs. Pat Stacy

orchestras in New York. In 1971 famed lead trumpeter, Zeke Zarchy, said, "Jess' son is quite a trumpet player in St. Louis. Plays the opera, the symphony and anything that comes through town requiring someone with chops, like the circus or big musicals."

Arriving in Los Angeles sometime in May, Stacy found work at the Haig on Wilshire Boulevard, across from the Ambassador Hotel, the first of the dozens and dozens of cocktail lounges he was to play until his retirement.

Down Beat (August 11, 1948) had reported that: "Lee Wiley and Jess Stacy aren't exactly in harmony these days." However, they seem to have travelled to the west coast together. *The Capitol News* for July, 1948 reporting that "Jess Stacy is pounding the keys at the Haig, small after dark spot on Wilshire in L.A. As a single, too. His wife, singer Lee Wiley, is doing Little Theater work under the name of 'Lee Stacy' . . ."

On July 15 the pianist moved to the St. Francis Room, on 8th Street, where he remained for the rest of the year. Occasional jam sessions enlivened his time there, but first the break-up of the Stacy-Wiley marriage must be confirmed. *Down Beat*, August 11, 1948 reported from Hollywood, "Vocalist Lee Wiley last month crushed the index finger of her right hand in a door, necessitating amputation of the digit."

There is conjecture that this incident happened because Wiley was in a rage, and that it was probably connected with the impending end of the marriage. Jess filed for divorce in Los Angeles on December 27, 1948.

John Lucas, who first met Stacy at the Palomar in 1935, was now a multi-instrumentalist, concentrating on trumpet, and he was more than happy that Stacy was settling in Los Angeles. In August 1948 he experienced a memorable evening at the St. Francis Room, "a jam session with my idol." And this was to be the first of many. Afterwards Lucas wrote a rave letter to *The Second Line*, mentioning that he played with trombonist Bill Williams for one set, and with Bruce Hudson, trumpet; Matty Matlock, clarinet; Eddie Miller, tenor; Nappy Lamare, guitar; Artie Shapiro, bass; for another.

At the St. Francis Room there was a small disc recorder on the piano, and Dick Reimer was one patron who obtained a cardboard record from Stacy – see discography.

Traditional jazz had made its mark in San Francisco in the early 1940s, with musicians like Lu Watters and Turk Murphy leading the revival, but it was a few years after this before two-beat jazz became the fashion in Los Angeles. One of the signs of this growing popularity was the first Dixieland Jubilee, organized by disc-jockeys Frank Bull and Gene Norman at the PanPacific Auditorium on Friday, October 29, 1948. "A continuous parade of great jazz began at 8:30 pm and wound up around 12.30 a.m.," noted Irving Jacobs, while *The Capitol News* reported: "They blew and they stomped and they paraded for four hours and 33 minutes and when they finished, 57 of the world's finest jazzmen wrapped up their horns, went home and started making plans for an even bigger Dixieland festival in 1949."

Featured were the bands of Louis Armstrong, Eddie Condon, Red Nichols, Pete Daily, Kid Ory, Charlie LaVere, Eddie Miller, and Ted Vesely, playing before an audience of 8,100. The concert was recorded by the Armed Forces Radio Service, who released some titles in the 'Just Jazz' series.

Stacy appeared with two groups, Eddie Miller and the Bobcats (Mannie Klein, trumpet; Warren Smith, trombone; Matty Matlock, clarinet; Doc Rando, alto; Eddie Miller, tenor; Nappy Lamare, guitar; Art Shapiro, bass; Ray Bauduc, drums) and Eddie Condon's band (Wild Bill Davison, cornet; Lou McGarity, trombone; Matty Matlock, clarinet; Art Shapiro, bass; Morey Feld, drums). (A review of the concert in the January 1949 issue of *The Record Changer* mentioned a band led by Stacy, with Nate Kazebier, Heinie Beau, George Van Eps, Art Shapiro and Nick Fatool, but this is unconfirmed.)

In November Stacy became a bandleader again: "Nate Kazebier took his trumpet down to the St. Francis Room in downtown Los Angeles and joined Jess Stacy's new band, along with Reuel Lynch, clarinet; Red Cooper, drums; and Weedey [Herbie] Harper, on trombone. Stacy had worked as a single at the spot for many months, and reportedly did such a bango job that his bosses agreed to up his ante to include the four sidemen."

The year ended on a sad note, when Stacy had to return to Cape Girardeau, where his father died on Tuesday, December 28, 1948, at the age of 86.

Stacy recalled that sometime in January he went to Casper, Wyoming, performing there until the end of February. In March he returned to Los Angeles, opening at the St. Francis Room and playing there until June. The next two months were spent in Omaha, Nebraska.

Much of the remainder of the year he played in Columbus, Ohio, at the Grandview Inn. That this was not a continuous engagement is indicated by two *Down Beat* news items: "[Jimmy McPartland] crew is now at the Grandview Inn . . . where they followed Jess Stacy." (November 4, 1949 issue) and "Jess Stacy working at the Grandview Inn . . . McPartland band returns for a second date on January 2." (December 30, 1949 issue).

Stacy spent the Christmas vacation in Cape Girardeau, and then: "[I] brought my mother and Aunt Johnnie out to L.A. with me. Played Radar Room Jan, Feb, and Mar on Santa Monica Blvd." On February 6, 1950, Stacy was a guest on Floyd Levin's weekly radio show, "Jazz On Parade", station KFMV in Hollywood. He confirmed being at the Radar Room, and talked of Johnny Lucas, Albert Nicholas and Archie Rosate dropping in to play. Stacy also made an appearance on the George Barclay radio show.

Recalling the Radar Room, trumpeter John Lucas: "There was no bandstand . . . the musicians who came to sit-in just gathered around the piano. I remember sitting up on the back of the seats of a booth, next to Lou McGarity [trombone]."

During the Radar Room engagement Stacy met Patsy Peck again, a meeting which led to marriage, and the major contribution to his happiness and well-being for the next 45 years.

After Pat Peck dropped in to see Stacy with a friend, Tony Newton, she and Jess began dating. Marriage was on the cards, but Stacy was concerned that he might have cancer. On August 1 he took his mother and aunt back to Cape Girardeau, where he underwent minor surgery for, according to Keller, the removal of a non-malignant fistular, or according to family friend, Walter Kempe Jr., D.O., hemorrhoids.

Freed of worry, Stacy telephoned Pat from the hospital and proposed. Years later he

Wedding Day – September 8, 1950.
Photo: courtesy of Mrs. Pat Stacy

celebrated her answer with a piano solo composition he recorded for Chiaroscuro, *Miss Peck Accepts*. They were married in Pat's parental home in Winnetka, on September 8, 1950.

Stacy told Whitney Balliett: "Pat and I married in 1950, even though I'd told her I was just a band pianist and that I had a miserable past. I couldn't ask for a better wife."

After the honeymoon, which included a stay in Cape Girardeau, they returned to Los Angeles. It was not long before they found 8700 Lookout Mountain Avenue, between Mulholland Drive and Laurel Canyon Boulevard, up in the Hollywood Hills, which was to be their home for the rest of their married life.

About three months before the wedding, when Stacy was playing at The Lark, Pat Stacy recalls, "We were sitting at a table when Lee Wiley came in and sat at the bar. Jess went over to speak to her briefly. When he came back to the table, I asked what she wanted. Jess said, 'She wants us to get back together, and I said 'No'."

In the period between appearing at the Radar Room and his operation, Stacy had played at the Track in Glendale, the Wedgewood Room on Wilshire Boulevard, and then the Lark, indicating the travels on the restaurant/bar circuit which Stacy was to endure into the 1960s. But there were exceptions to the routine of cocktail lounge soloing. For example, in March 1950: "Bernie Billings, tenor saxman and impresario for jazz concerts in eastern cities, inaugurated 'Jazz in the Afternoon' series at Hollywood's Florentine Gardens. Headliners at first of Sunday afternoon affairs, which started March 19, were Jess Stacy, Matty Matlock, Warren Smith, Joe Rushton, Nick Fatool, Dick Cathcart, Rico Vallese, Stan Wrightsman, Morty Korb *(sic)*, plus several promising newcomers. ('The admission price is only a buck, and the waitresses won't bother you if you want to make a coke last all afternoon', said Hal Holly.)"

It is not known if Stacy was present on any other Sunday afternoons, but the sessions did not last long. *Down Beat* for May 19, 1950, reported they were losing money.

A month or so later Stacy was reunited with more of the old Bob Crosby band, as Down Beat reported: "Gil Rodin, assigned to round up as many ex-Bob Cats as possible for crew backing Bob Crosby numbers in Columbia's "When You're Smiling", came up with five for the soundtrack session. They were Jess Stacy, Eddie Miller . . . Matty Matlock, Nappy Lamare and Zeke Zarchy. Others in crew especially assembled for Crosby numbers were Manny Klein, Lou McGarity, Manny Stein, bass; and Nick Fatool, drums."

In fact the "numbers" referred to were just one number, *If You Can't Get A Drum, With A Boom, Boom, Boom*, sung by Bob Crosby. Stacy, Matlock, Lamare, and McGarity are seen and heard; Eddie Miller is heard only, as is Country Washburne on tuba. The film, "When You're Smiling", starred Jerome Courtland, with specialty songs by, in addition to Crosby, Frankie Laine, Kay Starr, Billy Daniels, and the Mills Brothers.

127

Bassist Morty Corb and drummer Nick Fatool, plus George Van Eps on guitar, accompanied Stacy for a Capitol recording session on June 28, and the following month the same four players recorded for Columbia. This was to be Stacy's contribution to a series of 10" LP records under the title of "Piano Moods". The launch of the series was reported in *Down Beat* for August 11, 1950. Other pianists featured included Earl Hines, Teddy Wilson, Joe Bushkin, Bernie Leighton, and Cy Walters.

Jess Stacy at The Hangover

Photo: courtesy of Mrs. Pat Stacy

1950 closed with a band engagement. In November he took a group to San Francisco for a four-week stay at the Hangover Club, at Bush above Powell (as Joe Sullivan's composition has it). Stacy was replacing his old friend Muggsy Spanier, who ended a successful twelve-weeks on Saturday, November 11.

The personnel for "Jess Stacy and his Dixieland Band" was variously reported at the time: "Jess Stacy opened Nov 13 for four weeks for his first appearance in the Bay area since his Goodman days. With Jess are Lou McGarity, trombone; Albert Nicholas, clarinet; Smokey Stover, drums; and Rico D'Alles *(sic)*, trumpet. Nappy Lamare's group is slated to follow Stacy at the Hangover, opening Dec. 12." [Rico D'Alles was a misprint for cornetist Rico Vallese.]

A poster for the Hangover, owned by pianist and Stacy admirer, Ray Skjelbred, lists the musicians as: "Rico Vallese, Warren Smith, Albert Nicholas, Vince Muccillo, bass; Smokey Stover. Meade Lux Lewis was the intermission pianist."

However, the *San Francisco Chronicle* (November 20, 1950) reported: "Stacy has just opened at Doc Dougherty's jazz-hallowed Hangover hall on Bush Street – with Fred Greenleaf, trumpet; Warren Smith, trombone; Albert Nicholas, clarinet; Paul Sarmento, bass; Smokey Stover, drums." A broadcast from the club confirms this personnel for the later part of the engagement. All of which would suggest that Lou McGarity did not participate and that Vallese and Muccillo, if they did, did so only briefly.

At the end of 1950 the *Down Beat* readers' poll had Stacy in 21st position in the piano section, with 32 votes. In 1949 he had been placed higher at 17th, with fewer votes, just 19.

Early in 1951 Stacy began a long engagement at the Los Angeles Hangover Club, owned by Duncan Puett, at 1456 Vine Street. *Down Beat* for March 9, 1951 reported: "Jess Stacy now doing solo stint at Hangover Club (he followed Marvin Ash), also heads all-star jam combo at spot on Friday and Saturday nights. Regulars have included Reuel Lynch, clarinet; and Warren Smith, trombone."

Trumpeter Bob Higgins' memories of the Hangover were: "It was just an old three-story house converted, the downstairs was a bar and listening room, no dancing. They had food, and that was a very popular spot. It has a very special place in my memory, so many wonderful musical happenings took place there. We didn't make much money, but we had a hell of a good time." Higgins also recalled the number of jazz places within walking distance of the Hangover – Billy Berg's (where Louis Armstrong played), El Morocco (Red Nichols), Sardi's (Pete Daily), Brass Rail (Wingy Manone), and the Royal Room (Jack Teagarden). "I'll tell you, it was the heyday of dixieland jazz."

John Lucas recalled that: "It was so tiny that the tables were abutted right up to the little bandstand and the trombone slide would invariably drop condensation . . . into people's drinks, and they would be quite horrified, of course. That's how small and tight the bandstand was. I don't suppose the room held more than seventy people, maybe eighty. When you had to go to the can you had to go upstairs . . . Anyway, it was just an old house where they knocked out the walls and put in the bar. There were a lot of pictures and tiny tables."

While cornetist Tom Pletcher remembered the Hangover as: ". . . a small wood frame house about 1600 sq. ft. total. It had a patio outside and fence enclosure around patio. Typically small room and crowded tables – no dancing – dark and smoky – unusual feature was a balcony and railing that had several tables."

Lucas and Pletcher have different memories of the food served, the former recalling only the rudimentary sandwich, or similar, as required by law, whereas the latter mentions steaks, pizzas, and other Italian dishes.

Collector Larry Kiner recalled going to the Hangover to hear Stacy play solo piano, and ". . . on the weekends he'd be joined by the two Teagardens, Matlock, Miller, Corb, Fatool . . . great times!!!" And no doubt Duncan Puett's brother-in-law also sat-in. He was trombonist Elmer 'Moe' Schneider. (Puett and Schneider had married sisters.)

In March and April, again with George Van Eps, Morty Corb and Nick Fatool, Stacy recorded for Decca, making eight titles which appeared on a ten-inch Brunswick LP. Reviewing them, George Hoefer said: "Jess' relaxed, uncluttered style is shown to good advantage here as he slips easily through a pretty set of standards."

The hazards of playing solo piano were mentioned by critic Ted Hallock when he wrote a review of the Hollywood music scene in *Down Beat* for May 4, 1951: "Six barflies infested the Hangover doing their level best to out-talk Jess Stacy's pianistics."

Despite such interference the engagement at the Hangover was generally satisfactory, as the following *Down Beat* news item showed: "Hangover, Hollywood hotspot in which NBC staged publicity stunt to promote jazz airshow, 'Pete Kelly's Blues,' got such a lift it boosted Jess Stacy from single to trio with Charlie Teagarden and Ray Bauduc. Plus sliphornist Moe Schneider and clarinetist Matty Matlock joining festivities on Friday and Saturday nights."

Later, Sal Franzella, who had been playing with the Red Nichols band, replaced Matlock as the Friday and Saturday clarinetist. The Stacy trio continued its six nights-a-week schedule for the rest of the year, though the personnel is uncertain. Charlie Teagarden and Ray Bauduc were members of Jack Teagarden's band when it opened at the Royal Room on October 30. This may have been when Bob Higgins joined the trio on trumpet. Pianist Al Mack played on their Tuesday nights off, but he was replaced by Norma Teagarden towards the end of the year.

Jack Teagarden had only recently left the Louis Armstrong All-Stars. It was Teagarden, probably earlier in 1951, who had approached Stacy about joining the All-Stars. The pianist had declined: "I made two hundred and fifty dollars a week where I was, and I was not keen on going on the road again."

It is pointless yet fascinating to speculate how Stacy's career might have changed if he had accepted the offer to go with Armstrong.

In July Stacy had taken part in three sessions for Omega, a small and short-lived Hollywood record company. Excellent musicians accompanied less-than-excellent singers. The three titles known to have been issued were credited to either Jess Stacy or Matty Matlock. The *Down Beat* reviewer referred to the Stacy title: "Sounds like a fair hotel bunch, with a couple of strings sawing away." And of the vocalist on a Matlock title: ". . . a baby-voiced singer in the best Bonnie Baker tradition who cannot be described. You have to hear her to believe it. The name is Toni Roberts. Thank goodness she doesn't have a twin."

The annual Dixieland Jubilee, still organized by Frank Bull and Gene Norman, was held at the Shrine Auditorium in October. *Down Beat's* report (November 16, 1951) carried the heading:

CROSBY BAND REUNITED FOR FOURTH DIXIE JUBILEE
Huge Crowd On Hand For Event

The report referred to a turnout in excess of 6,500, with several hundred people turned away. Seat prices were set at a top of $3 plus tax, with the gross takings in excess of $15,000, tax deducted.

Billy Butterfield and Bob Haggart had flown in from New York to participate. Butterfield played with both the Crosby big band and with the Bob Cats, but Haggart played only with the small group, as did Jess Stacy. Stan Wrightsman played piano with the big band. Other bands in the show included those of Kid Ory, Rosy McHargue, Turk Murphy, Pete Daily, "Pete Kelly", the Firehouse Five Plus 2, and the Sextet from Hunger.

While Butterfield and Haggart were in Los Angeles, the Bob Cats also recorded for Capitol, and for Snader Telescriptions. Lou Snader made three-minute films for use as "fillers" by television stations. This material has since become available on video.

The Capitol recording session took place on October 3, and seven days later Stacy was again in the recording studio, making four titles for tenor-saxophonist Pud Brown's Westcraft label. Charlie and Jack Teagarden, plus Ray Bauduc, completed the band. *Down Beat* reported that the musicians played for scale because: ". . . they like Pud Brown and enjoyed the chance to play 'the way they wanted'."

Two of Stacy's associates. Left to right: Eddie Miller, Mickie Roy (singer) and Dave Dexter (who produced Stacy's solo Capitol records). c 1943

There was yet another opportunity for Stacy to play with the Teagardens when they opened the Royal Room on October 30, though in less happy circumstances. *Down Beat* reported: "Marvin Ash, pianist with the new Royal Room band headlined by Jack Teagarden, collapsed on the opening night as he prepared to mount the stand for the first number with what was first feared to be a heart attack. He was ready to leave the hospital at writing, however, and was expected to be back on the job by Nov. 13. Doctors said there was no sign of a heart ailment and that he seemed to have been the victim of nervous exhaustion.

Jess Stacy, who was on hand for the opening of the new band as a guest, took over the piano for Ash on the night. Norma Teagarden and others subbed for him until his return. Stacy also took Ash's place on his KFI-TV show, 'The Truth About Dixie.'"

The next issue of *Down Beat* contained the readers poll results, with Stacy improving his position in the piano section. He was 14th, with 55 votes – 671 less than the winner, Oscar Peterson.

Work at the Hangover was to continue for a little longer, and Stacy was in the routine he was to follow for the next ten years or so. There would be solo work in bars, usually solitary and unrewarding, though sometimes lightened by the presence of a fan or two; there would be special engagements or recording sessions to break the routine; and, most important, there would be a settled home life.

Anyone who has dined in a restaurant where there is a pianist in attendance must feel sympathy with the player, no matter the quality of the performance. As far as the customers are concerned, he might as well be invisible. To them he is the living equivalent of musak, just present in the background, "wallpaper music". The writer vividly recalls the truth of this being demonstrated one evening listening to Burt Bales, a fine pianist in the classic tradition. The noise level rose and fell in direct proportion to how loudly Bales played, the restaurant customers always keeping their sound level ahead of the pianist's.

Singer and pianist Bobby Short told Whitney Balliett: "And it's up to the audience, too. When you get a bad one, you work harder and harder and sing louder and louder to compensate, and they talk louder and louder to compensate for you." Billy Butterfield commented that solo jazz pianists either turned to drink or quit, while Alistair Cooke spoke of hearing Earl Hines in San Francisco playing in "a den of unheeding boozers."

Also suffered by solo pianists are swizzle-stick throwers, coat-pullers and amateur singers. These and other perils are discussed in detail in "Loose Shoes," the biography of the great stride pianist; Ralph Sutton, written by James D. Shacter. Unlike Stacy, Sutton's reactions to his customers' insensitivity were often profane, or even violent!

Floyd Levin had his memories of those jobs: "Most of the cocktail lounge jobs were dreadful for Jess as he hated to play for the drunks who crowded around him in piano bar style. I attended most of these dates but usually found Jess depressed to a point where he would talk to me while playing – completely bored with the job."

At least Stacy did not succumb to the temptation which the cocktail lounges offered. As he said: "The public makes certain demands on an artist, and about the only way you can survive is to do a fair amount of drinking. It got that way with me.

Sometimes in a club you can't even hear yourself play, and you have to drink in self-defense. Between the smoke and the noise, it's almost more than you can take."

Stacy gave up smoking in 1951 and he stopped being a heavy drinker: "All of a sudden I began to feel the pangs, the warnings. I started finding myself burning holes in the piano and I began to start feeling droopy, and I'd think I needed to get a cigarette. I sort of lost my appetite. I was also slowing down in my mind."

Another problem, in the beginning, was to build a suitable repertoire: "I had been a big band pianist for so many years, and when I played solos in recording studios, it had been mostly blues stuff, coming right out of my head. And now I had to work up a repertoire of regular and current tunes, so that I had at least something popular to offer people . . ."

The discography includes details of a 1953 performance privately recorded at the Holiday House. There is no reason to doubt that this was a typical evening's work by Jess Stacy, and the programme consists almost entirely of standards and ballads. Only *Ruby*, theme from the film, "Ruby Gentry", can be classified as current. Also heard is the feared customer who volunteers to sing.

Jess Stacy himself told Whitney Balliett something of the problems he faced during his Hollywood years: "I did have five or six years that were all right. The people in the bars would ask for *On Moonlight Bay* or *Clair de Lune*, which I always thought of as *Clear The Room*. But they'd pretty much leave me alone, and sometimes they'd even clap or some guy would lay a tip on me. But around 1955 TV began keeping the nicer people home and I came to feel those piano bars were snake pits. I had to walk around the block six or seven times every night to get up enough courage to go in. While I was playing, somebody would put a nickel in the juke box or some fellow would ask me if I'd play real quiet so he could watch the fights on the bar TV. Or else they'd all get drunk and sing along."

Bob Higgins, trumpet in the Jess Stacy Trio at The Hangover in L.A.　*Photo: courtesy of Bob Higgins*

1952 continued where 1951 had ended: ". . . Jess Stacy, who heads a trio at the Hangover, which is boosted to six or seven men on Friday and Saturday nights. Bob McCracken, recently of Chicago and now located in Hollywood, doing clarinet stint with Jess Stacy's augmented Friday-Saturday combo at Hangover. Other Stacy regulars at writing were Burt Johnson, trombone; and Bob Higgins, cornet."

On Monday nights there were "sit-in sessions", and one of the participants was clarinetist Heinie Beau: "I used to do off-night jam groups with Jess occasionally at the old Hangover on Vine St."

But changes were to come, as *Down Beat* for February 22, 1952, announced: "Jess Stacy, who has been heading a trio at the Hangover club, dropped back to solo, but heads combo on Friday and Saturday nights as formerly. Regulars on these stints now include Bob Higgins, Matty Matlock, Burt Johnson and Smoky Stover." Sometime in late spring Rosy McHargue's Ragtimers replaced Stacy at the Hangover and the pianist moved to the Astor Club in the valley.

John Lucas remembers the Astor, which was on the corner of Ventura and Laurel Canyon in North Hollywood, because of the evening he drove there from Pasadena, in his Hillman Minx, through torrential rain in order to be able to sit-in with Stacy. "It was still raining when we departed at two in the morning," Lucas said.

It should be mentioned that Knocky Parker (Professor John W. Parker) recorded the Jess Stacy composition, *Complainin'* for the Carleton Jazz Club on April 12, 1952. This was a rare instance of a Stacy work being performed by another pianist. Three years later Parker recorded Stacy's *Ec-Stacy*, issued on Audiophile AP28. It may have been around the same time that Steve Allen recorded an album of piano solos called "Steve Allen Plays The Piano Greats," issued on Dot DLP 3519. On this LP Allen paid tribute to such pianists as Fats Waller, Meade Lux Lewis, and Earl Hines, as well as Jess Stacy, playing *You Can Depend On Me* in Stacy's style.

On May 8, Bob Crosby compered another recording session of big band dixieland, at the CBS Vine Street Playhouse. Jess Stacy was due to be present, along with Jack and Charlie Teagarden, Ziggy Elman, Jimmy Dorsey, Red Nichols, Walter Gross, Johnny Mercer, Nick Fatool and Wingy Manone. No transcription release has been traced.

At the end of the year Stacy was back in the St. Francis Room. Wednesday was jam session night. John Lucas was a regular there, and he remembers musicians of the standing of Eddie Miller, Matty Matlock, Ray Bauduc, and Artie Bernstein sitting in. Lucas would also play duets with Stacy at the weekends, and he recalls one humorous occasion. They had arrived early and Stacy was watching the wrestling on television. One of the wrestlers was Gorgeous George, who had lovely, silken white hair and wore fancy robes. Then Jess realized it was nine o'clock and he started to play. The tune he unwittingly opened with was *The Man I Love*! He was ribbed a lot about that.

Left to right: Jess' Aunt Johnnie, Pat Stacy, Jess, Vada Stacy (Jess' mother), Muggsy Spanier. c.1953

Photo: courtesy of Mrs. Pat Stacy

Oscar Peterson was first in the piano section of the *Down Beat* poll of 1952, but Stacy was moved up to 16th.

In March 1953 the Muggsy Spanier band was booked into the Royal Room, from March 9 to April 5. During the engagement Ruth Spanier and Pat Stacy decided to share the cost of renting a studio, in order to record their husbands together. Muggsy Spanier was seldom in Los Angeles and this was a rare opportunity. Bassist Truck Parham and drummer Barrett Deems from the Spanier band provided the accompaniment. The session took place the day after the Spanier booking was completed.

Ruth Spanier, speaking to Bert Whyatt, referred to: "Those two funny, funny men. Rather alike, except that Jess has a very dry humor, very dry. But they got along beautifully. There's one point where Muggsy is just so busy listening to Jess he doesn't play. Jess is looking up with this basset-like face, and no Muggsy. It's so funny."

133

Perhaps this is an opportune point at which to confirm the impact which wives like Pat Stacy and Ruth Spanier made upon their husbands' life styles. Stacy's longevity may have been due in part to his genes, but the care he received at home was very important. In his later years Muggsy Spanier lived an orderly and comfortable life, thanks to Ruth Spanier. Joe Darensbourg and Wild Bill Davison were two other heavy drinkers who would have succumbed much earlier without a loving wife to care for them.

These musicians' last years were in marked contrast to those of Coleman Hawkins and Joe Sullivan, who drank themselves to death, with no one to slow them down or help them stop.

Trumpeter John Lucas
Photo: courtesy of Bill Williams

In May John Lucas achieved one of his great ambitions. He persuaded Jess Stacy to join his band, the "Blueblowers", for a weekly Monday night gig he had obtained at the Beverly Cavern. The Cavern, on the corner of Ardmore and Beverly Boulevard, was owned at that time by Sam Rittenberg and Rose Stanman, and was well-known for its employment of the George Lewis and Kid Ory bands.

On May 23, 1953 Lucas and Stacy appeared on, "Are You From Dixie", an hour-long program of music and conversation with George Barclay, on station KFI in Los Angeles. During the show it was stated that the band would start its engagement on May 25.

John Lucas, who was referred to by *Down Beat* as a "trumpet-vocal headliner on the Good Time Jazz label" (on the basis of a single recording session with the Firehouse Five Plus Two), remembered: "The Beverly Cavern was pretty big. I think it could hold a hundred and fifty people. It was not a very prepossessing place. It had a good size bandstand, and it did have almost a closet behind it, where the musicians could put their cases and stash a bottle or two. There were banners from colleges, U.S.C., U.C.L.A., Occidental, tacked on the wall behind the bandstand."

The personnel for the Blueblowers, which remained quite constant for the rest of the year, was confirmed by *Down Beat*: "Johnny Lucas into Beverly Cavern's off-nite (Monday) spot with band comprised of Jess Stacy (who also continues as single at the Holiday House), Lenny Esterdahl, guitar and banjo; Bob McCracken, clarinet; Mike Hobi, trombone; Bob Stone, bass; and Johnny Henderson, drums."

Trombonist Irvin Verret actually played the first two Monday nights with the band, until Mike Hobi was available. John Lucas again: "Irvin Verret, the marvellous trombonist, who's gotten so little recognition – I don't think he ever made any record other than singing his cajun blues – was on trombone occasionally, and Joe Darensbourg subbed for Matty [Matlock] quite a bit, too. Occasionally we'd have to have sub basses. Wellman Braud, Duke Ellington's bass player at one time, subbed for Bob. Bob was also working with the Los Angeles Symphony."

Matty Matlock replaced Bob McCracken as clarinetist fairly early on. There were quality substitutes for Stacy, too: "We had to get a sub for Jess once, because he went to Cape Girardeau, and we had James P. Johnson on two different occasions. Johnson was working in an all-black show on Las Palmas. Monette Moore was in it and she was a friend of mine. She said, 'Get James P.' So we did, and that was really exciting. Another pianist sat in for Jess – Ralph Sutton."

(The show 'Sugar Hill' opened at the Las Palmas Theater in Hollywood in June 1949. It is not known how long it ran. James P. Johnson had a major stroke in 1951, and it is reported that he was unable to play thereafter).

Another change in the band arose from Stacy's difficulties with drummers. John Lucas thought that John Henderson was "an awfully nice guy," but: "Jess had so much trouble with him that it was either Jess go or the drummer go. Of course, I was going to keep Jess, no matter what. I had the horrible job of telling the drummer . . . Anyway, I got Monte Mountjoy . . . and Jess was quite happy. Monte was a very solid drummer with a nice deep drop in his beat, the kind of thing that turned Jess on."

A happening at the Beverly Cavern which John Lucas particularly recalls concerned an arrangement of *I Found A New Baby*: "It was just an intro and a coda, and everything in between was regular dixieland style. We had all taken our solos, Jess Stacy was last, and he did his customary two choruses. But right on the bridge of the second chorus he started really moving. He kind of tucked his head down a little bit, shifted his body on the piano bench and started moving into that piano. I held up my finger for a third chorus . . . and he wound up taking five, six, eight, ten choruses, who knows, getting redder in the face all the time and the tension increasing all the time. The drummer had the good sense just to keep the rhythm going; he didn't try to join in. We came in and took about two choruses just flying high from that string of piano choruses. The only thing I remember about it is that each chorus seemed to get simpler and simpler. The phrases were just like bare bones. Typical trumpet-style piano, with that marvellous tremolo."

Parallel with the Monday night job at the Beverly Cavern, Stacy was working five nights, Tuesday through Saturday, at the Holiday House, on the Pacific Coast Highway, near Zuma Beach. Stacy said: "They have a beautiful patio there. You sit outside and look at the waves roll in. I think it's the most beautiful place around."

This engagement began on May 26 and lasted many weeks. The private recording which took place there on August 5 has already been mentioned.

The owner of the Holiday House was Dudley Murphy, who had his own connection with the world of jazz. He directed Bessie Smith in "St. Louis Blues" (her only appearance on film); Duke Ellington in another film short, "Black and Tan Fantasy"; and Paul Robeson in the full-length "The Emperor Jones".

At one time Local 47 of the American Federation of Musicians held an annual picnic in one of the Los Angeles parks. Tom Pletcher remembers going to these events with his father, trumpeter Stew Pletcher: "The union party was the annual Local 47 picnic that I and my neighborhood kids always looked forward to during the '40s and very early '50s. They used to have baseball games and all the musicians would play. Local 47 even back in the 40s and 50s was a huge organization and thousands of musicians showed up. They got great orchestras like the Dorsey orchestras, Harry James to play. It was really quite wonderful."

In 1953 Stacy was part of a small band, including Matty Matlock and Eddie

135

Miller, which appeared at the picnic and was caught on tape by collector Joe Boughton.

By November Stacy was playing at a club called The Falcon, and he ended the year by playing a band date, December 10-25. *Down Beat* reported on a new venue, the 22 Club, on Sunset Strip: "New ops kicked off with a string of two-beaters, with Jess Stacy heading a five-piece combo featuring Pud Brown. Announced to follow in a series of two week stands were Red Nichols, Jack Teagarden and Artie Shaw and the Gramercy Five."

Even if the other named groups did appear, the club soon folded.

When the *Down Beat* readers poll appeared, Oscar Peterson, Dave Brubeck and Bud Powell filled the first three places in the pianist section. Stacy was 21st, with Liberace 11th. The *Down Beat* issue for March 24 reported: "Jess Stacy, currently soloing at Lindy's, has decorated piano with candelabra set, says: 'Soon as my hair gets long enough, gonna get me a permanent, and make a try at television.'"

1954 was a quiet year. Work continued in the restaurants, steak houses and cocktail lounges of Los Angeles. One of the few known outside dates was an appearance on the Spade Cooley television show on February 6, 1954.

The Monday night dates at the Beverly Cavern with John Lucas and his Blueblowers continued during the first few weeks of the year, and in February the band recorded four titles for Jazz Man. Despite his star status with the group, Stacy's only solo is two choruses on *Hindustan*.

Another two recording sessions took place in April, 1954. These were by nine-piece bands under Jess Stacy's name, for the Atlantic label. Designed as a tribute to Benny Goodman, they were not issued until nearly two years later. This was after Stacy had recorded four piano solos in October 1955, allowing Atlantic to release a 12" LP to coincide with the film, "The Benny Goodman Story".

Heinie Beau cropped up here again, this time as arranger as well as reedman. His recollection of the 1954 sessions was: "Jess and Nesuhi Ertegun (producer of Atlantic) came to my house with the idea for the LP. The usual tight budget prevailed, so they decided on a small group. They suggested titles and we came up with a representative group. I arranged and played on the date. Jess himself outlined the numbers with only rhythm section. As to why I didn't write any solos for myself, I thought nothing of it at the time, but they apparently had envisioned this LP as being primarily a vehicle for Jess, and he would solo on every number. Secondly, they didn't want to make it an imitation of B.G. with another clarinet duplicating his solos. However I did write myself in on the closing *Goodbye*."

This Atlantic album by Jess Stacy and the Famous Sidemen was well received, and not just because of the story that: "Ziggy Elman felt so deeply about this album that he continued to play long after his lip had begun to bleed." Musically it is one of the highpoints of Stacy's later career, with an especially fine solo title, *Blues For Otis Ferguson*. The *Down Beat* reviewer of the album wrote: "Stacy throughout is superb, and it is a mystery why he has been recorded so seldom in recent years."

One concert to include Stacy was held in May, 1954. To quote *Down Beat*: "Bob Markus . . . is the impresario behind a series of Sunday afternoon concerts announced to start May 23 in Hollywood's Ivar theater, a small legitimate house. Announced for the opening event were Dick Cathcart and his 'Pete Kelly's Blues' band from the Jack Webb show; Jess Stacy; George Van Eps; Walter Gross; Kitty White; and Russ Cheever's Hollywood Saxophone Quartet."

John Lucas played at one of these concerts, with Jess Stacy and Nick Fatool. Bob Crosby was the compere. The few titles taped are listed in the discography. Lucas says: "I vaguely remember an afternoon session in the early or middle '50s in Hollywood in a big cement room off an alley, and put on by a Bob Marcus (sic) . . . he was a clerk in the record department of a local store in Pasadena."

The results of the Readers Poll in *Down Beat* for December 29, 1954 showed Oscar Peterson as the piano section winner again, with 837 votes. Liberace was 13th, and Jess Stacy was 26th, with 21 loyal votes.

In 1954 Universal Studios had had a screen success with "The Glenn Miller Story", starring James Stewart, so it was not surprising that in 1955 the company decided to make "The Benny Goodman Story". What was unexpected was that the lead role would be taken by Steve Allen. Goodman himself would play clarinet on the soundtrack, and recording began in mid-June at the Universal Studios in Hollywood.

From this arose an event in which Stacy gained much publicity in the musical press – without playing a single note.

At this time Stacy was working at The Garden of Allah, as a July 1955 *Down Beat* reported: "Garden of Allah Apartment Hotel, which houses many visiting notables, becomes Holiday House under new management policy, with Jess Stacy and piano holding forth at the pool-side bar."

Pat Stacy says Dudley Murphy was in charge of the Garden of Allah, and that Jess liked working there in one of the bungalows which had been converted into a tiny bar. "Jack Lemmon frequently was there playing the piano before Jess started to work. And this was where Billie Holiday came in one evening between her shows, sat on the piano bench with Jess and sang *Lover Man*.

Jack Lemmon is an accomplished, self-taught pianist. Keith Keller writes of Lemmon, at a Cannes Film Festival party, playing some Stacy trills, and saying: "Jess Stacy is the master. His playing always moved me and brought me peace of mind at the same time." Other film personalities who were Stacy admirers included Robert Mitchum and Pat O'Brien.

In "Oh, Jess!" Pat Stacy is quoted at length about the visit which Benny and Alice Goodman paid to Lookout Mountain Avenue, after Alice Goodman had seen the pianist at the Garden of Allah. Although the visit was requested by the Goodmans because of the forthcoming film, little was said about it during the evening: "Benny had touched only briefly on the picture, saying to Jess, 'We are making this picture, don't worry about a thing.'"

A contractor telephoned the following day, asking Stacy to report to the studio. When queried about conditions and payment, the studio employee pleaded that Stacy report at 10 a.m. the next morning. Stacy agreed, saying: OK, I'll come, but I won't play unless somebody down there offers me some kind of a deal, and so I went on down and was at the studio at 9:30, and the band was all set. A lot of them were my old buddies of the B.G. big time. Ziggy Elman was there, even if I knew him to have a bad lip so that he could only mime the original Elman solos that Mannie Klein would try to approximate on the soundtrack. [Others present included Harry James, Chris Griffin, Gene Krupa, Babe Russin, Hymie Shertzer, Allan Reuss, Lionel Hampton and Teddy Wilson.] And it was all like jolly old class-reunion time, that is, until I asked what my deal was . . . Why, I was to be paid scale, which is the lowest rate in the musicians' union accord . . . So I thought, well, I don't need the loot that bad. And I got ready to leave, when Benny Goodman came up to me and said, 'What's all this about, you are not going to give me a hard time, are you, Jess?', and I said, 'No, I believe not, because I'll be leaving right now.' And I turned around and just walked."

Stacy was also peeved when he discovered that: ". . . they have given most of the things I did with the band to Teddy Wilson, who was never actually a member of the band. And I was just supposed to do some little thing on one number – for flat scale for one session."

D. Russell Connor, in "Benny Goodman: Listen To His Legacy", blames the film producers for failing to agree terms with Stacy, but he also relates, in apparent contradiction, a story in which Goodman initially offered Harry James a ridiculously small amount to appear in the film.

It is certainly to be regretted that terms could not be agreed. Stacy's presence in the film would have added a little touch of authenticity to a typical Hollywood bio-pic, as well as increasing our opportunities to see him in action.

Around the same time there was a no doubt happier occasion, which *Down Beat*, July 27, 1955 reported: "Bob Crosby rounded up ex-Bob Cats Eddie Miller, Matty Matlock, Nappy Lamare, Jess Stacy and Ray Bauduc here [Hollywood], flew them to New York for a one-shot stint on the Jackie Gleason summer series."

In October Stacy recorded four piano solos, backed by Artie Shapiro on bass and Nick Fatool on drums, to provide the extra tracks needed to complete the Atlantic LP. The following month, on November 5, Stacy appeared on the George Barclay radio show, alongside Meade Lux Lewis and Edgar Hayes. Each pianist contributed his version of *St. Louis Blues*.

The ups and downs, the highs and lows, were to continue for a few years yet.

George Barclay's radio show – November 5, 1955.

Left to right: Edgar Hayes, George Barclay, Meade Lux Lewis, Jess Stacy and Adrian Tucker.

(Collector Adrian Tucker was an old friend from Benny Goodman's Palomar engagement)

Photo: courtesy of Mrs. Pat Stacy

1956 can be skated over rather quickly, there being few breaks from the saloon circuit. Stacy spent the year playing at locations such as the Black Angus Steak House and The Captain's Table. When *Down Beat* mentioned one engagement, it did so in the following form: "Jess Stacy, the 'forgotten man' of "The B.G. Story", is plying his trade at Gra-Jo's on South La Cienga." Working arrangements in these restaurants or cocktail lounges, were five or six nights a week, the average hours being 9 p.m. to 1:30 a.m. or thereabouts.

On March 3, 1956 Stacy recorded four original compositions, for Decca, with Nick Fatool on drums. This was to enable his 10" LP on Brunswick to be re-released as a 12" album. Three of the titles he had previously made for Commodore; the fourth, *Boo-Boos For Bob*, was named for Bob Thiele, who produced the session.

Reviewing the album, Brunswick BL54017, critic Nat Hentoff wrote: "One of the enduring individuals of jazz piano is represented here in one of the enduring piano LPs of recent years."

In July Stacy visited his son, who was teaching in St. Louis. The *St. Louis Globe Democrat* (July 27, 1956): "Jess Stacy in town for a visit with his son, Fred, who teaches the band at Lutheran High school."

Errol Garner was the top pianist in the *Down Beat* readers poll, with Stacy in 39th position.

By January, 1957, Jess Stacy was playing nightly, except Monday, at The Interlude on Sunset Boulevard, and he was probably still there when he was scheduled to appear at the Shrine Auditorium on February 22 in a Dixieland Jazz Festival. Bands on the bill included those of Jack Teagarden, Red Nichols and Barney Bigard, as well as the Dukes of Dixieland, the Bay City Jazz Band, and the Firehouse Five Plus Two.

In the July 11, 1957 issue of *Down Beat* there appeared an interview which Stacy gave to John Tynan. The pianist's comments on solo work at that time included: "I don't give a hang what the saloon crowd wants. I play what I like. To tell the truth, I figure if I satisfy two people out of 75 in this saloon, that's a good average . . . Personally, I like playing as a single. Some fellows can't do it; gets 'em down. For me, though, it seems easier – a lot easier – than band work. I don't do so bad either. Been working 49 weeks out of a year . . . Every place you work becomes a helluva rehearsal hall . . . I certainly don't expect everybody to love me. You can't please 'em all – that's impossible – so I don't try."

The famous humourist, S.J. Perelman, showed his sympathy for jazz by the mentions in his writings of such musicians as Benny Goodman, Kid Ory, Red Norvo and Pee Wee Russell. One of his stories is entitled, "And Thou Beside Me, Yacketing in the Wilderness" it includes an account of a visit, with his garrulous lady friend, to a club at which Jess Stacy is performing: "As it developed, the star turn at the club was one of the great modern masters, the incomparable Jess Alexandria Stacy, of Cape Girardeau, Missouri. His keyboard was bewitched that night; never has there been such a rolling bass, such superb arpeggios. I was in transport – destined, I should have known, to rank as the world's briefest . . . Desperately trying to staunch her rhetoric and at the same time pay homage to Stacy, who was doing a transcendant version of *Back Home In Indiana*, I made the fatal error of ordering double whiskeys . . . When Stacy stopped dead in the middle of *Riverboat Shuffle* and swung round ominously on his stool, I knew that jigwise, all was up."

Another literary mention of Stacy appeared in the 1960s, in a poem, "The Jazz Machine", by Richard Matheson, which included the lines:

I sat dummied in his coupe
My sacked-up trumpet on my lap
Listening while he rolled off words
Like Stacy runnings on a tinkle box.

A unique and splendid tribute to Stacy is contained in "For Jazz", Peter McSloy's book of 21 sonnets dedicated to notable jazzmen. The Stacy verse has such evocative phrases as "He owned the kind of lyrical command;" "Stacy sat easy, gathered in long-fingered hands;" and "In Goodman's band he was like a hidden spring."

"Stars Of Jazz" was a half-hour weekly television show which originated on Channel 7 (K.A.B.C.), Los Angeles, with Bobby Troup as the presenter. In July Stacy was featured on the show, alongside John Lucas, trumpet; Moe Schneider, trombone; Bob McCracken, clarinet; Bob Stone, bass; and Lou Diamond, drums. He appeared on the show again on September 9, 1957, with his "Benny Goodman All-Stars", Cappy Lewis, trumpet; Murray McEarchern, trombone; Heinie Beau, clarinet, alto; Dave Harris, tenor; Joe Koch, baritone; Allan Reuss, guitar; Morty Corb, bass; Nick Fatool, drums; Martha Tilton, vocals. The musicians were interviewed and Stacy was well featured.

In the *Down Beat* poll the top five pianists were Errol Garner, Oscar Peterson, Dave Brubeck, Horace Silver and Andre Previn. Stacy was not listed.

A January recording session for Good Time Jazz, accompanying singer and banjoist Clancy Hayes, got 1958 off to a good start. Six attractive titles resulted, but were not issued until five years later, when further songs were recorded with Ralph Sutton on piano.

To conclude the year, there was a recording session for Crown Records, a tribute to Benny Goodman. This was one of a number of "tributes" which the company organised. Stacy plays on five titles by the big band, which was conducted by Maxwell Davis, but is hardly heard. Heinie Beau appears again, sitting in the reed section, but the clarinet soloing is by Mahlon Clark.

And the December 22, 1958 issue of *Life* magazine contained a "When Jazz Was Young" feature. This included a few comments by Stacy, obtained when he was interviewed by Robert Campbell for the magazine. This short interview is held in the jazz archive at Tulane University in New Orleans.

An interesting discographical mystery arose during 1959. This concerns the film, "The Gene Krupa Story", which was retitled "Drum Crazy" for British release. Many sources, including the Verve soundtrack album sleeve-note, list Stacy as the pianist with the small group, which included Red Nichols, Benny Carter and Eddie Miller. However, it seems most likely that Stacy did not play on this soundtrack. This mystery is discussed in more detail in the appendix to the discography.

It was in June 1959 that *Down Beat* reported that Bob Thiele and Steve Allen were to start Hanover-Signature records. Since seeing Jess Stacy with the Bob Crosby band at the Blackhawk in Chicago, Steve Allen had become a major figure in the entertainment world, as comedian, presenter, and pianist. He had his own television show, made records and, as we have seen, even starred in a Hollywood musical. Bob Thiele was a jazz fan from the 1930s, started the Signature label in the early 1940s, and continued in the recording business right up until his death in 1996. It was Thiele who was in charge of operations for the new label.

140

Thanks to Steve Allen, and a little luck, Stacy was given the opportunity to record another piano album. Allen recalls the circumstances: "Jess was playing at a little restaurant in town [the Huddle-Bundy]. I had been told, by a friend of mine named Mike Gould, a music publisher, that he had discovered Jess's presence at the restaurant by accident, and since he knew I was a lover of good jazz music he thought I would like to go with him some night to hear Stacy. The two of us spent a couple of hours at the place, as I recall, and Jess was kind enough to play a great many requests for us. It must have been that night that I got the idea to do "The Return of Jess Stacy" album on the Hanover label. I was one of the owners of the label. It produced some good records but was not financially successful and so folded up after a brief period of operation. My strongest impression of Jess's jazz style is that he played the piano more like a trumpet than did any other pianist. His figures were usually played in octaves and his solos were, I think, closer to Louis Armstrong trumpet solos than they were to the playing of Art Tatum, Teddy Wilson, Bob Zurke or other good pianists of the 1930s."

Allen tells much the same story in his-sleeve note to Hanover HM-8010, The Return of Jess Stacy, on which the pianist is accompanied by Morty Corb, bass; and Nick Fatool, drums. He refers to the Huddle-Bundy as a combination restaurant and cocktail lounge in Santa Monica. Stacy had opened there on March 3, 1959.

In his sleeve-note Steve Allen writes of the post-war years: "Jazz itself was no longer of interest to the public, nor was big band swing music as commercial as it had been. There was nothing personal about Jess's decline during the war years; it was part of the decline of an industry and an art-form."

Another visitor to the Huddle-Bundy was an enthusiast from Canada named Paul Copeland. A merchant seaman, he had arrived in Los Angeles to join a freighter, only to discover that its sailing date had been delayed by one week. Discovering by chance where he could hear Jess Stacy, he made his way to Santa Monica: "I took a bus on a journey that seemed to last forever, and then . . . I had to walk for a couple of miles at least to the Huddle-Bundy, a quite attractive bar/restaurant located right across the street from the Santa Monica airport. I walked in and up eight steps to the bar on the mezzanine floor and immediately recognized Jess. He was playing a piano about which was placed a U-shaped "piano bar" where customers could sit just two or three feet away from Jess face to face . . . I spoke to Jess and he soon realized that I was quite aware of his place in American jazz. Jess laughed when I asked him if he had really said about his former wife, Lee Wiley: 'They didn't burn the last witch in Salem!' 'Yes,' he said, 'I said that. And I was right.'

That first night, Wednesday, September 30, 1959, I stayed with Jess listening to him play and talk until the Huddle-Bundy closed. He drove me not all the way back to my hotel, but nevertheless several miles out of his way, to a convenient bus stop. I returned every night that Jess appeared after that. And on every one of those nights I closed the Huddle-Bundy with Jess. The bar was closed on Sunday and Monday, so the last night I was there was on Tuesday, October 6, 1959. The next afternoon I boarded my freighter."

In December Stacy was invited to New York to be a member of the Benny Goodman Quartet, along with Lionel Hampton and Gene Krupa, for an appearance on a television show, "The Big Party." The broadcast took place on December 17. In his Goodman tome, D. Russell Connor tells how impressed he was by the search for

Some of Jess Stacy's advertising postcards

Hi Friend:

I am opening The Track Cafe, 1076 East Colorado Boulevard, Pasadena, Friday, April 14th. Drop in and say hello.

Sincerely,
JESS STACY

The Track Cafe, April 14, 1950

Beginning Tuesday, November 13, I WILL HAVE THE PLEASURE OF APPEARING AT THE WEST COAST'S MOST BEAUTIFUL RESTAURANT,

The Oyster House
666 NORTH LA CIENEGA BOULEVARD
LOS ANGELES

Hope to see you there —

† † *Jess Stacy* † †

Telephone
OL. 2-2900

NIGHTLY EXCEPT MONDAY
9:30 TO 1:30

The Oyster House, November 13, 1956

☆☆☆☆ OPENING FRIDAY, AUGUST 3rd ☆☆☆☆

Jess Stacy
"AMERICA'S FAVORITE JAZZ PIANIST"
NIGHTLY EXCEPT MONDAY, AT THE PIANO BAR IN THE SURF ROOM

Holiday House
27400 COAST HIGHWAY, MALIBU

GLENWOOD 7-2521   DINNER · COCKTAILS · SUPPER

Mr. Stacy's latest album for Atlantic Records No. 1225
"TRIBUTE TO BENNY GOODMAN"

Holiday House, August 3, 1956

Jess Stacy
"America's Favorite Jazz Pianist"
opening **Monday, January 9, 1961**

FRASCATI CHALET
2201 Wilshire Boulevard
Santa Monica

Nightly except Sunday   Phone EX 5178

Frascati Chalet, January 9, 1961

perfection during the rehearsals and how the last title played developed into an old fashioned jam session. He also admits that he and Stacy were less than kind in their comments on the film, "The Gene Krupa Story", which was privately screened for a few V.I.P.'s, including Gene Krupa, the evening of the rehearsals.

Stacy made another appearance with the Benny Goodman Quartet, this time with Rolly Bundock, bass; and Jack Sperling, drums, when the group appeared on The Dinah Shore Chevy Show on February 28, 1960. This show was taped in Burbank, California. Stacy told Keith Kellcr, with 'a wry smile,' "I know that Benny got ten grand for each of those shows, while I forgot my tough stance. I did them, damn it, for scale."

During 1960 Stacy had a lengthy engagement at Leon's Steak House at 10945 Victory Boulevard, at Vineland Avenue, in North Hollywood. When visited in 1979 it was typical of the establishments which used solo pianists to provide background music for its customers. It consisted of three main areas, a cocktail lounge, coffee shop, and dining room; a substantial and well-appointed business, which was opened by Leon Grown. The cocktail lounge, where the piano was situated, was only small.

Bob Ringwald played piano there from the late 1970s into the 1980s: "Leon's is a working-man's bar. It has been there about 40 years and many of the customers have been coming in for almost that long. I do well there because I'm willing to play what the general public like to hear. Jess walked out one night because of that reason. He couldn't stand to play what he considered pop music and he couldn't stand to play while people sang along."

One collector recalled listening to Stacy at Leon's and feeling for the pianist as he had to handle requests for tunes such as *Tie A Yellow Ribbon Round The Old Oak Tree*.

And so 1960, 1961 and 1962 passed, and the cumulative effect of the drunks, the stupid requests and the overall lack of interest were, as Stacy said, to weigh heavier and heavier upon him. Customers talking and laughing, accompanied by the rattle of cutlery and the clinking of china and glass, oblivious to the pianist, unless to pester him – was this the environment for a musician of great sensitivity? Undoubtedly, Stacy was asking himself this more and more.

A decade later pianists like Ray Bryant, Johnny Guarnieri, Art Hodes, Dick Hyman, Jay McShann, Sammy Price, Ralph Sutton and Dick Wellstood found their way onto the international jazz festival and jazz party circuit, which started at that time. These events gave the musicians enhanced prestige, allied to reasonable remuneration and attentive audiences. It happened all too late for Jess Stacy. By 1963 he was disillusioned with the music business and it is doubtful that he could have been persuaded to undertake a heavy traveling schedule.

Down Beat for May 23, 1963, contained a news item headed: "UNION PENSION PLAN HURTING LIVE MUSIC, JESS STACY SAYS" in which Stacy claimed that the live music business in Los Angeles clubs had been ruined by the club operators and Local 47. Stacy said: "The union pension fund is just not being bought by the club owners. They refuse to make the payments required for the musicians they hire. So they either hire less musicians and pay less into the fund or they cut out live music altogether. But it's not only the union, of course. It's the owners and the people you play for too. They're supposed to be listening, but they couldn't care less. That goes for the owners too. I played for one night with a Dixieland band recently, and I discovered that the club operator had stuck thumbtacks in the piano hammers. For that good old ricky-tick sound . . . It was the last straw. I didn't go back the next night."

Not long after this interview the long threatened crisis arose. As he told Jan Edward Wilson he felt that people, ". . . drove miles just to harass the piano player. I'd always loved what I did , but I was anxious to quit. I never was cut out for that kind of entertaining – I don't sing and really, I don't smile too much while I'm playing, and I don't drink with the customers. I was playing at a club in La Crescenta, and suddenly decided to stop it all and get a day job." He told Whitney Balliett that his last job was in a snake pit in La Crescenta on Friday and Saturday nights.

Here is how John Lucas remembers Stacy telling him about this: "He was working in a rotten little corner saloon in a rotten little hick town nortwest of Pasadena, up near the mountains. He had followed a pianoplayer (notice I did not say 'pianist') into this place. This joker had a bunch of wind-up dolls he'd parade on the piano-bar as he played. One night a boozy habitué of the place told Jess to wind up his goddamn dolls, and kept bugging him so that Jess, who had already been demoralized for the previous few years, slammed the keyboard cover down and walked out of the joint, never to come

143

back – even to pick up his check! International star, *Down Beat* poll winner, mentor of a generation of other pianists!. . ."

On September 3, 1963 Jess Stacy started work for the cosmetics firm, Max Factor & Co., in Hollywood. He was employed as a mail clerk. To quote the company, "Mr. Jess Stacy's primary duties were to deliver and collect company mail following an established route throughout Corporate Headquarters."

As Stacy told Whitney Balliett, "It was a lowly job and I'd guess you'd call it beneath my station. I walked ten miles a day delivering mail, but at least I enjoyed the first vacations with pay I'd ever had. I worked there six years and when I hit 65 they retired me."

Jess and Pat Stacy with Doll Face
Photo: courtesy of Mrs. Pat Stacy

Pat Stacy said that her husband "loved his job at Max Factor. The top corporate executives would ask him to sit down in their offices and chat with them when he delivered mail. He was sorry to leave when he reached the mandatory retirement age."

This loss to the jazz world was at least noted by fellow Chicago pianist, Art Hodes, who wrote in his *Down Beat* column: "It's a sad commentary on the music business and the musicians' union to see a player of the stature Jess Stacy enjoys having to find his livelihood in the cosmetic business."

Thus the full-time professional career of one of the great jazz pianists came to an end. He remained disillusioned about the music business for many years thereafter, but the nine-to-five job must surely have helped both his health and his peace of mind. The great days were over, but there were still occasional events to remind him of them – interviews, articles, concerts, recordings, a film soundtrack appearance, awards – all still to come during the next 30 years.

10

Retirement

Only a year or so after he went to work at Max Factor's Jess Stacy was interviewed again by *Down Beat.* This showed he was back playing weekends, Friday and Saturday nights, usually with Bob McCracken on clarinet and Ray Bauduc on drums, though the engagements were probably spasmodic. No locations were mentioned.

By 1966 public appearances were a rarity, as the following suggests, a recollection of the only time that drummer Bill French met Jess Stacy: "The occasion was in the summer of 1966, at a bar [The Swingin' End] owned by that fine trumpeter, Rico Vallese. On Monday nights Rico used to have sessions and all kinds of guys would drop in and either play or just listen. One night Jess came in (I think with Johnny Lucas) and tore the place up. As I remember, he didn't really *want* to, because he thought he was a little rusty. Anyway, he played so beautifully for most of the evening that I thanked my lucky stars that I happened to be there."

Benny Goodman celebrated the 30th anniversary of the first Carnegie Hall concert with a dinner party in the roof garden over his apartment in Manhattan. At this January 16, 1968, party, the following musicians from the Goodman band of the '30s were in attendance (as listed by D. Russell Connor): Ziggy Elman, Chris Griffin, Vernon Brown, Hymie Shertzer, George Koenig, Art Rollini, Jess Stacy, Gene Krupa, Lionel Hampton, Helen Ward, Martha Tilton. Stacy, Elman and Martha Tilton had flown in from the west coast, and Keith Keller tells how Elman fortified himself for the flight with a copious supply of various kinds of spirits.

Connor also writes: "Following a buffet dinner, Benny, Lionel, Jess, Gene and Ruby Braff jammed for more than an hour. (Photographer and ex-Goodman band boy 'Popsie' Randolph hadn't gotten Gene's drums set up when they began to play. Critic George Simon accompanied the group on cymbal before Gene could participate). Jess, especially, played beautifully, all the more remarkably because he had not performed professionally in a half dozen years." This jam session was taped by Russell Connor.

The June issue of *Esquire* magazine contained a two-page color photograph of the Goodman musicians, plus Buck Clayton, Bobby Hackett and Cootie Williams, who also participated in the Carnegie Hall concert.

During the party William B. Williams of WNEW radio taped comments from those attending, who also included Sol Hurok and John Hammond, and excerpts were broadcast on January 27. A couple of responses are worth quoting, including typically blunt Stacy.

Williams:	What is your reaction . . . to the musical sounds of today, the music that the kids dig today?
Stacy:	Personally, I don't listen to it.
Williams:	How can you avoid listening?
Stacy:	By working days. Turning off the radio.

This was followed by Gene Krupa saying: "If I may say one thing. I remember Stacy's attitude towards the music business in 1936 and 1937 and from what I heard just a moment ago it's still the same. This man believes music should be played a certain way, there should be a certain sincerity about it. I think Mr. Stacy's still the same way. I think everything he ever did musically proves that point."

The following year, on August 29, 1969, Jess Stacy left the employ of Max Factor, having reached retirement age.

Pat Stacy continued working, and her husband stayed home, keeping the house tidy and looking after the garden, watering, weeding and mowing the lawn; the kind of work so many retired men undertake. As for music, he said: "I get my kicks practising a lot and playing Bach." He bought himself an electric piano, but was never happy with it. "It's not quite human," he said.

Jess and Pat Stacy at home on Lookout Mountain Avenue, September 29, 1975.

Photo: courtesy of the late Donny McDonald

Two months after his retirement Stacy was lured to a jazz party in Pasadena, arranged for the Blue Angel Jazz Club. The party, organised by Dr. and Mrs. William A. MacPherson, at the University Club of Pasadena, lasted from 3 p.m. Saturday, November 1, to 2 a.m. Sunday, November 2, 1969. The proceedings were recorded and two albums were issued on the Blue Angel Jazz Club label, with Stacy playing solo and with a Clancy Hayes group. Other musicians present included Johnny Best and Tommy Thunen, trumpets; Dick Cary, trumpet and piano; Bob Havens and Abe Lincoln, trombones; Matty Matlock and Abe Most, clarinets; Don Lodice and Wayne Songer, reeds; Marvin Ash and Johnny Guarnieri, piano; Nappy Lamare and George Van Eps, guitar; Morty Corb, Ray Leatherwood and Art Shapiro, bass; Panama Francis, Jack Sperling, drums; Clancy Hayes, banjo, vocal; and Lyn Keath, vocal.

Jess Stacy at the Blue Angel Jazz Club,
November 1, 1969
Photo: courtesy of Bill Bacin

Left to right: Morty Corb, George Van Eps and Jess
Stacy at the Blue Angel Jazz Club.
Photo: courtesy of Mrs.Pat Stacy

Merrill Hammond's report in *Jazz Journal* included: "Making his first public appearance in seven years, Jess Stacy was sensational. Always a stickler for correct technique, Jess showed that although he hasn't worked as a musician for some time he still has that old touch which charmed dancers when he was with the Crosby and Goodman bands. He commanded the complete attention of musicians and guests as he tossed off with ease such favorites as *Lover Man* and *How Long Has This Been Going On*. There wasn't a dry eye in the house."

Despite the appreciation Stacy received at this party, he continued to feel sad about the changes in the music business. There is no reason to doubt John Hammond's comment that Stacy felt let down by history, though that feeling was to be soothed by the events of 1974. That year the painful memories of the Hollywood "snake pits" were to be eased and the jazz world was reminded that he should not be forgotten.

When pianist Jess Stacy and trombonist Nelson Riddle met in the Tommy Dorsey orchestra in 1945 it is unlikely that either expected that they would meet again in January 1974, on Paramount Pictures' sound stage in Hollywood.

F. Scott Fitzgerald's novel, "The Great Gatsby", was filmed mainly in England towards the end of 1973, much of it at Elstree Studios. Producer David Merrick and director Jack Clayton were determined that songs by Irving Berlin and other composers of the 1920s would be used on the soundtrack. Clayton, apparently, insisted that the music should be recorded in Hollywood, with as many veterans of the period as was possible. It has been suggested that there were differences with the original arranger. Whether that is true or not, Nelson Riddle was called urgently to England in November 1973 to look at the rough cut of the film and to begin scoring the music.

Five weeks later Riddle was back in Hollywood, starting to record the soundtrack. One result of this was that Jess Stacy was asked to participate. Nelson Riddle said, "I recommended Jess Stacy to Phil Kobgen. I kept seeing his name listed in the personnel of early bands, and, since I knew him and had worked with him with Tommy Dorsey, it was logical that I recommend him. Jess played only *Beale Street Blues*. Ray Sherman, a fine studio pianist, did the rest, including *Kitten On The Keys*. We did have Nappy Lamare on banjo, Nick Fatool on drums, Cappy Lewis on trumpet." Riddle also listed Mahlon Clark, clarinet; Shorty Sherock, trumpet; and Pete Lofthouse, trombone.

Dick Cary, though not mentioned by Nelson Riddle, was another of the musicians contacted: "I was just one of three trumpet players (John Best and Shorty Sherock [were the others]). 'Twas a very rainy day and I almost didn't get through the highway lakes – but did make it and was there from 9 a.m. to 7 p.m. I thought the score was terrible – not one jazz band piece all day and we had some fine guys, like Nick Fatool, Ray Sherman, Jess Stacy, Mahlon Clark, etc, etc."

Stacy is heard playing *Beale Street Blues* in a scene which features Robert Redford, Sam Waterston and Howard Da Silva having lunch in a restaurant. It is a lengthy scene, but the piano sound is obscured by the dialogue. This may not have been a bad thing, as the soundtrack album (on the Paramount label) confirms Stacy's complaints about the piano he had to play: "But for this they gave me a real curio item, a piano with metal pieces nailed or glued to the felt of its hammers. I guess it was supposed to make it sound real honky-tonkish, but I never in my life heard anything like it . . . I threw the soundtrack LP away after one hearing."

It was in the middle of 1974 that the major event of Jess Stacy's retirement occurred, one which resulted in much publicity and the opportunity to record again – The Newport Jazz Festival in New York.

As its name indicates, the Festival began in Newport, Rhode Island, in 1954. After a riot ended the 1971 festival it was moved to New York, where the musicians played in concert halls rather than on an outdoor stage.

In February, the World's Greatest Jazz Band – led by Yank Lawson and Bob Haggart, was playing at the Century Plaza Hotel in Century City, Los Angeles. Jess and Pat Stacy visited, to enjoy the music and meet their old friends. During a conversation with the band's pianist, Ralph Sutton, Stacy mentioned he had been invited to Newport, but was reluctant to go. Sutton said: " 'Listen, Jess, nobody plays like you. You go back there and get that money. Get it and it'll do you good.' In the meantime I got him to sit in with the band that night and he knocked everybody out."

When Marie St. Louis of the Festival office telephoned Stacy he was in the garden: "Fact, when I got to the phone from out in the backyard, where I was watering, I was puffing like a buffalo. I was really out of kilter. But I told her yes, I'd do it, because I figured it might be my last picture show."

To journalist Jan Edward Wilson, Stacy amplified on his response to that call: "It was a real surprise and my immediate reaction was: I didn't want to do it. So I searched for an excuse – and came up with a legitimate reason. I told them I wouldn't want to travel without my wife, and it wouldn't be financially feasible to take her at my own expense. But that reason died 10 minutes later with a second call, offering to pay Pat's expenses too, so I agreed to go."

Stacy's expression, "puffing like a buffalo," indicated he was out of condition. In recent years his weight had increased from a consistent 135 pounds to around 230, and playing at Newport meant intensive practising, dieting and exercising. Sitting at the piano for more than 20 minutes was a problem, so he began doing sit-ups. He and Pat took long walks each day. As a result of these efforts he was ready for New York.

Stacy was contracted to appear at two concerts, both in Carnegie Hall. The first, held on Sunday, June 30, was entitled "Solo Piano 1" and featured eight pianists: Eubie Blake, Bill Evans, Johnny Guarnieri, Eddie Heywood, Jess Stacy, Dick Wellstood and Teddy Wilson, with Marian McPartland as host. Eddie Heywood overran his allotted 15 minutes, but Marian McPartland refused Stacy's offer to reduce his set to ten minutes!

Opinions about Stacy's contribution varied, but he was enthusiastically received by the audience: "The audience bowled me off my feet, they loved it," he said.

Whitney Balliett reported: "One suspects that a good many people came to the first program to hear Jess Stacy, who has been in retirement on the coast for fourteen years. It was an auspicious moment when he stepped onstage . . . for it was the first time he had been back in the hall since that January night in 1938 . . . A little heavier, a little slower (he will be seventy later this summer), but with his handsome Irish face and sleek black hair intact, he sat down at once and reeled off *How Long Has This Been Going On, Lover Man* and *I Would Do Anything For You.* Some of his fingering was uneven and his harmony went out of whack once (Stacy calls lapses of this kind "meatballs"), but the famous style was all there – the little tremolos, the light, upper-register chords, the inner runs."

John S. Wilson, in *The New York Times*, was similarly impressed: "The melodists, who predominated on last year's single program and provided its essential merits, were, if anything, even better this year. A prime reason for this was the presence of Jess Stacy, the invaluable but largely overlooked pianist in Benny Goodman's orchestra at the height of its success in the mid-nineteen-thirties . . . Out of music he may have been, but he has obviously kept in shape musically. His three selections of Sunday's program had the edgy but lilting bounce that gives his playing a light insistent propulsion, and his phrasing was exquisite."

But Stanley Dance wrote: "Jess Stacy, nervous, probably rusty, lacks old incisive quality on three numbers." Judged by the Chiaroscuro recordings, recorded that same week, Stanley Dance's view was probably the most accurate.

The second appearance was on Friday, July 5, in a concert entitled "Friends of Eddie Condon and Ben Webster." Condon had died August 4, 1973, and Webster on September 20, 1973. Paying tribute to Eddie Condon were: Yank Lawson, trumpet; Wild Bill Davison, Bobby Hackett, cornets; Vic Dickenson, trombone; Barney Bigard, clarinet; Bud Freeman, tenor; Bob Wilber, soprano, clarinet; Joe Venuti, violin; Jess Stacy, Ralph Sutton, pianos; Bob Haggart, bass; Cliff Leeman, drums; Maxine Sullivan, vocal.

Bud Freeman and Jess Stacy played two duets, and Stacy was in the rhythm section which backed a Barney Bigard feature. The band in which Stacy appeared was Lawson, Hackett, Dickenson, Bigard, Venuti, Haggart and Leeman. Full details are shown in the discography, the concerts having been recorded by Voice of America. Again, opinions on the performance were not unanimous: "Jess Stacy and Bud Freeman, duo, do tentative *Don't Blame Me* . . . [Bigard] is featured on *Mood Indigo* with sensitive accompaniment by Stacy (probably his best of the fest.)", wrote Stanley Dance. Whereas Whitney Balliett's view was: "But the best came from Stacy, who, relaxed and all together, kept Bud Freeman's mind on his work . . . and played an accompaniment to Bigard's *Mood Indigo* that was a beautiful solo in itself (his accompanying was the one light that never failed in the Goodman band of 1935-38). Condon, though, would have been absorbed by a *Sweet Georgia Brown* in which the horns started in one key and the

Jess Stacy, 29 May 1975
Photo by Ed Lawless

rhythm section in another – a problem that Stacy said he solved by staying with Joe Venuti's key of F because Venuti was standing right beside him."

And from Steve Lake, a young writer, not very sympathetic to older forms of jazz came: "Most of Condon's old buddies seemed pretty shaky, but whether that's indicative of emotion or just advanced senility, I wouldn't care to opine. Bud Freeman, particularly, sounded as though he'd just dug his tenor out of the attic after a ten year lay off, although on the other hand violinist Joe Venuti played a slick enough *Sweet Georgia Brown*, and pianist Jess Stacey *(sic)*, despite a questionable penchant for kissing his fellow musicians whene'er opportunity allowed, appeared as comfortable as could be expected."

The day after the Solo Piano 1 concert, on July 1, Stacy recorded an album for Chiaroscuro Records, "Stacy Still Swings". On the following day he recorded again for Chiaroscuro, this time in a trio with Bud Freeman on tenor and Cliff Leeman on drums.   The Bud Freeman album, "The Joy of Sax" was not a success. Pat Stacy referred to "Oh, that Joy of Sax horror," and Jess Stacy said, "I hate to think about that Bud Freeman Trio LP."   But "Stacy Still Swings" is a satisfactory example of Stacy's playing in 1974, though any potential listener should not expect to hear the flowing, agile Stacy of 1940 or 1950. As Yank Lawson told the writer, this was not the Jess Stacy of old.

The other feature of the New York visit was the interview which Stacy gave to Whitney Balliett. "Back From Valhalla" appeared in *The New Yorker* for August 18, 1975, and was subsequently published in a book of Balliett profiles entitled "Improvising". Later it was included in the notes for the CD release of "Stacy Still Swings". It was very influential in bringing Jess Stacy's name to the fore again, and undoubtedly encouraged the other interviews which followed during the next few months.

Perhaps because of this, on February 16, 1975, The New Jersey Jazz Society honored Jess Stacy and Milt Gabler for their contributions to jazz. The award to Stacy was a plaque inscribed:

FOR FIFTY YEARS, FROM THE MISSISSIPPI RIVER BOATS TO CARNEGIE HALL, HE HAS PLAYED JAZZ PIANO IN HIS INIMITABLE CLASSIC, SWINGING STYLE AND WON THE ACCLAIM OF JAZZ LOVERS EVERYWHERE.

The event, at which Phyllis Condon, widow of Eddie Condon, was the guest of honor, was briefly reported by *The Melody Maker*: "Eight dixieland bands took turns entertaining over 1,200 people at the seven-hour sixth annual Pee Wee Russell Memorial Stomp which took place at the Martinsville Inn in Martinsville, N.J. Milt Gabler accepted a special award on behalf of Jess Stacy, who was unable to be present."

Three months later Stacy undertook a playing engagement at the Sacramento Dixieland Jubilee. The Jubilee had started in 1974, and the program for the long weekend was to mix 20 to 30 largely amateur bands with a dozen or so guests stars, playing in a number of locations in Old Sacramento. In addition to Jess Stacy, the guests for 1975 were Bobby Hackett, Teddy Wilson, Nick Fatool, Johnny Mince, Skeets Herfurt, Bill Allred, Dick Cary, George Probert, Cougar Nelson, Bill Napier, Barry Durkee, and a seven year old Molly Ringwald. Stacy's schedule was:

Saturday, May 24 (with the S.P.D.J. All Stars)	*1:15 pm*	*Grand Ballroom*
Saturday, May 24 (with Capitol City Jazz Band and Cougar Nelson)	*10:00 pm*	*49er Site*
Sunday, May 25 (with Gas House Gang)	*2:00 pm*	*Temple*
Sunday, May 25 (with Act of Providence)	*10:00 pm*	*Grand Ballroom*

To confuse matters, the program also shows Stacy playing at 10:00 pm on Saturday with the River City Express at the Firehouse.

The S.P.D.J. (The Society for the Preservation of Dixieland Jazz) was led by Stacy's old friend, trumpeter Johnny Lucas. Another trumpeter, Donny McDonald, leader of the band Act of Providence, had cause to remember his session with Jess: ". . . there was a bit of a mix-up. My own piano player, Wilda Baughn, who is blind, was somehow taken to the main outdoor stage . . . Her guide didn't know she was supposed to be at the main indoor ballroom with me. Jess was to be my solo guest star. As it turned out, I sent runners looking for Wilda, and Jess started out as regular piano player. The audience had been told of the problem and thought it was great sport. Then who should wander in, completely lost, but Teddy Wilson, looking for the main outdoor stage. Well, we made him our soloist, and he proceeded to 43 million great notes, prompting Jess to mutter, "Listen to that quick *** trying to cut me. I'll show him," after which he played *Lover Man* for eleven minutes. It was a great session, and finally my regular pianist, Wilda, found the right place and things got back to normal."

John Lucas recalled shortly after the event, "We played together last May in the Sacramento Jazz Festival for the first time in ten years . . . We had a seven-piece group and were playing for a room of about a 1000, an afternoon session, with booze, kids running all over, photographers, et al. He asked me if he could do *Lover Man*, all by himself, no rhythm section . . . He did about five choruses, so great, such fantasy, creativity, that not a soul stirred in that whole room! A moment to remember. When they asked him to come up here (500 miles north) he said, 'If they're crazy enough to ask me, I'm ridiculous enough to go.' He is really bitter about this awful business, but in such a comical way!"

Writer and promoter Floyd Levin, long an admirer of Jess Stacy, finally persuaded the pianist to appear in the third edition of "A Night in New Orleans" at the Wilshire Ebell Theatre in Los Angeles on September 20, 1975. Stacy played four solos, the three he

151

Jess Stacy and Nappy Lamare at the Dixieland Jubilee Festival, Sacramento, California, May 1976.

Photo: courtesy of Mrs. Pat Stacy

played at Carnegie Hall, plus *The One I Love Belongs To Somebody Else*, followed by two duets with Ralph Sutton. He received a standing ovation, but still declined to take part in the European tour of "A Night In New Orleans" which Levin and partner Barry Martyn organised for 1976.

If Stacy had made the European tour he would have missed appearing at the Old Sacramento Dixieland Jubilee again. The 1976 extravaganza was held between May 28 and 31, with Stacy a guest star, along with Bob Bashor, Billy Butterfield, Pud Brown, Dick Cary, Jack Crook, Joe Darensbourg, Pete Daily, Nick Fatool, Johnny Guarnieri, Connie Haines, Peanuts Hucko, Johnny Mince, Nappy Lamare, Ray Leatherwood, Abe Lincoln, Wingy Manone, Louise Tobin and George Van Eps. There were 41 bands appearing at numerous sites, with a total attendance of around 35,000 dixieland fans.

Stacy's schedule was:

Saturday, May 29   2:55 pm   *Temple*
Nappy Lamare and the Levee Loungers: (Joe Ingram, trumpet; Rex Allen, trombone: Abe Most, clarinet; Jess Stacy, piano; Nappy Lamare, banjo, vocal; Bill Spreter, bass; Nick Fatool. drums)

Saturday, May 29   8:10 pm   *49'er site*
Jess Stacy All Stars (Tom King, trumpet; Rex Allen, trombone; Peanuts Hucko, clarinet; Jess Stacy, piano; George Van Eps, guitar; Bob Hinman, bass; Cliff Swesey, drums)

Sunday, May 30   2:55 pm   *Depot*
Abe Lincoln All Stars (Bob Cooke, trumpet; Abe Lincoln, trombone; Johnny Mince, Jack Crook, clarinets; Jess Stacy, piano; Nappy Lamare, banjo; Charley Ahrens, bass; Frank Amoss, drums)

Billy Butterfield All Stars (Billy Butterfield, trumpet; Dick Cary, alto horn; Abe Lincoln, trombone; Peanuts Hucko, clarinet; Jess Stacy, piano; Nappy Lamare, banjo; Ray Leatherwood, bass; Nick Fatool, drums):

There is always a surfeit of banjo players at the Sacramento Jubilee, but Stacy seemed to survive, despite his dislike of them. As he commented in "Jazz Greats": "I guess the only pet peeves I've got are bad pianos and banjos. Holy mackerel, one group I played with had two of those mothers playing . . . What chance has a piano got when two banjos are whangin' away? I just put my hands in my pockets and said, 'That's it.' But I gave up that kind of gig years ago." He told Bill Mitchell that he was utterly exhausted afterwards.

The following summer, in July, Jess and Pat Stacy went on holiday to New York, and Hank O'Neal, owner of Chiaroscuro records, arranged for Stacy to record again. 15 titles were recorded over two days, July 19 and 20, nine of which appeared on the "Stacy Is Still Swinging" album.

1978 passed quietly, enlivened by attendance at sessions when old friends were playing. For one, the Stacys visited Eddie Miller when he played a college date with Jimmy and Marian McPartland.

The Second Annual Art and Jazz Celebration at the Hunterdon Art Center in Clinton, New Jersey, featured two concerts which took place on the Friday evenings of September 28 and October 5, 1979. The second concert featured the Dick Wellstood Trio (Wellstood, piano; Warren Vache, Jr, trumpet; Tony DiNicola, drums). Also included in the Celebration were displays of photographs taken by William Gottlieb, and memorabilia from Milt Gabler's Commodore Music Shop.

Jack Stine, of the New Jersey Jazz Society, telephoned Stacy and was able to persuade him to appear on the first evening. Stine was delighted; Stacy had in the recent past rejected offers from two New York clubs, the Village Vanguard ("What! Come back to that smoke-filled joint? No, I've had enough of that to last a lifetime.") and The Cookery.

Having accepted, Stacy, as ever, was again assailed with doubts, but he and Pat made it to New York, despite worries about the fires which had caused much damage in the Los Angeles hills that summer. Fortunately, they were under control before the end of September. (Later Stacy was to complain about gophers digging up his lawn, which he had neglected in order to practice for the concert).

The Stacys flew to New York on September 26, giving them the opportunity to visit Jess Stacy's son, Fred, and his wife, Beverly, now living in New York. Accordingly, Jack Stine was able to drive Jess and Pat Stacy, with Fred and Beverly Stacy, from New York to Clinton. Stine wrote afterwards: "Once at Clinton, and walking across the street from the parking lot to the Art Center, Jess began to sense that it was going to be allright after all. A gang of people were waiting outside to greet him and immediately he was surrounded by people for whom the name Jess Stacy was pure legend. Earlier I had asked Jess if he had a pen, and he said he didn't own one. I gave him mine. 'What's this for?' he wanted to know. I told him we were expecting around 200 people that night which meant that he would be signing about 200 programs. I knew he didn't believe me; I knew I was right. Once inside, he was mobbed even as he went up the stairs to the gallery proper. When he went into the main room, an even greater response awaited him while Pat, Beverly and Fred quietly sat at a table watched. I had told Fred that he probably did not understand what his old man's playing had meant for a whole generation of music fans, and seeing this reception must have given him a general idea. He looked as proud as any son would to see his father so received. Three sets later, during which Jess progressed from a a somewhat tentative beginning to a much more sure footed (handed?) conclusion, Jess received a much deserved standing ovation."

Stacy played a total of 12 tunes, typical of his repertoire at that time, including *Lover Man* and *How Long Has This Been Going On?*

Marty Grosz, who also appeared at the concert, playing guitar duets with Wayne Wright, wrote: ". . . it was a joy to see him at the piano. Unlike modern pianists, who appear to be handcuffed when they sit at the keyboard, his hands were about four or five octaves apart."

Two weeks later, on October 12, Bert Whyatt and this writer visited Jess Stacy and he was still delighted with the reception he had been given. He spoke of the standing ovation he had received and obviously felt this deeply. As he said: "I could have played *Chopsticks* and they would have loved me." But the travelling was very tiring and he would not undergo the trip to New York again. This concert was his final public performance.

Jess Stacy in his study,
October 12, 1979

Photo by Bert Whyatt

While the Stacys were in New York, Hank O'Neal again arranged for two days of recording for Chiaroscuro. 14 titles were taped, on September 30 and October 1, 1979, but none has yet been released.

"Bix: Ain't None Of Them Play Like Him Yet", a documentary about cornet player Bix Beiderbecke, was copyrighted in 1981. In this excellent film, made by Canadian Brigitte Berman, Jess Stacy is seen briefly, talking about his early hero. There is an amusing story in "Oh, Jess!" about the chaos which Miss Berman and her crew created in the Stacy household, when they visited in the late 1970s. Despite the upset caused, Pat Stacy considers it "a lovely, lovely film."

Left to right: Norma Teagarden, Marian McPartland and Jess Stacy, at Lookout Mountain Avenue.
Photo: courtesy of Mrs. Pat Stacy

At the end of 1981 Stacy was invited to take part in Marian McPartland's "Piano Jazz" radio shows. These 60 minute public service broadcasting programmes are now a long-running tradition. The format is for Marian McPartland to interview a pianist (or a musician who also plays piano), for her guest to play some solos, and for guest and host to play two or three duets. "Piano Jazz" has been broadcast by radio stations all across the U.S. and a few of the interviews were broadcast by the B.B.C.

Marian McPartland flew to Los Angeles to conduct interviews in November 1981, and Norma Teagarden came from San Francisco to participate on November 30. Miss Teagarden (Mrs Friedlander), sister to Jack and Charlie, recalled: "Jess Stacy had a party at his house when I made the Marian McPartland tape in Los Angeles. We all went out to his home after my day was over – Marian, Leonard Feather, and a couple from the radio company from the east. Jess was looking forward to taping."

During this December 1 interview Stacy again plays *Lover Man* and *I Would Do Most Anything For You*, but he also gives a short demonstration of how a calliope sounded and briefly attempts the "A minor chord thing" from *Sing, Sing, Sing*. Stacy sounds relaxed and cheerful throughout.

Two musicians of great importance to the Stacy story passed away in 1986. Benny Goodman died on June 13, and Teddy Wilson on July 31. In late 1985 Goodman had telephoned Stacy to ask if he would appear in what proved to be Goodman's final television appearance. This was a PBS telecast, recorded October 7, 1985, and broadcast in March 1986. Stacy appreciated the offer, but told BG that he hadn't played in a long time and he wasn't up to it. They reminisced for about 30 minutes and parted on good terms.

Each year the IAJRC (International Association of Jazz Record Collectors) convention is held in a different city. In 1987 the annual get-together took place in Los Angeles, which made it possible for Jess Stacy to be one of the honored guests. On August 15, he took part in a panel session with Albert Marx, in which he talked about the trip to the Palomar, rooming with Bunny Berigan, and the 1938 Carnegie Hall concert. Albert Marx discussed the recording of the concert, including Jess' *Sing, Sing, Sing* solo. Jim Lowe was in the audience, and said how moved Stacy was by the standing ovation which he received. There is an IAJRC video tape of the Stacy/Marx panel discussion, available to members.

Jim also commented that on another panel Martha Tilton was not happy to answer a question from the floor about what it was like to be accompanied by Jess Stacy!

Early in 1989 Jess Stacy was admitted into The Hospital of The Good Samaritan in Los Angeles for a colon cancer operation. This was followed by complications which necessitated further surgery. He was in the hospital for a total of two and a half months,

Jess Stacy at the IAJRC Los Angeles Convention, August 15, 1987.

Photo:
courtesy of Barry Schneck

finally returning home early in May. Recovery was slow; in August Pat Stacy was concerned for his weakness and depression, and a physical therapist was visiting three times a week, trying to build up Stacy's strength. In November he was writing to Keith Keller that he was finding it difficult to write, and was having to learn to walk all over again: "I have a long way to go, hope I can make it."

One hopes that he was cheered by two publications which appeared during the summer of 1989. In 1973 his old friend from Cape Girardeau, Peg Meyer, had become a published author when his "The Band Director's Guide To Instrument Repair" appeared. Then, in 1989, The Center for Regional History and Cultural Heritage at Southeast Missouri State University published Peg's "Backwoods Jazz in the Twenties", the story of his involvement with jazz and dance music in the Cape Girardeau area up to 1927, when: "I finally got out of the jazz band business. I was a little surprised when my wife told me about it." Naturally there are numerous mentions of Jess Stacy, the Agony Four, and their adventures in the silent movie era. This is essential and amusing reading for anyone wishing to know more of that time and place, and of Stacy's early days.

About the same time Keith Keller's "Oh, Jess!: A Jazz Life", published by the Mayan Music Corporation, appeared. To quote: "This book reflects research done prior to May 1989 and information supplied by the biographee in meetings and talks over the past six years." This Stacy biography, with a discography, is an interesting and informative account of Stacy's career, told in a non-chronological style.

1990 and 1991 continued as years of recuperation. Even in 1991 Stacy wrote to Keith Keller: "I have 3 doctors watching me like a hawk."

It was in 1990 that the American Federation of Jazz Societies inaugurated the Benny Carter Award, a "Benny", to be awarded annually to recognize a lifetime achievement in jazz. Benny Carter himself was the first recipient, followed by bassist Milt Hinton in 1991. Jess Stacy was the choice for 1992.

Jess and Pat Stacy at Saramento, May 20, 1992.

Photo by Derek Coller

Stacy was feeling well enough to make the trip to Sacramento, and on May 20 he received the award from Floyd Levin, on behalf of the AFJS. The presentation took place in the Martinique Room of Red Lion's Sacramento Inn, during the intermission in an evening of jazz films. Included in the program, prepared by Don Wolff, were clips from "Sweet and Lowdown", "Sarge Goes To College", and the Jack Teagarden and Bob Crosby Snader telescriptions.

The inscription on the "Benny", a bronze sculpting of Benny Carter by artist-musician John Heard, read:

The American Federation Of Jazz Societies
Presents The Third Annual Benny Carter Award To
Jess Stacy
In Deep Appreciation Of His Tremendous
Contribution To Jazz
May 20, 1992

This writer, along with Bert Whyatt, was pleased to be at the presentation. It was clear that Stacy enjoyed receiving the plaudits of the small but enthusiastic audience. He was walking with difficulty, having a problem with his balance, despite the aid of a stick, yet he was smiling and happy.

Two days earlier we had spent a pleasant hour or so at 8700 Lookout Mountain Avenue. We had been admitted by Stacy's "sitter," employed after Stacy had fallen while his wife was at work. Bert Whyatt noted: "Jess Stacy was waking from his post-lunch nap when we arrived . . . He was very cheerful and pleased to see us. It may be that he's pleased to have visitors anyway, for his wife, Pat, continues to go to her job each day. We had a pleasant chat in the course of which Jess showed his understandable forgetfulness

157

by telling us at least twice that he'd be 88 next birthday and thus his years would be the same as the number of keys on a piano. Pat left her work early to spend time with us before we left."

He also told us that since 1989 he had suffered, in addition to cancer, from pneumonia, hepatitis and heart problems. These continuing problems would have had a depressing effect and two visitors in 1993 reported that he felt "lousy", with the will to live fading.

However, he was in relaxed form for an interview in February 1993 which appeared in the television special, *Benny Goodman: Adventures In The Kingdom Of Swing*. This was produced and directed by Oren Jacoby, Eddie Condon's nephew. It is hard to disagree with Pat Stacy's summary that it is a wonderful documentary, with many shots of Jess telling about the early days of the Goodman band.

Early in 1994 he was in hospital again for a short stay, with a minor bladder problem.

Max Kaminsky died in New York on September 6, 1994. Stacy was stricken when he telephoned Virginia Kaminsky about her loss, but he was not to survive his old friend and colleague for long.

On December 23, 1994, Jess Stacy was again admitted to the Hospital of The Good Samaritan, suffering from breathing difficulties. He died peacefully in his sleep nine days later, at 6:35 p.m. on Sunday, January 1, 1995. The cause of death was congestive heart failure. His body was cremated, with the urn remaining at Westwood Village Mortuary.

His son, Fred, and daughter-in-law, Beverly, were able to fly to Los Angeles to be with him when he died. In addition to his wife and son, Stacy was survived by five grandchildren and five great-grandchildren.

During January, 1995, numerous press and radio tributes were made, and Pat Stacy received notes from many friends and fans – "even one from Tasmania."

Peter Watrous, in *The New York Times*, January 4, called Stacy one of the leading pianists of the swing era: "Mr. Stacy was a widely admired musician, even if he never received as much attention as some of his peers. His light, pensive touch, along with his lyricism, set him apart and made him a pianist who required careful listening. But his harmonic knowledge and his rhythmic grace made him a valuable asset to many bands."

While John Fordham, in his tribute in Britain's *The Guardian*, January 20, suggested that, "If Jess Stacy . . . had emerged in the 1980s as an upcoming youngster – playing the way he did around 1935 – he would have been a solo star. But Stacy arrived when the jazz world was dominated by keyboard geniuses like Art Tatum, Fats Waller, Teddy Wilson and Earl Hines, and his immense talent was largely overlooked, except as skilled assistance to powerful leaders. Stacy's style rolled up everything that was memorable about pre-bop piano playing into one polished, unfailingly apposite package."

Thus, at the age of 90, Jess Stacy departed this world, leaving behind a vast discography – piano solos, small band jazz, big band swing. These recordings, a very high proportion of which contain superb piano playing, will be his real memorium.

Sources

The sources used for each chapter, with the exception of those actually quoted with dates in the text, follow this introduction. All interviews and letters are with or to the author, except where shown otherwise.

Chapter I

Books
Paul E. Miller (editor):
   "Esquire Jazz Books" 1946 and 1947
Keith Keller: "Oh, Jess!"
Peg Meyer: "Backwoods Jazz in the Twenties"
Duncan Schiedt: "The Jazz State of Indiana"

Magazines
Cadence, May 1986 (Bob Rusch)
Down Beat, May 1938: May 6, 1949
The New Republic, Nov 24, 1937 (Otis Ferguson)
The New Yorker, Aug 18, 1975 (Whitney Balliett)
S&D Reflector, September 1965 (C.W. Elder)

Newspapers
The Los Angeles Herald Examiner, Oct 5, 1975
   (Jan Edward Wilson)
The Los Angeles Times, May 18, 1975
   (Leonard Feather)
The South East Missourian, Jun 23, 1919;
   Oct 18,1922 ; Nov 27, 1945

Sleeve Notes
Brunswick BL58029, "Jess Stacy" uncredited

Interviews
Dutch Estes, — Jun1984 (tape)
Peg Meyer, May 18, 1970; Oct 18, 1979
Dick Wellstood, Feb 16, 1976

Radio interviews
Jess Stacy on Marian McPartland's "Piano
   Jazz", Dec 1, 1981

Letters
Hugh Hudgings, Apr 17, 1980
Mary & Paula Kempe, Sep 26,'72; Sep 22, '80
Walter Kempe, Sep 23,1972
Joyce Lacey, Mar 31,1989
Peg Meyer, May 18, 1970
Florence O'Brien, Feb27, 1993
Jess Stacy, Jul 1 & Nov 13, 1972; Feb 17, 1993
Pat Stacy, Jan 31 & Mar 20, 1997; Apr 1, 1997
Streckfus Steamers, May 10, 1982
George Snurpus, Sep 8, 1993; Sep 25, 1993
Albert Uhl, Aug 8, 1984

Memoir
Vada Stacy; undated notes for proposed "This
Is Your Life" radio show.

Further information and other sources on the subject of steamboats, calliopes, the Streckfus brothers, and Fate Marable can be found in two articles by J. Lee Anderson in *The Mississippi Rag*, July 1994 and July 1996.

Hugh Hudgings, born 1910, also grew up in Cape Girardeau.

Dick Wellstood's version of *Poor Buttermilk* was on (LP) Jazzology JCE-73.

Of the shares which Fred Stacy received from the railroad, Jess Stacy said, "They must have been ate, because I never saw any of them."

Chapter 2

Books
Eddie Condon: "We Called It Music"
Richard Hadlock: "Jazz Masters of the 20s"
Art Hodes: "Hot Man"
Max Jones: "Talking Jazz"
Max Kaminsky: "My Life In Jazz"
Keith Keller: "Oh, Jess!"
Wingy Manone: "Trumpet On The Wing"
Artie Shaw: "The Trouble With Cinderella"
George Simon: "The Big Bands"

Magazines
Cadence, May 1986
Down Beat, Sep 23, 1949; Apr 21, 1950;
   May 4,1951; Feb 22, 1956
Jazz Hot, No. 9 (1935)
Jazz Journal, December, 1965
The Jazz Report, Vol. 8, No. 6 (1975)
The New Yorker, Aug 18, 1975
Record Research, No. 29, August 1960

Newspapers
The South East Missourian, Apr 6, 1925
Chicago Evening American Oct 22, 1927

Sleeve Notes
Columbia CLP632 "Chicago Jazz",
    by George Avakian
Hanover HM-8010 "The Return of Jess Stacy",
    by Steve Allen

Interviews
Bud Freeman, Aug 14, 1978
Buzz Knudsen with Jim Gordon, Jun 23, 1988
Muggsy Spanier with Steve Ross, 29apr39

Radio interviews
Eddie Condon 'Blue Network', Feb 3, 1945
Bud Freeman, BBC Radio, Aug 30, 1976
Art Hodes, BBC Radio, Oct 4, 1987
Jess Stacy, on Marian McPartland's "Piano
    Jazz" Dec 1, 1981
Jess Stacy, to Scott Ellsworth, KFI-LA,
    Aug 23, 1970

Letters
Jim Gordon, Jun 23, 1988
Marty Grosz, Jun 3, 1993
Catherine Jacobson, Apr 15, 1983
Ed Kusby, May 31, 1993
Frankie Laine, Oct 10, 1982
Dan Lipscomb, May 4, 1982
Bill Mitchell, Mar 18, 1996
Tut Soper (to Bert Whyatt), May 18, 1982
Jess Stacy, Jul 1 & Oct 1, 1972; Nov 13,1972
Jess Stacy (to Ruth Spanier), undated
Jess Stacy (to Norman Gentieu), Jul 4, 1976
Iris Town (to Paul Sheatsley), Dec 2,1987;
    Mar 3, 1988.

Frank Teschemacher: for a more detailed
account refer to "Giants of Jazz" 3LP set
sleeve notes by Marty Grosz; and to Cadence,
May 1986.

Bill Alamshah: for additional information
refer to Arcadia 2014 sleeve notes by Dick
Raichelson; and to *Record Research* 155/156,
July 1978.

The Midway Gardens ballroom was
demolished in 1929.

For further information on the cultural
background to the Chicago era and on the
musicians and institutions of that time, the
reader is referred to "Chicago Jazz: A
Cultural History, 1904-1930" by William
Howland Kenney.

Chapter 3

Books
Walter C. Allen: "Hendersonia: The Music of
    Fletcher Henderson and his Musicians"
James Lincoln Collier: "Benny Goodman and
    the Swing Era"
Stanley Dance: "The World of Swing"
Pee Wee Erwin: "This Horn For Hire"
    (with Warren Vache, Sr.)
Ross Firestone: "Swing, Swing, Swing"
Benny Goodman: "The Kingdom of Swing"
    (with Irving Kolodin)
John Hammond: "Hammond On The Record"
Max Jones: "Talking Jazz"
Nat Shapiro & Nat Hentoff: "Hear Me Talkin'
    To Ya"
George Simon: "The Big Bands"

Magazines
Cadence, May 1986
Down Beat, July 1936; Dec 15, 1939;
    Jan 1, 1940; Jul 11, 1957
Jazz Hot 18, (Jun/Jul 1937)
Metronome, February 1951
The New Republic, Dec 30,1936; Nov 24, 1937
The New Yorker, Aug 18, 1975; Dec26, 1977

Newspapers
The New York Times, Jan 17,1938
The Los Angeles Times, May 18, 1975

Sleeve Notes
Bluebird AXM2-5532/AXM2-5567
    "The Complete Benny Goodman"
    AXM2-5568 Volumes III, VII & VIII
    by Mort Goode
C.B.S. M67205 "Superchief" (Count Basie)
    (by Michael Brooks)
Commodore XFL15358 "Jess Stacy and
    Friends"

Interviews
Chris Griffin, Mar 21,1974
Jess Stacy at IAJRC Convention, Aug 15, 1987

Radio/Television* Interviews
Benny Goodman on BBC Radio 3, Dec 26, 1973
Rachel Goodman on "Benny Goodman
    (Adventures In The Kingdom of Swing)"*
Humphrey Lyttelton on BBC Radio 2,
    Oct 22, 1990
Jess Stacy to Don Chichester, WQLM-FM,
    Apr 9, 1987

Jess Stacy to Scott Ellsworth, KFI-LA,
    Aug 23, 1970
Jess Stacy on George Barclay show, KFI-LA,
    May 23, 1953
Bob Wilber to Gordon Cruikshank,
    Radio Scotland, Aug1987

Letters
Ernie Anderson, Apr 13, 1993
Harry Avery, Feb 27, 1980
Pee Wee Erwin, Jan 30, 1974
John Hammond, Dec 5, 1972
John Lucas, (on tape) Sep 16, 1986
Arthur Rollini, Aug 22, 1978
Jess Stacy (to Dan Mahony), Jan 13, 1989
Pat Stacy, Mar 20, 1997

Chapter 4

Books
John Chilton: "Stomp Off, Let's Go"
Doris Day: "Her Own Story"
Keith Keller: "Oh, Jess!"

Magazines
Cadence, May 1986
Down Beat, Oct 15, 1939: Jun 1, 1940:
            Aug 15, 1940: Jul 1, 1941
Metronome, October 1941

Newspapers
The Los Angeles Times, May 18, 1975
        (Leonard Feather)

Sleeve Notes
Giants of Jazz No.27 Joe Sullivan (3-LP set)
    booklet

Interviews
Billy Butterfield, Oct 1, 1975 (telephone)
Bill Challis to Norman Gentieu, 1986
Milt Gabler, Oct 25, 1979
Yank Lawson to Brian Peerless, 1986
Humphrey Lyttelton on BBC Radio 2,
    Jan 28, 1985
Jess Stacy, May 18, 1992
Jess Stacy to Bill Mitchell, Aug 30, 1988

Radio Interviews
Nappy Lamare to Scott Ellsworth, KFI-LA, 1971
Jess Stacy to Scott Ellsworth, KFI-LA,
    Aug 23, 1970
Jess Stacy to Phil Schaap, Mar 10, 87

Letters
Bob Haggart, Feb 20, 1976: Dec 11, 1996
Mary & Paula Kempe, Sep 26, 1972
Yank Lawson, Aug 11, 1972
Priscilla Rushton, May 23, 1987
John Steiner, Jul 6, 1993

Chapter 5

Books
James Lincoln Collier: "Benny Goodman and
    the Swing Era"
Bob Hilbert: "Pee Wee Russell: The Life of A
    Jazzman"
Keith Keller: "Oh, Jess!"
Barry Kernfeld (editor): "The New Grove
    Dictionary of Jazz"
    (entry by Dick Sudhalter)
Gunther Schuller: "The Swing Era"
Laurie Wright: "'Fats' In Fact"
    (chapter by Ernie Anderson)

Magazines
Cadence, May 1986
The Capitol News, April 1944
Down Beat, Jul 15, 1943; Apr 1, 1944;
            Dec 15, 1944; Feb 1, 1945
Jazz Journal International, November 1994
The Jazz Record, December 1944
Metronome, November 1944
The New Yorker, Aug 18, 1975
The Record Changer, March 1945

Newspapers
The Wall Street Journal, Apr 2, 1986
Variety, Dec 27, 1944

Interviews
Eddie Martin to Jim Shacter, Jun 11, 1977

Radio Interviews
Louis Bellson, BBC Radio 2, 1989
Bill Cronk to Sheila Tracy, BBC Radio 2,
    Jun 9, 1993
Buddy de Franco to Steve Voce, BBC Radio 2,
    Sep 20, 1981
Jess Stacy to Scott Ellsworth, KFI-LA,
    Aug 23, 1970
Jess Stacy to Don Chichester, WQLM-FM,
    Apr 9, 1987

Letters
Buddy Bergman, Jun – 1978

Murray Gaer, Jun 26, 1980; Jul28, 1980
Horace Heidt, May 7, 1975
Hugh Hudgings, Apr 17, 1980
John Lucas, Jan 15, 1994
Nelson Riddle, Jun 9, 1975
Jess Stacy, undated notes to Keith Keller
Gus van Camp, Nov 24, 1980

The Department of the Navy, Jul 1, 1993
Deane Kincaide, Feb 13, 1975
Gerry Martin, Sep –, 1977 (tape)
Peg Meyer, Nov 29, 1970
Bill Mitchell, Feb 10, 1993
Hank O'Neal, Dec 11, 1973
John Setar, Nov 29, 1977
John Steiner, May 7, 1992
Frank H. Trolle, Oct 30, 1983
Bus Watson, Mar 4, 1975; Jun –, 1975

Chapter 6

Much of the information about the Jess Stacy orchestra is based upon a lengthy interview which writer Jim Shacter conducted with Eddie Martin (Eddie di Martino), and his wife, Gerry. This chapter would be a shadow of itself without Jim Shacter's efforts, or without Eddie and Gerry Martin's generous co-operation in the interview on June 11, 1977, and subsequent letters and tapes to the author during 1977.

Books
Roger Cotterrell (editor): "Jazz Now"
    (Billy Butterfield/John Chilton)
Stanley Dance: "The World of Swing"
Bud Freeman: "Crazeology"
Keith Keller: "Oh, Jess!"

Magazines
American Jazz Review, April 1946
Cadence, May 1986
Down Beat, Jun 15, 1945; Jul 15, 1945;
            Sep 1, 1945; Oct 15, 1945
I.A.J.R.C. Journal, October 1983
Jazz Music, Vol. 5, No. 4
The Jazz Record, July 1945: November 1945.
The New Yorker, Aug 18,1975

Newspapers
The Los Angeles Times, May 18, 1975
        (Leonard Feather)
The Melody Maker, Jul 28, 1945
New York Amsterdam News, Aug 11, 1945

Interviews
Byron Baxter, Oct 21, 1979 (telephone)
Ed Hubble, Dec 17, 1974
Mario Toscarelli, Oct 27, 1979 (telephone)

Letters
Ernie Anderson, Oct 9, 1985
Buddy Bergman, Apr –, 1978; Jun 19, 1978
Earl Bergman, May 20, 1977; Jun –, 1977

Chapter 7

Books
Keith Keller: "Oh, Jess!"

Magazines
Cadence, May 1986
Down Beat, Jan 11, 1952 (Leonard Feather)

Interview
Eddie Martin and Gerry Martin, to Jim
        Shacter, Jun 11, 1977

Letters
Ernie Anderson, Oct 21, 1982
Byron Baxter, Oct 21, 1979
Buddy Bergman, Apr –, 1978, Jun –, 1978
Earl Bergman, May –, 1977
Deane Kincaide, Feb 13, 1975
Hank O'Neal, Dec 11, 1973
John Setar, Nov 29, 1977

Chapter 8

Books
D. Russell Connor: "Benny Goodman: Listen
        To His Legacy"

Magazines
American Jazz Review, November, December
        1946; January 1947.
Down Beat, Oct 21, 1946; Nov 18, 1946;
        Jan 1, 1947
Jazz Notes, January 1947

Newspapers
The Melody Maker, Jun 22, 1946, Jan 25, 1947
The New York Times, Oct 13, 1946;
        Nov 3, 1946

Chapter 9

Books
Whitney Balliett: "American Singers" (anthology)
Buck Clayton: "Buck Clayton's Jazz World"
    (with Nancy Miller Elliott)
Art Hodes: "Hot Man" (with Chadwick Hansen)
Holmes & Thompson: "Jazz Greats: Getting
    Better With Age"
Keith Keller: "Oh, Jess!"
Wingy Manone: "Trumpet 0n The Wing"
    (with Paul Vandervoort)
S.J. Perelman: "The Most of S.J. Perelman"
    (anthology)
Manfred Selchow: "Profoundly Blue"
    (Ed Hall biography)
Jim Shacter: "Loose Shoes"
    (Ralph Sutton biography)
Teddy Wilson: "Teddy Wilson Talks Jazz"
    (with Arie Ligthart & Humphrey van Loo)

Magazines
The Capitol News, July 1947; December 1948
Down Beat, many issues between 1948 and
    1956
The Jazzfinder, December 1948
The Jazz Record, April 1947
Jazz Journal, May 1952
The Mississippi Rag, May 1985
The New Yorker, Feb 21, 1948; Aug 18, 1975

Newspapers
Chicago Sunday Tribune, Oct 19, 1947
Los Angeles Herald-Examiner, Oct 5, 1975

Sleeve Notes
Atlantic 1225 "Tribute to Benny Goodman"
    (Jess Stacy), by George Frazier
Swaggie S1248 "Jess Stacy Piano Solos"
    by Bill Haesler

Interviews
Billy Butterfield, Oct 1, 1975
Buck Clayton, Nov 22, 1974
John Lucas, Oct 12, 1979
Jess Stacy, May 18, 1992
Zoot Sims, Jul –, 1975
unknown collector at IAJRC Convention,
    Aug 15, 1987

Radio Interviews
Alistair Cooke, on BBC Radio 3, Apr 24, 1977
Jess Stacy on George Barclay show, KFI-LA,
    May 23, 1953

Letters
Steve Allen, Apr 23, 1973
Heinie Beau, Aug 3, 1973
Paul Copeland, Dec 6, 1990
Bob Higgins, Apr 3, 1991
Gardner Hitchcock, Mar 25, 1991
Larry Kiner, Sep 6, 1985
Floyd Levin, Jan 3, 1975
John Lucas, May 1, 1976; May 19, 1977,
    Sep 15, 1986 (tape)
Max Factor Co., Feb 21, 1975
Peg Meyer, May 14, 1973
Tom Pletcher, Apr 1, 1983; Sep 21, 1983
Bob Ringwald, Sep 19, 1982
Ruth Spanier, Feb –, 1975 (to Bert Whyatt)
Jess Stacy, undated notes to Keith Keller
Pat Stacy, Mar 20, 1997; Apr 1, 1997
Zeke Zarchy, Sep 27, 1971

Chapter 10

Books
Keith Keller: "Oh, Jess!"

Magazines
Jazz Journal, January 1970; August 1974
Jersey Jazz, September 1979; November 1979
The New Yorker, Jul 29, 1974

Newspapers
Los Angeles Herald-Examiner, Oct 5, 1975
The Melody Maker, Jul 20, 1974
The New York Times, Jul 2, 1974

Radio Interviews
Ralph Sutton, on BBC Radio 2, Oct 11, 1975

Letters
Dick Cary, Oct 19, 1983
Bill French, Mar 23, 1993 (to Bert Whyatt)
Marty Grosz, Jun 30, 1993
Jim Lowe, Sep –, 1987
John Lucas, Jul 24, 1975
Donny McDonald, Oct 16, 1975
Nelson Riddle, Jun 9, 1975
Jess Stacy, Nov 20, 1972; Nov 8, 1989 & 1991
    (to Keith Keller);
Norma Teagarden, Feb 4, 1988
Bert Whyatt, Jul 14, 1992

Appendix I

Benny Goodman at The Palomar
by John Lucas

John Lucas first heard the Benny Goodman orchestra in 1935 as he was being driven down Mount Avenue, then turning into a side street at the rear of The Palomar to find a parking place. This is how he told the story on tape.

The whole back of The Palomar was open because it was summertime, August 1935, and it was open because they didn't have air-conditioning, of course. They needed all the circulation they could get. So we could hear the band as we drove past it looking for our parking place. The excitement in the pit of my stomach was almost like being afraid or some kind of terror or something.

We came down the sidewalk back to the Palomar to this long open space which was roped off with velvet-covered ropes, so that peepers had to go round to the front. As we were passing – mind you, I was 17 and my cousin and another fellow were about the same age, just teenagers, this man was standing at the ropes, checking that people didn't get through there. And he said, "Come on, boys, come in through here." He lifted one of the ropes and let us in. He introduced himself, saying "I'm Sid Masters, the manager here at The Palomar." He led us down behind the big shell of the bandstand, whereupon my stomach was doing even more flipflops.

He started to take us to a table way down to the right of the bandstand. We could see the sax section and Benny in his white uniform. The band had stopped playing and apparently it was intermission, because Benny came down off the stand and here came Mr. Masters leading Benny by the hand and saying, "Hey Benny, take these boys to a nice table." So Benny took us down to a table at the corner of the huge, huge dance floor. That Palomar was big enough to hold a blimp or two. Benny sat down with us and found out we were jazz fans. I was the true jazz fan because I was actually collecting records, the other two boys weren't.

Benny went backstage and got a glossy picture, which he autographed for me, and sat and talked during the whole intermission. He came back after the next set and said, "Say, you boys can't see too well, can you? The floor show's coming up and you'll certainly want to see it." The last thing we wanted to see was any floor show, but we didn't say so. He took us all around the dance floor, down into the V.I.P. section, across from the front of the bandstand. We could see everything. We were sitting next to Isabel Jewell and Pinky Tomlin. Jackie Cooper was at a table nearby, Andy Devine at another. They did the floor show and took another intermission.

This time Benny came back and brought Gene Krupa because by this time I had said that I was a drummer or essaying the job of being a drummer. We talked to Krupa and I remember he put a cigarette out, not quite, in an ashtray. After he left to go back on the bandstand we picked it up and passed it around and smoked GENE KRUPA'S CIGARETTE!

That evening, of course, was just a general, euphoric haze. To single out any one individual performance during the evening is well nigh impossible. Of course my eyes and ears were glued to Gene Krupa.

During one of his visits Benny said, "We're closing here pretty soon and we're going into the Paramount Theatre. Why don't you come and see us there? See us backstage during the movie and we can talk." Isabel Jewell was the actress ("The Tale of Two Cities", "Lost Horizon"). She kept watching us and I guess we kind of looked cute, or something. Pretty soon she said, "Could we join you at your table?" So they came over and she and Pinky Tomlin autographed the back of Benny's picture. She invited me over to the set where she was working on "The Tale of Two Cities" in the next few weeks. She gave me her phone number, Hampstead 8200, which I still remember and she said she would send her chauffeur over for me. It's still flabbergasting. I'm telling you, when we drove home back to Pasadena our whole car was about three or four feet off the ground. We were out of our brains with excitement and I guess I didn't sleep for three or four days.

I told my dad about it. He wouldn't let me play hooky to go see Isabell Jewell, but he said he'd take me to the Paramount. So we did and we went backstage and up to Benny's dressing room and talked about music [including Mozart and Joseph Schillinger]. Benny was around 24 or 25 then and intellectually active already. Amazing man.

I went back to The Palomar that following summer. Benny recognized me right away and called me, "John, hey John." By then the fans had gotten the idea of just standing around the bandstand, 40 deep, and the dancers had to dance around them. Being summertime, no air-conditioning, the sweat was streaming down everybody's face. Benny looked down, took pity on me, and, "Hey, come on up here". I don't know who hauled me up. Anyway, there I was on the bandstand, in front of this huge ballroom, sitting right next to Jess Stacy. That's where my friendship with Jess Stacy started. He was a fairly shy person then, and I was probably 30 times shyer, so we didn't say much to each other.

Then the following year, 1937, the band came back, this time with Harry James. Benny looked down at me in front of the bandstand, amongst the hundreds massed around him. "Hey, John," and there I was back on the bandstand, again beside Jess. This time Jess and I were able to talk without being too shy and he told me about some records he had made.

Appendix 2

Benny Goodman – A few selected comments

"Benny was kind of in his own world. Not hard to work for, but a lot of guys found him stand-offish."
(**Zeke Zarchy**, *Jazz Journal International.*, December 1983)

"He has always been practically incoherent when talking to his sidemen. Benny has a great ear, and can immediately spot a wrong note in an arrangement, but sorting it out was something else."
(**Billy Butterfield** to John Chilton, "Jazz Now")

"Benny was a puzzlement; it was always hard to figure out just what he was thinking . . . he would seldom couch a statement so that you knew exactly what he wanted; consequently a good deal of misunderstanding occurred with the people who worked for him, including me."
(**Chris Griffin** to Stan Woolley, *Cadence*, October 1976)

"He's eccentric, but he's got a lot of good qualities . . . Twenty-four hours a day he's not thinking or dreaming of anything but the clarinet . . . so somebody says something to him he's liable not to hear it, and he'll give you an answer that has nothing to do with what you asked.
(**Bobby Hackett** to Max Jones, "Talking Jazz")

"As Gene Krupa once told me, 'Just remember, baby, he's fired the best.'"
(Drummer **Dorothy Dodgion**, who was fired by Goodman the day after receiving great applause). ("American Women In Jazz")

"I never got The Ray, but one night I did not get a single solo, and for no reason that I could fathom."
(**George Masso** to author)

"He treated me wonderfully."
Louie Bellson to Stanley Dance, *Jazz Journal International*, September 1988)

165

"I think he had a lot of things to think about and sometimes he would be thinking about them and he'd look at you and he wouldn't see you."

(**George Koenig** on WNEW radio, January 16, 1968)

"When I first joined Benny, he called me 'Fletcher' for three months before he could remember my name . . . And then he told me I was the worst piano player he'd had since Frank Froeba."

(**Johnny Guarnieri**, "Hear Me Talkin' To Ya")

"He was a great leader. He knew what he wanted. He took great pains to get it right. He was a perfectionist and he never demanded more of his musicians than he demanded of himself."

(**Bob Wilber** to Gordon Cruikshank, Radio Scotland, August 1987)

"He always treated me OK. But he needed me worse than I needed the job . . . he was a cold man, didn't relate well to people, didn't understand them, and a lot of guys just couldn't work for him."

(**Yank Lawson** to Phil Atteberry, *The Mississippi Rag*, December 1992)

"Benny Goodman was by far the most unpleasant person I ever met in music and a slob!"

(**Helen Forrest** autobiography, "I Had The Craziest Dream")

"The guy was a boss and often you'll have a dim view of what a boss will do . . . He's lost in a fog all the time, has only a single thought in mind when the clarinet's in his hand."

(**Pee Wee Erwin** to Warren Vache, Sr., "This Horn For Hire")

"Benny Goodman was a strange man. It is always disappointing to discover that your idol had feet of clay – and a head of clay as well."

(**Bobby Rosengarden** to Peter Clayton, BBC Radio 1, July 13, 1980)

On Benny Goodman and party visiting the Ronnie Scott Club in London: "He'd have food and drink and whatever, and there was never any question of a bill. He just got up and left, as though it was his God-given right."

(**Ronnie Scott**, BBC Radio 2, March 30, 1991)

"I always got along fine with Benny – the only sideman who did, maybe."

(**Red Ballard**, of whom Arthur Rollini said: "timid Red Ballard, our second trombonist, was allowed to play one solo with Goodman, *Can't We Be Friends?*)

"Benny doesn't want anyone or anything to stand out above him and his orchestra. If it does, he doesn't just compete, he undercuts the opposition."

(**Anita O'Day**, telling of Goodman twirling his clarinet like Ted Lewis in order to distract attention away from Stan Getz and herself) ("High Times, Hard Times")

"I didn't have one bit of trouble with Benny."

(**Doc Cheatham** to James Lincoln Collier, "Benny Goodman and the Swing Era")

Goodman refused a $500 loan to Jimmy Maxwell, who wanted to pay for an operation for his father – but a few weeks later B.G. gave Maxwell $300 to replace money stolen from his jacket.

(**James Lincoln Collier**, "Benny Goodman and the Swing Era")

light and shadow

By Lillian Johnson

"Take It or Leave It," Benny Goodman Told the Man

The situation revolving around and about and in-between the Benny Goodman band provides a rich field for comment—pro or con.

First of all, there is the fact that Benny Goodman established a precedent when he hired colored musicians and put them before one of the largest publics in the world—the Benny Goodman public.

Next, there is the fact that although he hired, paid them well, and played music with them himself, never, up to a short time ago, was one of these colored musicians actually a bona fide member of the Goodman band.

They belonged exclusively to the Goodman quartet or quintet, except on occasions when the band was temporarily without a drummer, after Messrs. Gene Krupa, Dave Tough, and Buddy Schultz left, and Lionel Hampton was temporarily pressed into filling the spot.

However, as I said above, a few weeks ago, the latter situation was changed, for the famous Fletcher Henderson came into the Goodman camp, and soon afterward, it was announced that he would take the place of Teddy Wilson (who resigned from the quartet to form his own band), but that he would also take the place of Jess Stacy, white, as the regular Goodman pianist.

Now, this week, one Michael Levin, columnist, comes forward with an explanation and a dressing down for Benny from which dressing down, I respectfully beg to differ.

Jess Stacy, white, former pianist with Benny Goodman's orchestra, quit the orchestra because he thought he ought to have had the spot in the Goodman quartet that went to Fletcher Henderson.

It further seems that Stacy felt that he had been made to take a back seat for Teddy Wilson, and that after Wilson left, Goodman gave him the spot in the quartet until he could get someone else.

But Stacy had an idea that it should have been permanent.

Anyway, when Goodman told Stacy that Fletcher was going to do the piano work in the quartet, while Stacy went back to his regular job as pianist for the band, Stacy told Mr. G. that if he couldn't play with the quartet, he wouldn't play at all.

And Benny told him to take it or leave it. Well, Stacy couldn't back up then, so he left.

Levin goes on to say that Stacy is a good pianist, while Fletcher is not. And I beg to inform Levin, although I don't know how old he is, that the chances are that Fletcher was making a piano talk when he was in swaddling clothes.

And this is no reflection on Fletcher's age, either.

It's just that Fletcher Henderson was a piano playing wizard around Atlanta University years ago, and that Fletcher used to have a band that could stand head and shoulders with any of the biggies, today.

I won't go into why Fletcher's band declined somewhat, but it certainly wasn't Fletcher Henderson's piano playing.

And there's one thing that

BENNY GOODMAN

everybody can make sure of. Benny Goodman is a smart business man, and he didn't buy Fletcher Henderson's contract for fun. He bought it because he knew Fletcher would be an asset to his organization.

If Stacy feels the way Levin says he did, Stacy did right to bow out. He had a full share of publicity, with Goodman plugging him at every turn, and all the white columnists rooting for him.

Of course, if Levin is right, no colored musician, no matter how good he is, can hardly hope to get a place in Stacy's band. But Levin and Stacy could keep quiet. Perhaps they don't know it, but music is art, and there is no color line in art.

LUNCEFORD IN N.C.

RALEIGH, N.C. — Jimmie Lunceford and his orchestra played at the auditorium here Tuesday night.

The Afro-American,
August 19, 1939

Appendix 4

The Dartmouth

Reproduction of
an article from
"The Dartmouth",
April 27, 1939.

With acknowledgement to
The Dartmouth,
Hanover, New
Hampshire, "America's
Oldest College
Newspaper"
and to the editor,
Michael T. Reynolds.

Stacy, Goodman Pianist, Hides Light of Ability under Band's Bushel of Swing

Little-Known Key Man of Band's Rhythm Section Labelled 'Greatest White'

Unfortunately for Jess Stacy, Benny Goodman's band is composed of so many top-notch men, that, despite his fine abilities at the piano, he remains in the background of the outfit.

When, on May 1, at the Green Key Prom, you concentrate on Stacy, you will see why critics like Panassie and Hammond consider him among the best white musicians.

Solid Potent Beat

Along with Gene Krupa on the drums, Allan Ruess on the guitar and Harry Goodman on the bass, Stacy supplies what is generally recognized as the most potent beat in white jazz. These four constitute the Goodman rhythm section, solid foundation of the band.

The presence of Teddy Wilson on the piano of the Goodman quartet shades Stacy's recognition as regular pianist for the band and although Wilson is a greater jazzman than Stacy, the latter recently filled in on one of the quartet discs so capably that most listeners don't even notice Wilson is not playing.

Few Recordings

Although he has played piano for years, Stacy has not made many recordings. Well known in Chicago, he is a member of the small select group of musicians who play Chicago style. A strange personality, who lives in his music, he will improvise with his eyes shut, unable to keep the tears from his cheeks.

Liked Chicago Haunts

There is no doubt that he is one of the two best white pianists in hot jazz. Joe Sullivan is ranked by some a little higher because of his greater sensitivity, but Stacy's technical superiority make any such distinction futile.

Because Stacy liked Chicago, it was not until Goodman persuaded him, that the pianist would leave his haunts, where he was given to

spending most of the early morning hours improvising with small negro combinations.

In 1936, he waxed three sides with the young negro sensation Isreal Crosby on the bass, and Gene Krupa on the drums. Released only on English Parlaphone, the titles were: "Barrelhouse," "Go Back Where You Were Last Night" and "The World Is Waiting for the Sunrise."

Like most good men, Stacy is not given to the publicity needed by the corny outfits, the long hair boys. His playing is full and rich, and he pleases himself, as well as those to whom jazz means more than blowing ripples through a straw, and calling it rhythm.

Students Exhibit Works In Carpenter Showing

The annual exhibition representing the works of amateur Hanover artists and photographers will open Saturday in the Carpenter Galleries. Contributions for the exhibit must be in by Wednesday night, it was announced yesterday by Gobin Stair, the curator.

Original oil paintings, drawings and photographs by members of the student body and community will be included in the exhibition.

Court Releases Herndon

Washington, April 26, (AP)—The Supreme Court relieved Angelo Herndon, negro communist, of an 18-year prison sentence today, finding that his conviction under an ancient Georgia anti-sedition statute was unconstitutional.

By a 5-4 decision it held that in the Herndon case at least the law infringed upon constitutional liberties by placing "vague and indeterminate" limits upon the rights of freedom of speech and assembly. Herndon was convicted after the state accused him of possessing radical literature.

Appendix 5

Sing, Sing, Sing

Sing, Sing, Sing was composed – words and music – by Louis Prima, the trumpet player, singer and bandleader. He recorded it for Brunswick on February 28, 1936.

Jimmy Mundy made a standard three-minute arrangement for Benny Goodman, which was broadcast on March 18, 1936, with a vocal by Helen Ward. During the next twelve months or so the vocal disappeared and by the time of the Victor recording, July 6, 1937, the arrangement lasted nearly nine minutes.

Pee Wee Erwin ("This Horn For Hire", by Erwin, with Warren Vache Sr.) said that Mundy's arrangement was played every night on the job, with new riffs being added to the end of the chart. Erwin said that some of the riffs came from "classics like Holst's 'Planet Suite' and others were Rex Stewart riffs which Chris Griffin and I borrowed from Rex." (Griffin joined the band May 23, 1936 and Erwin left in August, so these changes took place in the space of two months or so).

Allan Reuss ("Stars of Jazz" TV show, September 9, 1957) said that the arrangement came when the band was at the "old Palomar" (i.e., late 1935), but that seems too early. He continued, "I remember Gene (Krupa) started continuing on with the drums, and Murray McEarchern started playing a bass figure (*Christoper Columbus*), and then we had Pee Wee Erwin (who) came in with licks. . ."

If the Reuss memory was correct, then the *Sing, Sing, Sing* music circulated before Prima recorded the song. If his memory was faulty, then the Christopher Columbus figure may have been part of the original arrangement.

To add to that we have James Lincoln Collier ("Benny Goodman and the Swing Era") saying that the number includes snatches of *Yankee Doodle Dandy* and a "waterfall" inspired by Stravinsky. The *Yankee Doodle Dandy* riff occurs 40 seconds into the arrangement.

On the Victor recording Jess Stacy does not solo, but he can just be heard behind the tenor sax solo. This hardly qualifies as an accompaniment, but what can be heard has the "feel" of his work in the Carnegie Hall version.

Goodman continued to feature the arrangement for the rest of his working life, and the last performance given in "Listen To His Legacy" is from a January 30, 1983 concert. But it is the 1938 Carnegie Hall version which will be remembered, thanks in large part to Jess Stacy's contribution.

Appendix 6

The Big Band intinerary 1945/1946

The following itinerary is based upon letters which Eddie Martin wrote to his wife-to-be, amplified with information from *Down Beat* and other individual sources.

1945

Jul 6	Band debuts at Seaside Park, Virginia Beach. for 4 weeks.
Aug 8	Poe Park, Bronx, New York
Aug 9	Central Park, Manhattan, New York
Aug 10	Prospect Park, Brooklyn, New York

there were possibly other New York park dates, all with pick-up personnels. These were followed by one-nighters, including:

	Hazelton, Pennsylvania
Aug 19	Danceland, Ocean Beach, New London, Connecticut
Sep 7	Casa Loma Ballroom, St. Louis. for 2 weeks.
Sep 21	Band Box, Chicago. for 10 weeks.
Nov 23	Colony Club, Cape Girardeau, Missouri. for 1 week.
Dec 1-12	one nighters in Oklahoma, Kansas, Missouri and Iowa, including:
Dec 7	Convention Hall, Enid, Oklahoma
Dec 14	Panther Room, Hotel Sherman,Chicago. for 2 weeks.
Dec 31	New Year's Eve in Hotel Sherman's grand ballroom.

Band then temporarily disbands.

1946

Jan/Feb	Band members jobbing around Chicago; some return home.
Mar 1	Band reforms in Boston. Plays one-nighters, including: Salem, Massachusetts *note 1* Lowell, Massachusetts *note 2* Manchester (State not given) Esquire Club, Boston Dover, New Hampshire
Mar (late)	Band folds again
Apr (mid)	Band reorganizes; rehearses in New York for about 10 days.
Apr 23 appx	Fills bookings in the Boston area, possibly including Symphony Hall, Boston. *note 3*
Apr 28	Danceland, Ocean Beach, New London.
May	college proms around New York, including Rochester University
May 23	Camden Park, Huntingdon
May 24	Athens, Ohio (perhaps Ohio University dance)
May 25	Erie, Pennsylvania
May 27	Rainbow Gardens, Fremont, Ohio *note 4*
May 29	Bradford, Pennsylvania *note 5*
May 30	Port Stanley Ballroom, London, Ontario
May 31	unknown, Michigan

Jun 1	Cleveland Hotel, Cleveland, Ohio
Jun 7-13	Sylvania, Ohio
Jun 14	Defiance, Ohio
Jun 15-21	Chippewa Lake Park, Ohio (amusement park)
?	Sun Valley, Worcester, Massachusetts
Jul 8-13	Lennie's Wagon Wheel, Old Orchard Beach, Maine
?	Palace Ballroom, Edgewater Hotel, ?
?	Boston
Aug 1-7	Trenton, New Jersey (dance floor of carnival)
Aug 9-22	The Sea Girt Inn, Sea Girt, New Jersey
	Band folds after this engagement.
Sep	It appears that more New York park dates were undertaken on a pick-up basis in an attempt to start again, but without success. One specific date is known, reported by Mike Romano:
Sep 8	Danceland, Ocean Beach, New London, Connecticut

Notes

1: perhaps at the Shribman Brothers' Charleshurst Ballroom. The Canodie Park Ballroom in Salem, New Hampshire, has also been suggested.

2: there was a Commodore Ballroom in Lowell.

3: Bus Watson thought he recalled the Symphony Hall concert included Billie Holiday and Horace Henderson. No other mention of a concert with Billie Holiday has been found, and this reference should be treated with caution.

4: the date may be May 26. Art Pilkington reported that the Rainbow Gardens closed its 1946 season on Sunday, May 26.

5: Bradford, Penn. seems the probable correct interpretation for "Bradworth" or "Bradforth Year" as suggested by Eddie Martin's handwriting.

6. The personnel for the Saxie Dowell Navy Band photograph on page 96 is, left to right: (first row) Eddie Slejko, Eddie Martin, Earl Bergman, Ray Beller, Dean Kincaide, Larry Molinelli (saxes), Saxie Dowell; (second row) Walt James, Tommy Oblek, two unknowns (tbs), George Vedegis (sp?) (g); Johnny Potoker (p) (third row) unknown, Eddie Hielika, Kenny Williams, Bob Kennedy, Ray Dorney (tps), Bob Radcliffe (d), Stanley Slejko (b) Bus Watson, sousaphone.

Appendix 7
Jess Stacy solo engagements - 1948-1964

Restaurants and Cocktails Lounges in which Jess Stacy played.
(All are in the Los Angeles area, except those in square brackets)

1948 May   The Haig (Wilshire Blvd)
Jul   St. Francis Room (3428 West 8th St) (from Jul 15)

1949 [Jan/Feb]   [in Casper, Wyoming]
Mar   St. Francis Room (3428 West 8th St)
May   The Kiru   (Wilshire Blvd)
[Jul/Aug]   [in Omaha, Nebraska]
[Sep-Nov]   [in Columbus, Ohio, at the Grandview Inn]
[Dec]   [in Cape Girardeau for Christmas]

1950 Jan-Mar   Radar Room,   (Santa Monica Blvd)
Apr 14   The Track Cafe, (1076 East Colorado Blvd., Pasadena)
May   The Wedgewood Room
Jun   The Lark   (6th St.)
[Jul-Sep]   [in Cape Girardeau; operation; then marriage]
[Nov]   [in San Francisco, at The Hangover]

1951   Hangover Club, Los Angeles (for most of the year)

1952 Jan-Feb   Hangover Club, Los Angeles
Mar 1-Apr 5   Astor Club (Ventura & Laurel Canyon)
Apr 15-Jul 12   King's Restaurant (Santa Monica Blvd)
Jul 24-Sep 20   Holiday House, Malibu
Oct 8-24   The Fairway   (9401 W. Pico Blvd)
Nov 19-   St. Francis Room (3428 West 8th St.)
Dec   St. Francis Room (weekends)

1953 (May)   Beverly Cavern (4289 Beverly Blvd) (on May 25th began Monday night gig with John Lucas band. Lasted into 1954)
Jul 25-Sep 8   Holiday House (Surfside Piano Bar, Pacific Coast Highway, Malibu)
Sep 9-Nov 26   The Falcon   (Pico & Sepulveda)
Dec 10-25   22 Club (8524 Sunset Blvd) (band date)
Dec 31   Holiday House, Malibu

1954 Jan 3-30   The Interlude (8572, Sunset Blvd)
Feb 14-Apr 18   Lindy's Steak House (3656 Wilshire) (from Feb 15th)
May 9-Jun 19   Harlequin Restaurant (224, S. Beverly Dr.)
Jun 28-Aug   Puppet Room (Melody Lane Restaurant, Wilshire Blvd at Beverly Drive)
Sep 7-Oct 23   Sip 'n' Surf, Santa Monica
Nov 1 on   Beecher's Restaurant (8505 Santa Monica Blvd)

1955 to Apr 30   Beecher's Restaurant (8505 Santa Monica Blvd)
May 3-16   Cypress Room
May   The Captain's Table (La Cienega Blvd) (2 weeks)
Jun 1-Sep 9   The Garden of Allah Room (Holiday House, 8152 Sunset Strip)
Sep 10-20   Holiday House, Malibu
Oct 25-Nov 6   The Keyboard (453 N Canon Dr) (trio)

	Nov 13-30	The Oyster House (La Cienega Blvd)
	Dec 1 on	The Elbo Room, Manhattan Beach

1956 to Jan   The Elbo Room, Manhattan Beach
Feb 10-Mar 8   Black Angus Steak House (8167 W. 3rd St)
Mar 9-Jul 14   Gra-Jo's (3560 S. La Cienega Blvd)
Aug 3-Sep 3   The Surf Room (Holiday House, 27400 Coast Highway, Malibu)
Sep 9-Oct 10   The Captain's Table (301 S. La Cienega Blvd)
Nov 11-Dec 9   The Oyster House (La Cienega Blvd)
Dec 10 on   Paul's New Silver Room (9045 Burton Way, Beverly Hills)

1957 to Feb 24   Paul's New Silver Room
Mar 11-Jul 24 The Open House (739 N. La Brea Ave)
Aug   The Pump Room (Ventura Blvd, Studio City)
Sep 23-Nov 30 The Open House (739 N. La Brea Ave)

1958 Jan 21- ?   Ile de France (6001, W. Jefferson Blvd., Culver City)
Mar 3-Jul 5   Pepy's Roman Room (La Cienega Blvd, Culver City)
Jul 28-Dec 23 Harlêquin Restaurant (224 Beverly Drive, Beverly Hills)

1959 Jan 19-Feb 21 Villa Frascati (Sunset Strip)
Mar 3-Oct 10   Huddle-Bundy Restaurant (3030 Bundy Dr. Santa Monica)
Oct 21-Nov 30 Motor Sport (Ventura Blvd, Encino)

1960 Jan 20-Nov 12 Leon's Steak House (10945 Victory Blvd, N. Hollywood)
Dec 1-Dec 21   The Elbow Room (Three Palms Restaurant, 9449 W. Pico at S. Beverly Drive)
               (not the same as The Elbo Room (December 1955)

1961 Jan 9-Feb 11   Frascati Chalet (2201 Wilshire Blvd)
Apr 19-May 21 Parisian Room (4960 W. Washington Blvd)
May 26-Nov 18 The Brown Derby (3377, Wilshire Blvd)
Dec 11 on   Lombardi's Restaurant (Law Building, Los Angeles)

1962 to Jan 31   Lombardi's Restaurant (Law Building, Los Angeles)
Feb 15-Mar 14 The Contessa (8751, Van Nuys Blvd, Panorama City)
May 9-Jun 16   The Ivory Tower (1610 26th St. Santa Monica)
Sep 13-Oct 24 The Steak-Out (3550 Wilshire Blvd)

1963 Feb 24-Mar 23 Paul's Steak House
Jun 8-18   The Embers
June 28 on   Intermezzo, La Crescenta (weekends)

1964 to Feb 3   Intermezzo, La Crescenta (weekends)

Jess Stacy opened at the Mural Room (5510 Hollywood Blvd) on Thursday, October 19th. This may have been 1956.

This listing was originally compiled from information provided by Floyd Levin, based upon the postcards which Jess Stacy mailed as he moved from one location to another. Additional data came from C.K. Bozy White and various magazines. Its present completeness is due solely to Pat Stacy.

Listing of Stacy associates

This is a selective roster of musicians, record producers, club owners and singers who impinged upon Jess Stacy's career, but have no entry in John Chilton's "Who's Who of Jazz" or in "The New Grove Dictionary of Jazz". All entries are, of necessity, brief, some because full details are not available.

VIC ABBS (trumpet)
In 1930 played with Jess Stacy's Aces. Worked with The Four Californians, 1934.

BASIL "BUZZ" ADLAM (sax/arranger) b. 1907 d. November 9, 1975
Born in Chelmsford, England; to Canada aged three. Worked with Jess Stafford and Phil Harris, 1933. Many years with Horace Heidt as arranger. Then worked (1945 on) for American Broadcasting Co. as west coast musical director.

WILLIAM "BILL" ALAMSHAH (trumpet/singer) b. July 20, 1909   d. 1974
Professional name: Bill Shaw. Born in Chicago, where he worked for Maurie Sherman, Julie Stein, Dave Rose, Henri Gediron and Jules Fasthoff. Moved to Los Angeles 1936. 1937/38 played with and managed Frankie Trumbauer's orchestra. Left music in 1938. After serving in WWII, became a teacher. Made private recordings with Jess Stacy.

DANIEL R. "DANNY" ALTIER (sax) b. September 14, 1902 d. May 16, 1984
Active in Chicago in the 1920s and 1930s. With Floyd Town's band, which included Jess Stacy, at the Midway Gardens and The Triangle, 1927/28.

ERNIE ANDERSON (promoter/publicist) b. May 25, 1910   d. June 12, 1996
Became a jazz enthusiast at an early age. As a student in Paris he dropped his studies and became a reporter on the *Chicago Tribune* (Paris edition). When the paper folded he returned to New York and joined an advertising agency. Meeting Eddie Condon,he went on to produce Condon's Town Hall & Carnegie Hall concerts, the Blue Network broadcasts and the Floor show television series. He produced Fats Waller's Carnegie Hall concert and the famous Town Hall concert by Louis Armstrong. As a press agent, his clients included film directors John Huston and Ingmar Bergman, and actors Jose Ferrer and Charles Bronson.

EDWIN "SQUIRREL" ASHCRAFT (piano/fan) b. 1907   d. Feb. 1981
Educated at Princeton; recorded on piano-accordion with the Princeton Triangle Jazz Club Jazz Band in 1926/27/28. Practicing as a lawyer, his home outside Chicago was a musicians' hangout Sunday or Monday nights from the mid-1930s to WWII. Recordings from these parties, plus some from the 1960s, were issued on the "More Informal Sessions" label. In Naval Intelligence during the war, then joined CIA until retirement in 1966. A Jess Stacy supporter; wrote sleeve note for Stacy's solo Chiaroscuro album.

BYRON BAXTER (trumpet) b. c. 1920
In U.S. Navy December 8, 1941 to August 1945, including two years with band led by banjoist Eddie Peabody. Played with Jess Stacy, approximately March to May, 1946. With Alvino Rey for one year; briefly with Ray McKinley; followed by two years at the Chicago theatre. On the Wayne King television show for two years, then 23 years in studios in Chicago, first radio, then television.

EARL BERGMAN (alto)   b. December 6, 1920
With Lou Breese in 1942. Joined Jess Stacy after navy service with Saxie Dowell. Then worked with Joe Sanders, 1946/47, followed by seven years as lead alto with Ray Anthony, 1948/54. Worked in Las Vegas thereafter. Brother of Buddy.

ELMER JEROME "BUDDY" BERGMAN (trumpet)   b. October 14, 1918   d. December 6, 1884
Worked with Charlie Teagarden 1938, Lou Breese 1939-42, Boyd Raeburn 1942, Horace Heidt 1943, Benny Strong 1944, Jess Stacy 1944/45, Bobby Sherwood 1947. Then left full-time music for a day job. Brother of Earl.

BERNIE BILLINGS (tenor/promoter)   b. December 11, 1914   d. December 25, 1995
With Bobby Hackett in 1938/39. In 1939 played on two of the Muggsy Spanier Ragtime Band sessions. During late 1940s, early 1950s played many Los Angeles clubs with his trio. Also worked with Pete Daily. Organized concert with Jess Stacy.

J. CLYDE BRANDT (music teacher)   b. February 10, 1887   d. April 9, 1973
Professor of piano and violin at South East Missouri State University in Cape Girardeau, from August 1919 until he retired in 1957. Gave Jess Stacy piano lessons shortly after his arrival in Cape Girardeau.

LEROY BUCK (drums)
Played with Jess Stacy's Aces, 1930. Recorded with Sleepy Hall's Collegians. Played with Frank Trumbauer orchestra May 1932 to May 1933.

JERRY BUMP (trombone)
Worked with Hitch's Happy Harmonists, 1922/24, then Charlie Davis. Recorded 1925 with Wingy Manone (OKeh unissued). With Al Katz at same time as Jess Stacy in 1927. See also Fred Rollison.

JOHN CARSELLA (trombone)
Worked with bands of Bill Grimm (on riverboat), Murph Podolsky and Carl Hoff. Also probably with Floyd Town during Jess Stacy's stay.

TONY CATALANO (trumpet, leader)   b. 1881   d. c. April 1950
Played on riverboats for most of his professional life, working with Carlisle Evans and Lee Stoeterau, and leading his own band, Tony's Iowans. Employed Jess Stacy 1924.

BILL CHANDLER (trumpet)
Recorded with Myron Schulz (1927) and Verne Buck (1928). With Jess Stacy's Aces, 1930.

BUDDY CLARK [Samuel Goldberg] (singer)   b. July 26, 1911   d. October 1, 1949
Active in Boston before moving to New York. Sang with Benny Goodman on "Let's Dance" radio show (1934). On Lucky Strike Hit Parade 1936-39. Thereafter successful on radio and records. Recorded over 500 titles. Dubbed vocals for movies, including Jack Haley and William Holden. Jess Stacy in accompaniment for one session. Died in a plane crash. (See *Record Research* 141. July 1976, et seq.)

CARLOTTA DALE (singer)
Worked with Jan Savitt (1939) and Will Bradley. Recorded with Jess Stacy All-Stars.

HELEN DANCE (see Helen Oakley)

EDDIE DI MARTINO (tenor)   b. November 2, 1922
Briefly with Ted Steel youth swing band, then Bob Allen. After war service with the Saxie Dowell Navy Band, joined Jess Stacy. Later worked with Will Osborne, Ray Anthony and for four years with Hal McIntyre. Left full-time music to work as woodwind repairman.

OTIS FERGUSON (writer/critic)   b. August 14, 1907   d. September 14, 1943
Worked for *The New Republic* magazine from 1934 to 1941. When the U.S. entered WWII he joined the merchant navy. Surviving a convoy to Russia, his next ship sailed for Salerno, where it was hit by a radio-guided bomb from a German plane. Ferguson was killed in the explosion. His writings are gathered together in "The Otis Ferguson Reader" (1982).

MURRAY GAER (drums) b. March 23, 1910

Worked with Larry Wagner, then with Abe Lyman 1937/42. Studio work 1942/44. One year in Army Air Corps, 1942/43. In mid-1944 replaced Frank Carlson in the Horace Heidt orchestra, when Jess Stacy was a member. Left Heidt in 1945, with Buzz Adlam, to join American Broadcasting Company. While on staff freelanced with Rudy Vallee, Paul Whiteman, Ray Noble, etc. Left full-time music and into insurance business in 1957.

FRED GREENLEAF (trumpet) b. September 17, 1915 d. January 1, 1979

Mainly worked in Detroit, including Hank Biagini band. Played in Chicago with Miff Mole (1947/8), Jazz, Ltd. (1950), and in Los Angeles with Ben Pollack (late 1951), and with Jess Stacy. Toured with Jack Teagarden, 1954. Recorded with Teagarden and with Art Hodes.

HORACE HEIDT (leader) b. May 21, 1901 d. December 1, 1986

Led a show/novelty band from 1923 to late 1940s. Hosted radio shows "The Pot of Gold", "Treasure Chest", plus "The Swift Show Wagon" for NBC-TV. In film "The Pot of Gold". Retired from music to concentrate on property management. Employed Jess Stacy.

BEN HELLER (guitar) b. January 21, 1906

Born in London, England. Played with Benny Goodman, alongside Jess Stacy, 1938/39, Teddy Powell, 1939, Harry James, 1940/45.

BOB HIGGINS (trumpet) b. October 13, 1916

First bands were those of Ayars Lamarr and the Amsler Brothers. Then with Dolly Dawn, 1940, Charlie Spivak, 1941, Carl Hoff, Teddy Powell, 1942, and Sonny Dunham, 1943. Two years of defense work. Moved to Los Angeles. Worked with Ted Vesely band, then five years at L.A. Hangover, 1949/1955, including 3 years with Rosy McHargue, and with Jess Stacy trio. With Ben Pollack and Jack Teagarden in 1956. From 1949 until he retired in 1979 he was working days and playing nights. After retirement continued to perform at concerts, parties and clubs. (See *The Mississippi Rag*, May 1984)

GARDNER HITCHCOCK (drums, singer) b. July 7, 1922

Worked with Don Ragon, Boots Randolph, Ish Kabibble, Kenny Sargent, and many other bands. Played many jazz gigs and recorded for GHB with Olive Brown, Don Ewell in 1972. Worked as piano tuner, and played with the Hot Cotton Jazz Band since 1982. Backed Stacy when he sat in with Don Ragon orchestra.

HUGH HUDGINGS (sax) b. October 7, 1910   d. December 1. 1983

Like Jess Stacy, he too grew up in Cape Girardeau. With Ben Pollack, 1938/39; Ted Fio-Rito, 1941; Jan Savitt, 1942; Horace Heidt, 1943/44; Skinnay Ennis, 1945/46. Used the name "Hugh Hudson" when leading small band at Los Angeles' clubs in late 1940s/early 1950s. Recruited Stacy for Horace Heidt orchestra.

JOE KAYSER (drums, leader) b. 1891 d. October 31, 1981

During WWI was in the Great Lakes Navy Band, conducted by John Philip Sousa. Worked with Earl Fuller (1917) and Meyer Davis (1919). Led his own dance band around Chicago from 1920 to 1935, when he became a booking agent, for NBC, GAC and then Music Corporation of America, until 1956 when he began his own agency. Was one of many drummers said to have invented the 'high hat' cymbal. Employed Jess Stacy.

ED KUSBY [Ed Kuzborski] (trombone) b. July 22, 1912 d. February 6 1995

Played with Clyde McCoy, Rudy Vallee, Hal Kemp (1935/40). Became studio musician, though with Bill Finegan army band in WWII. Left radio for film studio work with Columbia (1956/68) and Fox (1968/78), when he retired. Many recordings with Nelson Riddle, Billy May, Frank Sinatra, Spike Jones. Played short engagement in Joe Kayser band with Jess Stacy. Reviewing a Hal Kemp engagement George Simon referred to ". . .a brilliant trombonist named Ed Kusborski *(sic)*, who played many fine solos."

EASTWOOD LANE (piano, composer)   b. November 22, 1879   d. January 22, 1951
American composer whose works influenced Bix Beiderbecke and then Jess Stacy. (see *The Mississippi Rag*, February 1994; *Journal of Jazz Studies*, Spring 1971).

JOYCE LACEY (piano)   b. c. 1918
Worked in local bands around her birthplace, Malden, Missouri, then in Detroit. Tuition from Florina Morris, who gave some lessons to Jess Stacy. In 1949 began a long association with Doc Evans' band. Married to Johnny McDonald, who played sax with Evans. Played at Jazz, Ltd. on various occasions in late 1940s. In the 1980s played with The Tailgate Ramblers, led by Jim Joseph, tuba.

JOHN LUCAS (trumpet, drums, xylophone, singer)   b. March 15, 1918
Despite physical problems which would have floored a lesser man he became proficient on a variety of instruments, beginning with piano, mainly played trumpet, specially adapted to suit his disability. In late 1940s worked with San Gabriel Valley Blueblowers, which became the Firehouse 5 + 2. Played gigs with Pete Daily, George Lewis, the Old Standard Jazz Band and the New Imperial Jazz Eagles. Led own band, the Blueblowers, from June 1949 onwards. First met Jess Stacy in 1935, and played with him frequently in the 1950s/60s.

REUEL LYNCH (clarinet)   b. c.1915/20
A cult musician who floated from one group to another in Los Angeles. Worked with big bands of Seger Ellis, 1937; Merle Carlson, Vido Musso, Skinnay Ennis, 1938; Will Osborne, 1941; possibly Vido Musso again, 1945. With small bands, Daryl Harper, Bob Laine, 1940/41, and own group. Member of Red Nichols 5 Pennies 1949. Worked with Jess Stacy at St. Francis Room and Hangover Club.

JACK "MACHINE GUN" McGURN [Vincenzo Gibaldi] (gangster, club owner)
     b. 1903   d. February 15, 1936
Born in Sicily; to USA at one year old. Close friend of Al Capone, for whom he was chief gunman. Suspected of 22 murders. Probably planned the 1929 St. Valentine's Day Massacre. Owner of 100 Club where Jess Stacy played with the Danny Alvin band.

ALBERT MARX (record producer)
Married to singer Helen Ward. Worked for American Record Corporation. Arranged for Benny Goodman's 1938 Carnegie Hall concert to be recorded. Began Musicraft Records, Discovery and other companies.

EDDIE MARTIN (see Eddie Di Martino)

DONNY MacDONALD (trumpet)   b. September 11, 1918   d. March 9, 1991
Played with Lizzie Miles at the Club Hangover, San Francisco, 1953/54. Recorded in London in 1975. Worked with Jess Stacy.

JOYCE McDONALD (see Joyce Lacey)

RAYMOND F. "PEG" MEYER (tenor, clarinet) b. September 29, 1903   d. December 2, 1995
Worked in and around Cape Girardeau for his entire career, as musician, bandleader, music store owner, instrument repairer, teacher and local historian. Boyhood friend of Jess Stacy, with whom he formed his first band, The Agony Four. His autobiography, "Backwoods Jazz of the Twenties", was published by Southeast Missouri State University in 1989.

SIGMUND H. "SIG" MEYER (violin, leader)   b. 1893   d. September 22, 1982
Sig Meyer and his Druids played at the White City, Columbia and Wilshore ballrooms between 1919 and 1932. Briefly employed Jess Stacy. Left the music business during the Depression.

DUDLEY MURPHY (film director, journalist, bar owner)   b. 1897
Directed film shorts "Black and Tan Fantasy" (with Duke Ellington) and "St. Louis Blues" (with Bessie Smith), and the full-length "Emperor Jones" with Paul Robeson, 1933. In early 1940s made soundies for juke boxes. Owner of the Holiday House where Stacy played in 1955.

BILL MUSTARD (trombone) b. October 14, 1919   .
Prior to army service in WWII, worked with Charlie Spivak (1940/42), Woody Herman; then with Horace Heidt (at same time as Jess Stacy) and Teddy Powell. Later with Vaughan Monroe.

HELEN OAKLEY (writer, producer) b. c. 1915
An early jazz enthusiast; wrote jazz articles for *Down Beat* and *The Chicago Herald*. Helped form the Chicago Rhythm Club. Recommended Jess Stacy to John Hammond. Worked for Irving Mills, organized recordings for his "Variety" label. Initiated the small band Ellington recordings. Wrote biography of T-Bone Walker. Married, 1947, to British writer/producer, Stanley Dance. (See "American Woman In Jazz" by Sally Placksin)

LOUIS PANICO (trumpet) b. c. 1900   d. c. 1970
Born in Naples, Italy. Made name with Isham Jones 1922/24, then led own band until 1939. For next nine years with Chicago radio station WBBM. Employed Jess Stacy in Chicago.

CHARLES PARLATO (trumpet) b. c. 1915/20
Played with Horace Heidt in 1944, when Jess Stacy was pianist. On leaving Heidt joined Kay Kyser, then worked in radio, including the Dave Rose and Phil Harris shows. Joined Lawrence Welk in 1962 and was still with him in 1979.

RICHARD 'PAT' PATTISON (bass)   b. 1888   d. April 19, 1946
Arrived in Chicago 1920, with Joe Kayser. Worked with Spike Hamilton, Floyd Town, Coon-Sanders, Paul Mares, Boyd Raeburn, Lenny Esterdahl. Recorded with Danny Altier, Paul Mares & Muggsy Spanier.

JAMES C. PETRILLO (union leader) b. 1892   d. October 23, 1984
Leader of the American Federation of Musicians from June 1940. Responsible for the recording ban which began August 1, 1942, and was not fully resolved until 1944, with serious repercussions for the big bands.

DON RAFFELL (tenor) b. April 26 (c.1920)
Worked and recorded with innumerable big bands, including Charlie Barnet, Tommy Dorsey, Artie Shaw, Gerald Wilson and Nelson Riddle. Was in Horace Heidt band at same time as Jess Stacy. Also employed by Charlie Spivak, Billy May, Jerry Wald, the Tonite band. In the 1980s was still playing in the film/tv studios. Appears in Noni Bernardi's Band video, "The Way It Was" (1995)

JACK READ (trombone)
Worked with Art Kassel and Charles Agnew. Recorded with Elmer Schoebel and Charles Pierce. At Jazz, Ltd. in 1956.

FRED ROLLISON (trumpet)
Worked with Hitch's Happy Harmonists 1922/26; joined Al Katz, 1927/30, with a year out (1928) selling cars. Also played with Oscar Forster, Art Millerlei, and led own band. Recorded with Paul Freed (unissued), Wingy Manone, Hitch's Happy Harmonists and Al Katz. He and trombonist Jerry Bump frequently worked together. He and Stacy were in Katz's band together.

NICK RONGETTI (club owner, pianist) b. c. 1899   d. July 26, 1947
Graduated in 1927 from Fordham University of Law. After a year of studying medicine at Long Island University, Brooklyn, he ceased his studies to play piano in Greenwich Village night spots. Opened his own club, Nick's, in 1936.

JOE "POLACK JOE" SALTIS (gangster)   b. 1894   d. Aug. 1947

Came to Chicago from Hungary aged 11. Was 15th in list of "Public Enemies" when it was first issued by the Crime Commission in 1923. Was called "the most brutal gunman who ever pulled a trigger in Chicago." Believed responsible for attack on Mickey Rafferty, owner of the Triangle Cafe.

JOHN SETAR (reeds)   b. November 16, 1924

After leaving the Jess Stacy orchestra, worked with Buddy Morrow, 1946, Chuck Foster, Don Trenner, Freddy Martin 1949/54, and Jerry Gray, 1954/56. Moved to Los Angeles, and broke into television work in 1963, starting with two years on the Steve Allen Show.

TAL SEXTON (trombone)

In late 1923 was member of Hollis Peavey and his Jazz Bandits. Member of Carlisle Evans band with Jess Stacy.

MAURICE "MAURIE" SHERMAN (violin, leader) b. February 19, 1893   d. April 25, 1981

Father of pianist Ray Sherman. Began his professional career as a band leader at Chicago's Bismarck Hotel during early 1920s. Led bands at the Sherman Hotel, 1924/34, the Cafe DeAlex and the Oriental Gardens. The Maurice Sherman band was strictly a reading dance-band. Moved to Los Angeles in 1939, playing private parties on behalf of M-G-M. Stacy was with him briefly at the Sherman Hotel.

CHARLIE & SIMON "SY" SHRIBMAN

Based in Boston, the Shribmans owned and operated eight ballrooms throughout Massachusetts, Vermont and New Hampshire. They backed a number of bands in their early stages. In 1926 Charlie owned the Charleshurst Ballroom in Salem and managed the Mal Hallet band. He first booked Duke Ellington in June 1924. Ellington wrote: "I cannot imagine what would have happened to the big bands if it had not been for Charlie Shribman."

Sy Shribman died in Boston, June 2, 1946, aged 57.

CY SIMADEL (trombone)

Worked with Jess Stacy in Chicago with Floyd Town in the late 1920s. With Jess Hawkins' band at the Merry Gardens in 1936.

SAM SKOLNIK (trumpet)

With Tommy Dorsey, 1936; Charlie Barnet, 1940; Jess Stacy, 1945.

GEORGE MARSHALL SNURPUS (reeds)   b. June 27, 1906   d. December 27, 1996

Worked with Hitch's Happy Harmonists. Played with Walter Ford orchestra in Chicago, late 1928, alongside Wingy Manone and Frank Teschemacher, with whom, under Manone's name, he recorded two titles for Vocalion. Employed mainly in dance bands; Charles Agnew (1933-38), Jack Fulton, etc. Led own groups as George Marshall, until his retirement in 1973. (Refer *Storyville* no. 160, December 1994 and *IAJRC Journal*, Winter 1997).

FRANK MARTIN SNYDER (drums, leader) b. May 21, 1899   d. June 17, 1976

Was the original drummer with the New Orleans Rhythm Kings, 1921/22. Then worked with Elmer Schoebel, Arnold Johnson, Ralph Williams and Shorty Williamson, before leading small bands at various Chicago clubs. Jess Stacy worked with him briefly at The Subway in 1934. Left full-time music in 1947. (see *The Mississippi Rag*, June 1983).

MAURICE "MAURIE" STEIN (clarinet, alto) b. November 25, 1910   d. January 9, 1987

Brother of song-writer Jule Styne, with whose band he played. In his teens toured with Guy Lombardo. Worked with Benny Meroff and Phil Spitalny, 1930, then back with Lombardo. Led a band at Chicago's Chez Paree for many years in the 1930s. Jazz gigs included short dates with Jimmy McPartland (1940) and Bud Freeman (1942). Moved to Los Angeles, was briefly with Jack Teagarden late 1943. Ran Stein-on-Vine, a musical instrument store which became a popular hangout for AFM Local 47 musicians, whose offices were close by. Jess Stacy joined Benny Goodman from Stein's band.

HAROLD "SMOKEY" STOVER (drums)   b. c.1920   d. c.1974
Is first mentioned in connection with the Claude Thornill navy band which went to the South Pacific in late 1944. After his service Stover worked in numerous small bands, including Ted Vesely's. He recorded the drum sound track for Mickey Rooney in the 1951 movie, "The Strip." Became house drummer at Club Hangover in San Francisco, and can be heard on recordings from there by Meade Lux Lewis, Lee Collins, Lizzie Miles/George Lewis. Played engagement there with Jess Stacy. Also recorded with Joe Sullivan. With Wild Bill Davison's short-lived west coast band, 1966, and with Turk Murphy, 1967/70.

MARIO TOSCARELLI (drums)   b. c. 1920
Worked with bands of Bob Astor, Charlie Barnet, Jan Garber, Jess Stacy 1945, Boyd Raeburn, Ray McKinley, Ina Rae Hutton, Jerry Gray (1951), and five years with Vincent Lopez. Show drummer at the Copacabana until leaving full-time music.

BOB THIELE (record producer, writer)   b. July 27, 1922   d. February 6, 1996
Recorded Jess Stacy for Hanover-Signature. Edited "Jazz" magazine as a teenager, then ran "Signature" records until 1948. Worked for Decca-Coral, Hanover-Signature, and Impulse, then formed Flying Dutchman and Red Baron records. Wrote *What A Wonderful World* for Louis Armstrong and used the title for his autobiography. "One of the most respected and influential of jazz record producers."

FLOYD TOWN (tenor, clarinet, leader) b. October 20, 1899   d. March 4, 1968
In 1926 worked with Sig Meyer at Chicago's White City ballroom, then led own group at Midway Gardens, with Jess Stacy as pianist. Continued as leader at various clubs and ballrooms until 1929, when he joined Art Kassel. Organised his "Men About Town" seven-piece band 1935/37, then co-led four-piece The Embassy Boys until he left full-time music in 1942. Continued to play weekends. Was a member of the 1932 U.S. Olympic water polo squad. (See *The Mississippi Rag*, February 1990).

RICO VALLESE (cornet, guitar) b. c. 1915/20   d. early 1970s
Like Bobby Hackett, in whose style he played, Vallese came from Providence, Rhode island. Started out on guitar, then switched to cornet. Jobbed with Bud Freeman and then, after moving to Los Angeles in 1947, worked with Jack Teagarden, Rosy McHargue, Mike Reilly, Nappy Lamare, Kid Ory. For a while owned a bar called Swingtime and worked for Hughes Industries. Worked a four-week engagement with Jess Stacy at the Hangover in San Francisco. Recordings include Joe Alexander (Capitol) and Charlie LaVere (Jump).

P.L. "GUS" VAN CAMP (bass) b. August 4, 1912
Played with Stacy in both the Benny Goodman (1942/43) and Horace Heidt (1943/45) orchestras. Also worked with Ray McKinley, 1942; Skinnay Ennis, 1945/47; Frankie Carle, 1947/49. Plays intro to *Anywhere* by Horace Heidt (Columbia).

IRVIN "CAJUN" VERRETT (trombone, vocal)   b. 1906
Born in Bogalusa, Louisiana. Sang cajun-style. Worked with Fats Obenir. Was with Phil Harris c. 1941 and again in 1952 on NBC. Worked in the studios, and moonlighted with dixieland groups such as John Lucas and Ben Pollack's. Recorded with Eddie Miller and Nappy Lamare for Capitol in 1945 and 1949 respectively, and with Octave Crosby in 1954.

TED VESELY (trombone, leader) b. August 24, 1913   d. August 20, 1973
Worked with Cecil Gally orch; Fred Waring; then Ben Pollack, 1937, Artie Shaw, 1938, and Benny Goodman, the same time as Jess Stacy, 1939/40. With Claude Thornhill Navy Band 1944/45. During South Pacific tour was seriously injured in jeep accident. In Hollywood led a dixieland band during the 1950s, as well as working for Fred Waring, Bing and Bob Crosby. Ran a

music store in Las Vegas, founding the Las Vegas Youth Band in 1965.

CHARLIE VINAL (clarinet)   b. 1919   d. April 25, 1944
Suffered from infantile paralysis, and his Boston home was frequently visited by musicians, including Lionel Hampton and Jess Stacy, who were playing in the area.

JAMES KENNETH "BUS" WATSON (bass)   b. June 24, 1915
With the Saxie Dowell Navy Band, then with Jess Stacy. Worked for Jerry Wald. Three years with Hal McIntyre, also acting as business manager. Returned to New York and "did society circuit for Meyer Davis, Lester Lanin, Hugo Pedell, etc." Retired to Florida. Particularly recalls a short engagement playing with a Max Kaminsky sextet in 1952.

BILL WILLIAMS (trombone, leader)   b. July 22, 1912   d. April 9, 1989
Born in Orlando, Florida, he became a leader in Chicago. Moved to California. Worked for Warner Brothers as a copyist by day and led dixieland bands by night. Recorded for Alert. With Jess Stacy small band for short tour.

BENNY WINESTONE (tenor, clarinet)   b. December 20, 1906   d. June 10, 1974
Born in Glasgow, Scotland. In London played with Sidney Lipton, 1937, Lou Preager (1936/37), Eddie Carroll, Heralds of Swing, 1939. Emigrated to Canada. Worked with Frank Bogart, Louis Freeman, Louis Metcalf, Maynard Ferguson, then with own group and a variety of small combos. Often slipped across the Canada/U.S. border to play, which was how he came to join Jess Stacy in 1945.

PHIL WING (reeds)
With Jess Stacy in the Joe Kayser band 1924/25. Worked with Wayne King and in the NBC studios. Married Helen Stacy after her divorce. Stacy told Keith Keller, "Phil Wing was this good friend we had. He worked in all those cornball bands that I would rather starve than join."

Appendix 9

The Stacy Style (A 1970 treatise by John Steiner)

Stacy must have heard many of the 50 or 100 working jazz pianists around Chicago in the mid-20's to mid-30's when he was here. However, after much listening to their playing, and discussing Jess with the better jazz pianists, I have come to concur that stylistically Jess borrowed remarkably little from those whom he heard, and he left but little which the others could capably emulate.

There were in Chicago several jazz piano dynasties or style sequences:

Rag-to-swing	Confrey, then Bargy, then Gronwall
Wallerites	Blythe, later Don Ewell
Hinesmen	Tut Soper, Zinky Cohn, Cass Simpson, Bill Barbee
Bluesmen	Hodes, Melrose and the originators
Boogiemen	Ammons, Lewis

with Ammons lapping back over Jimmie Blythe, and the whole system being far more complicated than a simple tabulation might imply.

But not one Chicagoan became the New Stacy! The Easterner Dave Bowman did that a decade after Jess fully matured. When Jess' *World Is Waiting For The Sunrise* was imported by the shops in 1936, there was some stir locally. I recall hearing Stacy-inspired or -imitative versions of *World Is Waiting*, but that was about the extent of the Stacy influence. When some first generation jazzmen mentioned a resemblance of Dave North's playing to that of Jess, I questioned Dave, who said, "I don't recall that I knew Jess when I started using that roll (on the octave), and I can't imagine that I influenced him."

Where it had been Jim Thelman who opened jazz paths to Earl Hines, it became Earl who was the mentor to the Chicagoans. He pointed out the naturalness and forcefulness of treble octaves and led them toward the outer limits of improvisation. Jess at the very least must have derived inspiration from Earl. Yet at no place throughout their recording career would a knowledgeable listener confuse a four bar stretch of Jess with any four by Earl.

Once upon a time there was a hypothesis that Teddy Wilson sounded like Jess, and that idea was buttressed by the weak clay of their contemporaniety under Hines. It is true that like most other pianists of their period all three employed abundant and tasteful bass tenths and hard treble octaves, but each had his own figuration and filigree, and soon all three diverged in styles to where any 3-in-1 idea was unsupportable. Each man soon fathered his own jazz dynasty.

Jess recorded Bix' piano music in homage; his records show a maximum of Bix and a minimum of Stacy. Considering also that Bix' piano compositions are a distant department from the mainstream of jazz, it is surely clear that Jess' Bix recordings should not intrude on a critique of Jess the jazzman (no more than Goodman's classical forays should confuse an evaluation of Benny the jazzman).

By the early 40's Stacy had developed several styles into which he could shift allowing decided variation from one chorus to the next. Sharon Pease, the then piano columnist for *Down Beat*, related that as he attempted to transcribe some of Jess' ramblings, Jess would suddenly change to a new idiom. Despite the problem Pease was able to set down two of Stacy's styles, one in his transcription printed in the July 1940 issue and the other in November 1944. The first is sparse in bass tenths, the second is rich; the first is annotated in smooth time as indicated by triplets, the second in syncopated time shown by dotted eighths; the first has no octave or internal tremolos, the second is abundant with them.

Although it will be pretentious for me to attempt an analysis of Jess' style, it may be appropriate to discuss some of the elements here in the hope of forcing a fuller and more exact job from more competent hands.

The Stacy Style

Arpeggiatura – Short, interwoven arpeggios, usually unsyncopated but rhythm-accented, often in an upward direction, demonstrated in the published Stacy solo of *Don't Be That Way* and performed in the Freeman Trio's Commodore of *My Honey's Lovin' Arms*. Stacy's notes of the scales and accents (indicated by underlining) may be written 1232<u>3</u>434<u>5</u>456. More often the arpeggial unit consists of four or more notes, and the accents generally fall on harmony notes. Sometimes Jess may play counter arpeggios with both hands, an accomplishment I can hardly believe is improvised, as depicted in the transcription of *Sing, Sing, Sing* where

right hand		3	2	1	5	4	3	9	8	7
left hand				abc			def			ghi

(and having additional complications but which do not bear upon this point).   These arpeggios resemble familiar exercises for reed instruments. Buster Bailey, for one, used such exercises frequently in his improvisations. If we are content to call Hines' explosivity a *trumpet* style, we might then refer to Jess' style as a *reed* style.

In his early years Mel Powell and also Dick Cary showed some fondness for Stacyian arpeggios. Zurke worked out a weaving of small arpeggios in the bass. See his published solo on *Nickel Nabber* as an example.

Tremolo – The piano score of *Ec-Stacy* indicates treble octaves rocked at various tempos. They are used especially in the last, climactic choruses. Just the rocking of the octave was not, however, what set Stacy's sound apart from his pianistic relatives and imitators. His unique trick was a tremolo or trill of two notes within the played octave. Apparently this was not easy to achieve. Bushkin and Bowman acquired an ability to flutter two fingers while holding the octave, but for them it never came off as smoothly as in Stacy's hands. But perhaps this trick did not come full-blown to Jess either. Squirrel Ashcraft tells of observing Jess drill internal tremolos over and over, year after year. A variation which Jess uses and which his imitators find easier is to play the internal tremolo before striking the top and then the bottom of the octave. If Jess invented this device, it did not remain his personal property for long. In Jess' tremolos of all sorts there is generally a fast decay rate; this becomes more apparent if the records are played at a reduced speed.

Appoggiatura – Jess only occasionally uses grace notes, and he almost never smears. His anticipatory notes are usually 1/16ths given full value. In this and his runs I feel him shifting in and out of a 8/4 or 16/4 at will. Although his manner with tempo changing is less astonishing than the total rhythmic eccentricities of Hines, it does induce a pleasant change of bounce.

Spread – Jess is not large in stature, yet the sound of his tenths in both the right and left hands indicates that he reached them with ease.

Broken Chording – Jess, as well as many other jazzmen of the twenties, often uses broken chords; his are usually in a downward pattern such as

$$8 \quad 5 \; {}^{8} \; 5 \; 5 \quad 5$$
$$\qquad\qquad\qquad 3 \quad 3 \qquad \text{in even time}$$
$$3 \; {}_{1} \; {}^{3} \; 1 \; 1 \quad 1$$
$$\qquad\qquad\qquad 8 \quad 8$$

This figure might derive from his earlier ragtime playing. Although it is perhaps a lesser stylistic device, Jess uses it with exemplary taste to produce richly musical, almost harplike sounds.

Guitarist Marty Grosz appreciates Jess' opening up and lightly sketching his harmonies. This, Marty finds, yields "un-muddied" rhythm sections, it results in a more incisive piano sound, and it provides a clear track to a rhythm guitar. When Jess solos against full rhythm support, he often pares the treble to mere octave lines. In his World Transcriptions he did this. And at up tempos he retained openness and clarity by spreading wide his left hand, mainly laying in tenths as the chords changed.

Appendix 10

Influence and Style – Further thoughts

Reflecting upon John Steiner's treatise, perhaps there are other contributory factors to the Stacy style which can be discussed. Such factors would include his inate taste, personal stamina, power in hands and fingers, and willingness to practice.

In the biography there have been several mentions of Jess Stacy's addiction to practice and his habit of having a silent keyboard always to hand, in his hotel room and on the band bus. John Steiner's reference to this is amplified by Squirrel Ashcraft, in his 1974 sleeve note for Chiaroscuro CR-133, when he wrote: "I am not surprised that Jess' style and technique are so unchanged after so long. He has undoubtedly kept up his habit of practice (four hours a day when he was playing eight nightly with Benny). Once when he was spending a weekend with us I sneaked out on Sunday morning, when he was sitting at the piano in his bathrobe and looked as if he were likely to play, and turned on whatever recording gear we had then. I still have the result – a half-hour of scales and one short Czerny exercise."

Earl Hines told *Down Beat* that his normal reach was a tenth, an octave and two notes. Of Stacy's reach, Peg Meyer commented, "Jess had very long fingers and his hand spans 13 piano keys, the reason for those fine chords of his left hand." (A newspaper report quoted an octave and four, though another report said, ". . . has the most amazing hands you ever saw – can reach an octave and five notes." Derek Webster has pointed out that the length of Stacy's fingers can be seen in some of his photographs).

Squirrel Ashcraft provided what he thought was a clue to Stacy's special sound: "Jess Stacy has a unique piano vibrato because he has an unusually long middle finger, and he has worked out a flutter in the middle of the octave rather than by a vertical movement of his whole hand on the octave, from the wrist like Earl Hines, or a rocketing sort of action by practically everyone else. Listen carefully and you can't miss it; to me, it is almost a cornet lead."

James Lincoln Collier has commented that Stacy, instead of rocking his hand to produce the tremolo on the octave, would hit the octave as Hines did with thumb and little finger, and then play a trill on the interval of a second or third with the first two fingers inside the octave. A second important characteristic of Stacy's style was a pronounced use of accent, or dynamics, throughout his work, either on alternate notes, or more generally through the line, so that the music seems always to be coming and going. Stacy also divided the beat quite unevenly. These devices imparted to his work a tremendous swing. He was in my view one of the hardest swinging pianists in jazz."

Humphrey Lyttelton has rightly said that Stacy is one of that select and relatively tiny band of jazz players whose music can be recognized instantly within the first bar, the buoyant swing, the clearly defined melody line often expressed in octaves, and the subtle right-hand tremoloes that simulate the horn player's vibrato.

There can be no doubt that Stacy was possessed of both strength and stamina in order to cope with the strain of playing for long hours *and* to be heard through the sound of a big band. In the words of Otis Ferguson, his fingers just had to be "trained down to steel."

Stacy's taste is self-evident and all reports on this have confirmed his adherence to the highest possible standard, with no concession to commercialism. To quote trumpeter Zeke Zarchy, who worked with Stacy in both the Benny Goodman and Bob Crosby orchestras, "I will say that Jess is one of the most beautiful players I have had the pleasure of working with. His style is a joy to listen to, the most melodic and swinging all the time."

On the subject of improvisation, Stacy told Whitney Balliett, "When I play, it's mostly coming off the top of my head. Nothing is contrived ahead of time. I don't know what I'm doing and I can't explain it to anybody . . . I can hear what I'm going to do a couple of bars ahead, and when I get near the end of those bars a couple more open up . . . I think of the melody all the time and execute around it."

The vexed question of who influenced Stacy remains. Undoubtedly Fate Marable was a major figure, but the relationship with Earl Hines is not clear. There are no satisfactory recordings of Fate Marable playing piano to compare with Stacy's, but there is clearly a similarity between the work of Stacy and Hines as a young man. However, Stacy stated without equivocation that he was not influenced by Hines.

One can hear the Stacy touch in short solos and accompaniments by many pianists during the swing era, but presumably most of these could be traced back to the Hines influence. For example, listen to the Earl Hines solo on *Ann* by his big band. There is even Count Basie, if one judges by *Moten Swing* by the Moten band and *Listen My Children* by Basie's.

Stan Kenton's opinion, as expressed to Walter Kempe, was that he and Stacy were both addicted to Earl Hines. "Jess, he tried to copy Earl and so did I. Nat (Cole) did too. There were a whole bunch of us tried to copy Earl . . . Jess is one of the few white pianists that was able to get a similar sound like Earl."

Stacy's influence upon other pianists is also obscured by the effect that Earl Hines and Teddy Wilson had upon their contemporaries. Stacy stated he did influence Dave Bowman, whose style is the closest to his. This is surprising because Bowman, born in Canada in 1914, spent 1936 and 1937 in London. This would lead one to suppose that he would have heard little of Stacy during his formative years. Other examples of pianists apparently showing Stacy's influence are Bob Kitsis (behind vocal on *You're A Lucky Guy* by Artie Shaw) and Joe Bushkin (*Baby's Awake Now* by Lee Wiley; *Livery Stable Blues* and *Little Gates Special* by Bunny Berigan).

Mentioned in the biography are several pianists who have told of being influenced by Jess Stacy, players like Jane Jarvis, Steve Allen, Keith Ingham, Bill Mitchell, Ray Skjelbred, and Ray Sherman, but there were many others who admired him and in their formative years tried to emulate him. Dill Jones was one, as were Australians Dick Hughes and Rex Green. Lalo Schifrin has told how, as a young man, he was playing "the Jess Stacy Chicago style." In Norway there is Hans Olav Haugen, who has achieved a remarkable pastiche of the Stacy style.

Bob Greene, who is one of the foremost interpreters of the music of Jelly Roll Morton, said of Stacy, "It was his piano that got me interested in jazz piano when I was about 15, listening to the Goodman band. There was something about the way he played – there still is – that touched me, he had the knack of making a single note beautiful. He didn't need a lot of notes. Jess plays with spaces, too. There was beauty and form in his playing, and that wonderful sound he got when he hit a note he loved and gave it a tremolo. They say Hines and trumpet style, but that isn't Jess's secret. He just plays the good notes at the right time, with that special touch of his. He felt about a piano the way that Bix felt about the cornet. It should be beautiful and hot."

Of course, not every one was a Stacy admirer. Just two dissenting opinions were found during this research. Dick Cary, a fine pianist himself, said, "I honestly never thought much of his playing," while Byron Baxter, who played trumpet in Stacy's big band, said he was "only an adequate pianist."

Stacy said that he liked to "melt" with the band, and perhaps his band work was his greatest achievement. As Peg Meyer put it, "This is where Jess was great. Not only did he make the band sound good with his marvelous playing, but he kept the band alive, as he seldom played the same pattern twice, and all members of the band heard every note he played. He rode everything on the tip of the beat and you couldn't alter his tempo."

Milt Gabler, who produced many Stacy recordings for his Commodore label, summarized his feelings in a 1974 letter: "I recorded Jess for I loved what he did. You can always hear him coming through behind the band and soloists on the Goodman sides. He had a clean, free driving style that really made the band swing. He always listened to what the soloist was doing and backed them up with excellent taste, never getting in the way. He never tried to steal the show and he always inspired them to greater heights.

I made the solo sides because I never could get enough of Jess. He was very serious about what he did and even though he worked with BG every night, he practiced on a silent keyboard in his hotel room every morning for a couple of hours, going through Bach variations, etc. He was fond of Delius and Ravel as well. Jazzwise he liked Hines (who inspired him), Tatum, Waller, Wilson, Beiderbecke (on piano and cornet). Jess was a sensitive musician, and the beauty shows throughout his playing. The blues Jess recorded were spontaneous improvisations (as far as I know). However, I do believe that he did have pre-conceived ideas for melodies on the other compositions. My favorite Stacy is the Commodore 12" *Ec-Stacy*; not a pure blues, but something with an added dimension, the sensitive soul of a poet."

For further exploration of the Jess Stacy piano style reference can be made to the relevant chapters of the following works:

"The Essential Jazz Records"   (Stacy entry by Max Harrison)
"The Swing Era" (The Development of Jazz 1930-1945) (by Gunther Schuller)
"Annual Review of Jazz Studies 1" ('Refinement of Melody and Accompaniment in
    the Evolution of Swing Piano Style' by Eli H.Newberger)
"Benny Goodman and The Swing Era" (Chapter 12) (by James Lincoln Collier)
"Down Beat" (November 1937 and April 1, 1944: Sharon A. Pease column)

Appendix II

The compositions of Jess Stacy

1. **Solo**

Title	Date	Recording Company	Publisher
Ain't Goin' Nowhere	Jan 18, 1939	Commodore	Bregman, Vocco & Conn
Barrelhouse	Nov 16,1935	Parlophone	
Blue Fives	Nov 25,1944	Commodore	
Blue Notion	Oct 6, 1944	World	
Blues For Otis Ferguson	Oct 6, 1955	Atlantic	
Boo Boos For Bob	Mar 3, 1956	Brunswick	
Burnin' The Candle At Both Ends	Dec 16, 1940	Decca	Robbins
Complainin'	Apr 30, 1938	Commodore	Bregman, Vocco & Conn
Doll Face	Jul 1, 1974	Chiaroscuro	
Ec-Stacy	Jun 3, 1939	Commodore	Robbins
Evil Old Man	1959/1960	Hanover	
I Got A Load Off My Mind	—	unrecorded	Regent
Jess Stay	Sep 26, 1939	Varsity	
Jumpin' With Jess	Oct 6, 1944	World	
Lookout Mountain Squirrels	Jul 1,1974	Chiaroscuro	
Miss Peck Accepts	Jul 1, 1974	Chiaroscuro	
Old Ideas	1959/1960	Hanover	
Ramblin'	Apr 30, 1938	Commodore	Bregman, Vocco & Conn
Reno-vated	—	unrecorded	Regent
Ridin' Easy	Nov 25, 1944	Commodore	
Sell Out, The	Jun 13, 1939	Commodore	Robbins
Stacy's Still Swinging	Jul 1977	Chiaroscuro	
Stacy Still Swings	Jul 1, 1974	Chiaroscuro	
Steve's Blues	1959/1960	Hanover	
Young Ideas	1959/1960	Hanover	

2. **Collaborations**

Title	Date	Recording Company
Beat To The Socks (with Eddie Condon, Bud Freeman)	Jan 17, 1938	Commodore
Carnegie Drag (with Eddie Condon, Bud Freeman)	Jan 17, 1938	Commodore
Carnegie Jump (with Eddie Condon, Bud Freeman)	Jan 17, 1938	Commodore
Down To Steamboat Tennessee (with Willard Robison, Lee Wiley)	Jul 10, 1940	Commodore
Evelyn Waughbash Blues (with Bud Freeman)	Jul 2, 1974	Chiaroscuro
Kick In The Ascot (with Bud Freeman)	Jul 2, 1974	Chiaroscuro
Toad In the Hole, Part 2 (with Bud Freeman)	Jul 2, 1974	Chiaroscuro
Three Keyboards (with Willie Smith, Joe Bushkin)	Nov 30, 1938	Commodore
Three's No Crowd (with Bud Freeman, George Wettling)	Jan 17, 1938	Commodore

Stacy is also credited with the following published transcriptions:

1938   Camel Hop/Don't Be That Way   (Robbins)
1944   Two O'Clock Jump/Sing Sing Sing/I'm Coming Virgina/Jam Session/Lullaby In Rhythm/
            House Hop/Swingtime in the Rockies   (Robbins)

These 1938 and 1944 titles were included in a Robbins' folio entitled "Jess Stacy's Modern Piano Transcriptions."

1944   Flying Home/Reno-vated/I Got A Load Off My Mind/Nine Twenty Special/After Awhile
            (a Regent folio, "Jess Stacy Piano Solos")
1944   Eager Beaver   (Robbins)

        Moonlight Serenade   (Robbins)?

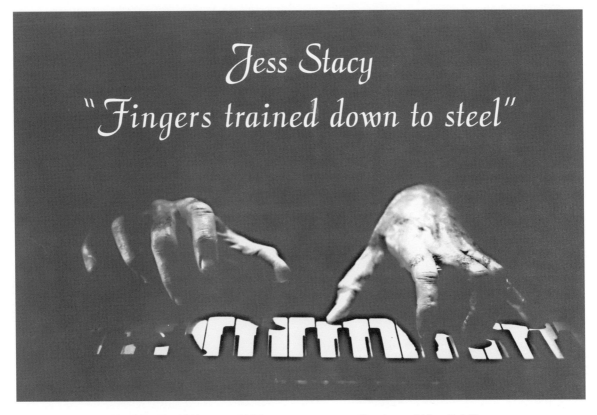

Photo by David Kovac – 1967   *Courtesy of Mrs. Pat Stacy*

Appendix 12

Other Awards & Tributes

*J*ess Stacy was inducted into the American Jazz Hall of Fame at Rutgers University in 1986, and into the *Jazz Beat* "All-Time Hall of Fame" in 1993.

A 1985 poll conducted for *Jazz Beat*, the quarterly magazine of the GHB Jazz Foundation, placed Stacy 14th in the piano section, with 220 votes. Quite a position for someone who was no longer a practicing musician, but not as surprising as his 16th place in the poll results published in the summer 1996 issue.

Musical tributes to Stacy have included the following:

1969 – Pianists Bob Greene and Don Ewell duetted on *Mr. Jess*, a Greene original, "born of his regard for Jess Stacy's work." This appeared on (LP) Fat Cat's Jazz FCJ-110. *Mr. Jess* was also recorded by The Swedish Jazz Kings in 1996 for (CD) Opus 3 CD19404.

1983 – On June 26, 1983, at the KOL Newport Jazz Festival, New York, pianist Keith Ingham and singer Barbara Lea performed a special tribute to Jess Stacy and Lee Wiley. Miss Lea sang songs associated with Lee Wiley, and Keith Ingham played several Stacy compositions, including *Ramblin', Complainin', Burnin' The Candle At Both Ends*, and *Ain't Goin' Nowhere*.

In November 1983 Bill Mitchell recorded an piano album called "Echoes of Chicago" for the Euphonic label (LP), ESR1225. With Hal Smith on drums, Mitchell paid tribute to Joe Sullivan, Art Hodes and Jess Stacy. The one original on the LP is *Cape Girardeau Shuffle*.

1984 – Pianist Ray Skjelbred recorded, again with Hal Smith on drums, for Stomp Off Records (LP), SOS1097. Included on the album was a Skjelbred original, a sequel to Stacy's *Complainin'*, titled *No Complaints*. (Skjelbred has written, "I take my foremost inspiration from Jess Stacy, a sweet man whom I first met in 1975").

1993 – In the notes to his Sackville CD (SKCD2-2033), Keith Ingham wrote: "One of my favorite piano players, Jess Stacy, knew 'a fine way to treat a Steinway'. Jess seemed to make the piano sing and I kept him in mind." Ingham was referring to his Stacy-ish treatment of *I Love A Piano*, the introduction to which is taken from Stacy's *Barrelhouse*.

1995 – Arbors Jazz (ARCD19152) by pianist Jane Jarvis contains her own composition and tribute, *For Jess*. In her notes, she writes: "He was my hero and my friend. All jazz pianists everywhere have been affected by his example of the role an ensemble pianist should play. He was the favorite pianist of every horn player he ever accompanied."

1996 – Ray Skjelbred recorded *Jess' Fine*, inspired by Stacy's record of *Ain't Goin' Nowhere*, with Hal Smiths' Roadrunners for Triangle (T-118 CD).

Two tributes which never materialized were a projected "This Is Your Life" program and a *Time-Life* "Giants of Jazz" LP set. Around 1950 a television producer toyed with the former idea for awhile, getting Jess Stacy's mother to write notes about her son, but eventually the idea was shelved. The *Time-Life* "Giants of Jazz" series consisted of three-LP boxed sets, appearing in the early 1980s. A Jess Stacy set (No. 31) was planned, with Marty Grosz chosen as note-writer, but before the production stage was reached the series ended, at No. 28, with a Bessie Smith collection.

There have been many radio tributes to Stacy, including a four-part recital by Vincent Pelote on station WGBO, Newark, NJ, starting in December 1985. Stacy was also well featured by Phil Schaap on station WKCR-PM, New York, talking by telephone each year around his birthdate, and during features on Bix Beiderbecke and Benny Goodman. Schaap presented a six-hour tribute after Stacy's death.

The Jess Stacy discography

This discography endeavours to list in chronological order all the recordings on which Jess Stacy appears. The term "recordings" has been interpreted to mean records, broadcasts and airshots which have appeared on 78 rpm (original issue only), microgroove and CD, radio transcriptions, and material from concerts and clubs which circulate among collectors. An exception to this approach has been with the Benny Goodman section, as explained in a following paragraph. The discography is based upon those indispensible standard reference works, Brian Rust's "Jazz Records 1899-1942" and Jorgen Grunnet Jepsen's "Jazz Records 1942 to 1968", and a Jess Stacy 'name' discography by Daniel L. Mahony, which appeared in *The Discophile* (No. 54, June 1957). Specialist works mentioned in the text have made a major contribution.

A standard layout of band or artist credit, personnel, recording location and date, followed by master and take numbers (where allocated), tune titles, and release details has been used, but with some breaks with tradition. Jess Stacy made his first recording seventy years ago and since that time the number of reissues of jazz material has grown continuously. Forty years ago all known issues could be listed in a discography; today it is still be possible to attempt this, but at the expense of space and clarity. The changes made here are in order to conserve that space and clarity. One variation has been to list only the original 78 r.p.m. issue. Anyone seeking further 78 r.p.m. details is referred to the works of Rust and Jepsen.

Abbreviations for the issue format are:
- (78) 78 r.p.m. recording, 10" or 12".
- (LP) $33^1/3$rd r.p.m. recording, microgroove long-play, 10" or 12"
- (EP) 45 r.p.m. recording, extended play, 7"
- (AC) audio cassette tape
- (CD) compact disc
- (Tx) Transcription produced for use by radio stations, $33^1/3$rd r.p.m., 12" or 16"
- (VC) Video Cassette

An attempt has been made to identify the band (quintet or larger) titles on which Jess Stacy can be heard soloing or accompanying. The identification method used is:
- **(A)** indicates a piano accompaniment to a singer, a soloist, or the reed section.
- **(I)** means there is a piano introduction to the tune.
- **(S)** indicates a piano solo.
- **(N)** means that the piano is inaudible or barely so.
- **( )** means that the title has not been auditioned.

It can safely be assumed that Stacy is heard both soloing and accompanying on duet, trio and quartet sessions. This annotation is subjective, in as much that on some titles marked **(A)** Stacy can be felt more than heard, whereas on other titles (Goodman's *House Hop*, for example) a few notes of interjection have been ignored. It should also be noted that the sound quality of the Benny Goodman Sunbeam releases is, as one would expect, well below that of the Victors, making it harder to detect Stacy's accompaniments. Recording balance and musical arrangements are also important; their effect helps to explain the impact of Stacy's accompaniments on Goodman's Victor records.

For reference purposes a four-figure number, starting with the last two figures of the year of recording, has been allocated to each session.

The Benny Goodman section for 1935 to 1939 was the source of much anxiety. It includes an enormous number of sessions and broadcasts, and thousands of record releases. In particular, with the advent of the Compact Disc there was an unholy scramble to release material from the 78 r.p.m. era in that format. The Victor titles by Benny Goodman were among the most popular to be selected, appearing on scores of labels, under Goodman's name as full CD's or as part of compilations. In the discography only the original issue numbers for the Benny Goodman Victor titles are shown. There are no reissue details.

Only titles from Benny Goodman broadcasts which have appeared on commercial discs, LP or CD, are listed. These broadcasts include numbers by the Goodman Trio and Quartet, with Teddy Wilson on piano, and these are not shown. No attempt has been made to list all the foreign issues given in D. Russell Connor's "Benny Goodman: Listen To His Legacy", the definitive BG discography, to which grateful acknowledgement is made.

Similarly, no airshots by Bob Crosby or Tommy Dorsey are shown, unless they were "issued" on transcription or on disc. Otherwise, all airshots, broadcasts and private recordings known to the compiler are listed.

Abbreviations: abbreviations used to indentify foreign issues of U.S. labels are: (E) = English; (F) = French; (G) = German; (Sw) =Swiss. RCABb refers to the RCA Bluebird series.

Instrument abbreviations used are:

acc	accordion	cl	clarinet	tb	trombone
as	alto saxophone	co	cornet	tp	trumpet
b	string bass	d	drums	ts	tenor saxophone
bar	baritone saxophone	frh	french horn	vl	violin
bb	brass bass	g	guitar	vo	vocalist
bj	banjo	p	piano	vtb	valve trombone
bsx	bass saxophone	ss	soprano saxophone	wh	whistling

My thanks are extended to the numerous contributors to the discography. If anyone is inadvertently omitted from the following list, my sincere apologies.

Tony Adkins, Walter C. Allen, Harry Avery, E.B. Woody Backensto, Arthur Badrock, Vic Bellerby, Trevor Benwell, Joe Boughton, Jerry Brown, Dave Carey, Nick & Jean Carter, Helene Chmura (Columbia Records), Ron Clough, Ian Crosbie, Charlie Crump, Helen Oakley Dance, Peter Darke, John R.T. Davies, William Dean-Myatt, Dave Dexter (Capitol Records), Allan Dixon, Frank Driggs, Frank Dutton, Wendell Echols (G.H.B. Records), Nesuhi Ertegeun (Atlantic Records), Barry Fleming, Milt Gabler (Commodore Records), Jim Gordon, Pete Goulding, Merrill M. Hammond, Bill Hardie, Ralph Harding, Pat Hawes, Jim Hibbits, Bob Hilbert, George Hulme, Malcolm Hunter, Trevor Huyton, Jorgen Grunnet Jepsen, Keith Keller, Tom Kelly, Lester Koenig (Good Time Jazz Records), Roger Krum, Eddie Lambert, John Leifert, Jack Lichfield, William Love, John Lucas, Harry Mackenzie, Dan Mahony, Tony Middleton, Gene Miller, Alun Morgan, Robert Morris, John Nelson, Art Neilsen, David Niven, Hank O'Neal (Chiaroscuro Records), John A. Payne, Brian Peerless, Tom Pletcher, Lothar Polomski, Bob Porter, Nolan Porterfield, Dick Reimer, Francis L. Rogers (Capitol Records), Howard Rye, Len Salmon, Walter Scott, Richard Sears, Ken Seavor, Manfred Selchow, Jim Shacter, Johnny Simmens. Daniel M. Simms, Hal Smith, Mike Sutcliffe, Eric Townley, Jerry Valburn, Howard J. Waters, Derek Webster, Bob Weir, Bozy White, Bert Whyatt, Laurie Wright.

The Bob Crosby section owes a great deal to the work of Jim Gordon, Frank Dutton and Charlie Crump, while the Tommy Dorsey listing can be credited to Harry Mackenzie, Lothar Polomski, Ken Seavor, and, for the RCA Victor data, Frank Driggs.

(2601) AL KATZ and His KITTENS (Eddie Kouden, Fred Rollison,tp; Jerry Bump, tb; Joe Magletti, cl, ss, as; Lou Storey, cl, as, vo; George Schectman, cl, ts, vl; Jess Stacy, p; Treg Brown, bj; Ray Kleemeyer, bb; unknown, d; Al Katz, director):

New York – Monday, May 3, 1926

35509-	**Somebody's Lonely** vLS			Victor rejected
35510-2	**Ace In The Hole**	**(N)**	(78)	Victor 20081
35511-	**Dynamite**			Victor rejected

other releases:
35510 (LP) T.O.M. 49, RCA(F) PM43267. Both are anthologies. Spoken introduction on 35510 by Katz and band members. reverse of Vi 20081-B, Coon-Sanders Original Nighthawk Orchestra.
Four takes made of 35510, and five each of 35509 and 35511.
Personnel from report in The Orchestra World, September 1926. Katz could be the drummer

(2801) FLOYD TOWN and his Band (Muggsy Spanier, co; Frank Teschemacher, cl; Floyd Town, ts; Jess Stacy, piano; George Wettling, drums; and others):
Chicago – circa early 1928

Wettling told collector Jim Gordon that the above musicians cut records which were never released. It has been suggested that if such a session took place it might well have been for Paramount, many of whose matrix numbers have not been traced.

(2802) DANNY ALTIER and His ORCHESTRA (Muggsy Spanier, co; Johnny Carsella, tb; Maurie Bercov, cl, as; Danny Altier, as; Phil Robinson, ts; Jess Stacy, p; Ray Biondi, g; Pat Pattison, b, bb#; George Wettling, d; Frank Sylvano, vo):
Chicago – Monday, October 22, 1928

C2466	**I'm Sorry Sally** vFS	**(A)**	(78)	Vocalion 15740
C2467	**My Gal Sal (They Call Her Frivolous Sal)** #	**(S)**	(78)	Vocalion 15740

other releases:
C2466/2467 also on (LP) Gaps 150, CJM 31, (CD) IRD C3, Village VILCD014-2
C2467 only on (LP) Swaggie JCS-114, (AC) Neovox 728

(3201) **BILL ALAMSHAH and JESS STACY** (Bill Alamshah, trumpet, vocal; Jess Stacy, piano):

Chicago – c. 1932

All Of Me		(LP)	Arcadia 2014
When It's Sleepytime Down South		(LP)	Arcadia 2014

These titles were originally discovered by collector John Leifert in a trunk in a Staten Island antique shop. They were on 13" aluminium discs, recorded at Green Recording Studios, 940 Lyon and Healy Bldg, apparently made as a present for singer Bee Palmer. Bill Alamshah, a Louis Armstrong admirer, was professionally known as Bill Shaw. Both musicians signed the label for *All Of Me*. The year of recording is estimated.

(3501) **PAUL MARES and His FRIARS SOCIETY ORCHESTRA** (Paul Mares, tp; Santo Pecora, tb; Omer Simeon, cl; Boyce Brown, as; Jess Stacy, p; Marvin Saxbe, g; Pat Pattison, b; George Wettling, d):

Chicago – Monday, January 7, 1935

C-870-B	**Nagasaki**	**(I/S)**	(LP)	Meritt 6
C-870-C	**Nagasaki**	**(I/S)**	(78)	OKeh 41574
C-871-B	**Reincarnation**	**(I/S)**	(LP)	Meritt 6
C-871-C	**Reincarnation**	**(I/S)**	(78)	Okeh 41575
C-872-B	**Maple Leaf Rag**	**(S)**	(LP)	Meritt 6
C-872-C	**Maple Leaf Rag**	**(S)**	(78)	Okeh 41574
C-873-B	**(When You Live In) The Land Of Dreams**	**(S)**	(LP)	Meritt 6
C-873-C	**(When You Live In) The Land Of Dreams**	**(S)**	(78)	OKeh 41575

other releases, all anthologies: (see notes for take details):
all -C takes on (LP) Columbia CLP632, Philips(E) BBL7061, (Eu) BO7095L.
all -C takes on (CD) IRD 1705, Gannet CJR1001. (AC) Neovox 819
C-870-C on (LP) Philips(E) BBR8110, (CD) Radio France 211761, (EP) Columbia 5-2094
C-871-C on (LP) Columbia CL2146, C3L32, CBS (E) BPG62237, C.S.P JC3L32, (EP) Columbia 5-2094
C-872-C on (LP) Folkways FP65, FJ2806. (CD) Millenium MILCD22, (EP) Columbia 5-2093
C-873-C on (LP) Columbia CL2146, C3L32, CBS(E) BPG62237, C.S.P JC3L32, (EP) Columbia 5-2093

Howard Rye has called this session "a discographical nightmare". The reasons for this nightmare include:
1. The use of both figures and letters for take identification. (At this time OKeh and Vocalion seem to have used numbers or letters indiscriminately to identify the takes recorded.)
2. Columbia's "dubbing" work on takes -1/-2 and allocating takes -C to the results.
3. George Avakian's efforts to improve the quality for LP reissue on Columbia by combining parts of takes -1 and -2 of C-870 and C-872.
Further details and comment on this 'nightmare', and on the "dubbing session" of January 26, 1935, are set out in an appendix to the discography.

(3502) **CHARLES LAVERE and His CHICAGOANS** (Johnny Mendel, Marty Marsala, tp; Preston Jackson, tb; Joe Marsala, cl, ts; Boyce Brown, as; Joe Masek, ts; Jess Stacy, p; Joe Long, g; Israel Crosby, b; Zutty Singleton, d; Charles LaVere, vo):

Chicago – Friday, April 5, 1935

C-955	**I'd Rather Be With You** vCLV	**(A)**	(LP)	Tax m-8007
C-956	**Smiles**	**(S)**	(LP)	Tax m-8007
C-957	**All Too Well** vCLV	**(I/A)**	(LP)	Tax m-8007
C-958	**Boogaboo Blues** vCLV & band	**(A)**	(LP)	Tax m-8007

Originally recorded for OKeh, but unissued.

other releases: all titles on (CD) IRD 1705, Gannet CJR1001

All listings, until the appearance of Gannet CJR1001, have shown LaVere as pianist and vocalist, a perfectly natural assumption. However, aurally the pianist for this session is Jess Stacy.

Bert Whyatt and this writer played these titles to Jess and Pat Stacy in 1979. Jess was uncertain, but Pat insisted it was his playing. Steve LaVere, on hearing the test pressings, realised it was not his father on piano, and Charlie LaVere later confirmed this.

There were two sessions by the LaVere band at this time, one on March 11, 1935, and the one of April 5. In his column in "Jazz Hot" for December 1938, trombonist Preston Jackson writes about the two recording sessions: "I remember about two years ago, I was recording with Charles Lavere *(sic)*. There was Jabbo Smith, Zutty, Jess Stacey *(sic)*, Huey *(sic)* Long (guitar), Boyce Brown, Joe Marsala, Leonard Bibbs and Marty Marsala. We recorded for Columbia or Brunswick. I know the records should have been good. We heard the test records, but the masters were ruined, why, bad machinery. We were asked to make them over, which we did, but Jabbo couldn't be found, he was in Detroit." Jackson is indicating that Stacy is also present for the March session, but this cannot be confirmed aurally. [It is interesting to note that six months earlier John Hammond wrote in *The Melody Maker* (September 29, 1934) of an all-star band which might record for Irving Mills, with Gene Krupa, Jabbo Smith, Jess Stacy and others.] During the 1940s LaVere, a fine jazz pianist in his own right, had a solo career as a singer, so the ambition to step away from the piano may have begun with this April 1935 session. The only dissenting voice here is that of Helen 0akley, who produced these sessions and the earlier Paul Mares date. She told her husband, Stanley Dance, that she was "positive that LaVere played piano on his own sessions."

(3503) **BENNY GOODMAN and His ORCHESTRA** (Nate Kazebier, Bunny Berigan, Ralph Muzzillo, tp; Red Ballard, Jack Lacey, tb; Benny Goodman, cl; Hymie Shertzer, Bill DePew, as; Art Rollini, Dick Clark, ts; Jess Stacy, p; Allan Reuss, g; Harry Goodman, b; Gene Krupa, d; Helen Ward, Joe Harris, vo):

broadcast, Palomar ballroom, Los Angeles – Thursday, August 22, 1935

[a]	**Goodbye** (theme)	
[b]	**At The Darktown Strutters' Ball**	**(N)**
[c]	**East of the Sun** vJH	**(A)**
[d]	**I Hate To Talk About Myself** vHW	**(A)**
[e]	**Star Dust**	**(N)**
[f]	**I'm In The Mood For Love** vJH	**(A)**
[g]	**The Dixieland Band** vHW	**(N)**
[h]	**Ballad In Blue**	**(N)**
[i]	**What A Little Moonlight Can Do** vHW	**(A)**
[j]	**Basin Street Blues** vJH	**(N)**
[k]	**Goodbye** (theme)	

Hymie Shertzer's name is frequently given as Schertzer.

other issues: all titles on (LP) Golden Era 15001; [e], [j], [k] on (LP) Sunbeam SB105

(3504) (same, except Joe Harris, tb, vo; for Lacey):

broadcast, Palomar ballroom, Los Angeles – summer 1935

	Sometimes I'm Happy	**(N)**

This broadcast title on (LP) Meritt 504

(3505) (same):

Los Angeles – Friday, September 27, 1935

BS 97015-2	**Santa Claus Came In The Spring** vJH	**(A)**	(78)	Victor 25195
BS 97016-1	**Good-Bye**	**(N)**	(78)	Victor 25215
BS 97017-1	**Madhouse**	**(S)**	(78)	Victor 25268
BS 97017-2	**Madhouse**	**(S)**	(78)	Victor 25268

(3506) JESS STACY (piano solos):

Chicago – Friday, November 15, 1935

C90445A	**In The Dark; Flashes**	(78)	Parlophone R2233

(Jess Stacy, p; Israel Crosby, b; Gene Krupa, d):   same session

C90446A	**Barrelhouse**	(78)	Parlophone R2187
C90447A	**The World Is Waiting For The Sunrise**	(78)	Decca 18110
C90447B	**The World Is Waiting For The Sunrise**	(78)	Parlophone R2233

other releases:
C90445A (LP) World Records SHB-39, Prestige 7646, Arcadia 2014, Sunbeam (unnumbered Bix set Vo.5), Swaggie
    S1248, Regal(E) REG2041, (CD) Classics 795, JazzTime(F) 797913-2, ASV Living Era AJA5073, AJA5172, Topaz
    TPZ1045, TPZ1050, Memphis Archives MA7015, (AC) Neovox 849
C90446A (LP) Music For Pleasure MFP1069, GX2509, World Records SHB-39, Prestige 7646,Folkways FP71,2809,
    Arcadia 2014, Swaggie S1248, (CD) Classics 795, JazzTime(F) 797913-2, ASV Living Era AJA5073, AJA5172,
    Topaz TPZ1035, TPZ1050, (AC) Neovox 849
C90447A (LP) Decca DL5133, BrE LA8544, World Records SHB-39, Arcadia 2014, Swaggie S1248, Prestige 7646,
    Regal (E) REG2041, (CD) Classics 795, ASV Living Era AJA5073, Topaz TPZ1050
C90447B (78) Decca 18110, Parlophone (Australian) A6561, (CD) Sunday Times STCD-211
C90447 (LP) Columbia KG32355, (AC) Neovox 849, (CD) JazzTime(F) 797913-2, MCA GRP18392

C90443/44 are "Tarzan In The Jungle" by Moderne Art Studios.
C90448 is by Peggy Walsh/Eleanor Kane

It has been reported that master C90448 is an unissued recording of *Go Back Where You Stayed Last Night* by Jess Stacy, but the "Decca Chicago Master Numbers" listing by Charles Garrod, whose introduction says, "the master numbers and dates were taken from the Decca recording sheets," gives C90444 and C90448 as shown above.
    In his notes to the 78 rpm album "Gems of Jazz", referring to *Barrelhouse*, Leonard Feather wrote of Jess Stacy

playing "a series of choruses improvised on the chord structure of an old tune, *Go Back Where You Stayed Last Night.*" Perhaps this was the source of the rumour about C90448.

A possible confirmation of the link between *Barrelhouse* and *Go Back Where You Stayed Last Night* may be found in a Hugh Porterfield auction listing in Joslin's Jazz Journal for February 1995. Porterfield included the following from the Peg Meyer estate: 90446-A *Go Back Where You Stayed Last Night* Decca unissued matrix, Porterfield stresses that 90446 is written twice on label and embossed in run-off.

Dealer and collector Larry Kiner had a Jess Stacy "to order" 'Nostalgia' cassette tape which included, allegedly, takes -A and -B of *Barrelhouse*, but no apparent difference between the two has been noted, although the claimed -B does seem to run about five seconds less than -A. 90447B is slightly slower than the -A take, with the bass a little more prominent. Pianist Pat Hawes considers take -B the better played version.

(3507) GENE KRUPA and His CHICAGOANS (Nate Kazebier, tp; Joe Harris, tb; Benny Goodman, cl; Dick Clark, ts; Jess Stacy, p; Allan Reuss, g; Israel Crosby, b; Gene Krupa, d):

Chicago – Tuesday, November 19, 1935

C90460-A	**The Last Round Up**	(N)	(78)	Parlophone R2268
C90461-A	**Jazz Me Blues**	(N)	(78)	Parlophone R2268
C90462-A	**Three Little Words**	(S)	(78)	Parlophone R2224
C90463-B	**Blues Of Israel**	(S)	(78)	Parlophone R2224

other releases:
C90460-A (LP) Music For Pleasure MFP1069, GX2509,Regal (Au,G) 1037, (AC) Ditto 103238, (CD) Past CD7008, Hallmark 300422
C90461-A (LP) Music For Pleasure MFP1069,Regal(Aug,G) 1037, (CD) Past CD7008
C90462-A (LP) Decca DL5134,Brunswick(E) LA8561, Capitol W2139,Regal, (E,G,Au) 2041,Time-Life STLJ05, Electrola(F) C 054-06 319, (CD) Sunday Times STCD-21
C90463-B (LP) Decca DL5134,Brunswick(E) LA8561,Parlophone PMC1222, Regal (E,G,Au) 2041,Music For Pleasure GFX2509, Electrola(F) IC 054-06 319, (CD) Past CD7008, Topaz TPZ1050
all four titles also on: (EP) Parlophone GEP8576, (AC) Neovox 870, (LP) World Records SHB-39,Prestige 7644,Ajax 101,Swing SW8458, (CD) Classics 754, JazzTime 797913-2,Swing CDSW8457/8

(3508) BENNY GOODMAN and His ORCHESTRA (Kazebier, Muzzillo, Harry Geller, tp; Ballard, Harris, tb; Goodman, cl; Shertzer, DePew, as; Rollini, Clark, ts; Stacy, p; Reuss, g; Goodman, b; Krupa, d; Ward, vo):

Chicago – Friday, November 22, 1935

BS 96299-1	**Sandman**	(N)	(78)	Victor 25215
BS 96500-1	**Yankee Doodle Never Went To Town** vHW	(A)	(78)	Victor 25193
BS 96501-1	**No Other One** vHW	(A)	(78)	Victor 25193
BS 96502-1	**Eeny Meeny Miney Mo** vHW	(A)	(78)	Victor 25195
BS 96503-1	**Basin Street Blues** vJH	(A)	(78)	Victor 25258
BS 96504-1	**If I Could Be With You (One Hour Tonight)**	(N)	(78)	Victor 25290
BS 96505-1	**When Buddha Smiles**	(N)	(78)	Victor 25258

(3509) (same personnel): NBC broadcast, Congress Hotel, Chicago – Monday, December 23, 1935

[a]	**Jingle Bells**	(N)
[b]	**Where Am I?** vHW	(N)
[c]	**Remember**	(N)
[d]	**The Music Goes 'Round And 'Round** vJH	(I/A)
[e]	**Get Happy**	(S)
[f]	**Basin Street Blues** vJH	(A)
[g]	**I've Got A Feelin' You're Foolin'** vHW	(A)
[h]	**That's You, Sweetheart** vHW	(N)
[i]	**Limehouse Blues**	(S)
[j]	**Someday, Sweetheart**	(N)

This broadcast was issued on (LP) Sunbeam SB 128.

Note: the majority of these broadcasts also open and close respectively with the band's themes, *Let's Dance* and *Good-Bye*.

(3510) (same personnel): NBC broadcast, Congress Hotel, Chicago – Sunday, December 29, 1935

[a]	**Alexander's Ragtime Band**	(N)
[b]	**The Dixieland Band**	(N)

These broadcast titles on (LP) Giants of Jazz 1005

(3601) (same personnel):   NBC broadcast, Congress Hotel, Chicago – Monday, January 6, 1936
  [a]   **Blue Skies**   **(N)**

[a]	**Blue Skies**	**(N)**
[b]	**With All My Heart** vHW	**(N)**
[c]	**Walk, Jenny, Walk**	**(N)**
[d]	**Rosetta**	**(N)**
[e]	**Bugle Call Rag**	**(N)**
[f]	**Thanks A Million**	**(N)**
[g]	**Truckin'** vHW	**(N)**
[h]	**On The Alamo**	**(A)**
[i]	**Eeny Meeny Miney Mo** vHW	**(A)**
[j]	**Madhouse**	**(S)**

This broadcast issued on (LP) Sunbeam SB 129, Cicala BLJ8026

(3602) (same personnel):   NBC broadcast, Congress Hotel, Chicago – Monday, January 13, 1936

[a]	**I Feel Like A Feather In The Breeze**	**(N)**
[b]	**I'm Shooting High** vHW	**(A/S)**
[c]	**Big John Special**	**(S)**
[d]	**Dear Old Southland**	**(S)**

This partial broadcast issued on (LP) Sunbeam SB 130.

(3603) (same personnel):   NBC broadcast, Congress Hotel, Chicago – Monday, January 20, 1936

[a]	**Farewell Blues**	**(N)**
[b]	**I'm Shooting High** vHW	**(A/S)**
[c]	**Stompin' At The Savoy**	**(N)**
[d]	**Basin Street Blues** vJH	**(A)**
[e]	**I'm Building Up To An Awful Letdown** vHW	**(N)**
[f]	**Transcontinental**	**(N)**
[g]	**You Hit The Spot** vHW	**(N)**
[h]	**I Surrender Dear**	**(N)**
[i]	**Yankee Doodle Never Went To Town** vHW	**(A)**
[j]	**Honeysuckle Rose**	**(N)**

This broadcast issued on (LP) Sunbeam SB 131.

(3604) (same personnel):   Chicago – Friday, January 24, 1936

BS 96567-1	**It's Been So Long** vHW	**(A)**	(78)	Victor 25245
BS 96568-1	**Stompin' At The Savoy**	**(N)**	(78)	Victor 25247
BS 96569-2	**Goody-Goody** vHW	**(A)**	(78)	Victor 25245
BS 96570-1	**Breakin' In A Pair Of Shoes**	**(N)**	(78)	Victor 25247

(3605) (same personnel):   broadcast, Congress Hotel, Chicago – Monday, February 3, 1936

[a]	**Dodging A Divorcee**	**(N)**
[b]	**The Day I Let You Get Away** vHW	**(A)**
[c]	**Sandman**	**(N)**
[d]	**Lights Out** vHW	**(A)**
[e]	**Alone** vHW	**(N)**
[f]	**Star Dust**	**(N)**
[g]	**Eeny Meeny Miney Mo** vHW	**(A)**
[h]	**King Porter (Stomp)**	**(N)**

This broadcast issued on (LP) Sunbeam SB 132.

(3606) (same personnel):   NBC broadcast, Congress Hotel, Chicago – Monday, February 10, 1936

[a]		**Remember**	**(N)**
[b]		**It's Great To Be In Love Again** vHW	**(S)**
[c]	**[JD]**	**I'm Gonna Sit Right Down And Write**	
		Myself A Letter	**(A)**
[d]		**Troublesome Trumpet** vHW	**(A)**
[e]		**Alone** vHW	**(N)**
[f]		**Oh, Sweet Susannah** vHW	**(A)**
[g]		**Goody-Goody** vHW	**(A)**
[h]		**Transcontinental**	**(N)**

This broadcast issued on (LP) Sunbeam SB 132.
[JD] this title by the JAM DANDIES, Kazebier, Harris, Goodman, Clark, Stacy, Reuss, Goodman, and Krupa.

(3607) (same personnel):   broadcast, Congress Hotel, Chicago – Monday, February 17, 1936

[a]	**Lost** vHW	**(N)**
[b]	**Goody-Goody** vHW	**(A)**
[c]	**Star Dust**	**(N)**
[d]	**Sandman**	**(N)**
[e]	**I Can't Give You Anything But Love, Baby** vHW	**(A/S)**
[f]	**Rosetta**	**(N)**
[g]	**You Hit The Spot** vHW	**(N)**
[h]	**Digga Digga Doo**	**(S)**

This broadcast issued on (LP) Sunbeam SB 130.

(3608) GENE KRUPA'S SWING BAND (Roy Eldridge, tp; Benny Goodman, cl; Chu Berry, ts; Jess Stacy, p; Allan Reuss, g; Israel Crosby, b; Gene Krupa, d; Helen Ward, vo):   Chicago – Saturday, February 29, 1936

BS 100012-1	**I Hope Gabriel Likes My Music**	**(N)**	(78)	Victor 25276
BS 100013-1	**Mutiny In The Parlor** vHW	**(A)**	(78)	Victor 26263
BS 100014-1	**I'm Gonna Clap My Hands** vHW	**(A)**	(78)	Victor 26263
BS 100015-1	**Swing Is Here**	**(N)**	(78)	Victor 25276

other releases:

all titles (LP) RCA Bluebird AXM2-5515, Victor LPV-578, RCA Camden 340, Ajax 101, Reader's Digest 3S, RCA International INTS1072, RCA(F) PM45354, 731,092, (EP) HMV 7EG8111, (CD) RCA Bluebird ND82180, Jazztime 797913-2, RCA Jazz Tribune(F) 74321 15521-2, Classics 754

100012 (LP) RCA(F) PM45350, NL89481(2), (EP) RCA(F) A75-492, (AC) Neovox 870, (CD) Past CD7008

100013 (LP) Neiman-Marcus 0456, First Edition DMM4-0456, RCA(F) NL89481(2), (CD) RCA Bluebird CDND86755

100014 (CD) Past CD7008

100015 (LP) Victor LPT26, WPT35, RCA Camden 368, Time-Life STLJ05, HMV DLP1054, BBC REB666, (EP) RCA(F) A75-492, (CD) BBC CD666, Radio France 211761, (AC) Neovox 870

(3609) BENNY GOODMAN and His ORCHESTRA (as November 22, 1935, except Pee Wee Erwin, tp; replaces Muzzillo):   broadcast, Congress Hotel, Chicago – Wednesday, March 18, 1936

        Sing, Sing, Sing vHW   **(N)**

This title on (LP) Sunbeam SB 105.

(3610) (Nate Kazebier, Harry Geller, Pee Wee Erwin, tp; Red Ballard, Joe Harris, tb; Benny Goodman, cl; Hymie Shertzer, Bill DePew, as; Art Rollini, Dick Clark, ts; Jess Stacy, p; Allan Reuss, g; Harry Goodman, b; Gene Krupa, d):   Chicago – Friday, March 20, 1936

BS100057-1	**Get Happy**	**(S)**	(78)	Victor 25279
BS100058-1	**Christopher Columbus**	**(N)**	(78)	Victor 25279
BS100059-1	**I Know That You Know**	**(N)**	(78)	Victor 25290

(3611) (same personnel)   broadcast, Chicago – Tuesday, April 21, 1936

[a]	**I've Found A New Baby**	**(N)**
[b]	**Prairie Moon**	**(S)**

These broadcast titles on (LP) Sunbeam SB 105

(3612) (same personnel):   Chicago – Thursday, April 23, 1936

BS 100379-2	**Star Dust**	**(A)**	(78)	Victor 25320
BS 100380-1	**You Can't Pull The Wool Over My Eyes** vHW	**(A)**	(78)	Victor 25316
BS 100381-1	**The Glory Of Love** vHW	**(A)**	(78)	Victor 25316
BS 100382-1	**Remember**	**(N)**	(78)	Victor 25329
BS 100383-1	**Walk, Jennie, Walk**	**(N)**	(78)	Victor 25329

(3613) (same personnel):   Chicago – Tuesday, May 12, 1936

[a]	**House Hop**	**(N)**
[b]	**The Dixieland Band** vHW	**(N)**
[c]	**Farewell Blues**	**(N)**

This broadcast on (LP) Sunbeam SB 153.

(3614) (same personnel, except Chris Griffin, tp; and Murray McEachern, tb; replace Geller and Harris):   New York City – Tuesday, May 26, 1936

        Sing Me A Swing Song vHW   **(N)**

This broadcast title on (LP) Aircheck 1.

(3615) (same personnel): New York City – Wednesday, May 27, 1936

BS 101255-1	**House Hop**	**(N)**	(78)	Victor 25350
BS 101255-2	**House Hop**	**(N)**	(LP)	Blu-Disc T-1015
BS 101256-	**These Foolish Things** vHW			unissued
BS 101257-1	**Sing Me A Swing Song** vHW	**(A)**	(78)	Victor 25340
BS 101258-1	**(I Would Do) Anything For You**	**(N)**	(78)	Victor 25350

(3616) (same personnel): New York City – Monday, June 15, 1936

BS 102214-2	**In A Sentimental Mood**	**(N)**	(78)	Victor 25351
BS 102215-1	**I've Found A New Baby**	**(N)**	(78)	Victor 25355
BS 102216-1	**My Melancholy Baby**			unissued
BS 102217-1	**Swingtime In The Rockies**	**(N)**	(78)	Victor 25355
BS 101256-4	**These Foolish Things Remind Me Of You**	**(N)**	(78)	Victor 25351

(3617) (same personnel):
New York City – Tuesday, June 16, 1936

BS 101255-3	**House Hop**	**(N)**	(78)	Victor 25350
BS 102066-X-1	**There's A Small Hotel** vHW	**(A)**	(78)	Victor 25363

(3618) (same personnel, except possibly Mannie Klein, tp; replaces Kazebier):

Hollywood – July/August 1936

	Bugle Call Rag	**(N)**

This title from the soundtrack of "The Big Broadcast of 1937" issued on (LP) Extreme Rarities 1002.

(3619) (same personnel, except Mannie Klein, tp; replaces Kazebier):
Hollywood –Thursday, August 13, 1936

PBS 97710-1	**You Turned The Tables On Me** vHW	**(A)**	(78)	Victor 25391
PBS 97711-1	**Here's Love In Your Eyes**	**(A)**	(78)	Victor 25391
PBS 97712-1	**Pick Yourself Up**	**(N)**	(78)	Victor 25387
PBS 97713-1	**Down South Camp Meeting**	**(N)**	(78)	Victor 25387

(D. Russell Connor suggests that Stacy is not present on 97712/97713.)

(3620) (same personnel, except Sterling Bose, tp; Vido Musso, ts; replace Klein and Clark):
Hollywood – Tuesday, August 18, 1936

	Sugar Foot Stomp	**(N)**

This early "Camel Caravan" broadcast title on (LP) Radiola 19, Sunbeam SB 149.

(3621) (same personnel, except perhaps Dick Clark, ts; added):
Hollywood – Friday, August 21, 1936

PBS 97748-1	**St. Louis Blues**	**(N)**	(78)	Victor 25411
PBS 97750-1	**Love Me Or Leave Me**	**(S)**	(78)	Victor 25406
PBS 97751-2	**Bugle Call Rag**	**(N)**	(LP)	Victor(G) LPM10022

(matrix 97749 was not used)

(3622) (same personnel as August 18, except Zeke Zarchey, tp; replaces Erwin):
probably New York City – Tuesday, September 1, 1936

	Sing, Baby, Sing vHW	**(N)**

This "Camel Caravan" broadcast title on (LP) Sunbeam SB 149, IAJRC 21.

(3623) (Chris Griffin, Ziggy Elman, Zeke Zarchy, tp; Red Ballard, Murray McEarchern, tb; Benny Goodman, cl; Hymie Shertzer, Bill DePew, as; Art Rollini, Vido Musso, ts; Jess Stacy, p; Allan Reuss, g; Harry Goodman, b; Gene Krupa, d; Helen Ward, vo): New York City – Wednesday, October 7, 1936

BS 0798-1	**When A Lady Meets A Gentleman Down South** vHW	**(A)**	(78)	Victor 25434
BS 0799-1	**You're Giving Me A Song And A Dance** vHW	**(N)**	(78)	Victor 25434
BS 02101-1	**Organ Grinder's Swing**	**(A)**	(78)	Victor 25442
BS 02102-1	**Peter Piper**	**(A)**	(78)	Victor 25442
BS 02103-1	**Riffin' At The Ritz**	**(N)**	(78)	Victor 25445
BS 02104-1	**Alexander's Ragtime Band**	**(N)**	(78)	Victor 25445

(Goodman plays alto on 02103. Masters 0799/02101 are consecutive.)

196

(3624) (same personnel):   CBS broadcast, New York City – Tuesday, October 27, 1936

        Jam Session   **(N)**

This broadcast title on (LP) Sunbeam SB 149.

(3625) (same personnel; Ella Fitzgerald, Benny Goodman, vo):

                                         New York City – Thursday, November 5, 1936

BS 02458-1	**Somebody Loves Me**	**(N)**	(78)	Victor 25497
BS 02459-1	**'Tain't No Use** vBG	**(A)**	(78)	Victor 25469
BS 02460-1	**Bugle Call Rag**	**(N)**	(78)	Victor 25467
BS 02461-1	**Jam Session**	**(N)**	(78)	Victor 25497
BS 02463-1	**Goodnight My Love** vEF	**(A)**	(78)	Victor 25461
BS 02464-1	**Take Another Guess** vEF	**(A)**	(78)	Victor 25461
BS 02465-1	**Did You Mean It?** vEF	**(A)**	(78)	Victor 25469

BS 02462 was not used for this session. Victor 25469 was withdrawn. Victor 25461 was also withdrawn, then re-issued using matrix BS 04235 *Goodnight My Love*, with vocal by Frances Hunt, backed with *'Taint No Use*. This happened because Ella Fitzgerald was contracted to Decca.

(3626) (same personnel):   Hotel Pennsylvania, New York City – Wednesday, November 25, 1936

        Jam Session   **(N)**
        'Tain't Good vHW   **(N)**
        Mean To Me   **(N)**
        Goodnight My Love vHW   **(A)**
        Pick Yourself Up   **(N)**

This CBS broadcast (from the Madhattan Room) on (LP) Jazz Archives 49.

(3627) (same personnel, except Irving Goodman, tp; replaces Zarchey):

                                   CBS broadcast, New York City – Tuesday, December 8, 1936

        Mean To Me   **(A)**

This title on (LP) Sunbeam SB 149.

(3628) (same personnel):   New York City – Wednesday, December 9, 1936

BS 03549-1	**When You And I were Young, Maggie**	**(A)**	(78)	Victor 25492
BS 03550-1	**Gee, But You're Swell** vHW	**(A)**	(78)	Victor 25486
BS 03551-2	**Smoke Dreams** vHW	**(A)**	(78)	Victor 25486
BS 03552-1	**Swing Low, Sweet Chariot**	**(N)**	(78)	Victor 25492
T-2435-1	**Smoke Dreams** (incomplete)	**(A)**	(LP)	Blu-Disc T 1015

(T-2435-1 was a test)

(3629) (same personnel):   Hotel Pennsylvania, New York City – Wednesday, December 9, 1936

        Swing Low, Sweet Chariot   **(N)**

This CBS broadcast title (from the Madhattan Room) on (LP) Sunbeam SB 149.

(3630) (same personnel):   CBS broadcast, New York City – Tuesday, December 15, 1936

        An Apple A Day   **(A)**

This title on (LP) Dr. Jazz W2X 40350, (AC) Dr. Jazz WTX 40350, (CD) Zeta ZET723

(3631) (same personnel; Margaret McCrae, Jimmy Rushing, vo):

                                   New York City – Wednesday, December 30, 1936

BS 03872-1	**He Ain't Got Rhythm** vJR	**(A)**	(78)	Victor 25505
BS 03873-1	**Never Should Have Told You** vMM	**(A)**	(78)	Victor 25500
BS 03874-1	**This Year's Kisses** vMM	**(A)**	(78)	Victor 25505
BS 03875-1	**You Can Tell She Comes From Dixie** vMM	**(A)**	(78)	Victor 25500

Notes: Before again listing the full personnel for the Benny Goodman orchestra it is perhaps relevant to comment that the saxophonists double on clarinets on some numbers (*Down South Camp Meeting, Wrappin' It Up,* etc). The sound quality on many of the Sunbeam albums is poor, particularly on those numbered SB-116 to SB-127. As a result it is often difficult to hear Stacy. The Madhattan Room was situated in the Hotel Pennsylvania in New York City. When the Goodman band is here listed on a broadcast from the Hotel Pennsylvania it also means the performance came from The Madhattan Room.

      For January 6, 1937, Connor lists a band version of *Stompin' At The Savoy*, from a short-wave broadcast to the BBC, via CBS, issued on (LP/AC) Dr. Jazz 40350.

      This is actually a quartet version, wrongly dated on the album sleeve.

(3701) **BENNY GOODMAN and His ORCHESTRA** (Harry James, Ziggy Elman, Chris Griffin, tp; Red Ballard, Murray McEachern, tb; Benny Goodman, cl; Hymie Shertzer, Bill DePew, as; Art Rollini, Vido Musso, ts; Jess Stacy, p; Allan Reuss, g; Harry Goodman, b; Gene Krupa, d; Frances Hunt, vo):

New York City – Thursday, January 14, 1937

BS 04235-1	**Goodnight My Love**	**(A)**	(78)	Victor 25461
BS 04236-1	**I Want To Be Happy**	**(A)**	(78)	Victor 25510
BS 04237-1	**Chlo-e (Song Of The Swamp)**	**(I/A/S)**	(78)	Victor 25531
BS 04238-1	**Rosetta**	**(N)**	(78)	Victor 25510

(3702) (same personnel):   Camel Caravan broadcast, New York City – Tuesday, January 19, 1937

[a]	**I Want To Be Happy**	**(N)**
[b]	**Swing Low, Sweet Chariot**	**(N)**

These CBS broadcast titles on (LP/AC) Dr. Jazz 40350, (CD) Zeta ZET723

(3703) (same personnel):   Hotel Pennsylvania, New York City – Wednesday, January 27, 1937

            Sometimes I'm Happy   **(N)**

This CBS broadcast title on (LP) Sunbeam SB 149.

(3704) (same personnel):   Hotel Pennsylvania, New York City – Wednesday, February 3, 1937

            Japanese Sandman   **(S)**

This CBS broadcast title on (LP/AC) Dr. Jazz 40350, (CD) Zeta ZET723

(3705) **LIONEL HAMPTON and His ORCHESTRA** (Ziggy Elman, tp; Hymie Shertzer, George Koenig, as; Art Rollini, Vido Musso, ts; Jess Stacy, p; Allan Reuss, g; Harry Goodman, b; Gene Krupa, d; Lionel Hampton, vb, d*, vo):

New York City – Monday, February 8, 1937

04582-1	**My Last Affair**	vLH	**(A)**	(78)	Victor 25527
04582-2	**My Last Affair**	vLH	**(A)**	(LP)	RCA(F) 430.665
04583-1	**Jivin' The Vibes**		**(N)**	(78)	Victor 25535
04584-1	**The Mood That I'm In**	vLH	**(A)**	(78)	Victor 25527
04585-1	**Stomp** (Hampton Stomp) *		**(S)**	(78)	Victor 25535

other releases:
all five takes: (LP) RCA(F) 430.655, NL89583(2), (CD) RCA Jazz Tribune(F) 74321 15525(2)
all takes -1: (LP) Bluebird AXM6-5536, RCA LPM-575, RCA(F) PM42393, (CD) Classics 524
04582-1   (LP) RCA(F) 741.077, RCA(G) LPM10024, (CD) ASV Living Era CD AJA5090
04583-1   (LP) Victor LPT-18, Camden CAL402, Camden(E) CDN129, First Edition DMM4-0456, RCA(F) 430.249,
                 730.640, Bluebird ND82433, (CD) Le Jazz CD1, Past CD9789
04584-1   (LP) RCA(F) 741.077, RCA(G) LPM10024
04585-1   (LP) RCA LPM6702-2. RCA(F) 741.077, Bluebird ND82433, (CD) ASV Living Era CD AJA 5090

(3706) **BENNY GOODMAN and His ORCHESTRA** (personnel as for January 14, except George Koenig, as; replaces DePew):   Hotel Pennsylvania, New York City – Wednesday, March 3, 1937

            Sometimes I'm Happy   **(N)**

This CBS broadcast title from the Madhattan Room on (LP) Columbia ML4590, CL818, Philips BBL7010, B07007L;
     (CD) Columbia 472990 2

(3707) (same personnel):   Hotel Pennsylvania, New York City – Thursday, March 25, 1937

            Down South Camp Meeting   **(N)**

This CBS broadcast title from the Madhattan Room on (LP) Columbia ML4590,CL818, Philips BBL7010, B07007L;
     (CD) Columbia 472990 2, Jazzmen 625-50-015

(3708) (same personnel):   Camel Caravan broadcast, New York City – Tuesday, April 13, 1937

            Minnie The Moocher's Wedding Day   **(N)**

This CBS broadcast title on (LP) Columbia ML4591, CL818, Philips BBL7010, B07007L; (CD) Columbia 472990 2

(3709) **LIONEL HAMPTON and His ORCHESTRA** (Cootie Williams, tp; Lawrence Brown, tb; Johnny Hodges, as; Jess Stacy, p; Allan Reuss, g; John Kirby, b; Cozy Cole, d; Lionel Hampton, vb, vo):

New York City – Wednesday, April 14, 1937

07792-1	**Buzzin' Round With The Bee**	**(S/A)**		Victor 22575
07793-1	**Whoa Babe** vLH	**(S)**		Victor 25575
07794-1	**Stompology** (I Got Rhythm)	**(N)**		Victor 25601

Mezz Mezzrow is listed as clarinet on this session, but cannot be heard.

other releases:
all titles: (LP) RCA LPM-575, RCA(F) PM42393, NL89583(2), Bluebird AXM6-5536, RCA(F) 730.640.
      (CD) RCA Jazz Tribune (F) 74321 15525(2), Classics 524, ASV Living Era CD AJA5090, Fremeaux & Associes FA211
07792-1 (LP) Camden CAL402, Camden(E) CDN129, Victor LPT-18, RCA(F), 430.655, 430.725
      (CD) Bluebird ND86458, Le Jazz CD1
07793-1 (LP) RCA LPM2318, RCA(F) 430.655, RCA(G) LPM10024
      (CD) RCA Jazz Edition CL89806, Phontastic PHONT-CD-7663, Best of Jazz 4010
07794-1 (LP) Victor LJM1000, HMV CLP1023, RCA(F) 130.214, 73.390, 430-725
      (CD) Bluebird ND86458, Le Jazz CD1, Past CD9789

(3710) (Buster Bailey, cl; Johnny Hodges, as; Jess Stacy, p; Allan Reuss, g; John Kirby, b; Cozy Cole, d; Lionel Hampton,
vb, d*, p#):   New York City – Monday, April 26, 1937

07864-1	**On The Sunny Side Of The Street** vLH	**(A)**	(78)	Victor 25592
07865-1	**Rhythm, Rhythm**	**(S)**	(78)	Victor 25586
07866-1	**China Stomp** #	**(N)**	(78)	Victor 25586
07867-1	**I Know That You Know** *	**(N)**	(78)	Victor 25592

on this title Stacy plays the bass part to Lionel Hampton's two-finger piano playing. *Rhythm, Rhythm* is based upon *I Got Rhythm* and *China Stomp* upon *Chinatown, My Chinatown*. Bailey does not appear to be present on 07864 and Hodges not on 07866.

Other releases:
all titles: (LP) RCA LPM-575, Bluebird AXM6-5536, RCA(F) 730.640, NL89583, PM42393; (CD) Classics 524
07864-1 (LP) Victor LPT-19, RCA LPM2318, RCA(F) 75.480, 430.725, Time-Life STL-J19, RCA CL89806, Readers Digest
      RDS6522, (CD) Bluebird ND86458, ASV Living Era CD AJA5090, Le Jazz CD1, Best Of Jazz 4010, Jazz Roots
      CD56056, Giants of Jazz 53050, Past CD9789, Fremeaux & Associes FA211
07865-1 (LP) Victor LPM1000, HMV CLP1023, RCA(F) 430.249, (CD) Bluebird ND82433, ASV Living Era CD AJA5172,
      Past CD9789
07866-1 (LP) RCA(F) 430.249, (CD) Bluebird ND82433, Giants of Jazz 53050
07867-1 (LP) Camden CAL402, CamdenE CDN129, RCA(F) 430.249, (CD) Bluebird ND82433, Jazz Roots CD56056,
      Giants of Jazz 53050

(3711) **BENNY GOODMAN and His ORCHESTRA** (personnel as for March 3, 1937):
      Camel Caravan broadcast, New York City – Tuesday, April 27, 1937

      Remember   **(N)**
This CBS broadcast title on (LP) MGM E3790, MGM(E) C810, Verve 2317056, Giants of Jazz 1028, Sounds Great 8004.

(3712) (same personnel):   broadcast, Hotel Pennsylvania, New York City – Wednesday, April 28, 1937

[a]	**Johnny One Note**	**(S)**
[b]	**Blue Hawaii**	**(N)**
[c]	**That Foolish Feeling** vFH	**(N)**
[d]	**Goodbye**	**(N)**
[e]	**Trust In Me** vFH	**(N)**
[f]	**Carelessly** vFH	**(N)**
[g]	**I Want To Be Happy**	**(A)**
[h]	**More Than You Know**	**(N)**

This CBS broadcast on (LP) Sounds Great 8004.

(3713) (same personnel):   WNEW broadcast, New York City – Thursday, April 29, 1937
      You Turned The Tables On Me vHW   **(A)**
This "Make Believe Ballroom" broadcast title on (LP) Columbia ML4591, CL818, Philips BBL7010, BBL7007L;
      (CD) Columbia 462990 2

(3714) (same personnel):   Hotel Pennsylvania, New York City – Thursday, April 29, 1937
      Alexander's Ragtime Band   **(N)**
      Big John Special   **(S)**
These Mutual broadcast titles on (LP) Sounds Great 8004.

(3715) (same personnel):   Hotel Statler, Boston – Friday, April 30, 1937
      Camel Hop   **(N)**
This broadcast (unknown network) title on (LP) Sounds Great 8004.

(3716) (same personnel):   CBS, Camel Caravan broadcast, New York City – Tuesday, May 11, 1937

   [a]   **Let's Dance**   **(N)**

   [b]   **Blue Hawaii**   **(N)**

[a] on (LP) Columbia ML/OL4613, CBS set 66429, Philips BBL7009, B07006L; (CD) Columbia 472990 2

[b] on (LP) First Time 1507, Jazztone 5114, Big Band Landmarks/Archives XXII, Onward To Yesterday ON1507,
      Festival 153, Musidisc MU153 & 30, Kings of Jazz KLJ-20005, Cicala BLJ8013, Black Lion INT127.034

(3717) (same personnel)   CBS, Camel Caravan broadcast, New York City – Tuesday, May 25, 1937

        Chlo-e (Song of the Swamp)   **(S)**

This broadcast title on (LP) MGM E3790, MGM(E) C810, Verve 2317056, (CD) Dejavu DVRECD08

(3718) (same personnel):   CBS broadcast, Los Angeles – Tuesday, June 29, 1937

   [a]   **Alexander's Ragtime Band**   **(N)**

   [b]   **When It's Sleepytime Down South**   **(N)**

[a] on (LP) MGM E3790, MGM(E) C810, Verve 2683055

[b] on (LP) MGM E3790, MGM(E) C810, Verve V8582, 2317056, 2428502.

(3719) (same personnel, plus Johnny 'Scat' Davis, vo):   Hollywood – summer 1937

   [a]   **Sing, Sing, Sing**   **(N)**

   [b]   **Hooray For Hollywood** vJD   **(N)**

These titles and other selections from the film "Hollywood Hotel" appear on (LP) Warners Bros. 3XX2736, United Artists
LA361H, Hollywood Soundstage 5004, Extreme Rarities 1002, EOH 99601 (CD) Great Movie Themes CD60008.

[a] on (VC) Jazz & Jazz Vid Jazz 25. [b] on (LP) RCA(G) ZL70136, (AC) ZK70136

(3720) (same personnel):   Hollywood – Tuesday, July 6, 1937

PBS 09569-1	**Peckin'**	**(N)**	(78)	Victor 25621
PBS 09570-1	**Can't We Be Friends?**	**(N)**	(78)	Victor 25621
PBS 09570-2	**Can't We Be Friends?**	**(N)**	(78)	Victor 25621
PBS 09570-3	**Can't We Be Friends?**	**(N)**	(LP)	RCA(F) 741.044
PBS 09571-1	**Sing, Sing, Sing** – Part 1	**(N)**	(LP)	RCABb AXM2 5568
PBS 09571-2	**Sing, Sing, Sing** – Part 1	**(N)**	(78)	Victor 36205
PBS 09571-3	**Sing, Sing, Sing** – Part 1	( )	(LP)	Time-Life STBB03
PBS 09572-1	**Sing, Sing, Sing** – Part 2	**(N)**	(LP)	Time-Life STBB03
PBS 09572-2	**Sing, Sing, Sing** – Part 2	**(N)**	(78)	Victor 36205
PBS 09572-3	**Sing, Sing, Sing** – Part 2	( )	(LP)	JAZ 41

(3721) (same personnel):   CBS, Camel Caravan broadcast, Los Angeles – Tuesday, July 6, 1937

   [a]   **Can't We Be Friends?**   **(N)**

   [b]   **Bugle Call Rag**   **(N)**

[a] on (LP) MGM E3788, MGM(E) C805, Verve 2317056

[b] on (LP) Columbia ML4591, CL819, CS8643, Harmony HS11271, CBS S63367, S52688, Time-Life STLJO5, CBS set
66420, Philips BBL7010, BO7007L, BO7665R; (CD) Columbia 472990 2

(3722) (same personnel; Betty Van, vo):   Hollywood – Wednesday, July 7, 1937

PBS 09576-3	**Roll 'Em**	**(S)**	(78)	Victor 25627
PBS 09577-1	**When It's Sleepytime Down South**	**(N)**	(LP)	RCABb AXM2 5568
PBS 09577-2	**When It's Sleepytime Down South**	**(N)**	(78)	Victor 25634
PBS 09578-2	**Afraid To Dream** vBV	**(A)**	(78)	Victor 25627
PBS 09579-2	**Changes**	**(N)**	(LP)	RCABb AXM2-5568
PBS 09579-3	**Changes**	**(N)**	(78)	Victor 25634

(3723) (same personnel):   Camel Caravan broadcast, Los Angeles – Tuesday, July 13, 1937

        King Porter Stomp   **(N)**

This CBS broadcast title on (LP) Columbia ML4591, ML/OL4614, CL818, CL820, CS8643, album P4M-5678, CBS S52688,
      Philips BBL7010, B07007L, set 66420; (CD) Columbia 472990 2

(3724) (same personnel):   Camel Caravan broadcast, Los Angeles – Tuesday, July 20, 1937

        Swing Low, Sweet Chariot   **(N)**

This CBS broadcast title on (LP) MGM E3788, MGM (E) C805, Verve 2317056

(3725) (same personnel):   Camel Caravan broadcast, Los Angeles – Tuesday, July 27, 1937

        Jam Session   **(N)**

This CBS broadcast title on (LP) Columbia JZ1, Philips BO7100l, Parlophone PMC1222, (CD) Jazzmen 625-50-015

(3726) (same personnel):   Camel Caravan broadcast, Los Angeles – Tuesday, August 3, 1937

           Always   **(N)**

This CBS broadcast title on (LP) Columbia ML4590, ML/OL4514, CL817, Philips BBL7010, B07007L, CBS set 66420;
    (CD) Columbia 472990 2

(3727) (same personnel):   Camel Caravan broadcast, Los Angeles – Tuesday, August 10, 1937

[a]	**Remember**	**(N)**
[b]	**Me, Myself and I** vBG	**(A)**
[c]	**Mother Goose Marches On** *	**(N)**
[d]	**Swing, Benny, Swing** *	**(N)**
[e]	**Sing, Sing, Sing** – Part 2	**(A)**

This CBS broadcast on (LP) Carib 810, Mirror 165, Sunbeam SB 146, (CD) Phontastic NCD8841/42
* Goodman does not play on these titles, which have vocals by the Meyer Alexander Chorus, plus Bloch & Sully on Swing, Benny, Swing.

(3728) (same personnel):   Camel Caravan broadcast, Los Angeles – Tuesday, August 17, 1937

[a]	**That Naughty Waltz**	**(N)**
[b]	**Satan Takes A Holiday**	**(S)**
[c]	**Chlo-e**	**(I)**
[d]	**Caravan**	**(N)**

These CBS broadcast titles on (LP) Mirror 165, Sunbeam SB 146, Carib 810; (CD) Phontastic NCD8841/42
[d] also on (LP) Columbia ML4591, ML/OL4613, CL819, Philips BBL7009, B07006L, B07665R, CBS set 66420; (CD)
Columbia 472990 2.

(3729) (same personnel; Martha Tilton, Pat O'Malley, vo):

                                           Camel Caravan broadcast, Los Angeles – Tuesday, August 24, 1937

[a]	**Sometimes I'm Happy**		**(N)**
[b]	**Minnie The Moocher's Wedding Day**		**(N)**
[d]	**Bye Bye Pretty Baby**	#	**(N)**
[d]	**Swing High, Swing Low** vPOM	#	**(N)**
[e]	**Sailboat In The Moonlight** vMT		**(N)**
[f]	**Roll 'Em**		**(S)**

These CBS broadcast titles on Sunbeam SB 147 (CD) Phontastic NCD8841/42
# indicates that Goodman not on these titles, which also have vocals by the Meyer Alexander Chorus.

(3730) (same personnel):   Camel Caravan broadcast, Los Angeles – Tuesday, August 31, 1937

[a]	**Camel Hop**	**(N)**
[b]	**La Cucaracha**	**(N)**
[c]	**The Blue Danube** vMAC	**(N)**
[d]	**Swing Song** vMAC, POM	**(N)**
[e]	**The Dixieland Band** vMT	**(N)**
[f]	**House Hop**	**(S)**

These CBS broadcast titles on (LP) Sunbeam SB 147 (CD) Phontastic NCD8841/42
MAC = Meyer Alexander Chorus.

(3731) **LIONEL HAMPTON and His ORCHESTRA** (Ziggy Elman, tp; Vido Musso, cl; Art Rollini, ts; Jess Stacy, p; Allan
Reuss, g; Johnny Miller, b; Cozy Cole, d; Lionel Hampton, vb, d*, vo):

                                              Hollywood – Sunday, September 5, 1937

PBS 09680-1	**The Object Of My Affection** vLH	**(S)**	(78)	HMV(Sw) JK2033
PBS 09680-2	**The Object Of My Affection** vLH	**(S)**	(78)	Victor 25699
PBS 09681-2	**Judy** vLH	**(N)**	(78)	Victor 25699
PBS 09682-2	**Baby, Won't You Please Come Home** vLH	**(A)**	(78)	Victor 25674
PBS 09683-2	**Everybody Loves My Baby** vLH	**(A)**	(78)	Victor 25682
PBS 09684-1	**After You've Gone** * vLH	**(S/A)**	(78)	Victor 25674
PBS 09685-1	**I Just Couldn't Take It, Baby** vLH	**(A)**	(78)	Victor 25682

other releases:
all takes: (LP) RCA(F) NL89583(2), (CD) RCA(F) Jazz Tribune 74321 15525(2)
all titles except 09680-1: (LP) RCA AXM6-5536, RCA(F) 430.655, PM42393, (CD) Classics 524
all titles except 09680-2: (LP) RCA(F) 741.077
09680-1 (CD) Bluebird ND82433
09680-2 (LP) Camden CAL402, Camden(E) CDN129, (CD) ASV Living Era CD AJA5090

09681-2 (LP) RCA(G) LPM10024
09682-2 (LP) Camden CAL402, Camden(E) CDN129
09683-2 (LP) Victor LEJ-5, (CD) ASV Living Era CD AJA5090, Le Jazz CD1, RCA Bluebird ND86458
09684-1 (LP) Victor LJM1000, HMV CLP1023, Camden CAL517,Camden(E) CDN138, (CD) RCA Bluebird ND82433,
      Affinity AFS 1036-4, Giants of Jazz 53050
09685-1 (LP) Victor LJM1000, HMV CLP1023, RCA(G) LPM10024; (CD) Past 9789

(3732) BENNY GOODMAN and His ORCHESTRA (personnel as for March 3, 1937):

Hollywood – Monday, September 6, 1937

PBS 09688-2	**Bob White** vMT	**(N)**	(78)	Victor 25683
PBS 09689-1	**Sugarfoot Stomp**	**(N)**	(78)	Victor 25678
PBS 09689-2	**Sugarfoot Stomp**	**(N)**	(LP)	RCABb AXM2 5568
PBS 09690-2	**I Can't Give You Anything But Love** vMT	**(S/A)**	(78)	Victor 25678
PBS 09690-3	**I Can't Give You Anything But Love** vMT	**( )**	(LP)	Veronica 1
PBS 09691-1	**Minnie The Moocher's Wedding Day**	**(N)**	(78)	Victor 25683

(3733) (same personnel):   Camel Caravan broadcast. Los Angeles – Tuesday, September 7, 1937
          Oh, Lady Be Good!   **(N)**
This CBS broadcast title on (LP) IAJRC 21, Sunbeam SB 149

(3734) (same personnel):   Camel Caravan broadcast, Dallas – Tuesday, September 14, 1937
          Peckin'   **(N)**
This CBS broadcast title on (LP) Columbia ML4590, ML/Ol4613, CL817, Philips BBL7009, B07006L, CBS set 66420;
    (CD) Columbia 472990 2.

(3735) (same personnel):   CBS, Camel Caravan broadcast, Kansas City – Tuesday, September 21, 1937
   [a]   **Madhouse**   **(S)**
   [b]   **Moten Swing**   **(N)**
[a] on (LP) MGM E3788, MGM(E) C805, Verve 2317056;
[b] on (CD) Columbia 472990 2.

(3736) (Harry James, Irving Goodman, Chris Griffin, tp; Red Ballard, Vernon Brown, tb; Benny Goodman, cl; Hymie
Shertzer, George Koenig, as; Art Rollini, Vido Musso, ts; Jess Stacy, p; Allan Reuss, g; Harry Goodman, b; Gene Krupa, d;
Martha Tilton, vo):   broadcast, Hotel Pennsylvania, New York City – Saturday, October 13, 1937
   [a]   **In The Shade Of The Old Apple Tree**   **(N)**
   [b]   **That Old Feeling**   vMT   **(A)**
   [c]   **Moonlight On The Highway**   **(S)**
   [d]   **The Moon Got In My Eyes** vMT   **(N)**
   [e]   **Chlo-e**   **(I/S)**
   [f]   **I'd Like To See Samoa of Samoa** vMT   **(S)**
   [g]   **Caravan**   **(N)**
   [h]   **Satan Takes A Holiday**   **(S)**
These CBS broadcast titles on (LP) Sunbeam SB 116; (CD) Viper's Nest VN171.
[c] on (CD) Columbia 472990 2.

(3737) (same personnel, except perhaps Ziggy Elman, tp; returns, replacing Irving Goodman):
           broadcast ,Hotel Pennsylvania, New York City – Saturday, 0ctober 16, 1937
   [a]   **House Hop**   **(S)**
   [b]   **So Many Memories** vMT   **(N)**
   [c]   **My Honey's Lovin' Arms**   **(S)**
   [d]   **Bob White** vMT   **(N)**
   [e]   **Marie**   **(N)**
   [f]   **Loch Lomond** vMT,BG   **(N)**
   [g]   **Roll 'Em**   **(S)**
These CBS broadcast titles on (LP) Sunbeam SB 117; (CD) Viper's Nest VN171.

(3738) (same personnel: Ziggy Elman definitely back):
           CBS, Camel Caravan broadcast, New York City – Tuesday, 0ctober 19, 1937
   [a]   **Sunny Disposish**   **(N)**
   [b]   **Rose Room**   **(S)**
[a] on (LP) Columbia ML4590, ML/OL4613, CL817, Philips BBL7009, B07006L, CBS set 66420; (CD) Columbia 472990 2.
[b] on (LP) Sunbeam SB 149.

(3739) (same personnel)   broadcast, Hotel Pennsylvania, New York City – Wednesday, October 20, 1937

[a]	**Stardust On The Moon** vMT	(N)
[b]	**Dear Old Southland**	(S)
[c]	**So Many Memories** vMT	(N)
[d]	**One O'Clock Jump**	(S)
[e]	**Me, Myself and I** vMT	(N)
[f]	**When It's Sleepytime Down South**	(N)
[g]	**Camel Hop**	(N)

These CBS broadcast titles on (LP) Sunbeam SB 118; (CD) Viper's Nest VN172

(3740) (same personnel):   broadcast, Hotel Pennsylvania, New York City – Thursday, October 21, 1937

[a]	**Minnie The Moocher's Wedding Day**	(N)
[b]	**Afraid To Dream** vMT	(N)
[c]	**Moonlight On The Highway**	(S)
[d]	**Once In A While** vMT	(N)
[e]	**Sugar Foot Stomp**	(N)
[f]	**More Than You Know**	(N)
[g]	**The Dixieland Band** vMT	(N)

These Mutual broadcast titles on Sunbeam (LP) SB 119; (CD) Viper's Nest VN172.

(3741) (same personnel, except Murray McEachern, tb; replaces Brown):

                                         New York City – Friday, October 22, 1937

BS 015535-1	**Let That Be A Lesson To You** vMT	(N)	(78)	Victor 25708
BS 015536-1	**Can't Teach My Old Heart New Tricks** vMT	(N)	(78)	Victor 25711
BS 015537-1	**I've Hitched My Wagon To A Star** vMT	(N)	(78)	Victor 25708
BS 015538-1	**Pop-Corn Man** vMT	(N)	(78)	Victor 25808

Pop-Corn Man was withdrawn one week after its release date.

Victor 25808 was subsequently re-released, coupling *Always and Always* with *oooOOOh BOOM!*

(3742) (same personnel, except Vernon Brown, tb; for McEarchern)

                     broadcast, Hotel Pennsylvania, New York City – Saturday, October 23, 1937

[a]	**In The Shade of the Old Apple Tree**	(N)
[b]	**You're My Desire** vMT	(N)
[c]	**Am I Blue?**	(S)
[d]	**Someday Sweetheart**	(N)
[e]	**Bob White** vMT	(N)
[f]	**Yours and Mine** vMT	(N)
[g]	**Jam Session**	(N)

These CBS titles on (LP) Sunbeam SB 120, Mirror 154, Strumthorpe Mews 193749; (CD) Viper's Nest VN173.

[a] on (CD) Columbia 472990 2. [g] on (LP) Sunbeam SB 119.

(3743) (same personnel):   broadcast, Hotel Pennsylvania, New York City – Wednesday, October 27, 1937

[a]	**When Buddha Smiles**	(N)
[b]	**Cherry**	(A)
[c]	**Swing Low, Sweet Chariot**	(N)
[d]	**Star Dust**	(N)
[e]	**The Lady Is A Tramp** vMT	(A)
[f]	**So Many Memories** vMT	(N)
[g]	**Swingtime In The Rockies**	(N)

These CBS broadcast titles on (LP) Sunbeam SB 121; (CD) Viper's Nest VN173.

[a] on (CD) Columbia 472990 2.

Cherry is actually from an undated broadcast.

(3744) (same personnel):   broadcast, Hotel Pennsylvania New York City – Tuesday, October 30, 1937

[a]	**Makin' Whoopee**	(N)
[b]	**Farewell My Love** vMT	(N)
[c]	**The Lady Is A Tramp** vMT	(N)
[d]	**Love Me Or Leave Me**	(S)
[e]	**Once In A While** vMT	(N)
[f]	**You And I Know** vMT	(S)

These CBS broadcast titles on (LP) Sunbeam SB 122; (CD) Viper's Nest VN174.

(3745) (same personnel):   CBS, Camel Caravan broadcast, New York City – Tuesday, November 2, 1937
   [a]   **Chicago (That Toddlin' Town)**   **(N)**
   [b]   **Ridin' High**   **(N)**
[a] on (LP) MGM E3788, MGM(E) C805, Verve 2317056. [b] on Columbia ML4590, ML/OL4613, CL817, P4M-5678, Philips
BBL7009, B07006L, Time-Life STLJ05; (CD) Columbia 472990 2.

(3746) (same personnel):   broadcast, Madhattan Room, New York City – Wednesday, November 3, 1937
              At The Darktown Strutters' Ball   **(N)**
This CBS broadcast title on Columbia ML4591, ML/OL4614, CL819, Philips BBL7010, B07007L, CBS set 66420;
(CD) Columbia 472990 2.

(3747) (same personnel):   broadcast, Hotel Pennsylvania, New York City – Thursday, November 4, 1937
   [a]   **Changes**   **(N)**
   [b]   **If It's The Last Thing I Do** vMT   **(N)**
   [c]   **Someday Sweetheart**   **(N)**
   [d]   **So Many Memories** vMT   **(N)**
   [e]   **Life Goes To A Party**   **(S)**
   [f]   **Farewell My Love**   vMT   **(N)**
   [g]   **In The Shade Of The Old Apple Tree**   **(N)**
   [h]   **Blossoms on Broadway**   vMT   **(A)**
   [i]   **Walk, Jennie, Walk**   **(N)**
   [j]   **I Can't Give You Anything But Love, Baby** vMT **(S)**
These Mutual broadcast titles on (LP) Sunbeam SB 123; (CD) Viper's Nest VN174.

(3748) (same personnel):   broadcast, Hotel Pennsylvania, New York City – Saturday, November 6, 1937
   [a]   **That Naughty Waltz**   **(N)**
   [b]   **Once In A While** vMT   **(N)**
   [c]   **Pop-Corn Man**   vMT   **(N)**
   [d]   **You Showed Me The Way**   vMT   **(N)**
   [e]   **Blue Skies**   **(N)**
   [f]   **If It's The Last Thing I Do** vMT   **(N)**
   [g]   **Life Goes To A Party**   **(S)**
These CBS broadcast titles on (CD) Viper's Nest VN175; [a], [g] on (CD) Columbia 472990 2. [a], [b], [c] on (LP) Sunbeam
SB 127; [d], [e], [f], [g] on Sunbeam SB 124.

(3749) (same personnel, except Will Bradley, tb; substituting for Brown):
                              Camel Caravan broadcast, New York City – Tuesday, November 9, 1937
              Someday Sweetheart   **(N)**
This CBS broadcast title on Columbia ML4591, ML/OL4613, CL819, Philips BBL7009, B07006L, CBS set 66420;
(CD) Columbia 472990 2.

(3750) (same personnel, except Murray McEarchern, tb; replaces Bradley):
                                     New York City – Friday, November 12, 1937

BS 017039-1	**You Took The Words Right Out**				
	Of My Heart vMT	**(A)**	(78)	Victor 25720
BS 017040-1	**Mama, That Moon Is Here Again** vMT	**(A)**	(78)	Victor 25720
BS 017041-1	**Loch Lomond** vMT,BG	**(A)**	(78)	Victor 25717
BS 017042-1	**Camel Hop**	**(A)**	(78)	Victor 25717
BS 017043-1	**True Confession** vMT	**(A/S)**	(LP)	RCABb AXM2 5557
BS 017044-2	**Life Goes To A Party**	**(S)**	(78)	Victor 25726

(3751) (same personnel, except Will Bradley, tb; replaces McEarchern):
                          broadcast, Hotel Pennsylvania, New York City – Saturday, November 13, 1937
              When Buddha Smiles   **(N)**
This CBS broadcast title on (LP) MGM E3788, MGM(E) C805, Verve(E) VLP9120

(3752) (same personnel):   Camel Caravan broadcast, New York City – Tuesday, November 16, 1937
   [a]   **Stardust**   **(N)**
   [b]   **If It's The Last Thing I Do** vMT   **(N)**
   [c]   **You Took The Words Right**
                  Out Of My Heart vMT   **(N)**
   [d]   **Laughing At Life**   **(S)**

[e]	**Mama, That Moon Is Here Again** vMT	**(N)**
[f]	**Big John's Special**	**(S)**

This CBS broadcast on (LP) Fanfare 13-113; (CD) Phontastic NCD8843/44. [f] on (LP) MGM E3789, MGM(E) C807, Verve V8582, 2317056, 2428502, Verve Special 2352 099 (CD) Deja Vu DVRECD08

(3753) (same personnel, except Vernon Brown, tb; replaces Bradley):

broadcast, Hotel Pennsylvania, New York City – Wednesday, November 17, 1937

	Camel Hop	**(N)**

This CBS broadcast title on (LP) MGM E3790, MGM(E) C810, Verve 2317056.

(3754) (same personnel):   broadcast, Hotel Pennsylvania, New York City – Friday, November 19, 1937

	Star Dust	**(A)**

This broadcast (unknown network) title on (LP) Columbia ML4591, ML/OL4613, CL819, Philips BBL7009, B07006L, CBS set 66420; (CD) Columbia 472990 2.

(3755) (same personnel):   broadcast, Hotel Pennsylvania, New York City – Saturday, November 20, 1937

[a]	**Laughing At Life**	**(S)**
[b]	**You Took The Words Right Out**	
	Of My Heart vMT	**(N)**
[c]	**Sweet Stranger** vMT	**(N)**
[d]	**Down South Camp Meeting**	**(N)**
[e]	**In The Still Of The Night** vMT	**(N)**
[f]	**Mama, That Moon Is Here Again** vMT	**(N)**
[g]	**Swingtime in the Rockies**	**(N)**
[h]	**Farewell My Love** vMT	**(N)**

This CBS broadcast on (LP) Sunbeam SB 125; (CD) Viper's Nest VN175.
[d] on (LP) Radiola 1314; [a], [f] on (CD) Columbia 472990 2.

(3756) (same personnel):   broadcast, Hotel Pennsylvania, New York City – Sunday, November 21, 1937

	Sugar Foot Stomp	**(N)**

This broadcast title (unknown network) on (LP) Columbia ML4590, ML/OL4614, CL818, Philips BBL7010, B07007L, CBS set 66420; (CD) Columbia 472990 2.

(3757) (same personnel, except Will Bradley, tb; replaces Brown):

CBS, Camel Caravan broadcast, New York City – Tuesday, November 23, 1937

[a]	**All Of Me**	**(N)**
[b]	**Vieni, Vieni**	**(N)**
[c]	**Clarinet Marmalade**	**(N)**

[c] on (LP) Columbia ML4591, ML/OL4613, CL819, P4M-5678, Philips BBL7009, BO7006L, CBS set 66420; (CD) Columbia 472990 2.
[a], [b] on (LP) First Time 1507, Jazztone 5114; other issues as for *Blue Hawaii*, 11may37.

(3758) (same personnel):   Camel Caravan broadcast, New York City – Tuesday, November 30, 1937

	St. Louis Blues	**(S)**

This CBS broadcast title on (LP) Columbia ML4590, ML/OL4613, CL817, Philips BBL7009, B07006L, B07665R, CBS set 66420; (CD) Columbia 472990 2, Jazzmen 625-50-015.

(3759) **HARRY JAMES and His ORCHESTRA** (Harry James, Buck Clayton, tp; Earl Warren, as; Herschel Evans, ts; Jack Washington, as, bs; Jess Stacy, p; Walter Page, b; Jo Jones, d; Helen Humes, vo):

New York City – Wednesday, December 1, 1937

B22083-1	**Jubilee** vHH	**(A)**	(78)	Brunswick 8038
B22083-3	**Jubilee** vHH	**(A)**	(LP)	Tax m 8015
B22084-1	**When We're Alone**	**(S)**	(LP)	Tax m 8015
B22084-2	**When We're Alone**	**(S)**	(78)	Brunswick 8035
B22085-1	**(I Can Dream) Can't I?** vHH	**(A)**	(78)	Brunswick 8038
B22086-1	**Life Goes To A Party**	**(S)**	(LP)	Tax m 8015
B22086-2	**Life Goes To A Party**	**(S)**	(78)	Brunswick 8035

Eddie Durham was arranger for this session. He is usually listed as trombonist also, but is not audible. Refer January 6, 1938 (3803) for query on remake session.

other releases:
all titles originally on Brunswick on (LP) Tax m-8015, LP7, TOM 36, (CD) Classics 903

all titles (takes unknown) on (CD) Hep CD1032, Jazz Archives No. 57
all seven takes on (CD) Affinity AFS1009
B22083-1 on (LP) CBS(F) 88493 (AC) Jazz Connoisseur Cassettes JCC77
B22083- on (CD) ASV Living Era CD AJA5120
B22084-2 on (LP) CBS(F) 88493, Big Band Archives BBA1206,
B22084-2 on (CD) Phontastic PHONT-CD-7663,
B22084- on (CD) Pro-Arte Digital CDD507, Kaz CD320
B22085-1 on (LP) CBS(F) 88493 (CD) Jazz Connoisseur Cassettes JCC77
B22086-2 on (LP) CBS(F) 88494, Columbia G31244, C31226 , CBS(E) M67205, M64223, Big Band Archives BBA1206;
    (CD) Delta 24 044
B22086- on (CD) ASV Living Era CD AJA5120, Pro-Arte Digital CDD507, Kaz CD320

(3760) **BENNY GOODMAN and His ORCHESTRA** (Harry James, Ziggy Elman, Chris Griffin, tp; Red Ballard, Vernon Brown, tb; Benny Goodman, cl; Hymie Shertzer, George Koenig, as; Art Rollini, Vido Musso, ts; Jess Stacy, p; Allan Reuss, g; Harry Goodman, b; Gene Krupa, d; Martha Tilton, vo):

New York City – Thursday, December 2, 1937

BS 017044-3	**Life Goes To A Party**	(N)	(78)	Victor 25726
BS 017452-1	**It's Wonderful** vMT	(A)	(78)	Victor 25727
BS 017453-1	**Thanks For The Memory** vMT	(N)	(78)	Victor 25727
BS 017453-2	**Thanks For The Memory** vMT	(S)	(78)	Victor 25727

(3761) (same personnel):

New York City – Friday, December 3, 1937

BS 017454-1	**If Dreams Come True**	(N)	(78)	Victor 25726
BS 017454-2	**If Dreams Come True**	(N)	(LP)	RCA(F) PM43173
BS 017455-1	**I'm Like A Fish Out Of Water** vMT	(N)	(LP)	RCABb AXM2 5557
BS 017456-1	**Sweet Stranger** vMT	(N)	(LP)	RCABb AXM2 5557

(3762) (same personnel):   Camel Caravan broadcast, New York City – Tuesday, December 7, 1937

[a]	**Hallelujah**	(N)
[b]	**I've Got My Love To Keep Me Warm**	(N)

These CBS broadcast titles on (LP), [a] on MGM E3789, MGM(E) C807, Verve 2317056; [b] on MGM E3790, MGM(E) C810, Verve V8582, 2317056, 2428502; (CD) Deja Vu DVRECD08

(3763) (same personnel, except Babe Russin, ts; replaces Musso):

Camel Caravan broadcast, New York City – Tuesday, December 14, 1937

[a]	**Three Little Words**	(N)
[b]	**Josephine**	(N)
[c]	**Dear Old Southland**	(S)
[d]	**I've Found A New Baby**	(N)

These CBS broadcast titles on (LP): [a], [b] on MGM E3788, MGM(E) C805, Verve V8582, 2317056, 2428502; (CD) Deja Vu DVRECD08. [b] on Columbia ML4591, ML/OL4613, CL819, Philips BBL7009, B07006L, CBS set 66420; (CD) Columbia 472990 2. [d] on (LP) Sunbeam SB 149.

(3764) (same personnel):   broadcast, Hotel Pennsylvania, New York City – Thursday, December 16, 1937

	One O'Clock Jump	(I/S)

This Mutual broadcast title on (LP) Sunbeam SB 127.

(3765) (same personnel):   broadcast, Hotel Pennsylvania, New York City – Saturday, December 18, 1937

[a]	**Big John Special**	(S)
[b]	**You Took The Words Right Out Of My Heart** vMT	(N)
[c]	**If Dreams Come True**	(N)
[d]	**Bei Mir Bist Du Schon** vMT	(S)
[e]	**At The Darktown Strutters' Ball**	(N)
[f]	**I've Hitched My Wagon To A Star** vMT	(N)
[g]	**I Wanna Be In Winchell's Column** vMT	(N)
[h]	**All Of Me**	(N)

This CBS broadcast on (LP) Sunbeam SB 126; (CD) Viper's Nest VN176.

(3766) (same personnel):   broadcast, Hotel Pennssylvania, New York City – Wednesday, December 22, 1937

[a]	**Life Goes To A Party**	(S)
[b]	**Sweet Someone** vMT	(N)

[c]	If Dreams Come True		(N)
[d]	Alice Blue Gown		(N)
[e]	Josephine		(N)
[f]	It's Wonderful		(N)
[g]	Rockin' The Town	vMT	(N)

This CBS broadcast on (CD) Viper's Nest VN176.
[a], [b] on (LP) Sunbeam SB 127; [c], [d], [e], [f], [g] on (LP) Sunbeam SB124.

(3801) (same personnel):   Camel Caravan broadcast, New York City – Tuesday, January 4, 1938

If Dreams Come True   **(N)**

This CBS broadcast title on (LP) MGM E3789, MGM(E) C807, Verve V8582, 2317056, 2428502.

(3802) **HARRY JAMES and His ORCHESTRA** (Harry James, Buck Clayton, tp; Vernon Brown, tb; Earl Warren, as; Herschel Evans, ts; Jack Washington, as, bs; Jess Stacy, p; Walter Page, b; Jo Jones, d; Helen Humes, vo):

New York City – Wednesday, January 5, 1938

B22249-1	Texas Chatter		(S)	(78)	Brunswick 8067
B22249-2	Texas Chatter		(S)	(LP)	Tax m 8015
B22250-1	Song Of The Wanderer	vHH	(A)	(78)	Brunswick 8067
B22251-1	It's The Dreamer In Me	vHH	(A)	(78)	Brunswick 8055
B22251-2	It's The Dreamer In Me	vHH	(A)	(LP)	Tax m 8015
B22252-1	One O'Clock Jump		(S)	(78)	Brunswick 8055
B22252-2	One O'Clock Jump		(S)	(78)	Columbia 37142

other releases:
all seven takes on Affinity AFS1009
all titles originally on Brunswick on (CD) Classics 903
B22249-1 on (LP) Tax m-8015, LP7, TOM 36, CBS(F) 88494; (CD) Delta 24 044
B22249-   (CD) Hep CD1032, Jazz Archives No. 57, Kaz CD320
B22250-1 on (LP) Tax m-8015, LP7, TOM 36, CBS(F) 88494, (AC) Jazz Connoisseur Cassettes JCC77
B22250-   (CD) Hep CD1032, Jazz Archives No. 57, Pro Arte Digital CDD507
B22251-1 on (LP) Tax m-8015, LP7, TOM 36, CBS(F) 88494, (AC) Jazz Connoisseur Cassettes JCC77
B22251-   (CD) Hep CD1032, Jazz Archives No. 57
B22252-1 on (LP) Tax m-8015, CBS(F) 88494
B22252-2 on (LP) Tax LP7, TOM 36, CBS(F) 88494
B22252-   (CD) Hep CD1032, Jazz Archives No. 57, ASV Living Era CD, AJA5120, Kaz CD320
(Note that the CBS(F) 88493/88494 LPs are in a double album numbered 88499.)

(3803) **HARRY JAMES and His ORCHESTRA** (same personnel):   New York City – January 6, 1938
B-22083-3	Jubilee	vHH			Brunswick 8038
B-22085-3	(I Can Dream) Can't I?	vHH			Brunswick 8038

These remakes from the December 1, 1937 session are listed thus in the 5th edition of Brian Rust's "Jazz Records 1897-1942". Earlier these titles were shown as probable rejects. It seems likely that this was yet another "dubbing" session, not an actual recording session. There is no trombone audible on B-22083-3 as issued on Tax m-8015, which would further suggest that this take was recorded at the December 1, 1937 session.

(3804) **BENNY GOODMAN AND His ORCHESTRA** (personnel as for December 2, 1937, plus following selected groups:
Sensation Rag/When My Baby Smiles At Me: Chris Griffin, tp; Vernon Brown, tb; Benny Goodman, cl; Jess Stacy, p; Gene Krupa, d:
I'm Coming Virginia: Bobby Hackett, tp; Vernon Brown, tb; Benny Goodman, cl; Babe Russin, ts; Jess Stacy, p; Allen Reuss, g; Harry Goodman, b; Gene Krupa, d:
Blue Reverie: Cootie Williams, tp; Johnny Hodges, ss; Harry Carney, bar; Jess Stacy, p; Allan Reuss, g; Harry Goodman, b; Gene Krupa, d: Carnegie Hall concert, New York City – Sunday, January 16, 1938

[a]	Don't Be That Way	(N)
[b]	Sometimes I'm Happy	(A)
[c]	One O'Clock Jump	(S/A)
[d]	Sensation Rag	(N)
[e]	I'm Coming Virginia	(N)
[f]	When My Baby Smiles At Me	(N)
[g]	Shine	(N)
[h]	Blue Reverie	(S/A)
[i]	Life Goes To A Party	(S)
[j]	Blue Skies	(N)

[k]	**Loch Lomond** vMT, BG	**(A)**
[l]	**Blue Room**	**(N)**
[m]	**Swingtime In The Rockies**	**(N)**
[n]	**Bei Mir Bist Du Schon** vMT	**(S/A)**
[o]	**Sing, Sing, Sing**	**(S/A)**
[p]	**If Dreams Come True**	**(N)**
[q]	**Big John's Special**	**(S)**

With the exception of [b] Sometimes I'm Happy and [p] If Dreams Come True (issued only on (LP) Sunbeam SB 127), which were rejected by Columbia for sound quality reasons, all the Carnegie Hall concert was issued by Columbia in 1950.

(LP) releases of this material included: Columbia ML/OL4341,ML/OL4342, ML4358/4359, CL814, CL815, CL816, CBS 62340/ 62341, CBS set 66202, 66420, Philips BBL7000/7001, BBL7441/7442,B070001/7001L. Refer to Connor for full details.
(CD) CBS CD450983 2, Giants of Jazz 53101/53102, Pilz FM8343-2. (The Pilz excludes [k], [l], [n], [q].
[a], [c] on (CD) Deja Vu DVREC08. [c], [e], [f], [h], [m] on (CD) Jazzterdays JTD102411

(3805) EDDIE CONDON and His WINDY CITY SEVEN (Bobby Hackett, co; George Brunis, tb; Pee Wee Russell, cl; Bud Freeman, ts; Jess Stacy, p; Eddie Condon, g; Art Shapiro, b; George Wettling, d):
Brunswick studios, 1776 Broadway, New York City – Monday, January 17, 1938

P-22306-1	**Love Is Just Around The Corner**	**(N)**	(78)	Commodore 500
P-22306-2	**Love Is Just Around The Corner**	**(N)**	(LP)	Commodore XFL14427
XP-22307-1	**Beat To The Socks**	**(I/A)**	(78)	Commodore 502
XP-22308	**Carnegie Drag**	**(S)**	(78)	Commodore 1500
XP-22309	**Carnegie Jump**	**(S/A)**	(78)	Commodore 1500
P-23310-1	**Ja Da No.2**	**(A)**	(LP)	Commodore XFL14427
P-23310-2	**Ja Da**	**(A)**	(78)	Commodore 500

other releases:
all takes on (LP) Mosaic MR23-123 (23 LP boxed set), London(E) DHMC 1, Commodore(G) 6.24054;
       (CD) Commodore(G) 8.24054
P-22306-1 on (LP) Atlantic SD 2-309, Commodore CCL7007, XFL14427, Time-Life STL-J17.
       (CD) Commodore CCD7007, Classics 742, Topaz TPZ1018, Jazz Roots CD56078, ASV Living Era AJA 5192,
       Commodore CMD24002, Giants of Jazz 53183, (AC) Commodore CCK7007, Time-Life 4TL-J17
P-22306-2 on (LP) Time-Life STL-J17 (CD) Commodore CMD14042, (AC) Time-Life 4TL-J17
P-22307-1 on (LP) Atlantic SD 2-309, Commodore CCL7007, XFL14427. (CD) Commodore CCD7007, Classics 742, Jazz
       Portraits CD14557, Topaz TPZ1026, Jazz Roots CD56078, (AC) Commodore CCK7007
XP-22308 on (LP) Ace of Hearts AHC 179, Commodore CCL7007, FL30.006, XFL14427, Jazztone J1216, Mainstream
       S/6010, 56010, Stateside SL10005, (CD) Commodore CCD7007, Classics 742, Topaz TPZ1018, TPZ1026,
       TPZ1050; (AC) Commodore CCK7007
XP-22309 on (LP) as for XP-22308, except Mainstream S/6010, 56010. (CD) Commodore CDD7007, Classics 742, ASV
       Living Era AJA5172, Topaz TPZ1026, ASV Living Era AJA5192, (AC) Commodore CCK7007
P-22310-1 on (LP) Commodore XFL14427
P-22310-2 on (LP) Atlantic SD 2-309, Commodore CCL7007, FL20,016, XFL14427, Book of the Month Club 10-5557,
       Franklin Mint 47, (CD) Commodore CCD7007, Classics 742, Jazz Roots CD56078, Topaz TPZ1034, Giants of
       Jazz 53183; (AC) Commodore CCK7007, Book of the Month Club 60-5561
reverse of Commodore 502 by Bud Freeman Trio. Commodore 1500 (12") labelled "A Jam Session at Commodore".
London DHMC 1 is record 1 of a double record set.

(3806) THE BUD FREEMAN TRIO (Bud Freeman, ts; Jess Stacy, p; George Wettling, d):
same session

P-22311-1	**You Took Advantage Of Me**	(78)	Commodore 501
P-22311-2	**You Took Advantage Of Me**	(LP)	Commodore XFL14941
P-22312-1	**Three's No Crowd**	(78)	Commodore 501
P-22313-1	**I Got Rhythm**	(78)	Commodore 502
(P-22440-1)	**I Got Rhythm**	(LP)	Meritt 11

other releases:
all takes, except 22440-1: (LP) London(E) HMC5032, Mosaic MR23-123, Commodore(G) 6.24061
P-22311-1 on (LP) Atlantic SD2-309, Commodore XFL14941 (CD) Classics 781
P-22312-1 on (LP) Atlantic SD2-309, Commodore XFL14941 (CD) Classics 781
P-22313-1 on (LP) Atlantic SD2-309, Commodore XFL14941
       (CD) ASV Living Era CD AJA5172, Classics 781, Topaz TPZ1035
The Meritt sleeve lists the recording date for P-22440-1 as February 16, 1938. The ARC/Columbia ledger lists this item as

"Commodore Trio", and Jerry Valburn, of Meritt Records, told Bert Whyatt this was some kind of audition thing, and not a recording for Commodore. Milt Gabler, of Commodore, advised Bert Whyatt that it was a rejected version from January 17, 1938, "probably sent to the factory for processing and entered into the ARC ledger on February 16. This was done without my knowledge. . ." Gabler's explanation seems the more likely, hence the acceptance of P22440-1 as an alternative version of P-22313. The two versions are different; Stacy and Freeman vary their solos, although following similar lines on each take. The main variations are:

P-22313-1 starts with a drum break, followed by Freeman in a brief improvisation, before he states the theme. After the piece has ended, there is muted applause, Stacy hits two single notes, and a voice is heard in the background.

P-22440-1 starts with a piano introduction, followed by Freeman introducing the theme.

(3807) **LIONEL HAMPTON and His ORCHESTRA** (Cootie Williams, tp; Johnny Hodges, as; Edgar Sampson, bar; Jess Stacy, p; Allan Reuss, g; Billy Taylor, b; Sonny Greer, d; Lionel Hampton, vb, vo):

New York City – Tuesday, January 18, 1938

018335-1	**You're My Ideal** vLH	(A)	(78)	Victor 25771
018336-2	**The Sun Will Shine Tonight** vLH	(A)	(78)	Victor 25771
018337-1	**Ring Dem Bells** vLH	(N)	(78)	Victor 26017
018338-1	**Don't Be That Way**	(N)	(78)	Victor 26173

other releases:
all titles: (LP) RCA Bluebird AXM6-5536, RCA(F) PM42393, (CD) RCA Jazz Tribune 74321 15525 2
018335-1 on (LP) Camden CAL517, Camden(E) CDN138, RCA(F) 430.249, 730.640;
        (CD) Bluebird ND82433, Classics 524, Le Jazz CD1
018336-2 on (LP) RCA(F) 430.249, 741.049, (CD) Classics 524, Fremeaux & Associes FA211
018337-1 on (LP) Victor LJM1000, HMV CLP1023, RCA LPM2318, RCA(F) 130.214, 430.725, 730.640, Readers Digest
        RS9676, RDS6526;
        (CD) Giants of Jazz 53050, Classics 524, Le Jazz CD1, ASV Living Era AJA5090, Jazz Roots CD56056, Bluebird
        ND86458, Phontastic PHONT-CD-7665, Past CD9789, JazzCD No.3, Fremeaux & Associes FA211
018338-1 on (LP) Victor LPT-18, RCA LPM1393, RCA(E) RC24002, RCA(F) 130.214, 430.725, 730.640;
        (CD) Bluebird ND86458, Classics 534, Le Jazz CD1

(3808) **BENNY GOODMAN and His ORCHESTRA** (personnel as for December 2, 1937):

Camel Caravan broadcast, New York City – Tuesday, January 18, 1938

Make Believe	(N)	

This CBS broadcast title on (LP) Fanfare 37-137

(3809) (same personnel):

Pittsburgh – February 15, 1938

Roll 'Em	(S)	

This broadcast title (unknown network) on (LP) Columbia ML4590, ML/OL4614, CL818, Philips BBL7010, B07007L, Time-Life STL-JO5, CBS set 66420; (CD) Columbia 472990 2, Jazzmen 625-50-015

(3810) (same personnel):

New York City – Wednesday, February 16, 1938

BS 019831-1	**Don't Be That Way**	(N)	(78)	Victor 25792
BS 019832-1	**One O'Clock Jump**	(S)	(78)	Victor 25792

(3811) **BUD FREEMAN TRIO** (refer to session 3806, January 17, 1938)

(3812) **BENNY GOODMAN and His ORCHESTRA** (same personnel, plus Lionel Hampton, vb):

Camel Caravan broadcast, New York City – Tuesday, February 22, 1938

I Know That You Know	(N)	

This CBS broadcast title on (LP) MGM E3788, MGM(E) C805, Verve(E) VLP9120, Verve 2317056.

(3813) (Harry James, Ziggy Elman, Chris Griffin, tp; Red Ballard, Vernon Brown, tb; Benny Goodman, cl; Hymie Shertzer, Dave Matthews, as; Babe Russin, Lester Young, ts; Jess Stacy, p; Freddie Green, b; Walter Page, b; Lionel Hampton, d; Martha Tilton, vo)

New York City – Wednesday, March 9. 1938

BS 021127-1	**Please Be Kind** vMT	(A)	(78)	Victor 25814
BS 021127-2	**Please Be Kind** vMT	(A)	(LP)	Victor LPM6703
BS 021128-1	**Ti-Pi-Tin**	(N)	(78)	Victor 25814
BS 021129-1	**oooOO-OH BOOM!** vMT,BG	(A/S)	(78)	Victor 25808
BS 021130-1	**Always and Always** vMT	(A)	(78)	Victor 25808
BS 021131-1	**Make Believe**	(N)	(78)	Victor 26088
BS 021132-1	**The Blue Room**	(N)	(78)	Victor 26088
BS 021132-2	**The Blue Room**	(N)	(LP)	Victor(G) LPM10025

(3814) (Harry James, Ziggy Elman, Chris Griffin, tp; Red Ballard, Vernon Brown, tb; Benny Goodman, cl; Hymie Shertzer, Dave Matthews, as; Bud Freeman, Art Rollini, ts; Jess Stacy, p; Ben Heller, g; Harry Goodman, b; Dave Tough, d):

broadcast, Hotel Pennsylvania, New York City – Thursday, March 31, 1938

Something Tells Me vMT **(A)**

This Mutual broadcast title on (LP) Sunbeam SB 152

(3815) (same personnel): Camel Caravan broadcast, New York City – Tuesday, April 5, 1938
[a] **Makin' Whoopee** **(N)**
[b] **I Fall In Love With You Every Day** vMT **(A)**

These CBS titles on (LP) Sunbeam SB152.

(3816) (same personnel): broadcast, Hotel Pennsylvania, New York City – Wednesday, April 6, 1938
[a] **Lullaby In Rhythm** **(N)**
[b] **When Buddha Smiles** **(N)**

Mutual broadcast. [a] on (LP) Sounds Great SG8004. [a], [b] on (LP) Sunbeam SB 152.

(3817) (personnel as for March 31, 1938, except Milt Yaner, as; replaces Shertzer):

New York City – Friday, April 8, 1938

BS 022414-1	**It's The Dreamer In Me** vMT	**(A)**	(78)	Victor 25846
BS 022415-1	**Lullaby In Rhythm**	**(A)**	(78)	Victor 25827
BS 022415-2	**Lullaby In Rhythm**	**(N)**	(LP)	RCABb AXM2 5568
BS 022416-1	**I Never Knew**	**(N)**	(78)	Victor 26089
BS 022417-1	**That Feeling Is Gone** vMT	**(A)**	(78)	Victor 25827
BS 022418-1	**Feelin' High And Happy** vMT	**( )**	(78)	unissued
BS 022419-1	**Sweet Sue – Just You**	**(A)**	(78)	Victor 26089

(3818) **THE BUD FREEMAN TRIO** (Bud Freeman, ts; Jess Stacy, p; George Wettling, d):

Brunswick Studios, New York City – Wednesday, April 13, 1938

P-22719-1	**Keep Smiling At Trouble**	(LP)	Commodore XFL14941
P-22719-2	**Keep Smiling At Trouble**	(78)	Commodore 503
P-22720-1	**At Sundown**	(78)	Commodore 503
P-22720-2	**At Sundown**	(LP)	Commodore XFL14941
P-22721-1	**My Honey's Lovin' Arms**	(78)	Commodore 504
P-22721-2	**My Honey's Lovin' Arms**	(LP)	Commodore XFL14941
P-22722-1	**I Don't Believe It**	(LP)	Commodore XFL14941
P-22722-2	**I Don't Believe It**	(78)	Commodore 504

other releases:
All 8 takes on (LP) Commodore XFL14941, Mosaic MR23-123, London(E) HMC5032, Commodore(G) 6.24061
The four titles originally on 78rpm on (LP) Atlantic SD2-309; (CD) Classics 781
P-22720-1 on (LP) Mainstream 56008/S6008 (CD) Sunday Times STCD-211

(3819) **BENNY GOODMAN AND HIS ORCHESTRA** (same personnel, except Noni Bernardi, as; replaces Yaner):

broadcast, Hotel Pennsylvania, New York City – Saturday, April 16, 1938

I Let A Song Go Out Of My Heart vMT **(A)**

This CBS broadcast title on (LP) Sunbeam SB152.

(3820) (same personnel): Camel Caravan broadcast, New York City – Tuesday, April 19, 1938
[a] **Sweet Sue - Just You** **(N)**
[b] **Ti-Pi-Tin** **(A)**
[c] **You Couldn't Be Cuter** vMT **(A)**
[d] **Ciribiribin** **(N)**

These CBS broadcast titles on (LP) Sunbeam SB 152.

(3821) (same personnel): broadcast, Hotel Pennsylvania, New York City – Thursday, April 21, 1938
[a] **Sometimes I'm Happy** **(A)**
[b] **You Went To My Head** **(A)**

These Mutual broadcast titles on (LP) Sunbeam SB 152.

(3822) (same personnel): New York City – Friday, April 22, 1938

BS 022487-1	**I Let A Song Go Out Of My Heart** vMT	**(A)**	(78)	Victor 25840
BS 022418-3	**Feelin' High And Happy** vMT	**(A)**	(78)	Victor 25840

BS 022488-1	**Why'd Ya Make Me Fall In Love?** vMT	**(A)**	(78)	Victor 25846
BS 022488-2	**Why'd Ya Make Me Fall In Love?** vMT	**(A)**	(LP)	Time-Life STBB03
'2359'	**Feelin' High And Happy** vMT	**(A)**	(LP)	Blu-Disc T.1015

(022418-3 is remake of title recorded April 8, 1938, and rejected. '2359' was a rehearsal disc.)

(3823) (same personnel):   Camel Caravan broadcast, New York City – Tuesday, April 26, 1938

[a]	**Don't Be That Way**	**(N)**
[b]	**House Hop**	**(S)**

These CBS broadcast titles on (LP) Queen-disc 060.

(3824) **HARRY JAMES and His ORCHESTRA** (Harry James, Ziggy Elman, tp; Vernon Brown, tb; Dave Matthews, as; Art Rollini, ts; Harry Carney, bar; Jess Stacy, p; Thurman Teague, b; Dave Tough, d):

New York City – Wednesday, April 27, 1938

22808-1	**Out Of Nowhere**	**(A)**	(LP)	Meritt 3
22808-2	**Out Of Nowhere**	**(A)**	(78)	Brunswick 8136
22809-1	**Wrap Your Troubles In Dreams**	**(S)**	(78)	Brunswick 8178
22810-1	**Lullaby In Rhythm**	**(S)**	(78)	Brunswick 8136
22811-1	**Little White Lies**	**(S)**	(78)	Brunswick 8178

other releases:
all 78 rpm titles on (LP) TOM 36, CBS (F) 84494. (CD) Jazz Archives No. 57, Classics 903
all five takes on (CD) Affinity AFS1009
22808-2 on (CD) ASV Living Era CD AJA5120.
22809-1 on (LP) CBS S67273
22810-1 on (CD) Phontastic PHONT-CD-7665, Pro-Arte Digital CDD507.

(3825) **JESS STACY** (piano solos):   Brunswick Studios, 1776 Broadway, New York City – Saturday, April 30, 1938

P-22828-1	**Ramblin'**	(LP)	Mosaic MR23.123
P-22828-2	**Ramblin'**	(78)	Commodore 506
P-22829-1	**Complainin'**	(LP)	Mosaic MR23.123

Commodore 506 as "A Piano Solo by Jess Stacy".

other releases:
P-22828-1 on (AC) Neovox 849
P-22828-2 on (LP) Commodore XFL15358, CCL7008, Mosaic MR23.123. Commodore(G) 6.24298; (AC) Neovox 849;
            (CD) Commodore CCD7008, Classics 795, Topaz TPZ1050
P-22829-1   (CD) Classics 795, (AC) Neovox 84

(3826) **EDDIE CONDON and His WINDY CITY SEVEN** (Bobby Hackett, co; Jack Teagarden, tb, vo; Pee Wee Russell, cl; Bud Freeman, ts; Jess Stacy, p; Eddie Condon, g; Art Shapiro, b; George Wettling, d):

Brunswick Studios, 1776 Broadway, New York City – Saturday, April 30, 1938

XP-22830-1	**Embraceable You**	**(A)**	(78)	Commodore 1501
P-22831-1	**Meet Me Tonight In Dreamland**	**(S)**	(78)	Commodore 505
P-22831-2	**Meet Me Tonight In Dreamland**	**(S)**	(LP)	Commodore XFL14427
P-22832-1	**Diane**	**(I/A)**	(LP)	Commodore XFL14427
P-22832-2	**Diane**	**(I/A)**	(78)	Commodore 505
P-22833-1	**Serenade To A Shylock** vJT	**(I/A)**	(78)	Commodore 1501
P-22833-2	**Serenade To A Shylock** vJT	**(I/A)**	(LP)	Commodore XFL14427

Commodore 1501, a 12" record, labelled "Jam Session At Commodore No. 2".
Diane on Commodore 505 labelled "Jack Teagarden and His Trombone".

other releases:
all seven takes on (LP) Commodore XFL14427, Mosaic MR23-123, London(E) DHMC 1/2, (LP/CD) Commodore(G)
            6.24054/8.24054
all four 78 rpm issues on (LP) Commodore FL20, 016,CCL7007; (CD) Commodore CCD7007, Topaz TPZ1026
XP-22830-1 on (LP) Atlantic SD2-309, Mainstream 56017, S/6017, Franklin Mint 47
            (CD) Classics 742, Commodore CMD14042, Giants of Jazz 53183
P-22831-1 on (LP) Book-of-the-Month Records 10-5557, London(E) HMC5007 Atlantic SD2-309   (CD) Classics 742
P-22832-2 on (LP) Atlantic SD2-309, London(E) HMC5007, Time-Life STL.JO8; (CD) Commodore CMD24002
P-22833-1 on (LP) Time-Life STL-JO8, Mainstream 56010, S/6010, Jazztone J-SPEC-100; (CD) Commodore CMD14042
P-22833-2 on (LP) Jazz Archives JA-1; (CD) Commodore CMD14042

(3827) **BENNY GOODMAN and His ORCHESTRA** (personnel as for April 16, 1938):

CBS, Camel Caravan broadcast, Boston – Tuesday, May 3, 1938

[a]	**I Can't Give You Anything But Love**	**(S)**
[b]	**Sampson Stomp**	**(S)**
[c]	**Wrappin' It Up**	**(N)**

[a], [b] on (LP) Queen-disc 060; [c] on (LP) Sunbeam SB 152. Queen-disc sleeve gives location as Waltham, Mass.

(3828) (same personnel):   CBS, Camel Caravan broadcast, Savoy Ballroom, New York City – Tuesday, May 10, 1938

[a]	**I've Found A New Baby**	**(N)**
[b]	**One O'Clock Jump**	**(I/S)**

[a], [b] on (LP) Queen-disc 060; [b] on (LP) Blu-Disc T-5001/2, Phontastic NOST-7625/6.

(3829) (same personnel):   Camel Caravan broadcast, New York City – Tuesday, May 17, 1938

[a]		**Star Dust**	**(A)**
[b]	SEPTET	**The Jazz Me Blues**	**(S)**
[c]		**I Let A Song Go Out Of My Heart** vMT	**(A)**
[d]		**Don't Be That Way**	**(N)**

SEPTET personnel: Harry James, Vernon Brown, Benny Goodman, Jess Stacy, Ben Heller, Harry Goodman, Dave Tough. CBS broadcast. [b], [d] on (LP) Fanfare 37-137; [a] on (LP) Blu-Disc T-5001/2, Phontastic NOST-7625/6; [b], [c] on (LP) Queen-disc 060.

(3830) (same personnel):   CBS, Camel Caravan broadcast, Boston – Tuesday, May 24, 1938

[a]	**Honeysuckle Rose**	**(N)**
[b]	**Lullaby In Rhythm**	**(N)**
[c]	**King Porter Stomp**	**(N)**

[a] on (LP) on Fanfare 37-137, [b] on (LP) Blu-Disc T-5001/2, Phontastic NOST-7625/6; [c] on (LP) Queen-disc 060.

(3831) (same personnel):   New York City – May 28, 1938

BS 023506-1	**Don't Wake Up My Heart** vMT	**(A)**	(78)	Victor 25867
BS 023506-2	**Don't Wake Up My Heart** vMT	**( )**	(78)	Victor 25867
BS 023507-1	**(I've Been) Saving Myself For You** vMT	**(I/A)**	(78)	Victor 25867
BS 023508-1	**Big John Special**	**(S)**	(78)	Victor 25871
BS 023509-1	**My Melancholy Baby**	**(N)**	(78)	Victor 25880
BS 023509-2	**My Melancholy Baby**	**(N)**	(LP)	RCABb AXM2 5568
BS 023510-1	**Wrappin' It Up**	**(A)**	(78)	Victor 25880
BS 023510-2	**Wrappin' It Up**	**(A)**	(LP)	RCABb AXM2 5568
BS 023511-1	**What Goes On Here In My Heart?** vMT	**(A)**	(78)	Victor 25878

(3832) (same personnel):   New York City – Tuesday, May 31, 1938

BS 023517-2	**A Little Kiss At Twilight** vMT	**(A/S)**	(78)	Victor 25878
BS 023518-2	**The Flat Foot Floogee** vband	**(A)**	(78)	Victor 25871

(3833) (same personnel):   CBS, Camel Caravan broadcast, New York City – Tuesday, May 31, 1938

[a]	**Alexander's Ragtime Band**	**(N)**
[b]	**I Never Knew**	**(N)**
[c]	**The Flat Foot Floogee** vband	**(A)**

[a] on (LP) Blu-Disc T-5001/2, Phontastic NOST-7625/6; [b], [c] on (LP) Queen-disc 060.

(3834) (same personnel):   CBS, Camel Caravan broadcast, Hotel Statler, Cleveland, Ohio – Tuesday, June 7, 1938

[a]	**Shine On, Harvest Moon**	**(N)**
[b]	**I Know That You Know**	**(N)**

[a], [b] on (LP) Blu-Disc T-5001/2, Phontastic NOST-7625/6; [a] on (LP) Queen-disc 060. The broadcast included a piano duet version of *She's Funny That Way* by Jess Stacy and Teddy Wilson. Unfortunately this has yet to be issued commercially.

(3835) (same personnel):   Camel Caravan broadcast, Boston – Tuesday, June 14, 1938

Swingtime In The Rockies	**(N)**

This CBS broadcast title on (LP) Blu-Disc T-5001/2, Nostalgia NOST.7625/6.

(3836) (same personnel):   Camel Caravan broadcast, Montreal – Tuesday, June 28, 1938

Clarinet Marmalade	**(N)**

This CBS broadcast title on (LP) Blu-Disc T-5001/2, Phontastic NOST.7625/6.

(3837) (same personnel): Camel Caravan broadcast, Williamsville, NY – Tuesday, July 5, 1938
      Minnie The Moocher's Wedding Day   **(N)**
This CBS broadcast title on (LP) Blu-Disc T-5001/2, Phontastic NOST.7625/6

(3838) (same personnel): New York City – Monday, July 11, 1938

BS 023511-2	**What Goes On Here In My Heart?** vMT	**( )**	(78)	Victor 25878
BS 024020-2	**I've Got A Date With A Dream** vMT	**(A)**	(78)	Victor 26000
BS 024021-2	**Could You Pass In Love?** vMT	**(A)**	(78)	Victor 26000
BS 023517-4	**A Little Kiss At Twilight** vMT	**( )**	(78)	Victor 25878

BS023511-2 remade from May 28, 1938 & BS023517-4 from May 31, 1938, although these titles from the original sessions were also issued.

(3839) **BUD FREEMAN and His GANG** (Bobby Hackett, co; Pee Wee Russell, cl; Dave Matthews, as; Bud Freeman, ts; Jess Stacy, p; Eddie Condon, g; Art Shapiro, b; Dave Tough, d): New York City – Tuesday, July 12, 1938

P-23233-1	**Tappin' The Commodore Till**	**(N)**	(78)	Commodore 508
P-23233-2	**Tappin' The Commodore Till**	**(N)**	(LP)	Commodore (G) 6.25894
P-23234-1	**Memories Of You**	**(A)**	(78)	Commodore 508
P-23234-2	**Memories Of You**	**(A)**	(LP)	Commodore (G) 6.25894
P-23234-NG	**Memories Of You**	**(A)**	(LP)	Mosaic MR23 134
P-23234-PB	**Memories Of You**	**(S)**	(LP)	Mosaic MR23 134

(same personnel, except Marty Marsala, d; replaces Tough):

P-23235-1	**Life Spears A Jitterbug**	**(S)**	(78)	Commodore 507
P-23235-BD	**Life Spears A Jitterbug**	**(S/A)**	(LP)	Mosaic MR23 134
P-23236-1	**What's The Use?**	**(S)**	(LP)	Mosaic (G) 25894AG
P-23236-2	**What's The Use?**	**(S)**	(78)	Commodore 507
P-23236-PB	**What's The Use?**	**(S)**	(LP)	Mosaic MR23 134

Recorded at the Brunswick Studios, 1776 Broadway. Milt Gabler told Bert Whyatt (23apr84), "Davey Tough was inebriated as was usual for him in those days. He only lasted two tunes. Marty Marsala was visiting to observe the session. Luckily he had been a drummer in his early days as a musician, only giving up traps when he injured his leg running beer in Chicago . . . He played fine on the date."

other releases:
all takes, except those on Mosaic MR23-134, are on (LP) Mosaic M23-123
all 78rpm issues on (LP) Atlantic SD2-309, Commodore CCL7007, (G) 6.25894AG. (CD) Commodore CCD7007, Classics 781
P-23233-1 on (LP) Time-Life STL-J17. (CD) Topaz TPZ1018
P-23234-1 on (CD) Fremeaux & Associes 022
P-23235-1 on (CD) Topaz TPZ1018

(3840) **BENNY GOODMAN and His ORCHESTRA** (personnel as for April 16, 1938, except Lionel Hampton, d; replaces Tough): New York City – Monday, August 8, 1938

BS 024472-1	**You Got Me** vMT	**(A)**	(LP)	Blu-Disc T.1015
BS 024473-2	**Blue Interlude** vMT	**(A)**	(78)	Victor 26021

(3841) (same personnel, except Dave Tough, d; replaces Hampton; and perhaps Art Rollini out): New York City – Friday, August 12, 1938

BS 02493-1	**When I Go A Dreamin'** vMT	**(A)**	(78)	Victor 26021

(3842) (same personnel, with Rollini): Camel Caravan broadcast, Coney Island, near Cincinnati – Tuesday, August 23, 1938
      Love Me Or Leave Me   **(S)**
This CBS broadcast title on (LP) Fanfare 37-137.

(3843) (same personnel): Camel Caravan broadcast, The Coliseum, Michigan State Fairgrounds, near Detroit – Tuesday, August 30, 1938

[a]	**The March of the Swing Parade** vMT	**(A)**
[b]	**I Used To Be Color-Blind** vMT	**(A)**
[c]	**At Sundown**	**(N)**
[d]	**Liza**	**(N)**
[e]	**Russian Lullaby**	**(N)**
[f]	**When I Go A-Dreamin'** vMT	**(A)**
[g]	**The Yam**	**(S)**

213

On *Liza* Goodman leads the saxophone section on alto. These CBS broadcast titles on (CD) Phontastic NCD8843/4. [a], [c], [e], [g] on (LP) Fanfare 37-137. [g] on (LP) First Time 1507, Jazztone 5114 & other issues as for *Blue Hawaii*, 11may37.

(3844) (same personnel):   broadcast, possibly Chicago – Thursday, September 1, 1938
   [a]   **Sugar Foot Stomp**   **(N)**
   [b]   **Honeysuckle Rose**   **(N)**
Both titles on (LP) Blu-Disc T-5001/2, Phontastic NOST-7625/6. Location uncertain. Both Chicago and Detroit have been suggested. Band opened in Chicago on September 2nd.

(3845) (same personnel):   Camel Caravan broadcast, Chicago – Tuesday, September 6, 1938
   [a]   **Chicago**   **(N)**
   [b]   **I've Got A Date With A Dream** vMT   **(A)**
   [c]   **Margie**   **(N)**
   [d]   **In A Mist**   (Stacy piano solo)
   [e]   **The Lambeth Walk**   vMT   **(A)**
   [f]   **You Go To My Head**   vMT   **(A)**
   [g]   **Madhouse**   **(S)**
all titles from this CBS broadcast on (LP) Soundcraft LP-1019; (CD) Jazz Hour JH-1038, Phontastic NCD8843/4.
[a], [d], [f] on (LP/AC) Dr. Jazz 40350. [a], [d] on (CD) Zeta ZET723.

(3846) (same personnel):   Chicago – Monday, September 12, 1938

BS 025466-1	**You're A Sweet Little Headache** vMT	**(A)**	(78)	Victor 26071
BS 025467-1	**I Have Eyes** vMT	**(A)**	(78)	Victor 26071
BS-025468-	**You're Lovely Madame** vMT	**( )**		unissued

(3847) (same personnel):   CBS, Camel Caravan broadcast, Chicago – Tuesday, September 13, 1938
   [a]   **Changes**   **(N)**
   [b]   **A-Tisket, A-Tasket** vMT & band   **(A)**
   [c]   **You're Driving Me Crazy**   **(N)**
   [d]   **Blue Skies**   **(N)**
   [e]   **I Used To Be Color-Blind**   vMT   **(A)**
   [f]   **Big John Special**   **(S)**
[c] on (LP/AC) Dr. Jazz 40350; [a], [b], [c], [d] on (LP) Soundcraft LP-1019; [e], [f] on (LP) Soundcraft LP-1020. All titles on (CD) Jazz Hour JH-1038, Phontastic NCD8843/4.

(3848) (same personnel):   Chicago – Wednesday, September 14, 1938

BS 025475-	**I Had To Do It** vMT	**( )**	unissued
BS 025476-1	**Margie**	**(N)**	Victor 26060
BS 025477-1	**What Have You Got That Get's Me?** vMT	**(N)**	Victor 26053
BS 025478-1	**Russian Lullaby**	**(N)**	Victor 26060

(3849) (same personnel):   Camel Caravan broadcast, Tower Theatre, Kansas City – Tuesday, September 20, 1938
   [a]   **Russian Lullaby**   **(N)**
   [b]   **I've Got A Pocketful of Dreams**   **(S)**
   [c]   **Moten Swing**   **(N)**
   [d]   **Oh, Lady Be Good!**   **(N)**
   [e]   **Margie**   **N)**
   [f]   **Star Dust**   **(N)**
(Jess Stacy, Lionel Hampton, p duet):
   [g]   **Space, Man** (China Stomp)
(full orchestra):
   [h]   **Bumble Bee Stomp**   **(S)**
All these CBS broadcast titles on (LP) Soundcraft LP-1020, (CD) Phontastic NCD8845/6. [a], [b], [c], [e], [f], [h], on (LP/AC) Dr. Jazz 40350. [c] on (LP) Fanfare 37-137, First Time 1507, Jazztone 5114 & other issues as for *Blue Hawaii*, 11may37, & (CD) Jazz Hour JH-1025, Columbia 472990 2. [g] on (LP) MGM E3789, MGM(E) C807, Verve(E) VLP9120, Sunbeam SB152. [c] on (LP) Black Lion Int.127.034. [h] on (CD) Columbia 472990 2. [a], [b], [c], [e], [f] on (CD) Zeta ZET723

(3850) (same personnel):   Camel Caravan broadcast, Congress Hotel, Chicago – Tuesday, September 27, 1938
   [a]   **Rose Of The Rio Grande**   **(N)**
   [b]   **Lullaby In Rhythm**   **(A)**
   [c]   **The Yam**   **(A/S)**
   [d]   **Ciribiribin**   **(N)**

[e]	Sometimes I'm Happy	(A)
[f]	One O'Clock Jump	(S)

All these CBS broadcast titles on (LP) Soundcraft LP-1021; (CD) Jazz Hour JH1025, Phontastic NCD8845/6.
[b] on (LP/AC) Dr. Jazz 40350, (CD) Zeta ZET723. [d] on (LP) Sunbeam SB 152.

(3851) (same personnel):   CBS, Camel Caravan broadcast, Minneapolis – Tuesday, October 4, 1938

[a]	You're Driving Me Crazy vMT	(A)
[b]	Clap Hands, Here Comes Charlie	(N)

[a] on (LP) Blu-Disc T-5001/2, Phontastic NOST-7625/6.
[b] on (LP) Fanfare 37-137, First Time 1507, Jazztone 5114 & other issues as for *Blue Hawaii,* 11may37.

(3852) (same personnel):   CBS, Camel Caravan broadcast, Chicago – Tuesday, October 11, 1938

[a]	Who Blew Out The Flame? vMT	(A)
[b]	Someday Sweetheart	(N)
[c]	Is That The Way To Treat A Sweetheart? vMT	(A)
[d]	Bumble Bee Stomp	(S)

All titles on (LP) Sunbeam SB 152.
[d] on (LP/AC) Dr. Jazz 40350, (CD) Zeta ZET723

(3853) (same personnel):   Chicago – Thursday, October 13, 1938

BS 025798-1	Is That The Way To Treat A Sweetheart? vMT	(A)	(78)	Victor 26082
BS 025475-3	I Had To Do It vMT	(A)	(78)	Victor 26082
BS 025468-3	You're Lovely Madame vMT	(A)	(78)	Victor 26053
BS 025799-1	Bumble Bee Stomp	(S)	(78)	Victor 26087
BS 025900-1	Ciribiribin	(N)	(78)	Victor 26087
BS 025901-1	This Can't Be Love vMT	(A)	(78)	Victor 26099

BS 025475 & 025468 are remakes from the sessions of 14sep38 & 12sep38. Masters 025799 and 025900 are consecutive.

(3854) ST. REGIS JAM SESSION

[a] (Max Kaminsky, tp; Mezz Mezzrow, cl; Bud Freeman, ts; Jess Stacy, p; Eddie Condon, g; Art Shapiro, b; Zutty Singleton, d):
[b] (Yank Lawson, tp; Tommy Dorsey, tb; Joe Marsala, cl; Bud Freeman, ts; Jess Stacy, p; Carmen Mastren, g; Art Shapiro, b; Dave Tough, d): (The number is introduced by Tommy Dorsey, speaking with Joe Marsala.)
[c] (Lee Wiley, vo; Bobby Hackett, co; Pee Wee Russell, cl; Bud Freeman, ts; Jess Stacy, p; Eddie Condon, g; Art Shapiro, b; Dave Tough, d):
[d] (Hot Lips Page, tp; Mezz Mezzrow, cl; Bud Freeman, ts; Jess Stacy, p; Eddie Condon, g; Art Shapiro, b; Zutty Singleton, d): (This number is introduced by W.C. Handy.)
[e] (Marty Marsala, tp; Joe Marsala, cl; Bud Freeman, ts; Jess Stacy, p; Eddie Condon, g; Art Shapiro, b; Zutty Singleton, d; with other musicians, including Sidney Bechet, ss; joining for the final choruses):

Introduced by Alistair Cooke from The Viennese Room of the Roof Garden of the St. Regis Hotel, New York City –
Saturday, November 5, 1938

[a]	Just The Blues	(I)
[b]	Someday Sweetheart	(I)
[c]	Sugar vLW	(N)
[d]	St. Louis Blues	(S/A)
[e]	You Took Advantage Of Me	(S)

These BBC broadcast titles on (LP):
[a] Jazz Panorama LP-9, Joker SM3114, Saga PAN6914
[b] Jazz Panorama LP-9, Saga PAN6914
[c] Black Jack LP3003, Joker SM3114, (LP/CD) Jass Nineteen
[d] Jazz Panorama LP-9, Saga PAN6914, Joker SM3114
[e] Black Jack LP3003
all titles on (LP/AC) Alamac QSR2445; (CD) Jazz Unlimited JUCD2029.
Keep Smilin' At Trouble and *China Boy* from this broadcast do not include Stacy. The "everybody play all-in" finale number, *I Found A New Baby*, has not been issued. Joe Marsala is not heard on [b] although announced. He may be in the ensemble. Pee Wee Russell announced on [e] but not heard.

Album titles have included: The Legendary St. Regis Jam Sessions (Alamac); Great Swing Jam Sessions (Jazz Panorama, Saga, Jazz Unlimited); Swingin' All Stars (Black Jack). Jass Nineteen is a Lee Wiley album.

(3855) **BENNY GOODMAN and His ORCHESTRA** (same personnel, except Lionel Hampton, d; replaces Tough):

                                          Camel Caravan broadcast, New York City – Tuesday, November 8, 1938
        Sing, Sing, Sing   **(N)**

This CBS broadcast title on (LP) Blu-Disc T-5001/2, Nostalgia NOST.7625/6.

(3856) (same personnel):   broadcast, Waldorf-Astoria, New York City – Wednesday, November 9. 1938
        Two Buck Stew   **(N)**

This broadcast (unknown network) title on (LP) Fanfare 37-137.

(3857) (same personnel):   New York City – Thursday, November 10, 1938

BS 028942-1	**Sing For Your Supper** vMT	**(A)**	(78)	Victor 26099
BS 028943-1	**Topsy**	**(S)**	(78)	Victor 26107
BS 028944-1	**Smokehouse**	**(N)**	(78)	Victor 26107
BS 028944-2	**Smokehouse**	**(N)**	(LP)	RCABb AXM2 5567

(3858) **WNEW JAM SESSION GROUP** (Yank Lawson, tp; Tommy Dorsey, tb; Artie Shaw, cl; Chu Berry, ts; Jess Stacy, p; Allan Reuss, g; John Kirby, b; O'Neal Spencer, d):

                                          Martin Block WNEW radio show, New York City – Friday, November 11, 1938
        Limehouse Blues   **(S)**

This title, the only one known from this broadcast, on (LP) Meritt 21. Al Hall has been listed as bassist.

(3859) **BENNY GOODMAN and His ORCHESTRA** (personnel as for November 1, 1938):
                                          CBS, Camel Caravan broadcast, New York City – Tuesday, November 15, 1938

[a]	**Sly Mongoose**	**(N)**
[b]	**Smoke House**	**(N)**

[a] on (LP) Black Lion Int.127.034, First Time 1507, Jazztone 5114, & other issues as for *Blue Hawaii,* 13may37.
[b] on (LP) Blu-Disc T-5001/2, Phontastic NOST-7625/6.

(3860) **BENNY GOODMAN and His ORCHESTRA** (Harry James, Ziggy Elman, Chris Griffin, tp; Red Ballard, Vernon Brown, tb; Benny Goodman, cl; Dave Matthews, Noni Bernard, as; Art Rollini, Bud Freeman, ts; Jess Stacy, p; Ben Heller, g; Harry Goodman, b; Buddy Schutz, d):   New York City – Wednesday, November 23, 1938

BS 028997-2	**I Must See Annie Tonight** vMT	**(N)**	(78)	Victor 26110
BS 028998-2	**Kind'a Lonesome** vMT	**(A)**	(78)	Victor 26110
BS 028999-1	**My Honey's Lovin' Arms**	**(S)**	(78)	Victor 26095
BS 028999-2	**My Honey's Lovin' Arms**	**(S)**	(78)	Bluebird 11056
BS 030308-1	**Farewell Blues**	**(N)**	(78)	Victor 26095
BS 030308-2	**Farewell Blues**	**(N)**	(LP)	RCABb AXM2 5568

(3861) (same personnel, except Lionel Hampton, d; for Schutz):
                                          Camel Caravan broadcast, New York City – Tuesday, November 29, 1938
        Honeysuckle Rose   **(N)**

This CBS broadcast title on (LP) Blue-Disc T-5001/2, Phontastic NOST.7625/6.

(3862) **BUD FREEMAN TRIO** (Bud Freeman, ts; Jess Stacy, p; George Wettling, d):
                                          Decca Studios, New York City – Wednesday, November 30, 1938

75957A	**Three Little Words**	(78)	Commodore 514
75958A	**Swingin' Without Mezz**	(78)	Commodore 514
75959A	**Blue Room**	(78)	Commodore 513
75960A	**Exactly Like You**	(78)	Commodore 513

other releases:
all titles on (LP) Atlantic SD2-309, Commodore XFL 14941, Mosaic MR23 123, London(E) HMC5032, Commodore(G) 6.24061; (CD) Classics 781, ASV Living Era AJA5172

(3863) **WILLIE THE LION SMITH** (Willie The Lion Smith, celeste; Joe Bushkin, Jess Stacy, p; George Wettling, d):
same date and session

75961A	**Three Keyboards**	(78)	Commodore C 520
75961B	**Three Keyboards**	(LP)	Mosaic MR23 123

other releases:
75961A also on (LP) Commodore XFL15775, CCL7012, Mosaic M23-123, Commodore(G) 6.25491; (CD) Commodore CCD7012, Classics 692. Stacy not present on *The Lion and The Lamb* from this session.

(3864) **BENNY GOODMAN and His ORCHESTRA** (personnel as for November 23, 1938, except Jerry Jerome, ts; for
Freeman):   New York City – Monday, December 12, 1938

BS 030390-1	**It Had To Be You**	**(S)**	(78)	Victor 26125
BS 030390-2	**It Had To Be You**	**(N)**	(LP)	RCABb AXM2 5568
BS 030391-1	**Louise**	**(S)**	(78)	Victor 26125
BS 030391-2	**Louise**	**(S)**	(LP)	RCABb AXM2 5568

(3865) (same personnel):   Camel Caravan broadcast, New York City – Tuesday, December 13, 1938

[a]	**It Had To Be You**	**(S)**
[b]	**Bach Goes To Town**	**(N)**

These CBS broadcast titles on (LP) Blu-Disc T-5001/2, Phontastic NOST.7625/6

(3866) (same personnel):   New York City – Thursday, December 15, 1938

BS 030701-1	**Whispering**	**(N)**	(78)	Victor 26130
BS 030702-1	**Bach Goes To Town**	**(N)**	(78)	Camden 624
BS 030702-2	**Bach Goes To Town**	**(N)**	(78)	Victor 26130
BS 030703-1	**I'll Always Be In Love With You**	**(S)**	(78)	Victor 26187
BS 030703-2	**I'll Always Be In Love With You**	**(S)**	(LP)	Blu-Disc 1004
BS 030704-1	**Undecided**	**(S)**	(78)	Victor 26134

(3867) (same personnel):   "Fitch Bandwagon" radio show, New York City – Sunday, December 18, 1938

	One O'Clock Jump	**(S)**

This CBS broadcast title on (LP) Blue-Disc T-5001/2, Phontastic NOST.7625/6

(3868) (same personnel):   CBS, Camel Caravan broadcast, New York City – Tuesday, December 20, 1938

[a]	**Whispering**	**(N)**
[b]	**Undecided**	**(S)**
[c]	**Hot Foot Shuffle**	**(N)**

[a], [b] on (LP) Blu-Disc T-5001/2, Phontastic NOST-7625/6; [c] on (LP) Fanfare 37-137 & other issues as for *Blue Hawaii,*
11may37.

(3869) (same personnel):   New York City – Friday, December 23, 1938

BS 030760-1	**We'll Never Know** vMT	**(A)**	(78)	Victor 26134
BS 030760-2	**We'll Never Know** vMT	**( )**	(78)	Victor 26134
BS 030390-	**It Had To Be You**	**( )**		unissued
BS 030391-3	**Louise**	**( )**		unissued
BS 030761-1	**Good For Nothin' But Love** vMT	**(A)**	(78)	Victor 26159

030390-/030391-3 are remakes of titles originally recorded 12dec38.

(3870) (same personnel):   Camel Caravan broadcast, New York City – Tuesday, December 27, 1938

	Bach Goes To Town	**(N)**

This CBS broadcast title on (LP) MGM E3789, MGM(E) C807, Verve V8582,2317056, Verve(E) VLP9120.

(3871) **ZIGGY ELMAN and His ORCHESTRA** (Ziggy Elman, tp; Dave Matthews, Noni Bernardi, as; Jerry Jerome, Arthur
Rollini, ts; Jess Stacy, p; Ben Heller, g; Harry Goodman, b; Al Kendis, d):
                                                                         New York City – Wednesday, December 28, 1938

030770-1	**Fralich In Swing**	**(A)**	(78)	Bluebird B10103
030771-1	**Bublitchki**	**(A)**	(78)	Bluebird B10103
030772-1	**29th and Dearborn**	**(S)**	(78)	Bluebird B10096
030773-1	**Sugar**	**(S/A)**	(78)	Bluebird B10096

Ben Heller, Arthur Rollini and Ernani "Noni" Bernardi himself have all confirmed that Bernardi made the arrangements for
the Ziggy Elman sessions. Rollini also advised: "I played the solos on *Sugar, Deep Night* [a non-Stacy session] and *Let's
Fall In Love.* Jerry Jerome did the others."
Fralich In Swing became And *The Angels Sing*

other releases:
all titles on (LP) Sunbeam SB-202, Ajazz 410
          (CD) Affinity AFS1006, Classics 900
030770-1 on (LP) RCA VPM-6043, DPS2019, (CD) Hallmark 300422, SMS SMS50
030771-1 on (LP) Victor LEJ-4. Camden CAL383, (CD) Bluebird(F) ND86753

(3901) **BENNY GOODMAN and His ORCHESTRA** (personnel as for December 12, 1938, plus Lionel Hampton, d; on -1;
Johnny Mercer, vo):   Camel Caravan broadcast, New York City – Tuesday, January 3, 1939
   [a]   **I Can't Give You Anything But Love, Baby** -1 **(S)**
   [b]   **Hurry Home** vMT   **(A)**
   [c]   **You Must Have Been A Beautiful Baby** vJM, BG **(N)**
   [d]   **Cuckoo In The Clock** vJM   **(N)**
This CBS broadcast on (LP) Fanfare 13-113, Giants of Jazz 1030.
Other titles from this broadcast feature pianists Meade Lux Lewis and Albert Ammons.

(3902) (same personnel, probably with Harry Goodman on b):
                                     Camel Caravan broadcast, New York City – Tuesday, January 10, 1939
   [a]   **Sweet Sue - Just You** -1   **(N)**
   [b]   **Could Be** vMT, JM, BG   **(A)**
   [c]   **Ciribiribin**   **(N)**
   [d]   **I Have Eyes** vMT   **(N)**
   [e]   **Sent For You Yesterday** vJM   **(I/S/A)**
This CBS broadcast on (LP) Giants of Jazz GOJ1030.

(3903) (same personnel, except Cy Baker, tp; for James; Hymie Shertzer, as; for Matthews; Billie Holiday, Leo Watson, vo):
                                       CBS, Camel Caravan broadcast, New York City – Tuesday, January 17, 1939
   [a]   **I Can't Believe That You're In Love With Me** **(N)**
   [b]   **Deep In A Dream** vMT   **(N)**
   [c]   **Fralich In Swing**   **(N)**
   [d]   **I Cried For You**   vBH   **(A)**
   [e]   **Jeepers Creepers** vMT, JM, BH, LW **(A)**
   [f]   **Hold Tight**   **(S)**
[d] on (LP) IAJRC 8, Queen-disc 16. [f] on (LP) First Time 1507 and other issues as for *Blue Hawaii,* 11may37.
The whole broadcast on (CD) Phontastic NCD8817.

(3904) **JESS STACY** (piano solos):
                            Brunswick Studios, 1776 Broadway, New York City – Wednesday, January 18,1939

P-23989-1	**Candlelights**	(78)	Commodore 517
P-23989-2	**Candlelights**	(LP)	Mosaic MR23.123
P-23990-1	**Complainin'**	(LP)	Mosaic MR23.123
P-23990-2	**Complainin'**	(78)	Commodore 506
P-23991-1	**Ain't Goin' Nowhere**	(78)	Commodore 517

other releases:
Commodore 506, 517 as "A Piano Solo by Jess Stacy"
all 78 rpm titles on (LP) Commodore XFL15358, CCL7008, London(G) 6.24298, Mosaic MR23-123
                    (CD) Commodore CCD7008, Classics 795,Topaz TPZ1050
P-23989-1 on   (LP) Sunbeam (unnumbered Bix set, Vol. 5)
                    (CD) ASV Living Era AJA5172, (AC) Neovox 849
P-23989-2/23990-1 on (AC) Neovox 849

(3905) **BENNY GOODMAN and His ORCHESTRA** (personnel as for January 17, 1939, with Lionel Hampton, vb-1; Joseph
Szigeti, vl-1; The Quintones, vo):   Camel Caravan broadcast, New York City – Tuesday, January 24, 1939
   [a]   **Gypsy Love Song**   **(N)**
   [b]   **My Heart Belongs To Daddy** vMT **(N)**
   [c]   **Undecided**   **(S)**
   [d]   **Shadrach**   vJM,TQ   **(N)**
   [e]   **Stompin' At The Savoy** -1   **(N)**
   [f]   **Wrappin' It Up**   **(N)**
This CBS broadcast on (CD) Phontastic NCD8817.

(3906) **JESS STACY** (piano solos):   Cape Girardeau – Friday, January 27, 1939
               The World Is Waiting For The Sunrise
               After You've Gone
These titles were listed for auction in "Joslin's Jazz Journal" (February, 1995) as part of R.F. Peg Meyer's estate. The first
title is on a 'PermaDisk' unnumbered 8" metal-base vinyl disc; the second on an 8" paperbased disc. They were recorded in
Peg Meyer's music store. In the light of Goodman's New York activities at this time, the date quoted from the 'PermaDisk'
label must be suspect.

(3907) **BENNY GOODMAN and His ORCHESTRA** (personnel as for January 17, 1939, plus Jack Teagarden, trombone-1, vocal): Camel Caravan broadcast, New York City – Tuesday, January 31, 1939

[a]	**And The Angels Sing**	(N)
[b]	**I Gotta Right To Sing The Blues** -1	(N)
[c]	**Basin Street Blues** -1, vJT	(A)
[d]	**Smoke House**	(N)
[e]	**Two Sleepy People** vJT/JM	(I/A)

[c] on (LP) Spook Jazz 6602, Giants of Jazz GOJ1038. [e] on (LP) Giants of Jazz GOJ1038. All above CBS broadcast titles on (CD) Phontastic NCD8817. (Pianist Pete Johnson guests on *Roll 'Em*, the final number on the broadcast.)

(3908) (same personnel, except Irving Goodman, tp; for Baker): New York City – Wednesday, February 1, 1939

BS 031873-1	**(Gotta Get Some) Shut-Eye** vMT	(A)	(78)	Victor 26159
BS 031874-1	**Cuckoo In The Clock** vJM	(A)	(78)	Victor 26175
BS 031875-1	**And The Angels Sing** vMT	(A)	(78)	Victor 26170
BS 031876-1	**Sent For You Yesterday** vJM	(I/A/S)	(78)	Victor 26170

(3909) (same personnel): Camel Caravan broadcast, State Theater, Hartford, Connecticut – Tuesday, February 7,1939

[a]	**Swingin' Down The Lane**	(N)
[b]	**(Gotta Get Some) Shut-Eye** vMT	(A)
[c]	**Estrellita**	(S)
[d]	**Cuckoo In The Clock** vMT	(A)
[e]	**Old Folks** (parody) vJM/BG	(N)
[f]	**Hartford Stomp**	(N)

[f] on (LP) IAJRC 8, First Time 1507 and issues as for *Blue Hawaii,* 11may37.
The whole CBS broadcast on (LP) Giants of Jazz GOJ1033, Sandy Hook 2102.

(3910) (same personnel): New York City – Thursday, February 9, 1939

BS 033710-1	**Estrellita**	(S)	(78)	Victor 26187
BS 033710-2	**Estrellita**	( )	(LP)	Blu-Disc 1004
BS 033711-1	**A Home In The Clouds** vMT	( )	(78)	Victor 26175
BS 033711-2	**A Home In The Clouds** vMT	(A)	(78)	Victor 26175

(3911) (same personnel): Camel Caravan broadcast, Earle Theater, Philadelphia, Pennsylvania – Tuesday, February 14, 1939

[a]	**Undecided**	(S)
[b]	**A Home In The Clouds** vMT	(N)
[c]	**Trees** vMT	(I)
[d]	**You're A Sweet Little Headache** vMT	(N)
[e]	**Hold Tight**	(S)
[f]	**Could Be** vMT, JM, BG	(A)
[g]	**Sent For You Yesterday**	(S)

These CBS broadcast titles on (LP) Giants of Jazz GOJ1033, Sandy Hook 2102. [c] on (LP) First Time 1507 and other issues as *Blue Hawaii,* 11may37. [g] on (LP) IAJRC 8.

(3912) (same personnel): Camel Caravan broadcast, Shubert Theater, Newark, New Jersey – Tuesday, February 21, 1939

[a]	**Honolulu**	(N)
[b]	**Hurry Home** vMT	(N)
[c]	**When Buddha Smiles**	(N)
[d]	**Good For Nothin' But Love** vMT	(N)
[e]	**Together** vMT	(S)
[f]	**Farewell Blues**	(N)

These CBS broadcast titles on (CD) Phontastic NCD8818.

(3913) (same personnel): Camel Caravan broadcast, Fox Theater, Detroit, Michigan – Tuesday, February 28, 1939

[a]	**Singin' In The Rain**	(N)
[b]	**Deep Purple** vMT	(A)
[c]	**In The Shade Of The Old Apple Tree** vMT	(N)
[d]	**Big John Special**	(S)
[e]	**(What's The Reason) I'm Not Pleasin' You** vJM	(A)
[f]	**Bugle Call Rag**	(N)

These CBS broadcast titles on (CD) Phontastic NCD8818.

(3914) (same personnel):　　　　　Camel Caravan broadcast, Lyric Theater, Indianapolis, Indiana – Tuesday, March 7, 1939

[a]		**Lulu's Back In Town**	**(N)**
[b]		**I Get Along Without You Very Well** vMT	**(N)**
[c]		**Indiana** vJM, BG ,band	**(A)**
[d]	TRIO	**Exactly Like You**	
[e]		**Estrellita** vMT	**(N)**
[f]		**(Gotta Get Some) Shut-Eye** vMT	**(A)**
[g]		**One O'Clock Jump**	**(I/S)**

TRIO: Goodman, cl; Stacy, p; Hampton, d.
This CBS broadcast on (LP) Giants of Jazz GOJ1036. [d] on (LP) Giants of Jazz GOJ1034.

(3915) (same personnel):

　　　　　Camel Caravan broadcast, Stanley Theater, Pittsburgh, Pennsylvania – Tuesday, March 14, 1939

[a]		**Oh, Lady Be Good!**	**(N)**
[b]		**Cuckoo In The Clock** vMT	**(A)**
[c]		**That Naughty Waltz**	**(N)**
[d]	QUARTET	**Pagan Love Song**	
[e]		**Begin The Beguine**	**(N)**
[f]		**You Oughta Be In Pictures** (parody) vJM/BG/band	**(A)**
[g]		**You Turned The Tables On Me** vMT	**(A)**
[h]		**Sent For You Yesterday**	**(I/S)**

QUARTET: Goodman, cl; Hampton, vb; Stacy, p; Schutz, d:
This CBS broadcast on (LP) Giants of Jazz GOJ1036. [c] on (LP) IAJRC 8; [d] on (LP) Giants of Jazz GOJ1034; [e] on (LP) IAJRC 8, First Time 1507 and issues as for *Blue Hawaii,* 11may37; [h] on (LP) Blu-Disc T-5001/2, Phontastic NOST-7625/6

(3916) (same personnel):　　　　　Camel Caravan broadcast, Earle Theater, Washington, D.C. – Tuesday, March 21, 1939

[a]		**Gypsy Love Song**	**(S)**
[b]		**I Get Along Without You Very Well** vMT	**(I/A)**
[c]		**Spring, Beautiful Spring**	**(N)**
[d]		**Bach Goes To Town**	**(N)**
[e]		**Them There Eyes** vJM	**(A)**
[f]	QUARTET	**Deep Purple**	
[g]		**The Kingdom of Swing**	**(S)**

QUARTET: Goodman, cl; Hampton, vb; Stacy, p; Schutz, d:
[g] on (LP) Blu-Disc T-5001/2, Phontastic NOST-7625/6.
[f] on (AC) Star Line SLC.61142.
All above CBS broadcast titles on (CD) Phontastic NCD8818

(3917) (same personnel):　　　　　Camel Caravan broadcast, Palace Theater, Akron, Ohio – Tuesday, March 28, 1939

[a]		**Clap Your Hands**	**(N)**
[b]		**And The Angels Sing** vMT	**(N)**
[c]		**Paradise** vMT	**(N)**
[d]	TRIO	**She's Funny That Way**	
[e]		**'Tain't What You Do** vJM, band	**(A)**
[f]		**Goodnight, My Love** vMT	**(A)**
[g]		**Swingtime In The Rockies**	**(N)**

TRIO: Goodman, cl; Stacy, p; Schutz, d:
[d] on (LP) IAJRC 8. [b], [c] on (LP) Sunbeam SB 152.
All above CBS broadcast titles on (CD) Phontastic NCD8819.

(3918) (same personnel, plus The Quintones, vo):　　　　　Camel Caravan broadcast, New York City – April 4, 1939

[a]		**Louise**	**(S)**
[b]		**That Sly Old Gentleman** vMT, TQ	**(A)**
[c]		**I'm Forever Blowing Bubbles** vMT	**(N)**
[d]	QUARTET	**Opus 3/4**	
[e]		**Kingdom of Swing**	**(S)**
[f]		**Hold Tight**	**(S)**
[g]		**Shadrach** vJM, TQ	**(N)**
[h]		**I've Found A New Baby**	**(N)**

QUARTET: Goodman, cl; Hampton, vb; Stacy, p; Schutz, d:
These CBS broadcast titles on (LP) Giants of Jazz GOJ1039. [d] on (LP) Giants of Jazz GOJ1034.

(3919) **BENNY GOODMAN QUARTET** (Benny Goodman, cl; Lionel Hampton, vb; Jess Stacy, p; Buddy Schutz, d):

New York City – Thursday, April 6, 1939

BS 035708-1	**Opus 3/4**		(78)	Victor 26240
BS 035709-	**I've Got Old-Fashioned Love In My Heart** vMT			rejected

It is assumed that the second title is by the Quartet. This master has been destroyed.

(3920) **BENNY GOODMAN and His ORCHESTRA** (personnel as for February 1, 1939):

New York City – Friday, April 7, 1939

BS 035713-1	**Show Your Linen, Miss Richardson**	vJM	**(A/S)**	(78)	Victor 26211
BS 035713-2	**Show Your Linen, Miss Richardson**	vJM	**(A/S)**	(78)	Victor 26211
BS 035714-1	**The Lady's In Love With You** vMT		**(A/S)**	(78)	Victor 26211
BS 035714-2	**The Lady's In Love With You** vMT		**( )**	(78)	Victor 26211
BS 035715-	**Them There Eyes** vJM				rejected
BS 035716-1	**The Kingdom Of Swing**		**(S)**	(EP)	Victor EPA5100
BS 035716-2	**The Kingdom Of Swing**		**(S)**	(LP)	RCABb AXM2.5568
BS 035717-1	**Rose Of Washington Square**		**(S)**	(78)	Victor 26230
BS 035717-2	**Rose Of Washington Square**		**( )**	(LP)	RCA(F) PM43173
BS 035718-1	**The Siren's Song**		**(N)**	(78)	Victor 26230

(3921) (same personnel; Lionel Hampton, d -1): Camel Caravan broadcast, New York City – Tuesday, April 11, 1939

[a]	**Honeysuckle Rose**	**(N)**
[b]	**Tears From My Inkwell** vMT	**(A)**
[c]	**Estrellita** vMT	**(N)**
[d]	**Don't Worry 'Bout Me** vMT	**(A)**
[e]	**Sing, Sing, Sing** -1	**(N)**

All these CBS broadcast titles on (LP) Giants of Jazz GOJ1039.
[a] on (LP) MGM E3789, MGM(E) C807, Verve V8582, Verve(E) VLP9120, Verve 2317056, 2428502.

(3922) (same personnel, except Corky Cornelius, tp; for Irving Goodman):

Camel Caravan broadcast, Jefferson County Armory, Louisville – Tuesday, April 18, 1939

[a]		**Rose of Washington Square**	**(S)**
[b]	QUARTET	**The Man I Love**	
[c]		**Show Your Linen, Miss Richardson** vJM	**(N)**
[d]		**Who'll Buy My Bublitchki?**	**(N)**
[e]		**Pic-A-Rib**	**(N)**

QUARTET: Goodman, cl; Hampton, vb; Stacy, p; Schutz, d.
[d] on (LP) Blu-Disc T-5001/2, Phontastic NOST-7625/6.
All above CBS broadcast titles on (CD) Phontastic NCD8819. [b] on (AC) Star Line SLC.61142.

(3923) (same personnel): Camel Caravan broadcast, Tobacco Warehouse, Asheville, N.C. – Tuesday, April 25, 1939

[a]		**Night Must Fall**	**(A)**
[b]		**You And Your Love** vMT	**(A)**
[c]		**The Beer Barrel Polka**	**(N)**
[d]		**Carolina In The Morning** vJM, BG	**(A)**
[e]	QUARTET	**Opus 3/4**	
[f]		**Don't Worry 'Bout Me** vMT	**(A)**
[g]		**Madhouse**	**(S/A)**

QUARTET: Goodman, cl; Hampton, vb; Stacy, p; Schutz, d:
These CBS broadcast titles on (CD) Phontastic NCD8819. [e] on (AC) Star Line SLC-61142

(3924) (same personnel, except Quinn Wilson, b; for Harry Goodman; Lionel Hampton, d; for Schutz):

CBS Airplay Theater, Camel Caravan broadcast, Chicago – Tuesday, May 2, 1939

[a]		**Jumpin' At The Woodside**	**(I/S)**
[b]		**The Lady's In Love With You** vMT	**(A/S)**
[c]		**Chlo-e**	**(S)**
[d]		**When Yuba Plays The Rhumba On The Tuba** vJM	**(N)**
[e]		**My Melancholy Baby**	**(N)**
[f]	QUARTET	**Chicago**	
[g]		**And The Angels Sing** vMT	**(A)**
[h]		**Clarinet Marmalade**	**(N)**

QUARTET: Goodman, cl; Hampton, vb; Stacy, p; unknown, d:
These titles on (LP) Giants of Jazz GOJ1042. [f] on (LP) Giants of Jazz GOJ1034.

(3925) (same personnel, plus Bruce Squires, tb):   Chicago – Thursday, May 4, 1939

BS 034649-1	**Pic-A-Rib**	**(I)**	(78)	Jazz Unlimited 11
BS 034650-1	**You And Your Love** vMT	**(A)**	(78)	Victor 26263
BS 034651-2	**Who'll Buy My Bublitchki?**	**(A)**	(78)	Victor 26263

(3926) (Ziggy Elman, Chris Griffin, Corky Cornelius, tp; Red Ballard, Vernon Brown, Bruce Squires, tb; Benny Goodman, cl; Hymie Shertzer, Noni Bernardi, as; Art Rollini, Jerry Jerome, ts; Jess Stacy, p; George Rose, g; Art Bernstein, b; Lionel Hampton, d; Martha Tilton, Johnny Mercer, vo):

Camel Caravan broadcast, Fox Theater, St. Louis, Missouri – Tuesday, May 9, 1939

[a]		**Trees**	**(N)**
[b]		**A Home In The Clouds** vMT	**(A)**
[c]		**Mighty Lak A Rose**	**(S)**
[d]		**St. Louis Blues** vJM	**(A)**
[e]	QUINTET	**Old Fashioned Love**	**(S)**
[f]		**Pic-A-Rib**	**(I)**

QUINTET: Goodman, cl; Hampton, vb; Stacy, p; Rose, g; Bernstein, b. These CBS broadcast titles on (LP) Giants of Jazz GOJ1042. [a], [b], [c] on (LP) Soundcraft 1021. [e] on (LP) Giants of Jazz GOJ1034.

(3927) (same personnel; Louise Tobin, vo):

Camel Caravan broadcast, Palace Theater, Cleveland, Ohio – Tuesday, May 16, 1939

[a]		**Don't Be That Way**	**(N)**
[b]		**Louise Tobin Blues** vLT	**(A)**
[c]		**Make Believe**	**(N)**
[d]		**Alexander's Ragtime Band** vJM	**(N)**
[e]		**It's Never Too Late** vLT	**(N)**
[f]		**Sent For You yesterday**	**(I/S)**

These CBS broadcast titles on (LP) Aircheck 32.
Some titles on Aircheck 32 and 34 are incomplete.

(3928) (same personnel, except Nick Fatool, d; for Hampton):

Camel Caravan broadcast, Palace Theater, Columbus, Ohio – Tuesday, May 23, 1939

[a]		**Blue Skies**	**(N)**
[b]		**If You Ever Change Your Mind** vLT	**(S/A)**
[c]		**Russian Lullaby**	**(N)**
[d]		**Boy Meets Horn**	**(N)**
[e]	QUINTET	**I Got Rhythm**	**(S)**
[f]		**Sugar Foot Stomp**	**(N)**

QUINTET: Goodman, cl; Hampton, vb; Stacy, p; Bernstein, b; Fatool, d:
These CBS broadcast titles on (LP) Aircheck 32.
[e] on (AC) Star Line SLC-61142.

(3929) (same personnel):   CBS, Camel Caravan broadcast, Elby Theater, Cincinnati, Ohio – Tuesday, May 30, 1939

[a]		**Three Little Words**	**(N)**
[b]		**Don't Worry 'Bout Me** vLT	**(A)**
[c]		**In A Little Spanish Town**	**(S)**
[d]		**Indianapolis Speedway Race** vJM	**(A)**
[e]	QUINTET	**Stompin' At The Savoy**	**(S)**
[f]		**Louise** vLT	**(A)**
[g]		**Bugle Call Rag**	**(N)**

QUINTET: as for May 23, 1939.
[a], [b], [c], [d] on (LP) Aircheck 32; [e], [f], [g] on (LP) Aircheck 34. [e] on (AC) Star Line SLC.61142

(3930) (same personnel):   Camel Caravan broadcast, Paramount Theater, Fort Wayne, Indiana – Tuesday, June 6, 1939

[a]		**Love Me Or Leave Me**	**(N)**
[b]		**The Lady's In Love With You** vLT	**(A/S)**
[c]		**Without A Song**	**(N)**
[d]	QUINTET	**Memories Of You**	**(A/S)**
[e]		**And The Angels Sing** vLT	**(A)**
[f]		**King Porter Stomp**	**(N)**

QUINTET: as for May 23, 1939.
These CBS broadcast titles on (LP) Aircheck 34. [d] on (LP) Giants of Jazz GOJ1034.

(3931) **ZIGGY ELMAN and His ORCHESTRA** (Ziggy Elman, tp; Hymie Shertzer, Noni Bernardi, as; Jerry Jerome, Art Rollini, ts; Jess Stacy, p; Ben Heller, g; Harry Goodman, b; Al Kendis, d):

New York City – Thursday, June 8, 1939

037604-1	**You're Mine, You**	(S/A)	(78)	Bluebird B10316
037605-1	**Let's Fall In Love**	(S)	(78)	Bluebird B10342
037606-1	**Zaggin' With Zig**	(I/S/A)	(78)	Bluebird B10316
037607-1	**I'll Never Be The Same**	(S)	(78)	Bluebird B10342

other releases:
all titles on (LP) Ajazz 410 (CD) Classics 900, Affinity AFS1006
037604-1 on (LP) Sunbeam SB 233
037606-1 on (LP) Readers Digest RS9673, RDS6526, Sunbeam SB 202.
037605-1/037607-1 on (LP) Sunbeam SB 202.

(3932) **JESS STACY – Piano, BUD FREEMAN – Tenor Sax A Duet**

Reeves Sound Studios, New York City – Tuesday, June 13, 1939

| R-2126-2 | **She's Funny That Way** | | (78) | Commodore 529 |

JESS STACY (piano solos):		same session		
R-2127-3	**You're Driving Me Crazy**		(78)	Commodore 529
R-2128-1	**The Sell Out**		(78)	Commodore 1503
R-2129-1	**Ec-Stacy**		(78)	Commodore 1503

R-2128 was listed in the recording ledger as *Yes! Jess*, and on Commodore supplements of the period as *Jess A Plenty*. Commodore 529 (R-2127) as "A Piano Solo by Jess Stacy". Milt Gabler (23apr84) told Bert Whyatt, "Bud Freeman was visiting us on the . . . session. He had his horn with him and felt like playing a chorus, so I let him do it. It was really supposed to be a piano solo date."

other releases:
all titles on (LP) Commodore XFL15358, CCL7008, (G) 6.24298, Mosaic MR23-123 (CD) Commodore CCD7008,
        Classics 795; (AC) Neovox 849
R-2126-2 on (LP) Atlantic SD2-309 (CD) Topaz TPZ1050
R-2127-3/R-2128-2 on (CD) Topaz TPZ1050
R-2129-1 on (CD) Commodore CMD24002

An entry in the Reeves Sound Studios ledgers indicated that these four titles had already been recorded on June 9, 1939. Milt Gabler told Bert Whyatt that this is incorrect. Details are given in the "Non Stacy Items" appendix at the end of this discography.

(3933) **BENNY GOODMAN's QUINTET** (Goodman, cl; Lionel Hampton, vb; Jess Stacy, p; Art Bernstein, b; Nick Fatool, d):

Camel Caravan broadcast, New York City – Tuesday, June 13, 1939

| | **Wishing** | (I/A) | | |

This CBS broadcast title on (LP) Giants of Jazz GOJ1034.

(3934) **BENNY GOODMAN and His ORCHESTRA** (same personnel as May 23, 1939, except Toots Mondello, as; for Bernardi):

Camel Caravan broadcast, Ritz-Carlton Hotel, Boston – Tuesday, June 20, 1939

[a]		**There'll Be Some Changes Made**	(N)
[b]	QUINTET	**China Boy**	(N)
[c]		**Class of '39**	(A)
[d]		**Wrappin' It Up**	(N)

QUINTET: Goodman, cl; Hampton, vb; Stacy, p; Bernstein, b; Fatool, d:
These CBS broadcast titles on (LP) Aircheck 34. [b] on (AC) Star Line SLC-61142.

(3935) **ZIGGY ELMAN and His ORCHESTRA** (Ziggy Elman, tp; Hymie Shertzer, Noni Bernardi, as; Jerry Jerome, Babe Russin, ts; Jess Stacy, p; Joe Schwartzman, b; Al Kendis, d):

New York City – Tuesday, August 29, 1939

041928-1	**You Took Advantage Of Me**	(S)	(78)	Bluebird B10413
041929-1	**I'm Yours**	(S)	(78)	Bluebird B10413
041930-1	**Am I Blue?**	(I/A/S)	(78)	Bluebird B10490
041930-2	**Am I Blue?**	(I/A/S)	(LP)	Meritt 7
041931-1	**I Have Everything To Live For**	(S)	(78)	Bluebird B10490

other releases:
all 78 rpm titles on (LP) Ajazz 410 (CD) Classics 900, Affinity AFS1006
041928-1/041929-1 on (LP) Sunbeam SB 233
041930-1/041931-1 on (LP) Sunbeam SB 202.
041928-1 on (CD) Vintage Jazz Classics VJC1009/2.

(3936) **JESS STACY and His ALL STARS** (Billy Butterfield, tp; Les Jenkins, tb; Hank D'Amico, cl; Eddie Miller, ts; Jess Stacy, p; Allen Hanlon, g; Sid Weiss, b; Don Carter, d; Carlotta Dale, vo; Noni Bernardi, arr):

New York City – Tuesday, September 26, 1939

US-1-D1	**What's New?** vCD	**(S/A)**	(78)	Varsity 8064
US-2-D1	**Melancholy Mood** vCD	**(S)**	(78)	Varsity 8064
US-3—	**Noni**	**(S)**	(78)	Varsity 8076
US-4—	**Jess Stay**	**(I)**	(78)	Varsity 8076

labels of both Varsity 8064 and 8076 are sub-titled: "Playing in the Honky Tonk", presumably inserted by Eli Oberstein, the head of U.S. Records.
Noni is related to *Muskrat Ramble*. Session produced by Warren Scholl.

other releases:
US-3/US-4 on (LP) Stinson SLP20. All titles on (CD) Classics 795.

Stacy has been shown on the Bob Crosby record date for October 2, 1939, *(Air Mail Stomp/High Society)*, but he did not join the Crosby orchestra officially until after that date. The pianist heard on *High Society* sounds like Joe Sullivan and there is no reason to think it is not he.

(3937) **BOB CROSBY and His ORCHESTRA** (Max Herman, Billy Butterfield, Shorty Sherock, tp; Warren Smith, Ray Conniff, tb; Irving Fazola, cl; George Koenig, Bill Stegmeyer, as; Eddie Miller, cl, ts, vo; Gil Rodin, ts; Jess Stacy, p; Nappy Lamare, g, vo; Bob Haggart, b, wh; Ray Bauduc, d; Bob Crosby, Teddy Grace, vo):

New York City – Monday, October 23, 1939

66791-A	**I Thought About You** vTG	**(A)**	(78)	Decca 2812
66792-A	**Happy Birthday To Love** vTG	**(A)**	(78)	Decca 2824
66793-A	**For Dancers Only**	**(A)**	(78)	Decca 3138
66794-A	**The Answer Is Love** vBC	**(N)**	(78)	Decca 2824

other releases:
all titles on (LP) Ajaz 254.
66793 on (LP) Swingfan SF1016,Sounds of Swing LP-109,MCA-Coral PCO.7995
66791/66792 on (CD) Halcyon DHDL130; HEP CD1054. 66793/66794 on (CD) Halcyon DHDL131

(3938) (same personnel):   New York City – Monday, November 6, 1939

66830-A	**It's A Whole New Thing** vTG	**(A)**	(78)	Decca 2839
66831-A	**Angry** vTG	**(A)**	(78)	Decca 2839
66832-A	**Complainin'**	**(S)**	(78)	Decca 3233

Complainin', composed by and a feature for Stacy, arranged by Haggart or Matlock – see Chapter 4.

other releases:
all titles on (LP) Ajaz 254. (CD) Halcyon DHDL131.
66830/66831 on (CD) HEP CD1054
66831 on (CD) Happy Days CDHD229.
66832 on (CD) MCA/GRP 16152.

(3939) **JESS STACY and His ORCHESTRA** (Billy Butterfield, tp; Les Jenkins, tb; Irving Fazola, cl; Eddie Miller, ts; Jess Stacy, p; Sid Weiss, b; Don Carter, d; Bob Haggart, arr):   New York City – Thursday, November 30, 1939

US-1110-1	**Breeze (Blow My Baby Back To Me)**	**(S)**	(78)	Varsity 8121
US-1111-1	**Breeze (Blow My Baby Back To Me)**	**(S)**	(78)	Varsity 8121
US-1112-2	**I Can't Believe That You're In Love With Me**	**(I/S)**	(78)	Varsity 8132
US-1113-2	**A Good Man Is Hard To Find**	**(S)**	(78)	Varsity 8140
US-1114-1	**Clarinet Blues**	**(I/A/S)**	(78)	Varsity 8132

Reverse of Varsity 8140 by Hal Bedell and his Orchestra; on some issues labelled as Jess Stacy. Session produced by George Simon. Queried about this session, Bob Haggart said: "I seem to remember doing some charts for one of Jess's own dates and I remember they did two versions of one tune - one medium tempo and the other slower – they released them as part I and II," . . . but the record labels say Fox-Trot and Blues, rather than Part I and II.

other releases:
All titles on (LP) Mosaic MR23-123; (CD) Classics 795
US-1110-1 on (LP) Mainstream 56011, S/6011.
US-1114-1 on (LP) Franklin Mint #20.

(3940) **BOB CROSBY and His ORCHESTRA** (personnel as for October 23, 1939):

New York City – Wednesday, December 6, 1939

66939-A	**Between 18th and 19th**			
	On Chestnut Street vEM, NL	(S/A)	(78)	Decca 2935
66940-A	**Pinch Me** vBC	(N)	(78)	Decca 2924
66941-A	**I Wanna Wrap You Up** vTG	(N)	(78)	Decca 2935
66942-A	**The Little Red Fox** vTG	(N)	(78)	Decca 2924

all titles on (LP) Ajaz 260; (CD) Halcyon DHDL131.
66939-A on (LP) Time-Life STBB14.
66941 on (CD) HEP CD1054

(4001) (same personnel):

New York City – Wednesday, January 10, 1940

	Nobody Knows	(A)

This broadcast title on (LP) Sunbeam SB 229

(4002) **GEORGE WETTLING'S CHICAGO RHYTHM KINGS** (Charlie Teagarden, tp; Floyd O'Brien, tb; Danny Polo, cl; Joe Marsala, ts; Jess Stacy, p; Jack Bland, g; Art Shapiro, b; George Wettling, d):

New York City – Tuesday, January 16, 1940

67059-A	**I've Found A New Baby**	(S)	(78)	Decca 18045
67059-B	**I've Found A New Baby**	( )	(78)	Decca 18045
67060-A	**Bugle Call Rag**	(S)	(78)	Decca 18044
67061-A	**I Wish I Could Shimmy Like My Sister Kate**	(A/S)	(78)	Decca 18044
67062-A	**The Darktown Strutters' Ball**	(S)	(78)	Decca(A) Y5857
67062-B	**The Darktown Strutters' Ball**	(S)	(78)	Decca 18045

other releases:
all takes except 67059B/67062A on (LP) Decca DL8029, Coral(E) CP38, Brunswick(E) LAT8042; (AC) Neovox 870
        (CD) Classics 909
67059-A/67060-A on (LP) Affinity AFS1026
67059-A on (CD) Sunday Times STCD-211
67062-A on (CD) ASV Living Era AJA5172
67062-B on (CD) Topaz TPZ1050

(4003) **BOB CROSBY and His ORCHESTRA** (same personnel as October 23, 1939):

New York City – Wednesday, January 17, 1940

	Embraceable You	(S)

This broadcast title on (LP) Sunbeam SB-216

(4004) (same personnel, Marion Mann, vo):

New York City – Tuesday, January 23, 1940

67095-A	**I've Got My Eyes On You** vMM	(A)	(78)	Decca 2991
67096-A	**Angel** vBC	(A)	(78)	Decca 2978
67097-A	**Ooh! What You Said** vMM	(N)	(78)	Decca 2992
67098-A	**Gotta Get Home** vBC	(A)	(78)	Decca 2991

other releases:
all titles   on (LP) Ajaz 260 (CD) Halcyon DHDL131
67097-A on (LP) Bandstand BS-7121, Smithsonian (no data), BBC BBC4000.2
67097-A on (CD) Aerospace RACD-7121

(4005) **BOB CROSBY'S BOB CATS** (Billy Butterfield, tp; Warren Smith, tb; Irving Fazola, cl; Eddie Miller, ts; Jess Stacy, p; Nappy Lamare, g; Bob Haggart, b; Ray Bauduc, d):

New York City – Tuesday, February 6, 1940

67172-A	**Do You Ever Think Of Me?** vNL	(A/S)	(78)	Decca 3040
67173-A	**Spain**	(A/S)	(78)	Decca 3248
67174-A	**All By Myself** vMM	(I/A)	(78)	Decca 3248
67175-A	**Jazz Me Blues**	(N)	(78)	Decca 3040

other releases:
all titles on (LP) Ajaz 260, (CD) Swaggie CD503, Halcyon DHDL131
67172-A on (LP) Swaggie S-1245, Decca DL8061, Brunswick(E) LAT8050
67173/74/75 on (LP) Swaggie S-1288, Affinity AFS.1014
67173-A on (LP) Ace of Hearts AH29, (CD) ASV Living Era AJA5097, AJA5172, MCA(E) MCFM2695
67174-A on (LP) Decca DL8061, Coral(E) CP110, Brunswick(E) LAT8050
67175-A on (LP) Decca DL8061, Coral(E) CP110, CPS6845,7360, MCA(E) MCFM2695
        (CD) Avid AVC530, Phontastic CD-7668, Topaz TPZ1054

(4006) **METRONOME ALL STAR BAND** (Charlie Spivak, Ziggy Elman, Harry James, tp; Jack Teagarden, Jack Jenney, tb; Benny Goodman, cl; Toots Mondello, Benny Carter, as; Eddie Miller, Charlie Barnet, ts; Jess Stacy, p; Charlie Christian, g; Bob Haggart, b; Gene Krupa, d):   New York City – Wednesday, February 7, 1940

CO 26489-A	**King Porter Stomp**	**(S)**	(78)	Columbia 35389
CO 26489-B	**King Porter Stomp**	**(S)**	(LP)	Phontastic NOST7610
CO 26489—	**King Porter Stomp**	**(S)**	(LP)	Blu-Disc T.1012

There are small variations between Stacy's solos on takes -A and -B.

METRONOME ALL STAR NINE (Harry James, tp; Jack Teagarden, tb; Benny Goodman, cl; Benny Carter, as; Eddie Miller, ts; same rhythm section):   same session

CO 26490-A	**All Star Strut**	**(I/S)**	(78)	Columbia 35389
CO 26490-B	**All Star Strut**	**( )**	(LP)	Sony(J), SONP50419
CO 26490—	**All Star Strut**	**(I/S)**	(LP)	Blu-Disc T.1012

The Blu-Disc titles were incomplete rehearsal takes (unnumbered). Little variation from complete titles.

other releases:
CO26489-A/CO26490-A on (LP) Columbia CL2528,Harmony HL7044, Queen-disc Q009, Tax m-8039
            (CD) CeDe International 66013
CO26489-A   on (CD) Phontastic CD-7668
CO26490-B   on (LP) Tax m-8039, CBS 67233

(4007) **BOB CROSBY and His ORCHESTRA** (personnel as for October 23, 1939, except Eddie Wade, tp; for Sherock):
                    New York City – Tuesday, February 13, 1940

67187-A	**Shake Down The Stars** vBC	**(A)**	(78)	Decca 3027
67188-A	**You, You Darlin'** vMM	**(A/S)**	(78)	Decca 3018
67189-A	**With The Wind And The Rain In Your Hair** vMM	**(N)**	(78)	Decca 3018
67190-A	**Reminiscing Time**	**(S)**	(78)	Decca 3054

other releases:
all titles on (CD) Halcyon DHDL131
67187-A on (LP) Ajaz 260, Sounds of Swing LP109
67188-A on (LP) Ajaz 260
67189-A on (LP) Ajaz 268
67190-A on (LP) Ajaz 268, Sounds of Swing LP109

(4008) (same personnel, except Bob Peck, tp; for Wade):   New York City – Monday, February 19, 1940

67204-A	**Up The Chimney Go My Dreams** vMM	**(A)**	(78)	Decca 3039
67205-A	**Run, Rabbit, Run** vMM	**(N)**	(78)	Decca 3039
67206-A	**Leanin' On The Ole Top Rail** vBC	**(A)**	(78)	Decca 3027
67207-A	**They Ought To Write A Book About You** vBC	**(N)**	(78)	Decca 3090

other releases:
all titles on (LP) Ajaz 268; (CD) Halcyon DHDL132.

(4009) (same personnel):   New York City – Tuesday, February 27, 1940

67231-A	**Tit Willow** vMM	**(A)**	(78)	Decca 3054
67232-A	**Ain't Goin' Nowhere**	**(S)**	(78)	Decca 3451
67233-A	**Sweet Genevieve** vBC	**(N)**	(CD)	Halcyon DHDL132
67234-A	**Where The Blue Of The Night**			
	Meets The Gold Of The Day vBC	**(S)**	(78)	Decca 3138

67232-A is a Stacy composition and feature. This matrix was renumbered 67985-A.
62733 was re-made March 26, 1940. A test of 62733-A exists.

other releases:
all issued 78 rpm titles on (LP) Ajaz 268; (CD) Halcyon DHDL132.

(4010) BOB CROSBY'S BOB CATS (personnel as for February 6, 1940)

New York City – Wednesday, February 28, 1940

67241-A	**Mama's Gone, Goodbye** vMM	**(A)**	(78)	Decca 3056
67242-A	**So Far, So Good** vMM	**(A/S)**	(78)	Decca 3055
67243-A	**A Vous Tout De Vey, A Vous** vMM	**(N)**	(78)	Decca 3056
67244-A	**You Ought To Hang Your Heart In Shame** vMM	**(A/S)**	(78)	Decca 3055

other releases:
all titles on (LP) Ajaz 268. (CD) Swaggie CD503; (CD) Halcyon DHDL132
67241-A on (LP) Swaggie S1245, MCA(E) MCFM2695

(4011) BUDDY CLARK (vo, with orchestra: Marty Marsala, tp Brad Gowans, vtb; Pee Wee Russell, cl; Bud Freeman, ts; Jess Stacy, p; Sid Weiss, b; Morey Feld, d):

New York City – March   , 1940

US-1457-1	**Nothing But You**	**(A)**	(78)	Varsity 8230
US-1458-1	**From Another World**	**(I/A)**	(78)	Varsity 8230
US-1459-1	**I Walk With Music**	**(A)**	(78)	Varsity 8233
US-1460-1	**This Is The Beginning Of The End**	**(A/S)**	(78)	Varsity 8233
US-1460-2	**This Is The Beginning Of The End**	**(A/S)**	(78)	Varsity 8233

US-1460-1 & US-1460-2 vary only slightly. On take -1 Clark sings, in the reprise, "Tell me what has become of the warmth of your smile". On take 2 "Tell me" is missing. He starts the next line of take -1 "And. . ."

other releases:
US-1460-2 on (LP) Sunbeam P513
all five takes on (LP) IAJRC 53

(4012) BOB CROSBY and His ORCHESTRA (personnel as for February 19, 1940):

New York City – Monday, March 4, 1940

67263-A	**My! My!** vBC, MM	**(S)**	(78)	Decca 3079
67264-A	**Moments In The Moonlight** vMM	**(N)**	(78)	Decca 3070
67265-A	**Say It** vBC	**(A)**	(78)	Decca 3079
67266-A	**Angel In Disguise** vMM	**(N)**	(78)	Decca 3070

other releases:
All titles on (CD) Halcyon DHDL132.
67263-A on (LP) Ajaz 268.
67264-A/65-A/66-A on (LP) Ajaz 280.

(4013) BOB CROSBY'S BOB CATS (personnel as for February 6, 1940):

New York City – Monday, March 11, 1940

67284-A	**It's All Over Now** vBC	**(I/A)**	(78)	Decca 3104
67285-B	**Adios Americano** vMM	**(A/S)**	(78)	Decca 3104
67286-A	**Tech Triumph** vBC	**(A)**	(78)	Decca 3080
67287-A	**V.M.I. Spirit** vBC	**(A)**	(78)	Decca 3080

other releases:
all titles on (LP) Ajaz 280. (CD) Swaggie CD503; (CD) Halcyon DHDL132.

(4014) BOB CROSBY and His ORCHESTRA (personnel as for February 19, 1940):

New York City – Monday, March 18, 1940

67335-A	**Fools Rush In** vMM	**(A)**	(78)	Decca 3154
67336-A	**From Another World** vMM	**(N)**	(78)	Decca 3091
67337-A	**Over The Waves**	**(N)**	(78)	Decca 3091
67338-A	**Cecilia** vBC	**(N)**	(78)	Decca 3090

other releases:
all titles on (LP) Ajaz 280. 67337-A on (LP) Coral CPS6845
67336-B has been listed in an auction.

(4015) **JAM SESSION AT COMMODORE No. 3** (Max Kaminsky, tp; Brad Gowans, vtb; Pee Wee Russell, cl; Joe Marsala, as; Jess Stacy, p; Eddie Condon, g; Art Shapiro, b; George Wettling, d):

Decca Studio, New York City – Saturday, March 23, 1940

76329-A	**A Good Man Is Hard To Find** Pt.1	(I/S)	(78)	Commodore 1504

(add Muggsy Spanier, co; Miff Mole, tb; Bud Freeman, ts):

76330-A	**A Good Man Is Hard To Find** Pt.4	(I/A)	(78)	Commodore 1505

(Spanier, co; Mole, tb; Marsala, cl; same rhythm section):

76331-A	**A Good Man Is Hard To Find** Pt.2	(A/S)	(78)	Commodore 1504

(Spanier, co; Kaminsky, tp; Gowans, v-tb; Russell, cl; same rhythm section):

76332-A	**A Good Man Is Hard To Find** Pt.3	(A)	(78)	Commodore 1505

Milt Gabler had Part 4 recorded out of sequence. He was concerned that the musicians should tackle the chart (sketched by Brad Gowans?) for this finale before tiredness and alcohol took their toll.

other releases:
all titles on (LP) Commodore FL30.006, XFL16568, Commodore(G) 6.25526, Ace of Hearts AHC179, Stateside SL10005,
      Mainstream 56024;S/6024, Top Rank 5003, Mosaic 23-123. (CD) Classics 759
76329-A on (LP) Fontana TFL5271, Mainstream 56026:S/6026, (CD) Commodore CMD24002
76330-A/76332-A on (CD) ASA Living Era AJA5192

(4016) **BOB CROSBY and His ORCHESTRA** (personnel as for February 19, 1940):

broadcast, New York City – Monday, March 25, 1940

[a]		**Summertime** (theme)	(N)
[b]		**Skater's Waltz**	(A)
[c]		**Shake Down The Stars** vBC	(A)
[d]	BOB CATS	**A Vous Tout De Vey, A Vous** vMM	(A)
[e]		**Complainin'**	(S)
[f]		**In The Mood**	(S)
[g]		**Where The Blue Of The Night**	
		Meets The Gold Of The Day vBC	(S)
[h]		**It's You, You Darling** vMM	(A/S)
[i]		**It's A Small World** vBC	(A)
[j]		**Wolverine Blues**	(A)

BOB CATS: Butterfield, Smith,Fazola, Miller,Stacy, Lamare, Haggart, Bauduc.
This Mutual Broadcasting System broadcast from the Terrace Room of the Hotel New Yorker, 34th Street & Eighth Avenue, on (LP) Aircheck 17.

(4017) (same personnel): New York City – Tuesday, March 26, 1940

67399-A	**Believing** vMM	(A/S)	(78)	Decca 3103
67400-A	**This Is The Beginning Of The End** vBC	(N)	(78)	Decca 3103
67401-A	**Ja Da**	(S)	(78)	Decca 3233
67402-A	**Sweet Genevieve** vBC	(S)	(78)	Decca 3668
67403-A	**Short'nin' Bread** vEM, whBH	(N)	(78)	Decca 3271
67403-B	**Short'nin' Bread** whBH	(A)	(78)	Decca 3271

Some sources incorrectly show 67403-B with an Eddie Miller vocal also.

other releases:
first three titles on (LP) Ajaz 280
67401-A on   (LP) Coral CRL57089,Coral(E) LVA9045; (CD) Happy Days CDHD229
67402-A on   (LP) Ajaz 287.
67403-B on   (LP) Ajaz 287, Bandstand BSR7111; (CD) Aerospace RACD7111

(4018) (same personnel): CBS "America Dances" broadcast, New York City – Friday, March 29, 1940

Over The Waves (N)

"Broadcast to Great Britain through the facilities of the British Broadcasting Corporation." The BBC Written Archives Centre advise that this broadcast was replaced by records. Of the dates for Crosby broadcasts to the U.K., this is the only one which fits the Stacy (who is announced) period. It is assumed that the broadcast took place but that reception in Britain was unacceptable.
This title on (LP) Fanfare 6-106, Jasmine JASM2512

(4019) (same personnel):
                Camel Caravan broadcast, Terrace Room, Hotel New Yorker, New York City – Saturday, March 30, 1940
            I Know That You Know   **(S/A)**
This title on (LP) Alamac QSR2403. (AC) Jazz Connoisseur Cassettes JCC74, JCC81
            (CD) Jazz Hour JH-1043, Fat Boy FATCD327

(4020) **JESS STACY and CHARLEY VINAL** (Stacy, p; Vinal, cl):
                            at Vinal's home in Quincy, Massachusetts – Tuesday, April 2, 1940
            Blues In Bedlam
            Exactly Like You (p solo)
privately recorded on acetate by Merrill Hammond. He titled the blues, *Blues in Bedlam*, because so many people talked while Stacy and Vinal played. Date taken from cover of record owned by Peg Meyer.

(4021) **BOB CROSBY and His ORCHESTRA** (same personnel as for February 19, 1940):
                                            New York City – Wednesday, April 3, 1940

67473-A	**Embraceable You** vBC	**(S)**	(78)	Decca 3271
67474-A	**I'm Nobody's Baby** vMM	**(N)**	(78)	Decca 3179
67475-A	**Sympathy**	**(N)**	(78)	Decca 3154
67476-A	**Speak Easy**	**(N)**	(78)	Decca 3179

other releases:
all titles on (LP) Ajaz 287.
67474-A   on (LP) Bandstand BSR7121.   (CD) Aerospace RACD7121
67475-A/67476-A on (LP) Bandstand BSR7111. (CD) Aerospace RACD7111

(4022) (same personnel):   broadcast, Chicago? – mid-April 1940
    [a]   **Between 18th and 19th**
                        On Chestnut Street vEM, NL   **(S/A)**
    [b]   **I'm Prayin' Humble**   **(N)**
Both titles on (LP) Sunbeam SB 229.

(4023) (same personnel):   broadcast, Blackhawk Restaurant, Chicago – Saturday, April 20, 1940
    [a]   **Alice Blue Gown**   **(N)**
    [b]   **Muskrat Ramble**   **(N)**
    [c]   **Tuxedo Junction**   **(S)**
    [d] BOB CATS **The March Of The Bob Cats**   **(A)**
BOB CATS: Butterfield, Smith, Fazola, Miller, Stacy, Lamare, Haggart, Bauduc.
The Blackhawk was at Wabash near Randolph.
[b] on (LP) Alamac QSR2403; (AC) Jazz Connoisseur Cassettes JCC74.
[a], [c], [d] on (LP) Alamac QSR2413. (AC) Jazz Connoisseur Cassettes JCC118.

(4024) (same personnel):   broadcast, Blackhawk Restaurant, Chicago – Monday, April 29, 1940
    [a]   **Boogie Woogie Maxixe**   **(S)**
    [b]   **Fools Rush In**   vMM   **(A)**
    [c]   **Cecilia** vBC   **(A)**
    [d]   **The Old County Down**   **(N)**
    [e] BOB CATS **Jazz Me Blues**   **(N)**
    [f]   **Reminiscin' Time**   **(S)**
    [g]   **Ooh! What You Said** vMM   **(A)**
    [h]   **The Starlit Hour** vBC   **(N)**
    [i]   **Sugar Foot Stomp** vNL*   **(S)**
BOB CATS: Butterfield, Smith, Fazola, Miller, Stacy, Lamare, Haggart, Bauduc.
* "Oh, play that thing!" *Boogie Woogie Maxixe* is a Stacy feature.
Note that clarinet voicings at this time were by four clarinets, plus Eddie Miller on tenor.
This Mutual broadcast on (LP) Aircheck 17.

(4025) (same personnel, except Doc Rando, as, cl; for Stegmeyer):
                            broadcast, Blackhawk Restaurant, Chicago – May , 1940
            I Found A New Baby   **(S)**
This title on (LP) Alamac QSR2403; (AC) Jazz Conoisseur Cassettes JCC74; (CD) Jazz Hour JH-1043, Fat Boy FATCD327

(4026) (Muggsy Spanier, co; Max Herman, Bob Peck, tp; Ray Conniff, Floyd O'Brien, tb; Hank D'Amico, cl; Doc Rando, Matty Matlock, as, cl; Eddie Miller, Gil Rodin, ts, cl; Jess Stacy, p; Nappy Lamare, g, vo; Bob Haggart, b, wh; Ray Bauduc, d; Bob Crosby, vo):   broadcast, Oriental Theater, Chicago – Saturday, June 1, 1940

   [a]   **The World Is Waiting For The Sunrise**   **(S)**
   [b] BOB CATS **Sister Kate**   **(N)**
BOB CATS: Spanier, O'Brien, D'Amico, Miller, same rhythm section.
[a] on (LP) Alamac QSR2413; (b) on (LP) Alamac QSR2403, Fanfare 6-106, Jasmine JASM2512;
      (AC) Jazz Connoisseur Cassettes JCC74
[a], [b] on (CD) Jazz Hour JH-1043, Fat Boy FATCD327

(4027) (same personnel):   broadcast, Indianapolis – Saturday, June 15, 1940
           King Porter Stomp   **(N)**
This title on (LP) Jazz Archives JA40

(4028) (same personnel):   broadcast, Strand Theater, New York City – Saturday, July 6, 1940
   [a]   **Diga Diga Doo**   **(S)**
   [b]   **The Big Noise From Winnetka**   **(N)**
   [c]   **I'm Prayin' Humble**   **(N)**

[a], [b] on (LP) Alamac QSR2403, Fanfare 6-106, Jasmine JASM2512.
[c]   on (LP) Alamac QSR2403.
[b], [c] on (AC) Jazz Connoisseur Cassettes JCC74.
[a]   on (CD) Jazz Hour JH-1043, Fat Boy FATCD327.

(4029) (same personnel):   broadcast, Detroit – July , 1940
           Jimtown Blues   **(N)**
This title on (LP) Sunbeam SB 229

(4030) **LEE WILEY** accompanied by Jess Stacy, piano; Muggsy Spanier, cornet
                            Reeves Studio, New York City – Wednesday, July 10, 1940
R-3111   **Down To Steamboat Tennessee**   (78)   Commodore 1507
R-3112   **Sugar**   (78)   Commodore 1507
This session continued into the early hours of July 11.

other releases:
both titles on (LP) Commodore XFL15358, CCL7008, (G)6.24298, Mosaic 23.123.
              (CD) Commodore CCD7008, ASV Living Era AJA5102, L'Art Vocal LA15, Topaz TPZ1050; (AC) Neovox 849
R3111 on   (LP) Mainstream 56010, S6010. (CD) ASV Living Era AJA5172
R3112 on   (LP) Mainstream 56009, S6009, Fontana TL5294
              (CD) Commodore CCD7000, CMD24002

(4031) **BOB CROSBY and His ORCHESTRA** (personnel as for June 1,1940)
                            broadcast, Thursday, August 1, 1940
           Somebody Loves Me   **(N)**
This title on (CD) Jazz Hour JH-1043, Fat Boy FATCD327

(4032) **BOB CROSBY and His ORCHESTRA** (personnel as for June 1, 1940, except Al King, tp; for Peck; plus Bonnie King, vo; The Bob-0-Links, vo):   Los Angeles – Tuesday, September 3, 1940
DLA-2106-A   **Two Dreams Met** vBK   **(N)**   (78)   Decca 3404
DLA-2107-A   **Drummer Boy** vBOL   **(A/S)**   (78)   Decca 3451
DLA-2108-A   **Cow Cow Blues**   **(S)**   (78)   Decca 3488
DLA-2109-A   **Down Argentina Way** vBK   **(A)**   (78)   Decca 3404

Cow Cow Blues is a feature for Jess Stacy. This Cow Cow Davenport composition was recorded by a Sammy Price band in March 1940 and the Crosby recording, a transcription by Bob Haggart, is based upon this.
The Bob-0-Links vocal group were Ruth Keddington, Johnny Desmond, Tony Paris and Eddie Lavine.

other releases:
all titles on (LP) Ajaz 287.
DLA-2107-A on (LP) MCA-Coral(E)PCO7995,622245.
DLA-2108-A on (LP) Bandstand BS-7121. (CD) Aerospace RACD7121

(4033) (same personnel):				Los Angeles – Friday, September 6, 1940
DLA-2124-A	**I'd Know You Anywhere** vBK	**(N)**	(78)	Decca 3434
DLA-2125-A	**Dry Bones** vNL, BOL	**(A)**	(78)	Decca 3488
DLA-2126-A	**I've Got A One-Track Mind** vBC	**(A)**	(78)	Decca 3434
DLA-2127-A	**You Forgot About Me** vBC, BOL	**(N)**	(78)	Decca 3417

other releases:
all titles on (LP) Ajaz 287

(4034) (same personnel):			broadcast, Catalina Island, CA – Sunday, September 8, 1940
[a]	**Complainin'**	**(S)**	
[b]	**Speak Easy**	**(S)**	
[c]	**Yancey Special**	**(S)**	

[a], [b] on (LP) Alamac QSR2403. [c] on (LP) Alamac QSR2413, Fanfare 6-106, Jasmine JASM2512;
    (AC) Jazz Connoisseur Cassettes JCC118; (CD) Topaz TPZ1050

(4035) (same personnel):				Los Angeles – Tuesday, September 10, 1940
DLA-2136-A	* **Don't Call Me Boy** vNL	**(S/A)**	(78)	Decca 3431
DLA-2137-A	**Gone But Not Forgotten** vBK	**(N)**	(78)	Decca 3417
DLA-2138-A	**Do You Know Why?** vBK	**(A)**	(78)	Decca 3445
DLA-2139-A	**Isn't That Just Like Love?** vBC	**(A)**	(78)	Decca 3445
DLA-2140-A	* **Take Me Back Again** vBC	**(A)**	(78)	Decca 3576
DLA-2141-A	* **I'll Come Back To You** vBC	**(A)**	(78)	Decca 3576
DLA-2142-B	* **You're Bound To Look**			
	Like A Monkey vNL & band	**(A)**	(78)	Decca 3431

* **BOB CATS**: Spanier, O'Brien, D'Amico, Miller, Stacy, Lamare, Haggart, Bauduc.

other releases:
all titles on (LP) Ajaz 294.   The Bob Cats titles on (CD) Swaggie CD503.
DLA-2142-B on (LP) MCA MCFM2695; (CD) ASV Living Era AJA5102.

(4036) (same personnel):		
	"Camel Caravan" broadcast, Mark Hopkins Hotel, San Francisco – Thursday, December 5, 1940	
[a]	**We're In The Money**	**(A)**
[b]	**Where's The Melody?**	**(A/S)**
[c]	**Oh! Susanna** vBOL	**(N)**
[d]	**Embraceable You** (fade)	**(S)**
[e]	**Panama**	**(N)**

These five titles on (LP) Blu-Disc T5004.
[a] on (LP) Fanfare 6-106, Jasmine JASM2512.

(4037) (same personnel):		
	"Camel Caravan" broadcast, Mark Hopkins Hotel, San Francisco – Thursday, December 12, 1940	
[a]	**Dry Bones** vNL, BOL	**(A)**
[b]	**Burnin' The Candle At Both Ends**	**(S/A)**
[c]	**The One I Love (Belongs To Somebody Else)**	**(N)**
[d] BOB CATS	**Jazz Me Blues**	**(A)**
[e]	**South Rampart Street Parade**	**(A)**

The Bob Cats personnel as for September 10, 1940.
These five titles on (LP) Blu-Disc T5004. [e] on (CD) Jazz Hour JHR73534

(4038) **BING CROSBY and CONNEE BOSWELL with Bob Crosby's Bob Cats** (vo, with personnel as for September 10, 1940, plus Max Herman, tp):

				Los Angeles – Friday, December 13, 1940
DLA-2271-A	**Tea For Two**	**(A)**	(78)	Decca 3689
DLA-2272-A	**Yes, Indeed!**	**(A)**	(78)	Decca 3689
DLA-2273-	**Xmas Greetings To Decca Employees**	**( )**	(78)	see note

other releases:
DLA-2271-A & 2272-A on (LP) Decca DL5390, Brunswick(E) LA8558; (CD) Swaggie CD503; (AC) Ajazz C-1607
DLA-2271-A   on (LP) MCA MCFM2721, Wave MFPL85601,
DLA-2272-A   on (LP) Decca DL4001, DL8075, DL9064, Brunswick(E) LAT8054/8382, MCA MCFM2739, MCL1689,
       GRO16032, Coral COP6240, Harlequin 80;

(CD) MCA GRF1 032, CDLM8012, Affinity CDAFS1021-2; (Tx) OWI Music of the Jazz Bands No. 6
DLA-2273- on (LP) Crosbyana LLM-023. Not originally for sale to the public, this title was just what it said, including greetings from Jack Kapp, with Bing and Bob Crosby and Connee Boswell, backed by the Bob Cats playing *Jingle Bells*. DLA-2272 has been reported on (78) Decca 25406 with take -C, but this is probably a dubbing from take -A.

(4039) BING CROSBY with Bob Crosby and His Orchestra (vo, with personnel as for September 3, 1940, except Elmer Smithers, tb; for Conniff):   Los Angeles – Monday, December 16,1940

| DLA-2274-A | **San Antonio Rose** | **(N)** | (78) | Decca 3590 |
| DLA-2275-B | **It Makes No Difference Now** | **(A)** | (78) | Decca 3590 |

DLA-2274-A has also been labelled as New San Antonio Rose.

other releases:
both titles on (LP) Decca DL5063, Ajaz 294; (AC) Ajazz C-1607
DLA-2274-A on (LP) Coral(E) CPS81

(4040) BOB CROSBY and His ORCHESTRA (same personnel):   same session

DLA-2276-A	**The Mark Hop**	**(S/A)**	(78)	Decca 3694
DLA-2277-A	**Burnin' The Candle At Both Ends**	**(S)**	(78)	Decca 3694
DLA-2277-B	**Burnin' The Candle At Both Ends**	**(S)**	(LP)	Swaggie S1248

Burnin' The Candle At Both Ends is a Stacy composition, transcribed by Bob Haggart as a feature for Stacy. Variations between the two issued takes are minor. Take -B has a clinker by one of the trumpet section in the early ensemble, and Spanier's cornet break is slightly different.

other releases:
DLA-2776-A on (LP) Vogue-Coral LVA9045, Sounds of Swing 109, Ajaz 294
DLA-2777-A on (LP) Ajaz 294

(4041) BING CROSBY with Bob Crosby's Bob Cats (vo, with personnel as for September 10, 1940, plus The Merry Macs, vo):   Los Angeles – Monday, December 23, 1940

DLA-2290-A	**Dolores** vBC,TMM	**(A)**	(78)	Decca 25349
DLA-2290-B	**Dolores** vBC,TMM	**(A)**	(78)	Decca 3644
DLA-2291-A	**Pale Moon (Pale Rider)** vBC,TMM	**(A)**	(78)	Decca 25349
DLA-2291-B	**Pale Moon (Pale Rider)** vBC,TMM	**(A)**	(78)	Decca 3887

other releases:
both -B takes on (CD) Swaggie CD503 (AC) Ajazz C-1617

(4042) BOB CROSBY and His ORCHESTRA (same personnel):   same session

| DLA-2292-A | **The Big Noise From Winnetka** vBC, BOL, whBH | **(N)** | (78) | Decca 3611 |
| DLA-2293-A | **Something I Dreamed, No Doubt** vBC, BOL | **(N)** | (78) | Decca 3815 |

other releases:
both titles on (LP) Ajaz 294.
DLA-292-A on (LP) Vogue-Coral LVA9099

(4043) (same personnel):   broadcast, San Francisco – Thursday, December 26, 1940

[a]	**Easy Rhythm**	**(A/S)**
[b]	**There'll Be Some Changes Made**	**(N)**
[c]	**Short'nin' Bread**	**(A/S)**
[d]	**Burnin' The Candle At Both Ends**	**(A/S)**
[e]	**The Mark Hop**	**(A/S)**

These "Camel Caravan" broadcast titles on (LP) Blu-Disc T5004.

(4044) (same personnel):   Los Angeles – Monday, December 30, 1940

DLA-2308-A	**Chick-Ee-Chick** vBK, BOL	**(N)**	(78)	Decca 3605
DLA-2309-A	**Blue Echoes** vBC, BOL	**(A)**	(78)	Decca 3605
DLA-2310-A	**Until You Fall In Love** vBC, BOL	**(A)**	(78)	Decca 3668
DLA-2311-A	**Much More Lovely** vBK	**(N)**	(78)	Decca 3762

other releases:
First three titles on (LP) Ajaz 294. DLA-2311-A on (LP) Ajaz 302.

(4045) (probably same personnel):

[a]	**Will You Still Be Mine?**	( )	(Tx)	Standard B111
[b]	**The Mark Hop**	( )	(Tx)	Standard B111
[c]	**If This Is Love**	( )	(Tx)	Standard B111
[d]	**Burnin' The Candle At Both Ends**	( )	(Tx)	Standard B111
[e]	**Do You Care?**	( )	(Tx)	Standard B111
[f]	**Nighty Night**	( )	(Tx)	Standard B111
[g]	**You Can Depend On Me**	( )	(Tx)	Standard B111
[h]	**Flamingo**	( )	(Tx)	Standard B111

These titles also appeared on World Transcriptions 4425/4432. They are "From this period", as listed in the Bob Crosby orchestra discography by Charles Garrod and Bill Korst (Joyce Record Club Publication, 1987).

(4101) (same personnel):   Camel Caravan broadcast, Los Angeles – Thursday, January 2, 1941

[b]	**Boogie Woogie Maxixe**	(S)
[b]	**Li'l Liza Jane**	(S/A)

Both titles on (LP) Blu-Disc T5004.

(4102) (same personnel, except Bob Goodrich, tp; for Spanier):   Los Angeles – Monday, January 6, 1941

DLA-2347-A	**Sunset At Sea** vBC, BOL	(A)	(78)	Decca 3611
DLA-2348-A	**I, Yi, Yi, Yi, Yi** vBK	(N)	(78)	Decca 3623
DLA-2349-A	**Chica-Chica-Boom-Chic** vBK, BOL	(N)	(78)	Decca 3623

other releases:
all titles on (LP) Ajaz 302

(4103) **HARRY LIM JAM SESSION (SUNDAY SWING SESSION)** (Muggsy Spanier, co; Bud Freeman, ts; Jess Stacy, p;
Bob Casey, b; Baby Dodds, d):   Hotel Sherman, Chicago – Sunday, March 9, 1941

Jazz Me Blues	(A/S)
Swinging Without Mezz	(S/A)
Exactly Like You	(I/S)
You Took Advantage Of Me (part)	(N)
Sister Kate	(A/S)
I Found A New Baby (fade)	(I/A/S)

These titles are from a concert promoted by Harry Lim. They were recorded on 12" 78 rpm acetate discs by Hugh Davis, with John Steiner acting as supervisor. Titles are as shown on the Jazzology CD, though the first title has also been listed as *A Good Man Is Hard To Find* on the Steiner-Davis acetates. The musicians do not state the melody.

These titles are on (CD) Jazzology Book CD No.2, issued with "The Lonesome Road", the Muggsy Spanier bio-discography by Bert Whyatt (1995).

(4104) **BOB CROSBY and His ORCHESTRA** (personnel as for January 6, 1941):   Chicago – Friday, March 28, 1941

93634-A	**Well, Well** vBC, BOL	(A)	(78)	Decca 3762
93635-A	**Call It Anything** vBC, BOL	(A)	(78)	Decca 3815
93636-	**Look At You, Look At Me** vBC, BOL	(N)	( )	unissued
93637-A	**Far Away Music** vBC, BOL	(N)	(78)	Decca 3752
93638-A	**Flamingo**	(N)	(78)	Decca 3752

93636-, from a test pressing, has circulated on tape.

other releases:
all 78 rpm titles on (LP) Ajaz 302

(4105) **BOB CROSBY'S BOB CATS** (Bob Goodrich, tp; Floyd O'Brien, tb; Hank D'Amico, cl; Eddie Miller, ts; Jess Stacy,
p; Nappy Lamare, g; Bob Haggart, b; Ray Bauduc, d; Bob Crosby, vo):   Chicago – Saturday, March 29, 1941

93639-A	**Those Things I Can't Forget** vBC	(A)	(78)	Decca 4398
93640-A	**I'll Keep Thinking Of You** vBC	(S)	(78)	Decca 3808
93641-A	**A Precious Memory** vBC	(A/S)	(78)	Decca 4398
93642-A	**I've Nothing To Live For Now** vBC	(A)	(78)	Decca 3808
93643-A	**Juke Box Judy**	(S)	(CD)	Swaggie CD504

other releases:
all 78 rpm titles on (LP) Ajaz 302; on (CD) Swaggie CD504

233

(4106) BOB CROSBY and His ORCHESTRA (personnel as for January 6, 1941; Liz Tilton, vo):

New York City – Thursday, May 29, 1941

69270-A	**Do You Care?** vBC, BOL	**(A)**	(78)	Decca 3860
69270-B	**Do You Care?** vBC, BOL	**( )**	(78)	Decca 3860
69271-B	**Will You Still Be Mine?** vLT	**(N)**	(78)	Decca 3860
69272-C	**You're A Darlin' Devil**	**(A)**	(78)	Decca 4305
69273-A	**Big Tom**	**(N)**	(78)	Decca 4403

other releases:
69270-A/69271-B on (LP) Ajaz 302
69272-C   on (LP) Ajaz 309
69273-A   on (LP) Ajaz 309, Sounds of Swing LP109

(4107) (same personnel):

New York City – Monday, June 30, 1941

69449-A	**It Was Only A Dream** vEM	**(N)**	(78)	Decca 4137
69450-A	**Elmer's Tune**	**(S)**	(78)	Decca 3929
69451-A	**The Angels Came Thru** vBC, BOL	**(A)**	(78)	Decca 3929
69452-B	**La Plus Que Lente**	**(N)**	( )	unissued

69452-B, from a test pressing, has circulated on tape.

(4108) (Yank Lawson, Max Herman, Lyman Vunk, tp; Floyd O'Brien, Elmer Smithers, Buddy Morrow, tb; Matty Matlock, cl; Art Mendelsohn, Doc Rando, as, cl; Eddie Miller, Gil Rodin, ts, cl; Jess Stacy, p; Nappy Lamare, g, vo; Bob Haggart, b, wh; Ray Bauduc, d; Bob Crosby, Liz Tilton, Bob-O-Links, vo):

Los Angeles – probably July   , 1941

[a]	**Mexicali Rose**	**(S)**	(Tx)	Standard P.173
[b]	**It Was Only A Dream** vEM	**(N)**	(Tx)	Standard P.173
[c]	**Catalina Jump**	**(S/A)**	(Tx)	Standard P.173
[d]	**This Love Of Mine** vBC	**(A)**	(Tx)	Standard P.173
[e]	**Boogie Woogie Maxixe**	**(S)**	(Tx)	Standard P.173

other releases:
[c], [e], on (Tx) Standard Z.236; (LP) Jazum 5. [a], [b], [c], [d] on (LP) Hindsight HSR.192. [a] on (CD) Hindsight MICH7126.

(4109) (same personnel):

Los Angeles – Thursday, September 4, 1941

DLA 2722-A	**A Gay Ranchero** vLT & band	**(N)**	(78)	Decca 4028
DLA 2723-A	**Something New** vBC, LT	**(N)**	(78)	Decca 4028
DLA 2724-A	**I'm Trusting In You** vBC	**(N)**	(78)	Decca 4027
DLA 2725-A	**From One Love To Another** vBC	**(N)**	(78)	Decca 4027

other releases:
all titles on (LP) Ajaz 309

(4110) (same personnel):

Los Angeles – Wednesday, September 17, 1941

DLA 2767-A	**My Imaginary Love** vBC	**(N)**	(78)	Decca 4049
DLA 2768-A	**A Sinner Kissed An Angel** vBC	**(N)**	(78)	Decca 4009
DLA 2769-A	**A Weekend In Havana** vLT	**(N)**	(78)	Decca 4049
DLA 2770-A	**Two In Love** vBC	**(N)**	(78)	Decca 4009
DLA 2771-A	**Take It Easy**	**(A)**	(78)	Decca 4137

other releases:
all titles on (LP) Ajaz 309
DLA 2771-A on (LP) Bandstand BSR7121. (CD) Aerospace RACD7121.

(4111) (same personnel):

Los Angeles – September   , 1941

| [a] | **Take It Easy** | **( )** | (Tx) | Standard P173 |
| [b] | **Will You Still Be Mine?** vLT | **( )** | (Tx) | Standard P173 |

other releases:
[a], [b] on (CD) Vintage Jazz Classics VJC-1046.

(4112) On October 23, 1941, the Bob Crosby orchestra, under the direction of Gil Rodin, recorded accompaniments for six Soundies (one-title juke-box films). Bob Crosby himself was not involved. Mark Cantor advises that Stacy is not heard. The titles and the featured artists were:

Abercrombie Had A Zombie (4306)		Liz Tilton/Lee Murray
Lazybones (4602)		Hoagy Carmichael/Dorothy Dandridge
Merry Go Round (4688)		Gale Storm/Dorn Brothers & Mary
Easy Street (4805)		Dorothy Dandridge
Jazzy Joe (4806)		Dorn Brothers & Mary
Hong Kong Blues (5705)		Hoagy Carmichael/Mi Chee

The catalogue number is shown in brackets after the title.

(4113) (same personnel):   broadcast, Los Angeles – Sunday, November 30, 1941
        Royal Garden Blues   **(N)**
This title on (CD) Jazz Hour JH-1043

(4201) (same personnel):   broadcast, Los Angeles – Sunday, January 18, 1942
  [a]   **Sugar Foot Strut**   **(S)**
  [b]   **Blue Surreal**   **(N)**
[a], [b] on (LP) Alamac QSR2403.
[a]   on (CD) Jazz Hour JH-1043, Fat Boy FATCD327

(4202) (same personnel):   Los Angeles – Tuesday, January 20, 1942

DLA-2834-A	**Vultee Special**	**(S)**	(78)	Decca 4397
DLA-2835-B	**Russian Sailors' Dance**	**(S)**	(78)	Decca 4397
DLA-2836-A	**A Zoot Suit** vNL	**(S)**	(78)	Decca 4169
DLA-2837-A	**Barrelhouse Bessie From Basin Street** vEM	**(N)**	(78)	Decca 4169
DLA-2838-A	**Brass Boogie** (Part 1)	**(S)**	(78)	Decca 18359
DLA-2829-A	**Brass Boogie** (Part 2) whBH	**(S)**	(78)	Decca 18359

The label for (78) Canadian Decca 10025 states: "featuring Jess Tracy, piano and (on side 2) Bog Haggart, whistling"!

other releases:
all titles on (LP) Ajazz 402
DLA-2834-A on (LP) Ace of Hearts AH-29, Joker SM3243, Franklin Mint 95
        (CD) ASV Living Era AJA5172, Topaz TPZ1054
DLA-2835-B on (LP) Bandstand BSR-7121, Swingfan SF-1016, Joker SM3243
        (CD) Aerospace RACD7121, Vipers Nest 1010
DLA-2837-A on (CD) Past Perfect PPCD78101
DLA-2838-A/DLA-2839-A on (LP) Bandstand BSR-7107, Coral COPS6845,
        (CD) Aerospace RACD7107

(4203) (same personnel):   broadcast, Los Angeles – Sunday, January 25, 1942
        Bashful Baby Blues   **(I/S)**
This title on (CD) Jazz Hour JH-1043

(4204) (same personnel):   Los Angeles – Tuesday, January 27, 1942

DLA-2851-A	**Sugar Foot Stomp**	**(S)**	(78)	Decca 4390
DLA-2852-A	**King Porter Stomp**	**(N)**	(78)	Decca 4390
DLA-2853-A	**Jimtown Blues**	**(N)**	(78)	Decca 25475
DLA-2854-A	**Eccentric**	**(N)**	(78)	Odeon 286027
DLA-2855-A	**Milenberg Joys**	**(N)**	(78)	Decca 25293
DLA-2856-A	**Original Dixieland One-Step**	**(N)**	(78)	Decca 25475

other releases:
all titles on (LP) Ajazz 402 (except for DLA-2854-A)
DLA-2851-A on (LP) Coral CRL56003, CRL57089, Coral-Vogue LVA9045; (CD) Kaz CD315
DLA-2852-A on (LP) Sounds of Swing LP-109, Swingfan SF-1016; (CD) Past Perfect PPCD78100, 78104
DLA-2853-A on (LP) Sounds of Swing LP-109, Swingfan SF-1016, Bandstand BSR7121, Joker SM3243;
        (CD) MCA/GRP 16152, Aerospace RACD7121
DLA-2854-A on (LP) Coral CRL57089, Coral-Vogue LVA9045
DLA-2855-A on (LP) Joker SM3243; (CD) MCA/GRP 16152
DLA-2856-A on (LP) Coral CRL57089, Coral-Vogue LVA9045, Bandstand BSR-7121; (CD) Aerospace RACD7121

(4205) **BOB CROSBY'S BOB CATS** (Yank Lawson, tp; Floyd O'Brien, tb; Matty Matlock, cl; Eddie Miller, ts; Jess Stacy, p; Nappy Lamare, guitar; Bob Haggart, b; Ray Bauduc, d): Los Angeles – Tuesday, January 29, 1942

DLA-2867-A	**That Da Da Strain**	**(S)**	(78)	Decca 25293
DLA-2868-A	**Sweethearts On Parade**	**(S)**	(78)	Decca 18355
DLA-2869-A	**It's A Long Way To Tipperary**	**(N)**	(78)	Decca 18355
DLA-2869-B	**It's A Long Way To Tipperary**	**(N)**	(CD)	Swaggie CD504
DLA-2870-A	**Tin Roof Blues**	**(I/A/S)**	(78)	Bruns(E) 04003

other releases:
all five takes on (CD) Swaggie CD504
DLA-2867-A on (LP) Joker SM3243, Swaggie S1288, MCA(E) MCFM2695, Ajazz 402
DLA-2868-A on (LP) Ajazz 402
DLA-2869-A on (LP) Ajazz 402, Coral COPS6845
DLA-2870-A on (LP) Ajazz 423, Coral CRL57089, Coral-Vogue LVA9045, Swaggie S1288, Affinity AFS-1014
        (CD) Charly Classic Jazz CDCD1241, Topaz TPZ1054

(4206) **BOB CROSBY and His ORCHESTRA** (personnel as for c. July 1941, session 4109; Gloria DeHaven, vo):
Los Angeles – c. January   , 1942

[a]	**Barrelhouse Bessie From Basin Street** vEM	**(N)**	(Tx)	Standard X116
[b]	**Mirage**	**(N)**	(Tx)	Standard P193
[c]	**Marcheta**	**(S)**	(Tx)	Standard P186
[d]	**Yank's Lament**	**(N)**	(Tx)	Standard P193
[e]	**Swingin' On Nothin'** vEM & band	**(N)**	(Tx)	Standard P187
[f]	**Soft Jive**	**(S)**	(Tx)	Standard P193
[g]	**A Zoot Suit** vNL	**(S)**	(Tx)	Standard P187

other releases:
all titles on (LP) Hindsight HSR.192
[b], [c] on (LP) Jazum 5. [c], [d] on (Tx) Standard Z236. [g] on (CD) Vintage Jazz Classics VJC-1046

[h]	**Vultee Special**	**(S)**	(Tx)	Standard P187
[i]	**Tell It To A Star** vGDH	**(N)**	(Tx)	Standard P187
[j]	**Livin' Lovin' Laughin'** vBC	**(N)**	(Tx)	Standard P187
[k]	**Russian Sailors' Dance**	**(S)**	(Tx)	Standard P187

other releases:
all titles on (CD) Vintage Jazz Classics VJC-1046.   [h] on (Tx) Standard Z236; (LP) Jazum 5.

(4207) **BOB CROSBY'S BOB CATS** (personnel as for January 29, 1942): Los Angeles – February 5, 1942

DLA-2885-A	**Way Down Yonder In New Orleans** vEM, NL	**(A/S)**	(78)	Decca 4403
DLA-2886-A	**You'll Be Sorry** vBC	**(S)**	(78)	Decca 18373
DLA-2887-A	**Tears On My Pillow** vBC	**(S)**	(78)	Decca 18373
DLA-2888-A	**I'll Be True To The One I Love** vBC	**(S/A)**	(78)	Decca 4357

other releases:
all titles on (LP) Ajazz 423 and (CD) Swaggie CD504.
DLA-2885-A on (LP) Swaggie S1245.

(4208) **BOB CROSBY and His ORCHESTRA** (personnel as for c. July 1941, session 4109):
Los Angeles – Tuesday, February 17, 1942

DLA-2907-A	**Black Zephyr**	**(N)**	(78)	Decca 4415
DLA-2908-A	**Blue Surreal**	**(N)**	(78)	Decca 4415
DLA-2909-A	**Chain Gang**	**(N)**	(78)	Decca 15064
DLA-2910-A	**Ec-Stacy**	**(S)**	(78)	Decca 15064

Ec-Stacy is a Stacy composition and feature, scored by Bob Haggart.

other releases:
all titles on (LP) Ajazz 423, MCA(E) MCFM2578
DLA-2907-A on (CD) Kaz CD315
DLA-2907-A/DLA-2908-A/DLA-2909-A on (LP) Sounds of Swing LP-109
DLA-2909-A on (LP) Time-Life STBB14; (CD) MCA/GRP 16152
DLA-2910-A on (LP) Ace of Hearts AH-29; (CD) ASV Living Era AJA5172, Topaz TPZ1050

236

(4209) (same personnel):   Los Angeles February   , 1942
    [a]   **Fighting Sons Of The Navy Blue** vBC   **(N)**   (Tx)   Standard P186
    [b]   **Black Zephyr**   **(N)**   (Tx)   Standard P186
    [c]   **Blue Surreal**   **(N)**   (Tx)   Standard P186
    [d]   **Two Timin' Gal** vBC   **(I)**   (Tx)   Standard P186

other releases:
all titles on (CD) Vintage Jazz Classics VJC.1046

(4210) (same personnel):   Hollywood – probably January to February, 1942
During this period the Bob Crosby Orchestra, with strings added, recorded for the soundtrack of the Irving Berlin musical,
"Holiday Inn". The band was not featured as a separate unit. Songs with backing by Bob Crosby included:
      I'll Capture Your Heart / You're Easy To Dance With / Happy Holidays / Let's Start The New Year Right /
      Be Careful, It's My Heart / Washington's Birthday March / Song of Freedom
      Vocals are by Bing Crosby, Fred Astaire and Marjorie Reynolds.   A Paramount film.
Soundtrack recordings appeared on (LP) Soundtrack STK-112 and (CD) Vintage Jazz Classics VJC-1012-2.
You're Easy To Dance With also on (LP) Jazz Archives JA-50.

(4211) (same personnel; Muriel Lane, vo):   Los Angeles – Tuesday, March 3, 1942
    DLA-2928-A   **Poor You** vBC & quartet   **(A)**   (78)   Decca 4316
    DLA-2929-A   **I'll Keep The Lovelight Burning** vBC & quartet   **(A)**   (78)   Decca 4290
    DLA-2930-A   **Don't Sit Under The Apple Tree** vBC & quartet   **(N)**   (78)   Decca 4290
    DLA-2931-A   **Last Call For Love** vBC & quartet   **(A)**   (78)   Decca 4316
    DLA-2932-A   **Dear Old Donegal** vML   **(N)**   (78)   Decca 4305

other releases:
all titles on (LP) Ajazz 423

(4212) (same personnel):   Los Angeles – March   , 1942
    [a]   **Don't Sit Under The Apple Tree** vBC   **(N)**   (Tx)   Standard X116
    [b]   **Last Call For Love** vBC   **(N)**   (Tx)   Standard X116
    [c]   **A String Of Pearls**   **(S)**   (Tx)   Standard P191
    [d]   **As We Walk Into The Sunset** vML   **(N)**   (Tx)   Standard P191
    [e]   **Somewhere, Sometime** vBC   **(N)**   (Tx)   Standard P191
    [f]   **Mary** vBC   **(N)**   (Tx)   Standard P191
Down Beat (May 15, 1942) reported that band was "currently" making transcriptions.

other releases:
[c] on (LP) Jazum 5. [f] on (LP) Jazum 49. [a], [b], [c], [d], [e] on (CD) Vintage Jazz Classics VJC.1046

(4213) (same personnel):   "Fitch Bandwagon" broadcast, Hollywood – Saturday, May 23, 1942
    [a]   **Jersey Bounce**   **(N)**
    [b]   **The Last Call For Love** vBC, quartet   **(N)**
    [c]   **Don't Sit Under The Apple Tree** vBC, quartet   **(N)**
    [d]   **Brass Boogie**   **(S)**
    [e]   **Smokey Mary**   **(S)**
all titles on (CD) Jazz Hour JH-1043. [a], [d], [e] on (LP) Sunbeam SB 229.
[b], [c], [d], [e] on (CD) Fat Boy FATCD327.
[d] on (LP) Alamac QSR2403, [d], [e] on (AC) Jazz Connoisseur Cassettes JCC.74
[e] on (LP) Fanfare 6-106, Jasmine JASM2512.

(4214) **BING CROSBY** (accompanied by Bob Crosby and His Orchestra: same personnel):
                                                                   Los Angeles – Monday, May 25, 1942
    DLA-2989-B   **Lazy**   **(N)**   (78)   Decca 18427
    DLA-2990-A   **Let's Start The New Year Right**   **(N)**   (78)   Decca 18429
    DLA-2990-B   **Let's Start The New Year Right**   **( )**   (78)   Decca 23823
    DLA-2991-A   **I've Got Plenty To Be Thankful For**   **(N)**   (78)   Decca 18426

other releases:
DLA-2989-B on (LP) Decca DL4256, DL8144, DL34002, Bing 7, Ace of Hearts AH17; (AC) AJazz C-1617
DLA-2990-A on (LP) Decca DL4256, DL5092, Brunswick(E) LA8592, Bing 7; (AC) AJazz C-1617
DLA-2991-A on (LP) Decca DL4256, MCA 65013, Bing 7; (AC) AJazz C-1617

(4215) **BING CROSBY, FRED ASTAIRE, MARGARET LENHART** (vocals, with Bob Crosby and His Orchestra: same personnel):   Los Angeles – Wednesday, May 27, 1942

DLA-2996-A	**I'll Capture Your Heart**	(N)	(78)	Decca 18427

        FRED ASTAIRE (vocal, with Bob Crosby and His Orchestra):   same date

DLA-2997-A	**You're Easy To Dance With**	(S)	(78)	Decca 18428

        BING CROSBY (accompanied by Bob Crosby's Bob Cats: Yank Lawson, Floyd O'Brien, Matty Matlock, Eddie Miller, Jess Stacy, Nappy Lamare, Bob Haggart, Ray Bauduc):   same date

DLA-2998-A	**When My Dream Boat Comes Home**	(N)	(78)	Decca 18371
DLA-2999-A	**Walkin' The Floor Over You**	(N)	(78)	Decca 18371

        FRED ASTAIRE (vocal, with Bob Crosby and His Orchestra: as before):   same date

DLA-3000-A	**I Can't Tell A Lie**	(N)	(78)	Decca 18428
DLA-3000-B	**I Can't Tell A Lie**	(N)	(78)	DeccaAus Y5793

other releases:
DLA-2996-A on (LP) Decca DL4256, DL5092, Brunswick(E) LA8592, Bing 7
      (CD) ASV Living Era AJA5147; (AC) Ajazz C-1617
DLA-2997-A on (AC) Ajazz C-1617
DLA-2998-A on (LP) Decca DL5323, DL8493, Brunswick(E) LA8579, LAT8228, Ace of Hearts AH31, Coral(E) CPS105;
      (AC), Ajazz C-1617
      (CD) Swaggie CD504, Happy Days CDHD229, Aerospace RACD7111, MCA GRP16032
DLA-2999-A on (LP) same issues, plus Decca DL5063, DL8076, DL9067, Brunswick(E) LAT8055; (AC) Ajazz C-1617
      (CD) Swaggie CD504, Happy Days CDHD229,MCA CDLM8013
DLA-3000-A on (AC) Ajazz C-1617
And no doubt many other issues of all the Bing Crosby and Fred Astaire recordings.

(4216) **MARY LEE** (vocal, with Bob Crosby's Bob Cat: Lawson, tp; O'Brien, tb; Matlock, cl; Miller, ts; Stacy, p; Lamare, g; Haggart, b; Bauduc, d):   Los Angeles – Friday, June 26, 1942

L-3059-A	**I Hung My Head And Cried**	(N)	(78)	Decca 4346
L-3060-A	**You're My Darling**	(N)	(78)	Decca 4346
L-3061-A	**The End Of The World**	(I)	(78)	Decca 4380
L-3062-A	**You Broke My Heart, Little Darlin'**	(N)	(78)	Decca 4422

other releases:
all titles on (CD) Swaggie CD504. L-3059/3060/3061 on (AC) Ajazz C-1617

(4217) **BOB CROSBY and His ORCHESTRA** (same personnel as September 17, 1941, The Wilde Twins, David Street, vo):   Los Angeles – June   , 1942

[a]	**We're Ridin' For Uncle**			
	Sammy Now vBC, DS, TWT, band	(N)	(Tx)	Standard P193
[b]	**I Remember You** vDS	(N)	(Tx)	Standard X117
[c]	**I'll Keep The Lovelight Burning** vBC & quartet*	(A)	(Tx)	Standard X117

*At this time the "quartet" consisted of David Street, Tommy Skeffington, and Lyn and Lee Wilde.

other releases:
These three titles on (CD) Vintage Jazz Classics VJC1046

(4218) (Yank Lawson, Max Herman, Lyman Vunk, tp; Pete Carpenter, Floyd O'Brien, Bruce Squires, tb; Matty Matlock, cl; Ted Klein, Doc Rando, as, cl; Eddie Miller, Gil Rodin, ts, cl; Jess Stacy, p; Nappy Lamare, g; Bob Haggart, b; Ray Bauduc, d):   Los Angeles – Monday, July 13, 1942

L-3090-A	**The Marines' Hymn** vBC & band	(N)	(78)	Decca 4385
L-3091-A	**Anchors Aweigh**	(N)	(78)	Decca 4395
I-3092-A	**Over There**	(N)	(78)	Decca 4368
L-3093-A	**When You Think Of Lovin',**			
	Baby, Think Of Me vBC, TWT & band	(N)	(78)	Decca 4357

other releases:
L-3092-A on (CD) Phontastic PHONTCD7670

(4219) (same personnel):   Los Angeles – Sunday, July 19, 1942

L-3109-A	**Where Do We Go From Here?**	(N)	(78)	Decca 4385
L-3110-A	**The Caissons Go Rolling Along**	(N)	(78)	Decca 4395
L-3111-A	**Semper Paratus**	(A)	(78)	Decca 4374

(4220) (same personnel):   Los Angeles – Monday, July 20, 1942

L-3112-A	(Pack Up Your Troubles In Your Old Kit Bag And) Smile, Smile, Smile	(N)	(78)	Decca 4368
L-3113-A	Army Air Corps (band shouts)	(N)	(78)	Decca 4374

(4221) **MARY LEE** (vo, with Bob Crosby's Bob Cats: Lawson, tp; O'Brien, tb; Matlock, cl; Miller, ts; Stacy, p; Lamare, g; Haggart, b; Bauduc, d):   Los Angeles – Thursday, July 30, 1942

L-3160-A	I Don't Care Anymore	(N)	(78)	Decca 4380
L-3161-A	It Makes No Never Mind	(N)	(78)	Decca 4402
L-3162-A	I Told You So	(N)	(78)	Decca 4422
L-3163-A	I'll Never Cry Over You	(N)	(78)	Decca 4402

Other releases:
all titles on (CD) Swaggie CD504. L-3160 on (AC) Ajazz C-1617

(4222) **BOB CROSBY and His ORCHESTRA** (same personnel as July 13, 1942):   Los Angeles – July   , 1942

[a]	I'm Gonna Move To The Outskirts of Town vNL	(N)	(Tx)	Standard X122
[b]	Don't Get Around Much Any More	(A)	(Tx)	Standard X121
[c]	Where Do We Go From Here?	(N)	(Tx)	Standard X121
[d]	Love Is A Song vDS	(S/A)	(Tx)	Standard P197
[e]	That Russian Winter vBC	(A)	(Tx)	Standard P197
[f]	Jingle, Jangle, Jingle vBC, DS	(N)	(Tx)	Standard X120
[g]	The Song Is You	(A)	(Tx)	Standard X122
[h]	You're Easy To Dance With vDS	(N)	(Tx)	Standard X120
[i]	Sugar Foot Stomp	(S)	(Tx)	Standard X122
[j]	When You Think Of Lovin', Baby, Think Of Me vBC, DS, band	(A)	(Tx)	Standard P197
[k]	I Left My Heart At The Stage Door Canteen vDS	(A)	(Tx)	Standard P197

other releases:
titles [a], [b], [c], on (LP) Hindsight HSR192
titles [d] to [k] inclusive on (CD) Vintage Jazz Classics VJC1046.

(4225) (same personnel; plus Gloria De Haven, Muriel Lane, vo):

                                              Los Angeles – between January and July, 1942

[a]	Skylark vBC	( )	(Tx)	Standard X116
[b]	Poor You vBC & quartet	( )	(Tx)	Standard X116
[c]	Arthur Murray Taught Me Dancing In A Hurry	( )	(Tx)	Standard X117
[d]	I Fell In Love With The Leader Of A Band	( )	(Tx)	Standard X117
[e]	Somebody Nobody Loves	( )	(Tx)	Standard X117
[f]	I've Got A Gal In Kalamazoo vBC	( )	(Tx)	Standard X120
[g]	South Wind vDS	( )	(Tx)	Standard X120
[h]	Lazy vBC	( )	(Tx)	Standard X120
[i]	Knock Me A Kiss vNL	( )	(Tx)	Standard X121
[j]	Hello Mom vDS	( )	(Tx)	Standard X121
[k]	Dearly Beloved vBC	( )	(Tx)	Standard X121
[l]	Twilight Till Dawn vDS	( )	(Tx)	Standard X122
[m]	You Were Never Lovelier vDS	( )	(Tx)	Standard X122
[n]	Dear Old Donegal	( )	(Tx)	Standard P173
[o]	Believe Me If All Those Endearing Young Charms	( )	(Tx)	Standard P173
[p]	Two In Love vBC	( )	(Tx)	Standard P173
[q]	Until I Live Again vGDH	( )	(Tx)	Standard P186
[r]	The Shrine Of St. Cecelia vBC	( )	(Tx)	Standard P186
[s]	It's Just A Mile From Treasure Isle vGDH	( )	(Tx)	Standard P186
[t]	The Light Of My Life vBC	( )	(Tx)	Standard P186
[u]	Hey Mabel! vBC	( )	(Tx)	Standard P186
[v]	Dreamsville, Ohio vBC	( )	(Tx)	Standard P187
[w]	Angel Beware vBC	( )	(Tx)	Standard P187
[x]	Love Turns Winter Into Spring vBC	( )	(Tx)	Standard P187
[y]	Kiss Me Tonight For Tomorrow vBC	( )	(Tx)	Standard P187
[z]	The Memory Of This Dance vML	( )	(Tx)	Standard P191

(4226) (same personnel): Hollywood – c. August, 1942
      Big Noise From Winnetka vBC, quartet, whBH **(A)**
This title from the soundtrack of the film "Reveille With Beverly" on (LP) Hollywood Soundtrack HS5014.

(4227) (same personnel): Hollywood – c. August, 1942
      When You Think of Lovin', Baby,
              Think Of Me vBC, TWT, band   **(N)**
This title from the soundtrack of the M-G-M film "Presenting Lily Mars" on (LP) Caliban 6038, Soundtrack STK117

(4228) (Yank Lawson, Lyman Vunk, Pete Castellano, tp; Floyd O'Brien, Blaise Turi, unknown, tb; Matty Matlock, Doc Rando, Ted Klein, as, cl; Bob Mario, Eddie Miller, ts, cl; Jess Stacy, p; Nappy Lamare, g; Bob Haggart, b; Cody Sandifer, d):
              broadcast, Lycoming Company,Williamsport, Pennsylvania – Thursday, December 3, 1942

[a]	**King Porter Stomp**	**(N)**	(Tx)	AFRS SB 64
[b]	**White Christmas** vBC	**(N)**	(Tx)	AFRS SB 64
[c] BOB CATS	**It's A Long Way To Tipperary**	**(N)**	(Tx)	AFRS SB 64
[d]	**Moonlight Becomes You** vBC	**(N)**	(Tx)	AFRS SB 64
[e]	**Paradise**	**(N)**	(Tx)	AFRS SB 64
[f]	**One O'Clock Jump**	**(S)**	(Tx)	AFRS SB 64

BOB CATS: Lawson, tp; O'Brien, tb; Matlock, cl; Miller, ts; same rhythm section.   AFRS = AFRS Spotlight Bands No. 64

other releases:
[a], [c], [e], [f] on (LP) Sunbeam SB 229.
[c] on (LP) Fanfare 6-106, Jasmine JASM2512.
[f] on (LP) Alamac QSR2413 and (AC) Jazz Connoisseur Cassettes JCC74.
all titles except [b] on (CD) Jazz Hour JH-1043. [c], [f] on Fat Boy FATCD327.
"The Victory Parade of Spotlight Bands" broadcasts were sponsored by Coca Cola.

D.R. Connor, in "Benny Goodman: Listen To His Legacy", has the Bob Crosby Orchestra disbanding in late November 1942 and Jess Stacy rejoining Goodman by December 2,1942. In fact the Crosby band broke up on December 17, 1942. Stacy joined Goodman the following day.

(4301) **BENNY GOODMAN and His ORCHESTRA** (uncertain personnel, but including Lee Castle, tp; Charlie Castaldo, Miff Mole, tb; Benny Goodman, cl; Hymie Shertzer, as; Jon Walton, Bob Taylor, ts; Joe Rushton, bsx; Jess Stacy, p; Dave Barbour, g; Louis Bellson, d; Peggy Lee, vo):
              Spotlight Bands broadcast, Chicago – Saturday, February 6, 1943
      Bugle Call Rag   **(S)**
This Blue Network title on (LP) Joyce LP-1073.

(4302) **BENNY GOODMAN and His ORCHESTRA** (probably Ray Linn, Bobby Guyer, Lee Castle, tp; Charlie Castaldo, Miff Mole, tb; Benny Goodman, cl; Hymie Shertzer, Leonard Kaye, as; Jon Walton, Bob Taylor, ts; Joe Rushton, bsx; Jess Stacy, p; Dave Barbour, g; Gus Van Camp, b; Louis Bellson, d; Peggy Lee, vo):
              film soundtrack, Hollywood February or March 1943

[a]	**Why Don't You Do Right?** vPL	**(A)**	
[b]	**Bugle Call Rag**	**(S)**	

Connor lists a personnel for this film ("Stage Door Canteen"), but it does not tally with that seen on screen. The personnel identified by Ian Crosbie would suggest that the filming and recording took place in Hollywood, rather than New York. These titles on (LP) Curtain Calls 100-12, Sandy Hook 2093.

(4303) (Lee Castle, Ray Linn, Bobby Guyer, tp; Charlie Castaldo, Miff Mole, tb; Benny Goodman, cl; Hymie Shertzer, Leonard Kaye, as; Jon Walton, Bob Taylor, ts; Joe Rushton, bsx; Jess Stacy, p; Bart Roth, g; Gus Van Camp, b; Louis Bellson, d; Peggy Lee, vo):
              Los Angeles – c. February or March 1943

[a]	**Air Mail Special**	**(N)**	(Tx)	AFRS DB 25
[b]	**You'd Be So Nice To Come Home To**	**( )**	(Tx)	AFRS DB 25
[c]	**9:20 Special**	**( )**	(Tx)	AFRS DB 25
[d]	**I Don't Believe In Rumours** vPL	**( )**	(Tx)	AFRS DB 25
[e]	**I Love A Piano** vPL, BG	**(S/A)**	(Tx)	AFRS DB 25
[f]	**I'm Just Wild About Harry**	**(N)**	(Tx)	AFRS DB 25
[g]	**Why Don't You Do Right?** vPL	**(A)**	(Tx)	AFRS DB 25
[h]	**Stealin' Apples**	**(S)**	(Tx)	AFRS DB 25

These titles were on Armed Forces Radio Service (AFRS) "Downbeat" No. 25 transcription.
[a], [e],[f], [g], [h] on (LP/AC) Swing House 46.

(4304) (same personnel, except Harold Peppie, tp; for Linn; Carmen Miranda, vo):

film soundtrack, Hollywood – March/April, 1943

[a]	**Minnie's In The Money**	**(N)**
[b]	**No Love, No Nothin'**	**(N)**
[c]	**Paducah** vBG,CM	**(S/A)**
[d]	**unidentified rhythm tune**	**(N)**

Eddie Miller, ts; is on the soundtrack, though not seen on screen.
All or some of these titles from the film "The Gang's All Here" on (LP) Sandy Hook 2009, Classics International Filmusic 3003.

(4305) (Lee Castle, Bobby Guyer, Ralph Muzzillo, tp; Charlie Castaldo, Miff Mole, tb; Benny Goodman, cl; Hymie Shertzer, Eddie Rosa, as; Bob Taylor, Herbie Haymer, ts; Joe Rushton, bsx; Jess Stacy, p; Allan Reuss, g; Sid Weiss, b; Ernie Austin or Les Braun, d; E'lane McAfree, vo):   broadcast, Princeton University, N.J. – Saturday, June 26, 1943

[a]	**After You've Gone**	**(N)**	(Tx)	AFRS DB 84
[b]	**Honky Tonk Train Blues**	**(S)**	(Tx)	AFRS DB 84
[c]	**But Not For Me** vEM	**(A)**	(Tx)	AFRS DB 84
[d]	**Henderson Stomp**	**(S)**	(Tx)	AFRS DB 84

[b], a feature for Jess Stacy, on (LP) Joyce LP-1073.
AFRS = AFRS "Spotlight Bands" No. 84.

(4306) (same personnel, except George Wettling, d):   broadcast, Hotel Astor, New York City – early July 1943

Stealin' Apples	**(S)**

This title on (LP) Jazz Society AA510, Giants of Jazz 1005, Jazum 27

(4307) **BENNY GOODMAN TRIO** (Goodman, cl; Stacy, p; possibly Ray McKinley, d):

"Broadway Bandbox" broadcast, New York City – Friday, July 16, 1943

Rose Room
Oh, Lady Be Good!

"Broadway Bandbox" was a Frank Sinatra radio show.
These two titles on (LP) Giants of Jazz 1002; and (AC) Jazz Connoisseur Cassettes JCC28.

(4308) **LEE WILEY** (vo; with Jess Stacy, p; Sid Weiss, b; Cozy Cole, d):   New York City – late September 1943

Sugar   V-Disc rejected

This is the only known title from a Gjon Mili Jam Session which included Jess Stacy. An all-star party at Mili's studio at 6 East 23rd Street was sponsored by LIFE magazine. Photographs appeared in LIFE magazine of October 11, 1943. Milt Gabler was supervisor for the recordings and Eddie Condon organised the music. Unfortunately, the party was too successful, with the noise and alcoholic atmosphere spoiling the recordings.

In *The Melody Maker* for December 18, 1943 a news item refers to a U.S. government recording session by Jess Stacy and Lee Wiley, organised by Milt Gabler and Eddie Condon. Gabler told Bert Whyatt: "I may have done so but I have no recall or notes on the session." However, it is probable that the news item actually referred to this Gjon Mili session.

(4309) **BENNY GOODMAN and His ORCHESTRA** (as for early July 1943, except Gene Krupa, d; for Wettling; Ray Dorey, vo):   Spotlight Bands broadcast, Cornell University, Ithica, NY – Saturday, September 25, 1943

[a]	**After You've Gone**	**(N)**	(Tx)	AFRS SB318
[b]	**Journey To A Star** vRD	**(N)**	(Tx)	AFRS SB318
[c] QUINTET	**Three Little Words**	**(S)**	(Tx)	AFRS SB318
[d]	**Minnie's In The Money** vBG	**(A/S)**	(Tx)	AFRS SB318
[e]	**I've Found A New Baby**	**(S)**	(Tx)	AFRS SB318

QUINTET: Goodman, cl; Stacy, p; Reuss, g; Weiss, b; Krupa, d.
AFRS = AFRS "Spotlight Bands" No. 318.

other releases:
all titles on (LP) Fanfare 27-127. [a], [c], [d], [e] on (LP) Jazz Society AA510, Golden Era 15078. [a], [c] on (LP/AC) Swing House 46. [d] on (LP) Jazz Society AA510. [e] on (LP) Swing Treasury 103
Part of this broadcast may be on (Tx) AFRS Spotlight Bands No. 162.

(4310) (same personnel):   Spotlight Bands, broadcast, Armory, Springfield, Mass. – Wednesday, September 29, 1943

[a]	**Sugar Foot Stomp**	**(A)**	(Tx)	AFRS SB 321
[b]	**No Love, No Nothin'** vRD	**(A)**	(Tx)	AFRS SB 321
[c] QUINTET	**Sweet Georgia Brown**	**(A/S)**	(Tx)	AFRS SB 321
[d]	**Sunday, Monday And Always** vRD	**(A)**	(Tx)	AFRS SB 321

| [e] | Paducah vBG | (A/S) | (Tx) | AFRS SB 321 |
| [f] | Clarinet A La King | (A) | (Tx) | AFRS SB 321 |

QUINTET: Goodman, p; Stacy, p; Reuss, g; Weiss, b; Krupa, d.

other releases:
(a), (c) on (LP) Queen-disc 042.
all titles on (LP) Fanfare 27-127. [a], [c], [f] on (LP) Swing Treasury 103
[a] on (LP) Dan 5002; (CD)Phontastic CD7671. AFRS = Spotlight Bands No. 321.

(4311) **BENNY GOODMAN QUARTET** (Goodman, cl; Stacy, p; Reuss, g; Weiss, b)
broadcast, Hotel New Yorker, New York City – Saturday, October 9, 1943

Honeysuckle Rose
This title on (LP) Joyce LP-1073.

(4312) **BENNY GOODMAN and His ORCHESTRA** (Lee Castle, Ralph Muzzillo, Charlie Frankhouser, tp; Bill Harris, Mark Bennett, tb; Benny Goodman, cl; Hymie Shertzer, Eddie Rosa, as; Bob Taylor, Al Klink, ts; Ernie Caceres, bar; Jess Stacy, p; Allan Reuss, g; Sid Weiss, b; Gene Krupa, d; Carol Kay, Ray Dorey, vo)
broadcast, Hotel New Yorker, New York City – Wednesday, October 13, 1943

[a]		Mission To Moscow	(A)	(Tx)	AFRS ONS 36
[b]		No Love, No Nothin' vRD	(I/A)	(Tx)	AFRS ONS 36
[c]		You're Driving Me Crazy	(N)	(Tx)	AFRS ONS 36
[d]		Henderson Stomp	(S)	(Tx)	AFRS ONS 36
[e]		Do Nothing Till You Hear From Me vBG	(A)	(Tx)	AFRS ONS 36
[f]	TRIO	Oh, Lady Be Good!		(Tx)	AFRS ONS 36
[g]		Speak Low vRD	(N)	(Tx)	AFRS ONS 36
[h]		Stealin' Apples	(S)	(Tx)	AFRS ONS 36

TRIO: Goodman, cl; Stacy, p; Krupa, d.

other releases:
[a] on (LP) Jazz Society AA510. [a], [c], [d], [e], [f] on (LP)Queen-disc 042.
[a], [c], [e], [f] on (LP) Magic AWE23. [f] on (CD) Phontastic CD7671.   AFRS = AFRS One Night Stand No. 36.

(4313) (same personnel):   broadcast, Hotel New Yorker, New York City – Thursday, October 21, 1943
[a]	I'm Just Wild About Harry	(N)	(Tx)	AFRS ONS 26
[b]	No Love, No Nothin' vRD	(I/A)	(Tx)	AFRS ONS 26
[c]	Minnie's In The Money vBG	(A/S)	(Tx)	AFRS ONS 26
[e]	Speak Low vRD	(N)	(Tx)	AFRS ONS 26
[f]	Don't Be That Way	(N)	(Tx)	AFRS ONS 26
[g]	I'll Be Around vCK	(A)	(Tx)	AFRS ONS 26
[h]	Stealin' Apples	(S)	(Tx)	AFRS ONS 26

other releases:
All titles on (LP) Donna 1100, King of Swing 1100, Mirro(?) 135. On (tape) Radio Yesteryear 1054.
[a], [c], [f], [h] on (LP) Queen-disc 042. [c] on (LP) Jazum 3. [h] on (LP) Swing Treasury 103.
AFRS = AFRS One Night Stand No. 26.

(4314) **BENNY GOODMAN SEXTETTE** (actually the Quintet: Goodman, cl; Stacy, p; Reuss, g; Weiss, b; Krupa, d):
broadcast, Hotel New Yorker, New York City – late 1943

| | Three Little Words | (S) | (78) | V-Disc 88 |

other releases:
on (LP) Spook Jazz 6605, Jazz Society AA509.

(4315) **BENNY GOODMAN and His ORCHESTRA** (as for October 13, 1943, except H. Collins, tb; for Bennett; Leonard Kaye, as; for Rosa; Zoot Sims, ts; for Taylor):
broadcast, Hotel New Yorker, New York – Thursday, November 4, 1943

[a]	Down South Camp Meeting	(N)	(Tx)	OWI/VOA 22
[b]	I'll Be Around vCK	(A)	(Tx)	OWI/VOA 22
[c]	Seven Come Eleven	(S)	(Tx)	OWI/VOA 22

Connor lists [c] with this date, but the three titles are listed for a separate broadcast sometime in November, 1943. As the two versions of [c] appear to be the same (Stacy is off-mike) it seems reasonable to treat as the same broadcast.

242

These titles appeared on two transcriptions, both labelled: "Outpost Concert Series No. 11, Music of the Jazz Bands No. 22"
OWI = Office of War Information. VOA = Voice Of America.

other releases:
all titles on (LP) Swing Treasury 103. (c) on (LP) Fanfare 27-127.

(4316) (same personnel):   broadcast, Hotel New Yorker, New York – Friday, November 5, 1943
      Mission To Moscow   **(A)**
This title on (LP) Swing Treasury 103.

(4317) (same personnel):   broadcast, New York City – Tuesday, November 9, 1943

[a]	**I'm Here**	**(N)**	(Tx)	AFRS ONS 45
[b]	**Dinah** vRD	**(A)**	(Tx)	AFRS ONS 45
[c]	**Do Nothing Till You Hear From Me** vBG	**(A)**	(Tx)	AFRS ONS 45
[d]	**Henderson Stomp**	**(S)**	(Tx)	AFRS ONS 45
[e]	**Sing, Sing, Sing**	**(N)**	(Tx)	AFRS ONS 45
[f]	**My Heart Tells Me** vCK	**(A)**	(Tx)	AFRS ONS 45

other releases:
[a] on (LP) Queen-disc 042. [d] on (Tx) AFRS ONS No.53 (LP/AC) Swing House 46. [d], [e] on (LP) Swing Treasury 103.
AFRS = AFRS One Night Stand No. 45

(4318) (same personnel):   broadcast, New York City – Wednesday, November 17, 1943

[a]		**At The Darktown Strutters' Ball**	**(S)**	(Tx)	AFRS ONS 53
[b]	TRIO	**Honeysuckle Rose**		(Tx)	AFRS ONS 53
[c]		**Tomorrow** vCK	**(N)**	(Tx)	AFRS ONS 53
[d]		**Do Nothing Till You Hear From Me** vBG	**(A)**	(Tx)	AFRS ONS 53
[e]		**Mission To Moscow**	**(N)**	(Tx)	AFRS ONS 53
[f]		**My Heart Tells Me** vCK	**(N)**	(Tx)	AFRS ONS 53
[g]		**I've Found A New Baby**	**(N)**	(Tx)	AFRS ONS 53
[h]		**Minnie's In The Money** vBG	**(A/S)**	(Tx)	AFRS ONS 53

TRIO: Goodman, cl; Stacy, p; Krupa, d.
other releases:
[b] on (LP) Queen-disc 042. [b], [d] on (LP) Swing Treasury 103.
[g] on (LP/AC) Swing House 46
Henderson Stomp on AFRS ONS 53 is from the November 9, 1943 broadcast.
AFRS = AFRS One Night Stand No. 53.

(4319) (same personnel):   broadcast, New York City – c. November 1943

After You've Gone	**( )**	(Tx)	AFRS P83/84
Dinah vRD	**( )**	(Tx)	AFRS P83/84

AFRS = AFRS Basic Music Library P83/84. Other cuts by other artists.

(4320) (same personnel):   broadcast, New York City – early December 1943

TRIO	**Limehouse Blues**		(Tx)	AFRS CP 4
	Air Mail Special	**(N)**	(Tx)	AFRS CP 4

TRIO: Goodman, cl; Stacy, p; Krupa, d.
AFRS = Navy Department AFRS Command Performance Unit 4. Also on (Tx) AFRS Command Performance No. 98.

(4321) (same personnel):   Recorded at Columbia's Liederkranz Hall, New York City – Thursday, December 9, 1943

[a]	**Dinah** vBG	**(A)**	(78)	V-Disc 159B
[b]	**Dinah** vBG	**(A)**	(CD)	VJC.1001.2
[c]	**Henderson Stomp**	**(S)**	(78)	V-Disc 159A
[d]	**Henderson Stomp**	**(S)**	(CD)	VJC.1001.2
[e]	**Henderson Stomp**	**(S)**	(CD)	VJC.1001.2
[f]	**'Way Down Yonder In New Orleans**	**(S)**	(CD)	VJC.1001.2
[g]	**'Way Down Yonder In New Orleans**	**(S)**	(CD)	VJC.1001.2

      BENNY GOODMAN, GENE KRUPA AND JESS STACEY *(sic)*   same session

(h)	**Limehouse Blues**	(78)	V-Disc 159A

VJC = Victorious Disc. This CD also contains two breakdowns (13 and 24 seconds each) of *Henderson Stomp*.

other releases:
[a] on (LP) Dan VC5022. [c] on (CD) Spectrum U4026. [c], [h] on (CD) Recording Arts JZCD304. [a], [c], [h] on (LP) Electra KV119, Jazz Society AA509, Spook Jazz 6605, Sunbeam 142. [c], [h] on (LP) Windmill 196. [h] on (AC) Jazz Connoisseur Cassettes JCC28.

(4322) BENNY GOODMAN and His ORCHESTRA (as for November 4, 1943, except that drummer is uncertain).

broadcast, Naval Academy, Annapolis, MD – Wednesday, December 15, 1943

[a]		**Mission To Moscow**	**(A)**	(Tx)	AFRS SB 232
[b]		**Seven Come Eleven**	**(S)**	(Tx)	AFRS SB 232
[c]		**Do Nothing Till You Hear From Me** vBG	**(A)**	(Tx)	AFRS SB 232
[d]		**No Love, No Nothin'** vRD	**(I/A)**	(Tx)	AFRS SB 232
[e]	TRIO	**Honeysuckle Rose** (part)		(Tx)	AFRS SB 232

TRIO: Goodman, cl; Stacy, p; unknown, d.
AFRS = AFRS One Night Stand No. 232.   [b] on (LP) Queen-disc 042.

(4323) (same personnel?):

broadcast, 1943

	King Porter Stomp	**(N)**	

This title on (LP) Swing Treasury 103. Source not indicated.

(4401) BENNY GOODMAN QUARTET (Goodman, cl; Jess Stacy, p; Sid Weiss, b; Morey Feld, d).

broadcast, Los Angeles – Tuesday, January 18, 1944

Rachel's Dream	(Tx)	AFRS ONS 188

There is a dispute about the source of this title. Most discographies allocate it as above to the January 18, 1944 relay to the Esquire All-American Jazz Concert at the Metropolitan Opera House in New York City. Connor gives the source as a Command Performance broadcast from mid-January. It should be noted that 21 titles from this Esquire concert, featuring such stars as Louis Armstrong, Art Tatum, Coleman Hawkins, Jack Teagarden, etc. appeared on three "One Night Stand" transcriptions (ONS 186/187/188).
AFRS = AFRS One Night Stand No. 188.

other releases:
On (Tx) AFRS Command Performance 155, 208, Spotlight Bands 261, Yank Swing Session 123. On (LP) Aircheck 27, FDC 1007, Joker 3132, Radiola 5051, Saga 6923, Sunbeam SB155, Swing House 46, Windmill 248. On (CD) Hot 'N' Sweet FDC25118, Music Memories 34019 PM527. (AC) on Swing House 46.

(4402) BENNY GOODMAN and His ORCHESTRA (Johnny Dee, Frank Berardi, Mickey Mangano, tp; Bill Harris, Al Mastren, tb; Benny Goodman, cl; Heinie Beau, Eddie Rosa, as; Al Klink, Zoot Sims, ts; Eddie Beau, bar; Jess Stacy, p; Allan Reuss, g; Sid Weiss, b; Morey Feld, d):

broadcast, Hollywood – mid-January 1944

I've Found A New Baby	**(N)**	(Tx)	AFRS CP 102

AFRS = AFRS Command Performance No. 102.
This title on (Tx) AFRS CP 208, (LP) Dan 5002.

(4403) BENNY GOODMAN and His ORCHESTRA (as for mid-January 1944; Lorraine Elliott, vo):

film soundtrack, Hollywood – February 1944

[a]		**Ten Days With Baby** vLE	**(A)**
[b]	QUARTET	**Rachel's Dream**	

QUARTET: Goodman, Stacy, Weiss, Feld.
From the film "Sweet and Lowdown". [a] is an alternative take to that used in the film. [b] the film version is edited.
Both titles on (78) V-Disc 779A; (LP) Jazz Society AA509, Spook Jazz 6605, Sunbeam 144, Dan VC5022. (CD) Recording Arts JZCD304. [a] on (LP) Windmill 196; (LP/AC) Swing House 46; and (CD) Spectrum U4026.

(4404) HORACE HEIDT'S MUSICAL KNIGHTS (possible personnel: Shorty Sherock, Charlie Parlato, Buddy Bergman, perhaps Jack Demello, tp; Jimmy Sims, Bill Mustard, unknown, tb; Abe Aaron, Tony Johnson, as; Hugh Hudgings, Don Raffell, ts; Joe Rushton or Fred Worrell, bsx; Jess Stacy, p; Gil Hintz, g; Gus Van Camp, b; Frankie Carlson, d; Buzz Adlam, ar; Bob Matthews, Virginia Reed, The Swingsters, vo; The Glee Club, vo; Fred Lowery, whistler):

broadcast, Trianon Ballroom, Southgate, CA – Wednesday, April 5, 1944

[a]	**Theme** (part) whFL	**(N)**	(Tx)	AFRS ONS 200
[b]	**I Love You**	**(I)**	(Tx)	AFRS ONS 200
[c]	**Tess's Torch Song** vVR	**(I/A)**	(Tx)	AFRS ONS 200
[d]	**Bells of St. Mary's**	**(I)**	(Tx)	AFRS ONS 200
[e]	**Just One Of Those Things**	**(N)**	(Tx)	AFRS ONS 200
[f]	**Brazil**	**(N)**	(Tx)	AFRS ONS 200
[g]	**Night and Day** vBM	**(I/A)**	(Tx)	AFRS ONS 200

[h]	**Rosetta** (piano solo, with b & d)		(Tx)	AFRS ONS 200
[i]	**I'm In The Mood For Love**	**(N)**	(Tx)	AFRS ONS 200
[j]	**Don't Sweetheart Me** vTS	**(I)**	(Tx)	AFRS ONS 200
[k]	**In The Still Of The Night**	**(I)**	(Tx)	AFRS ONS 200
[l]	**Theme** (part) whFL	**(N)**	(Tx)	AFRS ONS 200

AFRS = One Night Stand No. 200. The theme is *I'll Love You in My Dreams*.

(4405) (probably same personnel, except Murray Gaer, d; for Carlson):   broadcast – c. July 1944
[a]	**On The Sunny Side Of The Street**	**(N)**
[b]	**The Bells of St. Mary's** vBM, VR,TGC, TS, whFL	**(S)**
[c]	**The Day After Forever** vBM, VR, TGC	**(N)**

This is a double-sided acetate in Jim Gordon's collection.
On [b] Jess Stacy, Tony Johnson, Jimmy Sims, and Murray Gaer are announced.

On May 21, 1944, Eddie Condon began a series of afternoon broadcasts, normally of 30 minutes duration. Although unsponsored they continued almost weekly on the NBC Blue Network until April 1945. These radio shows were produced by Ernie Anderson and introduced by Fred Robbins and Eddie Condon.

Many of the broadcasts, complete or in part, were circulated to U.S. forces radio stations around the world on A.F.R.S. transcriptions. These were simply labelled "EDDIE CONDON". Jazzology have completed the release of these broadcasts, initially on LP, then on CD, including any available material which did not appear on the A.F.R.S. transcriptions.

Broadcasts are shown as ending with *Impromptu Ensemble*, a fast blues amalgam of *Ole Miss* and *Dippermouth Blues*, although it is announced under various titles. These include *Blues, Carnegie Leap, Muggsy's Serenade* and even *Why Is Leonard So Modest?*, a reference to critic Leonard Feather. Full personnels are not always announced, and aural evidence is not always reliable, particularly when the band is backing a singer or a featured soloist. Eddie Condon can be heard playing guitar on a few titles, but his presence in the rhythm section is otherwise uncertain. Lou McGarity was in the U.S. Navy at this time, so on occasion he is not announced; at other times he uses the pseudonym John Pesci. Dick Cary does play trumpet on a few numbers, but there is no aural evidence that he does so as often as he is listed in discographies. Such listing seems to be based upon announcements that he wrote the chart for a particular number.

On the broadcasts on which Jess Stacy appeared, sometimes he was the only pianist, on others he shared duties with Gene Schroeder or Joe Bushkin, or with a featured guest like Earl Hines.

Reissues are generally labelled as Eddie Condon, though there have been compilations under Jess Stacy's name (Aircheck 26) and Lee Wiley's (Totem 1033).

For the detailed story of these broadcasts and transcriptions, refer to "The Eddie Condon 'Town Hall Broadcasts' 1944-45" by C.K. 'Bozy' White.

(4406) **EDDIE CONDON**   broadcast, Town Hall, New York City – Saturday, August 5, 1944
(Max Kaminsky, tp; Benny Morton, tb; Pee Wee Russell, cl; Ernie Caceres, bar; Jess Stacy, g; unknown, b; Gene Krupa, d):
| [a] | **I Got Rhythm** | **(S/A)** | (Tx) | AFRS CONDON 9 |

(Stacy, p; Krupa, d):
| [b] | **Someone To Watch Over Me** | | (Tx) | AFRS CONDON 9 |

(Ed Hall, cl; Stacy, p; Krupa, d):
| [c] | **Oh, Lady Be Good!** | | (Tx) | AFRS CONDON 9 |

(Benny Morton, tb feature, with probably Bobby Hackett, co; Ed Hall, cl; Stacy, p; unknown b & d):
| [d] | **Summertime** | **(N)** | (Tx) | AFRS CONDON 9 |

(Lee Wiley, vo; with probably Hackett, co; Morton, tb; Caceres, cl; Stacy, p; unknown, b & d):
| [e] | **I've Got A Crush On You** vLW | **(I)** | (Tx) | AFRS CONDON 9 |

(as for (a) except Hackett, co; added; unknown, d; for Krupa; Lee Wiley, vo):
| [f] | **Sweet and Lowdown**   vLW | **(A)** | (Tx) | AFRS CONDON 9 |

C.K. Bozy White has suggested Joe Grauso for the unknown drummer.

other releases:
all titles on (LP) Jazzology JCE-1006 & (CD) Jazzology JCECD-1006.
[a] on (LP) Jazum 26. [b], [c], [d],[e], [f] on (LP) Jazum 52. [b], [c] on (LP) Aircheck 26. [e], [f] on (LP) Totem 1033,Baybridge UPS2280. part of [a] on (Tx) AFRS CONDON 18 and 20. [d] on (Tx) AFRS CONDON 18

(4407) **Unknown session** (Jess Stacy, p solo, with band closing at end):   broadcast – Saturday, August 12, 1944
Oh, Lady Be Good!

This is an acetate in Mike Sutcliffe's collection. Date (8/12/44) is handwritten on label. Possibly from a Horace Heidt broadcast, though perhaps not in the light of the announcer's comment: "By the way of saying welcome home, Jess Stacy takes off his hat to a fine man and a great member (number?). We finish with that famous Jess Stacy style, *Lady Be Good."*

(4408) **BOBBY HACKETT and His RHYTHM KINGS** (Bobby Hackett, co; Lou McGarity, tb; Pee Wee Russell, cl; Ernie Caceres, bar; Jess Stacy, p; Eddie Condon, g; Bob Casey, b; George Wettling, d):

WOR Studios, 1440 Broadway, New York City – Saturday, September 23, 1944

A-4805	**At Sundown**	**(N)**	(78)	Commodore C1523
A-4806-1	**New Orleans**	**(I/S/A)**	(78)	Commodore C622
A-4807	**Skeleton Jangle**	**(S)**	(78)	Commodore C622
A-4807-TK1	**Skeleton Jangle** #2	**(S)**	(LP)	Commodore 6.26171
A-4808	**When Day Is Done**	**(I)**	(78)	Commodore C1523
A-4808-1	**When Day Is Done** #2	**(I)**	(LP)	Commodore 6.26171
A-4809T	**Soon**	**(I/S)**	(LP)	Commodore 6.26171

other releases:
all 78 rpm issues on (LP) Commodore CCL7009 & on (CD) Commodore CCD7009 & on (AC) Commodore CCK7009.
all takes on (LP) Commodore(G) 6.26171, Mosaic MR23-128.
4805   on (LP) Book-of-the-Month Records 10-5557
4806-1 on (CD) Commodore CMD24002
4806-1/4807 on Commodore (LP) FL20.016; (45) 45-622, CRF-116; (EP) CEP-31
4808   on Commodore (LP) FL20-016; (45) 45-1526, CRF-116
4809T   on (CD) Commodore CCD7009
Commodore 1523 as "Jam Session At Commmodore No. 6".

(4409) **EDDIE CONDON**   broadcast, Town Hall, New York– Saturday, September 23, 1944
(Max Kaminsky, tp; Miff Mole, tb; Pee Wee Russell, cl; Ernie Caceres, bar; Jess Stacy, p; Sid Weiss, b; Gene Krupa, d):

[a]	**That's A Plenty**	**(N)**	(Tx)	AFRS CONDON 17

(Red McKenzie, vo; with group as [a], plus Bobby Hackett, co; Ernie Caceres, cl; for Russell):

[b]	**Sentimental Baby** vRM	**(A)**	(Tx)	AFRS CONDON 17

(as for [a], except Bobby Hackett, co; for Kaminsky):

[c]	**Easter Parade**	**(S/A)**		(not on AFRS)

(Ernie Caceres, bar; Stacy, b; Weiss, b; Krupa, d):

[d]	**untitled Caceres original**		(Tx)	AFRS CONDON 17

(Ed Hall, cl; Stacy, p; Weiss, b; Krupa, d):

[e]	**untitled**			(not on AFRS)

(Muggsy Spanier, tp; Mole, tb; Russell, cl; Caceres, bar; Stacy, p; Weiss, b; Krupa, d):

[f]	**Relaxin' At The Touro**	**(I/A/S)**	(Tx)	AFRS CONDON 17
[g]	**Poor As A Churchmouse**	**(A)**	(Tx)	AFRS CONDON 17

(Lee Wiley, vo; with group as [b])

[h]	**Wherever There's Love** vLW	**(I/A)**	(Tx)	AFRS CONDON 17

(all musicians)

[i]	**Impromptu Ensemble** (part)	**(I)**	(Tx)	AFRS CONDON 17

This was a 45-minute broadcast. [d] shown by Jazzology as *Crickett Jumps*.

other releases:
All titles on (LP) Jazzology JCE-1010 & (CD) JCECD-1010.
All titles, except [c], on (LP) Jazum 78.
[f] on (Tx) AFRS CONDON 22, 33, (LP) Jazum 52. [h] on (LP) Tono TJ6004

(4410) **PEE WEE RUSSELL and His HOT FOUR** (Pee Wee Russell, cl; Jess Stacy, p; Sid Weiss, b; George Wettling, d)

Recorded at WOR Studios, 1440 Broadway, New York – Saturday, September 30, 1944

A4818-TK1	**Take Me To The Land Of Jazz** #3	(LP)	Mosaic MR23.128
A4818-1	**Take Me To The Land Of Jazz** No.2	(LP)	Commodore XFL16440
A4818-2	**Take Me To The Land Of Jazz**	(78)	Commodore 596
A4819-TK1	**Rose Of Washington Square** #3	(LP)	Mosaic MR23.128
A4819-1	**Rose Of Washington Square** No.2	(LP)	Commodore XFL16440
A4819-2	**Rose Of Washington Square**	(78)	Commodore 627
A4820-TK1	**Keepin' Out Of Mischief Now**	(LP)	Commodore XFL16440
A4820-1	**Keepin' Out Of Mischief Now**	(78)	Commodore 627
A4821-TK1	**Wailing D.A. Blues**	(LP)	Mosaic MR23.128
A4821-TK2	**D.A. Blues** No. 2	(LP)	Commodore XFL16440
A4821-1	**D.A. Blues**	(78)	Commodore 596

other releases:
all takes on (LP) Mosaic MR23-128. Eight of these takes on (CD) Commodore CMD14042

all 78 rpm issues on (LP) Commodore FL20,014, XFL16440, (G)25490, Fontana(E) TL5271, London(E) HMC5005, Mainstream S/6026, 56026.
A4820-1 on (CD) Commodore CMD24002
A4818-1/A4818-2/A4819-1/A4819-2/A4820-1/A4821-TK2/A4821-1 on (LP) Commodore(G) 25490.
A4818-2 on (LP) Time-Life STL-J17.
A4820-1 on (CD) Commodore CMD24002.
A4821-1 on (CD) Topaz TPZ1035
A4818-1/A4818-2/A4819-TK1/4819-2/A4820-TK1/A4821-1/A4821-TK1/A4821TK2 on (CD) Commodore CMD14042.

(4411) **EDDIE CONDON** broadcast, Town Hall, New York City – Saturday, September 30, 1944
(Jess Stacy, p; Cozy Cole, d): (full band at coda)
   [a]   **Rosetta**   (Tx)   AFRS CONDON 18
(Ed Hall, cl; Stacy, p; Sid Weiss, b; Cole, d):
   [b]   **I Want To Be Happy**   (Tx)   AFRS CONDON 18
(Max Kaminsky, tp;Miff Mole, tb; Hall, cl; Ernie Caceres, bar; same rhythm):
   [c]   **Keep Smilin' At Trouble**   (S)   (not on AFRS)
(Muggsy Spanier, co; Max Kaminsky, tp; Miff Mole, tb; Ed Hall, cl; Ernie Caceres, bar; Stacy, p; Weiss, b; Cole, d):
   [d]   **Waitin' For The Evening Whistle**   (N)   (Tx)   AFRS CONDON 18
(as for [d] plus Gene Schroeder, p):
   [e]   **Bugle Call Rag**   (S)   (Tx)   AFRS CONDON 18
Waitin' For The Evening Whistle, a feature for Miff Mole, is the same tune as *Worrying The Life Out Of Me*, recorded by Ralph Sutton. It is not *Waitin' For The Evenin' Mail,* as misprinted in the discography by Bozy White. On [e] Schroeder plays the introduction.

other releases: all titles on (LP) Jazzology JCE-1009 & (CD) Jazzology JCD-1009
[d] on (Tx) AFRS CONDON 19 & 47. [a] on (LP) Aircheck 26. [b] on (LP) Chiaroscuro CR-113. [d], [e] on (LP) Jazum 74.

(4412) **RED McKENZIE with orchestra directed by Ernie Caceres** (Red McKenzie, vo; Billy Butterfield, tp; Lou McGarity, Buddy Morrow, Frank D'Annolfo, tb; Ernie Caceres, bar; Red Norvo, vb; Jess Stacy, p; Carl Kress, g; Bob Casey, b; George Wettling, d): New York City – Thursday, October 5, 1944

A-4826-1	**Sweet Lorraine**	(A)	(78)	Commodore C572
A-4826-TK1	**Sweet Lorraine** #2	(A)	(LP)	Mosaic MR23.128
A-4827-1	**It's The Talk Of The Town**	(A)	(78)	Commodore C562
A-4827-TK1	**It's The Talk Of The Town** #2	(A)	(LP)	Mosaic MR23.128
A-4828-1	**Through A Veil Of Indifference**	(A)	(78)	Commodore C572
A-4829-1	**Wherever There's Love**	(A)	(78)	Commodore C562
A-4829-2	**Wherever There's Love** #2	(A)	(LP)	Mosaic MR23.128

other releases: all titles on (LP) Mosaic MR23-128

(4413) **JESS STACY** (Stacy, p; Bob Casey, b; George Wettling, d): Decca Studios, New York City – Friday, October 6, 1944

N-2731-1	**Rosetta**	(Tx)	World JS38B
N-2732-5	**Oh, Lady Be Good!**	(Tx)	World JS38B
N-2733-2	**Keepin' Out Of Mischief Now**	(Tx)	World JS39A
N-2734-1	**Sweet Georgia Brown**	(Tx)	World JS38B
N-2735-1	**After You've Gone**	(LP)	Jazzology JCE90
N-2735-2	**After You've Gone**	(Tx)	World JS38B
N-2736-1	**Jumpin' With Jess**	(Tx)	World JS39A
N-2737-1	**Cherry**	(LP)	Jazzology JCE90
N-2737-2	**Cherry**	(Tx)	World JS39A
N-2738-1	**I Wish I Could Shimmy Like My Sister Kate**	(Tx)	World JS39A
N-2738-3	**I Wish I Could Shimmy Like My Sister Kate** (incomplete)	(LP)	Jazzology JCE90
N-2738-4	**I Wish I Could Shimmy Like My Sister Kate**	(LP)	Jazzology JCE90
N-2739-2	**Honeysuckle Rose**	(Tx)	World JS39A
N-2740-1	**Blue Notion**	(Tx)	World JS38B
none -1	**Someone To Watch Over Me** (incomplete)	(LP)	Jazzology JCE90
-2	**Someone To Watch Over Me** (incomplete)	(LP)	Jazzology JCE90
-3	**Someone To Watch Over Me** (incomplete)	(LP)	Jazzology JCE90

Decca Records/World Transcription studios were at 711, 5th Avenue.
The World "JS" prefix refers to the "Jam Session" series. All the above takes, including the unissued and incomplete, on (LP) Jazzology JCE-90. This album also contains the following: N-2732-1, -2, -3/ N-2733-1/ N-2738-2/ N-2739-1; which are all false starts.

other releases:
N-2732-5/N-2735-2/N-2737-1 on (Tx) World No. 371.
N-2733-2/N-2734-1/N-2736-1 on (Tx) World No. 353. Some titles also appear on (Tx) World R-585.
all titles originally on World on (LP) Esquire ESQ314.
N-2732-5/N-2733-2/N-2735-2/N-2736-1/N-2737-2/N-2738-1/N-2739-2 on (LP) Aircheck 26.
N-2736-1/N-2740-1 on (CD) Topaz TPZ1050

(4414) **EDDIE CONDON**   Ritz Theatre, New York City – Saturday, October 14, 1944
(Jess Stacy, p; George Wettling, d):
   [a]   **Sweet Georgia Brown**   (Tx)   AFRS CONDON 20
(add Ed Hall, cl; Bob Casey, b):
   [b]   **Honeysuckle Rose**   (Tx)   AFRS CONDON 20
(Lee Wiley, vo; Max Kaminsky, tp; Benny Morton, tb; Pee Wee Russell, cl; Ernie Caceres, bar; Stacy, p; Casey, b; Wettling, d): (band at close only)
   [c]   **Don't Blame Me** vLW   **(I/A)**   (Tx)   AFRS CONDON 20
(as for [c], plus Billy Butterfield, tp):
   [d]   **Impromptu Ensemble** (part)   **(I)**   (Tx)   AFRS CONDON 20

Jazzology notes list Stacy on *Sugar*, but aurally it is Gene Schroeder.
The Ritz Theatre, believed to be used as a radio studio, was on 48th Street.

other releases:
all titles on (LP) Jazum 26, Jazzology JCE-1011; (CD) Jazzology JCD.1011.
(c) on (Tx) AFRS CONDON 33, & (LP) Totem 1033, Baybridge UPS2280.

On this broadcast it is stated that the October 16 concert at Carnegie Hall would be recorded by the War Department, the Office of War Information, and The Office of the Coordinator of Inter-American Affairs for use on short-wave radio. Stacy was scheduled to be present.

(4415) **MUGGSY SPANIER and His V DISC ALL STARS** (Muggsy Spanier, co; Lou McGarity, tb; Pee Wee Russell, cl, vo; Boomie Richman, ts; Jess Stacy, p; Hy White, g; Bob Haggart, b,wh; George Wettling, d):
                                            Victor studios, New York City – Tuesday, October 17, 1944
D4-TC469-1C   **That's A Plenty**   **(S)**   (78)   V-Disc 424
D4-TC470-1A   **Squeeze Me**   **(S/A)**   (78)   V-Disc 475
D4-TC471-1A   **Jazz Me Blues**   **(S)**   (78)   V-Disc 507
D4-TC472-1   **Pee Wee Speaks** vPWR   **(A/S)**   (78)   V-Disc 344
D4-TC473-1A   **Pat's Blues**   whBH   **(I/A)**   (78)   V-Disc 394
The V-Discs shown above were U.S Army releases. There were also U.S. Navy releases, numbers 204/255/267/135/174 in above order. Producer George Simon said that one other title was recorded at this session.

other releases:
all titles on (LP) Spook Jazz SPJ6603, Connoisseur CR522, Saga 6917, Kiva Elec KV121, Joker SM3575, FDC 1020,
       Everybody's e1020. (CD) Classics 907; (AC) Holmia HM06, Jazz Connoisseur Cassettes JCC90
D4TC469 on (CD) Collection Hugues Panassie CTPL003.
D4TC470 on (LP) Cetra-Fonit/Vdisc Records VDL1006; (CD) Music Memories 30946
D4TC471 on (LP) Dan VC5008, Redwood Records RWJ1001.
D4TC472/473 on (LP) Discomania 101.
D4TC472 on (CD) Pickwick 54030

(4416) **EDDIE CONDON**   broadcast, Ritz Theatre, New York City – Saturday, October 21, 1944
(Ernie Caceres, cl; Jess Stacy, p; Bob Casey, b; Joe Grauso, d)
  [a]   **Three Little Words**   (Tx)   AFRS CONDON 21
(Lee Wiley, vo; Billy Butterfield, tp; Miff Mole, tb; Pee Wee Russell, cl; Caceres, bar; Stacy, p; Casey, b; Grauso, d):
  [b]   **Old Folks** vLW   **(I/A)**   (Tx)   AFRS CONDON 21
(as [b] plus Max Kaminsky, tp; Gene Schroeder, p):
  [c]   **Impromptu Ensemble**   **(I/A)**   (Tx)   AFRS CONDON 21
Stacy has been listed for *Struttin' With Some Barbecue* from this broadcast, but aurally this is not so.

other releases:
all titles on on (LP) Jazzology JCE-1012; (CD) Jazzology JCD-1012.
[c] part on (Tx) AFRS CONDON 44   [c] on Jazum 66. [a] on (LP) Jazum 37, Aircheck 26. [b], [c] on (LP) Jazum 38.
[b] on (LP) Baybridge UPS2280, Dan VC5020

(4417) **EDDIE CONDON'S JAZZ CONCERT ORCHESTRA** (collective personnel: Muggsy Spanier, co; Billy Butterfield, Max Kaminsky, tp; Lou McGarity, tb; Ed Hall, Pee Wee Russell, cl; Ernie Caceres, bar, cl; Jess Stacy, p; Eddie Condon, g; Bob Haggart, b; George Wettling, d; Lee Wiley, vo):

Muzak Studios, New York City – Tuesday, October 24, 1944

(Hall, Stacy, Haggart, Wettling)

zz-4166-1	**It's Been So Long** (breakdown 0:04)		(CD)	Stash ST.CD.530
zz-4166-2	**It's Been So Long**		(Tx)	Associated A60634B
zz-4166-3	**The Man I Love** (breakdown 0:20)		(CD)	Stash ST.CD.530
zz-4166-4	**The Man I Love**		(Tx)	Associated A60635B

(Butterfield, Hall, Caceres, Stacy, Condon, Haggart, Wettling):

zz-4166-5	**'S Wonderful** (breakdown 0:05)		(CD)	Stash ST.CD.530
zz-4166-6	**'S Wonderful** (breakdown 0:04)		(CD)	Stash ST.CD.530
zz-4166-7	**'S Wonderful**	(S)	(Tx)	Associated A60802B

(add McGarity): (see note 1)

zz-4167-1	**Just You, Just Me**	(S)	(Tx)	Associated A60802B

(add Kaminsky, Wiley):

zz-4167-2	**Old Folks** vLW (breakdown 0:33)		(CD)	Stash ST.CD.530
zz-4167-3	**Old Folks** vLW	(I/A)	(Tx)	Associated A60634B

(add Pee Wee Russell, cl):

zz-4167-4	**You're Lucky To Me** vLW	(A)	(Tx)	Associated A60635B

(Spanier, McGarity, Russell, Stacy, Condon, Haggart, Wettling):

zz-4168-3	**I Want A Big Butter And Egg Man**	(S)	(Tx)	Associated A60802B

(Spanier, Kaminsky, McGarity, Russell, Hall, same rhythm section):

zz-4168-5	**Carnegie Leap**	(I/A)	(Tx)	Associated A60634B

(Kaminsky, McGarity, Russell, same rhythm section):

zz-4168-6	**At Sundown**	(S)	(Tx)	Associated A60802B
zz-4169-1	**Sugar**			unissued
zz-4169-2	**Sugar**	(A)	(Tx)	Associated A60636B

(Spanier, Butterfield and/or Kaminsky, McGarity, Caceres, cl; Russell, same rhythm section):

zz-4169-4	**Muggsy's Serenade**	(A)	(Tx)	Associated A60635B

(Kaminsky, McGarity, Caceres, cl; same rhythm section):

zz-4170-2	**Back In Your Own Backyard**	(S)	(Tx)	Associated A60636B
zz-4170-3	**If I Had You**	(A)	(Tx)	Associated A60636B
zz-4170-4	**Indiana**	(A/S)	(Tx)	Associated A60636B

Note 1: Lou McGarity is usually shown as present from zz-4167-1, but he cannot be heard until zz-4168-3, *I Want A Big Butter and Egg Man*.

Carnegie Leap is another name for *Impromptu Ensemble*, as used on the Blue Network broadcasts. *Muggsy's Serenade* is linked to *Tin Roof Blues*. The unlisted takes are unused versions or, mainly, false starts of the titles shown.

other releases:
4166-2/4166-4/4166-7/4167-1/4167-3/4167-4 on (CD) Stash ST-CD-530
4166-2 on (Tx) Associated A61018, A61246, AFRS P369; (LP set) Murray Hill set. (LP) Everest FS-274, Gala GLP342, Design DLP47, Palm P30:08
4166-4 on (Tx) Associated A61015; (LP) Palm P30:08
4167-3 on (Tx) Associated A61246; (LP) Palm P30:08, Tono TJ-6004
4167-4 on (Tx) Associated A61015B; (LP) Palm P30:08, Tono TJ-6004;
4168-3 on (Tx) Muzak M-2425.
4168-5 on (Tx) Associated A61018, A61246, AFRS P368, (LP) Palm P30:08.
4169-2 on (Tx) Associated A60105B; (LP) Palm P30:08, Design DLP47, Gala GLP342.
4169-4 on (Tx) Associated A61015A, AFRS P368, (LP) Palm P30:08.
4170-2 on (Tx) Associated A61015A; (LP) Palm P30:08, Design DLP47, DLP213, Gala GLP342
4170-3 on (Tx) Associated A61015A; (LP) Palm P30:08
4170-4 on (Tx) Associated A61015A; (LP) Palm P30:08, Design DLP47, DLP213, Gala GLP342, Pickwick PR111, Everest FS274, Allegro ALL791,Spectrum DLP148, SDLP148, Murray Hill set, Palm Club 1652
4166-1 to 4167-4 inclusive on (CD) Jazz Classics JZCL5008.

(4418) **EDDIE CONDON**　　　　　　　　　　　　broadcast, Ritz Theatre, New York City – Saturday, October 28, 1944
(Max Kaminsky, tp; Lou McGarity, tb; Pee Wee Russell, cl; Ernie Caceres, bar; Jess Stacy, p; Sid Weiss, b; George Wettling, d):

[a]	**Sweet Georgia Brown**	**(S/A)**	(Tx)	AFRS CONDON 33
[b]	**I Ain't Gonna Give Nobody None**			
	Of My Jelly Roll	**(A)**	(Tx)	AFRS CONDON 33

(Jess Stacy, p; Sid Weiss, b; George Wettling, d):

[c]	**Keepin' Out Of Mischief Now**		(Tx)	AFRS CONDON 33

(Joe Marsala, cl; same rhythm section):

[d]	**Wolverine Blues**			(not on AFRS)

(as [a] except Russell out; Caceres, cl):

[e]	**'S Wonderful**	**(S/A)**		(not on AFRS)

(Red McKenzie, vo; with Kaminsky, tp; McGarity, tb; Marsala, cl; Caceres, bar; same rhythm section; Dick Cary, arr):

[f]	**It's The Talk Of The Town** vRM	**(A)**		(not on AFRS)

(as [a] plus Dick Cary, tp; Joe Marsala, cl):

[g]	**Impromptu Ensemble**	**(I/A)**	(Tx)	AFRS CONDON 33

other releases:
all titles on (LP) Jazzology JCE-1012 and (CD) Jazzology JCD-1012
[a] on (LP) Storyville SLP133, Jazum 52, [b] on (LP) Chiaroscuro CR108, Spook Jazz SPJ6607,Storyville SLP509
[c] on (LP) Jazum 52.   [e] on (LP) IAJRC 36.   [g] on (LP) IAJRC 38.

(4419) **EDDIE CONDON**　　　　　　　　　　　　broadcast, Ritz Theatre, New York City – Saturday, November 4, 1944
(Jess Stacy, p; Bob Casey, b; George Wettling, d):

[a]	**After You've Gone**		(Tx)	AFRS CONDON 23

(Pee Wee Russell, cl; same rhythm section):

[b]	**untitled** (Pee Wee Russell original)		(Tx)	AFRS CONDON 23

(Lee Wiley, vo; Billy Butterfield, and perhaps Dick Cary, tp; Lou McGarity, tb; Ernie Caceres, cl; same rhythm section):

[c]	**Wherever There's Love** vLW	**(A)**	(Tx)	AFRS CONDON 23

(Butterfield, Dick Cary, tp; Muggsy Spanier, co; McGarity, tb; Pee Wee Russell, cl; Caceres, bar; Stacy and Schroeder, p; Casey, b; Wettling, d):

[d]	**Impromptu Ensemble**	**(I/S)**	(Tx)	AFRS CONDON 23

[b] shown as *Pee Wee's Town Hall Stomp* on Jazzology and Chiaroscuro.

other releases:
all titles on (LP) Rarities 44,Jazzology JCE-1013; (CD) Jazzology JCD.1013.
[b] on (LP) Chiaroscuro CR108, Storyville SLP509.
[c] on (Tx) CONDON 36, (LP) Jazum 63, Tono TJ6004

(4420) **EDDIE CONDON**　　　　　　　　　　　　broadcast, Ritz Theatre, New York City – Saturday, November 11, 1944
(Max Kaminsky, tp; Pee Wee Russell, cl; Ernie Caceres, bar; Jess Stacy, p; Bob Casey, b; Joe Grauso, d):

[a]	**Easter Parade**	**(S/A)**		(not on AFRS)

(Caceres, cl; same rhythm section):

[b]	**Cherry**			(not on AFRS)

(as [a]):

[c]	**Someday Sweetheart**	**(S/A)**		(not on AFRS)
[d]	**Impromptu Ensemble** (fade out)	**(I/A)**		(not on AFRS)

All titles on (LP) Jazzology JCE-1013: (CD) Jazzology JCD-1013.
[b] on (LP) Aircheck 26

(4421) **EDDIE CONDON**　　　　　　　　　　　　broadcast, Ritz Theatre, New York City – Saturday, November 18, 1944
(Billy Butterfield, tp; Lou McGarity, tb; Pee Wee Russell, cl; Ernie Caceres bar; Jess Stacy, p; Bob Casey, b; George Wettling, d):

[a]	**'Way Down Yonder In New Orleans**	**(A)**		(not on AFRS)

(Jess Stacy, p; Bob Casey, b; George Wettling, d):

[b]	**Three Little Words**			(not on AFRS)

(as [a]):

[c]	**Song Of The Wanderer**	**(A)**		(not on AFRS)
[d]	**Impromptu Ensemble** (fade out)	**(I/A)**		(not on AFRS)

All titles on (LP) Jazzology JCE-1013, Jazum 74: (CD) Jazzology JCD.1013.

(4422) **JESS STACY** (piano; with Gordon "Specs" Powell, d):		New York City – Saturday, November 25, 1944	
A-4830-2	**After You've Gone**	(LP)	Commodore XFL15358
A-4830-1	**After You've Gone** #2	(LP)	Mosaic MR23.128
A-4830	**After You've Gone** #3	(LP)	Mosaic MR23.128
A-4831-2	**Old Fashioned Love**	(LP)	Commodore XFL15358
A-4831-1	**Old Fashioned Love** #2	(LP)	Mosaic MR23.128
A-4831	**Old Fashioned Love** #3	(LP)	Mosaic MR23.128
A-4832-	**Song Of The Wanderer**	(LP)	Commodore XFL15358
A-4832	**I Ain't Got Nobody**	(LP)	Commodore XFL15358
A-4833-2	**Blue Fives**	(LP)	Commodore XFL15358
A-4833-1	**Blue Fives** #2	(LP)	Mosaic MR23.128
A-4833-3	**Blue Fives** #3	(LP)	Mosaic MR23.128
A-4834-1	**Ridin' Easy**	(LP)	Commodore XFL15358
A-4834-2	**Ridin' Easy** #2	(LP)	Mosaic MR23.128

This was a Commodore recording session, but the titles did not appear on 78 rpm records. *Song Of The Wanderer* was dropped from the session after two unsuccessful takes and its matrix number (A-4832) re-allocated to *I Ain't Got Nobody*. When these titles were actually released some thirty-five years later, the two takes of *Song Of The Wanderer* were spliced together to make a composite and acceptable take for release.   (As advised by Milt Gabler to Bert Whyatt.)

other releases:
all takes appeared on (LP) Mosaic MR23.128.
Commodore XFL15358 was reissued on (LP) Commodore CCL7008, Commodore(G) 6.24298: (CD) Commodore CCD7008.
A-4830-2 on (LP) Mainstream 56008/S6008.
A-4832/A-4833-2/A-4834-1 on (CD) ASV Living Era AJA5172

(4423) **EDDIE CONDON**   broadcast, Ritz Theatre, New York City – Saturday, November 25, 1944
(Billy Butterfield, tp; Lou McGarity, tb; Pee Wee Russell, cl; Ernie Caceres, bar; Jess Stacy, p; Bob Casey, b; Johnny Blowers, d):

[a]	**September In The Rain**	(S/A)	(Tx)	AFRS CONDON 24

(Jimmy Dorsey, cl; same rhythm section):

[b]	**I Got Rhythm**		(Tx)	AFRS CONDON 24

(Ernie Caceres, bar; same rhythm section):

[c]	**I've Been Around**		(Tx)	AFRS CONDON 24

(as [a] except Muggsy Spanier, co; for Butterfield):

[d]	**The Lady's In Love With You**	(A)	(Tx)	AFRS CONDON 24

(as for [a], plus Lee Wiley, vo; Dick Cary, arr):

[e]	**Old Folks** vLW	(I/A)	(Tx)	AFRS CONDON 24

(as for [a] plus Hot Lips Page, tp, vo; Spanier, co):

[f]	**Uncle Sam Blues** vHLP	(I/A/S)	(Tx)	AFRS CONDON 24

All titles on (LP) Jazzology JCE-1014: (CD) Jazzology JCD-1014.
[a] on (LP) Rhapsody RHA6028, Jazum 38. [b], [c], [d] on (LP) Jazum 38.   [e] on (LP) Palm 30.08
[f] on (LP) Chiaroscuro CR-113, Foxy 9007.

(4424) **EDDIE CONDON**   broadcast, Ritz Theatre, New York City – Saturday, December 23, 1944
(Pee Wee Russell, cl; Jess Stacy, p; Bob Casey, b; George Wettling, d):

[a]	**D.A. Blues**		(Tx)	AFRS CONDON 29

(Jess Stacy, p; Casey, b; Wettling, d):

[b]	**Rosetta**		(Tx)	AFRS CONDON 29

(Bobby Hackett, co; Max Kaminsky, tp; Russell, cl; Ernie Caceres, bar; same rhythm sction):

[c]	**Ja Da**	(I/A)	(Tx)	AFRS CONDON 29

(as for [c], but omit Kaminsky; add Lee Wiley, vo):

[d]	**You're Lucky To Me** vLW	(I/A)	(Tx)	AFRS CONDON 29

(Kaminsky, Wingy Manone, tp; Russell, cl; Ernie Caceres, bar; same rhythm section):

[e]	**Impromptu Ensemble** (part)	(I)	

Jazzology and C.K. White list Stacy on *Jingle Bells/On The Sunny Side Of The Street/Blue Skies* from this broadcast, but aurally this is incorrect, despite Fred Robbins' apparent introduction of Stacy in the personnel.

All titles on (CD) Jazzology JCD-1015.
[a] on (LP) Aircheck 26, Chiaroscuro CR-108, Storyville SLP509. [b], [c], [d] on (LP) Jazum 74.

(4425) **EDDIE CONDON**   broadcast, Ritz Theatre, New York City – Saturday, December 30, 1944
(Max Kaminsky, tp; Benny Morton, tb; Pee Wee Russell, cl; Ernie Caceres, bar; Jess Stacy, p; Jack Lesberg, b; George Wettling, d):

[a]	Walkin' The Dog	(S/A)	(Tx)	AFRS CONDON 30

(Jess Stacy, p; Lesberg, b; Wettling, d):

[b]	I Ain't Got Nobody		(Tx)	AFRS CONDON 30

(as for [a]):

[c]	Strut Miss Lizzie	(A)	(Tx)	AFRS CONDON 30

(Sidney Bechet, ss; Stacy, p; Lesberg, b; Wettling, d):

[d]	I Know That You Know		(Tx)	AFRS CONDON 30

(as for [a], plus Bechet, ss):

[e]	Sweet Georgia Brown	(S/A)	(Tx)	AFRS CONDON 30

(Lee Wiley, vo; Jess Stacy, p: band at coda):

[f]	When Your Lover Has Gone vLW		(Tx)	AFRS CONDON 30

(as for [a], plus Bechet, ss):

[g]	Impromptu Ensemble	(I/A)	(Tx)	AFRS CONDON 30

other releases:
all titles on (LP) Jazum 53, Baybridge UPS2259, (CD) Jazzology JCD-1016.
[a] on (Tx) AFRS Condon 48: (LP) Rhapsody RHA6028, Good Music JRR3.   [c] on (LP) Rhapsody RHA6029.
[d] on (LP) Good Music JRR3.   [e] on (Tx) AFRS Condon 44: (LP) Good Music JRR3, Jazum 65, FDC 1012.   [f] on (LP) Good Music JRR3, Totem 1033, Baybridge UPS2280 .   [g] on (Tx) AFRS Condon 40: (LP) Good Music JRR3, Jazum 64

(4501) **EDDIE CONDON**   broadcast, Ritz Theatre, New York City – Saturday, January 6, 1945
(Billy Butterfield, tp; Tommy Dorsey, tb; Pee Wee Russell, cl; Ernie Caceres, bar; Jess Stacy, p; Sid Weiss, b; George Wettling, d):

[a]	Sunday	(S/A)	(Tx)	AFRS CONDON 31
[b]	How Come You Do Me Like You Do?	(S)	(Tx)	AFRS CONDON 31

(similar to [a], except Russell out; Dick Cary, arr; Jack Eberle, vo):

[c]	Every Night vJE	(A)	(Tx)	AFRS CONDON 31

(as for [a] except Max Kaminsky, tp; for Butterfield):

[d]	Keep Smilin' At Trouble	(S/A)	(Tx)	AFRS CONDON 31

(as for [a], plus Max Kaminsky, tp):

[e]	That's A Plenty	(S)	(Tx)	AFRS CONDON 31

(as for [c], except Lee Wiley, vo; Bobby Hackett, arr):

[f]	Sugar vLW	(I/A)	(Tx)	AFRS CONDON 31

(as for [e]):

[g]	Impromptu Ensemble	(I/A)	(Tx)	AFRS CONDON 31

other releases:
all titles on (LP) Rarities 37, Baybridge UPS2260 (CD) Jazzology JCD-1016.
[a] part, and [b], [e], [f] on (Tx) CONDON 46.   [b], [e], [f] on (LP) Good Music JRR 3.   [d] on (LP) Spook Jazz SPJ6607.
[f] on (LP) Memories Lightest LWIL403, Good Music JRR3; (AC) Jazz Connoisseur Cassettes JCC114
[g] on (LP) Chiaroscuro CR108, Storyville SLP509, Good Music JRR3

(4502) **EDDIE CONDON**   broadcast, Ritz Theatre, New York City – Saturday, January 13, 1945
(Billy Butterfield, tp; Tommy Dorsey, tb; Pee Wee Russell, cl; Ernie Caceres, bar; Jess Stacy, p; Sid Weiss, b; George Wettling, d):

[a]	September In The Rain	(S/A)	(Tx)	AFRS CONDON 32

(Tommy Dorsey, tb; with same rhythm):

[b]	Body and Soul		(Tx)	AFRS CONDON 32

(as for [a], except Muggsy Spanier, co; for Butterfield):

[c]	Rose Room	(S/A)	(Tx)	AFRS CONDON 32

(as for [a], plus Muggsy Spanier, co):

[d]	At The Jazz Band Ball	(S/A)	(Tx)	AFRS CONDON 32

(possibly as [a], plus Lee Wiley, vo; Dick Cary, arr):

[e]	How Long Has This Been Going On? vLW	(A)	(Tx)	AFRS CONDON 32

(as for [d]):

[f]	Impromptu Ensemble	(I/A)	(Tx)	AFRS CONDON 32

other releases:
all titles on (LP) Rarities 37, Sunbeam SB 231, Baybridge UPS2260; (CD) Jazzology JCD-1017.

252

[a], [b], [c], [d], on (Tx) AFRS CONDON 46. [b] on (Tx) AFRS CONDON 39.
[a] part on (Tx) AFRS CONDON 34, (LP) Good Music JRR3.   [c] on (LP) Baybridge UXP126.   [b] on (LP) Rarities 44.
[d] on (LP) Good Music JRR3, Joker SM3575, Saga PAN6917, Spook Jazz SPJ6603, (AC) Holmia HM06.
[e] on (LP) Totem 1033, (AC) Jazz Connoisseur Cassettes JCC91.

(4503) **EDDIE CONDON**   broadcast, Ritz Theatre, New York City – Saturday, January 20, 1945
(Wild Bill Davison, co; Tommy Dorsey, tb; Pee Wee Russell, cl; Ernie Caceres, bar; Jess Stacy, p; Sid Weiss, b; George
Wettling, d):

[a]	**Jazz Me Blues**	**(A)**	(not on AFRS)

(Tommy Dorsey, tb; with same rhythm):

[b]	**Smoke Gets In Your Eyes**		(not on AFRS)

(as for [a], except Max Kaminsky, tp; for Davison):

[c]	**At Sundown**	**(S/A)**	(not on AFRS)

(Sidney Bechet, ss; with same rhythm):

[d]	**Dear Old Southland**		(not on AFRS)

(Lee Wiley, vo; with Tommy Dorsey, tb; same rhythm: band, probably as [c], at coda):

[e]	**Don't Blame Me** vLW	**(I/A)**	(not on AFRS)

all titles on (CD) Jazzology JCD-1017.   [d] on (LP) Chiaroscuro CR113.

(4504) **TOMMY DORSEY and His ORCHESTRA** (probable personnel: George Seaberg, Mickey Mangano. Dale Pearce,
Roger Ellick, tp; Tommy Dorsey, Nelson Riddle, Red Benson, Collen 'Tex' Satterwhite, tb; Buddy De Franco, cl, as; Sid
Cooper, as; Al Klink, Gail Curtis, ts; Bruce Branson, as, bar; Leonard Atkins, Peter Dimitriades, Manny Fiddler, Joseph
Goodman, Alex Beller, Ruth Rubenstein Goodman, Bernard Tinterow, vl; Milton Thomas, David Uchitel, violas; Fred
Camelia, cello; Reba Robinson, harp; Jess Stacy, p; Bob Bain, g; Sid Block, b; Joe Park, tuba; Buddy Rich, d; Sy Oliver,
arr; Bonnie Lou Williams, Charlie Karroll, The Sentimentalists, vo):

broadcast, unknown Naval Station– Monday, January 29, 1945

[a]	**You're Driving Me Crazy** vTS	**(A)**	(Tx)	AFRS SB 739
[b]	**I Dream Of You** vCK	**(N)**	(Tx)	AFRS SB 739
[c]	**Buster's Gang Comes On**	**(S)**	(Tx)	AFRS SB 739
[d]	**Sleighride In July** vBLW	**(N)**	(Tx)	AFRS SB 739
[e]	**Well, Git It!** *	**(N)**	(Tx)	AFRS SB 739

* omit strings. "Jazz Records" incorrectly lists Milt Golden as pianist.
Dale Pearce is spelt as such on the Social Security sheets, though some sources show as Pierce.
AFRS SB = AFRS Coca Cola Spotlight Bands issue.
All these Blue Network broadcast titles also on (Tx) AFRS SB 584 and (LP) Giants of Jazz GOJ-1023.

Omitted from this listing is Tommy Dorsey's theme, *I'm Getting Sentimental Over You,* which opens and closes most
broadcasts by his orchestra. Stacy's solos with Dorsey are limited to two or four bars only.

(4505) **EDDIE CONDON**   broadcast, Ritz Theatre, New York City – Saturday, February 3, 1945
(Billy Butterfield, tp; Lou McGarity, tb; Ed Hall, cl; Ernie Caceres, bar; Jess Stacy, p; Sid Weiss, b; George Wettling, d)

[a]	**It's Been So Long**	**(A)**	(Tx)	AFRS CONDON 35

(Jess Stacy, p; Sid Weiss, b; George Wettling, d):

[b]	**Sweet Lorraine**		(Tx)	AFRS CONDON 35

(as for [a], except Max Kaminsky, tp; for Butterfield):

[c]	**Sunday**	**(A)**	(Tx)	AFRS CONDON 35

(Sidney Bechet, ss; with same rhythm):

[d]	**Don't Get Around Much Anymore**		(Tx)	AFRS CONDON 35

(as for [a]):

[e]	**Alice Blue Gown**	**(S/A)**	(Tx)	AFRS CONDON 35

(as for [c], plus Sidney Bechet, ss):

[f]	**My Blue Heaven**	**(A/S)**	(Tx)	AFRS CONDON 35

(probably as for [a], plus Lee Wiley, vo; Dick Cary, arr):

[g]	**How Long Has This Been Going On?** vLW	**(I/A)**	(Tx)	AFRS CONDON 35

(as for [a], plus Kaminsky, tp; Bechet, ss):

[g]	**Impromptu Ensemble**	**(I/A/S)**	(Tx)	AFRS CONDON 35

other releases:
[c], [f] on (Tx) AFRS CONDON 47.   [b] on (LP) Aircheck 26
all titles on (CD) Jazzology JCD-1018.
all titles, except [b], on (LP) Jazum 75, Baybridge UPS2261.

(4506) **TOMMY DORSEY and His ORCHESTRA** (personnel probably as for January 29, 1945, except Frankie Lester, vo):
broadcast, The Meadowbrook, Cedar Grove, NJ – Saturday, February 3, 1945

[a]	**More and More** vBLW	**(N)**	(Tx)	AFRS ONS 603
[b]	**Hawaiian War Chant**	**(N)**	(Tx)	AFRS ONS 603
[c]	**I Dream Of You** vFL	**(N)**	(Tx)	AFRS ONS 603
[d]	**Swing High** *	**(N)**	(Tx)	AFRS ONS 603
[e]	**The Minor Goes Muggin'** *	**(I)**	(Tx)	AFRS ONS 603

* omit strings. broadcast from the Meadowbrook Ballroom.

other releases:
[b] on (LP) First Heard FHR1974-3, Golden Era LP 15020. [d] on (LP) Jazum 3, Joyce 1086, First Heard FHR1974-3, Big Band Era 20127, Tobacco Road B/2654. [d] on (AC) Big Band Era F40127, Tobacco Road MB/92654.
[e] on (LP) Joyce 1086.

(4507) **TOMMY DORSEY and His ORCHESTRA** (personnel probably as for January 29, 1945):
broadcast, Staten Island, NY– Monday, February 5, 1945

[a]	**On The Atcheson, Topeka And Santa Fe** vTS	( )	(Tx)	AFRS SB 745
[b]	**Opus One**	( )	(Tx)	AFRS SB 745
[c]	**Nevada** vFL, TS?	( )	(Tx)	AFRS SB 745
[d]	**'Tain't Me** vTS	( )	(Tx)	AFRS SB 745
[e]	**Swing High**	( )	(Tx)	AFRS SB 745

These Blue Network broadcast titles also on AFRS Spotlight Bands 590.
AFRS SB = AFRS Coca Cola Spotlight Bands SB745.

(4508) **TOMMY DORSEY and His ORCHESTRA** (George Seaberg, Mickey Mangano, Dale Pearce, Gerald Goff, Sal La Pertche, tp; Tommy Dorsey, Nelson Riddle, Tex Satterwhite, Frank D'Annolfo, tb; Buddy De Franco, cl, as; Sid Cooper, as; Al Klink, Gail Curtis, ts; Bruce Branson, as, bar; Leonard Atkins, Peter Dimitriades, Manny Fiddler, Joseph Goodman, Alex Beller, Ruth Rubenstein Goodman, Bernard Tinterow, Sam Ross, vl; Milton Thomas, David Uchitel, violas; Fred Camelia, cello; Reba Robinson, harp; Jess Stacy, p; Bob Bain, g; Sid Block, b; Joe Park, tuba; Buddy Rich, d; Billy Usher, Bonnie Lou Williams, The Sentimentalists, vo):
Victor studio 2, East 24th St, New York City – Wednesday, February 7, 1945

D5-VB-85-1	**There's No You** vBU	**(N)**	(78)	Victor 20.1657
D5-VB-86-1	**Any Old Time** vBU	**(N)**	(78)	Victor 20.1648

"New Hot Discography" assumed that Milt Golden was the pianist for this session, as no pianist is shown on the recording sheets. However, Stacy is given on the Social Security list for the session. Salvatore La Pertche, Jr., is correct, but is usually given as La Perche. Session duration: 12.45 pm to 03.45 pm.

other releases:
D5-VB-86-1 on (Tx) AFRS Swingtime 45.

(4509) **EDDIE CONDON**   broadcast, Ritz Theatre, New York City – Saturday, February 10, 1945
(Muggsy Spanier, co; Lou McGarity, tb; Hank D'Amico, cl; Jess Stacy, p; Bob Casey, b; George Wettling, d):

[a]	**Should I?**	**(S/A)**	(Tx)	AFRS CONDON 36
[b]	**Song Of The Wanderer**	**(S/A)**	(Tx)	AFRS CONDON 36

(Sidney Bechet, ss; with same rhythm):

[c]	**Sister Kate**		(Tx)	AFRS CONDON 36

(as for [a], except Yank Lawson, tp; for Spanier):

[d]	**Indiana**	**(S/A)**	(Tx)	AFRS CONDON 36

(as for [a]):

[e]	**Relaxin' At The Touro**	**(I/A/S)**	(Tx)	AFRS CONDON 36

(Lee Wiley, vo; Stacy, p; Casey, b; Wettling, d):

[f]	**I Can't Get Started** vLW			(not on AFRS)

(all musicians):

[g]	**Impromptu Ensemble** (part)	**(I/A)**	(Tx)	AFRS CONDON 36

other releases:
all titles on (CD) Jazzology JCD-1019.
[a] on (Tx) AFRS CONDON 41, (LP) Jazum 38, 64(edited): Good Music JRR2. [b] on (LP) Jazum 38, Rhapsody RHA6028.
[c] on (LP) Jazum 38. [d] on (LP) Jazum 63, Rhapsody RHA6029, Baybridge Bonus E-1. [d] on (EP) Storyville SEP506
[e] on (Tx) AFRS CONDON 47, (LP) Jazum 63, Spook Jazz SPJ6603, Saga PAN6917, Joker SM3575, Rhapsody RHA6029, (AC) Holmia HM06. [f] on (LP) Totem 1033. [g] on (LP) Jazum 63.

(4510) TOMMY DORSEY and His ORCHESTRA (personnel as for February 7, 1945, with Dick Powell, mc & vo):

The Fitch Bandwagon broadcast, New York City – Monday, February 12, 1945

[a]	**Saturday Night** vDP,TS	**(N)**	(Tx)	AFRS Bandwagon
[b]	**Opus One**	**(S)**	(Tx)	AFRS Bandwagon
[c]	**You're Driving Me Crazy** vTS	**(N)**	(Tx)	AFRS Bandwagon
[d]	**I Should Care** vBLW, DP, TS	**(N)**	(Tx)	AFRS Bandwagon
[e]	**Alexander's Ragtime Band**	**(N)**	(Tx)	AFRS Bandwagon

The AFRS Bandwagon issue number has not been traced.

(4511) TOMMY DORSEY and His ORCHESTRA (similar personnel):

broadcast, Halloran General Hospital, Staten island, NY – Monday, February 12, 1945

[a]	**I'm Beginning To See The Light** vTS	**(N)**	(Tx)	AFRS SB 751
[b]	**I Dream Of You** vBU	**(N)**	(Tx)	AFRS SB 751
[c]	**Song Of India**	**(N)**	(Tx)	AFRS SB 751
[d]	**Sleighride In July** vBLW	**(N)**	(Tx)	AFRS SB 751
[e]	**Opus One**	**( )**	(Tx)	AFRS SB 751
[f]	**Any Old Time** vBU	**( )**	(Tx)	AFRS SB 751
[g]	**Swing High**	**(N)**	(Tx)	AFRS SB 751

This was a Blue Network broadcast. AFRS SB = AFRS Coca Cola Spotlight Bands.

other releases:
[a], [b], [c], [d], [g] on (Tx) AFRS SB 596. [c] on (LP) Giants of Jazz GOJ1023

(4512) TOMMY DORSEY and His ORCHESTRA (similar personnel, except Charlie Shavers, tp; Freddie Lester, vo; for Usher:

broadcast,400 Restaurant, 400 Fifth Avenue, New York City – probably Friday, February 16, 1945

[a]	**You're Driving Me Crazy** vTS	**(N)**	(Tx)	AFRS ONS 533
[b]	**Like Someone In Love** vBLW	**(N)**	(Tx)	AFRS ONS 533
[c]	**The Minor Goes Muggin'** *	**(I)**	(Tx)	AFRS ONS 533
[d]	**There's No You** vFL	**(N)**	(Tx)	AFRS ONS 533
[e]	**Opus One**	**(S)**	(Tx)	AFRS ONS 533
[f]	**I Should Care** vBLW, TS	**(N)**	(Tx)	AFRS ONS 533
[g]	**Alexander's Ragtime Band**	**(N)**	(Tx)	AFRS ONS 533
[h]	**Any Old Time** vFL	**(N)**	(Tx)	AFRS ONS 533
[i]	**That's It** *	**(N)**	(Tx)	AFRS ONS 533

This broadcast is believed to be from the opening night at the 400 Club, which has been variously reported as February 15th or, more likely, the 16th. [d] has a flautist. [e] has some doubling on clarinets. AFRS ONS = AFRS One Night Stand. *omit strings. All titles on (LP) Joyce Pix-2, LP1158.

(4513) EDDIE CONDON   broadcast, Ritz Theatre, New York City – Saturday, February 17, 1945
(Max Kaminsky, tp; Lou McGarity, tb; Pee Wee Russell, cl; Ernie Caceres, bar; Jess Stacy, p; Jack Lesberg, b; George Wettling, d):

[a]	**Strut Miss Lizzie**	**(S/A)**	(Tx)	AFRS CONDON 37

(as for [a], except Billy Butterfield, tp; added; Pee Wee Russell omitted; Dick Cary, arr; Red McKenzie, vo):

[b]	**Time On My Hands** vRM	**(A)**	(Tx)	AFRS CONDON 37

(as for [a], except Butterfield, tp; for Kaminsky):

[c]	**Ain't Misbehavin'**	**(S/A)**	(Tx)	AFRS CONDON 37

(Sidney Bechet, ss; with same rhythm):

[d]	**There'll Be Some Changes Made**		(Tx)	AFRS CONDON 37

(as for [a], plus Butterfield, tp; Bechet, ss):

[e]	**At The Jazz Band Ball**	**(S/A)**	(Tx)	AFRS CONDON 37

(as for [c], plus Lee Wiley, vo; Bobby Hackett, arr):

[f]	**Someone To Watch Over Me**	**(I/A)**	(Tx)	AFRS CONDON 37

(as for [e]):

[g]	**Impromptu Ensemble**	**(I/A)**	(Tx)	AFRS CONDON 37

other releases:
all titles on (LP) Baybridge UPS2261: (CD) Jazzology JCD-1019.
[a] on (Tx) AFRS CONDON 47, (LP) Jazum 75
[b] on (LP) Jazum 75, Palm P30:08
[c] on (Tx) AFRS CONDON 47, (LP) Jazum 76, Spook Jazz SPJ6607
[f] on (Tx) AFRS CONDON 40, (LP) Jazum 63, Totem 1033, (AC) Jazz Connoisseur Cassettes JCC91.
[d], [g] on Jazum 76 [g] on (LP) Jazum 76, Spook Jazz SPJ6607

(4514) **TOMMY DORSEY and His ORCHESTRA** (personnel as for February 7, 1945, except Charlie Shavers, Bob Guyer, tp; for Mangano, Pearce; Richard Noel, tb; for D'Annolfo; Livio 'Babe' Fresk, ts; for Curtis; omit string section, harp & tuba):

Victor studio 2, East 24th St, New York City – Friday, February 23, 1945

| D5-VB-112-1 | **After Hour Stuff** | **(S)** | (78) | Victor 20.3061 |
| D5-VB-113-1 | **That's It** | **(N)** | (78) | Victor 20.1710 |

Session duration: 01:30 pm to 04:30 pm. Both titles arranged by Fred Norman, who also wrote *That's It,* with Dorsey.

other releases:
D5-VB-112-1 on (Tx) AFRS GI Jive 2069, AFRS P-1159, P-GL-5; LP) Swing Era 1003, RCA Victor(E) DPM 2042
D5-VB-113-1 on (Tx) AFRS P-402; (LP) Sounds of Swing 106, Tobacco Road B/2654, Big Band Era 20127; (AC) Tobacco Road MB/92654, Big Band Era F40127

(4515) **EDDIE CONDON** broadcast, Ritz Theatre, New York City – Saturday, February 24, 1945
(Billy Butterfield, tp; Tommy Dorsey, tb; Jimmy Dorsey, cl; Ernie Caceres, bar; Jess Stacy, p; Sid Weiss, b; George Wettling, d):

| [a] | **Honeysuckle Rose** | **(S/A)** | (Tx) | AFRS CONDON 39 |
| [b] | **Baby, Won't You Please Home?** | **(A)** | (Tx) | AFRS CONDON 39 |

(Sidney Bechet, ss; with same rhythm):

| [c] | **China Boy** | | (Tx) | AFRS CONDON 39 |

(as for [a], except Max Kaminsky, tp; for Butterfield):

| [d] | **I Can't Believe That You're In Love With Me** | **(S/A)** | (Tx) | AFRS CONDON 39 |

(as for [a]):

| [e] | **Royal Garden Blues** | **(S/A)** | (Tx) | AFRS CONDON 39 |

(Lee Wiley, vo; Tommy Dorsey, tb; with same rhythm):

| [f] | **Any Old Time** vLW | | (Tx) | AFRS CONDON 39 |

(as for [a], plus Kaminsky, tp; Bechet, ss):

| [g] | **Impromptu Ensemble** (part) | **(I/A)** | (Tx) | AFRS CONDON 39 |

[g] the full version is on Jazzology, and includes a Stacy solo.

other releases:
all titles on (LP) Rarities 44, Baybridge UPS2262; (CD) Jazzology JCD-1020.
[a] on (LP) Jazum 53; [b] on Storyville SLP133, Good Music JRR2; [c] on (LP) Chiaroscuro CR113, Aircheck 26;
[d] on (LP) Jazum 63; [e] on (Tx) AFRS CONDON 48, (LP) Jazum 63; [f] on (Tx) AFRS CONDON 47, (LP) Jazum 63, Totem 1033, Memories Lightest LWIL403, Baybridge UPS2280, Dan VC5020; (AC) Jazz Connoisseur Cassettes JCC91, JCC114; [g] on (Tx) AFRS CONDON 48, (LP) Jazum 63.

(4516) **TOMMY DORSEY and His ORCHESTRA** (personnel probably as for February 23, 1945, plus string section, harp and tuba; as for February 7, 1945): broadcast, 400 Restaurant, New York City – Saturday, February 24, 1945

[a]	**I'm Beginning To See The Light** vTS	**(S)**	(Tx)	AFRS ONS 568
[b]	**More And More** vBLW	**(N)**	(Tx)	AFRS ONS 568
[c]	**Don't Ever Change** vFL	**(N)**	(Tx)	AFRS ONS 568
[d]	**Always**	**(N)**	(Tx)	AFRS ONS 568
[e]	**Song Of India**	**(N)**	(Tx)	AFRS ONS 568
[f]	**Any Old Time** vFL	**(N)**	(Tx)	AFRS ONS 568
[g]	**Midriff**	**(N)**	(Tx)	AFRS ONS 568
[h]	**I Should Care** vBLW,TS	**(N)**	(Tx)	AFRS ONS 568
[i]	**That's It** (part) *	**(N)**	(Tx)	AFRS ONS 568

AFRS ONS = AFRS One Night Stand. * omit strings.
Midriff is a Fred Norman composition, unconnected with the Duke Ellington recording.

[a], [b],[d], [g], [h] on (Tx) AFRS ONS 603. [a], [d], [g] on (LP) Joyce 1086, Tobacco Road B/2654, Big Band Era 20127;
(AC) Tobacco Road MB/92654, Big Band Era F40127. [f], [g] on (LP) Joyce 1086, Golden Era 15020.
[g] on (LP) First Heard 1974-3, Dance Band Days DBD08; (CD) Dance Band Days DBCD08.

(4517) **TOMMY DORSEY and His ORCHESTRA** (same personnel):
broadcast, AAFTC, New Haven, Connecticut – Monday, February 26, 1945

[a]	**Accentuate The Positive** vTS	( )	(Tx)	AFRS SB 763
[b]	**I Should Care** vBLW	( )	(Tx)	AFRS SB 763
[c]	**Three Little Words**	( )	(Tx)	AFRS SB 763
[d]	**Don't Ever Change** vFL	( )	(Tx)	AFRS SB 763
[e]	**Well, Git It!**	( )	(Tx)	AFRS SB 763

This Blue Network broadcast was from the Army Air Force Training Center at Yale, University.
Some titles on (Tx) Victory Parade of Spotlight Bands 608. (AFRS SB = Coca Cola Spotlight Bands)

(4518) **EDDIE CONDON**   broadcast, Ritz Theatre, New York City – Saturday, March 3, 1945
(Muggsy Spanier, co; Lou McGarity, tb; Sidney Bechet, ss; Ernie Caceres, bar; Jess Stacy, p; Sid Weiss, b; Johnny Blowers, d):
   [a]　　　　　**I've Found A New Baby**　　　　　**(S/A)**　(Tx)　　AFRS CONDON 40
(Dick Cary, tp, arr; McGarity, tb; Caceres, bar; same rhythm; Red McKenzie, vo):
   [b]　　　　　**Just Friends** vRM　　　　　　　**(A)**　(Tx)　　AFRS CONDON 40
(as for [a], except Max Kaminsky, tp; for Spanier):
   [c]　　　　　**That's A Plenty**　　　　　　　　**(S/A)**　(Tx)　　AFRS CONDON 40
(Bechet, ss; with same rhythm):
   [d]　　　　　**High Society**　　　　　　　　　　　　(Tx)　　AFRS CONDON 40
(as for [a], except Caceres, cl):
   [e]　　　　　**Someday, Sweetheart**　　　　　**(S/A)**　(Tx)　　AFRS CONDON 40
(as for [b], except Lee Wiley, vo):
   [f]　　　　　**The Man I Love** vLW　　　　　　**(I/A)**　(Tx)　　AFRS CONDON 40
(as for [a], plus Max Kaminsky, tp):
   [g]　　　　　**Impromptu Ensemble** (part)　　　**(I)**　(Tx)　　AFRS CONDON 40

[g] the full version is on Jazzology, and includes a Stacy solo.

other releases:
all titles on (LP) Baybridge UPS2262: (CD) Jazzology JCD-1020
[a], [b], [c] on (LP) Jazum 63.
[d], [e], [f], [g] on (LP) Jazum 64.
[a] part on (Tx) AFRS CONDON 42, (LP) Rhapsody RHA6029.
[c], [e] on (LP) Rhapsody RHA6029.
[e] on (LP) Baybridge UPS2280.
[f] on (LP) Totem 1033, Dan VC5020; (AC) Jazz Connoisseur Cassettes JCC91

(4519) **TOMMY DORSEY and His ORCHESTRA** (personnel as for February 24, 1945):
                                       broadcast, unknown location – Monday, March 5, 1945

[a]	**I'm Beginning To See The Light** vTS	( )	(Tx)	AFRS SB 769
[b]	**More And More** vBLW	( )	(Tx)	AFRS SB 769
[c]	**Opus One**	( )	(Tx)	AFRS SB 769
[d]	**Sleighride In July** vBLW	( )	(Tx)	AFRS SB 769
[e]	**That's It**	( )	(Tx)	AFRS SB 769
[f]	**Any Old Time** vFL	( )	(Tx)	AFRS SB 769
[g]	**After Hour Stuff**	( )	(Tx)	AFRS SB 769

AFRS SB = AFRS Spotlight Band.

other releases:
[a], [b], [c], [d], [e] also on (Tx) AFRS Victory Parade Of Coca Cola Spotlight Bands 614.

(4520) **TOMMY DORSEY and His ORCHESTRA** (Seaberg, William Moore, Guyer, Goff, tp; Dorsey, Karl De Karske, Noel, Satterwhite, tb; Gus Bivona, cl, as; Cooper, as; Klink, Fresk, ts; Branson, as, bar; Atkins, Dimitriades, Fiddler, Beller, Goodman, Ruth Goodman, Tinterow, Ross, vl; Uchitel, viola; Camelia, cello; Robinson, harp; Park, tu; Stacy, p; Bain, g; Block, b; Rich, d; Bonnie Lou Williams, Stuart Foster, The Sentimentalists, vo):
                                     Victor studio 2, East 24th St., New York City – Thursday, March 8, 1945

D5-VB-134-1	**A Friend Of Yours** vSF	( )	(78)	Victor unissued
D5-VB-135-1	**June Comes Around Every Year** vSF	**(N)**	(78)	Victor 20.1669

session duration: 10:00 am to 02:00 pm.

other releases:
D5-VB-135-1 on (Tx) AFRS P-319.

(4521) **TOMMY DORSEY and His ORCHESTRA** (same personnel, except Charlie Shavers, tp; for Guyer; Nelson Riddle, tb; for De Karske):　　　　　　　　Victor studio 2, East 24th St., New York City – Friday, March 9, 1945

D5-VB-134-2	**A Friend Of Yours** vSF	**(N)**	(78)	Victor 20.1657
D5-VB-136-1	**Nevada** vSF, TS	**(N)**	(78)	Victor 20.1710

session duration: 02:30 pm to 05:00 pm. Session should have started at 01:30, but Buddy Rich was late!
D5-VB-134-2 also includes a flautist.

other releases:
D5-VB-136-1 on (Tx) AFRS P-402.

(4522) **TOMMY DORSEY and His ORCHESTRA** (same personnel):

broadcast, La Guardia Field, New York City – Monday, March 12, 1945

[a]	**Saturday Night** vTS	**(A)**	(Tx)	AFRS SB 775
[b]	**All Of My Life** vBLW	**(N)**	(Tx)	AFRS SB 775
[c]	**Let Me Love You Tonight**	**(A/S)**	(Tx)	AFRS SB 775
[d]	**Any Old Time** vSF	**(N)**	(Tx)	AFRS SB 775
[e]	**Buster's Gang Comes On**	**(S)**	(Tx)	AFRS SB 775
[f]	**I Should Care** vBLW, TS	**(N)**	(Tx)	AFRS SB 775
[g]	**Hawaiian War Chant**	**(N)**	(Tx)	AFRS SB 775

broadcast from American Export Airlines. AFRS SB = AFRS Spotlight Band.

other releases:
[a], [b], [c], [f], [g] on (Tx) AFRS Victory Parade of Coca Cola Spotlight Bands 620.
[e] edited on (LP) Golden Era 15020, Big Band Archives 2204

(4523) **TOMMY DORSEY and His ORCHESTRA** (same personnel, less strings, harp and tuba):
JIMMY DORSEY and His ORCHESTRA (Bob Alexy, Irving Goodman, Ray Linn, Tony Picciotto, Red Solomon, tp; Nick DiMaio, Mickey Iannone, Sonny Lee, Andy Russo, tb; Jimmy Dorsey, cl, as; Jack Aiken, as; Frank Langone, ts; Bob Lawson, as, bar; Marvin Wright, p; Herb Ellis, g; Jimmy Schutz, b; Buddy Schutz, d; Sy Oliver*, Otto Helbig#, arr):

Liederkrantz Hall, New York City – Thursday, March 15, 1945

D5-TC-196	**Brotherly Jump** *	**(N)**	(78)	V-Disc 451
D5-TC-197	**More Than You Know** #	**(N)**	(78)	V-Disc 451

George Simon organised this session by the combined orchestras. The Jimmy Dorsey personnel is from the V-Disc Discography by Richard Sears, who quotes a slightly different personnel for the Tommy Dorsey band. *Down Beat* (15mar45) reported that Frank Sinatra was scheduled for the session, but forgot to show up. Both titles also on (78) Navy V.Disc 231.

other releases:
both titles on (LP) Joyce 2009, Sandy Hook SH2046.

(4524) **TOMMY DORSEY and His ORCHESTRA** (probably same personnel as for March 8, 1945):

broadcast, Naval Ammunition Depot, Lake Denmark, NJ – Monday, March 19, 1945

[a]	**You're Driving Me Crazy** vTS	**(A)**	(Tx)	AFRS SB 781
[b]	**Like Someone In Love** vBLW	**(N)**	(Tx)	AFRS SB 781
[c]	**Song Of India**	**(N)**	(Tx)	AFRS SB 781
[d]	**I Dream Of You** vSF	**(N)**	(Tx)	AFRS SB 781
[e]	**Tico, Tico**	**(S)**	(Tx)	AFRS SB 781
[f]	**I Should Care** vBLW, TS	**(N)**	(Tx)	AFRS SB 781
[g]	**Midriff**	**(N)**	(Tx)	AFRS SB 781

AFRS SB = AFRS Coca Cola Spotlight Band.   Blue Network broadcast.

other releases:
[a], [b], [c], [d] on (Tx) AFRS Victory Parade of Spotlight Bands 626.   [b] on (CD) Jass J-CD-14.

(4525) **EDDIE CONDON**   broadcast, Ritz Theatre, New York City – Saturday, March 24, 1945
(Billy Butterfield, Joe Bushkin, tp; Lou McGarity, tb; Pee Wee Russell, cl; Ernie Caceres, bar; Jess Stacy, p; Jack Lesberg, b; Danny Alvin, d; Bobby Hackett, arr):

[a]	**When Your Lover Has Gone**	**(A)**	(Tx)	AFRS CONDON 43

(as for [a], except Max Kaminsky, tp; for Butterfield & Bushkin):

[b]	**Jazz Me Blues**	**(A)**	(Tx)	AFRS CONDON 43

(Jess Stacy, p; Danny Alvin, d):

[c]	**You're Driving Me Crazy**		(Tx)	AFRS CONDON 43

(probably Butterfield, tb; McGarity, tb; Caceres, cl; same rhythm; Bobby Hackett, arr; Lee Wiley, vo):

[d]	**Wherever There's Love** vLW	**(A)**	(Tx)	AFRS CONDON 43

(as for [a], plus Max Kaminsky; Bushkin both tp & p):

[e]	**Impromptu Ensemble**	**(I/S)**		(not on AFRS)

other releases:
all titles on (CD) Jazzology JCD-1022.
all titles except [e] on Baybridge UPS2264.
[a], [b], [c] on (LP) Jazum 65.   [c] on (LP) Aircheck 26.

(4526) **EDDIE CONDON** (Max Kaminsky, tp; Benny Morton, tb; Pee Wee Russell, cl; Ernie Caceres, bar; Jess Stacy, p;
Eddie Condon, g; possibly Bob Casey, b; George Wettling, d):   concert, Town Hall, New York City – circa 1945
  Squeeze Me   **(S/A)**   (Tx)   NoJ 16A
(Ed Hall, cl; Jess Stacy, p; unknown b & d):
  It's Been So Long   (Tx)   NoJ 18A

Personnels are based upon notes which accompanied the transcriptions and upon aural evidence. Kaminsky, Morton,
Russell, Stacy, Condon and Wettling are mentioned in the notes for 16A. Stacy has also been suggested for *Cheri* (actually
Cherry), but it does not sound like him.
          It is not known if both titles listed above are from the same concert. Neither is it known when the concert(s) took
place. Manfred Selchow has proposed a March 11, 1944 concert for *It's Been So Long*. If this is correct then the pianist,
playing in Stacy's style, is Joe Bushkin, as Selchow suggests. Bob Hilbert has suggested Town Hall concerts recorded
between December 1943 and May 1944. But Stacy did not return to New York until late July 1944.
          The 16-inch "Notes On Jazz" transcriptions were released by the "Department of State – United States of America.
Information and Cultural Affairs, International Broadcasting Division."

(4527) **EDDIE CONDON**   World Broadcasting Studios – audition session, New York City – circa 1945
(Max Kaminsky, tp; Miff Mole, tb; Pee Wee Russell, cl; Ernie Caceres, bar; Jess Stacy, p; Eddie Condon, g; unknown b;
probably George Wettling, d):
  [a]   **Easter Parade**   **(A)**
(as for [a], plus Lee Wiley, vo; Dick Cary, arr):
  [b]   **Old Folks** vLW   **(I/A)**
(Jess Stacy, p; with d):
  [c]   **Rosetta**
(as for [a], plus Lee Wiley, vo):
  [d]   **On The Sunny Side Of The Street** vLW **(A/S)**
(as for [a], except Billy Butterfield, tp; for Kaminsky; Lee Wiley, vo):
  [e]   **'S Wonderful**   **(A/S)**
  [f]   **Someone To Watch Over Me** vLW   **(A)**
(Ed Hall, cl; Jess Stacy, p; unknown b & d):
  [g]   **Oh, Lady Be Good!**
(as for [e]):
  [h]   **Somebody Loves Me** vLW   **(A/S)**

Personnels given are based upon aural identification. Hal Smith suggests that George Wettling is the drummer, with Bob
Casey on bass on some titles. Ernie Anderson also suggested Wettling on drums. Jazzology insert lists probably Jack
Lesberg, g; George Wettling, d.
These titles were recorded as auditions for two Chesterfield Cigarette programmes, combining Condon's music and
Chesterfield advertising. To quote one line: "Eddie Condon and Chesterfield will be back again with the right combination. . . ."
          Ernie Anderson, who wrote the scripts, confirmed that these were auditions for which Chesterfield paid, but no
sponsorship resulted.
          Recording date is uncertain. 'Jazz Records' lists as "late 1944", and Bob Hilbert suggests "May 1944". Jazzology
insert suggests probably March 1945. See notes to session (4526).

[d] & [h] are followed by announcer Fred Robbins, then both titles are briefly reprised.
The four titles on Jazum 66 were from discs marked "Chesterfield Audition 1945".
All titles on (LP) a white label 10" Japanese issue; (CD) Jazzology JCD1023.
[a], [c], [e], [h] appeared on (LP) Jazum 66.

(4528) **TOMMY DORSEY and His ORCHESTRA** (probably same personnel as March 8, 1945):
                                              broadcast, Floyd Bennett Field, Brooklyn, NY – Monday, March 26, 1945
  [a]   **On The Sunny Side Of The Street** vTS **(A)**   (Tx)   AFRS SB 787
  [b]   **Opus One**   **(S)**   (Tx)   AFRS SB 787
  [c]   **Any Old Time** vSF   **(N)**   (Tx)   AFRS SB 787
  [d]   **That's It** *   **(N)**   (Tx)   AFRS SB 787
AFRS SB = AFRS Coca Cola Spotlight Bands.   *omit strings
Broadcast from the Naval Air Station at Floyd Bennett Field.

These Blue Network broadcast titles also on (Tx) AFRS Victory Parade of Spotlight Bands 632 and (CD) Jass J-CD-14.

(4529) **TOMMY DORSEY and His ORCHESTRA** (George Seaberg, Mickey Mangano, Cy Baker, Charlie Shavers, Gerald Goff, tp; Tommy Dorsey, Karle De Karske, Richard Noel, Tex Satterwhite, tb; Gus Bivona, cl, as; Sid Cooper, as; Al Klink, Babe Fresk, ts; Bruce Branson, as, bar; Leonard Atkins, Manny Fiddler, Joseph Goodman, Alex Beller, Ruth Rubenstein Goodman, Bernard Tinterow, David Uchitel, Kurt Dierterle, Raoul Poliakin, Seymour Miroff, Arnold Fidus, Leonard Posner, vl; Peter Dimitriades, Sam Ross, George Morgulis, Herbert Fuchs, viola; Fred Camelia, Armand Kaproff, cello; Reba Robinson, harp; Joe Park, tu; Jess Stacy, p; Bob Bain, g; Sid Block, b; Buddy Rich, d; Bonnie Lou Williams, Stuart Foster, The Sentimentalists, vo):　　　　　　　　　　　　　Lotos Club Studios, New York City – Friday, April 13, 1945

D5-VB-729-1	**Tales From The Vienna Woods**	**(N)**	(78)	Victor 20.1701
D5-VB-730-NP	**Out Of This World** vSF	**( )**		unissued

Note that the Viennese waltzes, on Victor 20-1698 through 20-1702, are played almost exclusively by the strings, plus Tommy Dorsey's solo trombone. There is a flautist (probably Louis Martin) on some titles.

other releases: D5-VB-729-1 on (Tx) AFRS SP-144.

These ten waltz titles were released in the Symphonic Popular series of the AFRS Basic Music Library.

(4530) (same personnel, except Jacques Margolies, Max Tartasky, Jack Fishberg, Harry Farbman, vl; for Dierterle, Poliakin, Fidus, Posner; Rudolf Sims, cello; for Kaproff):　　　　　　　　　　same date

D5-VB-730-NP	**Out Of This World** vSF	**( )**		unissued
D5-VB-731-1	**Emperor Waltz**	**(N)**	(78)	Victor 20.1699

Session durations: (4530) 09:25 am to 12:45 pm.

　　　　　　　　　　(4531) 04:00 pm to 07:00 pm.

other releases: D5-VB-731-1 on (Tx) AFRS SP-143

(4531) (same personnel, except Kurt Dierterle, Raoul Poliakin, Leonard Posner, vl; for Jacques Margolies, Tartasky, Farbman; plus Herbert Fuchs, cello):　　　　　　Lotos Club studios, New York City – Saturday, April 14, 1945

D5-VB-730-1	**Out Of This World** vSF	**(N)**	(78)	Victor 20.1669
D5-VB-732-1	**Roses From The South**	**(N)**	(78)	Victor 20.1702
D5-VB-733-2	**Vienna Life**	**(N)**	(78)	Victor 20.1699

other releases: D5-VB-730-1/D5-VB-733-2 on (Tx) AFRS SP-153

(4532) (same personnel, plus Louis Martin, flute):　　　　　　　　　　same date

D5-VB-734-1	**You Came Along (From Out Of Nowhere)** vSF	**(N)**	(78)	Victor 20.1722

Session durations: (4531) 10:10 am to 01:10 pm.

　　　　　　　　　　(4532) 02:45 pm to 05:45 pm (for one title!)

Take numbers are as advised by RCA Victor.

You Came Along is a re-titling of the song *Out of Nowhere*, also known as *(You Came To Me From) Out of Nowhere*.

other releases:

D5-VB-732-1 on (Tx) AFRS SP-153, AFRS SP-144, AFRS Swingtime H-52 #69.

D5-VB-733-2 on (Tx) AFRS SP-153, AFRS Swingtime H-52 #69.

D5-VB-734-1 on (Tx) AFRS BML P-467.

(4533) (probably same personnel, except Vido Musso, ts; for Klink):

　　　　　　　　　　　　　　　　　　　　broadcast, Rhodes General Hospital, Utica, NY – Friday, April 27, 1945

[a]	**You're Driving Me Crazy** vTS	**(A)**	(Tx)	AFRS SB 815
[b]	**I Should Care** vBLW, TS	**(N)**	(Tx)	AFRS SB 815
[c]	**Any Old Time** vSF	**(N)**	(Tx)	AFRS SB 815
[d]	**Hawaiian War Chant**	**(N)**	(Tx)	AFRS SB 815
[e]	**Fresh Money** *	**(S)**	(Tx)	AFRS SB 815

AFRS SB = AFRS Coca Cola Spotlight Bands.   *omit strings.

All these Blue Network broadcast titles also on (Tx) AFRS Victory Parade Of Spotlight Bands 660.

[d] on (LP) Sunbeam SB 211.

(4534) (Seaberg, Mangano, Baker, Shavers, Goff, tp; Dorsey, De Karske, Noel, Satterwhite, tb; Bivona, Cooper, Musso, Fresk, Branson, reeds; Atkins, Fiddler, Goodman, Beller, Ruth Goodman, Tinterow, Uchitel, Miroff, Fishberg, Arnold Fidus, Harry Farbman, Poliakin, vl; Dimitriades, Ross, Morgulis, Milton Thomas, viola; Camelia, Armand Kaproff, cello; Reba Robinson, harp; Park, tu; Stacy, p; Bain, g; Block, b; Rich, d; Stuart Foster, Bonnie Lou Williams, The Sentimentalists, vo):

　　　　　　　　　　　　　　　　　　　　Lotos Club studios, New York City – Monday, April 30, 1945

D5-VB-738-1	**Artists' Life Waltz**	**(N)**	(78)	Victor 20.1700

Session duration: 01:00 pm to 04:30 pm. (To record one title only?)

Also on (Tx) AFRS SP-143.

(4535) (same personnel): broadcast, Naval Hospital, Chelsea, Massachusetts – Thursday, May 3, 1945

[a]	On The Sunny Side Of The Street	vTS	(A)	(Tx)	AFRS	SB 820
[b]	Tico Tico		(S)	(Tx)	AFRS	SB 820
[c]	Let Me Love You Tonight		(S/A)	(Tx)	AFRS	SB 820
[d]	I Should Care	vBLW,TS	(N)	(Tx)	AFRS	SB 820
[e]	That's It *		(A)	(Tx)	AFRS	SB 820

AFRS SB = AFRS Coca Cola Spotlight Bands.   *omit strings.   On [b] & [c] announcer talks over Stacy's brief solos.

other releases: all titles on (Tx) AFRS Victory Parade of Spotlight Bands 665.   [b], [c], [e] on (CD) Jass J-CD-14.

(4536) (probably same personnel): broadcast, Indiantown Gap, Pennsylvania – Thursday, May 10, 1945

[a]	Any Old Time	vSF	(N)	(Tx)	AFRS	SB 826
[b]	I Should Care	vBLW, TS	(N)	(Tx)	AFRS	SB 826
[c]	Out Of This World	vSF	(N)	(Tx)	AFRS	SB 826
[d]	Midriff		(N)	(Tx)	AFRS	SB 826

AFRS SB = AFRS Coca Cola Spotlight Bands.

other releases: all titles on (Tx) Victory Parade Of Spotlight Bands 671, and (LP) Joyce 4008.   [d] on (LP) IAJRC 17.

(4537) (George Seaburg, Vito Mangano. Gerald Goff, Charlie Shavers, tp; Tommy Dorsey, Karl De Karske, Richard Noel, Tex Satterwhite, tb; Gus Bivona, cl, as; Sid Cooper, as; Vido Musso, Babe Fresk, ts; Bruce Branson, bar; Alphonse Schipani, Joschim Fishberg, George Morgulis, Joseph Reilich, Harold Kohen, Helen Janov, Kalman Reve, Jacques Margolies, Alex Beller, Leonard Atkins, Manny Fiddler, Peter Dimitriades, Bernard Tinterow, Sam Ross, vl; David Uchitel, Milton Thomas, viola; Harold Gomberg, oboe; David Greenbaum, Fred Camelia, cello; Tibor Shik, Philip Palmer, Adolf Schulze, Hugh Cowden, french horn; Reba Robinson, harp; Joe Park, tu; Jess Stacy, p; Robert Bain, g; Sid Block, b; Buddy Rich, d): Lotos Club studios, New York City – Monday, May 14, 1945

D5-VB-752-1	On The Beautiful Blue Danube	(N)	(78)	Victor 20.1698
D5-VB-753-1	You and You	(N)	(78)	Victor 20.1701

other releases:
D5-VB-752-1 on (Tx) AFRS SP-143, AFRTS APM 407.
D5-VB-753-1 on (Tx) AFRS SP-144

(4538) (same personnel):   same date

D5-VB-754-1	One Thousand And One Nights	(N)	(78)	Victor 20.1700
D5-VB-755-1	Voices Of Spring	(N)	(78)	Victor 20.1698
D5-VB-756-1	Wine, Woman and Song	(N)	(78)	Victor 20.1702

other releases:
D5-VB-754-1 on (Tx) AFRS SP-144.   D5-VB-755-1 on (Tx) AFRS SP-143.
D5-VB-756-1 on (Tx) AFRS SP-153.

(4539) (same personnel, except french horns & oboe omitted):   same date

D5-VB-757-1	There You Go	vSF	(N)	(78)	Victor 20.1715

other releases: also on (Tx) AFRS P-402.
On D5-VB-758-1 *The Minor Goes Muggin'* Jess Stacy is replaced by Duke Ellington.
Session durations: (4537) 01:30 **am** to 04.40 **am**
                    (4538) 07:35 **am** to 10.35 **am**
                    (4539) 11:25 **am** to 02:25 **pm** (one title only)

(4540) (same personnel, though string section personnel may vary; omit french horns):
broadcast, US Naval Base, Melville, Rhode Island - Saturday, May 19, 1945

[a]	Saturday Night	vTS	(A)	(Tx)	AFRS	SB 834
[b]	June Comes Around Every Year	vSF	(N)	(Tx)	AFRS	SB 834
[c]	All Of My Life	vBLW	(N)	(Tx)	AFRS	SB 834
[d]	Fresh Money *		(S)	(Tx)	AFRS	SB 834
[e]	Swing High *		(N)	(Tx)	AFRS	SB 834

AFRS SB = AFRS Coca Cola Spotlight Bands.   *omit strings

other releases: all titles on (Tx) AFRS Victory Parade Of Spotlight Bands 679.
[d] on Echo Jazz (LP) EJLP 01, (AC) EJMC 01, (CD) EJCD 01

(4541) (same personnel, though string section personnel may vary):

broadcast, unknown location – Monday, May 21, 1945

[a]	**I'm Beginning To See The Light** vTS	**(S)**	(Tx)	AFRS SB 835
[b]	**I Should Care** vBLW, TS	**(N)**	(Tx)	AFRS SB 835
[c]	**Let Me Love You Tonight**	**(A/S)**	(Tx)	AFRS SB 835
[d]	**Any Old Time** vSF	**(N)**	(Tx)	AFRS SB 835
[e]	**Well, Git It!** *	**(N)**	(Tx)	AFRS SB 835

AFRS SB = Coca Cola Spotlight Bands. All titles on (Tx) AFRS Victory Parade of Spotlight Bands 680.   *omit strings

(4542) (same personnel as May 14, 1945, (session 4537) less string sections, harp & tuba):

Victor studio A, Chicago – Saturday, May 26, 1945

D5-VB-336-1	**On The Atchison, Topeka And Santa Fe** vTS	**(N)**	(78)	Victor 20.1682
D5-VB-337-1	**In The Valley (Where The Evenin' Sun Goes Down)** vSF	**(N)**	(78)	Victor 20.1682

Session duration: 02:30 pm to 06:15 pm.

other releases:

D5-VB-336-1 on (Tx) AFRS P-365: Reader's Digest (LP) RD3/4-25-2, Reader's Digest(E) RDM/RDS 2176, (AC) KRD-025/A.
D5-VB-337-1 on (Tx) AFRS P-365.

(4543) EDDIE CONDON and His ORCHESTRA (Max Kaminsky, tp; Lou McGarity, tb; Joe Dixon, cl; Jess Stacy, p; Eddie Condon, g; Jack Lesberg, b; Johnny Blowers, d):

New York City – Thursday, June 14, 1945

72933A	**Oh, Lady Be Good!**	**(S)**	(78)	Decca 23431
72934A	**Swanee**	**(A/S)**	(LP)	Decca DL9234
72934B	**Swanee**	**(A/S)**	(78)	Decca 23433

other releases:

72933A/72934A on (LP) Decca DL9234, Brunswick(E) LA8518; (CD) MCA GRP16372.
72933A?/72934? on (LP) Decca DL5137

(4544) JESS STACY and His ORCHESTRA (Billy Butterfield, Pee Wee Erwin, Anthony Natoli, tp; Will Bradley, Jack Satterfield, tb; Sal Franzella, cl; Henry Ross, Hymie Shertzer, as; Larry Binyon, Julius Bradley, ts; Jess Stacy, p; Frank Worrell, g; Bob Haggart, b; Mario Toscarelli, d; Lee Wiley, vo):

New York City – Friday, June 29, 1945

D5-VB-451	**Daybreak Serenade**	**(S)**	(78)	Victor 20.1708
D5-VB-452	**It's Only A Paper Moon** vLW	**(S)**	(78)	Victor 20.1708

other releases:

both titles on (LP) RCA(F) 741.103; (CD) ASV Living Era AJA5172.
D5-VB-451 on (LP) Victor LEJ-11, Camden CAL328, Camden(E) CDN118, RCA Bluebird (LP) NL86754, (AC) NK86754,
        (CD) ND86754, Topaz TPZ1050
D5-VB-452 on (LP) Victor LPM1373, RCA Victor 74321 13035.2; (Tx) AFRS P-361; (CD) Bluebird(J) PDTD-1018, RST
        91566, Topaz TPZ1047

(4545) JESS STACY and His ORCHESTRA (probable personnel: Buddy Bergman, Eddie Downs, Sam Skolnik, tp; Ray Thomas, J.C. Wilson, tb; Johnny Setar, cl, as; Earl Bergman, as; Eddie Martin, Johnny Lewis, ts; Dick Voight, bar; Jess Stacy, p; Bus Watson, b; Jerry Rosen, d):

broadcast , Sherman Hotel, Chicago – December 1945

Air Mail Special	**(I/S)**	
unidentified (part)*	**(A)**	
Sweet Lorraine	**(S)**	

* The unidentified title is a very brief exposition of the band's theme.

This is the only known recording of the regular Jess Stacy big band. It is a double-sided acetate, made by an engineer in the radio room of the Sherman Hotel, and owned by Eddie di Martino (professional name, Eddie Martin). Unfortunately the acetate is heavily worn and almost unplayable.

(4601) BENNY GOODMAN and His ORCHESTRA (John Best, Nate Kazebier, Dick Mains, Dale Pearce, tp; Cutty Cutshall, Leon Cox, tb; Addison Collins, frh; Benny Goodman, cl; Larry Molinelli, Clint Bellew, as; Cliff Strickland, Zoot Sims, ts; John Rotella, bar; Jess Stacy, p; Barney Kessel, g; Harry Babasin, b; Louis Bellson, d; Eve Young, vo):

broadcast, 400 Club, New York City – Saturday, November 15, 1946

[a]	**Rosalie**	**(N)**	(Tx)	AFRS ONS 1260
[b]	**Somewhere In The Night**	**(I/A)**	(Tx)	AFRS ONS 1260
[c]	**Hora Staccato**	**(N)**	(Tx)	AFRS ONS 1260

[d]	SEXTET	**St. Louis Blues**	**(A/S)**	(Tx)	AFRS ONS 1260
[e]		**A Gal In Galico** vEY	**(N)**	(Tx)	AFRS ONS 1260
[f]	SEXTET	**Sweet Georgia Brown**	**(A/S)**	(Tx)	AFRS ONS 1260

SEXTET: Goodman, cl; Johnny White, vb; Stacy, p; Kessel, g; Babasin, b; Bellson, d. AFRS ONS = AFRS One Night Stand.

(4602) (same personnel):　　　　　　　　　　　　　broadcast, New York City – Tuesday, November 18, 1946

　　　　　　　　You Brought A New Kind Of Love To Me　　**(S)**

This NBC "The Victor Borge Show" title on (LP) Sunbeam SB 155.

(4603) (same personnel):　　　　　　　　　　broadcast, 400 Club, New York City – Saturday, November 22, 1946

[a]		**Somebody Stole My Gal**	**(N)**	(Tx)	AFRS ONS 1300
[b]		**For You, For Me, For Evermore** vEY	**(N)**	(Tx)	AFRS ONS 1300
[c]	SEXTET	**On The Sunny Side Of The Street**	**(I/S)**	(Tx)	AFRS ONS 1300
[d]		**Lonely Moments**	**(N)**	(Tx)	AFRS ONS 1300
[e]		**(I Sent You) A Kiss In The Night**	**(N)**	(Tx)	AFRS ONS 1300
[f]	SEXTET	**Honeysuckle Rose**	**(I/S/A)**	(Tx)	AFRS ONS 1300

SEXTET: Goodman, cl; White, vb; Stacy, p; Kessel, g; Babasin, b; Bellson, d. AFRS ONS = AFRS One Night Stand.
[e] Eve Young announced, but does not sing.

(4604) **BENNY GOODMAN QUINTET** (Goodman, cl; Stacy, p; Kessel, g; Babasin, b; Bellson, d):
　　　　　　　　　　　　　　　　　broadcast, New York City – Tuesday, November 25, 1946

　　　　　　　　September Song　　　　　　**(I/A/S)**

This NBC "The Victor Borge Show" title on (LP) Sunbeam SB 155.

(4605) **BENNY GOODMAN and His ORCHESTRA** (personnel as for November 15, 1945):
　　　　　　　　　　　　　broadcast, 400 Club, New York City – Saturday November 29, 1946

[a]		**Clarinade**	**(S)**	(Tx)	AFRS MC 812
[b]		**Love Doesn't Grow On Trees** vEY	**(N)**	(Tx)	AFRS MC 812
[c]	SEXTET	**On The Sunny Side Of The Street**	**(I/S)**	(Tx)	AFRS MC 812
[d]		**Whistle Blues** *	**(N)**	(Tx)	AFRS MC 812
[e]		**Stompin' At The Savoy** (part)	**(N)**	(Tx)	AFRS MC 812

SEXTET: Goodman, White, Stacy, Kessel, Babasin, Bellson.
AFRS MC = AFRS "Magic Carpet".　 * whistling by band.

(4606) **BENNY GOODMAN and His ORCHESTRA** (Nate Kazebier, Uan Rasey, Ray Linn, tp; Lou McGarity, Red Ballard, Tommy Pederson, tb; Benny Goodman, cl; Skeets Herfurt, Heinie Beau, as; Babe Russin, Jack Chaney, ts; Chuck Gentry, bar; Jess Stacy, p; Barney Kessel, g; Harry Babasin, b; Louis Bellson, d; Johnny White, vb; Eve Young, vo):
　　　　　　　　　　　　　　　　　broadcast, New York City – Monday, December 2, 1946

[a]		**Swanee River**	**( )**	(Tx)	AFRS BG 24
[b]	QUINTET	**I've Found A New Baby**	**(S/A)**	(Tx)	AFRS BG 24

QUINTET: Goodman, Stacy, Kessel, Babasin, Bellson.
AFRS BG = AFRS Benny Goodman Show. [b] also on (LP) Sunbeam SB 155.

(4607) (same personnel):　　　　　　　　　　broadcast, New York City – Monday, December 9, 1946

[a]		**Somebody Stole My Gal**	**(S)**	(Tx)	AFRS BG 26
[b]		**Hora Staccato**	**( )**	(Tx)	AFRS BG 26

AFRS BG = AFRS Benny Goodman Show.

other releases:
[a] on (Tx) AFRS Benny Goodman Show 27; (LP) First Heard FH-37, Quicksilver 5046; (CD) TKO CD.015, Double Play GRF124

(4608) (possibly Kazebier, George Wendt, Zeke Zarchey, Joe Triscari, tp; McGarity, Ballard, Bill Schaefer, tb; Goodman, cl; Herfurt, Beau, as; Russin, Chaney, ts; Gentry, bar; Stacy, g; Kessel, g; Babasin, b; Sammy Weiss, d; Johnny White, vb):
　　　　　　　　　　　　　　　　　broadcast, Hollywood – Monday, December 16, 1946

[a]		**I Never Knew**	**(A)**
[b]	SEXTET	**Where Or When**	**(I/A/S)**
[c]		**Benjie's Bubble**	**(S)**

SEXTET: Goodman, White, Stacy, Kessel, Babasin, Weiss.

These NBC "The Victor Borge Show" titles on (LP), [a], [c] on Sunbeam SB 156, [b] on Sunbeam SB 155.

(4609) (same personnel; Anita O'Day, vo):   broadcast, Hollywood – Monday, December 23, 1946
  [a]   **The Christmas Song** vAOD   **(A)**
  [b] SEXTET   **The World Is Waiting For The Sunrise**   **(S/A)**
SEXTET: Goodman, White, Stacy, Kessel, Babasin, Weiss.
These NBC "The Victor Borge Show" titles on (LP), [a] on Sunbeam SB 156, [b] on Sunbeam SB 155.

(4610) (same personnel; Jeannie McKeon, vo):   broadcast, Hollywood – Monday, December 30, 1946
          A Gal In Calico vJM   **(A)**
This NBC "The Victor Borge Show" title on (LP) Sunbeam SB156.

(4701) (same personnel):   broadcast, Hollywood – Monday, January 6, 1947
  [a]   **Great Day**   **(N)**   (Tx)   AFRS BG 27
  [b]   **Guilty** vJM   **(A)**   (Tx)   AFRS BG 27
  [c] QUINTET **Slipped Disc**   **(S/A)**   (Tx)   AFRS BG 27
QUINTET: Goodman, Stacy, Kessel, Babasin, Weiss.   AFRS BG = AFRS Benny Goodman Show.

other releases:
[a] on (LP) First Heard FH-23, Sunbeam SB 156, First Time Records 1974.1   [a], [b] on (LP) Yeri-Bean UNBN-467
[c] on Sunbeam SB 155, Swing House SH-17.

(4702) (same personnel):   broadcast, Hollywood – Monday, January 13, 1947
  [a]   **Lonely Moments**   **(N)**   (Tx)   AFRS BG 28
  [b]   **For Sentimental Reasons** vJM   ( )   (Tx)   AFRS BG 28
  [c] QUINTET **I'll Always Be In Love With You**   **(S/A)**   (Tx)   AFRS BG 28
QUINTET: Goodman, Stacy, Kessel, Babasin, Weiss.   AFRS BG = AFRS Benny Goodman Show.

other releases:
[a] on (LP) First Heard FH-23, First Time Records 1974-1.   [c] on (LP) Sunbeam SB 155, Swing House SH-17.

(4703) (same personnel, except Allan Reuss, g; for Kessel; Art Lund, vo):
                                     broadcast, Hollywood – Monday, January 20, 1947
  [a]   **The One I Love Belongs To Somebody Else** vAL **(A)**   (Tx)   AFRS BG 29
  [b]   **Dizzy Fingers**   ( )   (Tx)   AFRS BG 29
  [c] SEXTET **At Sundown**   **(A/S)**   (Tx)   AFRS BG 29
SEXTET: Goodman, cl; Ernie Felice, acc; Stacy, p; Reuss, g; Babasin, b; Weiss, d.   AFRS BG = AFRS Benny Goodman Show.

other releases:
[a], [c] on (LP) Yeri-Bean UNBN-467; [c] on (LP) Sunbeam SB 155.

(4704) (same personnel; Matt Dennis, vo):   broadcast, Hollywood – Monday, January 27, 1947
  [a]   **Clarinade**   **(S)**   (Tx)   AFRS BG 30
  [b]   **You Broke The Only Heart**
                         That Ever Loved You vMD   **(A)**   (Tx)   AFRS BG 30
  [c] SEXTET **Memories Of You**   **(I/S/A)**   (Tx)   AFRS BG 30
SEXTET: Goodman, Felice, Stacy, Reuss, Babasin, Weiss.   AFRS BG = AFRS Benny Goodman Show.

other releases:
[a] on (LP) First Heard FH-37; (CD) TKO CD.015.
[b] on (LP) Sunbeam SB 156.   [c] on (Tx) AFRS BG 36; (LP) Sunbeam SB 155.

(4705) (Kazebier, Wendt, Zarchey, Triscari, tp; Ballard, McGarity, Schaefer, tb; Goodman, cl; Herfurt, Beau, as; Russin, Chaney, ts; Gentry, bar; Stacy, p; Allan Reuss, g; Larry Breen, b; Sammy Weiss, d; Johnny Mercer, Matt Dennis, vo):
                                      Hollywood – Tuesday, January 28, 1947

1609-4L-1	**Lonely Moments**	**(A)**	(78)	Capitol 374
1609-alt	**Lonely Moments**	( )	(LP)	EMI(F) 1551563
1610-4R-2	**It Takes Time** vJM	**(A)**	(78)	Capitol 376
1611-	**Moon-Faced, Starry-Eyed** vMD	**(A)**	(LP)	Blue-Disc T1016
1612-2R-2	**Whistle Blues** *	**(N)**	(78)	Capitol 374
1619-4R	**Moon-Faced, Starry-Eyed** vJM	**(A)**	(78)	Capitol 376

Radio Recorders studios. 1619 probably recorded January 29, 1947, with Mercer vocal. Connor's "Listen To His Legacy" incorrectly gives Matt Dennis as vocalist on 1619. Intervening matrices are not by Goodman.   * whistling by band.

other releases:
1609-4L-1 on (Tx) AFRS P-771; (EP) Capitol EAP 1-409; (LP) Capitol T409, Capitol(E) LC6831, EMI(F) 1551563;
(CD) Capitol 7243 8320862 2 3**
1610-4R-2 on (Tx) Air Force G1-15, AFRS P-771; (LP) Capitol(E) LC6601
1612-2R-2 on (Tx) AFRS P-771; (EP) Capitol EAP 2-409;(LP) Capitol H409, T409, Capitol(E) LC6601, LC6831;
(CD) Capitol 7243 832086 2 3
** CD notes show matrix 1609-5.   They also show personnel variations, with Mannie Klein replacing Wendt; Tommy
Pederson, Ed Kusby, replacing Ballard, Schaefer; Gus Bivona replacing Herfurt.

(4706) (uncertain personnel, but including: Nate Kazebier, tp; Lou McGarity, Tommy Pederson, tb; Benny Goodman, cl;
Heinie Beau, as; Babe Russin, ts; Chuck Gentry, bar; Jess Stacy, p; Allan Reuss, g; Harry Babasin, b; Tommy Romersa, d;
Jeannie McKeon, vo):   broadcast, Hollywood – Monday, February 3, 1947

[a]		'S Wonderful	(S)	(Tx)	AFRS BG 31
[b]		Oh, But I Do vJMcK	( )	(Tx)	AFRS BG 31
[c]	SEXTET	The Anniversary Song	(S)	(Tx)	AFRS BG 31

SEXTET: Goodman, Felice, Stacy, Reuss, Babasin, Romersa.   AFRS BG = AFRS Benny Goodman Show

other releases:
[a] on (Tx) AFRS BG 47; (LP) First Heard FH-23.   [c] on (LP) Yeri-Bean UNBN-467.

(4707) BENNY GOODMAN SEXTET (Benny Goodman, cl; Ernie Felice, acc; Jess Stacy, p; Allan Reuss, g; Harry Babasin,
b; Tommy Romersa, d):   broadcast, near Los Angeles – February   , 1947

[a]	Sweet Georgia Brown	( )	(Tx)	AFRS CP 272
[b]	I Know That You Know	( )	(Tx)	AFRS CP 272

AFRS CP = AFRS Command Performance.   Broadcast early February from a military camp near Los Angeles.

(4708) BENNY GOODMAN and His ORCHESTRA (personnel uncertain; refer February 3, 1947):
broadcast, Hollywood – Monday, February 10, 1947

[a]		Jalousie	(A)	(Tx)	AFRS BG 32
[b]		Moon-Faced, Starry-Eyed vJMcK	(A)	(Tx)	AFRS BG 32
[c]	SEXTET	Sweet Georgia Brown	(S/A)	(Tx)	AFRS BG 32

SEXTET: Goodman, Felice, Stacy, Reuss, Babasin, Romersa.   AFRS BG = AFRS Benny Goodman Show.

other releases:
[a] on (Tx) AFRS BG 39, BG 45, BG 50; (LP) Sunbeam SB 156, Yeri-Bean UNBN-467.
[b] on (LP) First Heard 23.   [c] on (LP) Sunbeam SB 155.

(4709) BENNY GOODMAN QUINTET (Goodman, cl; Felice, acc; Stacy, p; Babasin, b; Romersa, d):
Hollywood – Wednesday, February 12, 1947

1631-6	Sweet Georgia Brown	(S)	(78)	Capitol 15768
1632-4	I'll Always Be In Love With You	(S/A)	(LP)	Capitol H479
1633-1	Sweet Lorraine	(S/A)	(78)	Capitol H441
1633-2	Sweet Lorraine	(S/A)	(LP)	Mosaic MQ6.148
1634-3	St. Louis Blues	(A/S)	(LP)	Capitol H479

other releases:
all titles on (LP) Mosaic MQ6-148; (CD) Mosaic MD4-148.
1632/33-1/34 on (LP) Swaggie S-1381.
All titles, except 1633-2, on (LP) EMI(F) 15515, Capitol(E) VMPM1002. (CD) Blue Moon BMCD-1042
1631 on (EP) Capitol EBF295; (LP) Capitol H295, P395, T395, T669, CapitolE LC6810, Amiga 850019, Swaggie S-1364.
1632/34 on (LP) Capitol H479, T669, Capitol(E) LC6680, LC6810; (EP) Capitol EAP1-479
1632 on (LP) Capitol(E) VMPM1002
1633-1 on (Tx) AFRS P-4224: (LP) Capitol H441, T441, Capitol(E) LC6620; (EP) Capitol EAP2-441

(4710) BENNY GOODMAN and His ORCHESTRA (personnel uncertain; refer February 3, 1947):
broadcast, Hollywood – Monday, February 17, 1947

[a]		'Way Down Yonder In New Orleans	(N)	(Tx)	AFRS BG 33
[b]		It Takes Time vBG	( )	(Tx)	AFRS BG 33
[c]	SEXTET	St. Louis Blues	(A/S)	(Tx)	AFRS BG 33

SEXTET: Goodman, Felice, Stacy, Reuss, Babasin, Romersa.   AFRS BG = AFRS Benny Goodman Show.

other releases:
[a] on (LP) Yeri-Bean UNBN-467. [c] on (LP) Sunbeam SB 155.

(4711) **BENNY GOODMAN QUINTET** (personnel as for February 12, 1947):

broadcast, Hollywood – Wednesday, February 19, 1947

| 1658-3 | **I Know That You Know** | **(S)** | (78) | Capitol B20130 |

      BENNY GOODMAN TRIO (Goodman, Stacy, Romersa):   same session

| 1659-4 | **I Can't Get Started** | | (LP) | Capitol H295 |

other releases:
both titles on (LP) EMI(F) 1551563, Mosaic MQ6-148; (CD) Mosaic MD4.148, Blue Moon BMCD-1042.
1658 on (LP) Capitol H479, Capitol(E) LC6880, Swaggie S-1381; (EP) Capitol EAP1-479.
1659 on (LP) Capitol P395, Capitol(E) LC6557

(4712) **BENNY GOODMAN and His ORCHESTRA** (personnel as for February 3, 1947):

broadcast, Hollywood – Monday, February 24, 1947

[a]		**Canadian Capers**	**(N)**	(Tx)	AFRS BG 34
[b]		**Maybe You'll Be There** vJMcK	**(A)**	(Tx)	AFRS BG 34
[c]	SEXTET	**I Know That You Know**	**(S/A)**	(Tx)	AFRS BG 34

SEXTET: Goodman, Felice, Stacy, Reuss, Babasin, Romersa.   AFRS BG = AFRS Benny Goodman Show.

other releases:
[a] on (Tx) AFRS BG 49; (LP) Sunbeam SB 156, Yeri-Bean UNBN-467.   [b] on (LP) First Heard FH-23, Sunbeam SB 156.
[c] on (LP) Sunbeam SB 155.

(4713) (personnel as for February 3, 1947; Beryl Davis, vo):   broadcast, Hollywood – Monday, March 10, 1947

| [a] | SEXTET | **You Turned The Tables On Me** vBD | **(A)** | (Tx) | AFRS BG 35 |
| [b] | | **Jack, Jack, Jack** | **(A/S)** | (Tx) | AFRS BG 35 |

SEXTET: Goodman, Felice, Stacy, Reuss, Babasin, Romersa: AFRS BG = AFRS Benny Goodman Show.
[b] announced as "Tuo Tuo Guerro"; listed as "Cu-Tu-Gu-Ru" on First Heard.

other releases:
[a] on (LP) Sunbeam SB 155, Swing House SH-17.
[b] on (LP) First Heard FH-23, Yeri-Bean UNBN-467, First Time Records 1974.1

There is uncertainty about the date when Jess Stacy left Goodman.
He may be present on the AFRS "Benny Goodman Show" transcriptions of March 17, 24, 31 and April 7.

(4714) **WINGY MANONE** (Wingy Manone, tp; Joe Venuti, vl; Jerry Wald, cl; Jess Stacy, p; Les Paul, g; Candy Candido, b;
Abe Lyman, d):   soundtrack recording, Hollywood – March 1947

| | **Jam Session Blues** | **(A/S)** | (VC) | JPS* WMV101191 |

* Jazz Pioneer Series (Canada) video cassette.
This title is from the soundtrack of the film "Sarge Goes To College".
Date based upon Manone's statement in his autobiography that he had to report to the Monogram studio on March 4, 1947.

(4715) **LEE WILEY with JESS STACY and his ORCHESTRA** (unknown trumpet; two saxes; Jess Stacy, p; unknown
guitar; bass; drums):   Lee Wiley, vo): New York City – c. May   , 1947

T1223M-2	**Sugar (That Sugar Baby O' Mine)**	**(I/A/S)**	(78)	Majestic 7258
T1224M-1	**Woman Alone With The Blues**	**(A)**	(78)	Majestic 7258
T1225M-2	**Memories**	**(I/A/S)**	(78)	Majestic 7259
T1225M-4	**Memories**	**( )**	(78)	Majestic 7259
T1226M-1	**But Not For Me**	**(A/S)**	(78)	Majestic 7259
T1226M-?	**But Not For Me**	**(A/S)**	(LP)	Allegro 4049

Full label name for Allegro is Allegro-Elite.
    Memories is actually *Memories Of You,* and is so given on Allegro-Elite, Tono, etc. *But Not For Me* on Halo has the
trumpet introduction deleted.
    The main difference between the two takes of *But Not For Me* lies in the vocal, with the version on Allegro-Elite
ending with a different lyric ("When Ev'ry Happy Plot. . .") to that on take -1. Also, at the close, Lee Wiley's voice breaks.
T1225M-4 has not been heard; apparently differences are minimal. . .
    This is another mystery session as regards recording date and personnel, as well as the difficulty of allocating the
alternative takes. There is much negative information, but no firm detail.
    The estimated date is usually given as June 1947, based upon a *Down Beat* report (June 4, 1947) which stated: "It
is understood that Miss Wiley will sign for Majestic and will be backed . . . by her husband . . ." However, Stacy was on tour

in California in early June. If the *Down Beat* report originated, say, in late April, then a May session would seem reasonable. It is just possible that the session took place in Los Angeles, but Majestic was a New York operation.

The only soloist heard, other than Stacy, is the trumpeter. Ernie Anderson thought it was probably Billy Butterfield, but when played these title by Brian Peerless, Butterfield suggested it could be Don Goldie. Don Goldie told the writer it was not he. Stacy himself thought it might have been Mannie Klein. Again, Klein said he was not present.

Ernie Anderson was advertising manager for Majestic during its short life. Although not officially involved on the production side, he managed to arrange for Lee Wiley and Bud Freeman to appear on Majestic. However, he could recall no personnel data for the Wiley session.

Bob Porter, whose listing of the Majestic sessions was serialised in *Record Research*, had no details of personnel or date.

Adjoining masters are T1222 by Victor Lombardo and T1227 by The Merry Macs.

other releases:
T1224M-1 on (CD) Music CD22727
T1223M-2/T1224M-1 on (LP) Allegro-Elite 4049, Halo 50269, Tono TJ6004; (EP) Royale 349
T1225M on (LP) Allegro-Elite 4049, Halo 50269, Tono TJ6004, Royale 6023, Showcase 106-3; (EP) Royale 349. All presumed to be take -2, though take -4 may be on Halo 50269.
T1226M-1 on (LP) Halo 50269 and, presumed take -1, Tono TJ6004; (EP) Royale 349.
T1226M-? on (LP) Allegro-Elite 4049 (this is an alternative take)
T1226M- on (LP) Tono TJ6004

(4801) **EDDIE CONDON** (Wild Bill Davison, co; Lou McGarity, tb; Matty Matlock, cl; Jess Stacy, p; Eddie Condon, g; Art Shapiro, b; Morey Feld, d):   Dixieland Jubilee, Pan-Pacific Auditorium, Hollywood – Friday, October 29, 1948

[a]	**The One I Love Belongs To Somebody Else**	(S)	(Tx)	AFRS JJ 28
[b]	**That's A Plenty**	(S)	(Tx)	AFRS JJ 29
[c]	**When Your Lover Has Gone**	(I)	(Tx)	AFRS JJ 30

AFRS JJ = AFRS Just Jazz.
[b] incorrectly labelled as *Sensation Rag*, and [c] as *Blues In B Flat*.
[b] incorrectly labelled as *Muskrat Ramble* on AFRS JJ40!

other releases:
[a] also on (Tx) AFRS Just Jazz 30,36,49; [b] on (Tx) AFRS Just Jazz 40, 50, 66: [c] on (Tx) AFRS Just Jazz 30, 49.

(4802) **EDDIE MILLER and The BOBCATS** (Mannie Klein, tp; Warren Smith, tb; Matty Matlock, cl; Eddie Miller, ts; Doc Rando, as; Jess Stacy, p; Nappy Lamare, g; Art Shapiro, b; Nick Fatool, d):   same concert

[a]	**Who's Sorry Now?**	(N)	(Tx)	AFRS JJ 29
[b]	**Yesterdays** (tenor &rhythm)	(I/A)	(Tx)	AFRS JJ 29
[c]	**At The Jazz Band Ball**	(N)	(Tx)	AFRS JJ 29

The date for this concert has been quoted also as October 5th and October 3Oth, but October 29 is believed to be correct. This was the first in the annual Dixieland Jubilee series run by Gene Norman and Frank Bull.

other releases:
all titles on (Tx) AFRS Just Jazz 40, 50 and 66.   #66 was labelled as Dixieland All Stars.

(4803) **JESS STACY** (p solo):   St. Francis Room, Los Angeles – late 1948
Barrelhouse

Recorded for Dick Reimer onto a cardboard disc at the St. Francis Room on 8th Street. Reimer recalled: "Jess had a small disc recorder on the piano . . . The record was about 7 - 10 inches and made of cardboard."

(5001) **JESS STACY** (p solo):   broadcast, Station KFMV, Los Angeles – Monday, February 6, 1950
Complainin'
In A Mist
Ja Da
Squeeze Me / Black and Blue
Sister Kate

These solos were recorded in the course of an interview on Floyd Levin's "Jazz on Parade" radio show.
The interview was transcribed and printed in *Joslin's Jazz Journal* (August 1985).

(5002) **JESS STACY and His TRIO** (Jess Stacy, p; George Van Eps, g; Morty Corb, b; Nick Fatool, d):

Los Angeles – Wednesday, June 28, 1950

6164-3	**Careless**	(CD)	Mosaic MD12.170
6165-4	**I'll Be Seeing You**	(78)	Capitol 15842
6166-2	**Can't We Be Friends?**	(78)	Capitol 1136
6167-1	**Imagination**	(78)	Capitol 1136

Capitol 1136 labelled as "Jess Stacy At The Piano".
Take details are as listed by Mosaic.
The Capitol 78's show, for example, 6166-2D3 and 6167-1D5, but D3 and D5 have no significance.

other releases:
All titles on (LP) Mosaic MQ19-170, (CD) Mosaic MD12-170.
6165   on (LP) Capitol H323, Capitol(E) LC6559
6166   on (LP) Capitol T795, T1034

(5003) **JESS STACY and His TRIO** (same personnel):

Los Angeles – Wednesday, July 5, 1950

RHCO4122	**Under A Blanket Of Blue**	(LP)	Columbia CL6147
RHCO4123	**I Can't believe That You're In Love With Me**	(LP)	Columbia CL6147
RHCO4124	**Lullaby Of The Leaves**	(LP)	Columbia CL6147
RHCO4125	**I'm Gonna Sit Right Down And Write Myself A Letter**	(LP)	Columbia CL6147

other releases:
RHCO4122/4124 also on (LP) Columbia CL603

(5004) (same personnel):

Los Angeles – Monday, July 10, 1950

RHCO4130	**Lover Man**	(LP)	Columbia CL6147
RHCO4131	**Keepin' Out Of Mischief Now**	(LP)	Columbia CL6147
RHCO4132	**Cherry**	(LP)	Columbia CL6147
RHCO4133	**In A Mist**	(LP)	Columbia CL6147

other releases:
RHCO4130 also on (LP) Columbia CL602.

(5005): **JESS STACY and His BAND** (Freddie Greenleaf, tp; Warren Smith, tb; Albert Nicholas, cl; Jess Stacy, p; Paul Sarmento, b; Smokey Stover, d):   broadcast, Hangover Club, San Francisco – Monday, November 27, 1950

| | **Muskrat Ramble** | ( ) | |

(5006) (same personnel):

November, 1950

	Clarinet Marmalade	( )	
	Tin Roof Blues	( )	
	High Society	( )	
	The World Is Waiting For The Sunrise	( )	
	In A Mist	( )	

(5007): (same personnel):

Monday, December 11, 1950

	Royal Garden Blues	( )	
	Sister Kate	( )	
	Way Down Yonder In New Orleans	( )	
	Muskrat Ramble	( )	
	At The Jazz Band Ball	( )	

These Hangover Club titles were recorded off-the-air by the late Alderson Fry on 7" reel-to-reel, 7 ips.
The tapes are now part of the William Love Estate.
The above details are as given by William Love, although the December 11th date is suspect, as the Nappy Lamare band was due to begin an engagement at the Hangover on that date, with the Stacy job ending on December 9th.

(5101) **JESS STACY and His TRIO** (Jess Stacy, p; George Van Eps, g; Morty Corb, b; Nick Fatool, d):

Los Angeles – Friday, March 16, 1951

L6158	**You Took Advantage Of Me**	(78)	Brunswick 80171
L6159	**Fascinating Rhythm**	(78)	Brunswick 80170
L6160	**I Can't Get Started**	(78)	Brunswick 80170
L6161	**I Want To Be Happy**	(78)	Brunswick 80171

other releases:
all titles on (LP) Brunswick BL58029, BL54017, Brunswick(E) LA8737, Ace of Hearts AH39, Affinity AFS1020, Swaggie S1248
L6159 on (LP) Decca DL79234.
L6159/L6161 on (Tx) Here's To Veterans 265

(5102) (same personnel):   Los Angeles – Tuesday, April 10, 1951

L6227	**Indiana**	(78)	Brunswick 80172
L6228	**Stars Fell On Alabama**	(78)	Brunswick 80172
L6229	**If I Could Be With You**	(78)	Brunswick 80173
L6230	**Oh, Baby**	(78)	Brunswick 80173

other releases:
all titles on (LP) Brunswick BL58029, BL54017, Brunswick(E) LA8737, Ace of Hearts AH39, Affinity AFS1020, Swaggie S1248
L6227/L6230 on (Tx) Here's To Veterans 265.
(On this transcription Stacy talks between the four tracks, stressing the importance of veterans advising any change of address.)

(5103) **JESS STACY and His ALL STAR ORCHESTRA** (Charlie Teagarden, tp; Ted Vesely, tb; Matty Matlock, cl; Eddie Miller, ts; Jess Stacy, p; George Van Eps, g; Morty Corb, b; Nick Fatool, d; Toni Roberts, Bob Albert, vo):
                                                        Los Angeles – Thursday, July 5, 1951

You Do Have Money, Don't You? vTR		Omega unissued
You Wonderful Gal vBA		Omega unissued
Why Not Admit It? vBA		Omega unissued
Try To Forget It vBA		Omega unissued

(5104) (Charlie Teagarden, Zeke Zarchy, Mannie Klein, tp; Ted Vesely, tb; Matty Matlock, cl; Jack Dumont, as; Eddie Miller, ts; Art Lyons, bar; George Kast, Erno Neufeld, Sam Cytron, vl; Jess Stacy, p; Nappy Lamare, g; Morty Corb, b; Nick Fatool, d; Toni Roberts, Bob Albert, vo):
                                                     Los Angeles – Wednesday, July 11, 1951

You Wonderful Gal vBA	**(N)**	(78)	Omega	OM109
Try To Forget It			Omega unissued	

(5105) **MATTY MATLOCK and His ALL STARS** (Teagarden, tp; Vesely, tb; Matlock, cl; Miller, ts; Stacy, p; Lamare, g; Corb, b; Fatool, d):   Los Angeles – Wednesday, July 11, 1951

Don't You Think It's About Time? vTR	**(A/S)**	(78)	Omega	OM110
You Do Have Money, Don't You? vTR	**(A/S)**	(78)	Omega	OM109

Omega OM110 (45-OM-110) has been reported from both a 45 rpm disc, apparently issued to radio stations, and a 78 rpm disc. Both have a Jack Teagarden group playing *Parasol* on the reverse, numbered OM-112. This appears to be a "mule coupling", ie; an erroneous coupling of 110 and 112.

(5106) **JESS STACY** (Stacy, p; Ray Bauduc, d):   Club Hangover, Los Angeles – 1951
                       Little Rock Getaway
(add Charlie Teagarden, tp):
                       Sugar
                       Charmaine
                       Three Little Words
recorded by enthusiast Elliott Jones on an early Magnacorder tape machine (15 ips).

(5107) **BOB CROSBY and The BOBCATS** (Billy Butterfield, tp; Elmer Schneider, Murray McEarchern, Ted Vesely, tb; Matty Matlock, cl; Eddie Miller, ts; Jess Stacy, p; Nappy Lamare, g; Bob Haggart, b, wh; Ray Bauduc, d; Bob Crosby, The Bob-O-Links, vo):
                                              Los Angeles – Wednesday, October 3, 1951

9112	**Bouquet Of Roses** vBC, BOL	**(A)**	(78)	Capitol 1850
9114	**Just A Little Lovin'** vBC, BOL	**(A)**	(78)	Capitol 1850

(Butterfield, tp; Warren Smith, tb; Matlock, cl; Miller, ts; same rhythm):   same session

9115	**Savoy Blues** whBH	**(A)**	(78)	Capitol 1894
9116	**Avalon**	**(S)**	(LP)	Capitol T293

Haggart's whistling is multi-tracked. Only four titles were made at this session. Matrix 9113 is *My Love* by Gordon MacRae. This reported by Frances Rogers of Capitol Records. Take details on the Capitol 78's are of no significance.

other releases:
9115 on (LP) Capitol T293, T1556, Pausa PR9034
9116 on (LP) Capitol T1556, SH-3301, Pausa PR9034

(5108) THE BOBCATS (Butterfield, tp; Smith, tb; Matlock, cl; Miller, ts; Stacy, p; Lamare, g; Haggart, b, wh; Bauduc, d):

Los Angeles – October   ,1951

[a]	**March Of The Bobcats**	**(S)**	Snader telescriptions
[b]	**Who's Sorry Now?**	**(S)**	Snader telescriptions
[c]	**Muskrat Ramble**	**(S)**	Snader telescriptions
[d]	**Panama Blues**	**(S/A)**	Snader telescriptions
[e]	**Savoy Blues** whBH	**(A)**	Snader telescriptions
[f]	**Complainin'**	**(S)**	Snader telescriptions
[g]	**Love's Got Me In A Lazy Mood**	**(N)**	Snader telescriptions

Backgrounds written, apparently, by Bob Haggart, except for Savoy Blues, which was by Paul Weston.
[f] & [g] are features for Stacy and Miller respectively.
Also recorded at this session was *The Big Noise From Winnetka,* the Haggart/Bauduc duet.

other releases:
all titles on (VC) Charly VID JAM 14, Storyville VVD758.
[b] on (VC) Charley VID SAM 100, [e] on (VC) Storyville 6008.
[a], [b], [c], [d], [e] on (LP) Camay 3035, New World NW/5035

(5109) PUD BROWN'S DELTA KINGS (Charlie Teagarden, tp; Jack Teagarden, tb, vo; Pud Brown, ts; Jess Stacy, p; Ray Bauduc, d):

Capitol studios, Hollywood – Thursday, October 10, 1951

DR-1001- –	**Lovin' To Be Done** vJT	**(N)**	(78)	Westcraft 1
DR-1002- –	**Jersey Bounce**	**(A)**	(78)	Westcraft 1
DR-1003-D1	**Pretty Baby**	**(S)**	(78)	Westcraft 2
DR-1004-D1	**Charmaine**	**(S)**	(78)	Westcraft 2

other releases:
all titles on (LP) Jazz Man LJ-334, New Orleans Jazz N.O.J.R.C. 002.
DR-1003 on (tape) Jazztape JT-1, Alphatape No. 1.

(5110) JESS STACY (p solos):

Club Hangover, Los Angeles – 1951

unidentified original
unidentified original

these titles are on a double-sided 12" acetate from an unknown source.

(5111) STACY, TEAGARDEN, LUCAS (Johnny Lucas, tp, vo; Jack Teagarden, tb, vo; Bob McCracken, cl, vo; Jess Stacy, p; Jimmy Pratt, d):

broadcast, Station KFI, Los Angeles – Saturday, December 22, 1951

[a]	**Way Down Yonder In New Orleans**	**(S/A)**		
[b]	**When It's Sleepy Time Down South**	**(I/A/S)**		
[c]	**Baby Won't You Please Come Home?** vJT	**(I/A)**	(CD)	Jazzology Press 4
[d]	**Big Butter And Egg Man**	**(I/S/A)**		
[e]	**Candlelights** (piano solo)			
[f]	**Basin Street Blues** vJT	**(A/S)**	(CD)	Jazzology Press 4
[g]	**Melancholy Blues**	**(I/A/S)**		
[h]	**Georgia On My Mind** vBM	**(A)**		
[i]	**Lover**	**(I/A)**		
[j]	**St. James Infirmary** vJT	**(I/A)**	(CD)	Jazzology Press 4
[k]	**Black and Blue** vJL	**(I/A)**		
[l]	**On The Sunny Side Of The Street**	**(I/S/A)**	(CD)	Jazzology Press 4

This broadcast from George Barclay's "Are You From Dixie?" radio show.
During the broadcast George Barclay mentions Jess Stacy playing *In A Mist* "when you were down last week." Barclay suggests the band should be called The Dixie Quintet.

(5201) BOB CROSBY (including Red Nichols, co; Ziggy Elman, Charlie Teagarden, Wingy Manone, tp; Jack Teagarden, vo; Jimmy Dorsey, cl; Jess Stacy, Walter Gross, p; Nick Fatool, d; Johnny Mercer, vo; Bob Crosby, compere):

CBS Playhouse, Vine Street, Hollywood – Thursday, May 8, 1952

No details are known of this free, public recording session, which was the subject of a news item in a Los Angeles newspaper for May 8, 1952. Presumably the session did take place, but it is not known if it was a recording for later broadcast or for a transcription, such as the "Dixieland Jamboree" session (5405). Such all-star dixieland transcriptions were popular at this time.

(5301) **MUGGSY SPANIER** (Muggsy Spanier, co; Jess Stacy, p; Truck Parham, b; Barrett Deems, d):

Radio Recorders, Los Angeles – Monday, April 6, 1953

tune 1, -1	**Rose Room**			
tune 1, -2	**Rose Room**	(false start)		
tune 1, -3	**Rose Room**		*(CD)	Jazzology Press 2
tune 2, -1	**untitled blues**			
tune 2. -2	**untitled blues**	(false start)		
tune 2, -3	**untitled blues**	(false start)		
tune 2, -4		(not used)		
tune 2, -5	**untitled blues**		*(CD)	Jazzology Press 2
tune 3, -1	**Do You Know What It Means To Miss New Orleans** (breakdown)			
tune 3, -2	**Do You Know What It means To Miss New Orleans**		*(CD)	Jazzology Press 2
tune 4, -1	**My Honey's Lovin' Arms**			
tune 4, -2	**My Honey's Lovin' Arms**			
tune 4, -3	**My Honey's Lovin' Arms**			
tune 4, -4	**My Honey's Lovin' Arms**		*(CD)	Jazzology Press 2

* Jazzology 2 = Jazzology Book CD 2, incorporated in the Jazzology Press book, "Muggsy Spanier: The Lonesome Road", a biography and discography by Bert Whyatt.

This is the private session which Ruth Spanier and Pat Stacy organised to give their husbands an opportunity to record together. Details will be found in the relevant chapter of the biography.

(5302) **JESS STACY and JOHNNY LUCAS** (John Lucas, tp, vo; Jess Stacy, p):

broadcast, station KFI, Los Angeles – Saturday, May 23, 1953

[a]	**Sleepytime Down South**	(CD)	Jazzology Press 4
[b]	**Melancholy Blues**	(CD)	Jazzology Press 4
[c]	**Oh, Baby** (piano solo)	(CD)	Jazzology Press 4
[d]	**Loveless Love** vJL	(CD)	Jazzology Press 4
[e]	**Stompin' At The Savoy** (piano solo)	(CD)	Jazzology Press 4
[f]	**Lover Man** (piano solo)	(CD)	Jazzology Press 4
[g]	**Study In A Minor** (the Sing, Sing, Sing solo) (piano solo)	(CD)	Jazzology Press 4
[h]	**Them There Eyes**	(CD)	Jazzology Press 4
[i]	**Big Butter And Egg Man**	(CD)	Jazzology Press 4

This is another broadcast from George Barclay's "Are You From Dixie?" radio show.
[a], [b] on (AC) "The Best of Johnny Lucas" privately issued cassette.

(5303) **JESS STACY** (piano): Holiday House, Los Angeles – Wednesday, August 5, 1953

A Sunday Kind Of Love
Complainin'
I've Got A Right To Sing The Blues
I Cover The Waterfront
Tenderly
I Can't Get Started
What's The Use?
Ruby
Someone To Watch Over Me
Sweet Georgia Brown
My Funny Valentine
I'll Remember April
Keepin' Out Of Mischief Now
New Orleans (part)
Have You Met Miss Jones?
Mary Lou (?) (part)
Do You Know What It Means To Miss New Orleans?
These Foolish Things
Autumn In New York
You Go To My Head
Sleepytime Down South
In A Mist
Lover Man
You Took Advantage Of Me
Body and Soul

What Is There To Say
Sweet Lorraine
Can't We Be Friends?
Peg O' My Heart
Melancholy
My Honey's Lovin' Arms
Manhattan
Penthouse Serenade
Black and Blue
Under A Blanket Of Blue
Lullaby Of The Leaves
If I Could Be With You One Hour Tonight
I've Got The World On A String
How Long Has This Been Going On?
Yesterdays
Tin Roof Blues
St. Louis Blues
Memories Of You
If I Had You
Have You Met Miss Jones?
Can't Help Lovin' That Man (unknown female vocal)
Don't Be That Way
Sister Kate
It's The Talk Of The Town
Stars Fell On Alabama
Lovely To Look At
Lazy River
Ain't Misbehavin'

Recorded at the Holiday House (hotel, restaurant, cocktail bar), 27400 Pacific Coast Highway, Malibu, right on the beach, by Joe Boughton, using a Pentron tape recorder.

   Sound is of low-quality, but the tape is no doubt a representative example of Jess Stacy's playing and repertoire, and the conditions he experienced, while performing in cocktail lounges

(5304) **EDDIE MILLER UNION BAND** (Irving Goodman, tp; Abe Lincoln, tb; Matty Matlock, cl; Eddie Miller, ts; Jess Stacy, p; Phil Stephens, b; Nick Fatool, d):   concert, Monterey Park, Los Angeles – August 1953

Struttin' With Some Barbecue	**(A/S)**	
The Sheik Of Araby	**(I)**	
St. Louis Blues	**(A/S)**	
Who's Sorry Now?	**(N)**	
For You (Lincoln feature)	**(A)**	
Royal Garden Blues	**(A/S)**	
Body and Soul (Miller feature)	**(I/A)**	
Sweet Georgia Brown	**(A/S)**	
In A Mist (piano solo)		
That's A Plenty	**(I/A/S)**	
My Inspiration (Matlock feature)	**(A)**	
Bugle Call Rag	**(S)**	
Panama	**(S)**	

Taped (possibly on Sunday, August 9th) by Joe Boughton at the annual open-air picnic of the American Federation of Musicians, Local 47.

(5401) **JOHNNY LUCAS and His BLUE BLOWERS** (Johnny Lucas, tp, vo; Mike Hobi, tb; Matty Matlock, cl, fl*; Jess Stacy, p; Lenny Esterdahl, bj, g#; Bob Stone, b; Monte Mountjoy, d):   Capitol studios, Hollywood – February   , 1954

[a]	**Lazy River**	**(A)**	(78)	Jazz Man 106
[b]	**Loveless Love Blues** # vJL	**(A)**	(78)	Jazz Man 106
[c]	**High Society** *	**(N)**	(78)	Jazz Man 107
[d]	**Hindustan** #	**(I/S)**	(78)	Jazz Man 107

[b] as *Careless Love* on Score.

other releases:
all titles on (LP) Jazz Man LJ-333B; (EP) Storyville SEP326, Tempo(E) EXA34.
[a], [b], [d] on (LP) Score SLP-4024.

(5402) JESS STACY and The FAMOUS SIDEMEN (Ziggy Elman, tp; Murray McEarchern,tb; Heinie Beau, as, cl*, arr; Vido Musso, ts; Chuck Gentry, bar; Jess Stacy, p; Allan Reuss, g; Art Shapiro, b; Nick Fatool, d):

Capitol Studios, Hollywood – Thursday, April 15, 1954

1277	**Roll 'Em**	(S)	(LP)	Atlantic LP1225
1278	**Where Or When**	(I/S)	(LP)	Atlantic LP1225
1279	**Sing, Sing, Sing**	(S)	(LP)	Atlantic LP1225
1280	**Let's Dance**	(N)	(LP)	Atlantic LP1225
1281	**Goodbye** *	(N)	(LP)	Atlantic LP1225
1282	**King Porter Stomp**	(S)	(LP)	Atlantic LP1225

other releases:
all titles on (LP) London(E) LTZ-K15012. (LP/CD) Atlantic Jazzlore 7-90664-1.
1279 on (EP) Atlantic EP571.
1277/78/82 on (EP) Atlantic EP570

(5403) (Ziggy Elman, tp; Ted Vesely, tb; Heinie Beau, as, arr; Babe Russin, ts; Joe Koch, bar; Jess Stacy, p; Al Hendrickson, g; Art Shapiro, b; Nick Fatool, d):

Capitol Studios, Hollywood – Thursday, April 29, 1954

1283	**Don't Be That Way**	(S/A)	(LP)	Atlantic LP1225
1284	**Sometimes I'm Happy**	(S)	(LP)	Atlantic LP1225
1285	**When Buddha Smiles**	(A/S)	(LP)	Atlantic LP1225
1286	**Down South Camp Meeting**	(S)	(LP)	Atlantic LP1225

other releases:
all titles on (LP) London(E) KTZ-K15012; (LP/CD) Atlantic Jazzlore 7-90664-1.
1285 on (EP) Atlantic EP570.
1283/84/85 on (EP) Atlantic EP571

(5404) JESS STACY (piano):

concert, Hollywood – May   , 1954

In A Mist

(Stacy, p; unknown, b; Nick Fatool, d):

Sweet Lorraine
Sunday

(add Johnny Lucas, tp: introduction by Bob Crosby):

Melancholy Blues

These titles are believed to be from a short-lived concert series, organised by Bob Markus at the Ivar Theatre, starting May 23, 1954.

(5405) "GUEST STAR" DIXIELAND CLAMBAKE No. 3 (Red Nichols, co; Ziggy Elman, Manny Klein, Andy Secrest, Charlie Teagarden, Zeke Zarchy, George Seaberg, tp; Jack Teagarden, Ted Vesely, King Jackson, Moe Schneider, Si Zentner, tb; Jimmy Dorsey, cl; Eddie Miller, ts; Matty Matlock, Skeets Herfurt, Babe Russin, Chuck Gentry, reeds; Joe Rushton, bsx; Jess Stacy, Marvin Ash, p; George Van Eps, g; Eddie Shrivanek, bj; Haig Stephens, b; Country Washburne, tu; Ben Pollack, Nick Fatool, Ray Bauduc, d; Johnny Mercer, vo; Bob Crosby, compere; Matty Matlock, arr-1):

Hollywood – c. July 1954

High Society	(N)	(Tx)	Guest Star 384
The Dixieland Ban vJM	(N)	(Tx)	Guest Star 384
Pagan Love Song -1	(S)	(Tx)	Guest Star 384

unison clarinets on "High Society".
Date based upon statement on "Guest Star" label, "not to be played before 1 August 1954".

other releases:
all titles on (Tx) Office of Price Stabilisation No. 20 as "Dixieland Jamboree; and (LP) Black Jack LP3009, Fanfare 2-102, Jasmine JASM2510.

(5501) (Jess Stacy, p; Art Shapiro, b; Nick Fatool, d):

Capitol Studios, Hollywood – Thursday, October 6, 1955

1692	**Sunny Disposition**		unissued
1693	**You Turned The Tables On Me**	(LP)	Atlantic LP1225
1694	**I Must Have That Man**	(LP)	Atlantic LP1225
1695	**Gee, Baby Ain't I Good To You**	(LP)	Atlantic LP1225
1696	**Blues For Otis Ferguson**	(LP)	Atlantic LP1225

other releases:
all titles on (LP) London(E) LTZ-K15012; (LP/CD) Atlantic Jazzlore 7-90664-1

(5601) **JESS STACY** (Jess Stacy, p; Nick Fatool, d):　　　　　　　　Los Angeles – Saturday, March 3, 1956

Boo-Boos For Bob	(LP)	Brunswick BL54017
Ec-Stacy	(LP)	Brunswick BL54017
Complainin'	(LP)	Brunswick BL54017
Ain't Goin' Nowhere	(LP)	Brunswick BL54017

other releases: all titles on (LP) Swaggie S1248.

(5701) **JOHNNY LUCAS SEXTET with JESS STACY** (Johnny Lucas, tp, vo; Moe Schneider, tb; Bob McCracken, cl; Jess Stacy, p; Bob Stone, b; Lou Diamond, d; Bobby Troup, presenter):

　　　　　　　　　　　　　　　　　　　　"Stars of Jazz" TV show, Los Angeles – Monday, July 15, 1957

theme: **Easy Rider**	**(N)**
Muskrat Ramble	**(I/S)**
Black and Blue　vJL	**(A)**
Complainin'　(piano solo, with drums):	
Walkin' With The King　vJL	**(I/A)**
them: **Easy Rider**	

Broadcast on Channel 7, KABC.

1958 has been suggested for this broadcast, but during it, when discussing Stacy's Atlantic album LP1225, Troup suggests to Stacy that he bring a Benny Goodman alumni band onto the show. This he did on September 9, 1957.

(5702) **JESS STACY and The BENNY GOODMAN ALL-STARS** (Cappy Lewis, tp; Murray McEarchern, tb; Heinie Beau, cl, as, arr; Dave Harris, ts; Joe Koch, bar; Jess Stacy, p; Allan Reuss, g; Morty Corb, b; Nick Fatool, d; Martha Tilton, vo; Bobby Troup, presenter):　　　　　　"Stars of Jazz" TV show, Los Angeles – Monday, September 9, 1957

Roll 'Em	**(S)**	(Tx)	AFRS SoJ 43
Please Be Kind　vMT	**(A)**	(Tx)	AFRS SoJ 43
Where Or When	**(S/A)**	(Tx)	AFRS SoJ 43
I Let A Song Go Out Of My Heart　vMT	**(A)**	(Tx)	AFRS SoJ 43
King Porter Stomp	**(S)**	(Tx)	AFRS SoJ 43

Broadcast on Channel 7, KABC.　　AFRS SoJ = AFRS "Stars of Jazz".

(5801) **CLANCY HAYES** (Pud Brown, cl; Jess Stacy, p; Clancy Hayes, bj, vo; Bob Short, tu; Shelly Manne, d):

　　　　　　　　　　　　　　　　　　　　　　　Los Angeles – Saturday, January 18, 1958

[a]	**You Took Advantage Of Me**	**(A/S)**	(LP)	GTJ M12050
[b]	**Dancing Fool**	**(A/S)**	(LP)	GTJ M12050
[c]	**After You've Gone**	**(I/A)**	(LP)	GTJ M12050
[d]	**Oceana Roll**	**(A)**	(LP)	GTJ M12050
[e]	**Waitin' For The Evenin' Mail**	**(I/A)**	(LP)	GTJ M12050
[f]	**Ain't She Sweet?**	**(A/S)**	(LP)	GTJ M12050

Hayes sings on all titles.　GTJ = Good Time Jazz.

other releases:
all titles on (LP) Good Time Jazz S10050, Vogue(E) LAG573; (CD) Good Time Jazz 10050.
[f] on (CD) Good Time Jazz 4416

(5802) **TRIBUTE TO BENNY GOODMAN** (Don Fagerquist, Irving Goodman, Mickey Mangano, Zeke Zarchy, tp; Hoyt Bohannon, Murray McEachern,　Tommy Pederson, tb; Mahlon Clark, cl, as; Les Robinson, Heinie Beau, as; Dave Harris, Babe Russin, ts; Jess Stacy, p; Allan Reuss, g; Sid Weiss, b; Nick Fatool, d; Maxwell Davis, conductor):

　　　　　　　　　　　　　　　　　　　　　　　Los Angeles – December　, 1958

[a]	**Bugle Call Rag**	**(N)**	(LP)	Crown CLP5090
[b]	**East Side West Side**	**(N)**	(LP)	Crown CLP5090
[c]	**King Porter Stomp**	**(N)**	(LP)	Crown CLP5090
[d]	**Sing, Sing, Sing**	**(N)**	(LP)	Crown CLP5090
[e]	**Jersey Bounce**	**(A)**	(LP)	Crown CLP5097

"Jazz Records 1942-80" also adds *Stompin' at the Savoy* to this session, although the original edition did not do so.　There are only snatches of background piano on this title, but these are not typical Stacy.

other releases:
[a], [b], [c], [d] on (LP) Crown CST121, Eros ERL50016.　[a] on (LP) Crown CLP5140, CST173; (tape) Omega 7-813.
[b], [e] on (LP) Modern M7001, MS801.　[d] on (LP) Crown CLP5126, CS159, Modern M7001, MS801
[e] on (LP) Crown CST129, Eros ERL50008, Bright Orange XBO718; (CD) Pickwick PWK027:　(tape) Omega 7-862.
[c], [e] on (AC) Pickwick HSC3273(?).　[a], [c], [d] on (LP) Bright Orange XBO704: (tape) Omega 7-813

(5901) **BENNY GOODMAN QUARTET** (Benny Goodman, cl; Lionel Hampton, vb; Jess Stacy, p; Gene Krupa, d):
"The Big Party" television show, New York City – Thursday, December 17, 1959

        Avalon
        Where Or When
        I Got Rhythm

These CBS television broadcast titles on (LP) Festival 246, Rarities 30, King of Swing (no number).

(6001) **BENNY GOODMAN QUARTET** (Benny Goodman, cl; Jess Stacy, p; Rolly Bundock, b; Jack Sperling, d; Dinah Shore, vo)   "The Dinah Shore Chevy Show", Burbank, CA - Sunday, February 28, 1960

        These Foolish Things
        That's A Plenty
        Slipped Disc   vDS
        After You've Gone   vDS

D.R.Connor gives location as New York City, but Pat Stacy advises that the show was made at Burbank.
These NBC television broadcast titles on (LP) Festival 246. Rarities 30, King of Swing (no number).

(6002) **JESS STACY** (Jess Stacy, p; Morty Corb, b; Nick Fatool, d):   Los Angeles – late 1959/early 1960

Way Down Yonder In New Orleans	(LP)	Hanover HM8010
St. Louis Blues	(LP)	Hanover HM8010
After You've Gone	(LP)	Hanover HM8010
Evil Old Man	(LP)	Hanover HM8010
Can't We Be Friends?	(LP)	Hanover HM8010
Memphis Blues	(LP)	Hanover HM8010
Tin Roof Blues	(LP)	Hanover HM8010
Steve's Blues	(LP)	Hanover HM8010
I Can't Believe That You're In Love With Me	(LP)	Hanover HM8010
Old Ideas	(LP)	Hanover HM8010
Up A Lazy River	(LP)	Hanover HM8010
Young Ideas	(LP)	Hanover HM8010

Also believed to be on (AC) Star Line SLC-61159.
Personnel given by Jess Stacy to Johnny Simmen. Hanover was founded in mid-1959. Stacy was playing at the Huddle Bundy at this period, and session is believed to have taken place sometime after October 6, 1959. This was the last time Paul Copeland saw Stacy at the Huddle Bundy and no mention of Steve Allen, owner of Hanover, or recording for Hanover was made during Paul's talks with Stacy.

(6901) **JESS STACY QUARTET** (Jess Stacy, p; George Van Eps, g; Morty Corb, b; Jack Sperling, d):
           Blue Angel Jazz Club party,   Pasadena – Saturday, November 1, 1969

How Long Has This Been Going On?	(LP)	BAJC 505
I Would Do Anything For You		unissued
Where Or When		unissued
I Guess I'll Have To Change My Plan		unissued
I'm Yours		unissued
Three Little Words		unissued
Lover Man		unissued

(add Bill MacPherson, cl):
I'll Never Be The Same	**(I/A/S)**	unissued

       JESS STACY (p solo):
Candlelights	(LP)	BAJC 506

(6902) **CLANCY HAYES and His TUNE TERMITES** (unknown, tp; Abe Lincoln, tb; Matty Matlock, cl; Jess Stacy, p; Clancy Hayes, bj, vo; Morty Corb, b; Panama Francis, d):   same date

[a]	**Melancholy Blues** vCH	**(A/S)**	(LP)	BAJC 506
[b]	**Dr. Jazz** vCH	**(I/S)**		unissued

(omit tp):
[c]	**Waitin' For The Evenin' Mail** vCH	**(S/A)**	(LP)	BAJC 506

BAJC = The Blue Angel Jazz Club. This jazz party, organised by Dr. William (Bill) A. MacPherson, with Dr. George C. Tyler, was held at the University Club of Pasadena. The trumpet player is not listed on the sleeve. Trumpet players in attendance were Dick Cary, John Best and Tommy Thunen. The player on [a] & [b] does not sound like Cary or Best.

other releases:
[a], [c] also on (AC) Jazz Connoisseur Cassettes JCC124.

(7401) **JESS STACY** (p solo): soundtrack recording, Hollywood – Monday, January 7, 1974
           Beale Street Blues

This title from the Paramount film, "The Great Gatsby", on (LP) Paramount SPFA 7006. In the film the playing is obscured by dialogue. The piano has been doctored. Recorded at Paramount Studios. Date confirmed by Pat Stacy.

(7402) **JESS STACY** (p solo): Warp Studios, New York City – Monday, July 1, 1974

take		timing		Chiaroscuro
	How Long Has This Been Going On?	(6:14)	(LP)	CR133
	Doll Face	(5:45)	(LP)	CR133
	Miss Peck Accepts	(8:15)	(LP)	CR133
	I Would Do Anything For You	(5:17)	(LP)	CR133
	Stacy Still Swings	(5:18)	(LP)	CR133
	Lover Man	(10:15)	(LP)	CR133
	Lookout Mountain Squirrels	(5:01)	(LP)	CR133
	Gee Baby, Ain't I Good To You	(5:20)	(LP)	CR133
	Memphis In June	(5:15)	(CD)	CR(D)133
	Riverboat Shuffle	(3:31)	(CD)	CR(D)133
	Miss Peck Accepts This Bum	(5:57)		unissued
	Miss Peck Accepts The Blues	(:)		unissued
-1	**I Would Do Anything For You**	(:)		unissued
-2	**I Would Do Anything For You**	(:)		unissued
	Blues For Eddie Condon *	(6:10)		unissued
	Lover Man	(6:28)		unissued
	Lookout Mountain Squirrels	(3:42)		unissued
	Gee Baby, Ain't I Good To You (medium tempo)	(5:11)		unissued
-4 ?	**Riverboat Shuffle**	(4:06)		unissued

* original title for *Stacy Still Swings*. *Lookout* shown as *Look-Out* on CR133
The above details, courtesy of Hank O'Neal, based upon the "rough notes", which are the only documentation for this session
This session probably continued on July 3. CR(D)133 notes quote the recording date as July 5.

(7403) **LAWRENCE FREEMAN with Jess Stacy and Cliff Leeman** (Bud Freeman, ts; Jess Stacy, p; Cliff Leeman, d):
         Warp Studios, New York City – Tuesday, July 2, 1974

Toad In the Hole, Part II		(LP)	Chiaroscuro CR135
She's Funny That Way		(LP)	Chiaroscuro CR135
I Got Rhythm		(LP)	Chiaroscuro CR135
'S Wonderful		(LP)	Chiaroscuro CR135
Don't Blame Me		(LP)	Chiaroscuro CR135
Somebody Stole My Gal		(LP)	Chiaroscuro CR135
Evelyn Wabash Blues		(LP)	Chiaroscuro CR135
The Birth Of The Blues		(LP)	Chiaroscuro CR135
Way Down Yonder In New Orleans		(LP)	Chiaroscuro CR135
Kick In The Ascot		(LP)	Chiaroscuro CR135

Label refers to *Evelyn Waughbash Blues*. Played at Carnegie Hall as *After Chicago Blues*.
Leeman, Freeman and Nod was recorded at this session without Stacy.
No recording sheets could be found. Various dates have been quoted by Chiaroscuro personnel, and these do not match with Whitney Balliett's report. Those shown here are based upon the Balliett report and the dates (July 1, 2, 3) supplied by Hank O'Neal (August 8, 1974) a few weeks after these sessions.

(7404) **NEWPORT IN NEW YORK** (Bud Freeman, ts; Jess Stacy, p): Carnegie Hall, New York City – Friday, July 5, 1974
  [a]   **Don't Blame Me**
  [b]   **After Chicago Blues**
(Yank Lawson, tp; Bobby Hackett, tp; Vic Dickenson, tb; Barney Bigard, cl; Joe Venuti, vl; Jess Stacy, p; Bob Haggart, b; Cliff Leeman, d): same concert
  [c]   **At The Jazz Band Ball** **(N)**
(Barney Bigard, cl; same rhythm):
  [d]   **Mood Indigo**
(as for [c], less Joe Venuti):
  [e]   **Baby Won't You Please Come Home** **(N)**
(as for [c]):
  [f]   **Sweet Georgia Brown** **(N)**
[f] is a Joe Venuti feature.

The above titles, recorded by Voice of America, were part of a concert entitled "Tribute To Eddie Condon and Ben Webster".

(7501) **JESS STACY** (p solo):   concert, Wilshire Ebell Theatre, Los Angeles – Saturday, September 20, 1975
      How Long Has This Been Going On?
      Lover Man
      I Would Do Most Anything For You
      The One I Love Belongs To Somebody Else

    JESS STACY and RALPH SUTTON (p duets on two pianos):   same concert
      Keepin' Out Of Mischief Now
      Ain't Misbehavin'

These titles taped at a "Night In New Orleans" concert promoted by Barry Martyn and Floyd Levin .

(7601) **NAPPY LAMARE and The LEVEE LOUNGERS** (Joe Ingram, tp; Rex Allen, tb; Abe Most, cl; Jess Stacy, p; Nappy Lamare, bj, vo; Bill Spreter, b; Nick Fatool, d):   concert, Sacramento – Saturday, May 29, 1976

[a]	**Blues My Naughty Sweetie Gave To Me**	(S)

(Stacy, p; Lamare, bj; Spreter, b; Fatool, d; band at coda):

[b]	**I Would Do Most Anything For You**	

(Abe Most, cl; same rhythm; band at coda):

[c]	**Exactly Like You**	(I/A)

(full band):

[d]	**I'm Gonna Move To The Outskirts of Town** vNL	(I/A)
[e]	**Lover**	(N)
[f]	**Body and Soul**	(A/S)
[g]	**Royal Garden Blues**	(I/S)
[h]	**Struttin' With Some Barbecue**	(I/S)

Taped by the late Art Nielsen, with Nappy Lamare's permission, at an afternoon session, at the El Rancho (?) cabaret, Capitol Street, part of the 1976 Old Sacramento Dixieland Jubilee.   [e] is a banjo feature, with band at coda. [f] is a trombone feature, with piano, bass, drums. [g] is a 10 minute version, with a four minute piano solo.

(7701) **JESS STACY** (p solo)   Downtown Sound Studios, New York City – Tuesday/Wednesday, July 19/20, 1977

take		timing		Chiaroscuro
	Stacy's Still Swinging	(5:40)	(LP)	Chiaroscuro CR177
-1	**Waiting For The Evening Mail**	(5:20)	(LP)	Chiaroscuro CR177
-1	**But Not For Me**	(5:18)	(LP)	Chiaroscuro CR177
	100 Years From Today	(5:58)	(LP)	Chiaroscuro CR177
-2	**The One I Love**	(4:37)	(LP)	Chiaroscuro CR177
-3	**So Glad I Found You**	(4:30)	(LP)	Chiaroscuro CR177
	I've Got A Crush On You	(3:30)	(LP)	Chiaroscuro CR177
-5	**After You've Gone**	(3:59)	(LP)	Chiaroscuro CR177
-1	**What Is There To Say?**	(4:50)	(LP)	Chiaroscuro CR177
-1	**St. Louis Calliope Blues**	(4:18)	(CD)	Chiaroscuro CRD133
-1	**Sunny Disposition**	(4:00)	(CD)	Chiaroscuro CRD133
-1	**Clap Yo' Hands**			unissued
-1 ?	**Barrelhouse**	(4:01)		unissued
-2	**Barrelhouse**		(IT)	unissued
-3	**Barrelhouse**		(IT)	unissued
-4	**Barrelhouse**	(4:02)		unissued
-1	**Squeeze Me**	(2:51)		unissued
-2	**Squeeze Me**	(3:10)		unissued
-1	**My Honey's Lovin' Arms**	(:)		unissued
-2	**My Honey's Lovin' Arms**			false start/unissued
-3	**My Honey's Lovin' Arms**	(3:46)		unissued
	Stacy's Still Swinging	(5:48)		unissued
-1	**The One I Love**	(5:16)		unissued
-1	**I've Got A Crush On You**	(3:38)		unissued
-2	**I've Got A Crush On You**			false start/unissued
-3	**I've Got A Crush On You**			false start/unissued
-4	**I've Got A Crush On You**	(3:37)		unissued
-1	**After You've Gone**	(:)		unissued
-2	**After You've Gone**			false start/unissued
-3	**After You've Gone**			false start/unissued
-4	**After You've Gone**			false start/unissued

These details supplied by Hank O'Neal of Chiaroscuro Records, based mainly upon the take sheets kept with the tape boxes.

(7901) **JESS STACY** (p solo)   Hunterdon Arts Center, Clinton, New Jersey – Friday, September 28, 1979

        Lover Man
        Sunny Disposition
        How Long Has this Been Going On?
        I Would Do Most Anything For You
        What Is There To Say?
        The One I Love Belongs To Somebody Else
        medley, including Autumn In New York

These titles, and five others, were recorded.
A tape is believed to be held by The Institute of Jazz Studies, Rutger's University, Newark, NJ.

(7902) **JESS STACY** (p solo):

        Downtown Sound Studios, New York City – Sunday, September 30, 1979 and Monday, October 1, 1979
(following possibly from September 30 session):

takes		timings		Chiaroscuro
-1	**untitled blues**	(6:50)		unissued
-1	**Fascinating Rhythm**			unissued
-2	**Fascinating Rhythm**	(4:50)		unissued
	Evalina ("bright")	(3:28)		unissued
	Evaline ("medium")	(3:42)		unissued
-1	**Sweet and Lowdown**	(4:21)		unissued
-1	**Autumn In New York**			false start/unissued
-2	**Autumn In New York**			false start/unissued
-3	**Autumn in New York**			unissued
-4	**Autumn in New York**			false start/unissued
-5	**Autumn In New York**			false start/unissued
-6	**Autumn In New York**	(3:24)		unissued

(session uncertain):

-1	**In A Sentimental Mood**	(2:44)		unissued
	Moon Mist			incomplete/unissued
	Moon Mist	(3:27)		unissued
	Moon Mist	(3:55)		unissued
-1	**Ship Without A Sail**	(3:11)		unissued
-2	**Ship Without A Sail**			unissued
-3	**Ship Without A Sail**	(4:08)		unissued
-4	**Ship Without A Sail**			unissued
-5	**Ship Without A Sail**	(3:30)		unissued

(October 1, 1979)

-1	**Keepin' Out Of Mischief Now**			false start/unissued
-2	**Keepin' Out Of Mischief Now**			false start/unissued
-3	**Keepin' Out Of Mischief Now**	(3:04)		unissued
-4	**Keepin' Out Of Mischief Now**	(:)		unissued
-1	**Oh, Baby**			false start/unissued
-2	**Oh, Baby**			false start/unissued
-3	**Oh, Baby**		(IT)	unissued
-4	**Oh, Baby**			false start/unissued
-5	**Oh, Baby**			false start/unissued
-6	**Oh, Baby**	(4:??)		unissued
-1	**Sunny Disposition**	(:)		unissued
-2	**Sunny Disposition**		(NG)	unissued
-4	**Sunny Disposition**	(:)		unissued
-5	**Sunny Disposition**	(3:48)		unissued
-6	**Sunny Disposition**	(:)		unissued
-7	**Sunny Disposition**	(3:48)		unissued
-1	**I Want A Little Girl**			false start/unissued
-2	**I Want A Little Girl**		(NG)	unissued
-3	**I Want A Little Girl**	(:)		unissued
-4	**I Want A Little Girl**	(2:47)		unissued
-5	**I Want A Little Girl**	(:)		unissued

-1	**I Ain't Got Nobody**		false start/unissued
-2	**I Ain't Got Nobody**	(2:30)	unissued
-3	**I Ain't Got Nobody**	(:)	unissued
-1	**untitled blues**		false start/unissued
-2	**untitled blues**		false start/unissued
-3	**untitled blues**	(:)	unissued
-4	**untitled blues**	(1:45)	unissued

These details supplied by Hank O'Neal, of Chiaroscuro Records, based upon his "recording diary".

Sunny Disposition has also been listed as *Sunny Disposish*. Take -3 of this number not shown on recording sheet. The September 30 session was scheduled from 01:00 p.m. to 05:00 p.m., and the October 1 session from 01:00 p.m. to 06:00 p.m. Only two of the take sheets are dated, hence the uncertainty about which title was recorded when.

(8201) **MARIAN McPARTLAND's PIANO JAZZ** (Marian McPartland -1, p; Jess Stacy-2, p):

Los Angeles – Tuesday, December 1, 1981

Dancing Fool	-2
Lover Man	-2
Oh, Baby	-2
Keepin' Out Of Mischief Now	-1, -2
Improvisation In A Minor	-2
Autumn In New York	-2
I Would Do Most Anything For You	-1, -2
Moon Mist	-2
St. Louis Blues	-1, -2

This interview for Marian McPartland's long-running "Piano Jazz" radio show was recorded December 1, 1981 and first broadcast June 20, 1982.

Marian McPartland plays one solo, *Heavy Hearted Blues*.

Oh, Baby is a short demonstration of how the calliope was played. *Improvisation In A Minor,* as it has been titled by Jazz Alliance, is a brief attempt at the A Minor chord effect from Stacy's *Sing, Sing, Sing* solo.

The interview has been issued on (CD) Jazz Alliance TJA-12017.

Cartoon by Peter Manders from the 1987
I.A.J.R.C. Convention in Los Angeles.
Reproduced by permission of the artist

Non Stacy items
and other queries

EARL BURTNETT and His Drake Hotel Orchestra

152609-1	Ridin' Around In The Rain	(78)	Columbia 2921D
152610-1	She Reminds Me Of You	(78)	Columbia 2922D
152611-2	Neighbors	(78)	Columbia 2922D
152612-1	Waitin' At The Gate For Katy	(78)	Columbia 2921D

Recorded in Chicago, May 11, 1934.
In Brian Rust's "American Dance Band Discography" (first edition) the personnel was stated to include Bruce Squires, Warren Smith, tb; Jess Stacy, p. There was little evidence for this statement and Stacy advised that he was not present.

BING CROSBY with The Andrews Sisters & Joe Venuti & His Orchestra

| 66632-A/B | Ciribiribin | (78) | Decca 2800 |
| 66633-B | Yodelin' Jive | (78) | Decca 2800 |

Recorded in New York City, September 20, 1939.
One source, the Decca-Brunswick-Vocalion Encyclopedia of Swing, printed in Britain in 1941, gave a personnel of: Bill Graham, Bobby Hackett, tp; Mike Riley, tb; Paul Ricci, cl; Joe Venuti, vl; Jess Stacy, p; Sammy Weiss, d.

However, this is not generally accepted as a Stacy session. The pianist cannot be identified aurally. Bing Crosby expert, Ralph Harding, understood the pianist to be Mel Grant, though it should be noted that Grant was a pianist active in Chicago, while Stacy was in New York in September 1939.

GENE KRUPA – film "THE GENE KRUPA STORY"

26230	Royal Garden Blues	(LP)	Verve 10202
26231	Indiana	(LP)	Verve 10202
26236	Way Down Yonder In New Orleans	(LP)	Verve 10202

Recorded in Hollywood, June 1959.
Also issued on (LP) Verve MGV15010, HMV CLP1352, Joyce LP3002, Sandy Hook SH2022

These small band titles from the movie "The Gene Krupa Story" ("Drum Crazy") present quite a mystery.

The personnel is usually listed as Red Nichols, co; Moe Schneider, tb; Heinie Beau, cl; Benny Carter, as; Eddie Miller, ts; Jess Stacy, p; Barney Kessel, g; Morty Corb, b; Gene Krupa, d.

The soundtrack album sleeve notes refer to Jess Stacy and Jimmy Rowles as pianists on the record. Stacy's presence is also noted in, among other publications, Jorgen Jepsen's "Jazz Records 1942-1969" Volume 4d; in the discography for "Benny Carter: A Life In American Music" by M & E Berger & J. Patrick; and in Michel Ruppli and Bob Porter's "The Clef/Verve Labels: A Discography".

Neither Benny Carter nor Eddie Miller remembered the session, when queried by this writer. Heinie Beau did, but could not recall Stacy being present, saying, "I don't remember Jess on any dates (for the film)."

In *Record Research* number 24 (September 1959) Woody Backensto reported:

At 10 a.m. on July 1, 1959, at Columbia Pictures, the following group recorded the (Red) Nichols sequence, "Indiana", for the Krupa story: Red Nichols, co; Moe Schneider, tb; Heinie Beau, cl; Skeets Herfurt, as; John Williams, p; Barney Kessel, g; Morty Corb, b; and, of course, Gene Krupa, d.

This would explain why Carter and Miller did not recall the session. Skeets Herfurt is not shown in the collective personnel on the album sleeve, but John Williams is shown as one of the drummers. Presumably this personnel from Backensto applies to all three small band titles. The only piano solo heard is on *Indiana* and this is not by Jess Stacy.

Pat Stacy says of the movie that Jess never mentioned it, "nor did either of us see the film." (Jess had seen it with Gene Krupa, of course)

LOUIS PANICO and his Orchestra

C-5379-C	Wabash Blues	(78)	Brunswick 4736
C-5380-C	Oh Doctor	(78)	Brunswick 4736

Recorded in Chicago, c. February 1930.

George Wettling, in "Record Research", number 24, gave the personnel for these titles as Panico, tp; Don Jones, tb; Frank Teschemacher, cl; Jess Stacy, p; Andy Panico, b; Wettling, d. This personnel, plus Putty Nettles on alto sax, was given in the first edition of Brian Rust's "Jazz Records 18971931", but was amended to show Maurie Bercov on clarinet and Pete Viera on piano in the fifth edition. Jess Stacy confirmed that he was not the pianist for these titles.

SEATTLE HARMONY KINGS

Some early listings quoted the pianist with this band, which was co-led by Eddie Neibauer and Ray Shields, as either Jess Stacy or Art Gronwall. In Jazz Journal, May 1949, Gronwall said the pianist was one Joey Thomas. Titles were:

33195-6	If I Had A Girl Like You	Victor 19772
33196-7	Darktown Shuffle	Victor 19772

Recorded in Camden, September 2, 1925.

MUGGSY SPANIER

There was a report by Jerry Valburn that he had acetates of Muggsy Spanier's big band with Jess Stacy sitting-in on piano at Jack Dempsey's in New York. However, Dave Bowman was Spanier's regular pianist and it is believed that Valburn was mis-led by Dave Bowman's stylistic similarity to Stacy.

JESS STACY and hiss *(sic)* All Stars

1503-2	Twelfth Street Rag	(78)	Polydor(F) 580.028
1506-3	Milenburg Joys	(78)	Polydor(F) 580.028

This record was mis-labelled. Titles are actually by Fletcher Henderson and his Orchestra, recorded in New York, c.October 1931, originally issued as Connie's Inn Orchestra on (78) Crown 3213.

JESS STACY (piano solos)

A small mystery surrounds the Commodore session (3932) of June 13, 1939. In the late 1940s Dan Mahony made some notes from the ledgers at Reeves Sound Studios in New York City. These included:

R158	June 9, 1939	Jess Stacy	Ec-Stacy
R159	June 9, 1939	Jess Stacy	Yes, Jess
R160	June 9, 1939	Jess Stacy	You're Driving Me Crazy
R161	June 9, 1939	Jess Stacy	She's Funny That Way

Reeves told Dan Mahony that these are listed as for Liberty Music and that they have no connection with R2126-R2129, which appear in the ledger under the correct date, June 13, 1939. But Milt Gabler told Bert Whyatt: "There was no Stacy session on 6/09/39. The Reeves book is wrong. The R158 thru R161 are actually Reeves Skating Rink Gammond Organ sides."

JESS STACY

Jazz Notes, May 1946, reported "Stacy waxed a solo album for Victor." Queried about this, RCA Victor (08may50) advised: "Jess Stacy did not record anything in 1946. His only recording was in June 1945, on which he made *Daybreak Serenade* and *It's Only A Paper Moon.*"

UNKNOWN ARTIST

In 1991 Bill Dean-Myatt saw a Cambridge Pianola Company catalogue which listed, on page 23, "Jazzmaster Music Rolls". Number 21 was *One O'Clock Jump* "arranged Jess Stacy".

The Cambridge Pianola Company's address was 3, Lyndewode Road, Cambridge LB1 2HL. Attempts to contact this address failed, as did a search for an apparently allied company, A.G. Trading.

It is most unlikely that Stacy cut the roll himself, so the significance of the "arranged Jess Stacy" is unknown.

UNKNOWN BAND

China Boy	(LP)	Arcadia 2014
Nobody's Sweetheart	(LP)	Arcadia 2014

The sleeve notes for Arcadia 2014 suggested that the pianist on these two titles could be either Jess Stacy or Dave Rose. The piano work did not sound like Stacy, and subsequent investigation by label owner Dick Raichelson indicated that these sides were recorded by members of the Henri Gendron band, with Ken Butler on piano.

THE PAUL MARES SESSION (3501)

Recorded for Okeh on January 7, 1935
Nagasaki / Reincarnation / Maple Leaf Rag / The Land of Dreams

The Columbia files show these four titles against dates of January 7, 1935 and January 26, 1935. From this data, Brian Rust's "Jazz Records 1897 -1942" showed the four titles (takes -1 and -2 of each) as made and rejected on the 7th, and remade (takes -C) on the 26th for issue. (The Chicago matrix listing, compiled by Helen F. Chmura of Columbia Records, also shows take *numbers* -1/-2 only.) The second date, however, actually refers to a "dubbing session", although it is unclear what work was carried out on the masters on this date. Howard Rye reported *(Collectors Items 38)* that the Columbia files state unambiguously that the issued takes -C are dubbings of take -A in each case. John R.T. Davies has investigated these titles, producing the following "map" in an attempt to show the changes made to C-870 and C-872, first by OKeh and then by George Avakian.

C-870   *Nagasaki*

4 bar intro	32	16	8	8	16	8	8	32	32	4	8	M8	8
piano	ens	as	cl	as	p	cl	p	tb	ens	d	ens	as	ens

-2   (complete performance)
-A   (alternative performance   until . . .)   as -2
-C   (identical with take -A)
CoLP (indentical with -A)   until) as -A*   then as -2
                                                                    *until four bars into the ensemble

C-872   *Maple Leaf Rag*
-2   (complete performance)
-A   (alternative performance)
-C   (identical with -A apart from loss of a turn of a groove in fourth bar of second clarinet solo)
CoLP (as -A until start of second clarinet solo which, together with the remainder, is as -2)

C-871 and C-873 do not appear to have been edited. JRTD also suggests that the first clarinet break on *Maple Leaf Rag* is suspiciously similar in take -2 and take -A.

Test pressings marked -A are known to exist for all titles.
The Meritt titles were listed on the LP insert as takes -B, although the tests, from which they were taken, are reported to have been marked -2. IRD have claimed their CD contains the "complete take -C" for *Maple Leaf Rag*, but this version has not been auditioned.

Other circumstantial evidence exists that there was no recording session on January 26. Helen Oakley, who produced the session, "feels sure there was only one session". In addition, the Mares band (without Simeon) was in regular employment on January 7, but it had disbanded by the 26th.

There are a number of small variations between the solos on the -B and -C takes, and George Wettling's drum rhythms vary. The most obvious difference is the tempo set for *Reincarnation*, which slower for take -B. (Take -C runs 2:45 minutes; take -B 3:23). During the first piano solo on take -B of *The Land of Dreams* there is a muffled shout, presumably to Stacy, which is not heard on take -C.

Index to the Discography

(references are to session numbers)

4003/05/07/10/12/13/14/16/21/26/31/
32/38/39/40/41/42, 4104/05/06/07/08
/12, 4205/06//07/08/10/14/15/16/17/
21/22, 5107, 5201, 5404/05

Crosby, Israel - b 3502/06/07, 3608

Curtis, Gail - ts 4504/08/14

Cutshall, Cutty - tb 4601

Cytron, Sam - vl 5104

D

Dale, Carlotta - vo 3936

D'Amico, Hank - as/cl 3936, 4026/35,
4105, 4509

Dandridge, Dorothy - vo 4112

D'Annolfo, Frank - tb 4412, 4508/14

Davenport, Cow Cow - p 4032

Davis, Johnny 'Scat' - tp/vo 3719

Davis, Maxwell - arr,leader 5802

Davison, Wild Bill - co 4503, 4801

Dee, Johnny - tp 4402

Deems, Barrett - d 5301

De Franco, Buddy - cl 4504/08

De Haven, Gloria - vo 4206/25

De Karske, Karl - tb 4520/21/29/34/37

Demello, Jack - tp 4404

Dennis, Matt - vo 4704/05

DePew, Bill - as 3503/08, 3610/23,
3701/06

Desmond, Johnny - vo 4032

Diamond, Lou - d 5701

Dickenson, Vic - tb 7404

Dierterle, Kurt - vl 4529/30/31

Dimaio, Nick - tb 4523

Di Martino, Eddie - ts 4545

Dimitriades, Peter - vl/viola
4504/08/20/29/34/37

Dixon, Joe - cl 4543

Dodds, Baby - d 4103

Dorey, Ray - vo 4309/12

Dorn Brothers & Mary - 4112

Dorsey, Jimmy - cl/as 4423, 4515/23,
5201, 5405

Dorsey, Tommy - tb 3854/58,
4501/02/03/04/06/07/08/l0/ll/12/14/15
/16/17/19/20/21/22/23/24/28/29/34/37

Downs, Eddie - tp 4545

Dumont, Jack - as 5104

E

Eberle, Jack - vo 4501

Eldridge, Roy - tp 3608

Ellick, Roger - tp 4504

Ellington, Duke - p 4539

Elliott, Lorraine - vo 4403

Ellis, Herb - g 4523

Elman, Ziggy - tp 3623, 3701/05/31/
37/38/60, 3813/14/24/60/71,
3926/31/35, 4006, 5201, 5402/03/05

Erwin, Pee Wee - tp
3609/10/22 4544

Esterdahl, Lennie - bj/g 5401

Evans, Herschel - ts 3759, 3802

F

Fagerquist, Don - tp 5802

Farbman, Harry - vl 4530/31/34

Fatool, Nick - d 3928/33/34, 4802,
5002, 5101/03/04/05 5201, 5304,
5402/03/04/05, 5501, 5601, 5702,
5802, 6002, 7601

Fazola, Irving - cl 3937/39,
4005/16/23/24

Feld, Morey - d 4011, 4401/02/03,
4801

Felice, Ernie - acc
4703/04/06/07/08/09/10/12/13

Fiddler, Manny - vl
4504/08/20/29/34/37

Fidus, Arnold - vl 4529/30/34

Fishberg, Joschim 'Jack' - vl
4530/34/37

Fitzgerald, Ella - vo 3625

Foster, Stuart - vo 4520/29/34

Francis, Panama - d 6902

Frankhouser, Charlie - tp 4312

Franzella, Sal - cl 4544

Freeman, Bud - ts 3805/06/11/14/18
/26/39/54/60/62/64 3932 4011/15,
4103, 4715, 7403/04

Fresk, Livio 'Babe' - ts
4514/20/29/34/37

Fuchs, Herbert - cello/viola 4529/31

G

Gaer, Murray - d 4405

Geller, Harry - tp 3508, 3610/14

Gentry, Chuck - bar 4606/08, 4705/06,
5402/05

Glee Club, The - vo 4404

Goff, Gerald - tp 4508/20/29/34/37

Goldie, Don - tp 4715

Gomberg, Harold - oboe 4537

Goodman, Benny - cl 3503/07/08,
3606/08/09/10/23/25, 3701/06/11/29/
32/36/60, 3804/08/12/13/14/19/27/29
/40/55/59/60/64, 3901/05/07/14/15/16
/17/18/19/20/22/23/24/26/28/33/34
4006, 4301/02/03/05/07/09/10/11/12/
14/15/18/20/21/22 4401/02/03,
4601/03/04/05/06/08/09,
4701/01/02/03/04/05/06/07/08/09/10/
11/12/13, 5802, 5901, 6001

Goodman, Harry - b 3503/08,
3606/10/23, 3701/05/36/60,
3804/14/29/60/71, 3902/31

Goodman, Irving - tp 3627, 3736/37
3908/22, 4523, 5304, 5802

Goodman, Joseph - vl
4504/08/20/29/34

Goodman, Ruth Rubenstein - vl
4504/08/20/29/34

Goodrich, Bob - tp 4102/05

Gowans, Brad - v-tb 4011/15

Grace, Teddy - vo 3937

Grauso, Joe - d 4406/16/20

Green, Freddie - g 3813

Greenbaum, David - cello 4537

Greenleaf, Freddie - tp 5005

Greer, Sonny - d 3807

Griffin, Chris - tp 3614/23
3701/36/60, 3804/13/14/60 3926

Gross, Walter - p 5201

Guyer, Bobby - tp 4302/03/05
4514/20/21

H

Hackett, Bobby - co 3804/05/26/39/54,
4406/08/09/24, 4501/13/25, 7404

Haggart, Bob - b/wh/arr 3937/38/39,
4005/06/16/23/24/26/35/40, 4105/08,
4202/05/08/15/16/18/21/28, 4415/17,
4501/44, 5107/08, 7404

Hall, Al - b 3858

Hall, Ed - cl 4406/09/11/14/17,
4505/26/27

Hampton, Lionel - vb 3705/09/10/31,
3807/12/13/40/41/49/55/61,
3901/05/14/15/16/18/19/21/22/23/24/
26/28/33/34, 5901

Handy, W.C. 3854

Hanlon, Allen - g 3936

Harris, Bill - tb 4312, 4402

Harris, Dave - ts 5702, 5802

Harris, Joe - tb/vo 3503/04/07/08,
3606/10/14

Hawkins, Coleman - ts 4401

Hayes, Clancy vo/bj 5801, 6902

Haymer, Herbie - ts 4305

Heidt, Horace - leader 4404/07

Helbig, Otto - arr 4523

Heller, Ben - g 3814/29/60/71, 3931

Hendrickson, Al - g 5403

Herfurt, Skeets - as 4606/08, 4705, 5405

Herman, Max - tp 3937 4026/38, 4108, 4218

Hintz, Gil - g 4404

Hobi, Mike - tb 5401

Hodges, Johnny - as 3709/10, 3804/07

Holiday, Billie - vo 3903

Hudgings, Hugh - ts 4404

Humes, Helen - vo 3759, 3802

Hunt, Francis - vo 3625, 3701

I

Iannone, Mickey - tb 4523

Ingram, Joe - tp 7601

J

Jackson, King - tb - 5405

Jackson, Preston - tb 3502

James, Harry - tp 3701/36/59/60, 3802/03/13/14/24/29/60, 3903, 4006

Janov, Helen - vl 4537

Jenkins, Les - tb 3936/39

Jenney, Jack - tb 4006

Jerome, Jerry - ts 3864/71, 3926/31/35

Johnson, Pete - p 3907

Johnson, Tony - as 4404/05

Jones, Jo - d 3759, 3802

K

Kaminsky, Max - tp 3854, 4015, 4406/09/11/14/16/17/18/20/24/25, 4501/03/05/13/15/18/25/26/27/43

Kapp, Jack 4038

Kaproff, Armand - cello 4529/30/34

Karroll, Charlie - vo 4504

Kast, George - vl 5104

Katz, Al - leader 2601

Kay, Carol - vo 4312

Kaye, Leonard - as 4302/03/15

Kazebier, Nate - tp 3503/07/08, 3606/10/18/19, 4601/06/08, 4705/06

Keddington, Ruth - vo 4032

Kendis, Al - d 3871, 3931/35

Kessel, Barney - g 4601/03/04/05/06/08/09, 4701/02/03

King, Al - tp 4032

King, Bonnie - vo 4032

Kirby, John - b 3709/10, 3858

Kleemeyer, Ray - bb 2601

Klein, Mannie - tp 3618/19/20 4705/15 4802 5104 5405

Klein, Ted - as 4218/28

Klink, Al - ts 4312, 4402 4504/08/20/29/33

Koch, Joe - bar 5403, 5702

Koenig, George - as 3705/06/36/60, 3937

Kohen, Harold - vl 4537

Kouden, Eddie - tp 2601

Kress, Carl - g 4412

Krupa, Gene - d 3503/06/07/08, 3606/08/10/23 3701/05/36/60, 3804, 4006, 4309/10/12/14/18/20/21, 4406/09, 5901

Kusby, Ed - tb 4705

L

La Pertche, Sal - tp 4508

La Vere, Charles - p, leader 3502

Lacey, Jack - tb 3503/04

Lamare, Nappy - bj/g 3937, 4005/16/23/24/26/35, 4105/08, 4205 /15/16/18/21/28, 4802, 5104/05/07/08, 7601

Lane, Muriel - vo 4211/25

Langone, Frank - ts 4523

Lavine, Eddie - vo 4032

Lawson, Bob - as,bar 4523

Lawson, Yank - tp 3854/58, 4108, 4205/15/16/18/21/28 4509, 7404

Lee, Mary - vo 4216/21

Lee, Peggy - vo 4301/02/03

Lee, Sonny - tb 4523

Leeman, Cliff - d 7403/04

Lenhart, Margaret - vo 4215

Lesberg, Jack - b 4425, 4513/25/27/43

Lester, Frankie - vo 4506/12

Lewis, Cappy - tp 5702

Lewis, Johnny - ts 4545

Lewis, Meade Lux - p 3901

Lim, Harry 4103

Lincoln, Abe - tb 5304, 6902

Linn, Ray - tp 4302/03/04, 4523, 4606

Long, Joe - g 3502

Lowery, Fred - wh 4404

Lucas, Johnny - tp/vo 5111, 5302, 5401/04, 5701

Lund, Art - vo 4703

Lyman, Abe - d 4714

Lyons, Art - bar 5104

M

MacPherson, Bill - cl 6901

Magletti, Joe - cl,ss 2601

Mains, Dick - tp 4601

Mangano, Vito 'Mickey' - tp 4402, 4504/08/14/29/34/37, 5802

Mann, Marion - vo 4004

Manne, Shelly - d 5801

Manone, Wingy - tp 4424, 4714, 5201

Mares, Paul - tp 3501

Margolies, Jacqes - vl 4530/31/37

Mario, Bob - ts 4228

Marsala, Joe - cl,as,ts 3502, 3854, 4002/15, 4418

Marsala, Marty - tp 3502, 3839/54, 4011

Martin, Eddie (see Di Martino)

Martin, Louis - flute 4529/32

Masek, Joe - ts 3502

Mastren, Al - tb 4402

Mastren, Carmen - g 3854

Matlock, Matty - cl,as,arr 3938, 4026, 4108, 4205/15/16/18/21/28 4801/02, 5103/04/05/07/08, 5304, 5401/05, 6902

Matthews, Bob - vo 4404

Matthews, Dave - as 3813/14/24/39/60/71, 3903

McAfree, E'lane - vo 4305

McCraeken, Bob - el 5111, 5701

McCrae, Margaret - vo 3631

McEarehern, Murray - tb 3614/23, 3741/42/50/51, 5107, 5402, 5702, 5802

McGarity, Lou - tb 4408/12/15/17/18/19/21/23, 4505/09/13/18/25/43, 4606/08, 4705/06, 4801

McKenzie, Red - vo 4409/12/18, 4513/18

McKeon, Jeannie - vo 4610, 4706

McKinley, Ray - d 4307

McPartland, Marian - p 8201

Mendel, Johnny - tp 3502

Mendelsohn, Art - as 4108

Mercer, Johnny - vo 3901/26, 4705, 5201, 5405

Merry Macs, The - vo 4041

Metronome All Star Band - 4006

Metronome All Star Nine - 4006

Mezzrow, Mezz - cl 37093854

Mi Chee - 4112

Miller, Eddie - ts,cl,vo 3936/37/39, 4005/06/16/17/23/24/26/35, 4105/08, 4205/15 /16/18/21/28, 4304, 4802, 5103/04

Miller, Johnny - b 3731

Miranda, Carmen - vo 4304

Miroff, Seymour - vl 4529/34

Mole, Miff - tb 4015, 4301/02/03/05, 4409/11/16, 4527

Molinelli, Larry - as 4601

Mondello, Toots - as 3934, 4006

Moore, William - tp 4520

Morgulis, George - viola 4529/34/37

Morrow, Buddy - tb 4108 4412

Morton, Benny - tb 4406/14/25, 4526

Most, Abe - cl 7601

Mountjoy, Monte - d 5401

Murray, Lee - 4112

Musso, Vido - ts,cl 3620/23, 3701/05 /31 /36/60/63, 4533/34/37, 5402

Mustard, Bill - tb 4404

Muzzillo, Ralph - tp 3503/08, 3609, 4305/12

N

Natoli, Anthony - tp 4544

Neufeld, Erno - vl 5104

Nicholas, Albert - cl 5005

Nichols, Red - co 5201 5405

Noel, Richard - tb 4514/20/29/34/37

Norman, Fred - tb 4514/16

Norvo, Red - vb 4412

O

O'Brien, Floyd - tb 4002/26/35, 4105/08, 4205/15/16/18/21/28

O'Day, Anita - vo 4609

Oliver, Sy - arr 4504/23

O'Malley, Pat - vo 3729

P

Page, Hot Lips - tp/vo 3854, 4423

Page, Walter - b 3759, 3802/13

Palmer, Philip - french horn 4537

Parham, Truck - b 5301

Paris, Tony - vo 4032

Park, Joe - tu 4504/08/20/29/34/37

Parlato, Charlie - tp 4404

Pattison, Pat - b 2802 3501

Paul, Les - g 4714

Pearce, Dale - tp 4504/08/14, 4601

Peck, Bob - tp 4008/26/32

Pecora, Santo - tb 3501

Pederson, Tommy - tb 4606, 4705/06, 5802

Peppie, Harold - tp 4304

Picciotto, Tony - tp 4523

Poliakin, Raoul - vl 4529/30/31/34

Pollack, Ben - d 5405

Polo, Danny - cl 4002

Posner, Leonard - vl 4529/30/31

Powell, Dick - vo 4510

Powell, Specs - d 4422

Pratt, Jimmy - d 5111

Price, Sammy - p 4032

Q

Quintones, The - vo 3905

R

Raffell, Don - ts 4404

Rando, Doc - as 4025/26, 4108, 4218/28, 4802

Rasey, Uan - tp 4606

Reed, Virginia - vo 4404

Reilich, Joseph - vl 4537

Reuss, Alan - g 3503/07/08, 3606/08/ 10 /23, 3701/05/09/10/31/36/60, 3804/07/58 4305/09/10/11/12/14, 4402, 4703/04/05/06/07/08,/10/12/13, 5402, 5702, 5802

Reve, Kalman - vl 4537

Reynolds, Marjorie - vo 4210

Rich, Buddy - d 4504/08/20/21/29/34/37

Richman, Boomie - ts 4415

Riddle, Nelson - tb 4504/08/21

Roberts, Toni - vo 5103/04

Robinson, Les - as 5802

Robinson, Phil - ts 2802

Robinson, Reba - harp 4504/08/20/29/34/37

Rodin, Gil - ts 3937, 4026

4108/12, 4218

Rollini, Art - ts 3503/08, 3610/23 3701/05/31/36/60, 3814/24/41/42/60/71, 3926/31

Rollison, Fred - tp 2601

Romersa, Tony - d 4706/07/08/09/10/11/12/13

Rosa, Eddie - as 4305/12/15, 4402

Rose, George - g 3926

Rosen, Jerry - d 4545

Ross, Henry - as 4544

Ross, Sam - vl/viola 4508/20/29/34/37

Rotella, John - bar 4601

Roth, Bart - g 4303

Rushing, Jimmy - vo 3631

Rushton, Joe - bsx 4301/02/03/05, 4404, 5405

Russell, Pee Wee - cl 3805/26/39/54, 4011/15, 4406/08/09/10/14/15/16/17/ 18/19/20/21/23/24/25, 4501/02/03/13/ 25/26/27

Russin, Babe - ts 3763 3804/13 3935 4606/08, 4705/06, 5403/05, 5802

Russo, Andy - tb 4523

S

Sampson, Edgar - bar 3807

Sandifer, Cody - d 4228

Sarmento, Paul - b 5005

Satterfield, Jack - tb 4544

Satterwhite, Collen 'Tex' - tb 4504/08/20/29/34/37

Saxbe, Marvin - g 3501

Schaefer, Bill - tb 4608 4705

Schectman, George - cl/ts 2601

Schipani, Alphonse - vl 4537

Schneider, Elmer 'Moe' - tb 5107, 5405, 5701

Schroeder, Gene - p 4411/14/16/19

Schutz, Buddy - d 3860/61, 3915/16/17/18/19/22/23/24, 4523

Schutz, Jimmy - b 4523

Schwartzman, Joe - b 3935

Seaberg, George - tp 4504/08/20/29/34/37, 5405

Secrest, Andy - tp 5405

Sentimentalists, The - vo 4504/08/20/29/34

Setar, Johnny - as/cl 4545

Shapiro, Art - b 3805/26/39/54, 4002/15, 4801/02, 5402/03, 5501

Shaver, Charlie - tp 4512/14/21/29/34/37

Shaw, Artie - cl 3858

Shaw, Bill (see Alamshah)

Sherock, Shorty - tp 3937, 4007, 4404

Shertzer, Hymie - as 3503/08, 3610/23, 3701/05/36/60, 3813/14/17, 3903/26/31/35, 4301/02/03/05/12, 4544

Shik, Tibor - f-horn 4537

Shore, Dinah - vo 6001

Short, Bob - tu 5801

Shrivanek, Eddie - bj 5405

Simeon, Omer - cl 3501

Sims, Jimmy - tb 4404/05

Sims, Rudolph - cello 4530

Sims, Zoot - ts 4315, 4402, 4601

Singleton, Zutty - d 3502, 3854

Skeffington, Tommy - vo 4217

Skolnik, Sam - tp 4545

Smith, Warren - tb 3937, 4005/16/23/24, 4802, 5005, 5107

Smith, Willie 'The Lion' - p 3863

Smithers, Elmer - tb 4039, 4108

Solomon, Red - tp 4523

Spanier, Muggsy - co 2801/02, 4015/26/30/35/40, 4102/03, 4409/11/15/17/19, 4423, 4502/09/18, 5301

Spencer, O'Neal - d 3858

Sperling, Jack - d 6001, 6901

Spivak, Charlie - tp 4006

Spreter, Bill - b 7601

Squires, Bruce - tb 3925/26, 4218

Stegmeyer, Bill - cl/as 3937, 4025

Stephens, Haig - b 5405

Stephens, Phil - b 5304

Stone, Bob - b 5401, 5701

Storey, Lou - cl/as/vo 2601

Storm, Gale 4112

Stover, Smokey - d 5005

Street, David - vo 4217

Strickland, Cliff - ts 4601

Sutton, Ralph - p 4411 7501

Swingsters, The - vo 4404

Sylvano, Frank - vo 2802

Szigeti, Joseph - vl 3905

T

Tartasky, Max - vl 4530/31

Tatum, Art - p 4401

Taylor, Billy - b 3807

Taylor, Bob - 4301/02/03/05/12/15

Teagarden, Charlie - tp 4002, 5103/04/05/06/09, 5201, 5405

Teagarden, Jack - tb 3826, 3907, 4006, 4401, 5109, 5111, 5201, 5405

Teague, Thurman - b 3824

Teschemacher, Frank - cl 2801

Thomas, Milton - viola 4504/08/34/37

Thomas, Ray - tb 4545

Thunen, Tommy - tp 6902

Tilton, Liz - vo 4106/08/12

Tilton, Martha - vo 3729/36/60, 3813, 3926, 5702

Tinterow, Bernard - vl 4504/0/20/29/34/37

Tobin, Louise - vo 3927

Toscarelli, Mario - d 4544

Tough, Dave - d 3814/24/29/39/40/41/54/55

Town, Floyd - ts/cl 2801

Triscari, Joe - tp 4608 4705

Troup, Bobby - compere 5701/02

U

Uchitel, David - vl/viola 4504/08/20/29/34/37

Usher, Billy - vo 4508/12

V

Van Camp, Gus - b 4302/03, 4404

Van Eps, George - g 5002,5101/03, 5405, 6901

Van, Betty - vo 3722

Venuti, Joe - vl 4714 7404

Vesely, Ted - tb 5103/04/05/07, 5403/05

Vinal, Charley - cl 4020

Voght, Dick - bar 4545

Vunk, Lyman - tp 4108, 4218/28

W

Wade, Eddie - tp 4007/08

Wald, Jerry - cl 4714

Walton, Jon -ts 4301/02/03

Ward, Helen - vo 3503/08, 3608/23

Warren, Earl - as 3759, 3802

Washburne, Country - tu 5405

Washington, Jack - bar 3759, 3802

Watson, Bus - b 4545

Watson, Leo - vo 3903

Weiss, Sammy - d 4608/09, 4701/02/03/04/05

Weiss, Sid - b 3936/39, 4011, 4305/08/09/10/11/12/14, 4401/02/03/09/10/11/18, 4501/02/03/05/15/18, 5802

Wendt, George - tp 4608, 4705

Wettling, George - d 2801/02, 3501, 3805/06/18/26/62/63, 4002/15, 4306/09, 4408/10/12/13/14/15/17/18/19/21/24/25, 4501/02/03/05/09/13/15/26/27

White, Hy - g 4415

White, Johnny - vb 4601/03/05/06/08/09

Wilde Twins, The (Lynn & Lee) - vo 4217

Wiley, Lee - vo 3854, 4030, 4308, 4406/09/14/16/17/19/23/24/25, 4501/02/03/05/09/13/15/18/25/27/44, 4715

Williams, Bonnie Lou - vo 4504/08/20/29/34

Williams, Cootie - tp 3709, 3804/07

Wilson, J.C. - tb 4545

Wilson, Quinn - b 3924

Wilson, Teddy - p 3834

Worrell, Frank - g 4544

Worrell, Fred - bsx 4404

Wright, Marvin - p 4523

Y

Yaner, Milt - as 3817/19

Young, Eve - vo 4601/03/06

Young, Lester - ts 3813

Z

Zarchy, Zeke - tp 3622/23/27, 4608 4705, 5104, 5405, 5802

Zentner, Si -tb 5405

Index to the Biography

(Listing names, bands, movies [in speech marks] and tune titles [in italics])

Notes on the Compact Disc
(Jazzology Press - Book CD 4)

(5302) Jess Stacy, piano; Johnny Lucas, trumpet & vocal:

Los Angeles – Saturday, May 23, 1953

1.   **Melancholy Blues**
2.   **Sleepy Time Down South**
3.   **Them There Eyes**
4.   **Loveless Love** vJL
5.   **Big Butter And Egg Man**

Jess Stacy, piano.   same location and date

6.   **Stompin' At The Savoy**
7.   **Lover Man**
8.   **Oh Baby**
9.   **Candlelights**
10. **Study In A Minor**

(5111) Jess Stacy, piano; Johnny Lucas, trumpet; Jack Teagarden, trombone & vocal; Bob McCracken, clarinet; Jimmy Pratt, drums.   Los Angeles – Saturday, December 22, 1951

11. **Basin St. Blues** vJT
12. **Baby, Won't You Please Come Home?** vJT
13. **St. James Infirmary** vJT
14. **Sunny Side Of The Street**